TEXAS HILL COUNTRY

LONE ★ STAR
TRAVEL ★ GUIDE

TEXAS HILL COUNTRY

Sixth Edition

RICHARD ZELADE

TAYLOR TRADE PUBLISHING
Lanham • New York • Boulder • Toronto • Plymouth, UK

Published by Taylor Trade Publishing
An imprint of The Rowman & Littlefield Publishing Group, Inc.
4501 Forbes Boulevard, Suite 200, Lanham, Maryland 20706
http://www.rlpgtrade.com

Estover Road, Plymouth PL6 7PY, United Kingdom

Distributed by National Book Network

ISBN 978-1-58979-609-6 (pbk. : alk. paper)
ISBN 978-1-58979-610-2 (electronic)

∞™ The paper used in this publication meets the minimum requirements of American National Standard for Information Sciences—Permanence of Paper for Printed Library Materials, ANSI/NISO Z39.48-1992.

Printed in the United States of America

CONTENTS

ACKNOWLEDGMENTS

In the thirty years spent putting together *Hill Country*, I've done a lot of listening, looking, and reading. Each experience, no matter how small, has increased in some way my understanding of the Hill Country and subsequently has enhanced this book. For this I am grateful. But I owe special thanks to a number of people. I would like to thank the staff of the Center for American History at the University of Texas at Austin, who spent hours shagging down all the files and books I was forever requesting.

The Texas State Historical Association's *Handbook of Texas*, considered to be the gold standard for Texas history, was used as a reference for all the trips. Material for all the trips also came from the archives of the *Austin Democratic/ Daily Statesman*, the *Galveston Daily News*, the *San Antonio Express, San Antonio Light, Llano News*, and others.

In putting together each trip, I found at least one book that proved to be a particularly valuable source of background information or quoted material. By trip, the books are as follows:

Take a Ride on the Fredericksburg and Northern Railroad: *Rails Through the Hill Country*, by F. A. Schmidt; *The San Antonio and Aransas Pass Railway*, by John W. Hedge and Geoffrey S. Dawson; *Charcoal and Charcoal Burners*, by Fritz Toepperwein; *Fredericksburg Self-Guiding Auto Tour*, by Joan Jubbard; and *Indian Wars and Pioneers of Texas*, by John Henry Brown.

Hermit of the Hills/Highland Lakes: *Pioneers in God's Hills*, by the Gillespie County Historical Society; *History of Burnet County*, by Darrell Debo; *Six Years with the Texas Rangers: 1875 to 1881*, by James B. Gillett; *Captain Jeff: Frontier Life with the Texas Rangers*, by Jeff Maltby; *The Life of John Wesley Hardin as Written by Himself*, by John Wesley Hardin; *Llano, Gem of the Hill Country*, by Wilburn Oatman; *Evolution of a State*, by Noah Smithwick; *Mills of Yesteryear*, by A. T. Jackson; and *Gold and Silver in Texas*, by Thomas J. Evans.

Mormon Trails: *The Lyman Wight Colony in Texas*, by J. Marvin Hunter; *Evolution of a State*, by Noah Smithwick; *Six Years with the Texas Rangers: 1875 to 1881*, by James B. Gillett; *100 Years in Bandera, 1853–1953*, by J. Marvin Hunter; *German Artist on the Texas Frontier: Friedrich Richard Petri*, by Wiliam W. Newcomb Jr.

Hill Country Rivers: *A Hundred Years of Comfort in Texas*, by Guido Ransleben; *Mountains of the Mind*, by Horace Morelock; *Unser Fortschritt: Our Progress*, by the Comfort Heritage Foundation Inc.; *A Journey through Texas*, by

Frederick Law Olmstead; and *With the Border Ruffians: Memories of the Far West, 1852–1868*, by R. H. Williams.

Enchanted Rock: *Blanco County History*, by John Moursund; and *Mills of Yesteryear*, by A. T. Jackson.

Many people have helped me over the years in assembling the material for this book. Their observations have made it truly special, something more than just another guidebook. Many are now deceased, but a bit of them lives on in these pages. Beginning with the first edition, back in 1983, my thanks go to Margaret Keidel, John and Edward Balcar, the Riskes, Gould Davis, Jimmy Nuckles, the Kliers, Mrs. Simek, Speedy, Emil, Joe, Cracker, Mr. Siems, Frank Wagner, C. W. Carlson, Clara Scarbrough, Max Theis, Red Casparis, Chuck Zelade, Irv and Mary Zelade, Susan and Jeff Reid, Brook Watts, Bill and Doris Bacon, Bob and Suzan Leggett, Kristin Brown, Odies Schatte, and Marianne Simmons. Thanks also to Emil Holtzer, Alton Koch, the Twin Sisters School Association, Rusty Vogt, Winnie Petty, and Walter Doebbler.

Subsequent edition thanks go to Marvin Finger, Andrew Sansom, Robin Giles, Edith Giles, Bill Stein, Buddy Rau, Louis Polansky, Helen Mikus, Joe Nick Patoski, Walt Falk, Gerald McLeod, Jim Shahin, Royce Nelson, and John Morthland.

Special, current edition thanks go to Curtis Clarke, faithful friend and driver, whose dedication and extra pair of eyes helped me concentrate on the finer details of updating.

My most heartfelt thanks go out to my deceased friend and mentor Anders Saustrup, who more than anyone else over the years helped me mold *Hill Country* into the substantial work that it is. His wealth of knowledge of Texas history and his dedication to historical accuracy saved me many times from potential embarrassment and made *Hill Country* more than just another guidebook.

INTRODUCTION

Texas, more than any other state, is the crossroads of America. Four major continental divisions come together here: the Rocky Mountains, the Great Western High and Lower Plains, and the Gulf Coastal Plains.

The farming woodland Caddoes, the cannibal coastal Karankawa, the roaming Apache and Comanche hunters, and the desert cliff-dwelling Pueblos—all of them once called Texas home. The cultures of Old Mexico and the Old South, the Wild West, and the Great Plains met and sometimes clashed here. English, German, Czech, and Scandinavian émigrés of the nineteenth century flocked to Texas in search of a new and better life, much like the northern snowbirds of today.

Birds from all corners of the North American continent meet here, more than six hundred different species in all. Rocky Mountain and Eastern species of oak and pine converge uniquely in Texas, which has at least five thousand species of plant life.

All these "roads" have led ultimately to Central Texas and the Hill Country—the heart of Texas—resulting in a singular cultural, geographical, and physiological potpourri which manifests itself in foods like chicken-fried jalapenos and wurst tacos; pronunciations like "Purd'nallez" (Pedernales), "Gwaddaloop" (Guadalupe), and "Manshack" (Manchaca); Texas-German words and phrases like "der Outlaw," "der Bollweevil," "die Fenz" (the fence), "das Stinktier" (the skunk), "der Mesquitebaum," and "die Kuh dehornen" (dehorn the cow); and Czech-Texan words like "rencak" (rancher), "polkat" (skunk), "akr" (acre), and "barbekue" (barbecue). And only in the Hill Country of Central Texas will you see the sacred Enchanted Rock and the limestone fences, houses, barns, and Sunday houses of the old German Texans.

Then there is the Balcones Fault, that great crack in the earth which bisects the whole of Texas—separating the western upland from the coastal lowland—but which manifests itself most notably in Central Texas, dividing the region yet ultimately binding it together.

Ironically, the name "Hill Country," for the book and the region, is misleading, as a University of Texas geology professor once pointed out. The more proper name should be "Valley Country," for our "Hill Country" has actually been formed from erosion rather than uplifts.

Tradition has it that the name "Texas" derives from a Caddo language word meaning "friends" or "allies." And Texans are a pretty friendly bunch of people.

Texas is also one of the most conservative states in the Union, and, Austin aside, the Hill Country and the rest of Central Texas is as conservative as the rest of the state. As never before, this book attempts to explain both phenomena by exploring the rich, varied, complicated, and intertwined histories of the region's ethnic, racial, national, and socioeconomic groups.

The trips in this book are meant to reflect the one-of-a-kind flavor that is the Hill Country. They take you out of the big cities, off the freeways and superhighways, away from the fast food franchises and shopping malls, and introduce you to the small towns and ghost towns, mountains and valleys, rivers and creeks, cafes and beer joints, and some of the fine folks of the Hill Country—the wonderful sweet cream that always rises to the top of a bottle of whole milk. But like good whole milk, that which is uniquely vintage Hill Country Texas gets a little harder to find each year.

Richard Zelade
Austin, Texas
October 2010

How to Use
This Book

We deliberately take to the tasty back roads so as to treat you to the most vivid flavors of the Hill Country. Getting to wherever you're going is always at least half the fun.

While this book takes you far and wide across the heart of Texas, it is not a comprehensive guide to the area and does not pretend to be. Trips are organized along themes, and it has not been possible to include every town in the region.

Although Texas is now predominantly urban, small towns and the open country are still the state's bedrock and the strongest links to our traditional, unique Texas past. There is a distinctly different mentality to our back-roads communities, an informal order of things. Hours and days open for businesses, while usually reliable, are still left largely to the whim of the proprietor, who may just decide to take the day off, open late, or close early.

The hours and days of operation given are designed to be as accurate and as up-to-date as possible but should not be blindly relied on. Places get sold, they close, or they burn down. Many places now have websites, which are usually useful for current information but are sometimes not updated as often as they should be. Calling ahead by phone is the surest way to confirm current hours of operation and other information.

Website addresses for restaurants, museums, visitor centers, and the like that have websites are given following each attraction's phone number, with the exception of Texas state parks and natural areas. For information on all state parks and natural areas, go to the Texas Parks and Wildlife Department's website: www.tpwd.state.tx.us.

Another important thing that has changed since this book first came out, in addition to the ubiquity of websites, is the improvement in road names, signs, and numbering, mandated by the universal 911 service. It's easier for me to publish concise, easy-to-follow directions now, but sometimes signs get knocked down or stolen, so it's still necessary at times to refer to local landmarks as direction aids.

Several of these trips can be easily done in one day, others take two days, and some can go either way. Distances are such that you should have to drive no more than thirty miles out of your way to find accommodations, since some of these small towns and villages have none. Usually towns with over one thousand population do. The countryside is now conveniently dotted, more than ever, with bed-and-breakfast facilities, but these generally do not accept drop-ins. There is also considerable turnover in B&B inns. Call the local chamber of commerce for a current listing of B&Bs in the area you're interested in.

Each city or town's listing begins with the name of the county in which it's located, the best estimate of the current population, and the telephone area code.

Because of the Americans with Disabilities Act, most places listed are now wheelchair accessible or partially accessible. Call ahead to make sure. Wheelchair accessibility is indicated by the letter *W*.

You should always carry a good state highway map with you, such as the free Texas Department of Transportation map, available at the state travel visitor centers scattered across the state, and at most local chambers of commerce and visitor centers. Mapsco's *The Roads of Texas Atlas* (www.mapsco.com) is my favorite travel companion; each public road, no matter how small, is shown and identified by its name and number, and many local landmarks, such as cemeteries, schoolhouses, community centers, and the like, are also identified.

If you just want to do part of a tour, or if you just want to visit a specific place, remember that about half of the towns and places in this book will be found on any good state highway map and are accessible by major highways.

With only a few documented exceptions, the road mileage in this book is over reasonably good to excellent paved roads. Perhaps thirty of the miles are gravel, and these are generally well graded, located in the arid uplift between Fredericksburg and Llano. They are sometimes rough and "washboarded" after bad weather, though.

Be careful when driving in rainy weather. Slow down on the winding roads, and be wary of low-water crossings. Any crossing with more than a few inches of running water can be dangerous, depending on the vehicle you are driving. When in doubt, "Don't Drown, Turn Around."

In concocting *Texas Hill Country*, I blended history, personal observations, folklore, and trivia, and then spiced it up with a little geology, geography, and humor. I hope you have as much fun exploring the Hill Country with this book as I had writing it.

Special Note: Due to the 2011 state budget crisis, the future of Texas state parks, including all state parks and natural areas in this book, was in doubt at press time. Please check the Texas Parks and Wildlife website for the latest status of each park or natural area.

Take a Ride on the Fredericksburg and Northern Railroad

Few of us today can fully appreciate the trials and tribulations of pioneer travel through the Hill Country. Overland trips that once took weeks now take hours. Certainly there has been no more revolutionary change in the modern lifestyle than this reduction in time. The average Roman family would have needed about two weeks to make the ox wagon trip from San Antonio to Fredericksburg, the same amount of time needed by the Adelsverein (a German colonization society in Texas) wagon trains a millennium later.

Then the railroad came along, and it turned the two-week journey from San Antonio to Fredericksburg into a one-day ride. Small wonder that people viewed the railroads with a mix of apprehension, awe, and admiration. As it turns out, the iron horse was merely the vanguard in a transportation revolution, the magnitude of which few of us can fully grasp.

Wondrously mighty as it was, the railroad had its problems in the Hill Country. Most lines just avoided this part of Texas entirely, and the few roads that dared enter the hills were arduously expensive to build. These railroads were highly coveted. Existing towns like Kerrville and Fredericksburg battled for routes, and developers looked forward to establishing new towns along the rights-of-way. In this southern section of the Hill Country, Kerrville won the first round for railroad service, becoming the western terminus of the area's first road, the San Antonio and Aransas Pass (SA&AP, or SAP) railroad in 1887. Later called the Texas and New Orleans (T&NO), the SA&AP became part of the Southern Pacific system in 1892, left it in 1903, and returned in 1925.

But progressive, persistent Fredericksburg was not to be denied, and although they had to wait nearly forty years and ended up building it themselves,

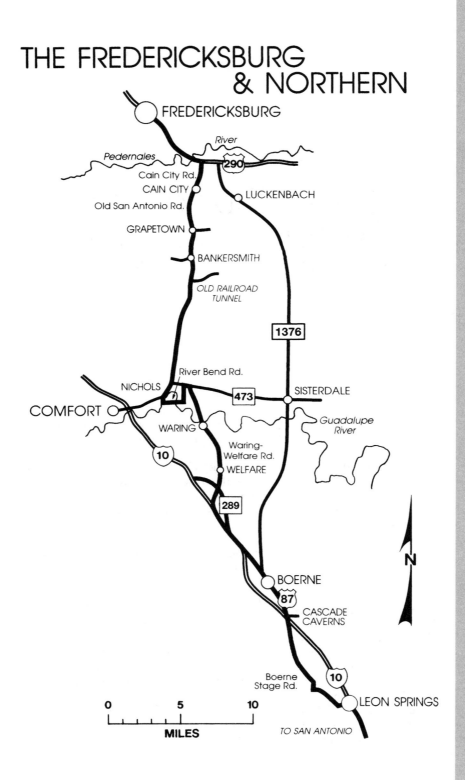

THE FREDERICKSBURG
& NORTHERN

FREDERICKSBURG

River

Pedernales

290

Cain City Rd.

CAIN CITY

LUCKENBACH

Old San Antonio Rd.

GRAPETOWN

BANKERSMITH

*OLD RAILROAD
TUNNEL*

1376

River Bend Rd.

NICHOLS

SISTERDALE

473

COMFORT

*Guadalupe
River*

WARING

Waring-
Welfare Rd.

10

WELFARE

289

BOERNE

87

CASCADE
CAVERNS

N

Boerne
Stage Rd.

10

LEON SPRINGS

0   5   10

MILES

TO SAN ANTONIO

the townspeople of Fredericksburg finally got their railroad in 1913. The San Antonio, Fredericksburg and Northern (SA F&N), as it was first incorporated (after bankruptcy and reorganization, it was renamed the Fredericksburg and Northern, or F&N), came into the world amid much ballyhoo and high expectations.

It never lived up to its advance billing. Ditto for the Kerrville branch of the SA&AP. The highways soon took away what business they had. And so the tracks of both were pulled up years ago and are now just dimming memories among the thinning ranks of Hill Country old-timers. But the towns they created and nurtured still hang on, even as ghosts, and if you look in the right places you can still catch glimpses of the ghost tracks themselves.

This trip takes you along the length of the Fredericksburg and Northern, from Fredericksburg to the southern terminus at Fredericksburg Junction east of Comfort. Here you transfer over to the SA&AP for the last leg of the excursion to San Antonio. It also takes you, as much as is possible, over the highway route that replaced it. And the scenery is pretty nice, too.

FREDERICKSBURG

Gillespie County Seat • 11,000 (approximate) • (830)
Unlike their free-thinking, intellectual compatriots in the German villages of Comfort and Sisterdale, and the "Dutch Settlements" of Castell, Leiningen, and Bettina, Fredericksburg's early settlers were practical-minded, God-fearing tradesmen and craftsmen, merchants and professional men, farmers and mechanics, who saw a chance to improve their quality of life in Texas. Most had joined the Adelsverein (Society for the Protection of German Immigrants in Texas) in Germany, finding the society's promises and terms irresistible.

Full of hopes and expectation, thousands of the immigrants landed on the Gulf Coast at Carlshafen (Indianola) in Calhoun County during the years 1844 through 1847. Hundreds of them never left the beaches of Carlshafen, falling prey to a host of plagues that burned through the crude tent-and-shack city like wildfire.

Several thousand managed to reach New Braunfels, the first way station on the trail to the Adelsverein's intended settlement area, the desolate three-million-plus-acre Fisher-Miller Grant. Prince Carl of Solms-Braunfels, the first commissioner general of the Adelsverein in Texas, founded New Braunfels in March 1845.

Less than three months later, Prince Carl was back in Germany, and the Adelsverein in Texas had a new commissioner general, John O. Meusebach. Meusebach was one of the few practical thinkers in the Adelsverein leadership and was a wise choice to succeed Prince Carl. Meusebach realized that to succeed in Texas the Germans would have to assimilate to the native culture rather than trying to recreate Germany in Texas. Meusebach accordingly dropped his title of nobility on the very day he sailed for Texas; Baron Ottfried Hans von Meusebach declared himself John O. Meusebach, Texan. Upon his arrival in New Braunfels, Meusebach found the Adelsverein's books hopelessly entangled and the society even more hopelessly in debt than previously feared. Meusebach also soon realized that another way station north of New Braunfels would have to be set up before the society's final push into the distant Fisher-Miller Grant could begin.

Meusebach commenced his search for land in August 1845, and by that winter he had bought ten thousand acres of wilderness on credit, eighty miles northwest of New Braunfels. The well-timbered tract was near the Pedernales River, but not on it, since that land was already owned and the price prohibitive. Two strongly flowing creeks coursed through the acreage. Surveyors sent to lay out a route to the embryonic settlement reached it in January 1846.

By the end of April, some 120 men, women, and children borne by twenty wagons and two-wheeled Mexican carts had commenced the sixteen-day journey to this new outpost, named Friedrichburg (Fredericksburg) in honor of Prince Friedrich (Frederick) of Prussia, an Adelsverein patron. Arriving on May 8, 1846, the colonists were on their own three days later. After helping pitch the tents and building a couple of huts, the teamsters, soldiers, and a few young able-bodied men returned to New Braunfels. Those who remained got to work laying out the new city and planting crops. They lived in tents or built huts consisting of poles rammed into the ground, like a Mexican jacal. The spaces between the poles were filled with clay and moss, and the roof was covered with dry grass. Militia companies were formed to protect the settlers from Indian attacks. Talk about culture shock—most of these groundbreaking pioneers had stepped off the boats from Germany only a matter of weeks earlier. But things got worse. Waves of disease swept through Fredericksburg during that first year, much as had happened on the beaches of Indianola and in nascent New Braunfels. Fever and dysentery prevailed, often terminating in dropsy, which usually proved fatal.

The death rate was highest during the hot months; on one day, the bodies of a father and three of his children were carted to the cemetery. A man and his wife died in their hut and rotted half away before their corpses were discovered. Often the dying were robbed by their neighbors, and any remaining belongings of the dead were considered common property that anyone could appropriate. But the survivors persevered, and with the subsequent wagonloads of reinforcements, their ranks had swelled to over five hundred by early 1847.

By the time the German scientist Dr. Ferdinand Roemer arrived in late January 1847, 156 settlers had died, and dysentery and "stomacacae" were still prevalent. Stomacacae, which spread to the throat and lungs, was often fatal. People died almost every day, despite the medicine and medical attention provided at no charge by the Adelsverein. (See Pioneer Place Garden, for William Hermes' detailed account of life and sickness in early Fredericksburg.)

Life became easier for the beleaguered Germans as 1847 wore on. Their first corn crop was good, and later that year, the breakaway Mormon leader Lyman Wight brought his flock from Austin to a spot near Fredericksburg on the Pedernales, where they established the community of Zodiac. The more experienced Mormons helped the Texas-green Germans learn many of the finer points of life on the frontier (see Mormon Trails).

After several months of negotiation, Meusebach signed a peace treaty with the Comanches in May 1847 regarding the country between the waters of the Llano and San Saba rivers. The treaty relieved Fredericksburgers of one of the deadliest headaches of frontier life: attacks by Indians who did not wish to make way for the white interlopers. Elsewhere in Texas, the Comanches would resist the Anglo onslaught fiercely, more so than any other Texas tribe. But the peace signed by Meusebach, U.S. agent Robert Neighbors, and the Comanche war chiefs on the banks of the Pedernales was largely kept, at least around Fredericksburg. The treaty allowed each group to travel freely and unmolested in each other's territory. In addition, "In regard to the settlement on the Llano the Comanches promise not to disturb or in any way molest the German colonists, on the contrary to assist them, also to give notice, if they see bad Indians about the settlement who come to steal horses from or in any way molest the Germans—the Germans likewise promising to aid the Comanches against their enemies, should they be in danger of having their horses stolen or in any way to be injured. And both parties agree, that if there be any difficulties or any wrong done by single bad men, to bring the same before the chiefs to be finally settled and decided by the agent of our great father."

The Comanches further agreed to allow the Germans to survey the country as far north as the Concho River and perhaps the Colorado. In return, Meusebach was to give the Comanches presents in the amount of $1,000, along with additional provisions to be given to the Comanches during their stay in Fredericksburg to amount to about $2,000 worth or more. Fifteen commercial establishments were in operation in Fredericksburg by the end of 1847.

The establishment of Fort Martin Scott by the U.S. Army in 1848 gave the people of Fredericksburg a chance to earn some desperately needed cash money. The town had previously subsisted on the barter system. The government paid in gold for its contracted supplies and services. Fredericksburg got an additional boost when the army established its primary military road west to California through the town. Fredericksburg was the last real outpost of civilization before El Paso, and most travelers bought supplies there before making the long push west. Things got even better when the forty-niners began rolling through, bound for the gold fields of California. But while their purchases swelled the town's coffers, the cholera germs these transients left behind filled the city cemetery with hundreds of new graves.

Gillespie County was created in 1848 from parts of Travis County and Bexar County, and Fredericksburg became its first and only county seat. Gillespie County was named for Richard Gillespie, a Texas Ranger who was killed leading the American charge on the Bishop's Palace in Monterrey, Mexico, on September 21, 1846, during the War with Mexico.

Fredericksburg became a regional trade center. Many of its industrious Germans became drovers, hauling in goods from San Antonio and the coast to supply the town and the string of army frontier forts just to the west, and hauling out locally produced cotton, grain, fresh fruits, and vegetables. The trip to San Antonio was at least a ten-day trudge for the lumbering ox wagons, and it often took a month to reach the coast.

It was a trip usually fraught with danger, and not one to be made alone, as illustrated by this account by "D. R." in April 1855, which followed the route we are about to embark on:

> I left Fredericksburg a day sooner than I intended, in company with an armed band whom I was glad to fall in with, as we had a long dreary route to travel through a country, at this time, by no means free from danger. At every place where we stopped, we heard of Indian depredations being committed; and found the whole country, along our route, in a state of alarm. Seldom a night passed without some

outrage, and though every precaution seems to be adopted, and no man thinks of leaving his own door without being armed, these wily savages have so far eluded every effort to detect them. They go mostly on foot in small bands, and from their thorough knowledge of the country, and their facilities for watching everything going on among the settlements, from the tops of the mountains, they can come down at any time in the night, and run off horses or cattle with impunity. In escaping with their booty, they invariably take to the mountains, where they scatter, so that it is impossible to trail them over the rocks. It was late in the morning when we started, and it being our intention to reach the Cibolo [present-day Boerne] that night, we had to push along. In passing Fort Martin Scott, about two miles below town, we could only take a hasty glance at it, from the road. Like all the other frontier posts I have visited, it is very beautifully situated, and must, at the time, have been an important point, as the building indicates that no expense has been spared by the Government to make it every way adapted to the accommodation of a large body of troops. Our route lay through a mountainous country, with but few settlements in sight of the road, though we passed occasionally through some fine valleys of rich lands. On the Perdinalis, we met a party from San Antonio, who had camped, for a short time, and were on their way to organize an Odd Fellows' Lodge at Fredericksburg. After interchanging a few courtesies, usual on such occasions, we kept along till we reached Grape Creek, where we encamped for an hour to rest our horses and partake of some refreshments.

Our next halting place was on the Guadalupe where we accidentally pulled up at the rancho of Mr. J. S. Brown [of whom we will soon learn more], who very courteously invited us to alight and in a few minutes had coffee, cigars, &c., placed before us, which we very gladly partook of. Here we learned the Indians had been down the night before and shot a horse belonging to Mr. J. W. Smith, a near neighbor of Mr. Brown's. While there, he sent over for the arrow which had been taken out of the horse and handed it to us. He remarked that arrows were so plentiful, the children used them to play with. He and his neighbors have employed men at thirty five dollars per month, to be out counting all the time, and scarcely a night passes without some depredation being committed in the neighborhood. The thing has become so common they scarcely think it worth speaking of, if a few horses or cattle are killed or run off, unless a stranger chance to come along at the time and make enquiries, in which case it may stand a chance of being published.

It was late in the night when we reached the Cibolo, where we met His Honor, Judge Devine, and several lawyers from San Antonio on their way to hold court at Fredericksburg, though there is not enough business to detain him more than a day or two. The room in which they were domiciled for the night, being well filled and guarded with a small armory of six shooters, we had to be staked out in another part of the house, not much adapted for sleeping. Consequently, we were up and on our horses before day break, as we resolved, on seeing our quarters, to take an early start in the morning, and ride to the Leon Springs to breakfast, a distance of twelve miles which we accomplished by eight o'clock. Here again, we heard of the Indians having been down the night before and stolen five horses from a Mr. Pleve, and two from McLellan, living at the Springs. The party who gave us information, at the house where we breakfasted, said there was now but one mule left in the whole neighborhood, as they had made a clean sweep at everything wearing a hoof. Here we fell in with a ranger returning home, who had that morning seen a horse with the skin taken entirely off both fore legs with a knife, which had been done a few nights previous by the Indians. He informed us that he had been with Capt. Calhoun's command, consisting of three companies of rangers and two of dragoons, accompanied by seventy-five wagons, and that they had traversed all the country bordering on the Wichita and Red River, for three months without seeing an Indian.

It is hardly to be supposed a body of 500 men, moving through the country, should be likely to see Indians, but this was Gen. Smith's order, that they should keep together, and it had to be obeyed. Immediately the troops quitted Fort Chadbourne, some 500 Indians who had been watching them on their route, came in and claimed protection, which was at once granted, thus the government were at the same time feeding and protecting the very savages they were sending out a force to chastise, at an enormous cost to the country. It is presumed part of those same Indians came down below, and have since been committing all those depredations, while the rangers and dragoons have been scouring a country where no Indian was to be seen.

In the spring of 1861, most Texas counties voted to secede, but 96 percent of Gillespie County's electorate voted against secession. No doubt there was strong Union sentiment in overwhelmingly German Gillespie County, but the final tally was also influenced by the voters' realization that secession meant war, and war meant both the loss of a major market for local products and the removal of protection against Indian attacks.

But the drovers managed to stay busy anyway. Many were conscripted to drive for the Confederate Army; others ran cotton down to Mexico, where the bales brought solid gold, not worthless Rebel paper money. The war actually spurred the Texas-Mexico cotton connection. At the height of the war, in 1863, the cotton wagons creaking through New Braunfels hauled the greatest volume in town history. Much of it was Gillespie County cotton. The payoff was good, but not without its dangers. Many Confederates regarded such border trade as treasonous and therefore punishable by death. Others with fewer scruples merely murdered the drovers for their money.

After the war, Fredericksburg again began to supply western-bound travelers and the reestablished frontier forts. As the iron horse crawled west across Texas after the war, Fredericksburg merchants began to hunger after some rails through their town. They hungered for about forty years. Meanwhile, the big ox wagons continued to roll over the hills to and from San Antonio.

As early as 1874, a bill was introduced in the Texas legislature petitioning for the incorporation of the San Antonio and Fredericksburg narrow-gauge railroad. It died on the vine.

In December 1882, The San Antonio Merchants' Exchange decided to try and induce Messrs. Peirce and Huntington of the Galveston Harrisburg and San Antonio Railroad to push forward the Fredericksburg road, and endeavored to get the Texas and St. Louis narrow-gauge railroad to build their road to that city. The Fredericksburg road was the subject of a great deal of indecision. It had been surveyed and begun several times, as recently as earlier that year. By June, a railroad to Fredericksburg was almost like a forgotten dream.

With railroad connections to Houston and points farther east, and Austin and points farther north, all San Antonio lacked were rail connections to the Gulf and to the west, which the recently organized San Antonio and Aransas Pass (SAP) railroad promised to provide. But the SAP had ambitions bigger than its pocketbook, and finance problems forced a reorganization of the railroad in 1885. Uriah Lott took over management of the road and in April 1885 signaled the road's interest in reaching out west. But money was short, and he needed the help of San Antonio's moneyed men, who as a class were as backward as spring was that year in coming forward. But prospects were at least brighter than they had been since the board of trade gave the project a black eye the previous summer.

When Fredericksburgers got wind of the San Antonio and Aransas Pass railway's plan to build a new road northwest out of San Antonio to the High Plains, they immediately formed a committee to confer with SA&AP manager Uriah Lott, to convince him to lay the rails through Kendall County to Fredericksburg. The committee was prepared to fork over right-of-way land and fat cash bonuses to the SA&AP. By December 1885 the race was on. And the advantage appeared to be tipped to a proposed line through Bandera to Kerrville. Lott was demanding $6,000 per mile from the people interested in the Fredericksburg route, and $1,000 from friends of the route via Bandera to Kerrville.

San Antonio's business community favored the Fredericksburg route for purely selfish reasons. They already had trade with Bandera and Kerrville in their pocket, with no very probable chance of it being lost, so building a road there would a useless defensive measure to protect interests not threatened.

But the Fredericksburg line was another matter. With Gillespie, Blanco, Mason, Llano, and the counties beyond, it was different; the bulk of their business went to Austin, Burnet, Lampasas, and Abilene. A line to Fredericksburg would attract business to San Antonio that was going elsewhere.

The Kerrville boosters talked time and again of the "miniature Alps" on the Fredericksburg route and the necessity of piercing tunnels through them. The Fredericksburg boosters in turn hired a civil engineer who assured them there was no more necessity for tunneling the divide between the Guadalupe and Pedernales rivers than there would have been for the Sunset folks to have tunneled Dignowty hill to get into San Antonio. He was confident that a competent engineer could locate a line from the Guadalupe to Fredericksburg crossing the "miniature Alps" and use no grade above 1 percent per mile.

But there was a big "but"—Kerrville's Captain Charles Schreiner, a bulldog of a man who caused even the most optimistic Fredericksburg boosters to admit, "If we had a few Captain Schreiners in our committee it would be better for us, and the prospects for the early completion of the road to Fredericksburg would be brighter."

By April 1886, Lott announced that if the people between San Antonio and Fredericksburg would take $289,000, 6 percent of the first mortgage bonds of the road, work would be commenced within thirty days from the time at which the money was raised.

In May, Austin businessmen were thinking about an independent line to Fredericksburg to protect their commercial interests.

By June 1886, it was all-out war between Kerrville and Fredericksburg. The Fredericksburg delegation, who had declared that the line should go by way of Sisterdale and directly to that city, had threatened to break up the whole scheme, if possible, in case it went by way of Kerrville. President Lott said it was his intention to supply all of the upper country with railroad facilities as far as possible, but he must first build his railway to Kerrville. There were engineering difficulties in the way of going into Fredericksburg from the south that would cost him $150,000 to overcome, and he did not have the money, nor would it pay if he had. He intended to build in the same general direction from Kerrville, and when he reached the Pedernales, he would be within fifteen to twenty miles of Fredericksburg and have a smooth valley route for his roadbed, and then if the people of that town wanted a branch road, he would be open to deal with them on the most liberal terms. It would look like the height of folly for Fredericksburg to undertake to throw any obstacles in the way, Kerrville boosters said. The road would come within a few miles of them anyway, and a half loaf would be better than no bread.

Kerrville boosters pointed out the roller flour mill that Captain Schreiner had erected to process the county's wheat crop and the other mill abuilding in Center Point, and the corresponding lack of such in Gillespie County.

Lott announced that there would be no railroad northwest from San Antonio until subscriptions of $180,000 to the first mortgage bonds of his road and guarantees of right-of-way and depots were forthcoming from the people along the line. Committees at San Antonio, Boerne, Comfort, Kerrville, and Fredericksburg went out among their townspeople to raise the necessary donations. After the majority of subscriptions had been pledged, Lott announced that he was ready to start projecting the right-of-way out of San Antonio.

On August 14, the Fredericksburg committee laid its and San Antonio's proposition before the SAP people in San Antonio.

Grading commenced on August 26, 1886, and by April of the following year trains were running to Leon Springs. The tracks pushed steadily through Boerne, Welfare, and Waring toward the Guadalupe River just north of Waring. Meanwhile, the people of Fredericksburg and Kerrville waited in suspense.

Construction halted in Fredericksburg until an immense wood-piling bridge was built across the river. From there, the rails turned toward Comfort, and there was much speculation as to which way they would veer from there: sharply north to Fredericksburg or south to Kerrville. When the big day of decision came, it was one of consternation for Fredericksburgers. The rails headed south for Kerrville. The first train arrived at Kerrville on October 6, 1887, and was received with a great celebration (see Kerrville).

Fredericksburg had courted Lott in earnest, but Captain Charles Schreiner and his city of Kerrville had been an even more determined competitor for the rails. Schreiner had been heard to say that Kerrville wanted a railroad really bad and that it should be obtained at any cost. Schreiner pointed out to Lott that the route to Kerrville did not include any high mountains; only easy grades would be encountered. The same could not be said of the route to Fredericksburg. Schreiner also guaranteed liberal cash bonuses and the promise of much freight tonnage in and out of the area.

Business looked great for a few years, but in the end the Kerrville branch proved to be a big disappointment, never shipping out enough tonnage to make the line profitable. The great High Plains route never made it past Kerrville.

In Fredericksburg, the Railroad Committee refused to be discouraged.

In January 1887, there was a rumor that railroad magnate Jay Gould would build a railroad to Fredericksburg from Kyle. Two months later engineers from the Fredericksburg and San Marcos Valley railroad started surveying.

Llano joined forces with Fredericksburg. In July 1888, there was a meeting at Fredericksburg regarding an SAP extension to Llano, to which the SAP appeared amenable as long as there was no actual loss to it.

At that point the SAP extension to Fredericksburg was considered a certainty, with $15,000 already secured. Lott told the Llano and Gillespie county committees that if they graded the road, the SAP would lay track, and equip and operate the same. By January 1889, Llano and Gillespie had raised $100,000, but San Antonio still lacked $15,000 of its $50,000 share.

Engineers surveyed the best route from below Comfort to Fredericksburg, and the grading was done by J. P. Nelson.

A long, sinuous route around the hills into Fredericksburg that passed at one point within eight miles of Kerrville was proposed. Charles Schreiner used his considerable influence to kill it.

In November 1890, boosters for the line came up with another reason for the line: access to the great iron ore beds in Llano. San Antonio desperately wanted to secure federal armaments manufacture, and with a coal supply already assured, Llano's iron ore would give San Antonio all it needed to become the Krupp's of America.

But this and all other deals fell through, almost always because of the high costs to be incurred by building through the Divide, the line of but-grudgingly penetrable hills south of town that separated the Pedernales and Guadalupe river watersheds.

In the meantime, mules had replaced oxen, but the big wagons continued to roll. They hauled in the big steam boiler for Fredericksburg's first electric light plant in 1896, and the bulky machinery for its first ice-making factory in 1907.

In 1903, Frisco railroad representatives were in negotiation for some time with the people of Mason and Fredericksburg concerning the purchase of the railroad grade that had previously been thrown up between Fredericksburg and the "big hill" but never completed. The Frisco was exploring the extension of their line from Brady to some point on the SAP, probably at Waring.

In October 1909, representatives from San Antonio and Fredericksburg signed a contract with J. P. Nelson to finally commence work on the road. But by the end of the year, he was spending just one hundred dollars a week on the payroll, with only a few teams and men working on the fill between Fredericksburg and Waring, and no one knew why. Nelson wasn't talking. In the meantime, interests in Austin were agitating for building a line to Fredericksburg, thus shutting out the San Antonio line.

In mid-January 1910, Nelson finally broke his sphinx-like silence when his efforts to interest moneyed men failed, saying that the Fredericksburg project was taken up at the request of E. H. Harriman, president of the Union Pacific and Southern Pacific railroads and the most powerful railroad man of his time, and he had been the backer behind J. P. Nelson in the Fredericksburg–San Antonio railroad project. For three hours and a half one afternoon under the shade of a giant pecan tree on the San Antonio River, behind the Hot Wells hotel, Mr. Harriman, while on his visit to San Antonio in the spring of 1909, went over the proposition with Nelson, giving it his endorsement and arranging details. Nelson was to raise the money for the grading, and the head of the Harriman lines was to do the rest. The San Antonio man fulfilled his part of the agreement, San Antonio and Fredericksburg both raising bonuses amounting to $110,000. Everything was ready to proceed when Harriman was brought back from Europe a very sick man. His death followed, and the deal was off.

"Had it not been for Mr. Harriman's death, the Fredericksburg road would now be nearly completed," Nelson declared.

"Mr. Harriman knew me when I met him at the Business Men's Club reception," said Mr. Nelson. "He asked if I was not the Nelson who had built the Aransas Pass line, and I replied half jokingly that I was the man who did it.

"I had my surveys of twenty years ago, profile maps, etc., and he was fully advised of the value of such a line, saying, 'A road will be built through there sooner or later and we might as well have it; not only does it appear to be a paying proposition, but it will build that territory. Do you think you can raise the money necessary to do the grading?'

"I responded I could. The matter was settled, and I immediately began work to raise the money. I appealed to San Antonio and Fredericksburg. The bonuses were raised. Then came Mr. Harriman's death."

Nelson could not perfect arrangements with the new powers in control of the Harriman lines, or with any of the several other institutions he was negotiating with to secure the $350,000 he needed.

He had not given up on raising the money, but if some other backer to build the road were found, he would waive all rights, for he said he wanted to see the railroad built and was willing to sacrifice his own interests to see trains in operation into Fredericksburg.

"While, probably, the contract has not been complied with morally, due to the crosses and disappointments I have had," Nelson said, "it has been legally. My payroll each week now amounts to more than $100, as I am engaged in putting in a base to the big fill between Fredericksburg and Waring. I have made the contract for derricks, hoists and all other machinery for the rock work, etc., and every dollar I am now putting in out of my own pocket is a benefit to the proposition. But what is the use of paying three times the cost of feed and other necessaries for a great force of workmen when the future, and my returns, are uncertain? I will not spend more money until every dollar for the building of the railroad is in the bank."

Upon Nelson's estimation that the road could be built for $350,000, the San Antonio and Fredericksburg parties decided to raise $200,000 more on their own rather than give up and possibly bolster the efforts of backers of an Austin to Fredericksburg road. The Fredericksburgers said they preferred a connection with San Antonio but, feeling increasingly anxious, would consider other propositions.

Nelson relinquished his contract a few weeks later.

In desperation, Fredericksburg's businessmen teamed up with their counterparts in San Antonio to build their railroad. By July 1911, it appeared as if the railroad dream would finally come true, despite Charles Schreiner. San Antonio and Gillespie capitalists decided that they would put up the necessary cash, after a failed attempt to secure financing in Chicago that involved the Chicago promoter telling Fredericksburgers that the San Antonio Chamber of Commerce was opposed to the project.

In order to repair the damage, several San Antonio chamber members took an automobile trip to Fredericksburg to reassure their partners. They took the same route you are starting, and although no one knew it at the time, their trip was a harbinger for the line's ultimate doom.

As part of the deal, J. P. Nelson signed a contract with Temple Smith to construct the road. By that time, grading from previous construction efforts had already been practically completed along seventeen miles of the road, including up to the big hill.

On March 12, the San Antonio Chamber of Commerce accepted a proposition from R. A. Love to build a railroad to Fredericksburg from Waring, agreeing to pay him a $50,000 bonus or take bonds for $150,000 to be issued by him on completion of the road. Fredericksburg had offered a gilt-edge bonus of $100,000, right-of-way, and depot grounds to anyone who would build the railroad to Fredericksburg. But Love had to give a satisfactory bond of at least $25,000 to show good faith and indemnify subscribers to the bonus for any expense they may have to incur in getting right-of-way and depot grounds and other expenses incident to the compliance with their part of the contract.

Finally, on November 14, 1912, Charles Nimitz, chairman of the Fredericksburg railroad committee (son of hotelier Charles Nimitz and father of future admiral Chester Nimitz), announced that a contract was signed for the road's long-awaited construction. To bring about the construction, the businessmen of Fredericksburg, who had just formed the Progressive Business League, agreed to give a bonus of $150,000 cash, right-of-way through Gillespie County, and terminal facilities in the town.

The Chamber of Commerce of San Antonio had pledged to give $50,000 toward the construction of the railroad, to be paid when through train service was established between San Antonio and Fredericksburg.

Businessmen of Fredericksburg had already subscribed $100,000 of the bonus asked of them. The remainder was to be raised within ten days. There was a great deal of enthusiasm over the signing of the contract, which the Fredericksburg committee believed ensured them a road, as the contractor, Foster Crane, was to put up a bond of $250,000 to ensure the construction of the road and begin work immediately after Fredericksburg had raised its entire bonus.

The bonus which Fredericksburg gave for the road was the largest ever offered in the state. It was equivalent to $6,000 a mile for the twenty-five miles that spanned the distance from that town to Comfort, where the connection with the San Antonio and Aransas Pass was anticipated to be made. Should the road be built to Comfort, the contractor would have the benefit of almost twenty miles of "dump" that was thrown up years before when a new railroad seemed to be in the making. That project, however, failed, but the dump still stood, and much of it could be used with but little additional work thereon.

Final construction began early in January 1913 on the 23.9-mile line from Fredericksburg to a junction with the SA&AP line about three miles east of Comfort. The route closely paralleled the wagon road to San Antonio laid out sixty years earlier, which is the road you will travel.

When the railroad committee opened negotiations to obtain right-of-way through property on the south side of the big hill, several owners refused to part with their holdings at a figure considered reasonable by the committee; ironically, some of them were men who had subscribed liberally to the railroad bonus when it was being raised. Some tracts had to be condemned. When the railroad project was formerly up, they gave right-of-way privileges, and the grade was built. Under the statute of limitations, land ownership reverted to them when the enterprise failed to materialize. Now they did not feel inclined to let go of the property a second time. Even so, the right-of-way was being graded on the south side of the big hill in places where it had been secured. A camp had been pitched on the big hill in preparation for making the big cut.

In February, contractor Foster Crane's grading gangs were at work on both ends of the line and in between, and making the cut through the big hill had commenced.

Toward the end of March, more than two hundred men were at work on the tunnel through the big hill, one hundred at each end.

By the end of May, four miles of track of the nine-mile stretch between the SAP connection and the big hill had been laid. The roadbed had been laid between Fredericksburg and the big hill. The Young Men's Business League was already hard at work planning a celebration the likes of which had never before been seen. Manager R. A. Love advised that the new road would probably be in operation by August 1.

On July 16, at 4 a.m., the tunnel opened, just four hours later than had been predicted for weeks.

Two weeks later, Crane declared his determination to get the railroad to Fredericksburg by September 1, even if he had to put on night crews, despite the fact that he had until January 1 to finish. The last stick of timber in the long bridge leading up to the tunnel's south entrance had been put in place. That bridge, of which you will learn more, was the biggest piece of construction on the line, at seven hundred feet and 272,000 board feet of timber. The first engine had arrived several months earlier, and the second engine was due any day. The first engine had been busy between Waring and the tunnel.

The people of Fredericksburg were anxious to have railroad connections at the earliest possible moment. They had been waiting patiently for nearly a quarter of a century, and now that the hour of success was at hand, their anticipation had been aroused to a high pitch, and Crane was desirous of pleasing them. Only for the fact that there had been a delay in the arrival of the bridge timber, it was probable that the road would already have been completed. Promise had been given that the material for construction of the four small bridges that remained would be delivered that week, and a crew of forty-two bridge men was waiting to slap the timbers into place.

One hundred of the best beeves in all of Texas had been secured for the great barbecue, the principal feature of the welcoming jubilee. Citizens had also raised $5,000 for the entertainment of their guests from the surrounding territory. Fredericksburgers had for months been accumulating products of all descriptions with which to give the road a good send-off, and an order of fifty-one carloads of lumber from San Antonio had already been placed. The prediction, just as it had been for the Kerrville extension twenty-five years earlier, was that it would be one of the busiest roads in the country.

By September 25, all but four miles of the railroad had been completed, and the celebration was being planned for October 22 through 24. Round-trip tickets from San Antonio would be $1.50, and the number of passengers was limited to four hundred on the first train. There would be another special train for the general public.

But into every life a little rain must fall, and the San Antonio, Fredericksburg and Northern was no exception. Heavy rains drenched the region during the last week of September, and it was nearly mid-October before the damage done by the rains had been repaired and track laying was resumed. If nothing serious happened, it was predicted that the track would be finished to the Fredericksburg depot grounds in a few days; one hundred hands were at work on the road.

Well, the first train finally pulled into Fredericksburg on November 11 at 1:10 in the afternoon and was greeted by a large number of citizens. A band played as the train drew up, and there was a scene of general jubilation. About thirty passengers were aboard, several San Antonians taking advantage of the opportunity to ride on the first train into the mountain town. The train consisted of two passenger cars and several freight cars. Sixteen Fredericksburg citizens arose early that morning and were on board when the train left at four o'clock for the trip to the junction with the SAP near Waring. This trip really inaugurated the passenger service. With the arrival of the SAP train, passengers for the Fredericksburg train transferred to the new line, and the return trip was made.

Until that train arrived, it was said that Fredericksburg was the largest town in the country without railroad connections.

The town celebrated the arrival of the iron horse with a three-day blowout affair, from November 18 to 20.

Bad weather failed to dampen the ardor of Fredericksburg's citizens, and the events of the celebration in honor of the completion of the new railroad took place as if the sun were shining brightly and the ground was dry. Despite the rain, the people of the community decided to celebrate the dawn of a new era, and they made the occasion memorable despite the handicap under which they labored.

The first day began with the firing of salutes at 5:00, 5:30, and 6:00 a.m., and music at the fairgrounds at 9:00, followed by the driving of the last spike by Temple D. Smith, who had been a member of the railroad committee since 1889, and the christening of the railroad by Miss Olga Priess, who had been chosen by a vote to be the queen of the celebration; she broke a champagne bottle over a driving wheel of the first engine.

Wagon-borne farm folks had bumped and rattled into town from miles around just to catch a glimpse of a "live" locomotive. They watched in awe as the great mechanical beast chugged to a halt. One of the farmers, who had traveled many hours to bring his family to view the spectacle, was filled with compassion. Walking over to the locomotive, he patted the tender gently and said, "Poor thing, you must be very tired."

The hundreds of San Antonians who took Fredericksburg by storm the first day in two special trains did not allow the rain to cool their enthusiasm or to prevent them from partaking of the good things the town had to offer. They made merry in royal fashion, participating in all the ceremonies of the day and arranging several "stunts" of their own to make Fredericksburg feel like they were glad to be there and didn't mind a little thing like bad weather. Fredericksburg appreciated that attitude and took special pains to afford entertainment which made the excursionists remember the trip for a long time to come.

When the Chamber of Commerce special drew in that first afternoon, the rain desisted long enough to allow Temple D. Smith to drive the last spike and Miss Olga Priess, queen of the celebration, to christen the road by breaking a champagne bottle over a driving wheel of the first engine, but it started again when the crowds adjourned to the fairgrounds to hear the address of welcome and listen to responses by speakers from San Antonio and Austin.

But the big grandstand protected the people from the downpour, and they listened attentively to the succession of speeches, which all predicted a bright and shining future for the mountain town, "unsurpassed for its picturesque scenery by any section of the United States" and that it would soon become a city of eight or ten thousand in population, a goal that was achieved seventy-five years later.

The grand, free barbecue was given at the fairgrounds, followed by speech-making by such luminaries as Governor Oscar Colquitt.

The second day was Old Settlers Day, which also featured live music throughout the day and afternoon speakers. During "Old Settlers Day," the pioneer residents of the town and of Gillespie County were in the limelight—not sunlight, for the elements again frowned on the quaint mountain town.

The third day was blessed by bright sun and the presence of more than five thousand visitors. It was capped off by a grand parade at two in the afternoon to show off settlement in Texas by the Germans. The parade, which was several blocks long, was formed in three divisions, the first led by a float representing Germania and comprising a reproduction of the march of the first Germans from Galveston to New Braunfels, Fredericksburg, and other points of destination.

After that float came a prominent citizen in the guise of Prince Solms von Braunfels attended by twenty aides, all garbed fittingly. A procession of ox carts, prairie schooners, and foresters with axes followed. Members of various German singing societies marched in this division.

The second division was headed by an impersonator of Baron von Meusebach, escorted by the "home guard," in half-German, half-American outfits. In this part of the parade came the Fredericksburg float showing a fair-haired girl with a miniature railroad at her feet. She was accompanied by a blacksmith, stockman, and farmer, symbolizing the industries of the community.

"Ceres," the goddess of plenty, led the last division, the float being in the form of a cornucopia. Other floats entered by businessmen followed, as well as floats entered by San Antonio and Austin.

The celebration closed with dances and other social events. It was the greatest celebration the Hill Country had yet seen, surpassing even Kerrville's extravaganza welcoming the SAP in 1887.

The rains that fell during the celebration failed to dampen the general enthusiasm but were a harbinger of things to come. The town's joy, and rail service, was short-lived. Early in December, heavy rains caused big floods throughout the Hill Country and played havoc with the roadbed, submerging thousands of yards of track; out of twenty-one bridges on the road, seventeen had been washed away or were severely damaged. One end of the tunnel was filled up with driftwood and dirt. Fredericksburg was a month without train service. Many of the roadbeds in the state had suffered from the recent high waters, but this new and unsettled bed was probably hit harder than any of the others. The SAP line from San Antonio to Kerrville was in extra bad condition, and trains running over it were making very poor time.

The SA F&N tracks ended at S. Adams, between E. Park and Walch Avenue. The depot stood between the tracks and E. Park, just west of the intersection of E. Park and Live Oak, across from the county fairgrounds. Evidently there was at least one spur that followed E. Live Oak briefly to service Southwest Granite Company on Granite Avenue/Comfort Road at Live Oak. The tracks left the city limits at the corner of S. Washington and Walnut. There were several sidings between Lincoln and Washington.

Fredericksburg businessmen welcomed the railroad enthusiastically. They could now ship and receive merchandise much more quickly and cheaply. There were great quantities of locally grown cotton to be shipped out, as well as produce, grain, and livestock. Perhaps most happy was the Nagel Brothers Quarry on nearby Bear Mountain, which could now ship its beautiful red granite out to the rest of the world. Before the railroad's arrival, it cost $125 to ship a wagonload of granite to Gonzales. On the San Antonio and Fredericksburg Northern, it cost only $20 to ship the same load.

Travelers were also elated. Heretofore, voyageurs to Fredericksburg anticipated a fatiguing trip. Detraining at Waring or Comfort, they boarded a stagecoach for the last twenty-five miles, rattling over large rocks and steep hills, through dust and mud. When they reached Fredericksburg, they were usually fit only for a long rest. Many weary travelers took their rest at the famous "steamboat" Nimitz Hotel.

It's time now to take a stroll down sprawling Main Street, Fredericksburg's traditional principal thoroughfare, which looks much as it did on that big day in 1913. Reflecting the town's heritage, Main Street now sports street signs that designate it as "Hauptstrasse." Start at Main Street's traditional anchor, the Nimitz Hotel, which is now the flagship of the Admiral Nimitz Museum.

ADMIRAL NIMITZ MUSEUM

340 E. Main • 997-8600 • www.nimitz-museum.org • Open daily • Fee • W variable • The Nimitz Hotel is detailed at some length in the Mormon Trails trip, but much about the place and its founder can be said here.

German-born Charles Nimitz put to sea at the tender age of fourteen as a member of the German merchant marine. He and his family came to America four years later, in 1844, first settling in Charleston, South Carolina. By May 1846, Nimitz was riding on that first wagon train to Fredericksburg. He opened a four-room hotel on this spot in 1852. By the advent of the Civil War, the Nimitz establishment enjoyed a far-flung reputation as the frontier's cleanest and most congenial lodgings. Weary travelers enjoyed the inn's hot baths, cold beer and wine, and tables loaded down with white bread and fresh vegetables.

Nimitz's hustling drive was typical of the Fredericksburg business community; if it couldn't be made here, it could always be wagoneered here. Despite the rugged journey to and from major market centers, Fredericksburgers and their guests enjoyed a standard of living unknown elsewhere on the frontier. The merchants' aggressive drive, plus the farmers' productivity, multiplied by the needs and appetites of travelers on the Upper Emigrant Road, were the reasons why.

Nimitz's reputation was not tarnished by the hard times of the Civil War, even though the "coffee" was a blend of parched sweet potatoes and toasted barley, and the cellar brewery had to be turned into a cistern. Nimitz organized the Gillespie County Rifles (one of several local frontier guard units) and served as the local conscription officer for the Confederate Army. Nimitz was one of the few Gillespie County residents who had voted for secession. The Unionist sentiments of the majority were to cause them much trouble. Nimitz and his men were honorable and evenhanded in their dealings with these reluctant Confederates, but others were not.

Perhaps most unsavory was J. P. Waldrip. He gathered around him a band of men who were anxious to avoid frontline duty but eager to murder and loot for personal gain. Soon Waldrip and his men were known and feared as Die Haengebande (the Hangman's Band). Die Haengebande prowled the countryside raiding and pillaging outlying German farms and dragging prospective noose victims from their houses, in the name of the Confederacy.

When Captain Nimitz sent conscription notices to some of Waldrip's men, the plunderers proved their patriotism by invading the Nimitz Hotel for the purpose of stringing up its proprietor. Nimitz evaded the noose by taking refuge in the dank brewery-cistern.

James Duff, late of San Antonio, was another thorn in the county's side. Commander of the irregular Confederate unit, Duff's Partisan Rangers, Duff was sent to Kerr and Gillespie counties following the declaration of martial law on the frontier in 1862. Duff conducted a reign of terror in the name of the Confederacy. Duff was probably responsible for the cold-blooded massacre called the Battle of Nueces. Duff's Rangers continued their depredations for some months thereafter before being recalled to San Antonio.

With the end of the war, many members of Die Haengebande were indicted for their actions. J. P. Waldrip died in the shadow of the Nimitz Hotel, felled in 1867 by a bullet fired by the vengeful son-in-law of a man killed by Waldrip's gang of ruffians and bandits. Life at the Nimitz Hotel then settled down to a more peaceful, though still lively, style.

Nimitz passed away on April 29, 1911.

Stroll west from the Nimitz on this, the north side of Main Street. A few doors west is the old Dietz Bakery.

OLD DIETZ BAKERY

312 E. Main

This building was constructed in about 1876 by George Wahrmund and served as a millinery shop and boarding house before becoming the Dietz Bakery. The bakery eventually moved on down the street, and the building served a variety of purposes before being restored to its original lines. Its mansard roof, lacy porch balustrade, and spindly, delicate porch posts bring a little French flavor to Main Street.

STRIEGLING HOUSE

310 E. Main

Next door to the old bakery is the old Striegling house. When built in 1908, this two-story limestone block house was one of the real showplaces on Main Street. An aggressive, progressive businessman, Robert Striegling was an officer of the committee that brought the railroad to Fredericksburg.

On to the 200 block of E. Main Street, where the Keidel family complex anchors the east end of the block.

KEIDEL FAMILY MEDICAL COMPLEX

248 and 250 E. Main

First you encounter the limestone Keidel Memorial Hospital, then the old two-story limestone Keidel family home, then the vintage Keidel Drug Store. Built in 1909, the latter was Fredericksburg's—and possibly the nation's—first medical arts complex. Keidel brothers Victor (physician) and Felix and Werner (dentists) maintained offices upstairs, while Kurt (pharmacist) ran the drugstore downstairs. Three distinguished generations of Keidel physicians served Gillespie County. Kurt's daughter Margaret Keidel owned and ran the drugstore until it closed a few years ago. Dr. Wilhelm Keidel was Gillespie County's first doctor and county judge. His grandson Victor is credited with performing the first blood transfusion in Texas. Son Albert was a schoolmate of X-ray pioneer W. C. Roentgen in Germany.

Wilhelm was trained in Germany and came to Texas in 1845 at age twenty. He enlisted in the U.S. Army for six months when the Mexican War broke out. He came to Fredericksburg to serve as the Emigration Company's doctor, although he wasn't a member of the first wagon train. Family legend has it that the job was to be only temporary. He was supposed to go to Johns Hopkins University in Baltimore for additional training. But he loved it here so much he decided to stay and was elected county judge the next year. A branch of the family still lives in Baltimore.

"The spring of 1847 was a good one, probably," Kurt's daughter, Miss Margaret Keidel, once observed. "The Hill Country—that is Mason, Willow City, Fredericksburg—was the only place you found bluebonnets then." But a friend of hers has always maintained that her grandmother brought the first lupinus (bluebonnet) seeds with her from Germany and then planted them here. "I was in Germany in August one year walking with a forest ranger in a preserve, and he showed me a patch of bluebonnets that were waist high," Keidel said, adding a final twist.

Wilhelm and the rest of the Germans were probably enamored with the babbling seasonal creeks and bowers of flowers. "German people are romantic," she declared, disputing the notion that Germans are a cold, reserved people. "The German language is romantic in that it paints pretty pictures. The romantic books about Texas and the Republic were as strong a lure as political or religious oppression at home." Some of the more optimistic emigrants kept mistaking the gnarled, twisted oaks for olive trees as their burdened wagons inched toward their new home at the southernmost edge of the Llano Uplift.

WHITE ELEPHANT SALOON

242 E. Main

Next door to the old Keidel Drug Store is one of Fredericksburg's most eye-catching buildings, the White Elephant Saloon, with its imported bas-relief carved white elephant above the front door. J. W. Kleck built this saloon back in 1888, when moonshine sold for fifteen cents a quart and thirteen saloons stood ready to slake a dusty throat's thirst. Most of Fredericksburg's gingerbread is wood, but elaborate wrought-iron filigree traces the White Elephant's roofline. A touch of old New Orleans, mais oui?

During the 1880s, White Elephant saloons appeared in towns and cities throughout Texas and the United States, acclaimed as "places of resort for gentlemen" and featuring long mahogany or cherrywood bars with elaborately carved ornamental details, above which hung numerous mirrors. Even little Brownwood, Texas, had its own White Elephant saloon. Wyatt Earp opened a White Elephant Saloon in Eagle City, Idaho, in 1883 or 1884. Austin, famous for its contrary nature in Texas, had its Black Elephant saloon, which, not surprisingly, catered to the city's black population. Bessie Smith began her singing career in front of Chattanooga's White Elephant saloon, about 1903, at the tender age of nine.

Fredericksburg's White Elephant was more docile than most; Fort Worth's White Elephant was best known for the famous shootout between "Little" Luke Short and "Long-haired Jim" Courtright, in 1887.

San Antonio's White Elephant Saloon, located on the city's main square, figured prominently in the assassination of Austin's most famous pistolero, Ben Thompson, in 1884. Bat Masterson wrote of Thompson, "It is doubtful if in his time there was another man living who equaled him with a pistol in a life-and-death struggle."

A. WALTER JEWELLER BUILDING

128 E. Main

In the 100 block of E. Main, you come to the old A. Walter Jeweller building. This common little structure is saved from anonymity by the exquisite center stone of its Alamo cornice. The smooth-as-glass red Bear Mountain granite bears an etched Roman-numeraled clock face set at ten o'clock and the surrounding words "A. Walter Jeweller." Alphonse Walter built the place in 1908. Dorer's specializes in antique watches and clocks.

OLD FREDERICKSBURG BANK

120 E. Main

The next point of interest west is the delightful, romantic old Bank of Fredericksburg building. Alfred Giles designed this turreted, castle-like bit of the Old World in about 1889, and the prominent local financier Temple Smith erected it that same year.

Most folks were rather suspicious of banks back then—after all, this was long before the advent of the FDIC and other federal regulatory agencies. So most bankers, Temple Smith included, erected miniature castles or cathedrals like this one to house their customers' money; "A mighty fortress is our bank," to parody Martin Luther. One of the most tireless railroad boosters in town, "Banker" Smith spent twenty-five years getting his rails, the quest for which he embarked upon almost as soon as he arrived in Fredericksburg.

At the end of this block, where it intersects Adams Street, E. Main becomes W. Main. Cross Adams. Walk a few more feet west on Main and you see a reproduction of the old Vereinskirche on your right, and the Gillespie County courthouses on your left. You are now on the Marketplatz, or Market Square.

VEREINSKIRCHE AND ARCHIVES MUSEUM

100 block of N. Main, in the Marketplatz • 997-7832 • Open Monday through Saturday 10–5 • Fee • W with assistance

Set back from Main Street, in the middle of the old market square is the Vereinskirche, whose coffee mill/Old World lines epitomize Fredericksburg's essential Germanness. Built a year after the Germans' arrival, the Vereinskirche (Society's Church) was the first public building erected. It served as a nondenominational church, school, and meeting hall. The cupola was used to watch the Indians during service. The church received its name from some cowboys who saw it for the first time.

This Vereinskirche is actually a faithfully rendered reproduction of the original (except the original had fachwerk, or "half-timber," walls), which stood in the center of Main Street, between the courthouse square and the market square. The first Vereinskirche was torn down shortly after Fredericksburg's Golden Anniversary Celebration in 1896. This reproduction was built in 1935–1936 in preparation for the Texas Centennial Celebration. The coffee mill church houses the Gillespie County Archives and local history collection, along with a collection of objects from early Gillespie County days, and rotating special displays.

Also in Market Square is a bust and plaque commemorating Jacob Brodbeck, an early aviation pioneer. Born in Germany in 1821, he immigrated to Texas in 1846. He taught school in the Vereinskirche in 1847, and later served as Gillespie County surveyor and district school supervisor. In 1863, he and his family moved to San Antonio. Before leaving Germany, Brodbeck had attempted to invent a clock that would run without winding. Once in Texas, he adapted his ideas to manned flight. By 1863, he had constructed a miniature airplane with a rudder, wings, and a propeller powered by coiled springs. The wings were partly movable. He also added a propeller screw for water navigation. He calculated that the plane's motive power and the wind's direction would allow for a flight speed of between thirty and one hundred miles per hour. By 1865, he was offering "certificates of interest" to potential investors in San Antonio and Gillespie County to finance his trial flight.

He gave some rather sketchy details of his air-ship to the *Galveston Tri-Weekly News*.

The air-ship consists of three main parts.

1. The lower suspended portion, formed like a ship with a very short prow to cut the air; it serves to hold the aeronaut, and also the power-producing engine with all the steering apparatus. This portion is shut up all around to prevent the rapid motion from affecting the breathing of the man within.
2. The upper portion, or flying apparatus, which makes use of the resistance of the air, consists of a system of wings, partly moveable, partly immovable, presenting the appearance of horizontal sails, but having functions entirely different from the sails of vessels.
3. The portion producing the forward motion consists either of two screws, which can be revolved with equal or unequal motion, so as to serve the purpose of lateral steering, or of wings of a peculiar construction. The preference to be given to one or the other depends on the force of the motive power. Another apparatus controls the ascending motion.

Supposedly he built a prototype and flew it several hundred feet, at an altitude "several feet higher than a tall tree," but crashed to the ground when the springs wound down. Brodbeck still hadn't solved the rewinding problem. He toured the eastern United States speaking publicly and seeking financial support but was unsuccessful. Some of his papers were stolen in Michigan. He returned to Gillespie County in 1870 and bought a farm at Luckenbach. Although unable to obtain a patent on his invention, he lived to see the Wright brothers validate his belief in man's ability to fly. Brodbeck died on his farm in 1910.

PIONEER PLACE GARDEN

Behind the Vereinskirche • Free • W

The Pioneer Place Garden is a quiet little green spot whose most obvious feature is the old wooden waterwheel, dedicated by the people of Fredericksburg to Lyman Wight's long-vanished Mormon colony at nearby Zodiac, in gratitude for the invaluable help given by the Mormons during the difficult early years.

OLD SCHMIDT HOTEL

218 W. Main

Old Charlie Nimitz's hotel was not without competition in early-day Fredericksburg. Located midway in the next block west is the double-porched two-story limestone building put up as a hotel in 1857 by Ludwig Schmidt. It served travelers for half a century. Since then, it has been a store, a saloon, a drugstore, and a doctor's office.

On to the 300 block of W. Main, where you first see a state historical marker.

The historical marker tells the story of Englebert Krauskopf, gunsmith, and Adolph Lungkwitz, silversmith, who together invented a guncap-making machine. 'Twas midway into the Civil War, and the Confederates were desperate for munitions. Little cottage industries were springing up all across Texas and the rest of the South. While Joseph Eubanks was building his cotton cards factory on the San Gabriel River down at Circleville, artisan Adolph Lungkwitz (brother of painter Hermann Lungkwitz) and mechanic Krauskopf were scheming a method of mass producing cheap and reliable firing caps. Their conception was sharpened by the leanness of frontier life, their execution equally hindered by it. But they persevered and were soon supplying the Confederate Army and their own Hill Country neighbors with thousands of caps marked with the factory's distinctive lone star. The old factory no longer stands, but other remnants of the Krauskopf family's business enterprises remain.

KRAUSKOPF STORE

312 W. Main

Englebert Krauskopf's boy, Oscar, ran a hardware store in this structure for years. All in all, four generations of Krauskopfs operated the hardware store, and three generations tended the general store next door. The building sports an attractive cast-metal cornice.

RUDOLPH ITZ SALOON

320 W. Main

Just a few feet farther west is the old Itz Saloon. Many early builders obscured their buildings' rocky origins by covering the rough rock surfaces with stucco, especially when the stone used was limestone rubble. Such was the case with Rudolph Itz, who built this place shortly after the Civil War. It was long a popular saloon; with the advent of Prohibition, it became a meat market.

ZION LUTHERAN CHURCH

426 W. Main

When Fredericksburg was founded, there wasn't a Lutheran congregation or pastor in the state. Six of Fredericksburg's founding families were Lutheran. They organized under the leadership of a layman, William Schumaker, a tailor and book dealer from Wuppenthal. The Lutherans weren't satisfied with the Vereinskirche minister and started to look for a minister. They heard of a fellow named Schneider, who lived in Victoria. He came to visit but turned out to be a Methodist missionary. Schneider organized a Methodist group, and some followed him. Some of the remaining Lutherans attempted to follow Gottlieb Burchard Dangers, pastor of the Evangelical Protestant Church at the Vereinskirche, who served from 1849 to 1869. But he disappointed them, and they pulled away again. In 1850, eleven Lutheran pastors came to Texas. In 1852, Pastor P. F. Zizelman came to Fredericksburg to organize Zion. The Zion congregation bought a lot on Main Street for forty-five dollars. The first rock church was built there in 1853. A second church was built 1884 and was then enlarged and remodeled in 1908.

Other Lutherans continued to worship at the Vereinskirche until 1893, when they built Holy Ghost Lutheran Church at 113 E. San Antonio. They hung a bell from the Vereinskirche in the tower of the new church, which was remodeled and enlarged to its present size in 1949. Holy Ghost was one of the last churches in Texas to hold regular German-language services, and German is still used occasionally in worship services.

Cross Main now, over to its south side, where you encounter the Uptown Welcome Center and Pioneer Museum complex.

UPTOWN WELCOME CENTER

325 W. Main • Open daily

This visitor center has maps, dining and attractions guides, and other useful information. The Dambach-Besier House stood at 515 E. Main Street for 135 years and was moved here in 2005 where it was reconstructed to form the entrance to the Pioneer Museum and serve as the Fredericksburg Convention and Visitors Bureau Uptown Welcome Center. F. Dambach built the limestone house in 1869. It was purchased by the Besier family for $400 in 1881.

PIONEER MEMORIAL MUSEUM

325 West Main • 990-8441 • www.pioneermuseum.net • Open daily during summer months, closed Sunday and Monday rest of year • Fee • W variable

The Pioneer Museum is actually a collection of buildings that includes the Weber family Sunday house, the Fassel home, the Kammlah barn, the Kammlah store and home, and the Fire Department Museum.

The Henry Kammlah family came to Texas in 1845 and to Fredericksburg in 1846. In 1849, Henry Kammlah the elder built the front four rooms and attic of this rambling family complex. Into this space were crowded both his growing family and his mercantile store. His son Henry Kammlah was a freight driver and survivor of the Battle of Nueces before he stepped into his father's storekeeping shoes. In the meantime, the house/store continued to grow; eight more rooms and a smokehouse were added. The store remained open until 1924. The Gillespie County Historical Society bought the house in 1955 and turned it into a museum. Today the front two rooms are filled with much of the store's old inventory. Some of the back rooms are filled with Kammlah family articles. Other rooms contain displays depicting pioneer life, centering on the Meusebach and Nimitz families. A wine cellar and three open-hearth kitchens round out the Kammlah house.

The Fassel house is furnished with period furniture. Its builder, Mathias Fassel, was a skilled wheelwright who helped keep Fredericksburg's rolling stock in repair. He was a busy man.

The Weber Sunday house was built in 1904 by August Weber. Most Sunday houses date between 1890 and 1920. German ranchers and farmers who lived far from town built them so that they might have a place to stay in town over the weekend, when they came in from the farm to shop and go to church, hence the name Sunday house. A typical Sunday house has one room with a lean-to kitchen out back and a sleeping loft up top, which is reached by an outside stairway or ladder. The boys in the family usually slept in the loft. Most Sunday houses were built of wood, but some were rock. It's important to remember that not every tiny house in Fredericksburg is a Sunday house; some people just had neither the money nor the inclination to build anything larger. Clusters of Sunday houses also developed around St. Paul Lutheran Church in Cave Creek and in the village of Harper. Sunday house use began to die out in the 1920s with the advent of motor vehicles and improved roads.

The story of the Fire Department Museum begins with Fredericksburg Social Turn Verein, established in 1871 in the tradition of German gymnastic clubs. The club opened with a gymnastics school and a nine-pin bowling alley. In 1883, the club sponsored a fire brigade that became the City Volunteer Fire Department.

The Fire Department Museum houses the town's turn-of-the century hand pumper, hose cart, chemical tank, and steam pumper inside a replica of the town's original fire station. The town's original fire-alarm bell is mounted atop the building. The oldest piece of equipment in the museum is a 1902 hand pumper that took six men to operate. A hose cart that dates to 1905 carried axes and a hose.

In 1909, the department purchased the chemical engine on display. It is not much more than a water tank on wheels. The tank contained a mixture of water and bicarbonate of soda (baking soda). When the wagon arrived at a fire, acid was added to the water and soda, which built up pressure in the tank and forced the water out through the narrow-diameter hose. Before the acid was added, a designated shaker man would shake the tank by means of a lever to thoroughly mix the water and soda. When it was mixed thoroughly, the acid was added. The chemical engine worked well when the fire was small and within reach. At larger fires, the chemical engine served as the "quick attack" rig while the steamer engine was set up.

The most interesting piece is the 1911 American LaFrance Cosmopolitan steam engine, which was pulled by hand, horse, or Model T truck. This steamer is one of seven still existing from the twenty-one that were completed between

1902 and 1912. With a capacity of 250 gallons, this was the smallest steamer manufactured. It is six feet high, seven feet long, three feet eight inches wide, and weighs 1,900 pounds. The engine's pumping capacity was 250 gallons per minute. It was a bit of a fire hazard itself, spewing red-hot cinders from its stovepipe exhaust. The Cosmopolitan and the chemical engine are still functional, though they are never activated. The rolling stock is brought out at least once a year for parades; call the museum for parade schedules.

The Walton-Smith log cabin was originally located near the Gillespie/Llano county line. Only the fourteen-by-fourteen-foot core of the cabin is original. The limestone chimney, front porch, and kitchen were added to duplicate the cabin's original appearance. The one-room White Oak School was moved here a few years ago. Children's educational and entertainment workshops are often held there.

At the southwest corner of the Pioneer Museum complex is the old First Methodist Church, which now serves as Historical Society offices and meeting room. It has displays of barbed wire and early Fredericksburg furniture. This is the oldest Methodist church in the Hill Country, having been built in 1855 of native limestone. Subsequent remodelings in 1912, 1923, and 1948 brought it to its current size and appearance. The original congregation split after the Civil War. The First Methodist Church stayed here, while the dissenters moved to Edison Street and founded the Edison Street Methodist Church. It only took a century, but the two congregations patched up their differences and reunited in 1970 as the Fredericksburg United Methodist Church. The new church kept the Edison Street sanctuary, and in the true Fredericksburg fashion of recycling buildings instead of tearing them down and building new ones, the congregation sold the old church building to the Historical Society in 1978.

ST. MARY'S CHURCHES

300 block of W. San Antonio

On the back side of the 300 block of San Antonio are located two of Fredericksburg's most imposing churches, the Marien Kirche (old St. Mary's) and the newer St. Mary's Church. They make a marvelous pair. Work on the Marien Kirche started in 1860 and was finished during the early days of the Civil War. The church's most distinctive feature is its stone spire, a strong reflection of the homeland Gothic. It has recently been restored. "New" St. Mary's supplanted the Marien Kirche in 1906, more finely detailed and delicate in appearance but equally Gothic. The interior paintings and stenciling rival those of the painted churches of Fayette County.

OLD FREDERICKSBURG POST OFFICE

125 W. Main

The attraction here is inside: the mural, "Loading Cattle," painted by Otis Dozier in 1942, depicting a cowboy on horseback shooing cattle into a railroad cattle car. Post office murals like this survive around the state as a reminder of the inspirational power of art during troubled times and the innovative ways in which the Franklin Roosevelt administration worked to dig America out of the Great Depression.

Completed between 1934 and 1943, and administered by the U.S. Treasury Department, the murals were paid for out of the 1 percent of construction costs reserved for building decorations. Beyond providing work for artists, the murals were meant to bring quality art to the American people and to tell the story of America. In Texas, mural subjects included Indians, Texas Rangers, Texas Longhorns, and cowboys. Only post offices built during the period were eligible to receive the murals. The artists were selected by anonymous competition, which gave women and minority artists a fair chance to receive a commission. Otis Dozier (1904–1987) also painted murals for post offices in Giddings and Arlington. Other Hill Country/Central Texas post offices with murals are located in Elgin, La Grange, Lockhart, and Smithville.

PIONEER MEMORIAL LIBRARY/OLD COURTHOUSE

Center of the courthouse square • 997-6515 • Monday through Thursday • Free • W

Fredericksburg has had three courthouses. The first stood where the post office is currently located. Of the two remaining, it is the second, limestone courthouse that catches the eye. Alfred Giles designed this 1882 edifice in the Romanesque Revival style, as evidenced by its formal balance, heavy decorative consoles, and classical roof slopes. The cut stonework at the corners and around the openings contributes to its stateliness while providing a pleasing contrast to the rougher, pitch-face stones that make up the main body. The roof ridges are topped with an intricate wrought-iron cresting. The limestone came from nearby quarries, which helped keep the building's final cost down to $23,000. Restored in 1967, the building's first story houses the Pioneer Memorial Library, while the second story contains a community hall and a beautiful wall tapestry depicting the history of Fredericksburg.

OLD GILLESPIE COUNTY JAIL

100 block W. San Antonio, directly behind the courthouse square • Open by appointment and on special occasions. Call the Gillespie County Historical Society, 997-2835.

This two-story limestone fortress is the second of Gillespie County's jails and was built in 1885. Abandoned as a jail in 1939, it stood various county duties until the late 1970s, when Fredericksburg Heritage Foundation funds, matched by Texas Historical Commission dollars, made its restoration possible. The ground floor housed a holding area and the sheriff's office and living quarters, which are authentically furnished. The second floor had two steel-clad cells located against the east wall and maximum security cells in the center and at the back. Graffiti decades old still mars the cell walls upstairs. The building is locked, but the wrought-iron gate to the jail yard is kept unlocked so that visitors may examine the building's exterior. You will shudder at the jagged glass shards sticking out along the top of the west rock wall, a crude but effective way to keep prisoners from scaling the wall, a security method often seen in Mexico.

BONN BUILDING

121 E. Main

The Nagel Brothers supplied much of the rich red granite used in Fredericksburg's buildings, as evidenced by Main Street cornerstones. The Nagels were not above the hard sell, as can be seen in several of the cornerstones. One of the best of these decorates the Bonn building, built by R. C. Bonn in 1913 and trimmed in Nagel red granite. An immaculately frocked lady and top-hatted gentleman flank the inscription "R. C. Bonn, 1913, A Convincing Fact That the Nagel Bros Have the Best Granite for Building and Monumental Work."

VAN DER STUCKEN BIRTHPLACE

123 E. Main

On down E. Main is the site where noted American composer and conductor Frank van der Stucken's birthplace once stood. Frank van der Stucken the younger was born on this spot in 1858. With the end of the Civil War, van der Stucken the elder sold out his business interests here and sailed his family to Belgium, where the gifted young Frank could receive the best musical instruction. He studied under the noted Austrian Franz Liszt, finally returning to America in 1884. He was promptly highly acclaimed here as both composer and conductor. Van der Stucken became the first musical director of the Cincinnati Symphony Orchestra in 1895. In the following years, van der Stucken received many international awards. He died in 1929 in Hamburg, Germany.

FREDERICKSBURG BAKERY

141 E. Main • 997-3254 • Tuesday through Saturday 8–5:15 • No Cr. • W

Next on this tour is the last of Fredericksburg's legendary bakeries, with the closing of Dietz Bakery. The building containing the Fredericksburg Bakery was erected by Louis Priess in 1889. Here he conducted his general store on the ground floor and raised his family on the second level. The two-story limestone structure is imposing yet coquettishly frilly with its rail-thin iron porch posts and lacy brackets and porch balustrades. Priess sold his building in 1923 to George Stucke, who turned the store into a bakery, which it has been ever since. The giant wood-stoked oven gave way in 1945 to more modern gas-fired ovens, and the ownership has changed. But the baked goods haven't suffered one whit over the years. All the white, wheat, and dark breads are good; the iced cinnamon-nut and banana loaves do anyone's breakfast table proud. You need to get here before noon for the best bread selection, for many Fredericksburgers will eat from no other loaf.

NIMITZ BIRTHPLACE

247 E. Main • Historical marker

On to the 200 block, where toward the end of the block you encounter the little whitewashed stucco cottage that was future Fleet Admiral Chester Nimitz's birthplace in 1885. Two of his uncles Henke operated meat markets on Main Street, and the old downtown Henke Meat Market stands next door to the Nimitz cottage, on the corner. The admiral's birth room contains old family photos.

Another block and you're back across the street from the Nimitz Museum. Residential Fredericksburg has just as much to see as Main Street Fredericksburg. Austin, Schubert, and Travis streets, running parallel to and north of Main, and San Antonio and Creek to the south, are lined with an extensive variety of vintage homes and businesses. This tour of residential Fredericksburg, which is admittedly just a sampling of the whole, starts with the 100 block of E. Austin, which runs parallel to Main one block north.

SCHANDUA HOUSE

111 E. Austin • Next to Fredericksburg Bible Church

In the 100 block of E. Austin, you see the tiny rock Schandua house, Fredericksburg's only fully authentic house restoration, right down to the absence of electricity and indoor plumbing.

VAN DER STUCKEN HOME

102 W. Austin at Adams

The stately two-story van der Stucken home stands guard over the market square, at the corner of W. Austin and N. Adams. Alfred van der Stucken, cousin of Frank van der Stucken the conductor, started work on this house in the 1890s. The house was originally one story, but van der Stucken added on a second story as his family grew. The white gingerbread porch trim and balustrades plus the heavy cornice provide a brilliant frosting contrast to the weathered gray limestone walls. Alfred was a prominent miller and backer of the railroad. Upon van der Stucken's move to San Antonio in 1912, the house and mill passed into the hands of others.

VAN DER STUCKEN HOME

114 W. Austin

On down at the west end of this block is another van der Stucken house. Felix van der Stucken built the one-story section of this limestone house soon after he bought the lot in 1864. The two-story section was added later. Its peculiar combination of Victorian and Greek Revival styles, along with its broad double front porch and markedly shallow roof, makes it one of Fredericksburg's most distinctive homes. Felix built a steam roller mill here in Fredericksburg during the postwar years, and it became famous as the Reliance Roller Mills.

The 400 block of W. Austin has several homes of interest.

JOHN WALTER HOME

408 W. Austin

First on your right is the John Walter home, a place that couldn't seem to stop growing once it got started. John Walter first built the little log cabin out front in 1867. Soon he added to the cabin a room behind and two on the side made of quarry-faced limestone blocks. Elected Gillespie County sheriff in 1876, Walter on occasion used his home as a jail, specifically the big one-room rock kitchen, which connected to the main house by a Durchgang (enclosed walkway). Its two windows are still barred. The latest addition, built in the late 1970s, is the imitation fachwerk section on the far side of the kitchen.

STRACKBEIN-ROEDER HOME

414 W. Austin

This simple, unassuming little house is typical of the second generation of Fredericksburg homes, the successors to fachwerk and log. The attic/sleeping gable is reached by an outside staircase, and two of the four original rooms lack windows.

BIERSCHWALE HOME

110 N. Bowie at Austin • B&B inn

Alfred Giles designed this home for William Bierschwale in 1889. Its style is distinctively Giles. County official, legislator, and banker, Bierschwale was an unwavering railroad booster.

Turn right on Bowie. At the end of this first block, you see on your left the distinctive double-chimneyed limestone house designed and built in 1856 by Johan Peter Tatsch.

TATSCH HOME

Bowie and Schubert • Historical marker

Tatsch's detailed blueprints for the house now reside in the Library of Congress, and the house is listed on the Historic American Builders Survey. Most noteworthy is the huge offset fireplace, which is large enough to roast a whole ox. A Tischlermeister (master furniture maker), Tatsch supervised the stonemasons' work and did the woodwork himself. Churns, buckets, barrels, bedsteads, wardrobes, rockers, and even spinning wheels—with nary a nail or screw in the lot—were turned out by his skilled hands. Today his solid handcrafted works command premium prices from collectors.

Turn left on W. Schubert from the Tatsch house; then turn left again onto Acorn 1 block later. Cross Main.

KLINGELHOEFER HOUSE

701 W. Main at S. Acorn

Just after you cross Main, on your right is the home begun by Johann Klingelhoefer soon after his arrival here from Germany in 1847. It began as a one-pen fachwerk cabin, expanding room by room as the family grew. Klingelhoefer was the other man in the county court judge controversy involving Mormon leader Lyman Wight. The final victor in their pitched battle for the office, Klingelhoefer served for many years thereafter.

Turn left on W. Creek, two blocks south of Main.

ST. BARNABAS EPISCOPAL CHURCH

S. Bowie and W. Creek • Historical marker

Peter Walter started work on this little fachwerk cottage soon after his arrival in 1846, making it one of the oldest houses in Fredericksburg still standing today. A wagoneer, Walter farmed the surrounding land between supply runs to Fort McKavett. St. Barnabas Parish bought the little house in 1952, restoring and consecrating it as a mission in 1954. It sits in the churchyard on your right.

KRIEGER HOUSE

512 W. Creek

Over in the next block on your left is the old bachelor Bude (shanty) of Adam Krieger and George Geyer. An 1848 whitewashed fachwerk cottage, the handsomely restored little house has an even older one-room log cabin out back.

PAPE AND DANGERS HOUSES

200 block of W. Creek • Historical markers

In the middle of the 200 block of W. Creek stand the old Pape log cabin and the little Dangers stone house, both of which sport historical markers. The Pape cabin is the older of the pair and is perhaps the oldest surviving structure in the town. The Friedrich Pape family arrived here in May 1846, one of Fredericksburg's first forty families. It had been a rough trip from Germany for the Papes. Three of the children had died on the boat over, and by the time the surviving Papes reached Fredericksburg, Mother Pape was very ill. The settlers communally built this little cabin for the ailing woman shortly after their arrival. They used post-oak logs cut nearby and probably topped it with a thatched grass roof until a shake roof could be constructed. Friedrich sold the lot and cabin to the Reverend Gottlieb Dangers a couple of years later, and Dangers then built the front section of the rock house in about 1851. He added two back rooms and a cellar in 1857.

JORDAN-TATSCH HOME

101 W. Creek

This is another 1850s vintage rock house, with subsequent frame additions.

The remaining three blocks of Creek are lined with a nice variety of old and not-so-old homes. Turn left on S. Lincoln at Creek's dead end. Turn right on Main Street/US 290.

KIEHNE HOME

405 E. Main • Historical marker

Friedrich Kiehne and wife Maria built this house in 1850, and it was Fredericksburg's first stone building, its first really permanent dwelling. Kiehne was a blacksmith, and he made most of the window hardware used in his home.

The double front porches with the connecting stairway give it a distinctive look. The Kiehne home is one of the most immaculately restored buildings in Fredericksburg.

DINING

ALTDORF RESTAURANT

301 W. Main • 997-7865 • Open daily • Lunch and dinner • W

Located inside an 1860 limestone house, Altdorf's dining room is pleasant enough, but in nice weather, take lunch or that afternoon break outside in the biergarten. It has an American-Mexican-German menu, with lots of sandwiches and finger foods, and a good beer selection.

ANDY'S DINER

413 S. Washington (US 87) • 997-3744 • Open daily Tuesday through Saturday for breakfast, lunch, and dinner; Sunday and Monday breakfast and lunch • No Cr. • W

Andy's is a favorite down-home eating spot for many locals, serving up home-style Anglo-German food in unpretentious, un-tourist surroundings.

ENGEL'S DELI

320 E. Main • 997-3176 • Open Monday through Saturday • Breakfast, lunch • V, MC

Engel's has good sandwiches, salads, soups, and pastries that are mostly made on the premises. Daily lunch specials are usually a good bet.

GEORGE'S OLD GERMAN BAKERY AND RESTAURANT

225 W. Main • 997-9084 • Closed Tuesday and Wednesday, open Thursday through Monday • Breakfast and lunch • W

They serve hearty German-Texas breakfasts, sandwiches and salads, and a variety of German main dishes. Good breads and pastries are baked on the premises.

HILL TOP CAFE

US 87, 10 mi. northwest of Fredericksburg • 830-997-8922 • www.hill-topcafe.com • Open Tuesday through Sunday, lunch and dinner • Cr. • W

Not your typical Texas highway cafe, the Hill Top serves a variety of American, Cajun, and Greek dishes for lunch and dinner, with an emphasis on fresh ingredients. It features a New Orleans-style Sunday brunch; live, lively (blues, jazz, boogie-woogie) piano music on weekends; and a casual atmosphere. Reservations are recommended.

SHOPPING AND OTHER ATTRACTIONS

DUTCHMAN'S MARKET

1609 E. Main (US 290), 2 miles east of the courthouse, just past Fort Martin Scott • 997-5693 • W

A variety of sausages, bacon, ham, jerky, jams, and jellies are cured or made using traditional Hill Country German methods. There are also cheeses and gift packages.

FREDERICKSBURG BREWING COMPANY

245 E. Main • 997-1646 • www.yourbrewery.com • Open daily, lunch and dinner

This brewpub dates only to 1994, but it fits in like an old-timer. A rotating variety of German-style lagers, pilsners, ales, and porters are brewed in the line of copper and stainless steel tanks. There is an enclosed beer garden out back. Lunch and dinner are served. B&B lodgings are located above the brewery.

Fredericksburgers have always been fond of their beer, and they weren't about to let Prohibition deny their thirst, as illustrated by the following joke: A visitor to Fredericksburg during prohibition asked a local where he might get a beer. He was told, "Any house where you see a light in the window, knock on the door. No use knocking at the other houses because there's nobody home."

FREDERICKSBURG HERB FARM

407 Whitney, off Milam • 997-8615 • www.fredericksburgherbfarm.com • Closed Monday • W

German gardens were the envy of their Anglo neighbors, who often bought the Germans' excess produce. The Fredericksburg Herb Farm carries on this tradition of urban farming. Hundreds of varieties of flowering, culinary, and ornamental herbs are organically grown and harvested for gourmet vinegars, olive oils, seasonings, teas, blossom potpourris, wreaths, bath potions, and body fragrances. A variety of old log, stone, and frame buildings house a B&B, restaurant, candle shop, and spa.

OPA'S SMOKED MEATS

410 S. Washington (US 87), 1 mile south of Main • 800-543-6750 • www.opassmokedmeats.com • Closed Sunday

Opa's Smoked Meats makes and sells a variety of smoked sausages, turkey, chicken, ham, bacon, and more. It has been in business since 1947.

GISH'S OLD WEST MUSEUM

502 N. Milam • 997-2794 • Open most afternoons, but call ahead to make sure

If it has anything to do with cowboys or lawmen, from the 1870s to the 1920s, Joe Gish has it or wants it. At his museum, you'll find badges, guns, hats, chaps, boots, saddles, clothes, movie posters, autographed photos, and more.

FREDERICKSBURG FUDGE

105 N. Llano • 997-0533 • www.fbgfudge.com • Open daily • W

Fredericksburg Fudge makes several flavors of creamy fudge and various varieties of hand-dipped chocolates and novelty candies. Those who are allergic to chocolate can indulge in white chocolate.

BERKMAN BOOKS

416 E. Main, 1 block east of Nimitz Museum • 997-1535 • www.berkman books.com • Open Monday through Saturday

Here you'll find new, used, and rare books, including local and Texana titles, as well as antique maps and prints.

SCHWETTMANN'S EMPORIUM

305 W. Main • 997-4448 • Open daily; Sunday afternoons

Schwettmann's is a stuffed zoo, with everything from ostriches to trophy jackalopes. Looking for deerskin shoes, a zebra skin, or a buffalo robe? You've come to the right place. How about a wild turkey, poised for flight, for your living room?

SIDE TRIPS

LUCKENBACH

Take US 290 east to FM 1376, then south to Luckenbach. 13 miles from Fredericksburg • 830-997-3224 • www.luckenbachtexas.com • W variable

Luckenbach, Texas, made world-famous by Waylon Jennings and Willie Nelson in the song of the same name, began its slow ascent to fame in the early 1850s, when brothers Albert, William, and August Luckenbach, along with other Germans from Fredericksburg, began to settle here in the hilly, blackland section of Gillespie County. William Luckenbach opened a post office in 1854, named "South Grape Creek," which operated for eleven years. August Engel opened a new post office in 1886 and named it Luckenbach. Engel and his descendants added a blacksmith shop, dance hall, general store, and cotton gin. In 1970, the Engel family sold the "town" to Hondo Crouch, Kathy Morgan, and Guich Koock. Hondo began to promote the town; Jerry Jeff Walker recorded his famous, live 1973 *Viva Terlingua* album here. Then came "the song," and the highway department quit putting up Luckenbach highway signs because people kept stealing them. Crouch was only briefly able to enjoy Luckenbach's international notoriety; he died of a heart attack in 1976. But the Luckenbach scene and lifestyle have persisted. The town is open daily, but the store is normally closed on Wednesdays. Dances take place occasionally, and weekend, shade-tree jam sessions often coalesce during peak season. Toss some washers or horseshoes, whittle, or drink a beer. The store sells T-shirts, cassette tapes, prints, and pottery. Barbecue is available on weekends.

LODGING

Fredericksburg can no longer boast of a Nimitz-class hotel, but there is no shortage of clean and pleasant accommodations in and around Fredericksburg. Bed-and-breakfast inns, unknown before 1980, have come on like Johnson grass or Kudzu; there are about three hundred now. Many are located in historic old homes.

BE MY GUEST LODGING SERVICE

997-7227

Be My Guest advertises a variety of accommodations in town and out in the country, by the day, week, or month.

COUNTRY COTTAGE INN

405 E. Main • 888-991-6749 • Cr.

Located inside the historic Kiehne Home, the inn offers two suites with king-size beds and German antiques. Complimentary continental breakfast. Outside patio in back.

GASTEHAUS SCHMIDT

1-866-427-8374 • www.fbglodging.com • Cr.

Gastehaus Schmidt can provide lodging in a wide variety of historic or modern homes and buildings in and around Fredericksburg, such as a rock house featured in the Willie Nelson movie *Barbarosa*.

Nearly a dozen motels are within walking distance of downtown, most of them locally owned and operated. Miller's Inn (910 E. Main, 997-2244) has kitchenettes available and accepts trained pets. Dietzel Motel (1141 US 290 W. and US 87 N., 997-3330, www.dietzelmotel.com) has a large pool. Some rooms have good views of the Hill Country.

TOURISM INFORMATION

FREDERICKSBURG CHAMBER OF COMMERCE/VISITOR INFORMATION CENTER

302 E. Austin, one block north of Main • 997-6523 • www.fredericksburg-texas.com • Open daily; check website for current hours • W

You can walk away from here with several armloads full of free information about things to see and do in and around Fredericksburg, including the *Fredericksburg Standard-Radio Post*'s quarterly *Visitors Guide*. Both the guide and the Visitors Bureau are the best places to go for information on the area's burgeoning B&B industry. Dozens of places have detailed, descriptive pamphlets available. If the Visitors Bureau is closed, a points-of-interest map is posted outside by the front door.

ANNUAL EVENTS

Throughout the year many special events and festivals are held in and near Fredericksburg, a tradition that dates to the town's and the county's founding. Among the oldest, though not the ones that draw large crowds, are the Schuetzenfest (shooting festival) on the weekend nearest August 1, and the Saengerfest (song festival) held in the fall.

The shooting fests were described in 1923 by Julia Estill:

The country people take special delight in the [shooting fests], for the festivities are held in some sylvan grove far from the city's dust and heat. The band, composed of country boys and men who blow lustily (and often discordantly!) on the wind instruments so dear to their hearts, entertains the multitude at intervals all day long. Between times, the crowd surges down to the rifle range, where boys and men try their skill at shooting the bull's-eye. There is a bounteous feast spread at noonday, of course, and the usual cake and coffee at four o'clock. The festivities wind up with a dance at night.

Nearly every community in Gillespie County has its choral club composed of men who sing the old German melodies taught to them by their fathers. Every spring or autumn there is a big gathering of all the singing clubs for a song festival. Then the hills re-echo the mighty sound. In the old days the fest smacked somewhat of a Dionysian festival, but now there is only music and song.

Besides Thanksgiving, Christmas, and New Years Day, there was "Second Christmas" (the 26th), "Second Easter" (Monday), and "Second Pentecost" (Monday), "when young and old came forth to play." The first of these holidays was for sacred observances, the second for festivities. Then there were merrymakings everywhere, and nothing could dampen the holiday spirit of the crowd.

Weddings, confirmations, and birthdays were feasted as well. There was roast pork, turkey, and goose; sausages (beef/pork, venison/pork, liver, and blood); homemade noodles and potato salads (Irish and sweet); and salads of beans, herring, or fruit. The herring salad was obligatory: boiled smoked herring, diced, with beets, boiled egg, pickle, apple, Irish potato, and vinegar. The four o'clock cake and coffee hour featured fifteen or twenty cakes along with cookies. But the cakes were preceded by sliced sausage, bread, butter, and several kinds of cheese. Sometimes there were cream cheese pies made with cheese, cream, butter, eggs, and raisins.

The Kaffee Klatsches featured a menu similar to the afternoon coffee and cake, along with jellies and jams (watermelon, wild plum, agarita) and cakes such as Mandel-brot (almond bread), Pfeffernuesse (pepper nuts), Zimmit-sterne (cinnamon stars), Lebkuchen (gingerbread), and Kaffee kuchen (coffee cake).

The Christmas season began on December 6 when St. Nicholas first visited homes, leaving candy and fruit and making sure the kids were minding their parents. He might return several times before Christmas. Santa Claus came on Christmas Eve, and on Christmas night the churches had enormous trees for the children, and after the evening program, kids got a bag of fruit, candy, nuts, and foten, a small present.

For the Kindermasken Ball, all the children would gather for a frolic at a local public hall, dressed as nymphs, fairies, butterflies, brownies, gnomes, witches, clowns, and flower girls and skip about until about 10 p.m., when they were whisked home or bedded down in the dressing room while the parents enjoyed an hour or two of dancing.

The farmers came to their city homes on Sunday morning and on Second Christmas, Easter Monday, and Pentecost Monday, when the young folks wanted to attend the balls that began promptly at 2 p.m. Also, they would stay here when they came into town to shop or get medical attention.

Some Protestant churches built houses in their churchyards for farmer members who didn't have Sunday houses. These combination kitchen-dining rooms had tables, benches, and a stove where lunches were reheated and coffee was boiled.

Some of the old festivities remain, but many newer ones now dot the calendar, a few of which follow.

MARCH OR APRIL

EASTER FIRES PAGEANT

Fairgrounds, SH 16 S. • Saturday night before Easter • Fee • W

The pageant in front of the fairgrounds grandstand depicts the history of the city's famed Easter Fires that burn every year on the hills around town. A cast of several hundred portray Easter bunnies, settlers, Indians, and wildflowers in a modern version of a legend that tells how a pioneer mother told her frightened children that the Indian fires on nearby hills were really just the Easter Bunny boiling dye to color his eggs (honestly). Food concessions are available.

MAY

FOUNDERS DAY AND INTERTRIBAL POW-WOW

Pioneer Museum Grounds, 309 W. Main • 997-2835 • Saturday nearest May • Free • Charge for tours • W

Sponsored by and for the benefit of the Gillespie County Historical Society, activities include demonstrations of pioneer crafts, cooking, baking, quilting, blacksmithing, musical entertainment, and food. A tour of old homes takes place in the afternoon. The event also celebrates the signing of the peace treaty between the people of Fredericksburg and the Comanches.

JUNE

STONEWALL PEACH JAMBOREE

Stonewall • Take US 290 to rodeo grounds • Approximately 12 miles east of Fredericksburg • 644-2735 • Third weekend In June • Admission to grounds free during the day; admission charged for rodeo • W

This annual salute to the famed Gillespie County peach features a parade, peach auction, various contests, a rodeo on Friday and Saturday nights, and the crowning of the Peach Queen on Saturday night, followed by a dance.

JULY

PARI-MUTUEL HORSE RACES

Fairgrounds, SH 16 S. • 997-2359 • www.gillespiefair.com • Third weekend in July • Fee • W

This event features horse races, bands, food, and beer. Races are also held in August; check website for dates.

A NIGHT IN OLD FREDERICKSBURG

Market Square (Marketplatz), 100 block of W. Main • 997-6523 • Third weekend in July • Fee • W

Lots of beer, food, games, contests, music, and dances (indoor and outdoor) provide a full evening of entertainment in a mixed German and country-and-western atmosphere. The fun begins at 5 p.m.

AUGUST

GILLESPIE COUNTY FAIR

Fairgrounds, SH 16 S. • 997-2359 • www.gillespiefair.com • Fourth weekend in August • Fee • W

The oldest county fair in Texas, it features livestock, handwork, sewing, home canning, baked goods, quilts, arts, crafts, and agricultural exhibits. There are also horse races, a carnival, refreshments, beer, and dances on Friday and Saturday nights in an outdoor pavilion.

OCTOBER

OKTOBERFEST

Market Square (Marketplatz), 100 block of W. Main • 997-4810 • www.oktoberfestinfbg.com • First weekend in October • Fee • W

There are crafts, quilts, collectibles, food, and entertainment, including a waltz contest and children's carnival.

DECEMBER

WEIHNACHTEN IN FREDERICKSBURG

Market square, 100 block of W. Main • 997-6523 • Ten days in early December • Fee • W

Patterned after German Christmas markets, this fair features gifts, imports, baked goods, food, and entertainment.

CANDLELIGHT HOMES TOUR

Various locations • 997-2835 • Second Saturday in December • Fee

Private homes and historic buildings are adorned with candles and old-fashioned seasonal decorations. It is an afternoon through evening tour.

★

The SA F&N was less than nine years old in 1922 when the San Antonio and Fredericksburg Auto Line offered daily, morning and afternoon, service between the two towns over the same route you are about to embark on, using seven-passenger Buick sedans. Similar service was offered to Kerrville, Bandera, Medina Lake, and San Angelo. By 1924, family motoring trips between San Antonio and Fredericksburg were the rage, further presaging the doom of passenger service on the railroad. In December 1924, the San Antonio Sunday Express ran a several-page feature story on an automobile touring trip through the "Texas Highlands" between San Antonio, Fredericksburg, and Austin. What follows is the "motorlogue" of the first leg of the tour, which was a two-day odyssey "back in the day." The route has changed in places, but you will get the idea.

The entire road is improved State highway and can be classed as good driving, except for about 10 miles of rough road in Kendall County, north of Waring. The rough stretch in Kendall County is graded and subject to State maintenance, but lacks a hard surface and remains rough in continued dry weather. These State highways are opening up some fine country. The new roads still need the seasoning that only time and some rain and maintenance work can give. But even now, like this Fredericksburg trip, they are throwing open to Texans and visitors many comfortable drives.

Coming out of Fredericksburg, with the courthouse on your right, proceed four miles, turn right at the signpost that points out the road leading to Luckenbach and to the San Antonio road (Old San Antonio Road).

9 miles—CAIN CITY. Turn right by the store, parallel to the railroad track. Avoid the road leading to Luckenbach and the new, modern road to Johnson City and Austin.

16.1 miles—Kendall-Gillespie county line. There has been a good road up to now; a rough road begins.

16.5 miles—Garage.

17 miles—Cross railroad.

17.3 miles—Water, dip.

19.1 miles—Steep hill (the Divide)

20.4 miles—Hilly country. Cross railroad again.

22.2 miles—Cross railroad.

23.9 miles—Cross railroad.

24.4 miles—Water. Pass under railroad bridge.

25.4 miles—Cross railroad.

25.7 miles—Cross railroad, hill.

25.9 miles—Sharp turn, water.

27.3 miles—Cross roads. The road to the left is the old road to Fredericksburg and is the shortest route, but bad in wet weather.

30.4 miles—Bridge over Guadalupe River. Fishing and camping.

30.5 miles—Turn right, road to left to Sisterdale.

30.8 miles—WARING. Turn right. Road to left to Comfort.

31.1 miles—Cross railroad.

31.4 miles—Steep hill and turn. Fine scenery.

32.4 miles—Cross railroad.

33.1 miles—S turn, low-water bridge.

34.3 miles—WELFARE. Store on left.

34.9 miles—Cross railroad.

38 miles—Turn left to Waring and Fredericksburg, by store. Road to right goes to Kerrville and Junction, OST route.

41.3 miles—Cross railroad.

43.3 miles—Cross railroad.

43.6 miles—End of paved road.

44.5 miles—BOERNE. Keep straight ahead.

45.1 miles—Turn left into Boerne. Road to right by store goes to Bandera.

53.4 miles—Keep on paved road, garage ahead. Road to left is famous Scenic Loop.

56.5 miles—LEON SPRINGS, right.

60.9 miles—Cross railroad.

61.4 miles—Steep hill and curve.

66.8 miles—Nine-mile hill.

73.1 miles—Cross railroad.

73.6 miles—Keep straight on Fredericksburg Road.

74 miles—Cross railroad.

74.2 miles—Keep straight ahead on paved road.

75.1 miles—North Flores Street, following OST markings, turn left into Houston Street, go east on Houston Street seven blocks and turn right on North Alamo Street, post office on the left. 75.6 miles.

Leave Fredericksburg on US 290, which parallels the old Fredericksburg and Northern tracks, which ran out of town east-southeast a mile or so to the south of US 290. About four miles out, you'll cross the Pedernales, and less than a mile later, you'll see the Cain City sign. Follow the Cain City Road south to the first of several towns that the F&N spawned.

Now located at the intersection of Cain City Road with US 290 is Timber and Stone (997-2280), a business that buys, sells, and restores antique and new log cabins. The cabins sit around like cars on a sales lot.

The railroad took this initial diversion east before turning to the business at hand—getting over the high hills to Comfort—in order to take advantage of a natural cut in the hills immediately south of the Pedernales. Indians following the Pinto Trail used this pass for centuries, and the Fredericksburg teamsters also plodded through, taking advantage of the range's easiest grades.

In two miles, Cain City Road dead-ends into the old road to Luckenbach. Turn right, and you enter what is left of downtown, ghost town Cain City.

CAIN CITY

Gillespie County • About 7 miles from Fredericksburg

Cain City is located right on the cut in the hills, smack dab on the Pinto Trail, the Old San Antonio Road, and the Fredericksburg and Northern railroad. Cain

City's location was not happenstance. It all started when J. C. Stinson moved from Kansas to San Antonio in 1913. Traveling west from Alamo City, Stinson fell in love with the Hill Country. Knowing that the F&N was pushing through the hills toward Fredericksburg, Stinson bought 324 acres here at Inspiration Point later that year. He immediately hired a surveyor to lay out lots, parks, and streets, streets with grandiose names like Main Street, Broadway, and Grapevine Terrace, in true Babbitt style.

Stinson's home was the first built in Cain City. Although Stinson fathered the town, it was named in honor of Charlie Cain, a San Antonio businessman who bailed out the railroad at a very critical time. An F&N depot was the second building in Cain City. Cain City was a boomtown in 1914 and 1915. A warehouse, lumberyard, post office, the two-story Mountain Home Hotel, a school, and two general stores, as well as a few dozen homes, went up. For the town's convenience, men, mules, and a steam-powered grader scratched out the present road to Luckenbach. A telephone system was installed, and a water system was established. The water system—a rare convenience for a town this size—employed simple gravitational pressure. A well was drilled, and the pure fresh water was pumped into a big steel storage tank on the crest of the steep hill overlooking the town. Water pressure for most of Cain City was thus provided by the water's downhill run.

That graded "high speed" dirt road to Luckenbach (now paved) drew a lot of trade to Cain City. Farmers from the Blanco and Pedernales valleys brought their cotton, corn, oats, and wheat here to have it shipped out to the waiting markets. Cain City saw no great cattle drives, but it did see some great turkey drives. Turkey growers from the Johnson City area, some twenty-five miles to the east, drove their thousands-strong flocks along the dusty, muddy road to the Cain City depot, where they were crated and hauled to San Antonio. Folks from Fredericksburg would ride out here from town, just for the novelty of the train ride. Often they'd stay long enough for a bite to eat in the Mountain Home Hotel dining room.

Stinson organized and built the Cain City Bank in 1917. The bank shared the ground floor with a drugstore; offices occupied the second story. A blacksmith and doctor settled here, and there was even talk of an electric light plant to serve the city. The cotton gin came in 1919.

But Cain City began a gradual decline starting in 1922, when Stinson moved his family back to San Antonio. Without his leadership, the bank sputtered along for another two or three years and then closed its doors forever. The Mountain Home Hotel changed hands, and shipping tonnage began to drop; people were leaving the old family farms in droves, and highway-borne trucks were commanding an increasingly larger share of the shipping that remained. Cain City died with the railroad. The hotel was torn down in 1942. The railroad shut down, and all its tracks were pulled up in 1944.

Just after you turn right at the T intersection with the Luckenbach road (two miles from US 290), you see all that's left of old Cain City. The bank was torn down in 1982. All traces of the railroad's path have been totally obliterated. The dance hall, the stores, the lumberyard, the gin, and even the old water tower have disappeared, leaving only a few houses scattered along the potholed, graveled paths that were once Main, Broadway, and Grapevine Terrace.

The bank ruins stood on your left at the corner where the old Luckenbach Road is intersected by Broadway. All that's left of the bank today are some red bricks from the vault in the yard of the one-story, frame ranch-style house which stands where the bank once stood.

Turn left on Broadway, which leads you over the top of the pass and then winds down to a junction 0.9 miles later with the western branch of the Grapetown Road, aka the Old San Antonio Road. Turn left at the yield sign. In 0.5 miles, you will see a section of the rail bed in the field to your left. Two and a half sparsely settled miles after you turn onto the Old San Antonio Road, AKA "Old No. 9 Highway," you pass another turnoff (to your left) to Luckenbach, and you're in the Grapetown neighborhood.

GRAPETOWN

Gillespie and Kendall counties • About 4 miles from Cain City

You're in Grapetown now, at least the far north end of it, for Grapetown in the older, larger sense stretches for another five miles down the road. In a few hundred yards, you pass on your right the entrance to the Doebbler Quarry, then on your left is downtown Grapetown, marked by the arching "Grapetown Eintracht Schuetzenverein, Est. 1887" sign.

Grapetown's first resident was John Hemphill, who began carving out his niche here in 1848. Subsequent settlers were overwhelmingly German. Other than in personal plots, not much farming was done in this rough country neighborhood. Most of the men were drovers or cattlemen. Actually, a man could be both drover and farmer without too much trouble. Since the roads were so poor, a trip to Indianola and back might take months.

A man could plant his spring corn crop, make a trip to the coast, return in time to cultivate his waist-high corn, make another trip, and return in time to harvest the crop. Two months for a round trip that one of our trucks can make in a day seems incomprehensible, but not when you remember that in wet weather the roads would get so sloppy that the high-wheeled wagons would sink waist deep in mud. A wagon train might progress so short a distance in a day that a man could run back to the previous night's campsite for a bucketful of still-burning coals. Remember also that they didn't have matches back then, either.

Apache and Comanche attacks plagued the isolated settlement, and then the Civil War pitted neighbor against neighbor. Some chose to fight or drive for the Confederacy; others hightailed it for Mexico or the thickets of the nearby High Hills.

Here at Grapetown, on the banks of School Creek, are the little limestone schoolhouse with its red tin roof, the shooting hall, and the old Rausch ranch house, down at the end of the little road past the school and shooting hall. The Rausches have been here from the beginning. The schoolhouse was built between 1882 and 1884 on land donated by Friedrich Baag with the provision that no religious or political meetings be held in the school. Should such a meeting be held, the property would revert to Mr. Baag. The teacherage was built nearby in 1887. Enrollment topped out at fifty in 1915. Children from as far away as seven miles into Kendall County attended. The school closed in 1944, when local students began to attend school at Cain City.

The Schuetzenverein (shooting club) was organized in 1887, along with a Liedertafel (singing club), but this rambling wooden hall was not built until

1893. The Liedertafel is now just a fading memory, but the Schuetzenverein remains active. Members still practice and compete here regularly in preparation for the annual two-day Bundes Schuetzenfest, a century-old Gillespie County tradition. The Schuetzenfest dates back to the days when good shooting kept meat on the table and thieves out of the livestock pens. Many of the men were proud of their marksmanship, and eventually they started getting together for shootin' matches so that they might determine to everyone's satisfaction just who was the best Scharfschuetze (sharpshooter). Shooting clubs like the Grapetown group were formed in almost all the little communities. Six clubs exist today, whose members compete for the title of Schuetzenkoenig, much as their grandfathers and great-grandfathers did.

From the Grapetown community center, continue south on the old Fredericksburg-to-San Antonio road. The aging Rausch ranch house is not the only remnant of old Grapetown; the road south is littered with century-old impregnable limestone houses and outbuildings. Many of the names on the mailboxes—Doebbler, Kallenburg, Leyendecker—have been here even longer.

You pass the quiet Grapetown cemetery on your right, then the Gillespie/Kendall county line a few yards south of an intersection with a gravel road (on your left), and finally, two miles south of the Grapetown community center, South Grape Creek.

Here on the north banks by the old wagon road, Friedrich Doebbler opened in his home a grocery, dry goods store, hotel, post office, and stage stop and named the complex Doebbler's Inn. The year was 1860, and Doebbler's place became an area gathering place and amusement center. Grapetown's first school and shooting hall were built across the creek from Doebbler after the Civil War. Tradition has it that the community's first school classes were held in 1859 in a small house belonging to Doebbler and taught by a Scotsman who would teach one week at Grapetown followed by a week at nearby Meusebach Creek settlement.

Very little of this rough country was fenced, and the settlers' cattle grazed on the wide open range of the High Hills as far east as Sisterdale and as far south as Comfort and the Guadalupe River. Each fall, the men and boys would round up the beeves and sort them out. They would usually sell the excess to Kerrville's Charles Schreiner, who drove area cattle to San Angelo, San Antonio, and Abilene, Kansas, during the postwar cattle-drive years. The big market-bound herds churned up a sea of mud or raised huge clouds of dust on the road through Grapetown.

Then the center of the neighborhood shifted north to its present location. All that remains today of early Grapetown are Doebbler's old stone stables near the creek.

BANKERSMITH

Kendall County • About 2 miles from Grapetown community center

During the thirty-one-year existence of the F&N, Grapetowners were served by a station named Bankersmith, after Fredericksburg's Temple D. "Banker" Smith. What used to be Bankersmith is off in the woods to your left, along the banks of South Grape Creek. Most of Grapetown's social life took place up the road at the school and shooting hall, but most of Grapetown's commercial activity remained down here around Doebbler's old establishment. A post office, dance hall, store, garage, and warehouse sprang up to keep the little depot company. The old wagon road eventually became the first paved road (Highway 9) north into Fredericksburg, and for a while Grapetown and Bankersmith enjoyed the best of these two transportation worlds. But just about the time that railroad traffic started dropping off, the main highway north (our present US 87) was rerouted a few miles west, through Comfort. Grapetown was left high and dry. All the buildings brought on by the railroad's advent were demolished following its demise.

Just after you leave what was once Bankersmith, you begin to catch glimpses of the old F&N roadbed, first on your left, then on your right. You parallel it for the next mile. An occasional tie litters the embankments, and an antiquated string telephone wire traces its path. The roadbed and your own asphalt path cross each other nine times in the next ten miles.

A mile or so south of South Grape Creek, you also notice that you are climbing a steady though unspectacular hill. You see on your right the prominent right-of-way embankment. You're about to crest the Divide of the Pedernales and Guadalupe rivers, the high hill the F&N chose to bore through rather than struggle over. For years it was the only railroad tunnel in Texas, not to mention a subject of local pride and thousands of picture postcards to boot. A state historical marker to your left atop this high hill marks the tunnel's crossing path, some sixty feet straight below. The marker has been stolen several times.

Stagecoach robberies all along the Fredericksburg-to-San Antonio line were common during the 1870s and 1880s, and the Divide, or "Big Hill," was a favorite ambush place, as well as Balcones Creek, five miles south of Boerne. Many of the robberies were carried out by a duo known as "Long" and "Short," or the "Tall Man" and the "Short Man." Whether it was always the same pair of men is open to debate; however, two young men, Pitts and Yeager, who were from the Leon Springs area, were convicted of robbing the mail stage here at the Big Hill in 1884 and were accused of the same crime at Balcones Creek.

THE TUNNEL

About 4 miles from Grapetown

Construction of the road had already commenced when engineers informed construction boss Foster Crane that a tunnel would have to be bored through the hill. They had earlier hoped that a forty-foot cut through the hill would suffice. No such luck. The tunnel was to be nearly one thousand feet long, and the north portal of the tunnel was prefaced by a cut five hundred feet long and forty feet deep. It would require the removal of over fourteen thousand cubic yards of limestone, blown out by eight carloads of blasting powder. The clear-out work was done by men wielding shovels and picks and by mules hauling scrapers and dump cars. It would take six months and $134,000 to complete the 972-foot tunnel, making it the most expensive piece of railroad construction in the whole state of Texas. It would remain Texas' only tunnel for years to come.

Work had started at both ends of the tunnel. Few believed that engineers could dig at both ends and meet in the middle, so considerable wagers were made as to how far off the shafts would be. When they met, it turned out to be a matter of a few inches. Men working deep inside the tunnel got their breath of life via a small shaft drilled from above ground to the top of the bore.

On July 16, at 4 a.m., the tunnel opened, just four hours later than had been predicted for weeks. An automobile party of men, including Temple Smith, went out to take a peep through the barrier. Smith was the first man to pass through the tunnel, followed by other members of the party. It would be ready in one week for ties and rails. Within ten miles of Fredericksburg, smoke could be seen from the engine hauling the material over the completed track on the south side of the Big Hill. It was expected that trains would be running by September 1. Work on the Pedernales bridge began next, as the material had already been unloaded at the junction and would be hauled by wagon to the river. This bridge was a small matter as there were several other more difficult pieces of bridgework south of the Big Hill. As soon as the tunnel was completed and the trestle work south of the hill connected with the tunnel, a night-and-day double force was put to work laying the track to Fredericksburg. Mr. Crane had purchased a sixty-five-ton engine as well as several passenger coaches and a number of freight cars.

Park up here by the marker, get out, and take a look at the south portal of this engineering feat. Standing at the upper edge of the cut, look down at the roadbed and opening forty feet below. Then look down the wild Block Creek Gorge, which leads into Rafter Hollow and had to be crossed in order to gain entrance to the south portal. This devilish depression was traversed by two trestles, known respectively as the Big Bridge and the Little Bridge. Big Bridge was seven hundred feet long, sixty feet high, and contained 272,000 feet of board lumber. The gap between Little Bridge and the tunnel entrance was occupied by a dump constructed of waste rock (rubble from the tunnel blasting) two hundred feet long. Men and mules built the trestles, just as they had carved out the tunnel. Only the overgrown roadbed remains today—the bridges were torn down nearly sixty years ago—but you cannot help but be impressed with the job these swearing men and beasts did with the terrain they had to tame.

MOUNT ALAMO/ALAMO SPRINGS

About 4 miles from Grapetown

In October 1913, Colonel W. W. Dexter of Houston, editor of the *Texas Bankers' Journal*, who had been in San Antonio on business, in the company of San Antonio's bankers and businessmen, spent a day in going to and returning from Mount Alamo. In speaking of his trip, which he described as delightful, he said in part,

> I had no idea that there were such mountains and valley scenes in Texas. This mountain is covered with majestic oaks and is a veritable greenhouse of foliage. It overlooks a verdant valley 600 feet below, is 2,300 feet above sea level and 500 feet higher than the famous Lookout Mountain of Tennessee.
>
> I was inspired and bewildered at the grandeur of the scenery. It was an apocalypse to me. It is free from bacterial life. No insects can abide on Mount Alamo. The climate is cool in summer, and protected from the chill winds of winter by a forest of oaks.

Garbed in rustic beauty it is an enchanted spot. On its summit is a fountain of pure water, coming as if directed by the will of the Creator. It forms a natural reservoir that is not unlike the fabled Parnassus where Apollo located after searching the world for a place of perpetual youth, and where he and the nine muses dwelt eternal.

My object in visiting Mount Alamo was to select a summer home site for myself and some of my friends.

When the new railroad to Fredericksburg is opened, and which tunnels Mount Alamo, we expect to bring a carload of capitalists from Galveston and Houston, who with the people of San Antonio will on Thanksgiving Day visit the inviting place.

The line of transit from San Antonio to Mount Alamo is two hours. While making this trip we flushed a magnificent drove of wild turkeys on the mountain, and saw evidences of wild deer and other game.

The waters of the Guadalupe and other streams course their way in the foothills of the mountains. We crossed no less than twenty streams between San Antonio and Mount Alamo. We predict for this enchanted spot a future no less famous than any in Colorado or California.

This beauty and the tunnel's novelty was strong enough to attract developers, who laid out the mountaintop pleasure resort community of Mount Alamo just adjacent to the tunnel's northern entrance, atop the broad plateau that forms the top of the largest hill in the Guadalupe Range. At an elevation of 2,300 feet, Mount Alamo was to cover a minimum area of 300 acres, and up to 1,500 acres at its zenith.

Promoters promised to install an electric lighting plant and water and sewage systems. A seventy-five-room clubhouse complete with bathhouses and screened sleeping porches was planned, as well as an eighteen-hole golf course. Surveyors laid out an elaborate system of streets and boulevards, the main artery of which was the two-hundred-foot-wide Berlin Boulevard. Special coaches ran from San Antonio to Mount Alamo, bringing out potential customers to see the sights. The F&N built a station here and hired the line's only female stationmaster, Alma Cowan, to staff it. The resort paradise of Mount Alamo folded in the aftermath of Wall Street's Black Friday in 1929. Mount Alamo, the train station, died with the railroad in 1944, and title to the land reverted back to its former owner, Alma Cowan's husband Otto.

Standing by the tunnel's historical marker, looking out and down the spectacular gorge to Rafter Hollow and beyond that to Block Creek, you can see why developers had such high hopes for Mount Alamo.

ALAMO SPRINGS CAFE

107 Alamo Rd. • 990-8004 • www.alamospringscafe.com • Open daily, lunch and dinner • W

It seems that there is no part of the Hill Country that can remain undisturbed from modern development. In this case, it is the ghost town of Alamo Springs, which is now the home of the Alamo Springs Volunteer Fire Department, Alamo Springs Christian Fellowship Church, and Alamo Springs Cafe, built next to the bat cave to take advantage of the stream of visitors to the Old Tunnel WMA. The cafe, which opened 2004, is in the transplanted old Fredericksburg saddle shop.

The cafe is best known for its hamburgers. The usual burger sides are served, along with evening dinner specials, beer, and Hill Country wines. They also have live music.

OLD TUNNEL WILDLIFE MANAGEMENT AREA

830-833-4333 • Open daily • W partial

After the railroad moved out, Mexican free-tailed bats moved in, and the tunnel's roadbed slowly deteriorated into a stew of dirt, limestone, water, and guano (the guano contains carnivorous beetles that strip the meat off the bones of a bat corpse in a matter of minutes) that is up to six feet deep in places. Up to three million bats roost in the tunnel from late spring to early fall. Pregnant bats arrive first, but then they leave the tunnel to give birth elsewhere in the Hill Country. Come midsummer, the mothers and their nearly mature offspring begin returning to the tunnel. The tunnel's population peaks in August and September. Experts believe that the tunnel is too drafty to be a successful bat nursery, which must have consistent warmth. In order to protect this important roost site, the Texas Parks and Wildlife Department acquired a 10.5-acre tract that included the tunnel in 1991. Local louts often came out at twilight to get drunk and fire their shotguns at the bats as they emerged to feed. Naturalists and conservationists believed the colony was in mortal danger from steadily increasing human activity on and around the site.

Around sunset each evening (the exact time varies depending on the time of sunset and other factors), the bats boil out of the tunnel entrance to spend the night feeding on the Hill Country's bounteous harvest of bugs. You can watch this dramatic exodus from an observation deck located high above the entrance. It's literally a river of life that flows out of the tunnel for half an hour in late summer when the population is at its peak. They may fly as far as thirty miles a night hunting dinner, mostly moths and little flying beetles. They may snag the odd mosquito, but mosquitoes aren't a major part of their diet. What they really like are the moths that are the adult forms of farmers' traditional enemies: corn borers, cutworms, and webworms. The colony collectively consumes twelve to fifteen tons of insects a night. Time spent dining nightly varies with the climate. During a drought, when insects are relatively scarce, they may hunt until dawn, or longer, until they are full. It is best to get here forty-five minutes to an hour before sunset on the day you go. With the first cold front of the fall, the bats hightail it out of here for their winter home in Mexico. While many of the old, traditional prejudices against bats are now being dispelled here in Texas and elsewhere in the United States, they still exist in Mexico, where people go to great lengths to drive the bats away, like burning old tires in bat caves. So while the bats' future in Texas is now somewhat more secure, continued persecution in Mexico may yet doom the species.

The tunnel's upper observation deck is always open, and Parks and Wildlife biologists are present nightly during bat season to answer questions. A lower viewing level is reserved for special bat tours.

★

Despite its spectacular tunnel and bridges, the SA F&N was a tooth-and-nail railroad, rivaled only by the Bartlett-Western railroad in Williamson County. The SA F&N may not have been the butt of derisive nicknames, as was the poor Bartlett-Western, but it did enjoy the same haphazard reputation among its patrons.

The SA F&N, once funded, was plagued with problems from the start of construction. Six hundred tons of steel rails had to be returned to their manufacturer, floods washed away large portions of the roadbed, and worst of all, as the surrounding cotton fields neared maturity, many of the gandy dancers deserted the road for the cotton fields. That didn't say much for working conditions on the F&N. The road owned outright only two locomotives; the rest of the locomotives and all the rolling stock were borrowed or leased from other railroads.

The first official train into an anxiously awaiting Fredericksburg was an hour late; the soft, shifting roadbed had kept the train's speed down. It had also experienced extraordinary difficulty in climbing the 2 percent grade that led up the gorge to the tunnel. Rain drowned out most of the town's three-day schedule of festivities. Once the party was over, the SA F&N set about to make a living. It soon snagged the local U.S. Mail contract, but a couple of years after its completion, the SA F&N sat in the hands of a court-appointed receiver, pockets-out busted. Meanwhile, the trains kept running, or at least tried to. It was not always easy.

The roadbed continued to settle, especially where the soft limestone rubble fills had been built up. At many of these soft spots, the rails would sink completely out of sight. There was a time when the twenty-four-mile trip from Fredericksburg Junction to Fredericksburg took eighteen hours. As many as a dozen derailments might occur during the course of a trip. Or the locomotive might run out of water, whereupon the engineer would hightail it as best he could to the tunnel, where he could drop a hose into the ditch where water always stood because of the constant tunnel seepage. In the wood-burning days, if the locomotive ran out of fuel, the crew would trudge into the woods with axes and cut enough wood to complete the trip. There was almost always a rifle or shotgun tucked away somewhere on the train, and when someone spotted a fat deer or turkey, the train would come to a screeching halt in order to give Robin Hood his chance. Even jackrabbits were considered targets worth stopping for.

The F&N could not afford a wrecking crane, so whenever a car derailed it was brought back to bear with block and tackle, ropes, jacks, and cables, plus the pulling power of a locomotive. Floods often destroyed or damaged bridges. Once, the daily mixed (freight and passenger cars) was trapped on the road. Having crossed a bridge that was washed away minutes later by a sudden raging torrent of floodwater, the on-moving train soon encountered a similarly washed-out bridge, thus leaving it isolated. Crew and passengers were forced to hike to a nearby farmhouse and stay the night with those hospitable folk. Another time, during the early 1920s, Little Bridge, leading to the tunnel's south portal, caught fire. An alarm was sent to the fire departments at Comfort and Fredericksburg, but they refused to send any of their equipment or men to help combat the blaze. So all road employees from the general manager on down piled aboard the little motorcars and sped down to the site to quench the flames.

Folks said that when riding the F&N the traveler had to begin his journey before the month of August in order to reach the end of the line by Christmas. A drummer who had to ride the F&N in order to reach clients in Fredericksburg complained about the slowness of the train to his first customer. "Well yes, that's one way to look at it," the German shopkeeper agreed, "but think how long you get to ride for a dollar." Actually, the train managed to maintain an average speed of close to twelve miles an hour.

It was also said that the road's financial grip was so precarious that it could not afford to have any of its trains hit a horse, cow, or goat. Crew members were warned to maintain a careful watch for livestock on the tracks, to stop the train immediately when straying animals were sighted, and not to move again until the offenders were removed from the right-of-way. Passengers were warned to bring along plenty of food, because there was a possibility that they would be suffering from hunger before their trip was over. A turtle stood a good chance of taking the F&N to a photo finish, they joked.

When passenger trains started running through the tunnel, it was the crew's custom to stop outside the portal and then check to see that no rocks had fallen from the ceiling onto the tracks. The conductor would request that all windows be closed before the train entered the tunnel, so that the choking black smoke would not flood the coaches. While passing through the tunnel, the engine exhaust would sometimes loosen small rocks, which would pepper the tops of the cars. During the winter, large icicles would form on the roof, sometimes growing to as much as a foot in diameter, making it impossible for the train to pass through until they were removed.

The road operated in receivership until December 26, 1917, when a group of San Antonio capitalists purchased it for $80,000. They promised to make many improvements and announced hopes of extending the road west to San Angelo and north to Llano. But as paved highways grew in length and number, along with the number of cars using them, the F&N's passenger and shipping business dropped off. It was not even able to pay operating expenses, much less the interest due on its bonds. With another change of ownership in the 1930s, the road lost all hope of turning a year-end profit, for its seven directors soon voted themselves annual individual salaries of $3,000. Attempts to sell the line to a larger company, like the Southern Pacific, failed. But still the trains bumped on, even though the passenger cars had been yanked from the daily mixed train. Which is not to say that passenger cars did not run on the tracks. James Krauter of Comfort said that during the 1930s, "we'd drive our cars down the railroad tracks. We'd deflate the tires, and they'd fit perfectly on the tracks."

Ironically, the same month that the railroad arrived in Fredericksburg, the businessmen who had worked so hard to bring it began the process that would kill it less than thirty years later; Progressive Business League was championing the cause of a county bond issue of $150,000 to put the roads of Gillespie County in first-class condition. The members were confident that they could convince voters of the advisability of such action. With the advent of the railroad, they reasoned, Fredericksburg would become the shipping point for a large territory, and they further reasoned that improved highways over which farmers could haul their produce were bound to add to the prestige and prosperity of the community.

Two road gangs were kept constantly at work keeping the county's highways in good repair. The roads were first graded and then topped so as to be of lasting quality. Residents along the roads being worked gave their assistance to the gangs, getting and performing actual labor to help the good cause along.

From the tunnel, resume your southward path, down the Divide, toward Fredericksburg Junction. You parallel the gorge; it's on your left. Just 1.8 miles past the tunnel marker, you cross paths again with the old railroad. In another half mile, you come to a private dirt road running off to the west, Giles Ranch Road. This road eventually leads to ranch headquarters, where

Giles family descendants still live and work. A mile later (a little over three miles south of the tunnel), you come to a low-water crossing over Rafter Hollow. On your left you see a gap in the railroad embankment where a wooden bridge once stood.

The old Hillingdon Ranch flag station stood near this low-water bridge, a flag station created primarily for the convenience of Hillingdon's illustrious owner, the prominent architect Alfred Giles, who commuted back and forth from San Antonio via the F&N/T&NO. Born in London, Giles immigrated to the United States in 1872, and by 1875 he was in business at San Antonio as Alfred Giles, architect, still barely twenty-two years old. By his early thirties, Giles had begun to design the dozens of courthouses (in the Hill Country: Bexar, Gillespie, Llano, Kerrville, and Kendall); jails (Bexar, Bandera, and Kerr); banks; and homes that marked his career. Many of them still stand today across Texas and northern Mexico. In the face of decreasing commissions in Texas, Giles operated a branch office in Monterrey, Mexico, during the 1910s. Buildings in Monterrey, Saltillo, Durango, Puebla, and Chihuahua attest to the firm's success. Notable extant structures in Monterrey are Banco Mercantil (1901), La Reinera (1901), and Arco de la Independencia (1910); in Chihuahua, the Palacio Municipal was constructed before 1908.

Frequent traveler as he was between San Antonio and Fredericksburg, Giles was one of the most gladdened travelers by the advent of the railroad. Not only was the ride marginally faster and more comfortable, but he no longer had to fear the depredations of highwaymen, such as on the evening of March 22, 1882.

That night, the outgoing and incoming mail on the San Antonio to Fredericksburg route were stopped and robbed by two men about three miles from Fredericksburg. The men went through the mails and then decamped. The northbound stage was held until the southbound one from Fredericksburg to San Antonio arrived. This was the favored way of operating. They went through both mails and got a fine gold watch from the southbound stage. Alfred Giles, on his way from San Antonio to Fredericksburg, was the only passenger on the northbound stage. The southbound stage had no passengers. Giles had been in San Antonio overseeing work on the new Bexar County courthouse, which he had designed.

Alfred said that he and the coach driver, Jim Brown, had come from San Antonio on the old Concord stage. As they neared Fredericksburg, Alfred asked if Brown had ever been robbed while driving, and Brown said, "No, somehow or other they have always missed me."

Within moments, they were waylaid by two men—one large and one small—who ordered them to put their hands up. Alfred froze.

"I shall never forget how big the gun in the large man's hand looked as the moonlight filtered through the trees and shone on the nickel plating. The men were not masked, but their hats were pulled low on their foreheads and the big man's sombrero was particularly large and the shadow from the brim entirely obscured his face."

Afraid to provoke them, Alfred and Brown offered no resistance as the men took their money and possessions. Alfred thought, "And I could not help but think of my wife and little girl, only a few months old, at home."

The robbers promised to let Alfred keep his watch if he agreed to help them rob the next coach. He and Brown agreed, first helping them sort through the mail. Then they heard the coach coming.

Once they had forced the coach to stop and rifled through its contents, which yielded few valuables, the robbers promptly fled into the night. As they departed, Alfred thought, "If I'd had my Winchester with me, I would probably have been able to get off a shot at one of them."

He later heard that the duo robbed other coaches and were dubbed "The Long and Short Men."

Giles told the *San Antonio Evening Light*,

> About 9:15 p.m., I was in front with the driver; it was a beautiful moonlight night, and just in passing the shade of some large trees, two men jumped out, and on presenting cocked pistols told the driver to hold up. He immediately stopped, and then the robbers asked him if there were any passengers; he answered, none inside, whereupon he ordered us to hold up our hands and get down, which we did; one of the men then gave his large six-shooter to his partner, and with a small derringer in one hand went to work with the other, searching me. The other man stood some three yards distant with his nickel-plated six-shooter gleaming in the moonlight, full cocked on us. The robber first took my watch, an English gold lever. I remarked that I hoped he would not keep the watch, nor a diamond ring I wore on my finger, as they were presents from my mother, and being easily identified would probably lead to his conviction. My money, some $20, I handed him; he thought awhile and then put back the watch and never touched the ring; he then searched all my pockets and satchel, even looking at letters, but getting nothing but the $20. I then asked if I could take my hands down as I was tired of holding them up. He said all right, and upon a request brought my overcoat from the stage, and even helped me on with it. He next went through the driver, Mr. James Brown, but only took his knife, saying he never robbed drivers. During all this time, some thirty minutes, the other man never moved, but kept his cocked pistol on us. The robber then went through the mail; he only made a water haul and did some general cursing for being in bad luck. He was about to open a box in the hind part of the stage when he thought he heard the stage from Fredericksburg coming this way. He asked me the time, and Brown if the stage was due, Brown answering yes, he at once began making preparations. They had already a rope stretched across the road, tied to trees on either side. We were then ordered to stay under a tree facing the coming stage, as he remarked if any shooting was to be done we would be killed first. I said I'll get behind the tree if I hear a shot, which caused quite a chuckle; such safety was only momentary as they ordered us to walk on in front of them to meet the coming stage. When the stage was a few yards from us, they called out, "hold up," much to the astonishment of the driver by name Ed.

The classically heavy second Gillespie County courthouse is one of his early major works, the Italianate Kendall County courthouse addition is one of his later works. But he was more than just a successful architect. Giles, together with father-in-law John James, owned this model thirteen-thousand-acre ranch called Hillingdon. Here Giles raised horses, mules, registered Aberdeen Angus cattle, and angora goats. He was active in a variety of stock raisers and breeders associations. Prominent journalist Richard Harding Davis paid the ranch lavish praise in his 1892 tome *The West from a Car Window*. Giles died here in 1920. Giles' grandson currently lives on and runs Hillingdon, which is several thousand acres reduced in size, but still very much a family operation. The old rambling ranch house hasn't changed much since Giles' death; old company portfolios with lovely illustrations of his work still adorn the desk in the front parlor, and blue ribbons from fat stock shows at the turn of the century still hang on the walls.

Giles designed a number of homes in what is now San Antonio's King William Historic District. One of the most prominent remaining examples of Giles' work is the Steves Homestead, home of San Antonio lumberman Edward Steves. The house was completed in 1877 for $15,000 and has been described as a "magnificent structure . . . which could not be duplicated for $25,000." The Steves Homestead is located on King William Street and is on the National Register of Historic Places. His fine home, along with others on King William Street, symbolized the success of German immigrants in frontier Texas. Giles also designed the Carl Wilhelm August Groos home (1880), and the motherhouse of the Sisters of Charity of the Incarnate Word on the campus of Incarnate Word College. In 1909, Giles altered the main facade of the Menger Hotel, adding Renaissance Revival details in stuccoed brick, pressed metal, and cast iron; he also designed an interior rotunda that provided light and served as a circulation hub.

A little over six miles south of the tunnel markers on your right, you see a strip of chest-high rock fence about 0.5 miles long, one of the best-preserved stretches of rock fence left in the Hill Country.

The Germans were the only ranchers in the west to build such fences, and the fences can be used to identify areas of German settlement. Ma, Pa, the kids, even Oma and Opa labored months and years to build the fences. They had to do the work themselves; hiring someone else to do it would run $300 to $400 a mile. The construction of rock fences came to an abrupt end, as you might well expect, with the introduction of barbed wire. But many of these centenarians are still functional. What was so slow in going up is now fittingly slow in coming down. Rock fence building is an art. Families sometimes used stone quarried from nearby limestone outcroppings. More often they employed rocks cleared from the fields before the spring plowing. Stones were often laid dry into a trench dug into the ground. This was the fence's foundation. A good stone fence had a smooth face, which made it hard for animals to climb over, and interlocking stones for strength. Fences with too smooth a face and a rubble fill in between were not nearly as strong. This stretch was obviously built to last.

Seven miles south of the tunnel marker, you see an old tin barn, set back from the road. The front half of it is up on stilts to facilitate loading goods in and out of the F&N boxcars. This now out-of-place building is our only clue that the railroad ran through here.

You cross Block Creek and its tributaries many times during these last few miles. Despite its former preeminence, the old Fredericksburg-to-San Antonio Road (Old Highway 9) was largely ignored by county and state authorities. Homemade warning signs done up in fluorescent red paint warned you of upcoming cattle and low-water crossings. At the water crossings, more of the red paint was daubed on posts, boulders, or whatever else was handy, as further warning to the motorist. Many of these crossings sported homemade flood markers, in contrast to the neatly executed five-foot graduated flood markers you see on state-maintained roads. But back then, all roads were similarly crudely marked. Early travel guides told you to "turn left at the red schoolhouse" or "right at the big oak tree with the red ring." Local residents erected signs that warned of various road hazards, identified the road, and told the traveler who lived in which direction. Travel was more an adventure, not just a means of getting from here to there. When you come to the junction with RM 473, a little over eight miles from the tunnel marker, continue straight ahead toward Comfort on RM 473. Now you're smack dab in the flat, richly green bottomlands of the Guadalupe, and it should be easy to see why the founders of Comfort chose that name, especially when you think back to the arid, hardscrabble hills of the Divide. All of this fertile land was once part of the sprawling Nichols neighborhood.

NICHOLS

About 10 miles from the tunnel marker

The first Anglo settlement here was named Brownsboro, after J. S. Brown, who settled at the mouth of Block Creek in 1848 or 1849. Folks began to call it Nichols starting in 1897, the year in which the Nichols Sanitarium for the treatment of pulmonary diseases was created. The Nichols Sanitarium, later the Nichols Ranch, was one of the world's first dude ranches. People from San Antonio and the rest of Texas came up from Alamo City on the T&NO and then made the switchover and the short, two-mile trip up to the Nichols Ranch flag station on the F&N. These visitors might spend the weekend or the entire summer taking the cure or just breathing in the country air here on the banks of the Guadalupe, staying in the big house or in one of the scattered guest cabins.

After traveling a little over a mile on RM 473, you see a stately steel truss bridge to your left, then a road, River Bend Road, running toward it off RM 473, marked by a sign for James Kiehl River Bend Park.

GUADALUPE RIVER BRIDGE

About 10.5 miles from the tunnel marker

One of the first things you notice about this big bridge that spans the Guadalupe is that it goes nowhere. There is no road to the bridge and no road from the bridge. It just stands like a giant Colossus of Rhodes, master of the Guadalupe, anchored at either end in uniformly lush green pastures. As such, it looks rather like some eccentric artistic extravagance, serving no purpose other than to decorate the countryside.

This current, purely aesthetic function is a fairly recently acquired role for the turn-of-the-century span. As late as 1973, it was the Guadalupe crossing of the T&NO line from San Antonio to Kerrville. Just west of the bridge, the F&N tracks met the T&NO rails at Fredericksburg Junction, which no longer exists. Here a small depot was built, which consisted of a small waiting room furnished with wooden benches, and a storage room for baggage and mail. The yards of the F&N's southern terminus consisted of a few dozen yards of storage tracks, a water tank, and a turning wye. San Antonio was a mere two hours and fifty miles away. If you were lucky, you had covered the twenty-four haphazard miles from Fredericksburg in about the same time.

As the Great Depression tightened its grip on Central Texas and the rest of the country, the F&N's position grew tenuous. When the Southern Pacific refused a chance to buy the F&N for $227,000, it was offered to the citizens of Fredericksburg for $75,000. They refused, declaring that it was impossible to raise even that amount during those hard times, besides balking at the idea of paying for the railroad again. So it remained unsold and limped along. By Pearl Harbor Day, the F&N belonged to one man, Dr. O. H. Judkins of San Antonio, all the other stockholders having bailed out. There was a great demand for scrap metal once the American war machine got rolling, and since the F&N had not been deemed essential to the war effort, Dr. Judkins saw a good chance to rid himself of an albatross. So he applied to the War Production Board and the ICC for permission to abandon the line and sell it for scrap. Permission was duly granted, and bids were invited. A Chicago firm won with the high bid of $77,000. This price included all steel rails, bridges, ties, rights-of-way, buildings, and land, everything but the toot of the locomotive whistle, essentially.

Fredericksburgers experienced a quick change of heart when they learned of the abandonment and sale, unsuccessfully appealing the government's decision, then offering to buy back the line from the salvage firm. The offer was declined. Removal of the rails started immediately, followed by the dismantling of the bridges and trestles. The wooden ties sold for up to a buck a piece. Six carloads of rail went to Australia, but most of the rail was sold to the War Production Board, which used it to build spur lines to all the new army camps. The big timbers went into new bridges across the country, some ending up along the Alcan Highway, which was to be our strategic lifeline to Alaska.

Faced with ever-increasing freight rates, Fredericksburg merchants began to rue the loss of their road. One merchant even went so far as to find out the cost of a replacement line. That figure came to $4,000,000. But highways and automobiles would have soon defeated that line, too, as soon as the travel-restrictive war was over. So the F&N died a rather ignominious though patriotic death, never really having lived up to the expectations of its builders and subsequent owners.

Out of sight, out of mind, goes the shopworn saying; this is exactly what happened to the F&N. It disappeared from the minds of the people it served almost as fast as its rails were ripped up. Its memory has faded just as completely as its physical presence, which is down to a swampy tunnel, some grassy embankments, and a few scattered ties.

Except for the big Guadalupe bridge, not much is left of the old Kerrville branch of the T&NO these days. When the tracks first pushed across the river in 1887, they crossed via a wood-piling bridge. This bridge was destroyed by a disastrous flood just after the turn of the century and was replaced by the current one. Funny thing, though—of the bridge's three steel-truss spans, one bears the date 1904, another reads 1906, and the third is blank. As you follow the road's dip down under the bridge and then its sharp veer to the left over the river, you may wonder why such a high bridge was needed to cross so little a river. In 1978, several consecutive days of heavy thunderstorms sent a wall of water crashing down the Guadalupe, engulfing the bridge and leaving brush caught thirty feet above you in the tree tops and the bridge's superstructure.

A San Antonio reporter gave the best description found yet of the T&NO's path from Boerne to the Guadalupe bridge, riding the first excursion train from San Antonio to the grand celebration at Comfort on August 27, 1887:

> One of the most notable features after leaving Boerne is the change in the aspect of the country and the difficulties that must have resulted in the construction of the road-bed and track. It is a comparatively level country that is passed through in

going from San Antonio to Boerne to that which is traversed from Boerne to Comfort. The undulations have become high mountains: The boulders have changed to huge masses of limestone rock: the rolling land has become rugged; high bluffs are on either side; the track passes through deep cuttings in the solid rock and over embankments ranging from 25 to 80 feet high, wide ravines are crossed by numerous bridges, and nowhere along the route is level country to be seen. At one point about 15 miles from San Antonio, the train passes over a track constructed on the face of a high bluff which has been blasted out. Far below, the river rushes along, overhead, the rock towers, the top scarcely visible. It is 115 feet from the extreme top of the bluff to the river and from the top to the track is 50 feet. Another feat of engineering skill is the massive bridge constructed over the Guadalupe river a few miles before Comfort is reached. It has a span of 1,011 feet and the river rolls along 50 feet below. This is the longest and the heaviest bridge on the Aransas Pass system with the exception of the Corpus Christi bridge. It is but a short time after passing this bridge before the point of destination is reached.

If the river is crossable here (don't attempt to cross if there's more than a foot of water flowing over the bridge), cross on over. Be alert and drive slowly and with caution; the road is paved but only one lane wide.

James Kiehl River Bend Park, located just over 0.5 miles after the low-water crossing by the old railroad bridge, is a brand new county park that offers free public access to a scenic stretch of the Guadalupe River.

You traverse the Guadalupe again about 0.5 miles later. Soon after this second crossing, 0.7 miles later, you pass by the old Brownsboro cemetery on your left, with graves that date from the 1870s to the 1940s. Just after the cemetery, River Bend Road dead-ends. Turn left here onto North Riverbend Road.

Turn right on RM Road 473 when this road dead-ends in 1.6 miles. After about 0.25 miles on RM Road 473, turn right on Waring-Welfare Road, marked by the "Waring 4" sign.

Note: If the river is too swollen to cross by the old railroad bridge, simply backtrack from the bridge to RM 473, and then turn right on RM 473 toward Sisterdale. After 2.5 miles on RM 473, you come to the Waring-Welfare Road. Turn right here to get to Waring.

As you drive through this thicketed bottomland, you'll notice another long stretch of aging, knee-high rock fence on your left.

You must cross the Guadalupe again to enter Waring. Most of the time, the Guadalupe placidly flows below this low-water bridge, but on occasion (most recently in October 1996) it rises spectacularly, as evidenced by the twenty-five-foot flood gauge attached to a towering cypress tree just to the left of the bridge. Immediately after crossing the rushing, cypress-shaded Guadalupe, bear to the right to enter Waring.

WARING

Kendall County • 73 • About 4 miles from the Waring-Welfare Rd./RM 473 junction

Waring, like dozens of other Texas towns, was a child of the railroads. Like dozens of other railroad towns, Waring put an older town—Windsor—out of business. Windsor was located across the Guadalupe River from Waring. The area was first settled in 1849, but Windsor didn't get a post office until 1880, although a stage stop was established earlier.

Waring was named for R. P. M. Waring, who donated the right-of-way land for the SA&AP (later known as the T&NO), when the line was being built to Kerrville in 1887. On October 2, 1887, the *Austin Statesman* announced that Waringford was the newest town on the northwest extension of the SA&AP and that it was intended to serve as the distribution point of freight and passengers to and from Fredericksburg, Blanco, and Sisterdale. In 1888, the post office was moved across the Guadalupe from Windsor, and the town was properly founded and named Waringford. It retained this name until 1901, when post office authorities shortened it. Today, Waring is a somnolent little river town composed of a couple dozen homes, a church, a store, and a post office. No matter where you are in Waring, you are always within earshot of the roaring Guadalupe.

The first thing you see as you enter Waring, if you look carefully, is the steeple of the old whitewashed Waring Baptist Church, which sits to your right. To reach it, turn right on Manning, the first street after you cross the river and enter Waring. It was originally a community church where all denominations worshipped on alternating Sundays. It was then abandoned, except for occasional community functions, until about World War II, when the Baptists took it over, an act that engendered hostility in some quarters. The antagonism has yet to die down. The present wooden-frame sanctuary is the second church building, built around the turn of the century; no one really knows exactly when.

The old Waring School sits across from the church on the riverbank, at Manning and Avenue E. The first wing of this wooden schoolhouse was built in 1891; the second in 1903, by public subscription. It is still used for the annual Waring Homecoming and as a polling and meeting place. The old Windsor stage stop is located directly across the river from the schoolhouse, up on the hill. All that remains are the rock stables, and they are on private property.

On adjoining corners, at the crossroads of FM 1621 and Waring-Welfare roads, are the Waring Store and the old Waring post office. The post office building began life in 1937 as the local Red and White grocery store and post office. The grocery closed several years ago along with the post office. Previous to settling down here, the Waring post office had changed locations eight times in only fifty years.

Waring still has some nice turn-of-the-century frame and embossed-tin farmhouses. From the Waring Store, head west about a quarter mile, up the hill, on RM 1621. Turn around, and from atop this hill you can see all of Waring spread out before you.

One of the buildings you see is the old Waring depot, sitting alone in the middle of a grassy field.

WARING DEPOT

One block west of Waring-Welfare Rd., corner of N. Front and Waring Rd.
• Not open to the public

A tin roof covers the older wood shingle one. At first glance, the abandoned Waring station looks like dozens of other rural Texas depots. Although these buildings were similar in size and the materials used, subtle individuality resulted from variations in detail and patterns of finish, such as ornamental shingle patterns or roof brackets. This depot's most distinguishing characteristic was the mustard color of its simple board-and-batten siding, some of which remains. The roof brackets are rudimentary A-line affairs. As you travel through the other little towns in this book, look at the few remaining old depot buildings, and you'll recognize these small variations. The Bertram depot is a good example.

The last train passed through Waring nearly forty years ago, and these days you can scarcely tell that the iron horse ever chugged through. The depot and adjoining grassy right-of-way are your only clues. The small frame house sitting across the street (to the east) from the depot was originally the hotel. Most of it was torn down years ago, leaving only this several-room section that is now a private residence.

Head back on RM 1621 to the Waring Store and junction, and turn right (south) on narrow little Waring-Welfare Road to reach Welfare.

The road to Welfare takes you through rolling, densely wooded ranching country; the trees are so thick that they form a canopy over the road in places. You also cross the old T&NO tracks twice; the silver rails lie embedded in the asphalt, and you see the raised roadbed on either side of you. Welfare sneaks up on you before you know it, four miles south out of Waring. There are no highway signs to warn you, only a handful of houses and the Welfare Store.

WELFARE

Kendall County • 36 • About 4 miles from Waring

Welfare, located in the fertile bottomlands of Big Joshua and Little Joshua creeks, was first settled by German immigrants in the 1840s and was known as Boyton or Bon Ton for several decades. The name was changed to Welfare when the railroad came through. But why the name was chosen is harder to pin down. Some say the surrounding rich fields caused people to regard it as a place where one could "fare well." Others say *Welfare* is a corruption of the German word *Wohlfahrt*, meaning "pleasant trip." Welfare, after all, had been smack dab on the main road west from old San Antonio de Bexar for centuries. Only with the comparatively recent construction of US 87 through Comfort has Welfare been bypassed by the mainstream of transcontinental traffic.

Indians traveling the Pinto Trail from the Northern Plains to south and central Texas closely followed what was later to be the path of the F&N, through the pass at Cain City and across the Divide. Then they continued on what would become the SA&AP's route across the Guadalupe near Waring and through the Spanish Pass south of Welfare, on through Boerne and San Antonio. The Spanish Pass provides a natural passage for travel through the range of high hills located about six miles north of Boerne. The pass was used by Spanish missionaries, miners, and soldiers bound for the San Saba de la Cruz Mission (located near present-day Menard), hence the name. Treasure hunters have been combing the Hill Country for the fabled San Saba mines ever since the mission was abandoned in 1758.

American teamsters, soldiers, and settlers continued to use the old Indian trail, and Welfare became a stage stop on the grueling San Antonio-to-San Diego run. The Camp Verde-bound camels also passed through Boyton/Bon

Ton on their way west from San Antonio in 1857. The "SAP," as the SA&AP was sometimes called, also chose this path of least resistance through the pass, and with its arrival in 1887, Boyton got a depot and a new name.

The main highway to Fredericksburg, old Highway 28, the Gulf-to-Panhandle highway, ran through Welfare until 1932. Highway 28, superseded by US 87, is now just the meandering county road you have been traveling on since the RM 473 turnoff.

The original Welfare store, a two-story building, was established in 1890, the post office in 1889. The building burned down in 1916 and was rebuilt that same year, a combination mercantile store, post office, cafe, saloon, and home (living quarters are attached out back). The Welfare Store was the heart of the Welfare business district. The saloon had its own private entrance, incidentally. No entrance was allowed from the room that housed the post office; federal law, you know.

Perry and Alma Laas operated the store and post office from 1920 or 1921 to either 1976 or 1978 (depending on which accounts you read). Then the store closed.

The store building was restored and reopened in 1998 as the Welfare Cafe and Biergarten, a fine dining establishment that is open Wednesday through Sunday (www.welfarecafe.com).

The cotton gin is gone, and the little whitewashed frame schoolhouse sits a hundred or so feet east of the road (to your left), even with the Welfare highway sign as you continue south out of Welfare. The school started life in 1890, about four miles from here, on Big Joshua Creek. The local men tore it down and rebuilt it here, across the railroad tracks from the store. Only a brace of houses stand in the immediate vicinity of the store, but folks from several miles around claim Welfare as their home, proudly proclaiming, "We're in Welfare, not on Welfare."

Just after you leave Welfare, continuing south on Welfare Road, you see the sad old roadbed on your left and then a collection of weather-beaten old homesteads as you continue on toward Boerne.

NICHOLAS ZINK HOMESTEAD

**About 5 miles south of Waring, look for a historical marker on your left •
Private property**

Born in Bavaria in 1812, Nicholas Zink came to Texas in 1844 with his wife, Louise. They came as part of the Adelsverein colonization scheme. Zink was a civil engineer and former Bavarian Army officer. According to Dr. Ferdinand Roemer, Zink had at one time been superintendent of road building in Greece and had come to Texas because his work in Greece had not been well received in Bavaria. He hoped to make a fortune in Texas through trading and speculation. Roemer described Zink as "a rather peculiar person with coarse, marked features, bald head, and spectacles on his nose, dressed in wide linen trousers stuffed into his boots, and wearing a short grey jacket."

From December 1844 to March 1845, he supervised the move of approximately half of the German immigrants from Indianola to New Braunfels. Once they had arrived at the site that would become New Braunfels, Zink supervised the construction of a log palisade, or fort, to protect the immigrants' temporary tent city. This fort was called Zinkenburg. Zink also surveyed the original town site and the surrounding farmland.

By 1846, Zink was hauling freight and passengers back and forth from Houston to New Braunfels. In 1847, he was divorced from Louise for "unhappy differences" and headed for Fredericksburg, but he changed his mind and settled on Sister Creek. There he built a large two-story log house, the first building in what would become Sisterdale. He remarried and gained a reputation as a good farmer. But he still wasn't satisfied, so in 1850, he and his new wife, Elisabeth, sold their house and land and moved to Fredericksburg to build and operate a gristmill on Baron Creek. By 1853, he had moved once again, this time to the Comfort area where he built Perseverance Mill on the Guadalupe River. Its first dam washed away, and then drought idled it for another year. In 1868, he moved here and built a limestone house, which is the center part of the current two-story ranch house you see from the road.

The 1870 Kendall County census listed Zink as a shingle maker. By this time he had married again, to an Englishwoman named Agnes who was young enough to be his daughter. When plans were announced to build the SA&AP line to Kerrville, Zink donated land for the railroad right-of-way and helped engineer it. His joy at its successful completion was short-lived, however; he died on November 3, 1887, less than a month after the first train steamed into Kerrville. Zink is buried in an unmarked grave on a knoll near this house.

Turn left onto FM 289 (about one mile past the Zink homestead), which soon becomes the I-10 frontage road.

PO-PO FAMILY RESTAURANT

US 87/I-10 frontage road, 8 miles north of Boerne and 3 miles from Welfare • 830-537-4194 • Open daily, lunch and dinner • Cr. • Beer, wine • W

The venerable Po-Po, with its famous, distinctive red neon "EATS" sign out front, started life as a dance hall built in 1929 by local rancher/dairyman Edwin Nelson. He had earlier established a gas station nearby, and this little motorist's oasis midway between Boerne and Comfort, at the junction of old highways 12 and 28, became known as "Nelson City." Nelson City still appears on official Texas Highway maps, although it has never had a post office or been incorporated.

The Nelson Dance Hall featured a dance every two weeks, and the musicians would play from 8 p.m. until 2 a.m. Admission started at twenty-five cents a head, but as the Depression deepened the price dropped to a dime and finally to the passing of a hat. People just couldn't afford to buy the gas to drive out there, so the dance hall failed.

The hall was sold in 1932 to Ned Houston, another local and very colorful rancher who exported cattle all over Central and South America. He converted the hall into a restaurant, naming it in all probability for the famous Mexican volcano Popocatepetl, whose nickname is Popo. Houston knew the volcano well, and he had been looking for a short, punchy name. Houston sold Po-Po in 1938, and it has changed hands several more times since. The plate collection (more than eight hundred plates now), which covers the inside walls, dates to the ownership of Luther and Marie Burgon (1950–1981).

Po-Po serves straightforward, simple American food: steaks, barbecue, chops, chicken, and seafood. Po-Po has a beer garden and outdoor music stage. It's wise to call ahead for reservations on Friday and Saturday nights.

From Po-Po, get on I-10 and head south toward Boerne. After four miles on I-10, take Business US 87 into downtown Boerne.

BOERNE

Kendall County Seat • 9,000 (approximate) • (830) • About 8 miles from Po-Po Restaurant

Townbuilder John James bought the land on which Boerne was built in 1840. Fourteen years later, he and Gustave Theisen laid out a town here and named it for Ludwig Boerne, a radical German political journalist and satirist. Boerne never came to Texas and was dead in Paris by 1837, but his writings maintained a measure of popularity, especially among the German radicals and idealists who immigrated to Texas in the 1840s and founded the communistic society of Bettina on the Llano River. (Read more about Bettina in the chapter "Mormon Trails.")

After the Bettina colony broke up, five of its founders migrated south to a spot near present-day Boerne. The *Handbook of Texas* states that "in 1849 a group of German colonists from Bettina camped on the north side of Cibolo Creek, about a mile west of the site of present Boerne. They called their new community Tusculum, after Cicero's home in ancient Rome." Like Bettina, Tusculum broke up after a couple of years. But some of the men stayed here individually, as Boerne's earliest settlers. Hundreds of Germans joined them, making Boerne and Kendall County one of the most thoroughly German regions in Texas. They built a dam across Cibolo Creek and used it to power a gristmill and shingle-making machinery. But these early comers were continually harassed by raiding, kidnapping Indians.

Boerne has been Kendall County's only county seat. Eighty citizens of Boerne and Sisterdale petitioned the state to create a new county as early as 1859, but Kendall County was not created until 1862, when the Confederate legislature carved it out of Blanco and Kerr counties. Boerne beat Sisterdale in the election to determine the county seat. At that time, the county's population was 81 percent German. They were primarily stock raisers, farmers, and cedar choppers. As late as 1877, a portion of the county's citizens were agitating in favor of removing the county from Boerne to Sisterdale, or thereabouts.

British immigrants began coming to the Boerne area during the 1870s and were not especially welcomed by the Germans. Many were inspired to come by William Gilliam Kingsbury, a dentist turned agriculturist and immigration agent for the Galveston, Harrisburg and San Antonio Railway company, which had a scheme for settling English immigrants in towns all along its line from Houston to San Antonio and beyond. Financial conditions were poor in England, and these men were attracted by promises of lots of money.

Kingsbury's speeches, pamphlets, articles, and books, published in several languages, are credited with having convinced thousands of people, mostly English, to immigrate to Texas. Editions of his pamphlet, "A Description of

South-Western and Middle Texas," were published in London in 1878 and 1883. His writings about Texas caused the governor to appoint him Texas commissioner of immigration. He represented several railroads in Europe and maintained a headquarters in London from 1875 to 1884, using the title of Texas Land and Emigration Agent. Kingsbury was active in agriculture and stock raising and was a pioneer in developing the modern silo system of storing feed. In 1872, Governor Edmund J. Davis named him one of Texas' three representatives at the 1873 Vienna World's Fair.

Kingsbury, who ranched in the Boerne area, encouraged the English immigrants to farm and to develop cattle ranches and lead herds of cattle north to market.

Like many immigrant guides of the nineteenth century, Kingsbury's pamphlet made grandiose promises about Texas that were at times outright lies, such as the claim that in the middle of the savage Texas July, "those of us who have farm work to do, or riding or driving upon the road, find no inconvenience in working ten hours per day. The heat is never oppressive as in England." Kingsbury's exaggerations had their negative consequences.

"Several hundred English families have been induced to come to Texas, during the last year or two, by the representations of Dr. Kingsbury," wrote the popular humorist Alex Sweet in about 1882. "Some of those people are doing well, some have gone back to England; and the rest lie around, and spend their leisure in writing letters to the *London Times and Telegraph*, abusive of Kingsbury and the State of Texas."

"Two Englishmen go into the store at Weimar.

"'Aw, 'ave you got henny Lea & Perrin's Wor'ster sauce?'

"'No: don't keep it, sir; never heard of it.'

"'Never 'eard of it! By Jove, what a blawsted country!'

"Turning to the other exile, "'Arry, let's go back to hold Hengland.'

"The English get homesick because they cannot get gooseberries and 'arf-and-'arf and Lea & Perrin's sauce, growing on every mesquite tree in Texas. They forget to give any credit to the watermelons, figs, and other good things that they get in Texas, and that they could not raise, even in a hothouse, in England."

Humor aside, so many of the English immigrants either went back home, or stayed and wrote home exactly what they thought of their experience, that Kingsbury and his minions went into spin control as early as 1880:

> We are aware that many of our countrymen have come here and returned dissatisfied. Some of them commenced cursing Texas before they lost sight of the shores of England because of some trivial inconvenience in their ship accommodations. Some have returned without landing from the ship and others after a stay of from twelve hours to as many days, and without having explored the country in some instances as much as one mile from the station or seen anything of it, except that little they could see from a car-window. We believe the fault in all these cases has been with the people and not with the country, and it is universally the case that those of us who have been here the longest like it the best and would not leave it for any country of which we have any knowledge. We have seen newspaper attacks by these returned and dissatisfied emigrants upon the descriptive writings of Dr. Kingsbury, the London agent at the GH and SA railway company, but we are satisfied, after verifying the statements made by him and the other gentlemen who contributed articles to his book, by our residence in the country, that every statement is fully warranted by the facts, and many of us think the country vastly

better than he has pictured it. Some of us know Dr. Kingsbury personally. He has been at our houses and we at his, and we have broke bread at each other's tables, and such of us indorse him as a man of sterling worth, honor and integrity, and respected by all who know him at home. Some men are dissatisfied wherever their lot is cast, and we have never known a country open to English emigration from which men have not returned and abused the agents who sent them.

By 1895, most of the English were gone from Kendall County and those further east along the GH&SA. They left behind a strong Episcopal Church in Boerne and the game of polo, which was, according to local lore, first played in the United States in the Boerne area.

Boerne became a stage stop on the road northwest from San Antonio, the Upper Emigrant Road. The SA&AP superseded the bumpy Concord stagecoaches in 1887, and all of a sudden the thirty-one miles between San Antonio and the romantic hills of Boerne were little more than an hour and ninety-five cents away. Boerne quickly grew into a popular tourist resort, famous, as noted in a tourist brochure of that era, for "the purest air God ever made for man or woman, either. The burg is principally noted for the unlimited quantity and excellent quality of its ozone, whatever that is, its surpassing beauty, its beer (imported from San Antonio), its public spirited citizens, pretty girls, good hotels."

The tourists also came here to climb the rugged hills, to drink the cold water bubbling from the iron and sulphur spring four miles out of town, to explore the caves along the Cibolo, or simply to sit around on the hotel porch and breathe the healthy air. Perhaps while they were here, the visitors also partook of some of the local fruit of the vine. Though the wild grapes and berries gathered around here bore little resemblance to the carefully cultivated grapes of the Rhine and Mosel, the immigrants nonetheless managed to produce a potable wine by adding large amounts of sugar to the juice. The quantities produced were generally quite modest, mostly intended for home consumption, but this was not always the case. Farmers around Boerne produced over fifty thousand gallons in one season during the 1870s. A few of the area's old Germans still make mustang grape and dandelion wines. A lot of charcoal burning was also done in and around Boerne, so much so that Boerne was often disparagingly called the "Charcoal Capital of the World" by neighboring towns.

Although the SA&AP was a big-time line compared with the F&N, it received its share of ribbing from its customers. They referred to the SA&AP as the SAP because it "went up in spring and came down in the fall." Of course, a round trip on the SAP didn't take quite that long, though it probably seemed that way sometimes to stranded passengers. The SAP also acted as colonization agent, bringing English settlers to Boerne via the Southern Pacific Colonization Company. (Southern Pacific bought the SAP but kept the old name.) The Texas and New Orleans (T&NO) didn't escape ribbing either; among blacks, at least, it was joked that T&NO stood for "Tramps and Niggers Only." Elsewhere in the state, the Houston East & West Texas was known as the "Rabbit" because its profile seemed to hop from hill to hill, and the ride was so unpleasant that it was "Hell Either Way You Take It." The Houston and Texas Central was called "Hoboes and Tin Cans."

On March 15, 1887, the *San Antonio Daily Express* described the SA&AP's inaugural run to Boerne in an article titled "First Train to Boerne over Northwestern Extension: A Pleasant Ride over a Beautiful Country; Day Spent in Romantic Hills around Boerne."

Those who had an opportunity of going out of San Antonio on the first train to Boerne over the Northwest Extension of the San Antonio & Aransas Pass road, realized perhaps for the first time that the 4-horse coach is a thing of the past. It has gone west where most needed, and San Antonians now travel luxuriantly in every direction by rail. With the departure of the stage coach San Antonio also bids an affectionate farewell to the old stage driver, a character much better known a few years ago than today. He was the boss once, and at a not very remote time when the prancing blacks or grays, "four-in-hand," danced into town from almost every direction, the driver was no mean character and was looked up to with as much deference as is usually accorded to the mayor of a country village. But he has gone now, his glory is departed, and the places which knew him once will know him no more forever. And there are none to mourn for him. In fact, the comfort and convenience of travel in a modern palatial railway coach over that afforded by the old time "Concord," leaving out of account the saving of time and money and the wear and tear of both body and mind, makes the stage drivers' demise and the advent of the iron horse in its place a blessing to suffering humanity. San Antonians think so, and all Boerne is now ready to echo "amen."

At 4:30, 10 minutes behind time, the train started, pulled by No. 11, the "Martin & Schryver" engine. Leaving out of the account the delay at the Balcones, in order to clear the way for the returning construction train, the trip was made in good time through as beautiful country as one would wish to see in a whole day's journey. The romantic scenery around Leon Springs, where there are lofty mountains and green valleys, was particularly admired by the travelers, many of whom had never been so far west of San Antonio before.

At Leon Springs, about the only suitable point on the route, on account of water, the Aransas Pass company expects to build a town. The site is a good one in every respect, with a flourishing country for miles around, and may one day not very remotely, either, become a busy, industrious village, furnishing more business for the merchants and manufacturers of San Antonio. One very noticeable feature of the trip was the superiority of the road bed. Though a new one just completed, it is as smooth as can be, making the short journey altogether one of rare pleasure and comfort. The . . . advent of the civilizing iron horse was made about . . . when a majority of the citizens of the town were found ready to welcome their guests, but more doubtless to see the puffing locomotive and hear the steam whistle for the first time in their lives. It was a great occasion, and as such was duly appreciated, although the lateness of the hour, no doubt, alone prevented our reception with a brass band at the head of the local militia company. The depot grounds are located about one mile east of town in an excellent situation for convenience and traffic, and the transfer of passengers and baggage is made from there in buses and hacks, though on this occasion many of the visitors were compelled to walk to town. It is the intention of the company to build one of its handsomest depots at once. It will be under the management of Mr. Theodore Grice, a young gentleman who has had large experience in the railroad business and has already made himself popular with the people of the village. At present he carries his office with him and does business wherever he finds it.

Boerne is situated among a dozen or more beautiful and romantic hills and from her throne of beauty rules Kendall County, 31 miles distant from San Antonio, by railroad count, and it costs you but the small sum of 95 cents to get to it and enjoy a whiff of the purest air God ever made for man or woman, either. The burg is principally noted for the unlimited quantity and excellent quality of its ozone, whatever that is, its unsurpassing beauty, its beer (San Antonio variety), its public spirited citizens, pretty girls, good hotels, for being the country home of the Herff family and the "One-Horse Farmer." Another thing your correspondent forgot to mention as among the noted institutions of Boerne, and that is the keno room. Cards are 3 for a quarter, and the game is played in the same old way. All sit around a rough pine table deeply absorbed in the numbers called out by the dealer, until one man yells "keno," and others say "Oh, h-ll!" only they say it in German and it doesn't sound so bad to English ears polite.

There is much of interest in and around Boerne for the stranger who may climb the rugged hills and drink in nature's magnificence in all its original undefiled beauty until he is footsore and weary, travel for 2 miles on the principal and only street in the city, drink the cold water of the iron and sulphur spring four miles distant, explore the hidden wonders of the caves and lofty bluffs along the Cibolo, or sit on the broad plaza of the Boerne Hotel and expand the lungs with deep draughts of ozone, or watch the slow and painful steps of the poor consumptive invalid who generally comes to West Texas when it is everlastingly too late for all the ozone in the world to do him any good.

Through the kindness of Capt. Brown, the livery man, your correspondent visited the iron and sulphur spring and tasted of its invigorating water. It is said to have some very superior medicinal qualities. It is kept in poor condition, however, without any care or attention, and only awaits the arrival of the enterprising Yankee to make a big "bonanza" out of it.

In the afternoon, after making the acquaintance of a number of prominent citizens, a pleasant and entertaining visit was made to the beautiful and substantial country home of Dr. F. Herff, in company with the entire family, when the afternoon was spent in riding over the doctor's vast possessions and examining the wonderful bluffs along the Cibolo river, where the water suddenly disappears in the ground, to rise no more. One noted feature in the doctor's pasture, besides these mysterious water caverns, is the Melakoff mountain, which rises to a height of several hundred feet above the fertile valley and affords perhaps the finest view in all the country. The residence is a handsome two-story, hard rock house, containing almost everything to make life worth living, and here it is that the doctor and his family, together with all his grandchildren go to spend a large portion of each summer. Altogether, Boerne offers a desirable place for excursionists, and it can be made one of the most popular health resorts in the South, if her people will exert themselves a little and make her advantages known to the great outside world. Nature has been most lavish in her gifts to Boerne and Kendall County. The ozone is there, but her people must do the rest.

The return journey was begun at 7 a.m. Monday and was made in good shape without accident in just two hours. The next excursion to Boerne will take place on Thursday, on which occasion there will be a grand barbecue.

The SA&AP brought hundreds of tourists and excursionists to Boerne, in what was called the Texas Alps. Resort hotels sprang up to accommodate them. The railroad also brought hundreds of tuberculosis sufferers, or "consumptives," as they were known. In the age before antibiotics, the preferred treatment for "consumption" was the open-air method, and Boerne had an excellent high, dry climate for this long-term treatment. A consumptive newly arrived in Boerne found too many invalids like himself, invalids who talked about themselves and their poor remnants of lungs, and coughed and groaned all night. The hotels and boarding houses smelled like drugstores, and the invalids drank to each other's better health in cod liver oil until they smelled like ancient fishermen. Many resorts did not accept consumptives, though.

Dr. Ferdinand Herff was instrumental in building the St. Mary's Sanitarium for tuberculosis suffers in Boerne and was also one of the primary supporters responsible for the branch line of the San Antonio & Aransas Pass Railway that ran from San Antonio to Kerrville, bringing thousands of patients to Boerne. Several other smaller sanitaria were built to accommodate all the patients.

In recognition for donating railroad right-of-way through his Herff Ranch and his other efforts in assisting the railroad, including donating land in San Antonio for the SAP roundhouse and car shops, SAP locomotive No. 10 was named the "Dr. Ferdinand Herff."

Just seventy years ago, Boerne was described as a "health and recreation resort ringed by wooded hillsides, spreading its winding streets past old stone houses. Narrow windows, outside stairways, steep gables, and prim little front-yard gardens show its Old World influence." With the completion of I-10 through Boerne, the sleepy German town became essentially a San Antonio bedroom town. But some of the old flavor remains. The Boerne Village Band is said to be America's oldest continuously active German music band, going back to 1860. It plays regularly at the Abendkonzerte Series at Boerne's Main Square.

A string of Victorian residences lines Business US 87 into town, harking back to the days when the SAP ran alongside.

A. S. TOEPPERWEIN HOUSE

612 N. Main

This one-story frame cottage with a distinctive porch turret was built in 1894 by a member of an unusually talented German immigrant family, of whom we shall shortly learn more. Family patriarch Lucian Ferdinand Toepperwein was born in 1810 in Westphalia, Germany, the son of a soldier and gate superintendent (surveyor of taxes) for the Prussian government. He became a teacher and in 1844 was appointed head magistrate of a girls' school where he authored several books for children. In 1849 he immigrated to Texas with his wife and their three oldest children.

The Toepperwein family farmed near Grapetown for several years. Lucien's daughter, Emma Marie, married Max Aue of Leon Springs in 1857. His second son, Wilhelm Herman, married Amalie Luckenbach on May 27, 1857, and that fall became the first public school teacher in Boerne. The oldest son, Gustav Adolph, married Charlotte Lohmann and ran a general store on Main Street. Arnold S. Toepperwein was the only son of the Gustav Toepperweins and became famous as a cabinet and furniture maker, remembered for his superb workmanship and the "Ringtail Rino" trademark inscribed on each piece of furniture. Examples of his work may be seen in the Kuhlmann-King House: the kitchen table and mantle, as well as the living-room bookcase, sport his unique Ringtail Rino signature.

Main at Blanco is the official center of town. Main Plaza is off to your right, the courthouse square to your left.

DIENGER STORE/ANTLERS INN

N. Main and Blanco

The two-story building immediately to your right at this corner was built in 1884 by local merchant Joseph Dienger. Distinguished by its broad two-story wraparound porches, the store was later famous as the Antlers Inn. It typifies the German tradition of fine craftsmanship and construction. The skill of its German masons is evident in the excellent workmanship of the walls. The square wooden porch columns framed with wooden moldings and jigsaw brackets are typically German. The ornate quatrefoil porch decoration contrasts nicely with the roughly polished limestone block walls.

Turn right on Blanco, so as to circle Main Plaza. On down at the end of the block is Ye Kendall Inn.

YE KENDALL INN

128 W. Blanco

The center section of Ye Kendall Inn is the old Reed house, built by Erastus and Sarah Reed, who purchased the land in 1859. The house and property changed hands several times during the next few years, and after 1869 its fame grew as the King place, under the ownership of Colonel and Senator Henry C. King. By 1878, the Boerne climate had begun to attract health seekers, mostly sufferers from asthma, tuberculosis, and sinusitis, who were willing to make the jolting thirty-one-mile stage ride from San Antonio. To accommodate the growing clientele, subsequent owners C. J. Rountree and W. L. Wadsworth enlarged the building to its present size and renamed it the Boerne Hotel. In 1909, owner Dr. H. D. Barnitz changed the hotel's name to its present appellation.

The original Reed house part of the inn is constructed of local limestone, with twenty-inch-thick walls. The building has a cellar, and there is evidence down there of a tunnel, which is rumored to connect the building with another building a block away. Story has it that the tunnel was dug for protection from raiding Indians. The courtyard out back is the old wagon yard, where passengers were loaded and unloaded from passing stagecoaches.

In 1996, several old buildings were moved onto the premises, including a 1920s schoolhouse formerly located on I-10; a carriage house; a 1922 Lutheran church first located in Dobrowolski, Texas; a turn-of-the-century Victorian cottage formerly located on Main Street; a cedar-log cabin from the Fredericksburg area; and an 1820s log cabin moved here from Virginia. Two reproduction storefronts were also constructed.

Follow San Antonio back to Main Street. Cross Main on E. San Antonio, past the courthouse and square.

KENDALL COUNTY COURTHOUSE

Main and E. San Antonio

The date on the limestone Kendall County courthouse reads 1909, but this date is only a half-truth. That was the year the front addition was built. Alfred Giles designed this shyly romantic Italianate addition during his later years, and it contrasts strongly with the severe lines of his 1882 Gillespie County courthouse. Yet both are distinctively Giles. The back half was built in 1870, which makes this the second oldest courthouse still in use as such in Texas. The jail next door was built in 1884, and the old sheriff's office is of the same era. It underwent extensive restoration in 2009.

Turn left at the eastern end of the courthouse block onto Saunders. Catercorner to the county jail is the Boerne City Utilities Office.

BOERNE CITY UTILITIES OFFICE

402 E. Blanco

Alfred Giles also designed the two-story limestone building that now houses the City Utilities Office. Built in 1910, it originally housed the Boerne High School. It bears a certain resemblance to the courthouse addition. An older one-story limestone block schoolhouse stands immediately behind it.

HISTORIC HOUSE MUSEUM/ KUHLMANN-KING HOUSE

400 E. Blanco, next to City Hall • 249-2807, 249-2469 • Museum open Sunday 1–4, Archives open Thursday 9–noon, 1–4 • Adults $1 • W variable

Upon the hill adjacent to the old school is a two-story limestone and cypress home turned museum. Built during the 1880s for local pharmacist and land baron William Kuhlmann, the house was sold in 1908 to Selina King, whose sons operated Boerne's King and King Lumber Company for many years. The Boerne ISD owned the house from 1920 to 1951, when it was purchased by the city of Boerne.

The Henry J. Graham Building, a simple frame turn-of-the-century store, has been moved from its original site in the 100 block of S. Main to its present location next to the museum. It started as a private bank (supposedly Boerne's first bank), then served as a real estate office, beauty parlor, barber shop, storage building, and telephone exchange.

Head on back to Main Street, and then turn left on it, toward the city of San Antonio.

Main Street Boerne today bears only passing resemblance to the Main Street of SAP days, but a few nice buildings still line the street.

FABRA SMOKEHOUSE

194 S. Main, behind Benefit Planners Building

Julius Fabra (1827–1910) came to Boerne in 1854 and worked as a freight hauler before opening a meat market here. His son, Ludwig, built the first story of this limestone smokehouse in 1887, and the second story in 1904. Ludwig's son, Henry, operated the market from Ludwig's death in 1929 until his retirement in 1962. The market itself made way for the current building.

BERGMAN LUMBER COMPANY

236 S. Main

The Bergman Lumber building is one of the nicest vintage structures left on Main Street. Two-story, buff brick with limestone trim, it is topped with a crenellated limestone parapet that bears the inscription "1902—H. D. Adler—1911." The front porch is supported by svelte cast-iron posts and lacy iron brackets, once all the rage.

THEIS HOUSE

200 block E. Main (Main and Newton) between Bergman Lumber and Plaza Package Store • Private residence

Just a few yards south of Bergman Lumber and a few more yards up an alley of a street named Newton is the little Theis house. Obscured from immediate view by a newer building on Main Street, this is one of Boerne's oldest residences, built in 1858. Originally a dogtrot cabin, its outer walls have been stuccoed and the dogtrot enclosed. But these improvements were made very long ago, and the home maintains a certain rustic look.

WENDLER HOUSE

302 E. Main • Currently commercial space

This simple one-story white stuccoed cottage is another of Boerne's oldest residences, built about 1855 by Henry Wendler, a master cabinetmaker from Germany. In 1865, he married a daughter of Albert Luckenbach, the namesake of both Luckenbach and Albert communities. They raised seven children in this house.

CIBOLO CREEK

Soon you cross Cibolo Creek. Over the centuries it has been known by a variety of names. Coahuiltecan Indians called it Xoloton; Tonkawas called it Bata Coniquiyoqui. The Spaniards knew it variously as Santa Crecencia, San Ygnacio de Loyola, San Xavier, and finally Cibolo. Cibolo is a Spanish-Indian term for "buffalo." The banks of Cibolo Creek are city parkland, from the Main Street bridge east along River Road/SH 46. It's a nice place to picnic or take a stroll.

ROBERT E. LEE HOUSE

S. Main and Evergreen • Private

Just after you cross the creek, at the corner of Evergreen and S. Main, you see on your left a tiny one-room limestone house. A front porch sign and a small Texas state historical plaque mark the cottage as the occasional quarters of Robert E. Lee, Colonel, Second U.S. Cavalry, back in his Texas frontier days. An interesting barrel-stave cistern surmounting a shingled turret stands a few yards behind the Lee quarters.

PHILLIP HOUSE MANOR

706 S. Main

You can't miss the old Joseph Phillip home, now known as the Phillip House Manor, located on your right a couple of blocks farther south from the Robert E. Lee house. Joseph Phillip built the core of this rambling limestone and mill-sawn lumber complex in 1860. It served as the family home for a few years, but as the years stretched into decades the little house was expanded again and again, serving as an inn (during the resort era), athletic and shooting club headquarters, and dance hall. Phillip's complex once included the old two-story Greek Revival Carstanjen building, built in 1901, located directly across the street.

RUDOLPH CARSTANJEN HOME

707 S. Main

This two-story, porched Greek Revival building dates to 1872, when it was built for early Sisterdale and Boerne settler Rudolph Carstanjen. According to John Henry Brown's *Indian Wars and Pioneers of Texas* (1880) and naturalization papers on file at the county courthouse, Rudolph Carstanjen immigrated from Le Havre, France, arrived at New Orleans on or about the end of July 1850, and headed for Texas, having told immigration authorities that he planned on living in Comal County.

He was born in 1827 in Duisburg, Prussia. His father, Charles, was a successful merchant who amassed a fortune. Rudolph was given a thorough German college education and at age twenty-one went to Buenos Aires, Argentina, where he went on to explore the country. His desire for adventure eventually led him to Texas.

In November 1855, he camped with seven other young men on the present site of Boerne. They built a log cabin, and thus the town began. The men were bound together as a commune and intended to perpetuate a colony along communistic lines. They acquired 640 acres, most of which eventually came under the control of member Croskey, who eventually became county surveyor. The original cabin was serving as his residence's kitchen by 1880. Carstanjen had no financial or material interest in the colony; he was just a traveler who had joined the idealists in search of health and pleasure. When it became evident that the scheme was impracticable, the group broke up and Carstanjen moved to Sisterdale where he bought 320 acres of land and settled down to the life of a farmer. Carstanjen's petition for U.S. citizenship was granted by the Gillespie County District Court during the September term of 1856. During his pioneer experience, he had $1,000 worth of horses and other stock stolen by Indians. In 1869, he married Miss Ottillie von Werder, who was born in New Braunfels, daughter of Hans von Werder, a lieutenant in the Prussian Army who came to New Braunfels as a companion of Prince Solms.

The Carstanjen family remained at Sisterdale until 1872, when they moved to Boerne. The Carstanjens had five children, and they lived in this house for several years before moving back to their farm near Sisterdale. Rudolph was comfortably wealthy (owing mostly to investments in Germany), which allowed him to accumulate numerous properties in Boerne and Kendall County and to lead a life free from having to earn a living. Which is not to say he did not endure the hardships of frontier life, having "roughed it" for two years without sleeping in a house, but he had the luxury of chucking hardship for the easy life whenever he pleased. His fortune enabled him and his family to travel the United States and Europe.

KRONKOSKY HILL

Kronkosky St., up from S. Main

This is the highest hilltop in Boerne, originally the estate of Albert Kronkosky Sr., who built the house between 1911 and 1917. It is currently a school and convent for Benedictine sisters. The tower (built in 1912) is now the school library and offers a great view. The grounds are open to visitors during daylight hours.

Family patriarch Lorenz Kronkosky moved to New Braunfels in 1859 from Germany. Albert Kronkosky Sr., the first of his five children, was born in New Braunfels in 1868. Albert Kronkosky Sr. moved from New Braunfels to San Antonio at the age of sixteen and began his career as a grocery clerk. He then became a clerk in a retail drugstore, which added a wholesale business. He later became chairman of the board of that business, the San Antonio Drug Company. As was the case with many San Antonians who could afford to do so, he built and maintained a home in Boerne. Albert Kronkosky Jr., an only child, was born in Boerne in 1908.

The family was also involved in the Gebhardt Chili Powder Company. Albert Kronkosky Sr. became involved in chili powder through a brother-in-law, William Gebhardt of New Braunfels. Gebhardt, who married Rosa Kronkosky, learned to dry Mexican peppers in his mother-in-law's oven, according to the Kronkosky family foundation. Gebhardt established the business and invented most of the machinery to manufacture the chili powders. But he was not a businessman, and Albert Kronkosky Sr. became owner and managed the firm's growth.

Albert Kronkosky Sr. died in 1944. Like his father, Albert Kronkosky Jr. was active in the drug and chili powder companies.

In 1961, Albert Kronkosky Jr. sold the family estate in Boerne, vacant for ten years, to the Benedictine sisters in San Antonio for $40,000, less than market value.

The main source of the family's wealth was stock in Merck and Co. Pharmaceuticals. Albert Kronkosky Sr. was one of the first investors in the company started by George Merck, a traveling wholesale drug salesman, who invited Albert Kronkosky Sr. to invest. When Albert Kronkosky Jr. died in 1995, he was largest single individual Merck stockholder. He and his wife used their considerable wealth to establish the Kronkosky Charitable Foundation to serve Kendall, Bexar, Bandera, and Comal counties.

OLD ST. PETER'S CATHOLIC CHURCH

S. Main at Kronkosky

Just south of the old Phillip House and up the hill a bit is the old St. Peter's Catholic Church, now dwarfed by the newer (1923) St. Peter's Church. In 1866, Galveston's Bishop Claude DuBois sent the young French emigrant priest Emil Fleury to Boerne to organize a congregation to serve the town and surrounding area. This simple, one-story, gabled limestone church was completed in 1867. Fleury left Boerne in 1869 but returned in 1923 to lay the cornerstone for the present St. Peter's. Except for the tin roof, the church retains its original exterior appearance, including the simple wooden steeple. The interior has been remodeled extensively and is of no historic interest.

THE KAISER HOUSE

902 S. Main

This unassuming limestone house was built by Alexander J. Kaiser, who was orphaned at age ten when his parents were killed by Indians at their farm on Little Joshua Creek between Boerne and Comfort. Shortly thereafter his older brother, Christopher, enlisted in the Confederate Army, and young Alexander went along to serve as a drummer boy. After the war, Kaiser was active in the village band, and built what is now the center of the house as a place for the band to practice in 1879. He later moved his growing family into the building and began to expand the home to its present size. Mr. and Mrs. Kaiser raised eight children here. The old water well, the lime kiln, the outside masonry bathtub, the smokehouse, and the tobacco house at the southwest corner of the property exemplify Kaiser's ingenuity and craftsmanship.

STENDEBACH HOUSE

103 Kronkosky • Open Mondays only

Behind the Beef and Brew Restaurant at S. Main and Kronkosky is another of Boerne's oldest residences, the Stendebach house. Now housing an antique shop, the Stendebach home is a good example of solid German workmanship, from the second phase of settling down here in the Hill Country, when sturdy rock houses replaced the initial log cabins. Field-dressed limestone blocks, a steeply pitched roof breaking stride over the backside-shed attachment, and casement windows are its distinguishing characteristics.

TOURISM INFORMATION

BOERNE CONVENTION AND VISITORS BUREAU

1407 S. Main, in the southern corner of the Wal-Mart parking lot • 888-842-8080 • http://visitboerne.org • Open Monday through Saturday

Located in the historic Kingsbury House, this is the place to go for tourist information.

LODGING

YE KENDALL INN

1-800-364-2138 • www.yekendallinn.com

Kendall Inn currently offers thirty-six rooms, suites, and cottages. There is an in-house restaurant (lunch and dinner daily), tavern, gift shop, and day spa.

AREA PARKS

BOERNE CITY PARK

**106 City Park Rd., off SH 46 East (River Rd.) about 1 mile east of Main •
249-9511**

The Boerne City Park complex has two areas of interest: the one-hundred-acre Cibolo Nature Center (249-4616, www.cibolo.org) and the Agricultural Heritage Center. The Nature Center has a series of walking trails which run along pretty Cibolo Creek, travel from grassland to creek bed, marshland to woodland, and offer a good cross-section of Hill Country habitats, flora, and fauna. The Nature Center Visitor Center is open Monday through Saturday. The trails are open daily.

The Agricultural Heritage Center (www.agmuseum.org) features a working blacksmith shop with a steam boiler powering a main drive shaft that drives various pieces of equipment. The Main Display Barn includes old farming and woodworking tools, antique wagons, a combine, and other displays. Outdoor equipment exhibits include old tractors, plows, combines, and more. The center is open on Saturday or by appointment.

GUADALUPE RIVER STATE PARK

The park is located at the north end of Park Road 31, 13 miles east of Boerne; take SH 46 from Boerne • 830-438-2656 • Open daily • Fee • W variable

Guadalupe River State Park (1,938 acres) is located along the boundary of Comal and Kendall counties. Bisected by the clear-flowing waters of the Guadalupe River, the park is notable for its ruggedness and scenic beauty. It has 4 miles of river frontage, 3 miles of hiking trails, and a 5.3 mile equestrian trail also open to mountain biking. The Guadalupe River's banks are lined by huge bald cypress trees, and the river is the park's most outstanding natural feature. On its winding path through the park, the river courses over four natural rapids; two steep limestone bluffs are evidence of its awesome erosive power.

Trees in the lower elevations and bottomlands include sycamore, elm, basswood, pecan, walnut, persimmon, willow, and hackberry. The uplands are typical Edwards Plateau limestone terrain with oak and juniper woodlands and interspersed grasslands. An old-growth ashe juniper woodland provides nesting habitat for the golden-cheeked warbler. Also living in the park are white-tailed deer, coyotes, gray foxes, skunks, raccoons, opossums, bobcats, armadillos, and other smaller species.

Outdoor activities include bird watching and nature study, canoeing, fishing, swimming, tubing, picnicking, hiking, and camping. The day-use area offers convenient access to the Guadalupe River and has picnic sites and ample parking. Campsites with water and electricity accommodate recreational vehicles and trailers; another area has campsites with water for tent campers and a separate area with walk-in tent campsites with water in the area.

HONEY CREEK STATE NATURAL AREA

Chipped stone tools and arrowheads found on this 2,293-acre property indicate that Honey Creek was favored by early hunter-gatherers and later Indian tribes who roamed the Edwards Plateau. The Doeppenschmidt family, which came from Bavaria, began to homestead in the area in 1866. Doeppenschmidt family members would acquire many parcels of land, including what would become Honey Creek Ranch. Adam Doeppenschmidt consolidated the various parcels in 1894 and sold them to Otto Weidner and Fred Rust in 1910. The tracts, which became Honey Creek Ranch, were worked by the Weidners until 1971. The area was opened for limited access in 1985.

Honey Creek is open for guided tours only and is periodically closed to visitors. There are two miles of trails. A two-hour, guided interpretive tour emphasizes history, geology, flora, and fauna. The tour is conducted on Saturday mornings; call Guadalupe River State Park to confirm. Access is through Guadalupe River State Park. The park has no facilities. Its vegetative diversity is one of its most attractive features. Ashe juniper, live oak, agarita, and Texas persimmon dominate the dry, rocky hills, and a few grasses such as little muhly and curly mesquite have found just enough soil in the cracks to hang on. The junipers are being removed from the upland flats, so the stands of native grasses are reestablishing themselves as the dominant groundcover. In the creek's canyon, there is an increase of cedar elm and older junipers; Spanish oak, pecan, walnut, and Mexican buckeye appear rather abruptly. The terrain levels out again in the narrow floodplain and the creek itself. The dominant species are sycamore and bald cypress. Texas palmetto, columbine, and maidenhair fern occur along the rock banks, spatter dock floats on the surface, and a number of emergent plants are visible in the clear, blue green water. The park's nine soil types have resulted in a varied and abundant fauna. All of the typical Hill Country species, from wild turkeys to fence lizards, ringtails to leopard frogs, plus many types of fish, are found, as well as several species with limited ranges, such as the threatened golden-cheeked warbler.

CASCADE CAVERNS

Cascade Caverns Rd., just off I-10 • When Business US 87 merges with I-10, get onto I-10 briefly toward San Antonio. Take the Scenic Loop/Boerne Stage/ Cascade Caverns Rd. exit off I-10 • 755-8080 • www.cascadecaverns.com • Open daily; check website for current hours • Fee

Carlsbad Caverns explorer Frank Nicholson made Cascade Caverns famous with exaggerated descriptions of his 1932 explorations. This story ran in the *Austin American* on March 26, 1932:

> Frank Ernest Nicholson, explorer of the Carlsbad cavern, Friday night announced the discovery of a 25 million-year-old Texas cave containing blind fish, white bats and milk-colored frogs. The cave is 20 miles northwest of here on the old Spanish Trail in the hills near Boerne. Its entrance has long been familiar to residents of the section but the cave was believed to end with a body of water 500 feet from the mouth. Giant formations hanging from the ceiling into the water give the impression of a back wall.

Nicholson said he and his party reached the far side of the water by diving beneath the formations and there found a grotto a mile in length leading to an underground lake of such great size that powerful flashlights could not distinguish the opposite bank.

"There are literally millions of glittering formations of infinite variety in size and shape," said Dr. Nicholson. "A subterranean stream flows from the first body of water on through the cavern with cascades at intervals. There is abundant animal life in the cave. We found crayfish, white beetles, white bats and white crickets. There were milk-colored frogs along the shore of the inner lake."

The water in the lake flows. A waterfall spills into it along the north shore. The main tunnel leads on and is larger than any other part so far explored. The ceiling at this point is 80 to 90 feet high and the grotto is from 75 to 100 feet in width. Indian arrowheads were found several hundred feet from the entrance. Immense deposits of fossilized sea shells were discovered along the lake shore. The cavern may rival any other on record in beauty and size.

Nicholson estimated the age of the cavern as 25,000,000 years by measuring the larger formations. These grow at the rate of an inch each 90 years. Some in the cavern are massive. Several chambers along the grotto are of great size.

The cave has been named "Cascade Cavern" by Nicholson. He will head an expedition sponsored by the San Antonio Chamber of Commerce which will go farther into the cave with stronger lights and complete equipment. The water in the outer cave will be drained to facilitate operations. For 60 years it has been known that a cave existed here, but it was always full of water. Recently Nature caused an opening deep down in the earth and all the water disappeared into the subterranean river, revealing the cave.

The blind fish, white bats, and milk-colored frogs were all figments of Nicholson's colorful imagination. Originally called Hester's Cave, the hole was commercially developed in 1933. It remained open until 1941. After a nine-year closure, it reopened in 1950. Evidence of ancient Indian life has been found, and legend has it that an early German settler lived a hermit's life here many years ago. The caverns take their present name from a waterfall that plunges almost one hundred feet from a shallow cave containing an underground stream into the main cave. Like most other commercial Texas caves, it is a water-formed cave and is considered 95 percent active. The stalactite/stalagmite formations grow about an inch every one hundred years. The tour takes about an hour. Recreational and camping facilities are located on the grounds.

ANNUAL EVENT

JUNE

Berges Fest • Kendall County Fairgrounds, US 46 • 888-605-9698 • www.bergesfest.com • Father's Day Weekend

This is one of the most colorful and diverse German festivals around. There are dances nightly, oompah music, children's olympics, a parade, and arts and crafts.

One last bit of trivia as we leave Boerne for Leon Springs. Perhaps the town's most famous citizen was Ad Toepperwein, better known as vaudeville's Dead-Eye Dick. Ad was so good with a shooting iron that even Buffalo Bill declined a match with him. It is said that during a ten-day shooting marathon in San Antonio, Toepperwein fired 72,500 times at 2.25-inch wooden blocks tossed into the air and missed only nine of them. The year was 1907, and the feat has yet to be equaled.

Adolph (Ad) Toepperwein was born in Boerne in 1869, the son of German immigrants Ferdinand and Johanna Toepperwein. Soon afterward, the family moved to Leon Springs, where Ferdinand worked as a gunsmith. When Adolph was thirteen, his father died, and the boy went to San Antonio, eventually becoming a cartoonist for the *San Antonio Express* newspaper. As fast with a pen as with a rifle, he won the lightning charcoal sketching contest at the Bexar Athletic Club's sport night in San Antonio in November 1896.

After seeing famed shooter "Doc" W. F. Carter give a marksmanship exhibition, Ad began practicing to perfect his shooting skills. In 1889, he quit his newspaper job and went to New York to find work in vaudeville. After touring with a circus for eight years, in 1901 Toepperwein began a fifty-year stint with the Winchester Repeating Arms Company as an exhibition publicity agent and sales representative. In 1903, he married Elizabeth Servaty. Although she had never before fired a gun, under Ad's supervision she developed into a superb shooter. Two years later, they were traveling as a team billed as "The Famous Toepperweins." They traveled throughout the world until Elizabeth's death in 1945.

Ad Toepperwein set his first official world record at the St. Louis World's Fair in 1904. In 1906, during a three-day exhibition, he hit 19,999 out of 20,000 hand-thrown wood blocks. In 1907, at the San Antonio fairgrounds, he set his most famous world record. At about twenty-five feet, shooting a 1903 model Winchester .22 automatic, he hit 8,000 hand-thrown wood chips in a row and missed only 4 out of the remaining 5,000 chips, during 68.5 hours of shooting. After his retirement in 1951, Toepperwein conducted a shooting camp in Leon Springs. He was elected to the Texas Sports Hall of Fame. Ad Toepperwein died in San Antonio in 1962 and was buried beside his wife in Mission Burial Park. A museum was opened in 1973 on the Lone Star Brewery grounds in San Antonio to house some of the Toepperweins' marksmanship memorabilia.

To resume your path to San Antonio, leave Boerne on Main Street/Business US 87. When Business US 87 merges with I-10, get onto I-10, briefly, toward San Antonio. Take the Scenic Loop/Boerne Stage/Cascade Caverns Road exit off I-10. To reach Leon Springs, the next station on the SA&AP/T&NO route, turn right at the T intersection on the road marked Boerne Stage Road/Scenic Loop Road.

The road sign does not lie; this is the old stage road, executed now in asphalt instead of rocks and ruts, yet still following the original sinuous and toilsome path. For decades traversing a rather lonely course, it can scarcely hold all of the traffic generated by recent area residential development. Still, it has a certain charm. In 2009, the nonprofit organization Preservation Texas Inc. named the ten-mile stretch of Boerne Stage Road/Scenic Loop Road between SH 16 and the Kendall County line as one of the state's top ten endangered historic places. The Scenic Loop was built in the 1920s as part of a forty-six-mile paved touring loop through the Hill Country. The Boerne Stage Road was paved as part of the Old Spanish Trail highway, the first paved cross-country highway, built in the 1920s, linking St. Augustine, Florida, and San Diego, California.

After about six miles, Boerne Stage Road comes to an intersection with Touton-Beauregard Road. Turn left here to reach Leon Springs, which has experienced explosive growth since the 1990s with the northward and westward expansion of San Antonio.

LEON SPRINGS

Bexar County • 9,000 (approximate) • (830) • About 12 miles from Boerne

Leon Springs' first settler was George von Pleve, a German nobleman and immigrant. Mr. von Pleve established a stage stop here in 1846 and was joined in 1852 by fellow immigrant Max Aue. A veteran of the 1848 Schleswig-Holstein War in northern Germany, Aue came to Texas shortly thereafter. He became a Texas Ranger soon after his arrival. Aue's services were rewarded with a 640-acre grant from the state, the plot being located here at Leon Springs.

At the time of his death in 1903, Aue owned more than twenty thousand acres. Upon marrying, he forsook the wild life and settled down to open the Leon Springs Supply Company. Soon he was postmaster, and the stage line was using his store as a horse-changing station and rest stop. His place got so popular that in 1879 Aue built the Leon Springs Hotel, located next to his store. This stage route between San Antonio and San Diego was the longest in the country and took nearly a month of day-and-night traveling to traverse.

Leon Springs was either the first or the last stop out of San Antonio, depending on which way you were headed. When the railroad came through in 1887, the station was named Aue Station in his honor. Aue's reputation with a gun followed him into civilian life. He was commonly acclaimed as the best hunter in the Hill Country. But even his formidable reputation did not render him immune to brigands.

On June 13, 1875, five young men rode up to Aue's station at noon. Aue didn't know their names but recognized them as former customers. They drew their guns, robbed Aue and his guests, and tied them up. They looted the store and ordered the stage company's hostler to saddle up fresh horses. Aue objected in colorfully vulgar language, so they put a pistol to his head, whereupon he shut up. The bandits headed for Boerne and then Comfort, taking the store's stock of clothing with them as well as Aue's money and horses. As soon as Aue got loose, he headed for Boerne and the sheriff's office. A posse was soon formed. The robbers took two horses at Comfort before proceeding to Kerrville, where they stole two more horses. At Kerrville, Captain Schreiner assembled a few men of his former minute company, and the posses gave chase and came up with them forty miles above Kerrville, where they demanded a surrender. The robbers replied by firing at the posse and then took to the brush on foot, leaving their horses. The posse also fired, mortally wounding one robber and killing one of the stage company horses, and capturing ten of the robbers' horses.

Before dying, the wounded bandit revealed the names of his partners and then smiled into the faces of his slayers and murmured, "Tell the old man [Aue] I died in his clothes."

Max passed his talent with a gun down to his sons and his nephew, "Dead-Eye Dick" Toepperwein. Good enough to turn Buffalo Bill gun-shy, Ad Toepperwein was still never good enough to beat his cousin—Max's boy—Rudolph Aue. Aue refused to shoot professionally because he felt it was just a waste of good ammunition. Toepperwein even acknowledged Rudolph's "deader eye" in a poem, which reads, "I've traveled around the world, but no one could shoot like Rudy could." That, from a man who could shoot your portrait in a matter of seconds into a square of tin.

But Rudy was busy running his business enterprises. Besides inheriting the family hotel and store, Rudolph Aue established five saloons to service thirsty troops at nearby Camp Stanley during World War I. It took a railcar load of Pearl beer a day, shipped in from the San Antonio Brewery, to slake their thirst.

Army tents stretched across the countryside during the war, and the troops used Leon Springs, which outcrops just off the Boerne Stage Road, as their laundry area. The camp, now known officially as the Leon Springs Military Reservation, has been closed off and on since its creation in 1917. It is currently in active use.

The end of World War I meant the first closing of the Leon Springs camp, and it also signaled the imminent demise of Charcoal City. Charcoal City was the collective name given to the charcoal burners who lined the banks of the Guadalupe River from just north of New Braunfels to just east of Sisterdale. A few of the burners sold or traded their charcoal to local storekeepers, but most of them drove their briquette-laden wagons down to San Antonio, where the burners sold their charcoal to wholesale dealers or plodded along the city streets, hawking it from their wagons. The charcoal market in San Antonio was variable. A wagonload might sell for as little as eight dollars or for as much as twenty-four dollars. But, as one burner put it, charcoal was always money in the pocket, unlike crops such as corn or cotton, which were often beaten down by hail, devoured by grasshoppers, or shriveled by drought.

The round trip from Charcoal City to San Antonio might take two days or a week depending on road conditions and how quickly the load could be sold. If the river was up, burners on the yonder side of the river were in a fix—there were no bridges back then—while burners on the San Antonio banks of the Guadalupe could laugh all the way to market, knowing that their loads would command premium prices.

Most people in San Antonio used charcoal stoves before 1920. One burner said, "Whenever I got to San Antonio with a load of charcoal that I could not sell, I would drive through the red light district, and in no time at all, they would buy every sack of charcoal. I never could figure out just what they did with that coal—and if I couldn't sell it, they were always ready to trade." At Christmas most burners would throw a few choice cedars on top to sell to the city folk.

Leon Springs was a favorite camping spot for the burners on their way to San Antonio. The loaded wagons' progress was slow, and very often ten to fifteen burners would end the day at Leon Springs. The water was good, and most of the surrounding land was open country, with good grazing for the hungry horses and mules. The men would make their camp for the night, telling stories, playing cards, drinking 'shine, fiddling, and fighting into the night. With an early start the next morning, they could be wandering Bexar's streets almost before the dew was dry.

Uriah Lott saw that the Leon Springs area was ideally suited for use as a picnic grounds, and he began running special weekend excursion trains here from San Antonio. He had a special place in his heart for orphan children and attached an extra coach at the end of the excursion trains for those kids. He paid for their food and drink and told his employees that these children were to be accommodated on any train at any time and at any place.

To see what's left of old Leon Springs today, cross under I-10 past Rudy's Country Store and turn right onto the Old Fredericksburg Road, into which Boerne Stage Road dead-ends. In a few yards you pass Max Aue's old Leon Springs store and hotel complex on your right.

Continue toward San Antonio on the Old Fredericksburg Road, past the blacksmith shop, and on to the Y intersection with the I-10 frontage road. Turn right on the frontage road so as to double back toward Boerne, past the Leon Springs schoolhouse and Max Aue's old store and hotel.

The quaint, cavernous limestone building that now houses a restaurant dates to 1932. It began life as a dance hall and bar and saw plenty of action during World War II—of the Saturday night cut-and-shoot variety—as the B-29 Club.

Now you're back at Rudy's Country Store (24152 W. I-10, 210-698-2141, www.rudys.com, open daily, lunch and dinner, Cr.), which Rudy Aue Jr. built in 1926. Rudy's claims to have the worst barbecue in Texas, and I've found that at times they live up to that claim. Many other folks love Rudy's meats (brisket, pork ribs, pork loin, sausage, chicken, and turkey breast). Take your choice, pay your money, and make up your own mind.

This completes the tour of Leon Springs, the last major stop before San Antonio on the old F&N/T&NO route. From Leon Springs, you can take I-10 into San Antonio, to the corner of South Alamo and South Flores streets where the SAP depot (long since razed) stood. Teddy Roosevelt and his Rough Riders boarded the train here for the long journey that eventually took them to Cuba and San Juan Hill.

If you wish to return to Fredericksburg, you can retrace the railroad tracks' path or take the following route through scenic, hilly, sparsely settled country.

Return to Boerne on Boerne Stage Road or I-10 and take Business US 87 into town. Continue on Business US 87 past the courthouse square and Market Plaza; 1.2 miles later, turn right on RM 1376. In 11.6 miles you come to an intersection with SH 473 and the hamlet of Sisterdale. Continuing on RM 1376, you again cross the Divide (about 6 miles east of the old railroad tunnel), and in about 17 miles you come to Luckenbach. From Luckenbach, go another 4.5 miles on RM 1376 to its dead end at US 290 at Rocky Hill. Turn left on US 290 to reach Fredericksburg, 5.6 miles to the west.

HERMIT OF THE HILLS/ THE HIGHLAND LAKES

APPROXIMATELY 180 MILES

White settlers started coming in numbers to the Texas Hill Country in the 1840s. The early comers liked what they saw: colorful spring flowers, fields of waist-high native grasses, sparkling rivers and bubbling springs, and live oaks that looked like olive trees from a distance. But this lushness was only skin deep. Only a thin layer of soil overlaid the limestone bedrock. The early pioneers' grazing and farming practices quickly destroyed this rich, but delicately balanced, ecosystem. Without the native grasses' thick root system to hold it together, much of what little topsoil the hills had was washed away by rain into the Colorado River and its tributaries, or was blown away by the wind. Wildfires, which had previously kept the growth and spread of ashe juniper and other species in check, were not allowed to burn by the settlers. The result has been the spread of the ashe juniper from its historical range of about three million acres to twenty-one million acres today. A very thirsty species, the ashe juniper literally sucks the land dry of moisture, drying up springs and depriving grasses of both sunlight and water.

The great cattle drives of the 1860s and 1870s also spread the mesquite tree from South Texas into the Hill Country via cattle dung. Cows like to eat mesquite beans, and as they walked from one place to another, they deposited the digested remains of what they had eaten miles earlier, including intact mesquite beans.

And then there was drought. Drought strikes the Hill Country periodically; some would say mostly. There are some wet years, to be sure, but mostly the Hill Country teeters on the brink of drought. The first settlers chanced to arrive during one of the Hill Country's rainy seasons. When drought inevitably returned to the Hill Country, they didn't know what to do; all the rivers and streams dried up. Would it ever rain again?

There was some doubt and much fear, until Jacob Kuechler (see Petri-Lungkwitz Farm) noticed that the growth rings of Hill Country trees alternated between thin and thick; there would be extended periods, even years, of drought, but the rains would eventually return.

HERMIT OF THE HILLS/
THE HIGHLAND LAKES

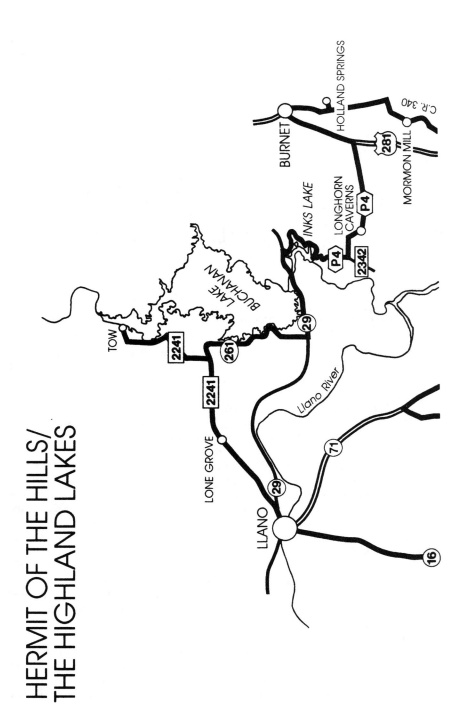

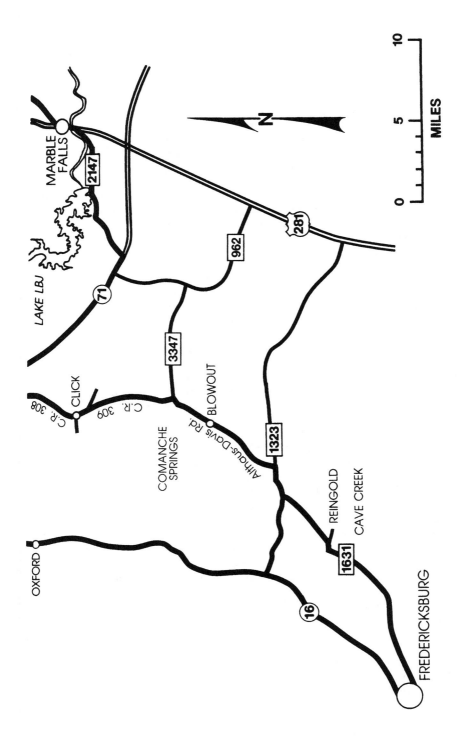

MARBLE FALLS

LAKE LBJ

71

2147

962

281

3347

CLICK

C.R. 308

C.R. 309

COMANCHE SPRINGS

BLOWOUT

Althaus-Davis Rd.

1323

REINGOLD

CAVE CREEK

1631

OXFORD

16

FREDERICKSBURG

N

0   5   10

MILES

While this promise of future rain gave at least scant hope to the folks who were already living here, it didn't attract very many more newcomers to the Hill Country. It took more land out here to sustain a family unit than it did east of the Balcones Escarpment, where it rained more and the dirt was deeper. Some families prospered, but most just managed to hang on. Scrimping and saving was a necessary part of life. Spendthrifts perished.

The old pioneer order began to fade in the 1920s as sons and grandsons of the pioneers, no longer willing or able to wrest a living out of this hard ground, began to flee to the cities. Dozens of villages began to fade from the maps. But by the 1960s, a new migration back out to the hills had begun. These newcomers did not depend on the land for a living, and so the sprawling old pioneer ranches and farms were split up into ranchettes, subdivisions, resorts, planned communities, and such. The mobile homes and California-style ranch houses of retirees and weekenders began to blanket the hills, beginning along the Highland Lakes.

Nothing has done more to change the face of the Texas Hill Country in modern times than the creation of the Highland Lakes chain of dams along 150 twisting miles of the Colorado River, from San Saba County down to Austin. The Highland Lakes brought flood control, drinking water, electricity, paved roads, and tourists to the scenic but hardscrabble Hill Country. The bright, sparkling Highland Lakes play such a large recreational role in our lives these days that we tend to forget their first, noble purposes.

The Texas legislature created the Lower Colorado River Authority (LCRA) in 1934. Before the LCRA's creation, droughts reduced the river's flow to a trickle, while a heavy rain could trigger horrendous floods that washed property and lives away all the way down to the Gulf of Mexico. Besides flood control and water storage, the LCRA's original mission included the generation of electric power. Each dam has its own generating station. Together, the hydroelectric plants provide more than 240 megawatts of capacity to LCRA's electric system. The arrival of electric power in the Hill Country transformed the difficult lives that most people led here only seventy-five years ago.

Without water and the air conditioning that electricity brings, most people would find Hill Country life unbearable. But with them, the region's population has exploded, creating power demands far beyond the hydroelectric plants' generating capacity. Once the LCRA's primary source of power, hydroelectricity today supplies, on the average, less than 7 percent of LCRA's needs. It is used during power emergencies and during power demand "peaks" in extreme weather because it is available at a moment's notice.

Austin, Marble Falls, and dozens of smaller communities depend on the lakes for their water. In the summer, the amount of water used is just about double the winter usage level. A multimillion-dollar-a-year rice farming industry downstream requires summer-long irrigation, using as much water in a single summer as the city of Austin uses in several years. Summertime lake levels are also affected by the customary lack of summer rain, which often amounts to two inches or less. Evaporation on hot sunny days adds further strain; even if lakes Buchanan and Travis released no water during the summer, they would lose a foot of water a month due to evaporation. Water levels at Lake Travis often drop sharply during the summer.

Water quality is an increasingly important mission for the LCRA. The LCRA's Colorado River Trail, which follows the Colorado River corridor through ten

Texas counties, from San Saba to the Gulf Coast, incorporates lakes, highways, parks, events, historic places, and other attractions in an effort to link cultural, historical, recreational, agricultural, and environmental interests to foster awareness and understanding of the importance of clean water and a healthy environment.

Despite all the lake-induced growth, traces of the old, isolated Hill Country still exist along the seldom-traveled back roads away from the lakes. This trip gives you a taste of both worlds.

FREDERICKSBURG

Gillespie County Seat • 11,000 (approximate) • (830)

Despite the passing of generations and the encroachment by "outsiders," Fredericksburg remains Texas' most enduringly German town and is increasingly popular with tourists and expatriate urbanites. Fredericksburgers tend to be protective of their historic landmarks; the town probably has more historic landmarks per capita than any other Texas municipality, and the number grows steadily. It is just one example of the conservatism that is embedded here as firmly as the granite mountains which overlook the town from the north.

Visitors to Fredericksburg are charmed by the abundance of rock houses and Victorian gingerbread, and by the traces of Old World customs and flavors that still hang on, such as the Schuetzenbundes and the annual county Schuetzenfeste, Maennerchor and Damenchor and the annual Saengerfest, the Easter Fires, and the Abendglocken. As recently as 1950, 75 percent of Fredericksburg's population was of German extraction, and German was spoken on the streets as often as English. Today the percentage of German extraction is down to about 50 percent, and only a few of the old folks still speak German among themselves on the street, often in hushed tones guaranteed not to attract the tourists' attention.

During World War II, Fredericksburgers quit speaking German—on the streets, in the churches, and even at home. Parents quit teaching their children German and never resumed the practice. Churches chose not to resume German-language services after V-E Day. Students in the public schools are now taking a renewed interest in learning German, but membership in the singing clubs (German language only) is still declining.

Fredericksburg is a friendly town, but there is a certain resentment among some of the old-timers. "We're glad they visit; we just wish they wouldn't stay," is an oft-echoed sentiment, even among merchants. Vintage Main Street commercial buildings and residences in the Historical District command six-figure prices, reasonable to someone from Austin or Houston, but bewildering to natives. Hundreds of old and new houses have been turned into B&Bs. The B&B business has gotten so hot that old buildings are imported from as far away as Indiana and Pennsylvania and reconstructed on plots of Hill Country pastureland. There is at least one local company that buys, sells, and reconstructs old log cabins and timber frame buildings, plus antique building materials salvaged from razed buildings. A couple of old Main Street businesses hang on, like Dooley's 5-10-25 Cent Store (131–133 E. Main), Crenwelge Motor Sales (301 E. Main), and Knopp & Metzger Department Store (231 W. Main), but most of

Main Street's storefronts are given over to antique and specialty shops, which is not to say that all of these newcomers or "auslanders" are ignorant of the customs and traditions of Fredericksburg. "Sometimes the newcomers are more German than we are," one native wryly admits.

A small but significant number are artisans and craftspeople who paint, sculpt, carve wood, or make toys, duck decoys, and gingerbread for Victorian restorations. "Handmade" is enjoying a renaissance in Fredericksburg.

Fredericksburg is still a small town but definitely growing, from 4,629 inhabitants in 1960 to nearly 11,000 in 2009. Is Fredericksburg in danger of losing its traditional identity?

To get the proper perspective, you have to climb to the top of Cross Mountain. All of Fredericksburg lays spread out just beneath you, some of it built with limestone from this weathered, scarred hillock. You see two Fredericksburgs, the old standing like Gibraltar in a sea of new. Some of today's old-timers may despair over the current state of affairs, but John Meusebach would probably approve. The very day he sailed for Texas to become the Adelsverein's new Texas commissioner, the Baron Ottfried Hans von Meusebach renounced his title to become John O. Meusebach, Texan. He knew you had to bend a little to fit into the new world.

Begin this trip at the Gillespie County courthouse, on US 290 in downtown Fredericksburg. Proceed east on US 290 to the intersection with FM 1631, about eight blocks east of the courthouse. Turn left here and head for Cave Creek.

As you leave town, you will notice acres of the trees that produce one of Texas' most famous and tasty products, the Hill Country peach. During a good spring, the trees are covered first with a riot of pink blossoms, then with dozens of succulent cling and freestone peaches. Subject as the peaches are to the vicissitudes of spring weather, some years we are blessed with bumper crops; other years the blossoms freeze on the trees, and the summer peach crop is barely large enough to feed the growers' families.

Gillespie County peaches are justly favored by connoisseurs. The trees favor the granite-sand soil and cool winter and spring nights. Approximately 1,400 Gillespie County acres are planted in peaches and nectarines. In a good year, the county produces 40 percent of the Texas peach crop. The earliest peaches ripen in May, and by the first of June the peach harvest is in full swing. The roadside stands are open, and peaches are being shipped to the big city supermarkets. Some of the orchards allow you to pick your own fruit, which is the most fun because you get to eat while you pick, and nothing beats a ripe peach or nectarine plucked from the tree.

Generally, May peaches are of the cling variety, the early June peaches are semi-freestone, and the late June and July varieties are freestone. Most of the roadside stands and many of the orchards are located along US 290 (see Enchanted Rock, Rocky Hill). For up-to-date information about Hill Country peaches, visit the Hill Country Fruit Council's website, www.texaspeaches.com.

B. L. Enderle, a Kerrville boy who moved to Fredericksburg in 1912 to become county surveyor and a schoolteacher at Fredericksburg High, is acknowledged as one of the fathers of the peach industry. Both of his parents were of pioneer German families and were involved in the founding of Comfort and Kerrville. An aunt married Captain Charles Schreiner. In Kerrville, Enderle's family lived on Earl Garrett Street near the courthouse and next door to

"Mother" Butt's grocery store. Mother Butt's husband was a TB victim, and he died shortly after the family's arrival in Kerrville to pursue his "cure." The store was established in 1905, and the widow Butt's boys helped out at the store. Her son Howard went on to establish the giant HEB supermarket chain.

In 1921, Enderle and his wife purchased 14.5 acres a mile east of Fredericksburg and began to plant peach trees. He had been growing peaches in his yard since 1915. By 1925, Enderle was producing more peaches than he could sell locally, and he had developed a peach sturdy enough to withstand commercial shipment to San Antonio. The delicacy of earlier-era Hill Country peaches had precluded such handling. Other growers were also developing commercially sized orchards. Because of his boyhood friendship with the Butt family, Enderle obtained the first sales outlet outside the area for Gillespie County peaches in San Antonio's H. E. Butt grocery stores. But it was not until after World War II that Gillespie County peaches began to muscle in on the state market.

Growing peaches is not easy work—the trees must be severely pruned each year, to say nothing of the work involved in picking and shipping them.

Antedating the peach trees out here was one of Fredericksburg's more memorable failed human blossoms, Peter Berg, called the Hermit of the Hills.

A few years after the founding of Fredericksburg, the young man Berg came to the new settlement from Coblenz, Germany. He was a splendid coppersmith and went to the farm of a man who befriended him to make the copper vessels for use on the farm. There he began to tinker with vessels for the manufacture of liquor. After a while, he came to town and built a still in the cliff at the side of Barons Creek, which runs through the town. The town authorities, knowing that he had no license, destroyed his plant, and he returned to the farm of his friend, who gave him a little piece of ground, located a few miles west of the junction of FM 1631 and FM 2721, where he built another still, vaulting in a cave in the side of a ravine and topping it with a hut in which he lived. The hut was entered from an upper level. It is told that this still was full of traps to catch inspectors when they came around. The front of the hut was two-storied; the back was built into the wall of the ravine. He also built a stone tower, which he used as his observation point for studying the stars and forecasting the weather.

Berg used to sell his wines and distilled whiskies on Sunday afternoons outside the old coffee mill church, to the farmers and ranchmen who came to town from miles around on Sundays for divine worship and trading in the afternoon.

A brother from Germany soon joined the hermit, but he was killed shortly after he arrived by the Indians while on his way to town with a barrel of whisky on his back. The barrel was later found with its contents untouched.

Berg had always boasted of the beauty of his fiancée who would soon come over from Germany to marry him. He sent her money to pay her passage and resigned himself to the necessarily long wait, travel in those days being so slow. In the meantime, the prospective bridegroom came to town and sold liquors outside the church. After weeks and weeks of waiting, at last came a teamster from Indianola, the place of landing, bringing the news that the girl had married very shortly after arriving. There were so many suitors, and she was told such harrowing stories of the Indians and the dangers of the overland trip to Fredericksburg, that she was prevailed upon to marry one of them. Berg withdrew to his cave and thenceforth led the life of a hermit, but he continued to sell his wines and whiskies which, they say, rivaled the best of Kentucky brands.

Berg was not a hostile man; he welcomed visitors willing to make the trip out and sold his product to them for thirty cents a gallon.

The sorrow and disappointment of losing his fiancée and the fact that he became quite deaf did not prevent Berg from carrying out one of his ambitions, which was to play the organ. No organ being available, he made one out of a box, with rolled newspapers pasted together serving as pipes. Persons who heard him play said he got good music from the crude instrument, and the organ was for many years still to be seen in Fredericksburg. Against Berg's wishes, the county gave him a pension, but as he did not spend it and did not put it in the bank, no one knew until after his death what he did with it. He frequently told his benefactor that he dreaded the day when he could no longer work, that when that time came he was going to put an end to himself because he did not wish to be a burden to others. He made good his threat. The report of the gun with which he killed himself was not heard, but the hut was set on fire and some hunters saw the smoke. After the fire was extinguished, a search was made and the pension money was found intact behind a loosened stone in the wall. There was money, too, hidden in the bottom of a trunk that had not burned.

From the fund, Berg was given a decent burial, and the balance was kept for relatives who might be located in Germany. Letter after letter, sent in search of some of his kin, remained unanswered, and the money was then turned over to the county treasurer.

Turn left at the FM 1631 and FM 2721 intersection and continue on FM 1631.

CAVE CREEK COMMUNITY

Gillespie County • About 12 miles from Fredericksburg

Cave Creek community was named for the creek that flows through the neighborhood and eventually enters the Pedernales River near Stonewall, and which has some naturally formed caves.

Almost every town and hamlet in the Hill Country has its Indian massacre story, and Cave Creek is no exception. In May 1861, Joe Stahl was killed, presumably by Indians. Born in Germany in 1821, Stahl came to Texas in 1852 with his wife, Louisa, and three children. After working in Fredericksburg as a carpenter, Stahl built a log cabin for his family at Cave Creek, on 160 acres. The family cleared fourteen acres for cultivation. On the morning of May 10, Stahl left home to look for a stray cow and calf. He carried a lunch, pocketknife, and long whip. He told his wife that if he had not found the stock by nightfall he would stay with the Eckert family (fourteen miles away) and search again the next day. When he had not returned by Wednesday, Mrs. Stahl grew upset and told a neighbor that Stahl had disappeared. A search party combed Cave Creek and the environs until Friday, when they found Stahl's body at Rocky Branch, three miles northeast of Stonewall. He had two arrows in his back and one in his neck. The killers took everything but his shoes, which were carried to Mrs. Stahl for identification. Given his advanced state of decomposition, he was buried on the spot. Mrs. Stahl continued to run the farm with the help of her seven children.

About three miles past the FM 1631 and FM 2721 junction, you encounter Hermit Hill Road to your left and then a narrow paved road on your right and a sign reading "Cave Creek Rd." Turn right on this little road to reach the old Cave Creek schoolhouse, 0.5 miles down this country lane from FM 1631.

CAVE CREEK SCHOOLHOUSE

John Ebert donated eight acres for a school in 1865, which was organized in 1870. This one-story building, which dates to 1896, is a fine example of vintage Hill Country folk architecture. A frame structure covered with brick-sized patterned-tin siding, the schoolhouse was originally roofed with hand-cut cedar shingles, some of which are still visible under the current corrugated tin roof. The fireplace with its stucco limestone-rubble chimney has been supplanted by a wood-burning stove. A record of eighty-two students attended in 1917. Students often explored nearby Berg's Cave after his death. The pavilion was built in the 1920s or 1930s.

The end of the school year was marked by an all-day community celebration. Meat donated by local families was barbecued in pits dug in the ground. Students performed plays, and the day ended with a dance. Admission was charged, and the proceeds paid for improvements and repairs. Local merchants treated the students to refreshments and ice cream. The school closed in 1950, but the still-tidy schoolhouse serves as a community center and an area polling place on election day. The community club meets at the schoolhouse on the third Friday of each month to play pinochle and enjoy the refreshments they bring. Visitors are welcome.

Return to FM 1631 and continue north. In another mile you come to Cave Creek community's spiritual center, St. Paul's Lutheran Church.

ST. PAUL'S LUTHERAN CHURCH

About 13 miles from Fredericksburg

St. Paul's Church is the oldest rural Lutheran church in Gillespie County. The sanctuary was built of rough boxing planks, with a forty-foot steeple, in 1884. In 1890, the building was enlarged and a beaded ceiling was installed. The building was covered with its present skin of embossed-tin siding in 1928–1929. Its simple style epitomizes the spirit of the hardworking, God-fearing people who settled Cave Creek. The weathervane atop the tinned steeple bespeaks their practicality. As in Fredericksburg, clusters of Sunday houses developed around the church.

As you continue north on FM 1631 from St. Paul's Church, it's easy to see why the area was first settled. Cave and North Grape creeks water the land well. Some fields are cultivated, others are lush with rich green Bermuda, and the remainder are just good grazing.

A little less than four miles beyond Cave Creek, you see a sign reading "North Grape Creek Rd.," another sign directing you to turn right to reach Rheingold School, and a paved road running off FM 1631 to your right, the first paved right since Cave Creek. Turn right on North Grape Creek Road, and at the T intersection turn right, as per the Rheingold School sign, to reach the school.

RHEINGOLD COMMUNITY

Gillespie County • About 17 miles from Fredericksburg

Rheingold means "pure gold" in German, and the community was so named because almost all the early-day inhabitants of the neighborhood were from the Gold family. In 1873, for example, seven out of the ten children enrolled at the local school were Golds. The Gold family first moved to the area in the 1850s, coming from Germany via New Braunfels. Descendants of Peter and Jakob Gold owned most of the land, and the gin, store, and school in Reingold, also known as the Gold community.

The Rheingold school still stands at the end of Rheingold School Road. William Gold donated two acres of land here in 1891 for the school. The first school building was the house now standing behind the present school. It began as a log cabin that was later stuccoed over. To this, a frame room was added, followed by a rock addition to the back, making this one of the more architecturally interesting buildings in Gillespie County. When the present frame school building was built, the house became the teacherage. The pavilion was built and used for Christmas programs and school closings, which featured a barbecue and dance. "Free school" lasted about six months, and "pay school" finished out the school year. Up to eight grades were taught, and one teacher taught as many as seventy-four students. The school was closed and consolidated with the Fredericksburg Independent School District (ISD) in 1949. Today the school serves as a local polling place and community center. Community gatherings are the last Friday evening of each month, and visitors are welcome; dominoes is the game of choice. Several barbecues are held during the year, and the school is still used for reunions and other celebrations.

Continue on FM 1631 to the intersection with FM 1323. Turn right on FM 1323 about three miles north of the Rheingold turnoff; in less than two miles you turn left off FM 1323 onto Althaus-Davis, the first paved road to your left since turning onto FM 1323.

Althaus-Davis Road owes the first half of its name to Christian Althaus, a pioneer doctor who was born in Germany in 1821. He received medical training in the Prussian army and came to Texas in 1846. He was in Fredericksburg by the time town lots were distributed in 1847. That year he married Anna Maria Elisabetha Behrens, whose mother brought her and her brother to Fredericksburg with the first colonists after her father died on the boat. They would have seven children.

In the spring of 1847, Althaus was one of the signers of the Meusebach-Comanche Treaty, which brought peace for a time to the Hill Country frontier (see Fort Martin Scott). He gave the Comanches medical treatment and followed the advice of his friend Chief John Carnor to "be friendly and never pull a gun." Althaus spoke several Indian dialects and worked for a time at Fort Martin Scott distributing food to the Indians as a U.S. government agent. He also made and sold saddles and other supplies to the forty-niners on their way to California. In 1857, he moved his family to Cave Creek to start ranching. He built the family home over a spring to provide water inside the house and a cool place to store his medicine. Althaus opposed slavery and secession, but he organized the home guard during the Civil War and was a Gillespie county commissioner several times during and after the war.

He worked as a doctor until the 1880s, under difficult circumstances. The Althaus home served as a makeshift hospital and orphanage. Medical instruments were scarce; when Althaus needed to amputate an arm, he had to have the saw (now at Pioneer Museum, Fredericksburg) made by a local blacksmith. He made his own medicines from locally grown herbs, roots, and bark. When he went to Bandera to treat diphtheria patients, he used medicine he made from honey, almond juice, and blackjack tree bark; thirty-four out of thirty-five of his patients survived. Elizabeth and the children tended the farm during the doctor's trips, which sometimes lasted for weeks. Althaus died in 1915 and was buried in the St. Paul Lutheran Church cemetery.

After a few miles on this narrow road, and just west of the "big" branch of Youngblood Creek, you pass through a "devil's playground" of great gray granite boulders strewn and stacked helter-skelter over several acres of rolling pastures. You experience a sort of caveman-primeval sensation as you drive among these room-sized boulders, reminiscent of the legendary great elephant dying grounds, only these massive chunks double as both corpse and monument. Few spots in the Hill Country evoke such ominous feelings. As one local has said, "The world's just plain cockeyed out here."

As you cross from Gillespie County into Blanco County, Althaus-Davis Road becomes County Road 310 and continues paved for a short distance before the hard surface peters out and you are soon driving on clean, well-drained and graded granite gravel.

For the next few Blanco County miles, you pass through the old Blowout and Comanche Springs communities. Each is more a frame of mind now than a town with an identifiable center. Comanche Creek is the stream that flows through Blowout and Comanche Springs. You cross four of its branches in as many miles.

BLOWOUT COMMUNITY

Blanco County • About 25 miles from Fredericksburg

After about a mile and a half on gravel, you pass a set of corrals and a ranch house on your left, marked by an A. Davis Ranch sign. This is the Davis Ranch (private property, not open to the public), all that remains of Blowout today. No trace of the post office, or store, or anything else remains.

Perhaps you're wondering where Blowout got its name. Did an oil well blow out here? Or was there a big party or feud here, once upon a time? Well, after passing the Davis corrals and house on your left, start looking to your right, at the hills. In a half mile or so, you just might see a big black hole up in the side of one of these hills. It is from this hole that the name Blowout derives.

One story has it that back when Comanches still roamed the area, a band of hunters tracked a bear into a cave. Failing to draw the bear out any other way, they decided to smoke it out, lighting a huge brushfire at the cave's entrance. Sparks from that fire ignited several centuries' worth of volatile bat guano (like many other Hill Country caves, this cave was a bat roost). The resulting explosion blew out the mouth of the cave to such a size that it became a landmark to travelers—known as the Blowout Cave. And Blowout Cave became the namesake for the community that grew up nearby. We do not know what became of the bear or the Indians.

True story or not, we do know that Blowout Cave was dissolved out by running groundwater and was at one time the site of gushing springs similar to others found in the Hill Country. Millions of bats still live there. According to local rancher Arthur Pressler, the name "Blowout" came from when lightning exploded an accumulation of ammonia and other gases generated from guano.

Regardless, we do know from reading the *Austin Democratic Statesman* that on May 3, 1878, Albert Hutchins arrived in Austin from the "bat guano cave 60 miles west of Austin," where he was in charge of a party of men getting out guano for a shipment to Europe. He said that the cave extended through a mountain for a distance of a quarter mile with a width of one hundred feet. The guano was one hundred feet deep and could only be estimated by the millions of pounds. Just before dark each night, he said, the bats commenced to fly out of the cave in a solid volume, and it took them about five hours to fly out of the cave, whose opening measured about twenty feet square. In Hutchins' opinion, the cave seemed to have been a volcano, and it contained many chambers and passages. His men had managed to haul out two carloads of guano during their first day or two of work. The harvest continued through at least the following year; in early May 1879, ten or fifteen laborers started up to the guano caves from Austin.

Neighboring Comanche Springs has its heart about two miles north of the Davis place, just before the intersection with the road to Click.

Remnants of an old rock fence on the left side of the road begin just after the Davis ranch and continue for several miles, in various stages of preservation. The best preserved stretches of fence come just before the fence ends.

COMANCHE SPRINGS

Blanco and Llano counties • About 27 miles from Fredericksburg

As you cross Comanche Creek, you notice on your left a little springhouse built over the creek. This is the Comanche Spring. Nearby is an old ranch house. Private property! This is Comanche Springs today. Period. It was not always this way.

Twenty-three members of the Anderson, Shelley, and Hardin families came here from Kentucky and Tennessee in the fall of 1854. They found here a broad fair valley where grass waved five feet high, the soil was deep and fertile, and springs watered every draw. It reminded them of home, and they decided to stay. Their cattle grew sleek and fat on the tall grasses that have been replaced by the mesquite, scrub cedar, and oaks of today. The school was built the next year, in 1855, from native timber that they hauled to Cypress Mill to be cut and then hauled back. This was the second school in Blanco County.

The land was fertile and well watered, but the surrounding hills were full of Comanches, who raided, burned, and killed at their leisure. When the Civil War came, nine of the eighteen young men here were immediately drafted; the other nine stayed at home as members of the frontier rangers. This was, after all, the very edge of the frontier, and with so many of the men gone to war, the Indian raids became more daring and frequent. But eventually even the second nine were drafted, and life in Comanche Springs was burdensome indeed. Ready-made cloth was unobtainable. Many of the women had to trade for raw cotton, ride ten or fifteen miles over to a neighbor who had a spinning wheel, loom the cotton, spin the thread, and then weave the cloth. When the surviving menfolk marched back home, they came with empty pockets, with no money to rebuild their shattered farms. They had to barter for the goods they needed, tan hides, make furniture, and brew moonshine to survive.

After four years of cashless living, the men of Comanche Springs planned a desperate adventure: they would pool all the cattle in the region and drive them across the desert to California, where investors made rich from the gold mines were begging for cattle with which to stock their pastures. The drive went well until they crossed the Pecos River into Geronimo's territory. Silas Gipson was killed in the first Indian attack, and though the Comanche Springs men won the battle, they were ready to turn back for home until Tom Shelley talked their spirits back up. They persevered and eventually did reach California, where their longhorns sold for forty dollars each, paid in hard gold. Flushed with success, some of the men stayed for years thereafter. Others returned to Comanche Springs two years later, in 1871, with the first hard money the community had seen since the early days of the war.

But the Indian attacks continued through the 1870s, and the school had to be abandoned because of them. By 1876, however, the Indians had ceased to be a factor, a post office was established, and both Blowout and Comanche Springs prospered, situated as they were on this, the Austin-to-Fredericksburg mail and stage road, which passed through Dripping Springs and Round Mountain before dipping southwest to pass through here. It seems hard to imagine now, but this narrow little gravel road, which alternates between a coarse red granite surface and a powdered sugar-like limestone sand surface was the road west in its day, the US 290 of its time.

Blowout and Comanche Springs were obviously bypassed over the years by the march of modern civilization, and all that remains now of the hamlets are some nice old stone fences, the two old ranches with rail fences and loading pens, and their accompanying weathered outbuildings. Drive slowly to avoid hitting the many roadside cattle and deer. Look closely as you cross Comanche Creek, and you may see a fat nutria or beaver cutting a path through the water. This is the Hill Country of a past generation, still present.

Several miles past Comanche Springs, you come to a three-way intersection. Turn left here onto Blanco County Road 309, aka Lynn Hardin Road. (Immediately beyond this point, County Road 310 becomes FM 3347.) You continue on well-drained, smooth granite gravel, easily drivable in all but the very worst weather.

In front of you, on the east side of the road, is Red Mountain, its granite baldness relieved by only occasional stands of cedar and oak. This is about as far south and east as the Llano Uplift extends. Depending on the light and time of day, Red Mountain's color ranges from the palest of pinks, to orange, to a rich red. Yet the name fits only this western side of the high hill. The other side is almost completely green, covered with cedars and oaks. Members of the Hardin family have lived and ranched in its shadows for over one hundred years. You also get a good view of Packsaddle Mountain, with its loaf-shaped silhouette, off in the north. You cross the path of Comanche Creek several more times as you drive toward Click.

Although you are still in the Comanche Creek neighborhood, you are now in Llano County, and during the Civil War, A. E. Edgeworth operated a saltpeter works here on Comanche Creek. The saltpeter was used to make gunpowder for Confederate troops. The saltpeter was made from bat guano mined from the caves (like Blowout Cave) that honeycomb the nearby hills.

A little over five miles from the intersection of Click Road and FM 3347, you cross Sandy Creek. Aptly named, a thin silver thread of water courses down the middle of a bed of pink granite sand as wide as the Colorado River. Flakes of gold and silver are occasionally found in the sand, along with fool's gold (iron pyrite) and the occasional arrowhead.

Legend has it that the fabulous lost Los Almagres, or Bowie, Mine was located atop nearby Packsaddle Mountain, and that several of the ore smelters were located along Sandy Creek.

CLICK COMMUNITY

Llano County • About 2 miles from Sandy Creek

Contrary to what you might guess, the origin of Click's name is unimaginative: it was named for early settler Malachi Click. Prior to the establishment of the post office in 1880, the settlement was known as Sandy Valley, situated as it was in the bottomlands of Sandy Creek. After George Byfield built his store, Click was also known as Byfield's Store. In those days, Click had a school and Cumberland Presbyterian Church in addition to the post office/store. Joe Smith, born in 1855 in Blanco County, nine miles west of Round Mountain, trailed herds to Kansas and Colorado and otherwise worked cattle until 1911, when he bought the store at Click and became postmaster.

Now only the stripped-of-paint, shuttered store remains at the crossroads, still used as a deer-hunting hut. A gaunt windmill completes this picture of once prosperous desolation. Members of the Click family still live nearby on Sandy Creek. The equally weather-beaten, once elegant clapboard farmhouse that stood nearby is now gone.

About six miles north of Click and after the road has turned to pavement, you cross Honey Creek, which, in the words of one old settler, "never ran dry, even during a drought; it flowed with water as fresh and sweet as honey." Even during the great drought of 2009, when all other area streams were dry to the bone, or nearly so, Honey Creek still flowed, and sizeable bass and perch were seen in its waters.

On your left is Riley Mountain, whose summit is Dancer Peak, named for the Reverend Jonas Dancer, who established a Methodist church on nearby Honey Creek, which rises from several sources along the base of Riley Mountain. Dancer moved from Austin to Llano County in 1852, attracted by tales of the mineral wealth said to abound there. After several years of prospecting, according to J. W. Wilbarger, he settled on Honey Creek. Others soon followed. On May 23, 1859, he and other men of the neighborhood had planned to gather at a certain spot to cut out a new road from Llano to Austin. Dancer, a punctual man, arrived at the appointed time with his tools. But no one else came. Dancer decided to start working by himself. While working, a group of Indians attacked. Unarmed, he fled to a ravine. The Indians ran up to the bluffs above and rained arrows down on him. Wounded in several places, he staggered around bleeding for a while before sitting down on a rock bench in the bluff and dying. The attackers scalped and mutilated him. A search party found his corpse the next day. Ironically, his daughter, Mathilda Friend, was killed in the infamous Legion Valley massacre of 1868, of which you will read later in this chapter.

When the Click Road dead-ends into SH 71, turn right. After about three miles, and just after you have passed Packsaddle Mountain, you encounter a historical marker and a road running off to your left, skirting the edge of Packsaddle Mountain.

PACKSADDLE MOUNTAIN

About 10 miles from Click

Though not particularly beautiful or awe inspiring, there is perhaps no other mountain or hill in all of Texas that has more adventure and romance associated with it than Packsaddle Mountain. Legend and fact have become inextricably intertwined over the centuries. The legends surrounding Packsaddle Mountain begin with the lost Los Almagres gold and silver mine. According to stories, Don Bernardo de Miranda discovered a rich vein of gold and silver on top of Packsaddle Mountain in 1757. Peons worked the shafts atop old Packsaddle unceasingly until 1775, when the mine workers were attacked by an overwhelmingly large band of Indians. Seeing that they were going to be massacred, the Spaniards filled in the mine shafts so that the Indians could not work them.

Another story has the Indians in possession of the mines, working them for tremendous amounts of wealth. The Spaniards, ever eager to acquire quick wealth, were determined to drive the Indians away and gain possession of the fabulous mine. In the course of the battle, the Indians killed all the Spaniards and then filled all the shafts with earth and rock. They then abandoned the mine, fearing another, more successful attack from a Spanish settlement on the San Saba River. Both stories agree that for years thereafter the top of Packsaddle was covered with human bones.

There is similar ambiguity regarding the origins of Packsaddle's name. Old-timers said it was so named for the depression or gap in the mountain, making it resemble an old-fashioned packsaddle. Others say that the first settlers found an abandoned packsaddle left by some earlier traveler on the mountain and named it accordingly.

Tradition says that the last Indian battle fought in Llano County was atop Packsaddle Mountain, in August 1873. A band of Comanches (or Apaches, as some tellers insist) had slipped into Llano County during the summer of 1873 and established a camp atop Packsaddle, from which they proceeded to attack and plunder ranches in the valley below.

Mrs. A. C. Bowman provided the following account in 1936, passed down to her by two of the battle's participants.

> The Indians had made raids in the neighborhood of the J. R. Moss ranch, in the southern part of Llano County, the day and night before the battle, stealing a number of horses from the white settlers. Late in the evening of Aug. 3, an arrow was found piercing the leg of a gentle milch cow on the Moss ranch, and it was this incident that precipitated the fight.

Help was quickly obtained from the nearby ranchmen, and early the next morning a party of eight men [W. B., J. R., and L. B. Moss; Eli Lloyd; Archer Martin; Pinckney Ayers; Robert Brown; and L. B. Harrington] set out to follow the Indians' trail, which led in an easterly direction to Packsaddle mountain, a distance of some 25 miles.

Leading their horses up the mountain, the Moss party suddenly came upon the Indians, grouped around a campfire eating roasted beef. Some were lying about asleep. The white men placed themselves between the Indians and their horses, and the fight began. The redskins were not shooting arrows, but were armed with guns and pistols the same as the white men were.

They fell back behind a ledge of rocks on the side of the mountain 3 different times, rallying and making a new attack in each instance. Finally, however, they retreated down the mountain, chanting as they went. Three dead Indians were found on the battlefield. It was estimated that there were 17 men, two women and one boy in the Indian band.

Four of the white men were wounded, namely, Bill Moss, Arch Martin, Eli Lloyd and Pink Ayres, all of whom recovered. They were carried to the John B. Duncan ranch home, located on Honey creek in Llano county, about three miles from Packsaddle mountain. This then stately two-story structure, which housed a pioneer Llano family and which was perhaps the finest residence in that part of the country during the early days, stood in its original state until a few years ago, when fire destroyed all except the walls.

Harrington was sent to Llano on horseback for a doctor, borrowing a fresh horse from Mr. Duncan. Traveling a distance of about 12 miles, he obtained Dr. C. C. Smith, a pioneer Llano doctor, who returned to the ranch with him, the two arriving shortly after 9 o'clock that night.

Bill Moss, due to his strong constitution, recovered and was able to return home within a week. The other three wounded men also recovered. Bill Moss went to his grave in 1926, carrying the lead from an Indian's weapon—the wound inflicted at the time of the Packsaddle fight and which caused him much pain and discomfort until his death 53 years later.

Harrington, who was left behind to bring up the horses after the battle, tells this experience: "I turned to getting the Indians' and our horses together. When I started them north, they went up beside the battleground, so I went up there to turn them back. At that time, I saw the old chief on the ground. I said, 'Old boy, when you folks kill our people, you always take their scalps.' I stepped off my pony, went into my pocket for my knife, and scalped him, taking his ears. By the time I hung it on the horn of the saddle and stepped on my pony, the horses had gone back down the battle line. When I had gotten down that way, I saw another Indian, the one that Bob and I killed, and I said to myself, 'One scalp is lonesome.' So I put in a few minutes and got a mate to the chief's scalp.

"By this time the horses were all around the Indians' camp, so I went to picking up and putting on horse bows, quivers, shields, blankets, Indian lariats and anything else that I could, including the old chief's breast plate. When I had gotten as much as I could handle, I rounded up the horses and started off the mountain. When I got to the brakes, to where I could look off, I saw the boys about two miles ahead. I battled the 24 horses with all the power that I could and finally got them off the mountain. After that I had no trouble until I got to Honey creek. The horses were so dry that I had some trouble in getting them started from the creek. But I soon put them to Duncan's ranch, where the rest of the boys had stopped."

The Packsaddle fight may have been the last major fight between Indians and whites in Llano County, but it was not the very last fight, nor did it signal the end of Indian troubles in Llano County, as my research of contemporary accounts has revealed.

In late August 1874, a party of nine Indians, supposed to be a part of a larger number, made their appearance in Llano County and took a lot of stock from the Hinton Rancho. They were trailed from there to the Little Llano River, within a few miles of Bluffton, and were attacked by five citizens on Tuesday evening, who were driven back, with one man wounded in the hand. After the attack, the passes were being closely watched for the Indians' escape. It was thought they would pass through Hoovers or Backbone Valley, which was being closely guarded. Court was in session at Llano, and it was reported that the grand jury men and others had their horses stolen by the Indians.

Only a little more than a week later, the Indians that had been in Llano town stole several head of horses from the A.G. Roberts outfit. They also took a fine horse from Frank Holden. Sixteen Indians were seen near the Putnam Rancho, traveling toward House Mountain. A body of Indians stole fourteen head of horses from the San Fernando Creek country, a few miles north of Llano town. They were followed by eight or ten of the boys. The Indians hid in a thicket and when the boys came up fired on them, wounding three and causing them to retreat.

The Packsaddle mine is claimed by some to be the famed Los Almagres mine, based on research by Dr. Herbert E. Bolton, an early-Texas history authority, in which he had identified Miranda's mine with the "Boyd shaft" on nearby Honey Creek. Based on this coincidence, some think it logical that Miranda also operated a mine, or mines, on Packsaddle Mountain, as he would have been likely to prospect the entire vicinity.

In 1926, in the *Austin American Statesman*, David J. Morris wrote about a pair of modern-day treasure seekers in "Rich Llano Gold Mine, Old as Nation, Is Found."

Discovery of the historic old gold and silver mine, discovered by Don Bernardo de Miranda, seems a pretty sure fact after following numerous old Spanish marks directing to the location where the present shaft struck ore. This rich vein of ore, at one time the means of the Spanish riches in Texas, was located by G. W. Burton and W. P. Bankston of Austin.

Young Burton has been a mine prospector for several years, much of his early life being spent in Mexican mines. Seven years ago he became interested in the stories of Spanish mines on the famous Packsaddle mountains of Llano county. Working more or less for different individuals he did much prospecting on this chain of mountains, but found that the showing was not promising enough to hold the financial backing necessary to put the project through.

He also felt that there must be markings put there by the Spanish to show the location of the mine. Knowing their methods and capable of reading their signs from experiences in Mexico, Burton, with the aid of Bankston, started out in earnest to find the old mines.

"Stories I had heard about the mines was that the Indians and Spanish had a battle on the top of Packsaddle mountain years and years ago. Old timers say that many bones of humans once lay around the mountain top. The old stories further state that the Indians, in an endeavor to conceal the mines filled them with dirt from other crevices in order to make the mountain top look the same. Recent discoveries of crevices which appear to have been filled by human hands makes me more positive than ever that old stories were true."

Burton undertook about a year ago to see if he could find any old Spanish signs on rocks or trees. One day on the very tip edge of the mountain top he prized up a large flat rock. Carefully rubbing his finger over the surface of the rock underneath, Burton found a Roman cross cut on the rock. There was the evidence that at one time the Spanish really roamed over the mountain. Other strong evidences he had already found were the old Spanish smelters located in the surrounding valleys. These showed positive evidence of ore having been smeltered years ago. There was one smelter on Honey creek and two on Big Sandy, all in sight of Packsaddle mountain.

After finding the cross, Burton spent a year wandering over the mountain top searching for other signs. He found them both on rocks and trees. In all he found four different signs pointing to the cross he first found and where he sunk the shaft that unearthed the rich vein of ore. Not only did each set of signs show the direction of the mine, but pointed to the others, in case one was destroyed there would be others.

On the top of a rock was found another cross, five dots and an "X" mark. The dots described the distance from the spot to the mine and the "X" mark meant that the mine was exactly in the opposite direction to which the dots pointed. On a tree a large spot, a mining spike and a notch was cut, on another a notch and on still others initials, arrows, daggers, &c. All of these had a story which Burton could read or figured out after finding the others. A couple of notches cut in different trees at different places, were such that a rifle barrel or straight stick laid in them would point directly to the mine.

This search was buoyed up by the account given by Miranda. Another idea which Burton had and which he has found true is that the richest deposits of ore will not be found in the valleys but in the mountains. The formations he has found on Packsaddle mountain are almost the same as the rich mining area in Durango, Mexico.

"In starting my search, I was interested in lead and silver. Very little gold is around here, although the vein I have struck has considerable gold in it, lots of silver and lead.

"Lead comes up from the ore in the bottom of the mountain like a vapor. It rises slowly and settles on the surface and the silver and gold remain beneath. When I first struck the vein I am now mining, it had an abundance of lead in it and for this reason, although the vein was only about one-fourth inch thick I kept digging.

"At the depth of 40 feet the vein came to the first pocket. The first pocket I struck assayed about $200 mineral per ton. Going on down to the depth of 60 feet my vein of mineral had increased to three inches in thickness and here I struck another pocket that gave forth about $800 per ton. The next pocket I strike will possibly yield $1,000 a ton. The $200 per ton is too small to work, but the others could be worked with fine profit.

"I am hopeful that I will not strike the bed of ore until I reach a shaft depth of about 100 feet which will give me a valley level and the ore a chance to spread out in every direction without limit. If any one goes down by shaft and looks up, they will see the air is full of white smoky vapor, the lead vapor coming forth from the ore and floating upward.

"The old story about this mine states that it was located just left of the Old Spanish trail on top of the mountain. That is exactly where mine is located. In fact my trail, leading up the mountain top is the old trail itself. When Bankston and myself started working here in December we had to build our road and cut our path wider to the top and to haul up the machinery. We have air blowers, an eight horsepower engine, derrick and everything needed.

"Don Miranda's account states that he located and discovered on the Main Almagres mountain, a rich deposit of mineral, lead, gold and silver, the veins running in every direction.

"An interesting discovery of Spanish markings which proved true, was made by myself a few years ago on Ratliff ranch. In helping to mine soapstone here for a lime furnace in Austin, I came across two stones bearing the Roman number seven and eight. The next day I came across a Spanish map cut in the soapstone and saying in direction language, go three mountains and three creeks west and three mines will be found. These directions have been followed and one shaft located. This stone was marked by ten stones set in the ground 10 feet apart, the figures in Roman numerals and the 10 being the fartherest from the map. These directions located the mines on the Albert Smith place, 10 miles west of Oxford.

"I have found gleanor ore in several caves around here and Spanish coins have also been found. I can vision a great rush to this region just as soon as we strike the ore deposit. There is almost every kind of mineral in these mountains and a possibility of this region becoming one of the greatest mining and smeltering sections of the world. It has taken years of painstaking work, the cost of many a human life to discover what we believe at last to be the long lost mines of gold and silver of the 17th century Spanish accounts, and if they prove to be, Texas will become the richest mining state in the United States."

But in the end, their Packsaddle mine never got off the ground, the magic vein still undiscovered.

Much of the mountain is six-hundred-million-year-old sandstone in horizontal layers which rests on even older Packsaddle schist, which is exposed in the bed of Honey Creek at the foot of the mountain, by SH 71. Traces of gold, silver, and other metals are mixed in the sands of Honey Creek.

All these rich legends and stories notwithstanding, it's almost certain that Los Almagres mine was located on nearby Riley Mountain, above Honey Creek. A brochure published in about 1915 by the Llano Real Estate & Investment Company has a photo of the operations of the Los Almagres Mining Company and the following commentary:

The Los Almagres Mining Company owns and controls the minerals on about 1600 acres of land on Honey Creek, about ten miles southeast of Llano town, on which it has done some development work. This work was done along the contact between the Cambrian and Pre-Cambrian rocks, on the side of what is known as Riley Mountain. From the limited work done the Company can show at least one and one-half million tons of soft hematite iron ores of very fine quality, along with which is found gold, silver, lead, manganese and other metals. From the extent of the outcroppings it is quite probable that from five to twenty million tons of this iron can be found and easily worked. And it is also quite probable that the precious metals exist in paying quantities.

The Los Almagres Mining Company was formed by J. Farley of Dallas, after retracing Miranda's 1756 expedition in 1907 with historian Herbert Bolton, who had obtained a copy of Miranda's journal from a Mexican archive. Their interpretation of Miranda's narrative led them to what was then known as the Boyd shaft on Honey Creek. The company's optimism flew in the face of the opinions of members of the United States Geological Survey who visited the site in 1909 and described the mine as unproductive.

Rumors of valuable minerals in the Llano River country had their beginnings in about 1731, when Spanish soldiers and citizens of San Antonio began the first of three expeditions against the Apaches who had attacked Spanish missions and settlements. The heart of the Apacheria, or Apache homeland, was the San Saba River valley. On their way to the San Saba country, the Spanish expeditions passed through the Llano River country, where they heard of interesting mineral deposits. In the summer of 1753, an expedition explored the Pedernales, Llano, and San Saba river valleys seeking a mission site for the

Apaches. The Comanches (who were even fiercer than the Apaches) had begun to enter the Apacheria and wreak terrible destruction. In desperation, the Apaches began to look toward the Spanish as allies and told the Spanish priests that they would give mission life a try.

As that 1753 expedition traveled through the Central Mineral Region, Lt. Juan Galván heard Indians tell of a *cerro de almagre*, a hill of red ocher. Ocher is a naturally occurring mix of iron oxide, sand, and clay, which indicates the presence of mineral-bearing ores, including silver and gold. The Indians used it for decorating themselves and their possessions.

Upon his return to San Antonio, Galván informed his superiors. Since the Spanish empire was financed on silver and gold mined in the New World, any report of new sources of wealth was taken seriously. Several groups of San Antonio citizens went looking for the mines; Apache Indians led one group to the hill in 1753, but they found no valuable ore. Texas Governor Jacinto de Barrios y Jáuregui decided to send an official expedition, led by Lt. Governor Bernardo de Miranda y Flores, to explore the Llano and Colorado valleys in search of the Cerro del Almagre and the Almagre Grande. On February 17, 1756, Miranda left San Antonio with sixteen soldiers, an Indian interpreter, five citizens, and some peons.

After locating the cerro de almagre, which Miranda described as a "silver mountain," his men opened a shaft and found "a tremendous stratum of ore." The ore veins were so abundant that Miranda guaranteed "a mine to each of the inhabitants of the province of Texas." The five citizens denounced ten mine claims on the spot. On the way back, at the Guadalupe River, an Apache told him of great silver deposits six days above the Llano in Comanche country. After Miranda's return to San Antonio, a three-pound ore sample went to two mine owners in Pachuca for assay. They said the samples were rich but wanted to see more ore. They suggested that Barrios send thirty mule loads of the ore to Mazapil, a mining town between Zacatecas and Saltillo, for further testing.

Miranda asked the viceroy to finance the ore extraction and to build a fort to protect the workers, with himself as captain, and his request was granted in November 1757. But nothing further came of the project. In the meantime, the Apache mission and a presidio were established on the San Saba River near present-day Menard. The presidio captain, Diego Ortiz Parrilla, seeking permission to move his garrison to Los Almagres to work the mine, obtained ore samples and smelted them at his post. He calculated a yield of one and one-half ounces of silver from seventy-five pounds of ore. After hostile Indians destroyed the San Saba Mission in March 1758, Ortiz Parrilla was reassigned. The mine was never officially opened. But Miranda's report and Parrilla's subsequent interest gave birth to an enduring legend. The slag heap that Ortiz Parrilla left on the bank of the San Saba River fired the imagination of later treasure seekers, who assumed that the mine was nearby.

Interest in the mines resurfaced periodically throughout the colonial period, but for a variety of reasons nothing happened.

Stephen F. Austin, on his first trip to Texas, heard of a rich silver mine on the San Saba River and a gold mine on the Llano. Hearing again in Mexico City of the unworked ore deposit called Los Almagres "in the territory of Sansava," he sent men to inspect it, but they probably went to the wrong place. In 1829, the mythical "lost" silver mine of San Saba began appearing on Austin's maps. Austin, realizing the value of the legend in attracting immigrants, mentioned the mine in an 1831 promotional pamphlet. For years afterward it was mentioned in nearly every book about Texas.

James and Rezin Bowie's searches reinforced the legend. Los Almagres became known as the "lost Bowie mine."

In 1842, two Anglo-Texans found the old Spanish diggings on the *cerro de almagre* but failed to link them with either the nearby Arroyo de los Almagres (Honey Creek) or the legendary San Saba mine. That year Prince Carl von Solms-Braunfels, commissioner general of the Adelsverein, heard the old Spanish silver mine stories and found a Mexican who promised to guide him to the mines. He called on the Adelsverein to send him fifty miners. After John Meusebach had taken over as commissioner, he asked the Berlin Academy of Sciences to help find a geologist who could survey the Adelsverein's Texas grant and find the mineral deposits. Dr. Ferdinand von Roemer was chosen and came to Texas late in 1845. When he got to the old Spanish fort on the San Saba in 1847, he saw no signs of any geologic formation that contained precious metals.

From the mid-1870s through the mid-1880s, there was renewed interest in these legendary mines, with several "forty-niners" reporting promising results, but which were subsequently dismissed by state geologist S. B. Buckley after a geological survey of the area: "Much time and money had been uselessly spent for want of a knowledge of geology and mineralogy." He had not found a single good specimen of either gold or silver ore. Only after Herbert Bolton stumbled across the name Almagres in 1904 did modern-day goldbugs, beginning with Farley, refocus on the Riley Mountain site. But to this day, both Packsaddle and Riley mountains have proved far richer in folklore than in proven mineral wealth.

Continue on SH 71 another nine miles to the junction with FM 2147. Turn left onto FM 2147. This road offers several good views of Lake LBJ, and then Lake Marble Falls.

LAKE LBJ

Originally named Granite Shoals Lake, this stretch of the Colorado was renamed in 1965 for then-president Lyndon Johnson in gratitude for his efforts on behalf of the LCRA. Construction of Wirtz Dam, which forms the lake, began in 1949. It was originally called Granite Shoals Dam and was built mainly to generate electrical power for short periods to meet peak demands. There are ten floodgates as well. The dam was renamed in 1952 to honor Alvin C. Wirtz, the LCRA's first general counsel and "father."

The lake covers 6,375 acres. Most of the area's power needs are now met by the LCRA's Thomas C. Ferguson Power Plant at Horseshoe Bay, and the lake provides cooling water for the plant. Limestone cliffs give way to granite along the lake's 21.5 mile course. Skiers like the absence of obstructions and the stretches protected from high winds. The many caves and coves make for good fishing. There are many private campgrounds and boat-launch facilities and one LCRA primitive area along the lake.

COTTONWOOD RECREATION AREA

On Lake LBJ, adjacent to the south side of Wirtz Dam, off FM 2147, about 5 miles from the SH 71/FM 2147 intersection • Open daily • Free

This seventeen-acre tract (part of the LCRA's Primitive Recreation System) offers a boat ramp, parking, observation area, fishing, picnicking, and hiking, but no camping, running water, or restrooms. Day use only is allowed. Cottonwood has about 2,100 feet of Lake LBJ shoreline. Granite rock formations protrude throughout. The spring wildflowers are nice out here.

Continue east on FM 2147 toward Marble Falls. Below Alvin Wirtz Dam is Lake Marble Falls.

LAKE MARBLE FALLS

Lake Marble Falls is the smallest of the Highland Lakes, 5.75 miles long and covering about 780 surface acres. The dam was constructed from 1949 to 1951 for electrical power generation and has ten floodgates. The dam was originally called Marble Falls; it was renamed in 1962 to honor Max Starcke, LCRA general manager from 1940 to 1955. Lake Marble Falls is a popular destination for fishers, boaters, skiers, swimmers, and campers. There are several private campgrounds and boat-launch facilities, as well as a cluster of small city parks in downtown Marble Falls, just upstream from the US 281 bridge.

To reach Marble Falls, turn left at the intersection with US 281 after 7.5 miles on FM 2147. But a trip over to Max Starcke Dam should precede your entry into Marble Falls. To reach the dam, turn right onto US 281 and travel about a mile until you see the highway sign reading "Max Starcke Dam." Turn left here and follow the twisting road about two miles across scenic Flat Rock Creek, bearing right at each of three forks in the road until you are on a gravel road overlooking the Colorado River, a power substation, and the Max Starcke Dam just to your left.

MAX STARCKE DAM OVERLOOK

Off US 281

The falls that gave Marble Falls its name were submerged by the completion of Starcke Dam in 1951. Max Starcke was the LCRA's first general manager. Even though the beautiful falls are gone, the view from up here of the Colorado River and its layered, weather-grayed limestone cliffs is nonetheless striking. Once every decade or so, the LCRA lowers Lake Marble Falls for one reason or another, and the first ledges of the stair-stepped Marble Falls are exposed for a few weeks.

The creation of Lake Marble Falls also submerged Sulphur Springs, located on the north side of the Colorado River, just downstream from the US 281 bridge and above Starcke Dam. J. G. Michel said that many people came from far away to drink the water, which was believed to have healthful properties, and fill their jugs.

Return to US 281, turn right, and drive into Marble Falls.

MARBLE FALLS

Burnet County • 7,000 (approximate) • (830) • About 17 miles from Pack-saddle Mountain

The US 281 bridge across the Colorado River passes over the now submerged Marble Falls. The falls were long prized for both their beauty and their industrial potential, falling twenty-two feet down a series of slick marble ledges, forming a three-mile-long lake above. For all its potential, Marble Falls—the city—was a long time in coming to life. A Colonel Charles J. Todd was the first to attempt to "bring in" Marble Falls, buying a tract of land on the east side of the river at the great falls in 1851 for eighty dollars. Todd laid out a town but failed to attract any buyers. Then, in 1854, young Adam Johnson happened onto the falls and began the project that was to take up the rest of his life, the founding and promotion of a great city and industrial complex at the Marble Falls. Johnson had recently moved to Hamilton's Valley, which would soon become Burnet, the county seat. He became a surveyor and also worked as a guard/driver for the overland mail along the U.S. government's frontier mail routes. He had been sent down from Fort Mason (in Mason County) to inspect the falls.

Johnson wrote, "Simply as the central figure of beautiful scenery, these magnificent falls interest and delight all who visit them; but it is only when their immense power for moving machinery and serving the needs of man is considered that their importance is realized. The practical observer cannot look upon this splendid volume of water, dashing and leaping from ledge to ledge, and hear its ceaseless roar, without being impressed with the thought that nature has fashioned this seeming irregularity and concentrated such titanic power for some grand purpose and that it only waits for man to see the opportunity and turn it to account."

Johnson immediately set out to acquire title to as much of the land around the falls as possible, spending every penny he could get. Imagine his disappointment when he discovered that the titles he held were invalid and he would have to start over again.

The Civil War interrupted his quest, and Johnson enlisted in the Confederate Army, rising to the rank of general under the noted cavalry commander Nathan Bedford Forrest. Johnson was blinded during a battle in his home state of Kentucky. After the war he returned to his wife and family in Burnet. He resumed his real estate dealings, acquiring vast acreage in Burnet County and plotting the birth of his city by the falls. He and his son Robert often traveled by carriage down to the falls, the elder Johnson giving directions through the wilderness maze from memory.

And the journey to the falls was truly a-maze-ing, as recounted in this article from the *Burnet Bulletin*, dated May 17, 1881:

A Visit to the Noted Marble Falls. A party of Burnetites visited one of the three great waterpower sites of the county, last Friday. The Marble Falls are located on the Colorado, 16 or 17 miles south west of Burnet in a wild, mountainous country. As usual with everybody except those who live there, our crowd got lost hunting them, and in all travelled over eight or ten miles of extra spider-web roads, hog trails and sheep ranges before we came in sight, and then it was through the courtesy of Mr. Geo. Lacy, who had his nephew to pilot us there, which he kindly did, though suffering from an attack of the mumps at the time. It is a disgusting thing to get lost, only you have a chance to see the country and cultivate your patience. Did you ever see so many left-hand roads in your life as in this region? At first sight, the visitor, who anticipates something sublime or majestic, is disappointed with the Marble Falls. As Joe Gaston says, "he expects a little Niagara," and finds instead an aggregate descent of 40 or 50 feet (we visited the upper falls), a broad river, and a considerable roar through fissures of slate rock in dozens of places. But there is no doubt it is one of the grandest factory and mill powers of the world. There is enough water going over those 200 yards of ledges, it does seem, to furnish bread for the universe, and the beauty of it is, the current can be controlled at comparatively little expense. The banks are high, the volume shallow and broken in many places, with a world of material to construct dams and foundations to be had on the spot. The ledges over which the river falls are slate rock; below in the bed and on the banks, solid masses of building marble, so stained by the elements as not to show without blasting what it really is. We are informed that there are two other falls below these within one and one-half miles distance, where the river is narrow, the banks higher, and the descent more concentrated. Wildness and ability are the characteristics of the Marble Falls. They are owned by the Todd heirs of Kentucky, and at present held in the market at $7,500. For a real live, healthy, exfoliating shower-bath, we commend to our readers one of the sports of the Falls. Stand under it, and you have a scrubbing and harrowing equal to the far-famed baths of Turkey.

Less than two months later came the announcement of the purchase of the Marble Falls by the St. Louis and Mexican Narrow Gauge, which put a new complexion on railroad prospects in this section. This was especially the case since this company had applied for a change in its charter, by which its route would be made to pass through Burnet. Leaving the town of Lampasas, the line of the St. Louis Narrow Gauge would, it was more than probable, enter Hamilton Valley, pursuing which southward it would pass naturally through the town of Burnet, and entering Backbone Valley follow it to the falls. Should the survey, then in progress, of the Northwestern Narrow Gauge locate its line through the town of Burnet, the town would become the intersecting point of these two roads, the one placing Burnet in communication with the Gulf on the southeast and the great undeveloped country on the northwest; the other with the North and west on the one hand and the great tropical Southwest on the other. The significance to this place of the great marble industry to be developed here by such railroad construction was universally understood.

One of the keys to success in Johnson's grandiose plan was railroad service to Marble Falls, and the fate of Marble Falls was intertwined with that of the new state capital. The Austin and Northwestern railroad had reached Burnet by the spring of 1882. The old limestone capitol building had burned in November 1881, and state fathers were wrangling over the construction of a new statehouse. Plans had originally called for the building to be built with native limestone from near Austin, but the stone proved to be unfit for exterior use. A fight ensued over what stone to use. Some favored limestone from Indiana; others insisted on native stone. Owners of Granite Mountain just west of Marble Falls (see the Mormon Trails trip) offered the state all the granite needed to complete the capitol, free of charge. But Granite Mountain was sixteen miles from the closest railhead at Burnet, and the granite could be hauled to Austin no other way.

In the summer of 1885, Adam Johnson spoke to the legislature and offered seven miles of right-of-way over his land, between Burnet and Granite Mountain, free of charge to the state for the construction of a branch line over which to haul the granite. He assured the state that his fellow landowners would similarly oblige. They did, and the state built the spur using convict labor. With the Granite Mountain spur's completion in the winter of 1885, Johnson could at last see his dream beginning to unfold.

In 1886, Johnson began laying out his town from memory, beginning from a spot on the riverbank near the northwest corner of the present US 281 bridge. Lot sales began in July 1887 at a brisk pace, reported Marble Fall's first newspaper, the *Daily Texas Nutshell*.

The thousands of Colorado River Valley acres surrounding Marble Falls were prime cotton acreage, and part of Johnson's dream was the construction of a giant cotton mill powered by the falls to process the bumper harvests. To build the factory, he and several other men formed the Texas Mining and Improvement (TM&I) Company in 1887 and began building a three-story factory on the north banks of the river next to the falls (northwest corner of the US 281 bridge). Among his partners in the Texas Mining and Improvement Company was Fielding Holloway, who began building a large tannery and boot and shoe factory at the falls late in 1887.

Johnson sank every penny he had into the project, but TM&I ran out of money just as workers were ready to roof the giant building. Work ground to a halt as Johnson schemed to raise the rest of the money. Finally a rich cousin from Kentucky came through, and the shell was completed. But TM&I ran out of money again, and there wasn't a lick of machinery inside the imposing edifice. Johnson went back east to try and raise money for the machinery but met with failure; the building was not tall enough to accommodate existing cotton mill machinery, and then the Colorado went on one of its forty-foot rampages, gutting the building. The eastern capitalists turned Johnson down stone cold. Johnson went home and somehow raised the money to rebuild the factory, taking advantage of massive infusions of free labor courtesy of the local Farmers Alliance, who had a large stake in Johnson's dream. But TM&I continued to suffer from capital problems and eventually went bankrupt. The giant factory building housed a variety of businesses before it went down in a spectacular blaze on a cold night in 1964. Its mill race, however, can be seen whenever the lake level is lowered.

During those early, flush years of expectation, hundreds of folks were drawn here by brochures touting Marble Falls as "The Manufacturing Center of the Southwest," but many were also drawn here on the promise of a healthy, disease-free life. One land company bragged, "No location in the world surpasses this for benefiting those afflicted with those dreaded diseases so common at this day and time in the crowded cities and harsher climates elsewhere. Here we see daily living evidences of the beneficent results of prolonged residence of those coming here in the last stages of disease, men and women who, as a forlorn hope, have given this place a trial, regained their health, become permanent citizens and reared families of robust boys and girls."

General Adam Johnson's last grandiose plan, which he was promoting in 1922 (the year of his death), was the relocation of the entire Texas prison system to Burnet County. Naturally, the new prison complex was to be located near Marble Falls. "More water flows down the Colorado than any other Texas River," he said. Development of the river could provide cheap electricity for much of the state. Prisoners could build the power plants, and the electricity could then be used in the mining of copper, iron, and graphite. A large graphite deposit was located near the proposed prison site, so the prisoners could mine graphite. In addition, Johnson proposed that the convicts quarry granite, gravel, and crushed stone after they were through building the electric plants. The state graciously declined.

ROPER HOUSE

Third St. at US 281 • Private offices

Among the expectant early comers were George Roper and his wife, Elizabeth. Roper was a charter member of the Texas Mining and Improvement Company. In 1888, he built the Roper Hotel, which served as a stop for traveling salesmen and vacationing Texas politicians, including Governor James Stephen Hogg and his family. An ad for the hotel in the *Marble Falls Messenger* in 1899 read,

> The Hotel de Roper is a building quite neat,
> And the fare they give you is hard to beat.
> The drummers say Uncle George is clever and kind.
> And Mrs. Roper as hostess is just to one's mind.

A few blocks north of the Roper House on US 281 is the old Marble Falls Railroad Depot.

OLD MARBLE FALLS RAILROAD DEPOT/VISITORS CENTER

2607 US 281 at Broadway • 800-759-8178

This depot was built in 1893. The iron rails reached from Austin to Granite Mountain by 1885, but they didn't enter Marble Falls until 1889, when the Granite Mountain and Marble Falls Railroad built the necessary four miles of track. With the completion of this line, there commenced a flood of vacationers that continues to this day.

Marble Falls' historic homes district is located behind the old depot in the quadrangle formed by Broadway (north), Avenue E (east), Third Street (south), and Avenue H/US 281 (west). Among the twenty-odd old homes, one of the most attractive is the Otto Ebeling home, 601 Avenue F at Sixth Street, a frame Victorian house. The most historically significant house is Liberty Hall (119 Avenue C). Adam Johnson had this spacious house built on high ground, facing south with a view of the falls, at the time of Marble Falls' founding. From the second-story front porch, his son Robert could survey all the goings-on and provide the general with daily reports on the building of the blind man's town, as Marble Falls came to be called.

From the old depot, cross Avenue H/US 281 on Broadway and turn left on Main. In one block, you come to the O. M. Roberts cottage.

O. M. ROBERTS COTTAGE

Seventh St. and Main • Not open to the public

Former Governor (1879–1883) Oran M. Roberts was one of the many Texans lured to Marble Falls in its early years. Roberts retired here in 1893 from his law professorship at the University of Texas and built this whitewashed cottage, which originally stood at Third and Main. Mr. and Mrs. H. E. Fabion bought the place in 1903, moved it to its present location, and altered the front porch and roofline, adding Victorian touches such as the tin gingerbread along the roof's peak. A state historical marker is posted in the front yard.

Continue south on Main through downtown Marble Falls.

   A good dozen of the old downtown buildings—limestone, brick, and granite—still stand largely unchanged, notably the city hall at Second Street and Main.

MICHEL'S DRUG STORE

216 Main • 693-4250 • Open Monday through Saturday • W

The original Michel's Drug Store was built in 1891 and burned down with the rest of the west side of Main Street in the big fire of 1927. It was replaced by the present store; the attraction here is the old-fashioned soda fountain, which still serves old-time fountain Cokes, floats, sodas, and milkshakes.

Turn right on Second Street to reach the old Marble Falls jail.

OLD MARBLE FALLS JAIL

On Second St., one and a half blocks east of US 281 • Not open to the public

One of Marble Falls' oldest still-standing structures, and one that is thankfully no longer used, is the old jailhouse. Located on Second Street in the middle of the block between Main and Avenue J, next door to the GTE offices, the low-slung gray concrete blockhouse served for many years as a temporary home for local errants. A two-cell affair, the jail has a pair of barred slit-hole windows per cell and a cast-iron-strip front door, altogether a most dismal place to spend one's time. The jail is firmly closed to the public, but you can still catch a peek at its gloomy interior through the slit windows.

From the jail, return to Main and turn right on Main to North First. Turn right on North First and go another block to the intersection with Avenue J, which is marked by a stop sign. The road takes you through part of the Marble Falls municipal park complex, located on a branch of Lake Marble Falls. Avenue J becomes Pecan Valley Road after the road makes a ninety-degree bend to the right in the park. As you leave the parks complex, turn right on Johnson Street and go another couple of blocks to reach the home of Brandt Badger, cofounder of Marble Falls.

BRANDT BADGER HOUSE

Johnson St., between Aves. M and N • Private residence

Brandt Badger, Confederate veteran, in the 1880s moved from Gonzales to Burnet, where he established a store. Soon after, he sold the store and partnered with Adam Johnson, Robert Johnson, Fielding Harper, and others in the Texas Mining and Improvement Company to found the town of Marble Falls. He built this two-story house in 1888 of granite from Granite Mountain. In fact, the stones were cut from quarry rubble remaining after the shaping of the stone blocks used in the state capitol. Badger lived here until his death in 1920, and the house remained in the family until 1943.

From the Badger House, continue on Johnson to its dead end at Avenue S and the Marble Falls Cemetery. Turn right on Avenue S to reach the old Marble Falls Alliance University. Avenue S dead-ends into Broadway; turn left on Broadway, which immediately places you in front of the old university.

MARBLE FALLS ALLIANCE UNIVERSITY

2005 Broadway

Part of Adam Johnson's big plan for Marble Falls included a university. In February 1890, he donated several acres for the school. In August he donated several more lots, the sale of which was to help finance the construction of the school building and a wooden dormitory. In addition, $15,500 was borrowed from TM&I to construct and furnish the buildings. The buildings were finished in 1891, but by the end of that year the university was so deep in debt that in December the property was sold in a sheriff's sale to TM&I for $605. TM&I owned it until November 1895, when it sold the school property to the Marble Falls Land and Power Company for $100,000. From 1893 to 1907, it was operated as an elementary and secondary school on a tuition basis by the Marble Falls Common School District, which rented the facilities for $100 a year. After voters approved the creation of a free public school system in 1907, the Marble Falls Land and Power Company sold the school buildings and property to the school district for about $6,000. The sturdy granite school has served local students ever since, but the dormitory, which stood on the banks of Backbone Creek, has long since disappeared.

From the old university, go to the end of the block, to Avenue U, and turn right. At FM 1431, turn right and proceed to the intersection with US 281. Turn right on US 281 to get to the Blue Bonnet Cafe.

THE BLUE BONNET CAFE

211 US 281 S. • 693-2344 • www.bluebonnetcafe.net • Open Monday through Saturday breakfast, lunch, dinner; Sunday breakfast and lunch • No Cr. • W

The Blue Bonnet is a fifty-year tradition here, although you wouldn't know it once inside. Breakfasts feature great biscuits and homemade doughnuts. Later in the day, fried catfish and homemade pie are popular choices. Chicken-fried steaks, hamburger steaks, fried chicken, burgers, and such complete the menu. Overall, the starches are great and the vegetables okay. The best time for vegetables is at lunch. Still, it's worth the tab.

INMAN'S RANCH HOUSE

707 Sixth St. at US 281 • 693-2711 • Tuesday through Sunday • Lunch, dinner

They have a limited menu, but it's worth the stop: turkey sausage (lean but moist, nicely coarse texture), beef brisket, slaw, and beans.

TOURISM INFORMATION

MARBLE FALLS CHAMBER OF COMMERCE

916 Second St. • 693-2815 • www.marblefalls.org

MUSEUM

THE FALLS ON THE COLORADO MUSEUM

905 Third St. • 798-2157 • www.fallsmuseum.org • Open Thursday through Saturday

This relatively new museum is dedicated to preserving local history and features changing exhibits. Across from the museum (910 Third Street) is the other surviving hotel from the early days, the old Bredt boarding house, later bought and run for many years by the Wallace family, and currently a B&B inn.

PARKS

Marble Falls has three adjoining parks at the foot of Main Street that offer access to Lake Marble Falls, as well as other standard city park amenities, plus kayak and paddle boat rentals: Falls Creek Park, Lakeside Park, and Johnson Park.

ANNUAL EVENTS

APRIL

HIGHLAND LAKES BLUEBONNET TRAIL

Trail winds from Austin through Marble Falls, Burnet, Buchanan Dam, Kingsland, and Llano • First two weekends in April

Features oceans of bluebonnets, historic and scenic sites, local art exhibits, and festivals.

MAY

SPRING FEST

Early May • 693-2815

Spring Fest features street dances, a parade, arts and crafts, sports tournaments, and a carnival.

To continue the trip, go to the intersection of US 281 and FM 1431. Proceed two blocks north on US 281 to the intersection with Mormon Mills Road, marked by a four-way light, and turn right, and then immediately veer left to get to Mormon Mills.

If all of this sounds complicated, well, it is. But the trip north to Burnet on the old Mormon Mills Road is one of the most scenic back roads in Burnet County and the Hill Country. This narrow and winding paved road wanders in and out of Hamilton Creek valley, past the site of the old Mormon mill and settlement on Hamilton Creek (see the Mormon Trails trip). Watch for wandering cattle and goats. Just south of the Mormon Mills site, you cross Hamilton Creek, and the low-water crossing often has one or two inches of the creek flowing over it. You may very well have to share the bridge with several of the neighborhood's stolid Brahma cattle. It's easy to see why the Mormons settled here: the creek flows wide, cool, clear, and blue, while tall sycamores line the banks like sentinels.

You should drive slowly for the next several miles past the old Mormon Settlement site and Hamilton Falls (which you can catch a glimpse of from the road), for there are often some big chuckholes in the road that you will need to dodge.

Somewhere along this road, between Mormon Mills and Burnet, was held Burnet County's first camp meeting. These summertime evangelistic gatherings were social as well as religious events, as Noah Smithwick described in his memoir, *Evolution of a State*:

> The first one held in Burnet County was by the Methodists at Sand Springs on the road midway between Burnet and the Mormon mills, in 1855, Parson Whipple, an old Texas pioneer, being the chief priest. The hungry, both spiritually and physically, were freely fed at these meetings, the preachers dispensing the stronger spiritual meat of fire and brimstone first and tapering off the feast with milk and honey, while outside at every camp long tables were spread, provided with comfort for the physical man, where all were welcomed, an invitation to that effect being extended from the pulpit in the name of the campers whose hospitality was grossly abused in consequence. As other denominations took up the work, a regular chain of camp meetings every fall, with the incidental dispensation of free grub, induced many not overthrifty people to become regular camp followers, and most of them being quite forehanded with children, they became a heavy tax on the good brethren. The meetings, however, were not then drawn out indefinitely, five days being the usual limit.
>
> There finally sprung up a sect in Backbone valley that discounted all others in spiritual manifestations. Protestant Methodists they styled themselves, though just what the name implied I never learned. They had meetings every night, singing, shouting and going into trances, during which they spoke with tongues and played on imaginary harps, and, as a grand finale, springing to their feet and running as if pursued by the emissaries of Satan. Crowds of curious sightseers flocked to see the performance as though it were a circus.
>
> The men of the sect all felt themselves called to preach, and as the emoluments of office were not sufficient to support the whole neighborhood, they had to make up the deficit by hook and by crook. A whole batch of them were once summoned as jurors. One after another they arose and pleaded the statutes in their favor as ministers of the gospel. The judge finally arose and blandly inquired if there were any men in their neighborhood who were not ministers of the gospel. Shiftless at best, their hallucinations rendered them even more so; they had worked their credit for all it was worth and were almost on the verge of starvation. They had gotten into me for various amounts of breadstuffs and I decided to shut down on them, the more especially as crops were short that year and mill stuffs commanded cash.
>
> One old fellow who had a large family had been particularly troublesome. Seeing him coming, I told the miller not to let him have anything more. With

an empty bag in one hand and leading a thin, ill-fed looking little boy by the other, he assaulted my fortress with the usual request for a bushel of meal on credit, reciting the failure of his crop, which, by the way, he had neglected to plant, and the destitute condition of his family in consequence. Without daring to look at the child, I put on a severe look and replied: "I can sell every dust in the mill for cash, Mr. ——. It is therefore impossible to accommodate you." The poor creature turned away, and taking the little boy by the hand, said in tremulous tones: "Well, son, we might as well go." I involuntarily glanced at the child, whose appealing eyes were raised to my face; tears stood in the blue baby eyes, tears of hunger. "Here, John, give Mr. —— a bushel of meal," I said to the miller. I never got a cent for the meal, but the joy that lit up that little wan, pinched face and sparkled through the tears in those little eyes amply repaid me. I knew that the father was improvident, but the child was not to blame for that. Verily, "the sins of the fathers," etc. That same man denounced me as an "infidel." "Well," said one of his neighbors, "he's better than you are anyway, for the Bible says, 'He that provideth not for his household is wuss'n an infidel.'" Had it not been for the large number of cattle that were being pastured in the country, many of the poor people would have certainly suffered; but milk will sustain life, and milch cows were to be had for the asking. My old-time friend, Peter Carr, who had obtained large landed possessions in Burnet and moved his immense herd of cattle thither, was certainly a great benefactor in allowing the poor people to milk his cows.

About twelve miles north of Marble Falls and three miles south of Burnet you see a rambling white one-story ranch-modern house and assorted barns off to your left, and a historical marker immediately to your left on the side of the road.

HOLLAND SPRINGS

Burnet County • About 12 miles from Marble Falls

Located three hundred yards to the west on Hamilton Creek are the Holland Springs, named after Samuel Holland, the first permanent white settler in Burnet County. Indians had visited these cool clear springs for centuries before Ben McCulloch established a Texas Ranger camp here in 1847. Samuel Holland, a Mexican War veteran and recent Georgia émigré, visited the Ranger camp here in 1848 and liked the lush Hamilton Creek valley so much that he bought 1,280 acres here and settled down. Holland helped create Burnet County in 1852 and was the first county treasurer, a state legislator, and an investor in business projects such as the Texas Mining and Improvement Company, the Marble Falls Textile Mill, and the Marble Falls Ferry Company. In 1869, Holland bought the Mormon Mills property. The springs are on private property and may only be visited with special permission from the owners.

Several hundred yards past the Holland Springs marker, you come to a Y intersection. Take the right fork, which is County Road 340, not the left fork (County Road 340A). To enter Burnet, you pass under two railroad tracks, follow the road's veer ninety degrees to the left, and then take the first right, which is S. Pierce. S. Pierce takes you right to the courthouse square in downtown Burnet.

BURNET

Burnet County Seat • 7,100 (approximate) • (512) • About 15 miles from Marble Falls

The town of Burnet (pronounced "Burn-it") got its start in 1849, when the U.S. Army established Fort Croghan, located in what are now the western outskirts of Burnet. The fort was one of a string of eight frontier forts, located about sixty miles apart and stretching from the Rio Grande to the Upper Trinity River, built to protect frontier settlements from Indian depredations. It superseded the old outpost at Holland Springs. With the protection of Fort Croghan's soldiers, the little settlement first known as Hamilton Valley began to grow, attracting such notable early Texans as Noah Smithwick and Peter Carr (from Webberville), and Adam Johnson.

Burnet County's greatest feud took place soon after the county was organized in 1852, as the new county's inhabitants tried to decide where the county seat would be located. The two principal contending sites were the Hamilton Creek location near Fort Croghan and the Oat Meal Creek site (now Oatmeal). Controversy raged until Peter Carr tipped the balance in favor of Hamilton by donating 160 acres of land for the county seat. County commissioners graciously accepted Carr's offer, and Hamilton became the seat of Burnet County. Hamilton/Hamilton Valley became Burnet in 1858, in honor of David Gouverneur Burnet, the provisional president of the Republic of Texas.

On December 21, 1861, three days before his death, Peter Carr wrote his will, which gave the city of Burnet 6,359 acres of land and $23,500. His gift was to be used to build a college here. Carr's heirs took the will to court, and in 1868 the Texas Supreme Court ruled in their favor, leaving Burnet County with only two acres for a public school.

Burnet grew as a regional trade center until the Civil War and Reconstruction brought unrest to the area. The Burnet County Troubles, as they were known, had their roots in the vote over secession in 1861. Up to this time, no murder had been recorded in the young county, other than the unfortunates killed in Indian attacks.

Burnet County voted against secession by a wide margin, which did not sit well with the Confederate government. Many of the counties that voted against secession, such as Gillespie, Mason, and Travis, did so on the strengths of their German American communities. But Burnet County was settled in large part by men and families from the Old South states, few of whom owned slaves. In 1857, the county counted only 150 slaves worth $82,000. Little of the land in Burnet County was fit for slave-system farming. The soil was thin and the terrain rugged, fit only for stock raising. It was poor land settled by poor people.

Indians had killed white settlers in sporadic raids during the 1850s, but with the onset of the Civil War, their attacks increased and would last another ten years, until the big fight on Packsaddle Mountain. Indians entered the town of Burnet itself to steal horses at least as late as October 1872, and instead of enjoying the beautiful full-moon nights, fears were entertained that the Indians would raid.

A healthy number of men volunteered and fought in the Confederate Army, but many more stayed home to serve in an assortment of frontier and home guard companies. They had plenty of Indians (mostly Comanche, with allies from other tribes) to fight, plus white men called "bushwhackers" and "renegades." These companies seem not to have been very effective in protecting their fellow citizens and were held in accordingly low regard, if contemporary correspondence is to be believed.

A letter from Burnet in April 1862 read as follows:

We have any number of Indians in our county this moon, killing, and stealing horses. They murdered a little boy in this county, and attacked a gentleman and lady in a buggy. The man managed to get into a thicket with his wife and child, where they were followed by the Indians shooting arrows at them. The man was armed; but did not fire till an Indian charged up to the thicket, when he shot and killed him.

The people outside of us are moving together, and some of them are leaving this part of the country altogether. There was a family of them murdered in Mason Co., on the Llano river, and their house burned. Two Germans near Fredericksburg, and a negro boy this side, was killed by them.

A party of Capt. McMillan's company of Rangers, numbering fifteen, at first fought 10 Indians, had several skirmishes with them, and at the last had twenty-six men, while the Indians had dwindled down to eleven. In every one of the skirmishes the Indians are said to have whipped them. The captain, it is reported, could not make more than five or six of his men to fight at all. One man broke at the commencement and told the others to run or they would be killed. Most of them took this advice and left their captain and three or four others to do the fighting, though the captain was dangerously and three or four others slightly wounded.

A. T. Nicks, of Burnet County, Boyce's settlement, about thirty-five miles from Austin, arrived in Austin on the morning of July 9, 1863, bringing two arrows taken from the body of a Mr. Cook, who was shot in the cow pen of James Boyce on the previous Monday night evening. There were about fifteen Indians in the settlement at the time. Noah Taylor, of the town of Burnet, was shot through the shoulder but not killed on the morning of the same day, and his horse was shot from under him and died. The Indians were in considerable force in Burnet, Blanco, and Williamson counties and had been seen within fifteen miles of Austin, at Bagdad, having killed several horses there. Nicks strongly recommended that measures be taken at once to prevent their further advance, or the capitol of the state might "be invaded by the savages in a few days." Nicks handed over the fatal arrows to the governor to prove his point.

J. T. C. wrote a letter published in the *Galveston Daily News* in July 1863 about another in the string of attacks that month:

Round Mountain, Blanco County

Twenty-eight Indians made a raid last night into the north western part of this county, 15 miles hence and stole and killed all the horses they could lay their eyes upon. Also into Llano (the town) and took off all they could, and killed twenty odd horses. This I heard from my neighbor, Mr. M. Moss, who is just from Llano with his family. If the frontier regiment keeps on hauling cotton, making dancing parties, visiting their families, &c., &c., it may as well disband at once.

I was informed yesterday by Mr. Evans, of Uvalde, that the citizens of that county have represented the company stationed in that vicinity as a nuisance and requested its removal by the Governor. Certainly it is, that these frontier counties have never been protected by any troops stationed on our frontier.

J. T. C.

Bushwhackers were a varied bunch, and the term was widely abused. Some who were considered bushwhackers had been officially commissioned by Confederate authorities. Others were masquerading opportunists who harassed, robbed, and sometimes killed those accused of opposing secession, men like Burnet County's first judge, John Scott, or John Hubbard, nephew of Noah Smithwick, who left Burnet County for California in April 1861 because he didn't like what he saw coming. He warned Hubbard about the dangers of staying, but Hubbard hung on until he was threatened to the point of fleeing in 1863. A few days before his departure he was killed.

John Scott had come to Burnet County in 1851, pockets flush with gold from the California gold fields. He was a northerner, but he had four sons in the Confederate Army and had been supplying food to the Confederate Army. Despite these contributions to the southern cause, bushwhackers had threatened him, so he decided to flee to Mexico with $2,000 around his waist. He and another Unionist named McMasters were ambushed, robbed, and killed at the Colorado River crossing between Marble Falls and Smithwick, their bodies tossed into Dead Man's Hole.

Indian raids had increased during the war, but the raiding "Indians" were not always Native Americans. Near the end of the Civil War, some of the bushwhackers and outlaws began to dress up like Indians for their misdoings. It would be a favored disguise for more than a dozen years. In May 1873, a party of eight "Indians" were captured in Llano County with stolen horses. They were discovered to be white men painted and were hung; as late as the night of August 31, 1876, Captain W. H. Sims, commanding officer of Texas Rangers Company O, was kidnapped by six or more men painted as Indians. His kids escaped to the woods. Sims and his wife begged for his life, but they strung him up from a tree anyway about three-fourths a mile away from where the Sims family had been camping.

Conrad and Wilhelm Fuchs enlisted in the Third Frontier District service under Captain Christian Dorbandt in January 1864. A childhood friend, who was a secessionist, warned them that despite their enlistment into the frontier service, their lives were no longer safe and that they should move out of the area. They moved their young families to Black Jack Springs, and Willie went on to make hats for soldiers in La Grange while Conrad went to Houston and joined an artillery unit there, where he reported being well received even by well-to-do slaveholders, wearing his artillery cap with red trim.

Christian Dorbandt was born in Denmark and came to America in 1834 at age sixteen. He fought in the Mexican War and eventually landed at Fort Croghan. He retired from the army and settled at Smithwick. A Texas Rangers captain, in 1861 he became a lieutenant in the Confederates' Burnet Guards. In the fall of 1863, General Rip Ford sent him up and down both banks of the Colorado for fifty miles from Burnet toward Austin to round up "Unionists" camped in the wild country along the twisting river. These "Unionists" were accused of all sorts of wrongdoings. They captured a number of men and ran the rest off. A few weeks after becoming captain of the new Third Frontier District in January 1864, Dorbandt and his citizen soldiers killed two "renegades," as non-Indian bad boys were then being called. His son, Christian Dorbandt, born 1857 in Backbone Valley, moved to Burnet in the mid-1880s, where he was appointed deputy sheriff by Sheriff John Wolf, who was later killed in a gun battle by Constable John Taylor of the Bertram Precinct. Christian Jr. would go on to be Burnet City marshal and Burnet County sheriff, beginning in 1890.

William Jeff Maltby, born in Illinois in 1829, was the best known member of the Burnet home/frontier guard companies. After a year's service in the Arkansas Volunteers, he became a civilian employee of the United States Army in Fort Smith, Arkansas, serving as a carpenter, wagon master, scout, dispatch bearer, teamster, and hunter from 1849 to 1855. He helped build and supply several Texas frontier forts. In 1856, Maltby operated a stage stop at Fort Clark on the road from San Antonio to El Paso. He married Mary Francis McKinney and moved to Burnet County in 1857, where they began ranching. That July, the settlers organized to defend themselves from the many Indian raids that were occurring. Maltby was elected an officer, and they immediately began scouting.

During the Civil War, Maltby served a year with the Seventeenth Texas Volunteer Infantry. But by February 1863 he was so sick that the regiment's doctor told him that only the healthy air of West Texas would save him, and he gave Maltby a medical certificate to exit the service. After several months' recuperation at home, Maltby reentered military service. In August 1863, Col. John S. (Rip) Ford, state commandant of conscripts, ordered him to organize a "minuteman" company to arrest bushwhackers and deserters and kill Indians. Indians had been raiding Burnet County during every full moon of 1863, led by a man they named Big Foot. Many of the county's men had already gone into the Confederate Army, so all the boys who were old enough to ride and shoot were required to scout the country for Indians. Big Foot struck three days after the company was organized, stealing all the work and saddle horses. Maltby gave chase unsuccessfully. The next full moon they raided again, killing the Wofford Johnson family. These were probably Penateka, or Southern, Comanches. Maltby's men gave chase again, without success. Three moons passed without a raid. Then came another raid and unsuccessful chase. Big Foot raided Llano and Mason counties, killing Mrs. Blalock and her children, Tom Miligan, and Miss Todd.

At this point, Maltby joined Ford's company on the Colorado fifty miles above Austin to sweep this rough country of deserters and bushwhackers who were hiding in its many caves. According to Maltby, those not killed in battle were taken prisoner. The Civil War ended in April 1865, but it was several months before federal authorities actually took Burnet County under control. In the meantime, Maltby's minutemen continued to police the county.

Once federal control was established, soldiers were sent from Austin to disband the minutemen and arrest Maltby and fifty-nine other Burnet County men who had hunted down bushwhackers, deserters, and Indians during the war. The wanted men included prominent citizens such as Professor W. H. Holland, Tom and John Moore, and Christian Dorbandt. Several of them were arrested and imprisoned in Austin, including Dr. Tom Moore, who had served in the 1861 Secession Convention and as a receiver in the Confederate court at Austin. He was imprisoned for seventy-eight days. A few months later, the Moore family moved to Waco.

Jeff Maltby escaped capture. In 1906, Maltby published the adventures of his adult life in *Captain Jeff, Frontier Life with the Texas Rangers*.

Warned of his imminent arrest by federal troops, Maltby took to the brush. When the federal troops couldn't capture him, they ransacked his house. They marched back to Austin with the prisoners they had captured, including Tom Moore. Maltby returned to his house, reasoning that it would take the soldiers a while to get back to Burnet County. He kept his horse saddled for a quick get-away. One evening after supper, a neighbor boy warned him that the Yankees had marched onto his property. Maltby jumped on his horse and rode pell-mell through the troops, who tried to give chase but gave up and then went on to Burnet. Maltby returned home, talked with his wife, and decided to ride into Austin to surrender. When he got to Liberty Hill, he met up with a friend who persuaded him to ride to the soldiers' camp near Burnet and give himself up. With Maltby in custody, the commander ordered every man in Burnet County to report to the camp so that a jury of twelve could be selected for a sort of court-martial. The commander, a lawyer, wanted the whole bloody truth about the murders committed in Burnet County during the war and subsequently reported by loyal Union men. But the government lawyer couldn't come up with any incriminating evidence. The jury had no questions for Maltby and left the room, leaving the government lawyer and Maltby alone. When Maltby asked about his fate, the officer said, "I don't know what to do; there have been so many hard reports to General Oaks against you that he sent me here to arrest you and some others, and to leave no stone unturned to prove your guilt. If it was left to me, I would do as Christ did when the hypocrites brought the woman to Him to be rebuked. He said to them: 'He that is guiltless let him cast the first stone,' and they all sneaked off just as your accusers have done this evening. When I gave them the opportunity to question you there was not one of them that had the courage to ask you a question but that old hypocritical preacher, and the question he asked had nothing whatever to do with your guilt or innocence."

The officer decided that Maltby should post a bond of $1,000 for thirty days. No one called for him during that time, and Maltby was free, for a while. He went into the cattle business again, trailing his beeves and those of his neighbors to New Orleans and Kansas. But then a federal judge, prosecuting attorney, and sheriff were appointed for Burnet County. A grand jury indicted Maltby and his fifty-nine associates for murder and robbery during the war. Maltby posted bond, hired a lawyer, and waited for trial. The time came, and the state postponed the trial until the next session. This was followed by another postponement. When the third term began, the judge threw out the cases.

Despite Burnet County's decisive vote against secession, Reconstruction brought no relief to the county, as the *Galveston Daily News* noted in May 1868: "Burnet, owing to Indian depredations, grasshoppers and other causes, has degenerated for the last seven years. There is neither church nor hotel in the place. The iron works near by are played out, wheat destroyed by grasshoppers, no sale for beef and great scarcity of money. All these things conspire to dishearten its people."

By the early 1870s, a gang of tough men troubled the expanse from Burnet over into Llano County and up into Mason County. Criminals and cattle thieves controlled Burnet County at least part of the time from 1865 to 1876. The rustlers often masqueraded as Indians. A settler near the Sage community told of nearby settlements being plagued by the attacks of a single Indian. But when members of a minuteman company formed in 1869 chased him down and killed him, they found that he was a white man in disguise.

On the night of April 10, 1874, the Burnet County courthouse burned, just hours after the April session of district court had closed. Brand records, meeting records, and some probate papers went up in flames. It was universally assumed to have been an act of arson committed by men recently convicted or indicted by the court. Fortunately, the district clerk had removed the records pertaining to their cases before leaving the courthouse that afternoon. The clerk had abandoned the courthouse as an office several months earlier, using instead a building on the northeast corner of the square.

After the courthouse fire, court was held under the shade trees on Burnet's public square, hardly a secure place to try desperate criminals who had equally unscrupulous friends. Judge Emanuel Sampson would not hold court until the court could be adequately protected. Other judges in the district followed his lead. Colonel Samuel Holland, Burnet County's first settler, was appointed to direct a force to see that law and order prevailed and justice was administered. The judge, knowing of what stuff Holland was made, said to him, "Holland, I look to you to protect this court, else I can't hold it."

Holland had about twenty determined and well-armed men with which to protect the judge and court. The leader of the opposition party said he would kill the man who swore against him in court. Colonel Holland put a nephew of his behind this man with a five-pound bowie knife and ordered him to cut the renegade's shoulder down if he drew a weapon. The man did not draw, and the trial went on peaceably.

The new courthouse would not be finished until 1875.

Judge William Blackburn came to Burnet in July 1865. Hailing from Tennessee, where he had served in the legislature, he had been a captain in the Confederate cavalry. He had a few U.S. cents in his pockets and was smoking mullein leaves for tobacco when he arrived. Trained as a lawyer, he set up a school to earn a grubstake. A year later, his wife and son had joined him, and he had established a law practice. He practiced law with James Cook, so famed as a prosecutor that one outlaw said that when Cook was about, he could have all the sidewalk he wanted.

In April 1876, Blackburn was elected judge of the Seventeenth Texas Judicial District, which included Burnet, "a section of country infested with Indians and other desperate characters who looked upon officers of the law as enemies and the enforcement of law and order as infringement of their rights. That he possessed a physical danger and a determination to meet every danger and difficulty in the discharge of his duties is the unanimous verdict of all those associated with him in those days."

T. E. Hammond came to Texas in 1871 from South Carolina and ended up in Burnet where he went to work for Adam Johnson. He studied law and was admitted to the bar in 1876. He also edited and managed the *Burnet Bulletin* for a year. He served as captain of the company of frontier guards formed in the 1870s to guard against marauders and would go on to help found Marble Falls in 1887 as a member of the Texas Mining and Improvement Company.

As Mrs. Nannie Moore Kinser remembered, "Burnet had quite a gang of tough men in the 1870s. . . . They terrified Llano and Burnet counties. Some were killed, some went to the pen, and some left for parts unknown. I remember [Scott] Coolie well. He was a small man but Dynamite and not afraid of anyone. His hands were smaller than his wrists and they could not handcuff him." Coolie and his ilk started rounding up cattle after the war without regard to ownership and driving them off to market. A number of men were indicted for this crime, but they were so strong in number that the local judge refused to conduct their trials unless he was protected.

In fact, the reign of terror associated with Cooley extended into neighboring Mason County, and clear down to Austin and Travis County.

In 1873, the German majority in nearby Mason County elected John Clark as sheriff and Dan Hoerster as county brands Inspector. The Germans and the American-born residents were being plagued by cattle thieves. Little is known of John Clark's life before or after his term as Mason County sheriff. Born in Georgia in 1823 or 1824, he and his wife lived in San Saba during the 1860s where she died. He then remarried. At some point, Clark moved to Mason County and became very popular among the Germans. He was supposed to have been a Union soldier, since Captain Dan Roberts of the Texas Rangers referred to him as "one of the blue hen's chicks." Hoerster was a well-known local German, a big man who would not run from a fight. Clark was aggressive in dealing with anyone accused of—or merely suspected of—livestock theft, including lynching or shooting them. Although the Germans and the born Americans were suffering from a common problem, an enmity rose between them.

On May 13, 1875, Sheriff Clark sent Deputy Sheriff John Wohrle (Worley) to Castell to bring Tim Williamson to Mason to make bond on a charge of cattle stealing. Wohrle and his prisoner were attacked by twelve men with blackened faces. The deputy refused to defend Williamson from the crowd. When Williamson attempted to escape as the mob descended on him, Wohrle shot his horse. The mob then made short work of Williamson. No trial was held for this murder.

This vigilante murder angered Scott Cooley (Coolie), an ex-Texas Ranger, who vowed revenge. Williamson had befriended Cooley when Cooley was a young boy, and Mrs. Williamson had nursed him through a serious bout with typhoid fever. Cooley grew into a stout, powerful young man who had served with distinction in the Texas Rangers. He was known to suffer from fits, or "brain fever," supposedly from a snake bite, but he was a well-liked young man. He had officially resigned from the Rangers at the time of Williamson's death, but he was still camping with them.

Cooley made a list of the names of the men he thought responsible for Williamson's death and surrounded himself with a band of desperadoes, including George Gladden; Moses and John Baird, two cowboys of dubious reputation from Burnet County; and a drifter known as Johnny Ringo. The band made their headquarters at Gladden's place in Loyal Valley and proceeded to terrify the surrounding area. Cooley's revenge resulted in the killing of at least a dozen men.

John Wohrle was shot in the head and killed on August 10, 1875, while he was working on his well, and then was scalped. The consensus was that Cooley did it. After killing Wohrle, Cooley was a different man. He wore his hat down low over his eyes and avoided eye contact with strangers. He refused to shake hands for concern that his gun hand not be available for a second.

After Wohrle's death, Cooley and the boys stopped off at a saloon operated by a man named Eckert one day, where Cooley ordered a round of drinks. When Eckert demanded payment, Cooley reached into his pocket and tossed Wohrle's scalp on the bar. The stunned bartender backed away and said that the drinks were on the house. Later some of the gang barged into John Meusebach's store and fired several shots at the feet of the dignified old German statesman, one of which grazed his leg.

Carl Bader, whose brother Peter had been part of the group that had killed Williamson, was the next target of Cooley's gang. On August 19, Cooley's band showed up at Bader's Llano County farm where he was working in the field. Cooley and Ringo shot him down where he stood. It is here that versions of what happened next fork for a month or so.

According to one version, when word of Bader's death reached Mason town, Sheriff John Clark hired a local gambler named Jim Cheyney to go to Gladden's place and get the band to come to Mason. Cheyney found Gladden and Moses Baird, who agreed to make the trip to Mason. Cheyney left Gladden and Baird behind him and raced back up the road to Mason. As Gladden and Baird approached Keller's Store on the Llano River east of Mason on September 7, 1875, they saw Sheriff Clark standing outside. A gun battle erupted, and Gladden and Baird were badly wounded by Clark's posse. They managed to ride about a mile back toward home with Clark's men pursuing them. There Baird died and Gladden was found too badly wounded to fight. Carl Bader's brother, Peter, wanted to finish Gladden off, but John Keller swore he'd kill anyone who attempted to shoot the wounded man. Bader assuaged his anger by removing a gold ring from the hand of dead Moses Baird, along with the finger itself.

On September 25, 1875, Cooley helped John Ringo and a man named Bill Williams revenge Moses Baird's death by killing James Cheyney. A Texas Ranger report stated, "John Ringgold and another man of the Gladden-Cooley party killed Cheyney in the presence of his family while he was arranging breakfast for them, then Gladden, Cooley, Ringgold and others of the party rode into town and ate their breakfast at the hotel and boasted publicly at the table of what they had done, telling those present that they had 'made beef of Cheyney and if someone did not bury him he would stink.' They remained in town some time and one of them, Gladden, had an interview with Justice Hey during this time. The fact of their having done the killing is of public notoriety, and yet no warrants was or has been issued for their arrest. I asked the Justice why no warrants had been issued for their arrest, his reply was, no complaint had been made against them, though he held the inquest."

The citizens of Mason asked Governor Richard Coke to send in the Texas Rangers for protection.

On September 28, the Ranger report states, Company A and part of Company C of the Texas Rangers reached Coal Springs in Mason County for the purpose of quelling disturbances in that county. Reaching Keller's Store, on the Llano, the Rangers were surprised to see Clark and about twenty of his men rise up in a fighting attitude from behind a stone fence; they had mistaken the command for the Gladden-Cooley party of Cold Springs, and the Beard party of Burnet, who they figured would be coming into Mason that day "to burn up the town."

Either that day or the next day, September 29, Dan Hoerster was ambushed and killed by John Baird (Moses Baird's brother), Gladden, and Cooley in downtown Mason. Another version of the story states that on that day, Peter Jordan (a friend of Hoerster's) and Gladden were wounded. Ranger Captain Jones checked out the scene at Cold Springs, and then he and Ranger Sgt. Daniel Roberts tried to get down to the bottom of things. During a gunfight at Keller's store on the Llano River, Clark and Keller's son wounded Mose Beard and George Gladden. Beard died, but Gladden was sent to his home at Loyal Valley to recover.

During October, the Rangers made twenty-two arrests, twelve of them for offenses committed in Mason County, and others from adjoining counties. Two parties showed fight, and one man in each was wounded. Peace in Mason County had been restored, they declared.

Early in December 1875, Burnet County Sheriff A. J. Strickland arrested John Ringo (Ringgold) based on a disturbing the peace indictment from April 1875. On December 6, 1875, after posting a $150 bond, Ringo was released from jail. His sureties were J. R. Baird and George Gladden. At the end of December, Ringo and Cooley were arrested and jailed for threatening the lives of Sheriff Strickland and his deputy. Their arrest caused serious concern that their friends would try to bust them out of the Burnet jail.

On January 2, 1876, the *Austin Statesman* reported that fifty men were guarding the jail while another twenty men were dashing around town threatening to break open the jail to liberate the prisoners. The situation was so tense that the sheriff refused to receive a prisoner from Austin in the morning for fear of attack. The prisoner was received later in the day, but as the Austin man who had escorted the prisoner, an ex-policeman named Johnson, began his return ride to Austin, he met many armed men along the road. A feeling of dread and insecurity pervaded the community, and strangers were eager to get out of town.

To prevent any attempt to free Ringo and Cooley, the authorities decided to take the men to the Austin jail. While en route to Austin, the men received a great deal of attention in the newspapers.

Sheriff Strickland and ten to twelve men took the two prisoners to Austin on January 3 for safekeeping until the next meeting of the Burnet District Court on the fourth Monday of the month. The group stopped at Salge's Restaurant before heading to jail, and a large crowd gathered to see the two men who had, for the past few months, "been on the rampage" in Mason and Burnet counties. "They were cool and reserved and chatted as easily as any of the guards and each recognized a person or two in the crowd," the *Austin Statesman* reported.

Cooley was charged with killing Wohrle and taking his scalp. Ringo was charged with threatening the Sheriff of Mason County and Strickland.

With Cooley and Ringo locked up and the Rangers on the hunt for the others, it appeared as if the violence was at an end. Hardly so.

Peter Bader had been hiding out around San Fernando Creek in Llano County. When Gladden and John Baird found out where he was, they prepared an ambush on the road between Llano and Castell. As Bader traveled up the road one evening in January 1876, the two waited behind a granite outcrop, and John Baird got his revenge for his brother Moses' death. He later proudly displayed the gold ring Bader had taken from his dead brother, saying "Bader cut my brother's finger off to get it, and I cut Pete's finger off to get it back."

That same month, the Cooley party in the great vendetta in this county were charged with another murder. A foreigner by the name of Bourbon was riding along the public road when he was attacked by a party of men and shot. The party, then seeing some men approaching and supposing them to be friends of their victim, told them to take up the man and take care of his valuables, as they (the assassins) did not want money but his life. Bourbon had $400 and a gold watch when he was shot.

Cooley and Ringo were held in the Travis County jail until late January 1876, when they were taken by ten men to Burnet to appear before the Grand Jury, which indicted them for threatening the sheriff and his deputy. Ringo and

Cooley applied to have their court case transferred to another county. After pleading not guilty, their case was transferred to Lampasas County. They were released on bond on February 4, 1876, and were ordered to appear at the next session of the Lampasas court.

Ringo and Cooley surrendered to Burnet authorities in March 1876 and were taken under heavy guard to Lampasas County. In March 1876, John Ringo was tried and convicted in Lampasas County for threatening the Burnet sheriff and his deputy. An appeal was filed, and the conviction was reversed, but not until 1877; Ringo remained in custody waiting for the result of the appeal.

On April 1, 1876, the *Austin Statesman* editorialized, exasperatedly: "If the sheriffs of several counties of Texas, authorized as they are to call out the posse comitatus, were removable by the governor, there would be infinitely better order maintained in western counties. Now and then a sheriff is chosen by the disorderly elements of society. His sympathies are with those that delight in excitements of rapine, violence, and disorder, and there is no local restraint upon ebullitions of villainy and crime is openly riotous. If Gov. Coke's hand were mailed with iron force enough to choke the official life out of sheriffs of counties in which murderers go unwhipt of justice, murders would soon be very rare."

In May 1876, several men freed John Ringo and Scott Cooley from the Lampasas jail, and in the summer of 1876, Ringo and the rest of Cooley's band were again reported stealing livestock in the Mason area. Citizens organized to go after them and issued a call to Gillespie County for the Mounted Rifles to help capture them.

Many residents remembered Cooley's vow to kill Sheriff Clark. But Cooley had missed his chance. Sheriff Clark had left office and left town. He had been implicated with the cattle rustlers he had been charged with exterminating. While Cooley and Ringo were in jail, Sheriff Clark had been indicted for complicity in the disappearance of Bill Coke while on his way, under guard, to the Mason jail. Coke had been arrested by a mob at a ranch on Mill Creek, southwest of Mason. Support for Sheriff Clark had declined, while desire to avenge the recent deaths increased. The charges fell through, and Clark resigned his position, vanishing from Mason County as mysteriously as he had arrived. By the time of the 1880 U.S. census, he was living in Burnet. Rumor has it that he and his wife were killed sometime between 1880 and 1884 and left seven orphans.

On June 18, 1876, a San Saba man reported that he overheard two men talking in church about a gunfight in Llano County between stockmen and desperadoes from Scott Cooley's party, in which sixteen men were killed. True? Probably not. But such was the tenor of the times.

Cooley's rampage came to an end sometime in the summer of 1876, after his escape from jail. Cooley had eaten dinner at the Nimitz Hotel in Fredericksburg when he suddenly fell ill. For a time it was believed that he had been poisoned by Germans, but it's more likely that the "brain fever" that had plagued him most of his life had now ended it. It also may explain many of his actions in the latter days of his life. William Scott Cooley died at about twenty-one years of age and was buried in Blanco County's Miller Creek Cemetery.

John Baird fled Texas to Lincoln County, New Mexico, where he met with a violent end. George Gladden, Neil Cain, and Johnny Ringo were both captured in a hut where they were living, at the Moseley Ranch near Castell some miles above Cold Springs, during the first week of November 1876, by Sergeant Robinson, commanding a detachment of seven men of Company C, Texas Rangers, assisted by Sheriff Bozarth of Llano and six men. They were placed in the Llano County jail. It was said at the time that the Ranger commands of Major Jones and Captain McNelly had brought not less than fifty desperados and stock thieves to grief during the previous three months and had perhaps frightened as many more out of the country.

About a week later, Gladden, Ringo, and Cain (see Mormon Trail, Llano) were brought to Austin to be held in the Austin jail until the courts convened in the respective counties where they were to be tried for the crimes committed. Gladden had been indicted in Llano County for the murder of Peter Bader, and five capiases charging him with theft had been issued for his arrest. Gladden was convicted of the murder of Peter Bader and was sentenced to ninety-nine years in the state pen in December 1876.

While Ringo was in the Travis County jail, he was indicted by the Mason County Grand Jury in November 1876 for killing James Cheyney. The original indictment was destroyed by a fire. On May 18, 1877, a substitute indictment against Ringo was filed.

On October 29, 1877, an arrest warrant was issued against Ringo in Mason County, and the sheriff took Ringo into custody on November 1, 1877. He was placed in jail at Mason until his court date. At court, the judge ordered that fifty men should be prepared to serve as a jury pool. Ringo's case was continued, and on November 19, seven Texas Rangers set out to take him back to the Travis County jail, but while en route to Austin, Ringo was apparently detained briefly in the Llano County jail by Sheriff Bozarth for some reason.

The *Austin Daily Statesman* on December 4, 1877, reported on his return to Austin:

> George Gladden, recently committed to the State prison for life, will be confined to a felon's cell here-to-day. John Ringo, charged with all manner of crimes, will cross the bridge this morning with Gladden. The pretty pair will rest for a time in the jail of this city. Sheriff Bozarth, of Llano, had these terrible fellows in charge. The people will be curious to see these two men, famous for the devilish deeds they have done.

While in the Travis County jail in Austin, Ringo became friends with the notorious John Wesley Hardin. In December 1877, Ringo's attorney filed a writ of habeas corpus and demanded that a bond be set for his client. Ringo was brought back to Mason and on December 20, 1877, was released on a $2,500 bond. He was ordered to appear before the court on May 10, 1878.

While on bond, on February 4, 1878, Ringo was arrested by five Texas Rangers in Junction City, Kimble County, for disturbing the peace. He was released after giving a bond. On April 18, 1878, Ringo appeared in Mason and filed a sworn affidavit that several men were needed as witnesses in his case. On May 15, 1878, the district attorney for Mason County requested that the case against John Ringo for the murder of James Cheyney be dismissed. No witnesses were willing to testify against John Ringo.

After the murder charge against him was dismissed, he settled at Loyal Valley, Mason County. In November 1878, Ringo was elected constable for Precinct Four at Loyal Valley. Whether Ringo ever took the position is not known.

It is believed that he left Texas in 1878, and by 1879 he was in the Arizona Territory. In December of 1879, Ringo was arrested for his participation in a bar shooting in Safford, Arizona Territory. Ringo then briefly left the territory and journeyed to Texas and Missouri before returning to the Arizona Territory in July 1881, where he took up residence at the Grand Hotel in Tombstone.

We know from the following article dated May 3, 1881, published in the *Austin Daily Statesman*, that when Ringo was visiting Austin, he proved no match for Austin's famous city marshal, Ben Thompson.

> Mr. John Ringo was in town early Sunday morning and was passing his time down in a house in the jungles. Along about 4 o'clock he missed his purse, and stepping out in the hall where some three or four of Austin's nice young men were seated, he came down upon them with his little pistol and commanded them to "up hands," he quietly searched the whole tea party. Not finding his purse he smiled beamingly upon the young men, and retired to his room while they quietly slid out and reported the facts to the police. Marshal Thompson in person went down to the house, but was refused admission to the room, whereupon he cheerfully kicked open the door, and to the infinite disgust of Mr. Ringo, scooped him in. He was disarmed, and Officer Chenneville, who had arrived, marched him to the station and yesterday he was fined $5 and costs for disturbing the peace, and $25 and costs for carrying a pistol. He settled with the city and left a wiser if not sadder man.

He returned to the Arizona Territory, where he got involved in a feud with the Earp Brothers in Tombstone. On July 13, 1882, he was found in Morse's Canyon leaning against a tree with a bullet wound in his head. Some historians believe he was slain by the notorious gunman Buckskin Frank Leslie, but others say he took his own life.

George Gladden was pardoned in 1884, after which it is said that he left the state. But Gladden could not stay away from Texas, evidently: on June 22, 1887, Uvalde County Sheriff Baylor arrested Gladden and lodged him in the county jail upon a capias from Eagle Pass. Captain Jones of Texas Rangers Company D had some time ago received a telegram from the sheriff of Kimble County to arrest Gladden with a bunch of stolen horses.

Then, the *San Antonio Light* reported on April 21, 1888, that Gladden, "a notorious character throughout western Texas," had been extradited from Mexico by authorities of Piedras Negras and turned over to Maverick County Sheriff Cooke, who lodged him in the county jail at Eagle Pass. Gladden was wanted in various western Texas counties but was extradited on an indictment for horse stealing from Williamson County.

George Gladden, alias George Lee, was charge for a forged note in Prescott, Arizona, on February 15, 1894. The *Rio Grande Republican* newspaper of Las Cruces, Territory of New Mexico, reported on March 23, 1895, that Gladden had received a sentence of thirty days in jail plus costs, for unspecified crimes.

By May 23, 1895, Gladden was in El Paso, according to Robert K. DeArment's *Deadly Dozen* and Leon Metz's *John Wesley Hardin*, where he had resumed his friendship with his old Travis County jail mate John Wesley Hardin. That evening, Charley Perry, sheriff of Chaves County, New Mexico, entered the Wigwam Saloon, one of Hardin's favored watering holes, demanding to see Hardin. Gladden, who was present, told him that Hardin was not there but that he was a friend of Hardin's and asked if he could be of help. Perry, who was drunk, responded that Gladden and Hardin had murdered some of his friends and that he was ready to square accounts with them.

Gladden declined the offer, noting that he was unarmed. Perry put two revolvers on the bar and told Gladden to take his choice. Gladden again declined the challenge, whereupon Perry slapped his face, called him a coward, and promised to return the next day to settle up with Gladden and Hardin.

After giving his account of their meeting, Gladden had lawyer Hardin swear out a warrant against Perry and had him arrested on various charges, including threatening to take a life, assault, and battery. Perry pled guilty to two of the charges the next day and paid a ten-dollar fine. Perry did not follow up on his threat to kill Gladden and Hardin, but Hardin would die three months later at the hands of Constable John Selman. After this episode, Gladden disappears from history.

Llano County Sheriff J. J. Bozarth died in November 1880. He had served three terms and took sick to death the day that he was elected the fourth time. He was very popular and had but fifty-three votes against him. His death was deeply lamented.

Burnet County Sheriff Strickland resigned from office in January 1878 and in June 1880 was convicted by a Travis County jury and sentenced to two years in the state pen.

In late summer 1879, D. S. Ogle, editor of the *Burnet Bulletin* and treasurer of the county, turned up missing, along with $2114.17 of public funds, leaving the county and his private creditors to mourn his sudden disappearance. He ostensibly left for Austin to deposit some public money, but he forgot to do so, though he arrived safely in that city. There he announced his intention of proceeding to Galveston on a trip for the "good of his health." This was five or six weeks earlier, and he was probably still looking after his health, as nothing further was heard from him. In the meantime his creditors, including General Adam Johnson, took charge of the *Bulletin*, and constituted Mr. T. E. Hammond editor and publisher, until the paper was sold at a sheriff's sale a few months later to Col. James A. Stevens, who had moved to Burnet in 1879.

The paper had gone through a number of editors during its first six years, beginning in 1873. Subscribers often complained that the paper never reached them. Presumably the outlaws were tampering with the mail and its carriers.

Colonel Stevens, who had served in the Confederate Army, edited and published the *Bulletin* for nearly twenty years. He built a reputation for the paper as a clean, fearless periodical. When Colonel Stevens bought the *Bulletin*, it required courage for an editor to condemn the wrong and uphold the right, as in those days this country contained many desperate characters who were intolerant of criticism, and ofttimes men would be shot and killed upon the slightest provocation. Colonel Stevens knew this, but it did not deter him from vigorously starting and carrying on the fight in this section of the state for what he considered good government and civic righteousness.

He had not been a resident of Burnet long before some of his articles offended some of the desperate characters, and they called upon him with the intention of scaring him into silence, but they soon found out they were attempting to bluff the wrong man. Their personal violence was vigorously resented, and to protect himself from attack by firearms, he carried his gun to his office with him thereafter. He continued to publish the truth, regardless of who was offended or whom it pleased, and he continued this policy as long as he was connected with the paper. His enemies, and he made many, in leading the fight to stamp out lawlessness in Burnet County, soon learned to respect him and came to realize that only death or disability would stop him in his crusade for right.

Burnet was not a pretty town in those years either, as one old-timer related:

> For many years Burnet remained just a somnolent little town, so much so that a horse-and-buggy drummer, who while spending a night in the one hotel, sat smoking and looking out over the unpaved, mud-puddled, littered square, and quipped, "When God created the world, he must have raked up the refuse, piled it, and said 'Burn-et here.'"

In February 1881, as plans were advancing to build a new state capitol building in Austin, and railroad mania was sweeping over Texas and the rest of the country, a group of ambitious thinkers in Burnet were agitating for the construction of a narrow-gauge railroad from Austin to Burnet to haul the region's best granite to build the new state capitol. If the legislature would only give them $4,000 per mile to build the line, they said, "The building of our narrow gauge road to Burnet would secure at once the finest material for the main body of the house at but little more than it would cost to wagon the material from adjacent hills," referring to the Oak Hill limestone first chosen by the capitol's building committee.

"A large part of the stone work can be done by convict labor. A capitol can be built at a cost of one fourth less money than the same can be built by general contract. If these are facts, would it not be wise to at once make suitable legislation granting the company a loan of the four thousand dollars per mile, and secure the finest material in the State at so small a cost of money?"

Two months later, a group of Austin and Hill Country capitalists, plus two investors from Dubuque, Iowa, met in Austin to form the Austin and Northwest Railroad Company. Adam Johnson offered five hundred city lots, together with other property to the amount of $100,000, to encourage the road to come to Burnet.

In the counties above Burnet, the Austin and Northwestern railway boom was causing quite a flutter among the population. Stock was being taken, and other donations were being made, and all were anxious to see the road put through San Saba and then on through McCulloch, Coleman, Runnells, and Taylor counties, terminating at Abilene, in the last-named county.

"What would be the effect of a railroad coming to Burnet?" wrote one booster to the *Burnet Bulletin*.

> One of the leading objections we have heard is that it would bring a great deal of the riff-raff of society—cut throats, professional gamblers and idlers, and soiled doves. We should remember, also, that it would bring a still larger number of good men and their families into the place. In every community, however bad, the law abiding and virtuous are always in the majority. This majority in some sections may be for a while over awed and neutralized in its influence, but in the end, the right prevails, and the community settles down into peace and order, and churches and court prevail where once lawlessness and dens of infamy were dominant. We believe upon the coming of a railroad to Burnet, freight transportation would be quickened and regulated, if not cheapened; the freighters would all get into more profitable business; newcomers would arrive and stop, and some remain while others would go on further; new

houses would spring up by dozens; the mechanics would get plenty of work; the farmers could more readily dispose of their produce; the schools would improve; new churches would be built; real estate would be greatly enhanced in value; and every business and profession would feel the benefit. The greatest evil of a railroad is when it becomes a monopoly, and grinds the public with exorbitant charges, but even that may be remedied.

Apart from the advantages to be derived by the farmer, the merchant, the professional man, the laborer, and all others, a railroad to Burnet will prove a blessing in another respect. It will be the death of the village gossip and back-biter. Like all other small places, our excellent community is afflicted with a few tale-bearers and petty slanderers, who from the very scarcity of their victims grow bold and correspondingly venomous from having to go over the same ground so often. It has been suggested that the railroad will open up such a flood of sunshine, and novelty, and strange faces and new ideas, that the dirt throwers and poison mongers will forget their venom and meanness amid the clatter and thunder of the cars and be buried forever out of sight beneath the wave that "goes rolling on."

On December 3, 1881, the surveying party completed their preliminary survey to Burnet, in the presence of a small but enthusiastic audience of the natives. They reported a good route all the way from Austin except for the hill three or four miles east of town. The distance by line surveyed from Austin to Burnet was just fifty-four miles.

Despite Adam Johnson's generous offer, the railroad wanted more from Burnet: the right-of-way from Williamson County line to Burnet, the necessary depot grounds, and $50,000 bond for the $10,000 of company stock taken by Burnet's citizens. The railroad, in turn, agreed to build and operate the road to Burnet by the first of May. The depot would be less than half a mile from the public square. Dr. W. H. Westfall, a Burnet banker and one of the road's biggest backers, stated that the crisis had come and it was for the people to say whether they would let the opportunity pass or not. The people of Burnet came up with the goods, and a contract with the railroad company was signed.

With the signing of the contract came this "Warning to Immigrants" in the *Burnet Bulletin*:

Persons intending to come to Burnet town to live had better bring their houses along with them. There is not an unoccupied cabin, tent, pig-pen, umbrella, hogshead, hollow stump, or roosting tree inside of the town and the cry is still for more rooms. Men wait for men to vacate, and those expecting others to get out, are in turn counting the days before they take leave to occupy some other palatial rat-harbor. The tenant that can hope to "hold the fort" where he is now through the winter is looked on as enviously as a bloated bond-holder. The question with renters is not "how is your health?" but "when do you move?" The condition of things causes rents to be paid down promptly to the day, lest the horrors of Irish eviction be theirs, although the landlords are as forbearing as they can be. The trouble is, Burnet is now a town with 600 population with house covering enough for only about 400 persons. Lumber is scarce and high and the railroad is coming. That's what's the matter.

By New Year's Day 1882, work along the line to Burnet was booming, and it was confidently predicted that Burnet was bound to become, in a few years, a town of 2,500 inhabitants.

Underscoring Dr. Westfall's importance to the A&NW, by January 7, the road's first engine, the *Dr. Westfall*, had been painted and burnished up, and quoting the *Austin Statesman*, "It is now a perfect little beauty. F. A. Hill, civil engineer, and M. C. Hurley, contractor, H. M. McNeill and Wm. Brueggerhoff have returned from a three-day trip up the Austin and Northwestern line. They made the final location of the main line from here to Burnet and report a great boom in the section of country they visited. Track laying has commenced and iron is arriving daily for the Austin and Northwestern. Frog-Stool Row has now but a little space left, and when that is filled up, the west side of Burnet's Public Square will look business-like and gorgeous."

But just a month later, the national railroad boom was turning into a bust. The Texas and St. Louis Railway, on which Burnet had so confidently counted, announced that the company had temporarily suspended all active work below Coryell County in order to concentrate all of its forces in Arkansas.

But this disappointment was soon replaced by prospects of a branch of the Missouri Pacific dipping down from Belton, through Burnet, to the Marble Falls.

An overwhelmingly bright future still seemed in store:

> Now that the county is soon to have railroad communications with the outside world, the prospect of Burnet county is a bright and prosperous one. The granite of the country stands next to that of Vermont, and soon the 2 granite arms of the United States reaching from Vermont to Texas will be connected by steel bands of railway, and Burnet may be called upon to supply granite to the southern and western states.
>
> Our marble rivals that of Italy for hardness, durability and great variety of coloring.
>
> The tar springs in the vicinity of Burnet have already been leased with the intention of developing their wealth as soon as the railroads will furnish transportation. Our streams of ever-flowing water and the marble falls will furnish the cheapest power for mills and factories. Our hills covered with the unrivaled mezquit will furnish the finest pasture for cattle, sheep, and goats. Our fertile valleys will afford food enough for consumption and for export.
>
> So with our pastures, farms, quarries of marble, granite, iron and the water powers, all that Burnet county needs is capital and energy to develop it into one of the richest in the Lone Star State. We believe there are men now in the county willing and able to develop all this latent wealth, and soon the railways will bear from it trains loaded with marble, granite, iron, petroleum, cattle, sheep, wool, cotton, corn, wheat and manufactured articles, and will in return cause a golden stream of wealth to flow into our midst.

But prosperity brought its dark side. In March 1882, Burnet experienced its first robbery and small pox scare, courtesy of all the new immigrants.

Would the Austin and Northwestern reach Burnet by its May 1 deadline?

It was expected that the iron rails would be run into Burnet by six o'clock on the afternoon of May 1, but in fact they reached the town at 11:35 p.m., with twenty-five minutes to spare, thus securing the $10,000 bonus and avoiding forfeiture of the aforementioned bond. The last spike was driven by W. H. Westfall, of Burnet, at 11:40 p.m. The spot was at the edge of the city cemetery, in the presence of about five hundred citizens. Contractor Mike Hurley rolled out a dozen kegs of beer for the boys, and a rousing, but quite sober, glorification was had in toasts and kind hopes for the success of the enterprise. The *Burnet Bulletin's* reporter would have preferred that they had taken cold water, but everything went off without any indecency or excess, he noted.

Freight shipments between Austin and Burnet began several days later: lumber, furniture, and groceries from Austin, and wool from Burnet.

With the whistling of the evening train, there was a simultaneous movement on the part of many Burnet citizens to take a walk in the eastern suburbs—not to see the cars, of course not—but just to get an airing, you know. The narrow-gauge train and the stagecoach started from Liberty Hill together on May 23 and got into Burnet "neck and neck." "Won't that do for speed?" the *Burnet Bulletin* commented. With the trains now running into town, it looked quite citylike down on Jackson Street.

Burnet's honeymoon with the railroad was short-lived. On May 23, a town meeting was held to consider the condition of the burial ground and to take action for its enclosure and improvement. The coming of the railroad had thrown it open to the depredations of the stock. There were plenty of boys idling their time playing on the railroad. The fear was that somebody's boy was going to get killed.

Late on the evening of May 20, at about eleven o'clock, a burglar or burglars entered Smith & Robinson's hardware store, going in the front door by false keys, and broke open the combination safe and took all the money there was in it, about eighty dollars. They also helped themselves to two pistols, one of them a twenty-dollar ivory-handle, the other an English bulldog. The safe lock was broken all to pieces, showing practiced hands and the necessary tools. The neighbors heard the noise made in the store but did not suspect the cause of it. The same night, Culbertson and Brownlee's grocery store was opened the same way, it appears, and some two dollars was taken from the cash drawer. The citizens began talking about employing a night watch or incorporating the town.

By June 1, a good deal of anxiety was being felt over the remarkable delay of the narrow-gauge road in getting its daily freight and passenger trains to Burnet. Burnet had suffered some loss by the condition of her road, especially when it came to lumber prices vis-à-vis communities like Lampasas, but it was felt that Burnet prices would become more competitive when the narrow-gauge was in a condition to take lumber over the track safely by the carload.

The problem was that the Austin and Northwestern had been built on the cheap, accomplished by skimping on the quality of the roadbed and operating on the false assumption that the lighter narrow-gauge cars and engines could carry and pull just as much freight as standard-gauge roads built on sound road-beds. Washouts were a problem on the A&NW from the beginning.

In June, trains were running weekly at best, as crews struggled to get the roadbed into runnable condition. Finally, on June 28, the first regular through passenger train left Austin and reached Burnet at noon. A number of citizens were present to witness the arrival. That same day, people in Austin were talking with those in Burnet for the first time via the telephone, in a "perfectly satisfactory" experiment.

On July 3, a daily schedule was started on the narrow-gauge. The trains were "mixed," leaving Austin at 7 in the morning, arriving at Burnet at 12 noon, and departing for Austin at 1 p.m. Persons in Austin could now visit Burnet, transact business, and return the same day, except on days like July 6, when the train was delayed several hours because the baggage car jumped the tracks. No one was hurt, and very little damage was done.

The depot agent's office was at first a boxcar. By August 29, the Austin and Northwestern was building a cotton platform in Burnet for the coming season, and Austin was doing a good business with Burnet and other towns along the rail line.

A couple of days later, a skeptical Austin rider took his first ride up to Burnet:

From the abuse that had been heaped upon the Narrow-gauge road, we expected to have our back-bone dislocated by the first trip. To our surprise, we find it with the exception of a few miles a very good road. It rocks instead of jolts you. Last Wednesday noon, we boarded the train on the Austin and Northwestern narrow gauge, with the shrinking reluctance with which a bob-tail politician accepts a nomination for office; for we had heard the road so much abused for its rough and dangerous condition, that the anticipation of a pleasant ride was considerably leavened with the foreboding of a broken leg. To our grateful surprise, it proved very much smoother than we expected, although by no means like ice. Beyond Liberty Hill, but little objection can be made to the road bed, while on the home stretch to Austin, after you cross the International, it is charming. The peculiarity of the narrow-gauge is that the passenger is rocked from side to side as in a cradle, as contra-distinguished from the churning of the Central and the leaps and plunges of the I. and G. N. Even the scenery along the route was better than expected, with its long swells of shin-oak, precipitous ledges of rock along the Gabriel, occasional spots of hanging moss, and lovely mountain perspectives in the hazy distance. The new town of Bertram (once South Gabriel) is located on a high, level ridge, and will eventually become the prettiest, as it will continue the best business point between the termini of the road. Liberty Hill is growing. The other intermediate stations, Leander, Brueggerhoff, and Cummings, are as yet nothing more than a house, a man, a yellow dog, and pure air.

On December 7, Dr. Westfall, who owned extensive quarries of the fine marble and granite in Burnet County, tendered, free of charge, in behalf of the citizens of Burnet County, all the granite and marble for building in entirety the new capitol. But it would be a while before the Austin and Northwestern would be capable of safely transporting it.

In October 1882, it was reported that the A&NW's roadbed was being put in excellent condition and in a few more months the company would have as good a roadbed as could be found in the state. That goal had obviously not been achieved by January 12, 1883, when news reached Austin that there had been a serious accident on the Austin and Northwestern railroad the day before. As the passenger train, bound for Burnet, was about one and a half miles from Cummings, a wheel on one of the coaches broke, and the car jumped the track and turned over on its side. Major H. M. Holmes, chief clerk in the attorney general's office, who was going to his home in Mason City, had his shoulder dislocated, and he was otherwise seriously, though not dangerously, hurt. Two ladies and a little child were hurt also, the latter and one of the ladies badly, it was said. The cause of the accident was the long and unusual spell of wet and cold weather which had soaked the roadbed and made it soft and bad for traveling. Major Holmes could not be moved from Leander, whence he was taken for medical attention.

There was another terrible accident on the afternoon of February 3, 1883, about two and a half miles south of Liberty Hill. At about three o'clock the passenger train from Burnet left Liberty Hill with fifteen passengers and was running at a slow rate on account of the engine being broken. A broken rail caused the coach to jump the track, and the car partly turned over, there being a slight embankment there. The stove fell on Mrs. Robert H. Ward of Burnet, hurting her foot and setting her clothing on fire. This was promptly extinguished, but not before she had received painful burns on her legs, and she was otherwise hurt. Mrs. Burroughs, of Weatherford, had her hand cut by the breaking of the window through which her arm was forced by the fall; a piece of glass lodged in her hand, causing great pain. Several other parties were more or less bruised, skinned, and hurt, one man having his shoulder badly mashed. It seemed this road was a regular shoulder-splitter when it started—vide Maj. Holmes' injury. It is fortunate the engine was disabled, as it prevented the train from running fast, in which case the accident would have undoubtedly proved fatal. The officers did everything possible for the injured and procured medical attention for Mrs. Ward and Mrs. Burroughs.

The road's bed was eventually stabilized, the gauge was changed from narrow to standard, and it eventually became part of the Southern Pacific system. With the railroad's arrival and the resulting boost to the local economy, stone and brick buildings began to replace the less permanent wooden ones around the courthouse square, and many still stand today.

Burnet was named the Bluebonnet Capital of Texas by the Sixty-seventh Texas Legislature. Appropriately, Burnet's big annual celebration is the Bluebonnet Festival, held the second weekend in April, with dances, arts and crafts, and lots more.

BADGER BUILDING

S. Pierce and Jackson • Monday through Friday 9–4:30 • Free • W

On the southeast corner of the courthouse square stands the Badger building, a two-story cut-limestone-block edifice completed in 1883. The historical marker on the building reads in part: "This two-story limestone building is representative of other commercial buildings on the courthouse square in the 1880s. Built for local financier Dr. W. H. Westfall and Captain Brandt Badger, who had served in the Civil War from Texas. Badger and son operated a wholesale and retail drugstore on the ground floor. The second floor, divided into five rooms, was used as office space. Badger sold the business in 1885 and later, in conjunction with Adam Johnson, helped establish Marble Falls."

Since that time, the Badger building has housed a hardware store, a bank, the state Parks Board, the Burnet Rural Telephone Company, the post office, and other businesses before it became a museum and youth and community center in 1966 that houses a collection of Burnet County memorabilia and locally crafted goods.

WORLD'S SMALLEST CITY PARK

Outside the Badger Building, S. Pierce and Jackson • W

Located outside the Badger building, this tiny park consists of a small gazebo and a big chunk of granite squeezed onto a several-square-foot plot of grass, with a sign identifying the thumbnail plot as the "World's Smallest." Who would dispute it?

Circumambulating the square, you notice that although many of the structures are essentially vintage, most of the facades have been modernized over the years, detracting somewhat from the desired nineteenth-century effect. The stone building on the corner of Main and Jackson (for many years Dilbeck's Department Store, now an antique mall) is one of the few essentially unaltered structures on the square, as a look at the old pictures of the square displayed inside the Badger building will reveal.

D. L. EMMETT BUILDING

123 E. Jackson

This two-story limestone building dates to 1883 and features some nice keystone window arch work and a smooth facade, owing to the highly polished, closely fitted stone blocks. Traces of a previous occupant's advertisements, Seidensticker's Men's Store, still linger across the front of the second story.

BURNET BULLETIN

101 E. Jackson, at Main • Newspaper office

The rougher, quarry-dressed limestone block exterior of this simple two-story building contrasts with the Emmett building's smoother skin. This one was built in 1872. The newspaper inside was founded a year later. But the newspaper, Burnet's oldest, didn't move in here until 1979. It was a general store until 1900 and then was variously a furniture store/mortuary and a telephone company office. The second story was used as a courtroom during the 1930s when the current courthouse was under construction.

A. I. HABER BUILDING

236 S. Main, at Jackson

Dating to 1883, this two-story rusticated limestone block commercial house was for many years Dilbeck's Department Store. Its facade is essentially unaltered.

OLD MASONIC LODGE

309 S. Main and League • Not open to the public

Located one block south of the Haber building is the old Masonic temple, built in 1854 and the oldest commercial structure in Burnet. Logan Vandeveer, a hero of San Jacinto, came here in 1849 as the beef supplier to Fort Croghan. He became the first postmaster when the Hamilton post office was established about 1850. After this two-story limestone edifice was completed, Vandeveer ran a store in the bottom story, while the Masonic Lodge met upstairs. The Valley Lodge No. 175 used the building from 1855 to 1969 and still owns it.

According to Noah Smithwick, the lodge was dedicated on June 24, 1855, and was celebrated with a grand barbecue and ball. The dinner was free, and there was more than enough food for everyone, with plenty of leftovers. It was a veritable freeloaders' paradise, Smithwick recalled:

> I saw one fellow who I knew had not contributed one cent to the dinner riding off on horseback with a quarter of roasted beef on his shoulder, upon which, with the assortment of cakes, pies, etc., his thrifty helpmeet had collected from the table, the family no doubt feasted several days.
>
> The houses of the early Texans were small, but their hearts were large enough to cover all deficiencies. No candidate for hospitality was ever turned away. After the danger from the Indians was over we had all outdoors in which to entertain our friends. If there was a wedding everybody was invited and a long table set out in the yard, around which the guests stood while partaking of the cheer with which it was loaded.
>
> These free-for-all dinners were discontinued after a few years; the hungry hordes that swarmed in from all parts of the country, not content with a hearty dinner, filled their pockets, reticules, baskets and handkerchiefs with the dessert provided by the ladies, till they went on strike against the imposition, and thereafter only those having the password gained admittance.

THE GALLOWAY HOUSE

108 E. League, at Pierce

A block east of the Old Masonic Lodge is this rather common-looking two-story frame house with double wraparound porches. The original part of the house was built in 1856 out of adobe-covered stone by Major Hugh Calvert. It served as an inn for a few years. Enoch Brooks bought it in 1885 and made major changes. W. C. Galloway bought it in 1899 and enlarged it still more. Galloway helped organize the First State Bank of Burnet and served as county tax collector and mayor of Burnet. The old two-story brick First State Bank building still stands a few feet away, catercorner to the Brandt building, on the courthouse square, at the corner of Pierce and Jackson, with the bank's name still on the street side of the building, fading away with time.

GEORGE WHITAKER RESIDENCE

802 S. Main • Not open to the public

Several blocks south of the Masonic Lodge, on Main, is the Whitaker house, built in 1870. Whitaker's hand-hewn limestone block house features an inside cistern. With the water supply inside the house, Whitaker and family could withstand Indian attack almost indefinitely, and Indian raids continued well into the 1870s here. A 1939 addition to the house is built of limestone salvaged from the old Burnet County courthouse, predecessor to the present granite monolith. Whitaker was the first editor of the *Burnet Bulletin*. He spent only one year at the job.

J. C. COOK HOME

200 N. Main

Heading back north on Main, you see the J. C. Cook home, which was built in 1873 in the early Victorian style and features a staircase and other fittings brought in by ox wagons all the way from New Orleans.

Continue north on Main to Taggard to see other old homes. Return to the square and turn left on Washington (on the north side of the square).

BURNET COUNTY JAIL

Washington and Pierce

Located at the northeast corner of the courthouse square is the county jail, designed by noted architect F. M. Ruffini and built in 1884 of hand-hewn limestone blocks. The roof features elaborate period cast metal work. The jail was used through 1981.

From the jail, proceed north on Pierce one block to SH 29 and turn left to reach old Fort Croghan, a few blocks past the hospital and marked by a highway sign.

FORT CROGHAN

703 Buchanan Dr. (SH 29) • 756-8281 • Call for hours • Fee • W

The land for Fort Croghan was first leased from John Hamilton, for whom the town of Burnet was originally named, and then from Peter Carr. The fort was named for George Croghan, an illustrious career army officer, but was also known as Fort Hamilton.

Noah Smithwick worked briefly at Fort Croghan:

Finding a pastoral life unsuited to my taste, and the sparsely settled condition of the country in my vicinity rendering a blacksmith shop unremunerative, when the commander at Fort Croggin advertised for an armorer, I went up and worked a short time, long enough, however, to get an insight into the workings of the government machinery. There was a little upstart of a noncommissioned officer, who, having been made a sergeant, appropriated another fellow's wife and put on more airs than did the department commander. He set up a carriage and his wife had to have a servant and fine clothes. As his regular pay would not nearly pay his expenses he made up the deficit by cheating the government. He came into my shop one day with his scales, saying:

"I wish you would fix these scales for me so they will weigh a trifle light. The men all draw more rations than they can eat and it is just wasted. Now, if I could manage to save a little from each one they would never miss it, and where I issue several hundred a day it would amount to a good deal to me."

I told him that I was not employed to do that kind of business.

"Oh," said he, unable to understand my reason of refusal, "I'll pay you well for it."

In rather forcible language I rejected his offer, and he went away, a sadder if not wiser man.

Relating the incident to Logan Vandever, he laughed heartily at my verdancy.

"Why, that's nothing," said he. "When you've been here as long as I have, you will see that they all, from the commandant down, steal, each according to his opportunity. That man is only a poor little cuss. He has to steal by the ounce; others steal by the ton." A statement which I had an opportunity of verifying shortly after.

Some parties who had taken a contract for supplying corn for the horses drove up to the quartermaster's department late one afternoon and began to unload. The grain was put up in cotton bags supposed to contain 2 bushels. The "slack" of the bags, however, was so conspicuous that the commandant ordered them all weighed, calling on me as a civilian to witness the attempted fraud. Not one of those weighed fell short less than a peck, and some more. The quartermaster, with righteous indignation, ordered the guilty parties to reload the corn and take it away. Seemingly but little disturbed by the exposure of their dishonesty, the contractors drove across the creek and camped for the night. Early the next morning they drove back to the fort, where the corn was received without more ado, though the bags were just as slack as on the previous day. My observations since that time have not tended to disprove Vandever's assertion.

There was, however, one notable exception. Lieutenant Givens stands out in bold relief against this background of speculators and schemers. When the division headquarters were removed to San Antonio the quartermaster general arbitrarily usurped the functions of the local quartermasters, buying up supplies at San Antonio and hiring teams to distribute them among the posts, some of which were several hundred miles distant. The post at Burnet had been abandoned and the company to which Lieutenant Givens was attached moved out to some of the outside posts, where Givens was assigned the position of quartermaster, the responsibilities of which he accepted in good faith. Finding he could buy corn delivered to his post at a smaller cost to the government than that being sent out by the quartermaster general he proceeded to act on the information. This did not suit his highness, the quartermaster general, and seeing that corn in San Antonio was cheaper than corn nearer the post he sent on an accusation against Givens, charging him with fraud, also annulling Givens' contracts and placing him under arrest. The lieutenant was courtmartialed and dismissed from the service. He then sent on his report, showing the fraud that was being perpetrated, and having influential friends in congress his case was taken up in that body and resulted in his reinstatement and promotion.

As the Texas frontier moved further west, the soldiers stationed in this line of forts also moved westward. Most of the soldiers left in 1853, and the army officially abandoned the fort in 1855. Fort Croghan did not fall into disuse, however. Local frontier guards used the old fort as a rallying point whenever Indian attacks occurred, and many early county residents lived in the old fort buildings until they could move onto their own land. Most of the buildings disappeared over the years until only the stone structure, known locally as the "powder house," remained.

In 1957, the Burnet County Historical Society bought 1.6 acres of the fort's original grounds and moved four old stone-and-log buildings from Burnet's past onto the property. Local families donated hundreds of everyday items used by their ancestors, and the resulting conglomeration is now the Fort Croghan Museum.

From Fort Croghan, head back toward Burnet and US 281.

BURNET COUNTY BBQ

616 Buchanan/SH 29 W. • 756-6468 • Open Wednesday through Monday, lunch and dinner, closed Tuesday • No Cr. • W

Here you'll find good brisket, and also chicken, Elgin sausage, and ribs, cooked with live oak.

At the junction of SH 29 and US 281, turn right on US 281 and go three blocks to the corner of S. Water (US 281) and League to reach the first of two houses built by Adam Johnson in Burnet. "Rocky Rest" is set back several hundred feet from Water Street.

ROCKY REST

404 S. Water, at League St.

Adam Johnson built this spacious two-story Greek Revival home on the west bank of Hamilton Creek for his bride, Josephine Eastland, in 1860. They were married on New Year's Day 1861. Built of ashlar limestone and hand-hewn logs, the house's thick walls and high, narrow windows gave extra protection in the event of Indian attacks. Johnson organized a local "minuteman" company at nearby Fort Croghan upon the army's divestiture of the fort. The house later served as a school, which Johnson helped organize.

From Rocky Rest, return to the US 281/SH 29 intersection and turn right on SH 29. Proceed about 1.5 miles east on SH 29 to reach "Airy Mount," Johnson's second home, which will be on your right about 0.75 miles east of town. If you cross the railroad tracks, you've gone too far.

AIRY MOUNT

SH 29 • B&B inn

The massive limestone barn with attached cistern and nearby house are the principal components of Airy Mount and have been landmarks for generations of travelers. Long in ruins, both house and barn were restored by Dr. and Mrs. Joe Shepherd, longtime owners of Johnson's Rocky Rest. In attempting to rebuild the Airy Mount house almost from scratch, the only guides they had to rely on were a few fading exterior photographs and the recollections of several Burnet old-timers.

What prompted the Johnsons to leave Rocky Rest for Airy Mount? After two of their children died at Rocky Rest, Adam and Josephine said enough is enough and decided to build a new home in a healthier location. Low-lying, creek-side locations such as Rocky Rest were thought to be unhealthy. The healthiest spots were thought to be on high ground, well drained, and exposed to the wind, which Airy Mount certainly is. Johnson was so slight of build that locals say he had to walk around with rocks in his pockets to keep from being blown away, so airy is this hill. Story also has it that the barn was built first and that the Johnsons lived in it for several years as they waited for the new house to be built. One of their children was born in the barn, but when Mrs. Johnson was expecting again, she categorically refused to bear another child in the barn, Johnson was forced to hurry up construction of the house to the point that he wasn't able to add the originally intended second story. The way the house is constructed hints that Johnson had planned for a second story. The main entrance to the house faces toward the railroad tracks and away from the highway, since there was no Highway 29 when the house was finished in 1884.

From Airy Mount, return to Burnet on SH 29.

OTHER AREA ATTRACTIONS

BURNET CHAMBER OF COMMERCE

229 S. Pierce, Burnet 78611 • 756-4297 • www.burnetchamber.org

This is the source for local information, including the annual Bluebonnet Festival.

HAMILTON CREEK PARK

Along Hamilton Creek, south of SH 29 and west of US 281 • Open daily • Free • W

This linear park lies along both sides of Hamilton Creek. There's a walk-over bridge, a playground for kids, fountains, and a gazebo.

HIGHLAND LAKES AIR MUSEUM/COMMEMORATIVE AIR FORCE MUSEUM

US 281, at the Burnet Municipal Airport on the south side of town • 756-2226 • Open Saturday and Sunday • Fee

Several World War II and Vietnam War–era fighters are permanently based here; plus firearms, photos, and other memorabilia.

THE HILL COUNTRY FLYER

Runs from Cedar Park to Burnet seasonally • 512-477-8468 • www.austin-steamtrain.org • Reservations recommended • W with assistance

Burnet is the western terminus for this entertaining train, which leaves (during season) from its home station in Cedar Park and rides the old A&NW rails. Round trip is thirty-three miles, taking you through Leander across the San Gabriel River, through Liberty Hill and Bertram, and down into the Hamilton Creek valley and Burnet. The spring wildflowers are lovely, as is the fall foliage, and you'll see longhorn cattle along the way, as well as Airy Mount, home to land tycoon Adam Johnson. You will see big blocks of pink granite lying alongside the tracks, destined for the state capitol's construction, which fell off along the way to Austin. You'll have a couple of hours to kill eating lunch, visiting museums, browsing the antique and gift shops, or just walking around.

Weekend service was inaugurated in 1992, and the train has been a popular ride ever since. Number 786, a restored Southern Pacific Mikado-class steam locomotive built in 1916 by the American Locomotive Company, is the train's namesake, but it has been undergoing accident-caused restoration for several years and its future return to service was undetermined at press time. Number 786 used to haul freight between Houston and Austin before being retired in 1956. Upon retirement, it ended up on display in a downtown Austin park. The City of Austin acquired it in 1986. A few years later, Austin-area steam-train enthusiasts began restoring the engine and acquiring rolling stock. In the meantime, a vintage diesel engine pulls an assortment of cars: 1920s passenger coaches, air-conditioned passenger coaches and streamlined Pullmans from the 1950s, a club car, and a caboose. There are three levels of service on each train ride: coach class, excursion class, and first-class Pullman lounge. Coach cars are not air conditioned or heated. Ticket prices and seasonal schedules vary, so it's best to visit the website, www.austinsteamtrain.org, or call 477-8468 for up-to-date details.

NORTH SIDE OF LAKE BUCHANAN

From Burnet, take SH 29 west about three miles to FM 2341, then north (right) approximately fifteen miles. FM 2341 is very twisty and hilly, so take it easy and enjoy the views of Lake Buchanan and the surrounding countryside. Spring wildflowers are excellent.

The world's biggest graphite mine (inactive for at least thirty years) is located several miles northwest of Burnet, off FM 2341, on the way to Canyon of the Eagles Nature Park. The county's graphite deposits were discovered in 1916, and the Southwestern Consolidated Graphite Company began operation shortly thereafter. During World War I, graphite was used in enormous quantities in munitions manufacture. Mining stopped during the Great Depression but began again at the request of the War Production Board in 1942.

Burnet County has diverse mineral deposits; we have already read of its richness in graphite and granite. But who among us has heard of ichthyol (pronounced "ICK-thee-all")? In about 1920, Burnet was bursting with pride over its supply of ichthyol, claiming to have the country's greatest deposits. Ichthyol's future looked bright, in the days before penicillin. Ichthyol is derived from limestone rock asphalt, which is porous limestone filled with bitumen, or asphalt. It is a trademark name for ichthymol, a thick, smelly brown liquid distilled from bituminous stone (containing fish remains) that was formerly used for treating all sorts of skin problems and disorders, such as tenderness or breaking of tissue, abrasions, and massage. Its beneficial effect is due to its mild irritant, stimulant, antiseptic, anti-infective, and analgesic action. Noted psychic Edgar Cayce highly recommended ichthyol, calling it the "best application for bed sores," and also recommending it for treating scratches and itching of the vulva.

But Burnet's purported ichthyol deposits were as inflated as its hopes for ichthyol-derived riches. The *Handbook of Texas* notes that the only limestone rock asphalt of marketable quantity and quality in Texas is located on 75,000 to 100,000 acres in southwest Uvalde County and southeast Kinney County. From 1885 to 1895, the Lathe Carbon Company extracted the bitumen from this deposit of stone for extraction of the ichthyol. But so far as is known, there was no ichthyol mining in Burnet. Limestone rock asphalt has proved enduringly useful as road paving material, beginning about 1898, when the contracting firm of Parker-Washington surfaced several blocks of San Antonio's Market Street with material from the Uvalde County deposit, very crudely handled, which nonetheless made a smooth and impervious surface for approximately twelve years.

VANISHING TEXAS RIVER CRUISE

16942 FM 2341 • From Burnet, take SH 29 west about 3 miles to FM 2341, then north (right) approximately 14 miles to Canyon of the Eagles Park • 800-4RIVER4, 512-756-6986 • www.vtrc.com • Cruises daily (except Monday and Tuesday) year round, weather permitting • Reservations required • Fee • W call ahead

Vanishing Texas River Cruise attracts visitors from around the world. Bring your camera. The *Texas Eagle II*, a seventy-foot, two-hundred-passenger vessel, has an enclosed all-weather deck and two observation decks. The tours begin and end at the Canyon of the Eagles Park Store on Lake Buchanan. The lake's diverse waterfowl population includes great blue herons, American white pelicans, egrets, osprey, roseate spoonbills, and from November to March, American bald eagles. Spring brings a riot of wildflowers to the banks. The standard two-and-a-half-hour scenic wilderness cruise goes up and down the Colorado River canyon, past scenic waterfalls and sheer cliffs. Bald Eagle Cruises run November through March, allowing glimpses of one of Texas' largest colonies of bald eagles. This two-and-a-half-hour cruise departs daily except Tuesday. The Saturday four-hour Ultimate Eagle Cruise offers greater viewing opportunities. Saturday Sunset Dinner Cruises run May through October. This two-and-a-half-hour cruise is a great way to view Lake Buchanan's beauty in the context of a glorious Texas sunset while enjoying a good meal on Saturday evenings.

CANYON OF THE EAGLES NATURE PARK

From Burnet, travel west on SH 29 to FM 2341. Travel north on FM 2341 for about 14 miles to the entrance • 800-977-0081 • www.canyonoftheeagles.com • Open daily • Fee • W partial

Canyon of the Eagles' 940 acres include a rugged tree-covered ridge, granite bluffs overlooking Lake Buchanan, and sandy beaches. A network of trails runs through an eight-hundred-acre nature preserve with protected habitat for the golden-cheeked warbler, black-capped vireo, and bald eagle; a portion of the trails are closed each year from March 1 to September 1. The brightly colored golden-cheeked warbler is a small, migratory songbird on the Federal Endangered Species List. These picky birds build nests from only fine, shredded ashe juniper bark. Broad-leaved trees and shrubs provide habitat for the caterpillars, spiders, and insects they feed upon; habitat loss is the greatest threat the warblers face. Black-capped vireo are nervous little songbirds that nest in dense oak trees and juniper thickets. They sing and chirp frequently but can be difficult to spot. They are often observed hanging upside down from small branches or twigs while foraging for food. The Lakeside Trail follows the park shoreline, passing through American bald eagle habitat. These famous winter Texans roost along the waterfront and hunt unsuspecting fish swimming too near the surface. The eagles flush with foot traffic, so visitation into the area is closed. A limited number of visitors can view the area and the birds with a docent and learn more about ongoing protection and recovery efforts. Hikers learn about the birds' life history and how to protect their natural habitats. The rest of the park contains primary-use trails, a day-use area, a beach and park store, camping, and lodge and dining facilities. The park store has the usual supplies, plus gifts and outdoor items, such as nature books. Relax in one of the many rocking chairs and enjoy a spectacular sunset. The park has multiple fishing docks and piers along three miles of lakefront. Lake Buchanan is famous for striper, white bass, and catfish. Stargazers can enjoy the two-telescope observatory at star parties (call ahead for schedule). There is a restaurant, a sixty-four-unit lodge, RV sites, campgrounds, and a swimming pool (for lodge guests only). To reserve an RV or camping site, call the Texas Parks and Wildlife's central reservation center at 512-389-8900.

BURNET COUNTY PARK (WHITE BLUFF)

On the north side of Lake Buchanan, on FM 2341, about 15 miles west of Burnet • 512-756-4297 • Open daily • Free

This five-acre park offers a boat ramp, camping, lake access, picnicking, and restrooms.

From Burnet, go south on US 281 toward Marble Falls. About five miles south of Burnet, turn right onto Park Road 4 toward Longhorn Caverns and Inks Lake. Park Road 4 is very dramatically hilly to Longhorn Cavern State Park.

LONGHORN CAVERN STATE PARK

Park Rd. 4, 6 miles off US 281 • About 11 miles from Burnet • 1-877-441-CAVE • Open every day except Christmas Eve and Christmas Day; visitor center opens at 9 a.m. daily • Fee, group rates available

The Longhorn Caverns were at least a million years in the making, beginning during the Ice Age when the northern part of the United States was covered by glaciers. As the glaciers receded, the Texas climate became drier, and the groundwater level began to drop, dissolving the limestone as it fell. Underground rivers flowing through the cave helped to carve out the labyrinthian passageways and huge rooms.

People have used the cave since their earliest days in Texas; flints and other crude tools have been found. More recently, stories have it that in 1840 young officer Robert E. Lee captured bands of Indians by driving them into the gaping mouth of the cavern. A secret Confederate powder factory was operated in the cavern's 183-foot main room during the Civil War. Local legend relates that outlaw Sam Bass hid out in the cave during the 1870s. The cavern is said to be the third largest in the world, and it became a state park in 1932.

The cave tour takes about an hour and a half, through rooms filled with stalactites and stalagmites, sparkling displays of calcite crystals, unusual flint formations, and the unique Hall of Marble. Rubber-soled shoes are recommended. Tours are conveniently scheduled throughout the day. Call for current tour times. The park grounds include picnic areas, nature trails, rock formations, and a plethora of wildflowers each spring. Most of the quaint rock buildings dotting the ground were built by WPA workers in the 1930s.

From Longhorn Caverns, continue west on Park Road 4. From this point to the road's dead end into SH 29, Park Road 4 twists and turns back on itself through miles of granite boulders strewn about as casually as toys inside a baby's playpen. About four miles past Longhorn Cavern, Park Road 4 encounters FM 2342 and takes a hard right. Turn right here and follow Park Road 4's path north.

HOOVER VALLEY

Burnet County • About 4 miles from Longhorn Caverns

Very soon after you turn to the north on Park Road 4, you see a state historical marker on the right side of the road. Hoover Valley was settled in 1850 by Reverend Isaac Hoover, who established a church here, next to the Hoover Valley Cemetery. The cemetery is located several hundred feet west of the historical marker, on the paved road running to your left off Park Road 4, across from the marker.

HOOVER VALLEY CEMETERY

Off Park Rd. 4

Graves here date back to 1850, but the stone with the most tragic story behind it marks the resting place of F. M. and Susan Whitlock and children. The simple limestone slab reads "Sacred to the memory of F. M. & Susan Whitlock killed by the Indians, Dec. 7, 1870." On that fateful day, at the foot of nearby Long Mountain, a band of unknown Indians attacked the Whitlock cabin. Attracted by the smoke, neighbors found the slain Mr. Whitlock lying in the field where he had been surprised. They found the children scattered about the yard, stripped of their clothing. Mrs. Whitlock lay burning in the cabin, which was made of cedar logs. Fire had burned the logs until they had fallen in, and it was not possible to retrieve her body until the next morning, by which time it had been reduced to ashes.

Albert K. Erwin was among the Whitlocks' neighbors: "We found the house burned and the entire family dead, with the exception of two young lads who happened to be hunting at the time of the depredating. Every one of the dead people was scalped. We started to ride after the Indians and went in the direction of their trail so long as we could follow it. We lost the trail at the end of the first day, but continued to scout the surrounding country.

"A little past noon of the second day Indians were sighted. J. Bell spied a party of Indians by the use of his spy glass. The Indians were lying on the ground in the shade of a tree. We calculated they were asleep and they were. We didn't know whether or not they were the Indians which did the depredating. But there were no questions asked of them. Our party quietly surrounded the crowd of Indians and when we all were in good shooting range we poured the lead into them."

Proceeding north from Hoover Valley, you enter Inks Lake State Park.

INKS LAKE STATE PARK

**3630 Park Rd. 4 West; about 8 miles from Longhorn Cavern • 512-93-2223
• Open daily • Fee**

Located in the Llano Uplift, the park is marked by outcroppings of colorful pink gneiss and granite, many of which are covered with colorful lichens: green, yellow, orange, black, and gray. Several varieties of oaks and myriad wildflowers thrive on the coarse sandy soil derived from the rock.

A great scenic overlook on Park Road 4 looks out on the Devil's Waterhole, an arm of Inks Lake. There is a delightful waterfall that flows practically year round. The casually placed giant pink boulders, seemingly tossed about the landscape, probably inspired the waterhole's hellish name, but perhaps the buzzards had something to do with the name, too. They hover by the dozens in the late afternoon sky, riding the thermals, plunging and rising hundreds of feet in a matter of seconds as they wheel in lazy, mile-wide circles, sometimes dropping down just low enough to let you catch a glimpse of their red or black wrinkled, featherless heads.

Inks Lake State Park is 1,201 acres and was acquired by deeds from the Lower Colorado River Authority and private owners in 1940 and opened to the public in 1950. The water level of Inks Lake is usually unaffected by drought and is maintained at a normal level most of the time. During flooding situations, the lake level can rise as the flood waters are passed through Inks Lake to other lakes downstream. Visitors enjoy camping, backpacking, hiking, and golf. The golf course, locate alongside the lake, is one of the most beautiful in the state. Since Inks is a constant-level lake, droughts do not affect water-related activities such as lake swimming (unsupervised beach), boating, water skiing, scuba diving, and fishing. There are limited-use mini-cabins for rent, and the park offers wireless Internet access (Wi-Fi) to park visitors. Tours and guided activities include nature walks, geology hikes, fish seining, lakeshore ecology, Junior Ranger programs, and the Devil's Waterhole Canoe Tour.

At 4.2 miles in length and containing about eight hundred surface acres, Inks Lake is the second smallest of the Highland Lakes. It was created in 1938 with the completion of Arnold Dam, subsequently named Roy Inks Dam, in honor of Llano resident Roy Inks, who was a director of the LCRA board.

Turn left on SH 29 when Park Road 4 comes to an end in a little over seven miles. In a couple of miles you cross Inks Lake. The Depression-era four-span cantilever bridge has been replaced by a new bridge, but it still stands to your left. Continue west on SH 29 past Buchanan Dam.

BUCHANAN DAM

About 1 mile from the Inks Lake bridge

Lake Buchanan, formed by Buchanan Dam, (pronounced "Buck-annon," not "Bew–cannon") is the oldest and largest of the Highland Lakes, thirty-two miles long and eight miles wide. On windy days, whitecaps break over the lake, and it looks more like the ocean than an inland lake. At 11,200 feet in length, Buchanan Dam was the largest dam of its type in the world when finished in 1938. Named for Congressman James Buchanan, this is still one of the largest multiple-arch dams in the world. The village of Buchanan Dam sprang up after the dam's completion and is a resort, retirement, and fishing community.

An interesting tidbit about Buchanan Dam: In 1854, while surveying the area for public school land, young Adam Johnson came to the Shirley Shoals on the Colorado River and said, "Here we should build a dam." At this same exact spot in the spring of 1931, construction of Hamilton Dam, as it was originally called, commenced.

A small industrial town, with all the modern conveniences, including electric lights and refrigeration, running water and a sewage system, and a hospital, was built at the construction site, on the Llano County side of the Colorado River, where four hundred engineers and employees and their families resided. A road from Llano to the dam site, a distance of twenty-two miles, was built, and a daily bus line was in operation. A five-mile railroad spur was built from the Austin-Llano branch of the Southern Pacific Line to the dam site.

The Hamilton Dam was the first of a series of six dams on the Colorado River planned by the Emery, Peck and Rockwood Company. In 1932, bankruptcy forced the closing of the project. U.S. Congressman Buchanan secured federal funds to revive the project in 1934, whereupon the dam, post office, and town were renamed in his honor.

BUCHANAN DAM MUSEUM

Located inside the LCRA building at dam headquarters • SH 29 • Open daily • W

There is a nice view of Lake Buchanan from this building by the dam; the museum has displays on the dam's construction and local history that include a living history video presentation and lots of old photos. There's a Xeriscape garden outside, and the kids can feed the huge school of carp that gathers below the observation deck (when lake levels are normal). Visitors can walk along the top of the dam; it is two miles long. Tours of the dam are given on weekends during the summer. Call the Lake Buchanan-Inks Lake Chamber of Commerce for the latest schedule. The Lake Buchanan-Inks Lake Chamber of Commerce (512-793-2803, http:// buchanan-inks.com) is located at the same site. It is open daily except Tuesdays.

The LCRA, Llano County, and Burnet County operate several parks on Lake Buchanan.

BURNET COUNTY PARK AT BUCHANAN DAM

North side of Buchanan Dam, off TX 29, about 10 miles west of Burnet • 512-756-4297 • Open daily • Free

This tiny five-acre park has a boat ramp, lake access, primitive camping, and picnicking.

Turn right onto SH 261 two miles past Buchanan Dam and proceed toward Bluffton.

Option: You can shorten the trip at this point by about twenty miles by continuing west on SH 29 to Llano. About six miles west of the SH 261 turnoff, you begin to parallel the picturesque, boulder-strewn Llano River. You catch frequent glimpses of the river for the next five miles. The City of Austin now owns the old Southern Pacific railroad tracks that run alongside the highway to Llano; visionaries foresee the day when commuter and light excursion trains once again run this scenic route.

On the way to Bluffton on SH 261, you catch many glimpses of Lake Buchanan and pass many outcroppings of pink granite. This is prime resort area, as the numerous fishing camps, motels, and resorts attest.

BLACK ROCK PARK

On Lake Buchanan, on TX 261, just off FM 1431, about 15 miles west of Burnet • 512-793-3138 • www.lcra.org • Open daily • Fee

This twenty-five-acre park offers lake access for swimmers, waders, and anglers (great for stripers), hiking, picnicking, a play area, camp sites, RV sites, heated and air-conditioned cabins, potable water taps, dump station, restrooms, and picnicking. It is very popular on summer weekends. Reservations for Black Rock Park facilities can be made by calling Texas Parks and Wildlife Reservation Center at 512-389-8900 more than forty-eight hours in advance.

LLANO COUNTY PARK

On Lake Buchanan, next to LCRA's Black Rock Park • 915-247-4352 • Open daily • Free

This five-acre park has a single-lane public boat ramp for sailboats and motor-boats. There's camping, picnicking, fishing, and swimming.

BARRINGER HILL

Underneath Lake Buchanan

Buried beneath the waters of Lake Buchanan near the dam is the legendary Barringer Hill. Only a small mound of rock and dirt thirty-four feet taller than the surrounding country, Barringer Hill was not even remotely interesting in appearance, but in the words of the U.S. Geological Survey, "Few if any deposits in the world, and certainly no others in America, outside of the localities where monazite is found, have yielded such quantities of rare earth metals as that at Barringer Hill."

Barringer Hill was named for John Barringer, a carpenter who acquired the land in 1886 when its owner was unable to pay Barringer fifty dollars for a house he had built for the man. At that time, the Llano area was gripped with dreams of mineral wealth, especially iron. A few months later, Barringer, while out prospecting his newly acquired land, stumbled upon an outcropping of heavy, greenish black ore. No one in the neighborhood knew what the mineral was, and later that year, Professor N. J. Badu of Llano (see Llano in "Mormon Trails") sent ore samples to Philadelphia and New York. Meanwhile, Mr. Barringer had taken out a quantity of gadolinite estimated at 800 to 1,200 pounds, which was largely picked up and carried off by persons in the neighborhood as curiosities. Some of the choicer pieces, showing crystal form, found their way into various museums. Specimens were sent to a number of places before it was finally identified.

The samples were found to be composed primarily of a radioactive yttria mineral, known as gadolinite, that had previously only been found in small amounts in Russia and Norway. Yttria minerals were extremely valuable. In 1887, pure yttrium brought $144 an ounce, at a time when pure gold brought only $19 an ounce on the London exchange. The minerals from this deposit were so valuable that they were wrapped in tissue paper, packed in iron-bound boxes, and shipped by Wells Fargo express at one hundred pounds a box. At best, obtaining each pound of ore cost ten dollars.

The discovery of gadolinite at Barringer Hill attracted the interest of Thomas Edison and George Westinghouse. William E. Hidden, a Newark, New Jersey, mineralogist with connections to both companies read a newspaper account about the discovery and obtained a piece. At that time, Edison and Westinghouse were looking for gadolinite to use in the creation of a filament for electric lightbulbs but had found no accessible sources of the mineral. Hidden sent Dr. William Niven, a Scottish-born Texan, to investigate Barringer Hill in 1889. Niven identified forty-seven minerals there, including five previously unknown rare earth elements.

Hidden commissioned Niven to buy the land. In 1889, Barringer agreed to sell his land to Edison's Piedmont Mining Company. Depending on who's telling the story, the company paid Barringer either $5,000 or $10,000 in gold. The gold was sent to Burnet via the Austin and Northwestern Railroad, where Barringer picked it up accompanied by a strapping young bodyguard.

Edison experimented with all forty-seven Barringer Hill minerals, but by 1903, the company could find no use for any of them. Meanwhile, German chemist Hermann Nernst, working for Westinghouse, had developed a street lamp that used raw gadolinite as a filament. Nernst had patented the lamp that bore his name in 1897, but his original design for the lamp was commercially useless, because the lamp had a life of only two hours. Another Westinghouse engineer, Marshall Hank, was able to increase this number to seven hundred hours. The improved lamp's design featured a filament consisting of 25 percent yttria and 75 percent zirconia. These ingredients were made into a paste, squirted into strips, baked, and then cut into the proper lengths. When the mixture was cold, it was nonconductive, but after being heated, it became a conductor that gave off a brilliant light with wavelengths penetrating deep into the infrared.

With its technical problems solved, the Nernst Lamp Company decided to put the lamp into production and bought Barringer Hill through William E. Hidden.

George Westinghouse had developed and introduced the Nernst lamp to the commercial market in the United States, organizing the Nernst Lamp Company in 1901. Production took place in Pittsburg in a five-story factory building with a total floor area of 101,000 square feet. By 1904, a total of over 130,000 Nernst glowers had been placed in service throughout the country.

During the winter of 1902–1903, the Nernst Lamp Company sent Hidden to begin excavation. In 1903, Marshall Hanks, the engineer who had improved the Nernst Lamp, arrived to run the mining operation. According to *The Story of Barringer's Hill* by Jean Hackett and Robert Wilkes, Hanks was unpopular with the miners because he kept secrets from them. Hanks had heard many stories about what murderers and scoundrels Texans were and took them seriously. The miners, not surprisingly, took every opportunity to play pranks on Hanks. Among the miners were Barringer and his young bodyguard, Tad Casner.

A little gadolinite went a very long way in those days, and only sporadic mining was necessary. When large-scale mining began, it lasted only a year. The incandescent lightbulb had been invented, and the need for gadolinite was fading in the face of a much cheaper wire filament. The Barringer Hill mine ceased large-scale operations in 1904, and a man nearly lost his life as a result—or did he?

Marshall Hanks had been sent down by Westinghouse to supervise mining operations in 1903. Then he received orders to close the mine. The miners were boiling mad at the prospect of unemployment, and Hanks had faced nothing but trouble with them from the beginning of his stay. The miners had not been told what they were extracting, and they imagined they were mining radium. So they struck for hazardous duty pay. Hanks solved that problem but soon afterward received the closing orders.

It took thirteen boxes to hold all the mining equipment that was being shipped back to company headquarters in Pittsburgh, but there were fourteen boxes on the Austin and Northwestern railroad station loading dock in Kingsland. That last box contained Hanks, who believed that his former employees were out to kill him. Secreted in his box, he could hear the ex-miners rampaging through the streets of Kingsland in search of him. As they searched, workers loaded the crates onto the train. The miners marched to the station and demanded to search the boxes, but they didn't get past the Wells Fargo Express agent. Soon after, the train pulled out of Kingsland, and once it was out of the county the conductor pried open the right box and set Hanks free. Conversely, there are those who claim the miners were just having a bit of fare-thee-well fun with their disliked, but gullible, ex-boss.

Hanks always believed the miners had wanted to kill him. He went on to have an illustrious engineering career in Pennsylvania. Nernst went on to discover the Third Law of Thermodynamics, for which he won a Nobel Prize in 1920.

At any rate, only sporadic mining was done at Barringer Hill thereafter, and it was one of the first areas to be covered by Lake Buchanan.

BLUFFTON

Llano County • 75 • About 11 miles from Buchanan Dam

Bluffton is located at the junction of SH 261 and FM 2241, and the community's center is the store at the crossroads and the nearby church. Bluffton has moved around quite a bit since it was first founded in 1852. Along with the Tow Valley community, Bluffton was one of Llano County's first permanent settlements. First located five miles from Tow Valley on the west bank of the Colorado River, it faced a high bluff across the river. Bluffton's first settlers were "Uncle" Billy Davis and his wife, two daughters, and four sons, Ben, Caleb, Henry, and Ned. The Davises were soon joined by I. B. "Uncle Ike" Maxwell, who rode here from Arkansas on a mule and named the village for his hometown of Bluffton, Arkansas. When Ike Maxwell arrived, Henry Davis gave him one hundred acres of his section of land. Uncle Ike's first wife was a daughter of Billy Davis, while his third wife was a daughter of Caleb Davis.

In 1857, Henry Chadwick built a gristmill on the river, followed by a cotton gin. Bluffton's first store was opened by one-legged John Pankey, who lost his limb in the Civil War. After he settled in Bluffton, some of the residents chipped in to buy him a wooden leg and to get his store started.

Located on the Austin-to-Mason road, Bluffton was a stage stop and a prosperous town through the 1880s. Teamsters from as far west as Fort Mason and Fort McKavett passed through Bluffton, taking loads of cotton and other commodities to Austin, from where they brought back supplies and provisions for the people living in those then far-removed western outposts of civilization. The stagecoach rumbled over the road daily, carrying passengers and the mail.

At that time, people crossed the Colorado River, which separated Bluffton from points east, including Burnet and Austin, by fording it, some of the most historic crossings being the Davis, Salt Works, and Gooch fords. Ferry boats were used across the river when the stream was up and at deeper points in the river, the ferries and the natural fords being the only available means of crossing the river until a bridge was built at Bluffton by Llano and Burnet counties in 1911.

Bluffton had a saltworks, a Masonic Lodge, a saloon/hotel, and a ten-pin bowling alley during its heyday. Lots of cotton was grown in the fertile Tow Valley, and Bluffton attracted desperate men, men who made a practice of robbing stages, lone travelers, and gold-laden farmers returning home from market.

One night in November 1883, a bunch of cowboys came to old Bluffton to get drunk and ended up burning the whole town down except for the hotel, school, lodge, saloon, and a couple of houses. Undaunted, Bluffton folks moved the remaining buildings and otherwise rebuilt their town a short distance upriver. Two days after the saloon had been moved, it burned to the ground. But "new" Bluffton again became a busy trading center, its stores, saloon, and blacksmith shops having a large local and traveling patronage. This continued to be the main road between Llano and Burnet, and on east to Austin, and was heavily traveled.

But when the route of the Austin-to-Mason road changed, and the railroad came through this section of the country in the early 1890s, Bluffton began to decline. The remains of old Bluffton were submerged by Lake Buchanan in 1937, and the town moved to its present location. Today it is scarcely more than a store and a few houses dotting the modern highway.

The year 1936 signaled the end of a way of life in the Hill Country, the hillbilly way, when the LCRA acquired large holdings along the Colorado preparatory to building the dams that comprise the Highland Lakes. Bluffton and Tow Valley had to be moved from what is now the bed of Lake Buchanan. Hundreds of folks had to move to higher ground or Austin. They had led simple, self-sufficient lives, growing or hunting almost everything they needed. To raise cash money for luxuries such as coffee and shoes for the children, they cut cedar and burned charcoal for sale in Austin, Cedar Park, or Burnet. One woman described how it was: "I ain't had a new dress in many a day. I could get a real prutty dress for a dollar down in Austin, but seems like ever time I get a dollar saved up the truck breaks down, and the old man has to have the money. But I don't mean to complain. Selling the charcoal is his only way of making a livin'."

It's not surprising that his truck broke down when you consider the rocky "roads" these people traveled. Until 1933, the only road to the Bull Creek settlement twelve miles from Austin was a trail that forded Bull Creek ten times in twelve miles and hugged steep bluffs on both sides of the creek. Small wonder that hardly anyone in Austin ever made the effort to visit the Hill Country. It was terra incognita, just twelve miles from Austin.

A wide-brimmed felt hat was often the first thing a boy turning man bought. He generally earned his money trapping animals and selling their skins. Skunks were real moneymakers, and the scents of a boy's profit might linger with him for days.

Families were large, with six to twelve children. Children were valuable workers who helped contribute to the family's well-being. Everyone worked, but nobody worked too hard, because life was also about having fun, such as extended family visits and reunions, play parties, dances, school plays, and summertime "camp" meetings. The Hill Country folk intermarried extensively, so friends and family often dropped in to visit for a couple of days. The floors at night were packed tightly with slumbering bodies, but nobody minded. The clans often fought among themselves but presented a united front to the outside world.

Play parties were hosted by different families, and invitations were spread up and down the valley by word of mouth. Refreshments weren't a problem because there weren't any. Folks played singing games like "Old Dad Tucker" and "Shoot the Buffalo," and listened to chanteuses singing the old ballads and some newer songs about the hardships and simple pleasures of life.

Dances were held weekly in homes, halls, and pavilions. Fiddlers and square dances were the order of the night, and the whole family came. Camp meetings were held under a brush arbor, such as the one at Oatmeal, for one, two, or three weeks, with all-day meetings on Sunday that featured a basket dinner and fire-and-brimstone preaching.

School "plays" often consisted of students performing recitations and songs and usually featured a box supper afterward, where the girls' and ladies' box lunches were auctioned off to the highest bidders. But kids seldom went to school for more than a few years. Book learning only went a little ways in the Hill Country way of life. If you could read the Bible and cipher your accounts at the stores in Austin or Burnet or Llano, you knew enough.

Families who lived near the river faced the menace of flood, which could come any time of year, or even several times a year, any time the vast Colorado River watershed upstream got anything more than a healthy rain. After fleeing the floodwaters, they often returned to find crops and livestock swept away.

Along the Colorado and tributaries such as Bull Creek, there were narrow fertile valleys where fine crops of fruits and vegetables were grown. One woman whose farm was covered by Lake Buchanan allowed that she had been paid enough for her land, but when she thought of the fine watermelons that she raised, she got plumb homesick. Her home was in an area that regularly flooded. During one especially bad flood, a rescue party rowed to her house. They found the water nearly to the level of the front porch, where she sat, fishing.

At the Bluffton Store, located at the junction of SH 261 and FM 2241, turn right on FM 2241 and proceed north to Tow.

Located between old Bluffton and old Tow was one of Llano County's earliest industries, David Cowan's saltworks. David Cowan was a surveyor in Burnet County when he was granted permission by friendly Indians to survey this area. The Indians told him of a salt bank along the west bank of the Colorado. Cowan settled near the salt bank shortly thereafter and started working the bank in 1852. During the Civil War, Cowan made salt for the Confederacy, producing twenty to thirty bushels per day. The first Llano district court was held at the saltworks, now submerged under Lake Buchanan.

CEDAR POINT RECREATION AREA

On upper Lake Buchanan, off FM 3014, near Tow Community, about 25 miles from Burnet

Part of the LCRA's Primitive Recreation System, this area consists of about 350 acres of undeveloped land for those who like to rough it. There are access roads, parking areas, a single-lane boat ramp, fire rings for campsites, but no tables, running water, or restrooms. There are over three miles of shoreline, but no designated swimming areas. Old roads and pathways serve as hiking trails. There are lots of nice lake views. Birders and other nature lovers can see blue herons, double-breasted cormorants, roadrunners, and osprey, but the bald eagles that winter on Lake Buchanan rarely come here; you need to go by boat farther up the Colorado River canyon.

TOW

Llano County • 305 • About 5.5 miles from Bluffton

David and Gideon Cowan were Tow's first settlers, in 1852, but the resulting village was named for early resident William Tow. Some of the finest hats made in early Texas came from Tow. Early settler John Morgan first worked at the saltworks, but he soon started his own hattery, using the pelts of beavers and other animals he trapped. He charged eight and ten dollars for his distinctive, wide-brimmed hats, but in a gesture of patriotism he gave them away free to Confederate soldiers.

Tow was also forced to relocate when Lake Buchanan covered its original location. It now centers around the old white school, church, and fire department on FM 2241. By the way, you pronounce Tow like "cow" rather than "tow" as in "tow the car." Locals are very particular about this, and it's best to pronounce Tow correctly.

Tow is most famous for its pan barbecue, a barbecuing technique invented here more than fifty years ago and practiced publicly only once a year until 1991 at the annual Memorial Day weekend Tow Fish Fry and Pan Barbecue. To make pan barbecue Tow style, brisket or other favorite meats are cooked over mesquite coals in big pans, rather than resting directly on the grill. The meat still acquires the wonderful mesquite-smoked flavor, but instead of dripping into the fire, the meat juices accumulate in the pan, making a wonderful gravy. This annual event was suspended because the volunteer fire department had reached its fund-raising goals. But now that you have the recipe, why not try pan barbecuing for yourself?

From the Tow community grounds, continue north on the road to Tow Village. FM 2241 ceases as a state-maintained road, but a smaller paved road continues north to Fall Creek Vineyards and Tow Village.

FALL CREEK VINEYARDS

Tow Village, 2.2 miles north of the Tow post office • 325-379-5361 (winery), 512-476-4477 (office) • www.fcv.com • Open daily; tasting room • Free

Vineyards and wineries have sprouted up all over the Hill Country in the last twenty years, beginning with Fall Creek Vineyards in 1975. While in France in the early 1970s, Fall Creek's founder, Ed Auler, noticed that parts of the French wine country were remarkably similar to the soil, terrain, and microclimate of this lakeside ranch. Being Texas' most geologically and climatically diverse region, the Texas Hill Country possesses countless soil varieties and a hot day/cool night growing season pattern, perfect for growing the finest grapes of a great many varieties.

Fall Creek wines began winning medals in wine competitions in the early 1980s, proving that the Hill Country could make world-class wines. Fall Creek wines have been served at the White House; President George H. W. Bush took some to Beijing to serve at a state barbecue. So many wineries have opened since then that "the Texas Hill Country" is now officially recognized as a wine-producing region.

From Tow, retrace your route back to Bluffton and turn right on FM 2241 toward Llano.

A little less than three miles west of the Bluffton store is the Bluffton Cemetery, with a picturesque local-stone fence, entryway, chapel, and well. Buried here are Ike Maxwell and John Barringer, owner of Barringer Hill. This stretch of FM 2241 is part of the Texas Hill Country Trail and is flanked on both sides by bowers of wildflowers each spring.

LONE GROVE

Llano County • 50 • About 5 miles from Bluffton

Lone Grove was established as a post office in 1876 and had one store here on the north side of the Austin-to-Mason road, on the banks of the Little Llano River near Dreary Hollow. The store and post office later moved to the east bank of the Little Llano and were joined by a gin, a sawmill, a couple of saloons, and a gambling house. These houses of ill repute went out of business when the new road bypassed Lone Grove. The old school still serves as a community center.

Just west of Lone Grove, five miles northeast of Llano, is the old Heath gold mine, located on your right. Gold was discovered accidentally in the early 1890s on land owned by a Mr. Heath. Serious mining commenced in 1896. In 1901, two cars of ore were shipped to a smelter in Pueblo, Colorado, where it assayed at about 1.75 ounces ($35) of gold per ton. Several different optimists sank shafts, dug pits, and cut trenches here, but they never found sufficient concentrations of gold to make extraction truly profitable, not even with cyanide, which is used to leach low-density micro-gold particles from rock formations. In 1911, the Llano Gold and Rare Metal Mining Company, operator of the Heath Mine, built a new mill designed to handle fifty tons of ore per day. By 1942, it had produced more than eight thousand fine ounces of gold.

A couple of miles outside of Llano, FM 2241 runs into SH 29. Take SH 29 to enter Llano.

LLANO

Llano County Seat • 4,000 (approximate) • (325) • About 8 miles from Lone Grove

Llano is covered at length in the Mormon Trails trip, so only a few notes of passing interest will be mentioned here.

MALONE MANSION

SH 29 • Not open to the public

A few hundred feet east of the city limits on SH 29, you can see a driveway flanked by twin granite gateposts. The house that stands beyond the gate, atop the hill overlooking the beautiful Llano River valley, is the Malone mansion. Built during the boom days of the late 1880s, this one-and-one-half-story limestone mansion was one of Llano's early-day showcases. Eastern capitalists like F. J. Malone poured into Llano in anticipation of the big iron boom. When the boom subsided and the Malones and their ilk were gone, the Malone mansion became a tuberculosis sanatorium. In 1916, granite magnate Tom Norton bought the house and moved his wife Agnes and five daughters in. Two of the daughters, Cordelia and Catherine, lived in the house until their deaths, two days apart in February 1988, from arsenic poisoning at the hands of a young family friend. He was convicted of their deaths and went to prison.

Turn left onto SH 16 at the junction of SH 29 and SH 16.

As you pass through town, consider these pieces of Llano trivia:

- After the big iron boom went bust, Llano was widely promoted as a place "unsurpassed in health." An Austin reporter wrote in 1911, "Llano is great on mines and minerals—the common talk of the day deals in veins and strata of earth and rock; but the mine of vast wealth to the visitor from the hot lands is that stratum of delicious and life-giving ozone to which the face of the earth was projected in those past eons of time. The blessed ozone, nature's own free champagne, with which you may become intoxicated, yet feel better instead of worse the morning after.

  "In this ozone-charged air the newcomer recognizes the cause as well as the effect, and the sluggish blood accelerates its pace in a seeming desire to get quickly a full supply of it for fear the supply will run out. The delightful ozone laden air of the Llano region is the constant topic of conversation by visitors and has no relation to 'hot air' talk, which, if stirring, will be found out of town among the prospectors and mining camps."

- One of Texas' foremost sculptors, Frank Teich, spent the last thirty-eight years of his life in Llano. Teich has been called the father of the granite industry in Texas. He worked on many buildings and monuments throughout Texas and the South, many of them Confederate monuments. His Teich Monumental Works in Llano was a small town in its own right. He was known far and wide as the "Sculptor of the Hill Country," and his work in many states was known to thousands of people.

  Born in Lobenstein, Germany, in 1856, he took private drawing lessons from famous German painters and attended the ancient Art School of Nuremburg. While studying with the German sculptor Johannes Schilling, he worked on the German national monument "Die Wacht Am Rhein." One year was spent with the Franciscan Brothers at Dedelbach on the Main. He came to America in 1878, and his first work was with an architect in Chicago.

  He superintended the granite cutters and inspected the granite used in the building of the present state capitol. In 1885, he came to San Antonio where he carved the columns used on several bank buildings. His marble yard prospered, but his health failed. After warnings from physicians, he moved to Fredericksburg, where he operated a granite quarry. He moved to Llano in 1900 and established the Teich Monument Works, which he operated until his death.

- Llano County has had perhaps more nicknames than any other county in Texas: Rockhound's Paradise (241 different rocks and minerals are found in the county), Deer Capital of Texas, Land of Legend and Lure, Gem of the Hill Country, Iron Capital of Texas, Birmingham of Texas, Granite Capital of Texas, Colorado of Texas, and Livestock Capital of Texas (Llano County brings more hogs to market each year than any other county in Texas). Whew!

OXFORD

Llano County • 33 • About 10 miles from Llano

A little more than nine miles from the intersection of SH 16 and SH 71 south of Llano, you come to the ghost town of Oxford, marked by a closed gas station/store. The cemetery sits in a field directly across the road from the store, and a roughly paved road runs off to your right by the store, identified by a sign directing you to the Inks Ranch.

Oxford was a bustling village with nearly three hundred inhabitants by 1896. Folks had lived here for years scattered along Lost and Hondo creeks. One winter in the 1870s, Tom Sims took a load of bacon to Waco to sell. There he met A. J. Johnson, who wanted to come to Llano County. He came in 1880 and laid out the town of Oxford, naming it for his hometown of Oxford, Mississippi, where he had graduated from Oxford University. Soon Oxford had a gin, a post office, a couple of stores, a drugstore, a doctor, and a blacksmith. The nearby Bedford Academy boasted over one hundred pupils. An incident one night earned Oxford its nickname, Cat Town; some young men attending a schoolhouse dance got drunk and threw a cat into a large cauldron of boiling coffee. Oxford was also home to C. T. and John Moss, members of one of Llano County's greatest ranching families. The cemetery was established in 1881, with the earliest known burial in 1883. Resting here are A. J. Johnson (1832–1912) and James Moss (1843–1924), Confederate veteran and leader of the cowboy band at the nearby Packsaddle Mountain battle in 1873.

Oxford's most famous inhabitant was Francis A. "Frank" Hamer. Born in 1884, Hamer grew up on a ranch in San Saba County. In 1894, Hamer's family moved to Oxford, where he worked at his father's blacksmith shop. In 1901, he hired out as a wrangler on the Pecos County ranch of Barry Ketchum, brother of outlaw Tom "Black Jack" Ketchum. In 1905, Hamer captured a horse thief and was recommended by the county sheriff for a position with the Texas Rangers. Hamer enlisted as a Texas Ranger in 1906 and soon became known as an expert shot. During World War I, he patrolled the Texas-Mexico border from Brownsville to the Big Bend, chasing bandits, bootleggers, and arms smugglers.

During the 1920s, he restored order in violent oil-boom towns such as Mexia and Borger. Hamer retired from active duty in 1932 but retained his commission. On February 1, 1934, Hamer became a special investigator for the Texas prison system, assigned to track down Bonnie and Clyde. After a three-month search, he trapped them near Gibsland, Louisiana, on May 23, 1934, and with the aid of several local policemen shot and killed them. Congress awarded Hamer a special citation for his work. In 1948, he returned to duty as a Ranger at the governor's request to help check the election returns in Jim Wells and Duval counties in the controversial U.S. Senate race that resulted in Lyndon Johnson's election. Hamer retired in 1949 and lived in Austin until his death in 1955. He had been wounded numerous times and had killed an undetermined number of felons.

From SH 16, turn right on the roughly paved road by the old Oxford store and proceed a little more than a mile until you come to a collection of old stone buildings to your right dominated by the massive burned-out bulk of a once-proud stone home.

C. T. MOSS RANCH

One mile west of Oxford • Not open to the public

This is the old C. T. Moss ranch. The big burned-out main house was built in 1888 and burned in 1968, all ten rooms of it, leaving only the walls. C. T. Moss built the county's first barbed-wire fences, and with his father and brothers he owned most of the land and cattle in the southern half of Llano County. Brother Jim led the cowboy band in the battle on Packsaddle Mountain, by the way.

James R. "Jim" Moss was born in Fayette County in 1843. In 1857, he moved with his parents to Llano County. James served in the Civil War, and when he returned, he and his brother Charles worked their father's cattle. They also raised many hogs. Since there was no local market, they killed and baconed about two hundred hogs one winter and the next summer loaded the meat into ox wagons and hauled it to Austin, Bastrop, La Grange, and Washington-on-the-Brazos to sell. It was so hot that they traveled at night and rested during the day. During the late 1860s, they drove herds of cattle to Louisiana and then once to California.

The collection of stone buildings surrounding the big house is one of the most impressive in the Hill Country, and the fancy wrought-iron fence and gate still encircle the crumbling Moss homestead. Jim Moss's frame Victorian house also stands nearby.

A correspondent for the *San Antonio Herald* wrote in the fall of 1876, "In some portions of the valley there are enterprising and thrifty ranchmen engaged primarily in the cattle traffic. Among those we have met are the Moss brothers and they are all successful in their pursuits. There are four brothers located in different valleys and they all have comfortable and commodious houses, and possess in their surroundings evidences of thrift and industry not found in all the ranchos in this county."

Return to SH 16 and continue south toward Fredericksburg.

In another few miles you cross Sandy Creek and enter Legion Valley, the site of one of the worst Indian massacres in the Hill Country. On February 6, 1868, Legion Valley was locked in winter's icy grip. Mrs. Boyd Johnson, Mrs. Babe Johnson, Miss Amanda Townsend, and four children were spending the day with neighbor Mrs. Mathilda (John) Friend. The menfolk were away that day, believing their families were safe from Indian attack in such intemperate weather.

At about three o'clock that afternoon, the four children, who were snowballing in the dark, saw a group of horsemen approaching and began to scream.

Correctly appraising their identities as Indians, the women rushed the children into the house and bolted the door. Once inside, the women—save Mrs. Friend—went into a state of hysteria greater than the children's. The Indians, hearing the screaming, rightly surmised that there were no men inside and began to batter the doors down. Once they were inside, only Mrs. Friend fought, whereupon she was shot, scalped, and left for dead. The Indians took the other seven hostage and rode off.

Mrs. Friend, an arrow sticking from her chest, bound her scalped head and managed to drag herself one and a half miles through the snow to her nearest neighbor. There she begged him to remove the arrow. He failed, and then he and his family fled for the cedar brakes, fearing an attack on their house, too. They left Mrs. Friend alone by the fire with a bucket of water, her wounds undressed, not even her bloody clothes removed.

A posse did not start after the Indians until thirty-six hours later. They followed a gruesome trail. Five miles from the Friend home, they found one of the babies, its skull bashed in. Several hours later they found another baby, its throat cut ear to ear, next Mrs. Boyd and Mrs. Babe Johnson, ravaged and mutilated, and finally Miss Townsend in a similar horrible condition. The Indians' trail had wandered zigzag over to Hell's Half Acre in Gillespie County, back through Blowout community, and then up by Kingsland, where they murdered another man before escaping for good with two of the children, Mrs. Friend's boy and another girl.

In June 1869, the little girl, named Melinda, who was carried off by the Indians that tried to kill Mrs. Friend and captured her little son, was recovered from the Comanche Indians at Fort Arbuckle and was put in the charge of a woman in Grayson County who treated her very kindly and sent her to school. She said at the time that her parents were named Green and Clementine Cordel, but she could not tell where they might be addressed.

Melinda and the boy were restored to their families several years later, and Mrs. Friend miraculously recovered from her wounds and moved to Missouri. The tragedy could have been averted if only the women had been able to maintain a measure of restraint; the Indians attacked only when they realized the men were gone.

On February 12, 1870, the Comanches returned to Legion Valley, "bold as lions and having declared that Texas did not belong to the whites." They came to old man Moses that morning and had a fight. They waylaid Dan Moore and Riley Walker and shot Riley Walker dead, two balls passing through his body and six or seven arrows found in his body. His face was brutally mutilated. The Indians were hid behind a big rock about twenty feet distant, seven miles southeast of the Enchanted Rock. Dan Moore was shot in the arm, just above the elbow, the ball passing through and breaking the bone, and the same or another struck his side making a bad wound.

"To give some idea of the fear folks lived in every minute those days," writes Albert K. Erwin,

I want to relate a laughable deal that happened near Pack Saddle Mountain. The muzzle loading gun was still the tops in guns and most people moulded their bullets. The women folks generally did the moulding during their spare time. They used a ladle into which solid lead was placed, then heated until it would pour. When the lead would pour it was poured into a bullet mould.

One time Mr. James, if I recall the name correctly, was sitting before the fireplace moulding bullets. Mr. James was seated in a rocking chair fogging his pipe and feeling contented. Suddenly their tranquility was broken by hearing a noise under the house. The noise came from a spot under where the couple were setting. Mrs. James at that moment held a ladle full of hot lead. The first thought which entered the couple's heads was that Indians were under the house for the purpose setting it afire. Mrs. James poured the molten lead through a crack in the floor. The moment the lead went through the floor a loud cry of pain emitted from a human, followed by the sound of a scrambling person.

Mr. James rushed out and saw the forms of Indians departing. He investigated under the house and there found a pile of tender wood ready to be fired.

In this area you notice an obvious change in the landscape—the gray-and-pink granite and oak trees have given way to white limestone, marl, and juniper trees. This sudden change takes place fourteen miles north of Fredericksburg, caused by a large fault that dropped the Cretaceous Trinity limestone into contact with the older pre-Cambrian metamorphic rocks and granite.

BELL MOUNTAIN/OBERHELLMANN VINEYARDS

463 Bell Mountain Rd., about 13 miles from Oxford • 830-685-3297 • www.bellmountainwine.com • Open Saturdays, March through mid-December • Free tour • W variable

Located at the base of Bell Mountain, this vineyard began in 1974 on abandoned farmland. Johannesberg Riesling, Gewurztraminer, Chardonnay, and Pinot Noir are among the grapes grown. After the tour, enjoy a complimentary tasting of the wines made here.

From Oberhellmann Vineyards, continue south on SH 16 to Fredericksburg.

Mormon Trails

Texas has been attracting dreamers and schemers for centuries: brigands like Jean LaFitte; treasure hunters like Jim Bowie; empire builders like Philip Nolan, Augustus McGee, Henry Perry, and Dr. James Long; utopians like Nicholas Zink of Sisterdale, Gustav Schleicher of Bettina, and Victor Considerant of La Reunion; religious leaders like Johann Kilian and his Wendish Lutheran flock, and Lyman Wight and his Mormon faithful. Few Texans know anything of these men and their dreams, perhaps because most of them failed. Lyman Wight, one of the Latter-day Saints' original Quorum of Twelve, followed his dream to Texas. This trip traces the wanderings of Wight and his followers through the Hill Country.

Before we start traveling, we need to look at the events that led to Wight's migration to Texas. The Latter-day Saints movement traces its beginnings back to 1820, when young Joseph Smith received a vision from God. The fifteen-year-old Smith was attending a Baptist-Methodist revival in his hometown of Palmyra, New York, when a voice from heaven told him not to join any sect, but rather to await a second vision from God.

This second vision came in 1823, when a heavenly messenger revealed to Smith the location of some ancient plates buried in a field near Palmyra. These plates supposedly contained the record of ancestry of the American Indians, who were supposed to be the remnants of the ancient House of Israel. Accompanying the plates were two stones, the Urim and the Thummin, which held the key to the plates' translation. Smith was allowed to see the plates during this second vision, but was not allowed to take possession of them. Four years later the messenger visited Smith again, and this time Smith got to keep the plates. Smith then translated the plates to several scribes, including his new wife, Emma, and a schoolteacher, Oliver Cowdery. When completed, the revelations were printed at Palmyra in 1829. This is the Book of Mormon, which Mormons hold in equal esteem with the Bible.

Smith began to attract followers, one of whom was Lyman Wight. Wight was born in New York or Connecticut in 1796. He fought with distinction in the War of 1812. In 1823, Wight married Harriet Benton; they moved in 1826

MORMON TRAILS

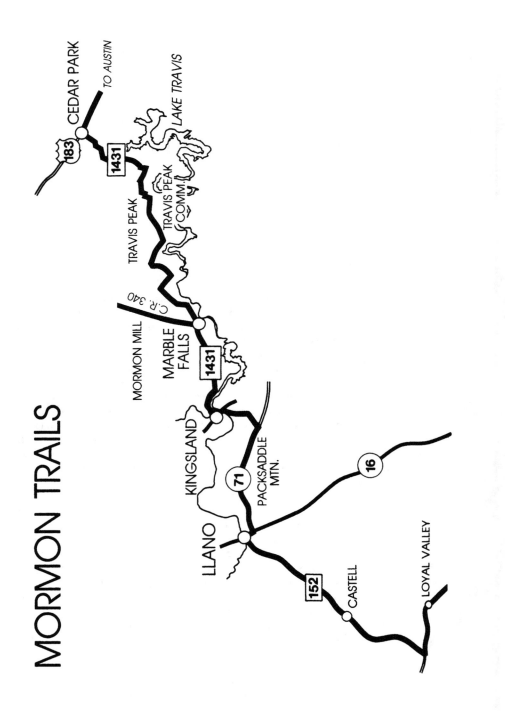

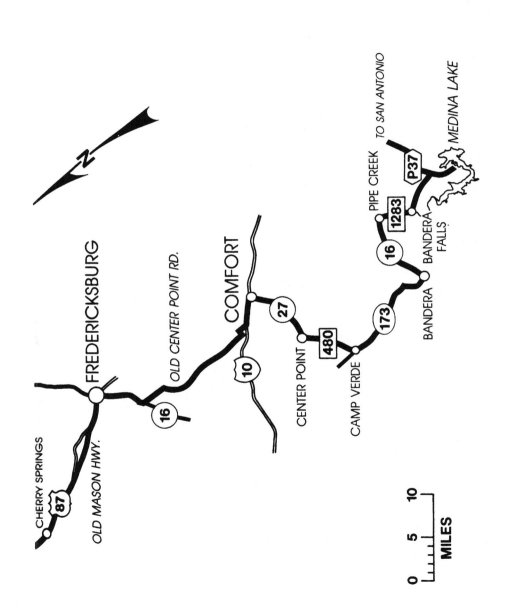

CHERRY SPRINGS

87

OLD MASON HWY.

FREDERICKSBURG

16

OLD CENTER POINT RD.

COMFORT

27

10

CENTER POINT

480

CAMP VERDE

173

BANDERA

16

BANDERA FALLS

1283

PIPE CREEK

TO SAN ANTONIO

P37

MEDINA LAKE

N

0   5   10

MILES

155

to Cuyahoga County, Ohio, where Wight joined the Lord's flock under the tutelage of a Baptist-turned-Campbellite preacher named Sidney Rigdon. Rigdon's converts formed a commune, twelve families strong, which had interests in farming and mechanics. A year later, the commune members were baptized into the Latter-day Saints church. Wight became a Latter-day Saints elder just six days after his baptism.

While in Kirtland, Ohio (their first gathering place), the Mormons adopted the "stewardship plan." The stewardship plan is the economic basis for Mormonism. By its terms, each man gives all his properties to the church, whereupon he is given stewardship over certain properties, usually the same that he has just given over to God. Out of these properties he keeps only enough for his "just wants and needs" and turns over the surplus to the church's general fund, administered by a bishop. This was a different proposition from Rigdon's "common stock" system; Wight employed the common stock system in Texas.

Neighbors in Kirtland did not appreciate the presence of the Latter-day Saints, so it was decided that the main mass of Mormons would move to the western edge of Missouri, the edge of America's western frontier, according to a vision received by Smith. Wight was specifically mentioned in one of Smith's visions as one of those chosen to carry the gospel to Missouri. At the conference of June 3–6, 1831, Joseph Smith laid his hands on Wight and ordained him to the High Priesthood, after the holy order of God, and the spirit fell upon him. But that same month, God, through Smith, also warned, "And let my servant Lyman Wight beware, for Satan desireth to sift him as chaff." Wight would prove to be a theological loose cannon. At one church meeting a few years later, John Corrill complained that Lyman Wight was teaching that "all disease in this church is of the devil, and that medicine administered to the sick is of the devil; for the sick in the church ought to live by faith," a charge that Wight acknowledged to be true. The more practical-minded president told Wight to keep this belief strictly to himself, and affirmed the utility of church-approved roots and herbs as medicine, especially when administered by a church member.

Wight and four other elders came to Independence, the seat of Jackson County, Missouri, in 1831. Smith and other church officials arrived soon after and announced that this section of Missouri had been revealed as Zion, the promised land of the Mormons. They bought forty acres of land and laid the cornerstone for a temple that was never constructed. They established a Mormon newspaper, *The Evening and the Morning Star*, in 1832. By 1833, the Mormon population in Jackson County was nearly 1,500, about one-third of the county's population. The Mormons organized their Missouri Zion as a collective and lived every minute of their lives according to the church's evolving doctrine, which stood in sharp contrast to the individualistic, loosely structured character of most frontier communities. The Mormons' economic success, their ability to control local elections, their clannishness, their church secrets, and their rapid growth in numbers aroused the anger and fear of their mostly Southern, Anglo neighbors, who also objected to the Mormons' abolitionist beliefs and their belief that the American Indians were the lost tribes of Israel.

Tensions between Mormons and gentiles grew. The Mormons saw Jackson County, Missouri, as their final gathering place, the sacred place to which Christ would come for the second resurrection. If this sacred plot were lost to them, the Mormons were to redeem it by force if necessary. There were minor persecutions and personal conflicts, and then mob violence erupted. The Mormons' printing facilities at Independence were destroyed, and the Mormons as a group were driven from the county in 1833. Lyman Wight claimed that 203 Mormon houses and one mill were burned. He also said, "I saw 190 women and children driven 30 miles across the prairie in the month of November, with 3 decrepit men only in their company. The ground was thinly crusted with sleet and I could easily follow on their trail by the blood that flowed from their lacerated feet on the stubble of the burnt prairie."

In one instance, he was chased by seven men about six miles; they were fully armed and came upon him so suddenly that he had to mount his horse with a blind bridle, without any saddle or arms, except a pocketknife. His horse being fleet, he escaped by outrunning them and leaping a deep wide ditch, where none of his pursuers dared follow.

On July 23, 1833, he signed an agreement that the Saints would leave Jackson County before the first day of January 1834; but before that time they were all driven out. After the Saints were driven out of Jackson County, volunteers were called for to go and visit the prophet in Kirtland. Bishop Partridge asked several of the elders to go, but they made excuses. Lyman Wight then stepped forward and said he could go. The bishop asked him what situation his family was in. He replied that his wife lay by the side of a log in the woods with a child three days old, and he had three days' provisions on hand, so he thought he could go very well. Parley P. Pratt next volunteered, and they went together to Kirtland in February 1834. On their arrival at Kirtland, the prophet obtained the word of the Lord, and they were commanded to gather up the strength of the Lord's house to go up to Zion, and it was the will of the Lord that there should be five hundred men, but not to go up short of one hundred. In fulfillment of this commandment, Lyman Wight went through Pennsylvania, and on the fifteenth day of March, he attended a conference at Avon, New York. He also went through Michigan, northern Indiana, and Illinois, and assisted Hyrum Smith in gathering up a company of eighteen, who joined Zion's Camp at Salt River, Missouri, on June 8, where the camp was reorganized, and Lyman Wight was appointed the second officer. He walked the whole journey from Michigan to Clay County without stockings on his feet. By the appointment of Joseph Smith, he gave a written discharge to each member of the camp when they were dismissed.

On July 3, 1834, he was ordained one of the high council of Missouri, and he was one of the signers of an appeal to the world making a proclamation of peace in Missouri that month. He spent the summer of 1834 in Clay County, Missouri. He took a job of making one hundred thousand bricks and building a large brick house for Colonel Michael Arthur in Clay County.

He was counseled to go to Kirtland and get his endowments. He started in the fall of 1835 and preached his way through to Kirtland, baptizing such as would receive his testimony. While on the journey, he called at the city of Richmond, Indiana, and announced he would preach in the courthouse. He walked through the city and being a stranger was unknown, but wherever he went, the people were blackguarding the "Mormons," and many declared they would tar and feather the preacher when he came to meeting that night. At the time of appointment, Brother Wight was at his post. There being no light provided, he went and bought candles and lighted the room. The house was soon filled with men who brought tar and feathers for the "Mormon" elder.

He preached about two hours, reproving them most severely for their meanness, wickedness, and mobocratic spirit. At the close of the meeting, he said, "If there is a gentleman in this congregation, I wish he would invite me to stay with him overnight." Whereupon, a gentleman stepped forward and tendered him an invitation, which he willingly accepted. His host said, "Mr. Wight, it is astonishing how you have become so well acquainted with the people here, for you have described them very correctly." He was kindly entertained and furnished with money in the morning to aid him on his journey.

He spent the winter of 1835–1836 in Kirtland and received his endowment. He returned to Missouri in 1836.

The Mormons had fled over into neighboring Clay, Ray, and Daviess counties, but they did not abandon their claim to Zion. They would do whatever it took to get their legally purchased property back. When a barrage of letters to the governor proved fruitless, the Mormons began to take stronger measures. By May 1834, the Mormons in Clay County had established an armory where they made swords, knives, and pistols, and repaired rifles and shotguns. Wight, who had held a colonel's commission in the Missouri militia, became the Mormons' chief military commander. General Wight was truly a soldier's general. On June 18, 1834, the Mormon band had to cross a slough that was half a mile wide. The soldiers had to wade through waist-deep mud and water. According to one compatriot, "General Wight, who had traveled from Kirtland [Ohio] without a stocking on his foot, carried Brother Joseph Young on his back." Breakfast that day was watery-thin cornmeal gruel.

On August 16, 1834, Joseph Smith wrote Wight from Kirtland and told him to "enter complaint to the Governor as often as he receives any insult or injury, and in case that they proceed to endeavor to take life, or tear down houses, and if the citizens of Clay County do not befriend us, to gather up the little army and be sent over immediately into Jackson County, and trust in God, and do the best he can in maintaining the ground."

The Clay Countians at first welcomed the Mormons, as refugees, with Christian charity, but the Mormons soon wore out their welcome, and on June 29, 1836, the gentiles of Clay County called on the Mormons to leave the county, for roughly the same reasons given by the Jackson County gentiles. The Mormons could move elsewhere (they recommended Wisconsin) or the gentiles would commence a civil war against them. At least partly in response to this threat, the Missouri legislature created Caldwell County, just north and east of Clay County, on December 29, 1836, as a Mormon refuge.

Within a few months of its creation, most of the Mormons moved to Caldwell County, where they founded the towns of Salem and Far West. Far West became the county seat. A temple site was selected in 1837, and the population swelled to 4,000. Again, friction developed between the Mormons and their gentile neighbors. Quarrels gave way to shootings, which in turn begat a guerilla war, known as the Mormon War, in 1837.

Meanwhile, Lyman Wight settled in 1837 on a great bend of the Grand River in Daviess County (located above Caldwell County) and established a ferry. In May 1838, Joseph Smith visited Wight's settlement and named it Adam-ondi-Ahman, which in the Reformed Egyptian language means "Adam's Consecrated Land." According to church history, this is the valley where three years before his death Adam gathered all the patriarchs—Seth, Enos, Cainan, Mahalaliel, Jared, Enoch, and Methuselah—and gave them his final blessing. As he blessed them, the heavens opened up, and the Lord appeared. Here, Smith prophesied, the judgment will sit and the Son of Man will appear and issue a decree that his dominion will be everlasting. At the brow of a hill above the village, Smith discovered a ruined stone altar where he said the patriarchs had worshipped.

David W. Patten preferred a charge against Brother Wight for teaching false doctrine. He was tried before the high council at Far West, April 24, 1837, and it was decided that he did teach false doctrine. He made the required acknowledgements.

Adam-ondi-Ahman grew rapidly. By October 1838, nearly two hundred houses had been built, and forty more Mormon families were living in wagons while waiting for more houses to be built. But the end was near. The Mormons had problems with the gentiles in Daviess County almost from the beginning. Adam-ondi-Ahman was located just four miles north of the county seat of Gallatin. Gallatin was a ragged row of ten houses, three of which were saloons. Almost overnight, the Mormons outnumbered the gentiles in Daviess County, and their thriving town quickly left Gallatin in the dust.

When a group of unarmed Mormons came to Gallatin to vote on August 6, 1838, they were met by a mob controlled by Col. W. P. Peniston, a member of the county's founding family and a candidate for office whom the Mormons opposed. A drunkard picked a quarrel with one of the Mormon leaders, and a fight began. Pistols weren't used, but rocks, clubs, and the occasional butcher knife were pressed into service. Men dropped like flies on all sides. Major Joseph H. McGee saw a Mormon pursued by two Missourians. The Mormon had a butcher knife sticking out between his shoulders. As they chased him, another Mormon seized a large club, rushed in between them and their victim, and knocked the gentiles senseless into the dirt. The Mormons retreated, but on October 11, 1838, they attacked Gallatin and sacked and burned the town's storehouse and tailor shop. Adam-ondi-Ahman came to resemble a fort.

In 1838, Governor Lilburn W. Boggs ordered the state militia to either exterminate the Mormons or drive them from Missouri. When some Mormons moved over into Carroll County (just east of Caldwell County) in the summer of 1838, a civil war with the gentiles soon flared. The Mormons left Carroll County in September rather than face massacre by their neighbors. On October 30, 1838, two hundred Missouri militia attacked a small group of Mormons who had taken refuge at Haun's Mill in Caldwell County. About eighteen Mormons were killed, and the militia threw the bodies down a well.

After the Haun's Mill massacre, the state militia was dispatched to Far West. The Mormons at Far West surrendered. The leaders were tried by court-martial and were ordered shot, but the sentence wasn't carried out. They were jailed instead. On November 8, 1838, shortly after the Mormons surrendered at Far West, Brigadier General Robert Wilson went to Adam-ondi-Ahman to hold an inquiry into the alleged Mormon transgressions. After a three-day hearing, every Mormon was acquitted, but Wilson ordered the town to be vacated in ten days. The Mormons were allowed to spend the winter in Caldwell County, but they had to leave Missouri as soon as it warmed up. The abandoned town quickly fell into ruin, and by 1940, only one crumbling log house—said to be the house of Lyman Wight—remained. Elder Lyman Wight joined his fellow Mormon leaders in jail. On December 1, 1838, Prophet Joseph Smith, his brother Hiram Smith, Lyman Wight, Sidney Rigdon, and two others were placed in the Clay County jail in Liberty. The town was abuzz with wild rumors of poisoning attempts, gruesome punishments, threats of lynching, and attempted escapes. Joseph Smith had a series of revelations while the other prisoners denounced any townspeople who came within shouting distance.

Peter Burnett described the Mormon captivity:

When the March 1839 term of the District Court of Davis County came on, the sheriff of Clay removed the prisoners, under a strong guard, from the jail in Liberty to Davis County, to be present at the impaneling of the grand jury. It was apprehended that the prisoners would be mobbed by the irritated people of Davis, and the sheriff of Clay was determined to protect his prisoners if he could. Mr. Rees and myself went to Davis County as their counsel. The courthouse at the county seat having been burned the fall before by Lyman Wight's expedition, the court was held in a rough log school-house, about 25 feet square. This house was situated on the side of a lane about a quarter of a mile long. It being immediately after the annual spring thaw, this lane was knee-deep in mud, especially in the vicinity of the court-house.

The people of the county collected in crowds, and were so incensed that we anticipated violence toward the prisoners. In the daytime the Court sat in this house, the prisoners being seated upon a bench in one corner of the room; and they were kept under guard there during the night. In the end of the room farthest from the fireplace there was a bed in which the counsel for the prisoners slept. The floor was almost covered with mud.

The prisoners arrived on Saturday evening, and the Court opened on the following Monday. They were fully aware of their extreme danger. As I slept in the room, I had an opportunity to see much of what passed. The prisoners did not sleep any for several nights. Their situation was too perilous to admit of repose. Smith and Wight talked almost incessantly. Smith would send some one for a bottle of whisky; and, while he kept sober himself, Lyman Wight would become pretty well drunk, and would kindly invite the guards of Davis County (into whose keeping the prisoners were then committed) to drink with him, which invitation was cordially accepted. Some of the guards had been in the combats between the Mormons and the people of Davis County.

The subject of incessant conversation between Wight and these men was the late difficulties, which they discussed with great good nature and frankness. Wight would laughingly say, "At such a place" (mentioning it) "you rather whipped us, but at such a place we licked you." Smith was not in any of the combats, so far as I remember. The guard placed over the prisoners in Davis, after the sheriff of Clay delivered them into the hands of the sheriff of that county, did not abuse them, but protected them from the crowd. By consent of the prisoners, many of the citizens of Davis came into the room and conversed with them hour after hour during most of the night. Among others, I remember two preachers, who had theological arguments with Smith, and he invariably silenced them sooner or later. They were men of but ordinary capacity, and, being unacquainted with the grounds Smith would take, were not prepared to answer his positions; while Smith himself foresaw the objections they would raise against his theory, and was prepared accordingly.

Joseph Smith Jr. was at least six feet high, well formed, and weighed about 180 pounds. His appearance was not prepossessing, and his conversational powers were but ordinary. You could see at a glance that his education was very limited. He was an awkward but vehement speaker. In conversation he was slow, and used too many words to express his ideas, and would not generally go directly to a point. But, with all these drawbacks, he was much more than an ordinary man. He possessed the most indomitable perseverance, was a good judge of men, and deemed himself born to command, and he did command. His views were so strange and striking, and his manner was so earnest, and apparently so candid, that you could not but be interested. There was a kind, familiar look about him, that pleased you. He was very courteous in discussion, readily admitting what he did not intend to controvert, and would not oppose you abruptly, but had due deference to your feelings. He had the capacity for discussing a subject in different aspects, and for proposing many original views, even of ordinary matters. His illustrations were his own. He had great influence over others. As an evidence of this I will state that on Thursday, just before I left to return to Liberty, I saw him out among the crowd, conversing freely with every one, and seeming to be perfectly at ease. In the short space of 5 days he had managed so to mollify his enemies that he could go unprotected among them without the slightest danger. Among the Mormons he had much greater influence than Sidney Rigdon. The latter was a man of superior education, an eloquent speaker, of fine appearance and dignified manners; but he did not possess the native intellect of Smith, and lacked his determined will. Lyman Wight was the military man among them.

Joseph Smith Jr. was a very stout, athletic man, and was a skillful wrestler. This was known to the men of Davis County, and some of them proposed to Smith that he should wrestle with one of their own men. He at first courteously objected, alleging substantially that, though he was once in the habit of wrestling, he was now a minister of the gospel, and did not wish to do anything contrary to his duty as such, and that he hoped they would excuse him upon that ground. They kindly replied that they did not desire him to do anything contrary to his calling; that they would not bet anything; that it was nothing but a friendly trial of skill and manhood, for the satisfaction of others, and to pass away the time pleasantly; and that they hoped he would, under all the circumstances, comply with their request. He consented; they selected the best wrestler among them, and Smith threw him several times in succession, to the great amusement of the spectators. Though I did not witness this incident, I heard it stated as a matter of fact at the time, and I have no doubt of its truth.

Rigdon was paroled; the other five Mormon leaders remained in the Liberty jail until April 15, 1839. The grand jury having indicted the prisoners, Burnett applied to the court for a change of venue to some county where the prisoners could have a fair trial. The court changed the venue to Boone County and committed the prisoners to the sheriff of Davis, with instructions to convey them to the jail in Columbia, the Boone County seat. While being transferred to Columbia, Joseph Smith and most of the prisoners escaped; the rest of the Mormons escaped from the Columbia jail and fled to Illinois, where most of their followers had settled after leaving Missouri. The escapes were probably arranged.

The Mormons built a city—Nauvoo—in Illinois and there enjoyed prosperity and peace for a few years, bringing in thousands of converts, the result of the massive proselytizing efforts of the missionary arm of the church, known as the Quorum of Twelve. Wight became a member of the Quorum in 1841. He also became president of the Black River Lumber Company, which the Mormons formed to acquire lumber for the construction of a temple at Nauvoo.

By 1843, the Mormons were having trouble with their Nauvoo neighbors and were looking for a new Zion. The Republic of Texas seemed to offer great possibilities as a place to found a nation all their own, so the church began to make plans for a colony in Texas. Wight was at the head of this company. Come 1844, the Texas plan was sidelined for a time while the church organized a harebrained attempt to elect Joseph Smith president of the United States. Should Smith be defeated, the Texas plan would take effect.

The Texas plan provided for the purchase of territory "north of a west line, from the falls of the Colorado River to the Nueces River, thence down same to the Gulf of Mexico and along the Rio Grande and up the same to the United States territory." The Mormons expected to be recognized here as a sovereign nation and to help the struggling Texas republic to defend herself from Mexico. The Black River Lumber Company was to take possession of the new territory. At the time, the Mormons' desired territory was part of the land in dispute between Mexico and Texas. A Mormon representative went to Texas to negotiate with the government and returned in 1844 with treaty approval by the president's cabinet. Three more men were then appointed commissioners to meet with the Texas congress to ratify the treaty, after which Wight and George Miller were to lead the colony to this territory.

The plan to elect Smith president of the United States ended in Carthage, Illinois, on June 27, 1844, when Smith was killed by a mob that broke into the jail where he was being held. Confusion followed at Nauvoo, and Brigham Young, president of the Quorum of Twelve, assumed control of the church and declared himself to be the successor to Smith. The Quorum followed his lead, save Wight and two others. Most of the faithful followed Young out to Utah, while other smaller groups went their own way, including Lyman Wight. Wight was not called the Wild Ram of the Mountains for nothing.

When Wight refused the leadership of Brigham Young, he decided to lead the Black River Lumber Company to Texas, following the council's 1844 directive. On March 25, 1845, Wight and 150 followers started down the Mississippi for Texas. They landed near Davenport, Iowa, from which point they prepared for the rest of the trip, which was to be overland.

Enter Texas.

After Indian problems, disease, and death, they crossed the Red River into Texas on November 10, 1845, and spent the winter in Fort Johnston, an abandoned Republic of Texas fort in Grayson County. They resumed their journey south on April 24, 1846, crossing the Trinity River at Dallas, the Brazos River near Marlin, and the Little River near Rockdale, before arriving at Webberville, east of Austin, on June 6 of that same year.

They didn't stay long. Noah Smithwick, chronicler of early Texas and the Mormons' neighbor at Webberville, wrote:

> They were a novelty in the religious world, and curious to know something of their peculiar views, I permitted the elder to preach in my house. Preaching of any kind was so rare that the neighbors all gathered in and listened with respectful attention while the elder expounded the doctrine of the Latter-day Saints, being careful to leave out its more objectionable features. But among most people the idea obtained that they were a lawless band, and the subject of rising up and driving them from the country was strongly advocated. They were in sufficient numbers to stand off the Indians, and, it being their policy to isolate their communities, which relegated them to the outskirts of civilization, I was willing to utilize anything that formed a barrier against the savages. I therefore counseled suspension of hostilities till some overt act called for their expulsion.

Smithwick's advice was not heeded, and the Mormons soon moved to a spot on the Colorado River a few miles above Austin by the "Great Falls," near the present location of Tom Miller Dam. Here they settled down to the business of making a living. They took the contract for the first jail in Austin.

AUSTIN

At the falls of the Colorado, the Mormons built the area's first gristmill. According to Heman Hale Smith, a great-grandson of Lyman Wight, it took the colony seven weeks to build a dam across the Colorado, put up a mill building, and construct the wooden machinery. The waterwheel was made of cypress, oak, and some iron parts. "Cog workers" carefully carved the teeth of the various wooden gear wheels using sharp knives made by the colony's blacksmiths. Wight had brought a set of French millstones but did not use them in Austin, holding them in reserve until the colony established a permanent home. Millstones were made of local limestone, which were satisfactory for grinding corn, although they required frequent sharpening. Disaster struck a few months later.

Smithwick relates, "Up to this time we were under the necessity of grinding our corn on steel mills run by hand—a tedious and wearying process, so that in building the mill the Mormons became public benefactors and it was a great catastrophe when a rise in the river swept their mill away. They gathered up the machinery, but, discouraged with the prospect, began to look about for a better location."

One report has them moving up the river to Bull Creek, where they established another mill. At any rate, during their stay in Austin, they proved to be prodigious workers, building several houses in addition to the jail and several miles of roads to their mills. We know these roads now as Scenic Drive, which runs along the banks of Lake Austin from Enfield Drive to Pecos Street, and Lakewood Drive/Spicewood Springs Road, which runs along Bull Creek. Most of Lakewood Drive has now been obliterated by Loop 360. These roads are among the most visually pleasing in Austin.

Hard work notwithstanding, the Mormons had managed to indebt themselves to the tune of $2,000 to Austin merchants. About three weeks after the flood, Wight led an exploring party west to scout for a new colony location. It found a favorable location in Gillespie County on Grape Creek "with plenty of good water and timber, abounding with game and honey."

Wight had heard of the German settlement at Fredericksburg and hoped that he and his flock might be able to live harmoniously with the mostly abolitionist and Free-Soiler Germans. In November 1846, three of the colony's elders visited Adelsverein commissioner John Meusebach in New Braunfels, asking permission to settle forty-six families in Adelsverein territory. According to Dr. Ferdinand Roemer, the three elders weren't given an unqualified promise to their petition, but they did sign a contract with Meusebach whereby they agreed to build a mill at Fredericksburg similar to the one they built in Austin. And so the Mormons prepared to move again, into the valley of the Corderillas, or Cordilleras Mountains, as the hills ringing Fredericksburg were variously called (*corderilla* means "lambskin dressed with the fleece" in Spanish; *cordillera* means "mountain range").

ZODIAC

Wight authorized a few families to move immediately to Gillespie County, clear land for a farm, and build a dam across the stream. But before the dam was completed, Grape Creek ran dry. By May 1, 1847, another mill site had been selected four miles below Fredericksburg on the Pedernales, and six weeks later the advance guard had a gristmill in operation. Crops were planted, the Austin mill site was sold, and the whole colony moved to the new settlement, named Zodiac by Wight. Soon the Mormons had constructed a sawmill, general store, temple-storehouse, school, blacksmith and wagon shop, cabinet and furniture shops, shingle mill, and houses for the twenty-odd Mormon families.

Wight's colony was a godsend to Fredericksburg; the Mormons supplied the Germans with seed, lumber, and shingles from their mill, cornmeal from their gristmill, and furniture from their shops. The Mormons also helped the Germans adjust to the idiosyncrasies of farming on the edge of the Great American Desert. Many of the German immigrants were becoming farmers and herders for the first time. The colony also supplied grain and lumber to nearby Fort Martin Scott. The colony earned extra money by building mills for others. Nat Lewis, who lived in San Antonio, visited Zodiac while on a freighting trip to El Paso. Impressed by the Mormons' mill, he asked Wight to build him a mill on the San Antonio River, and the mill became operational in 1849.

On December 13, 1848, two men from Brigham Young's headquarters came to Zodiac, their mission being to persuade Wight to journey to Salt Lake City to counsel with his brethren on the Quorum of Twelve. They threatened him with excommunication should he refuse. Wight replied, "Nobody under the light of the heavens except Joseph Smith or John Smith, the president of the Fifty, can call me from Texas to come to Salt Lake City," and he said that he had as much authority to call one of the Twelve—or rather Eleven—to Texas, as they had to call him to Utah. The Wild Ram of the Mountains was excommunicated a year later.

Wight apparently tried to get along with his neighbors, both red and white. Chief Buffalo Hump and his Comanches visited Zodiac several times during 1849 and 1850 and gave the Mormons the privilege of traveling anywhere through their nation. Wight tried to discuss Mormonism with them, which seemed to please the Comanches greatly. At one point, a large band of Comanches camped near Zodiac, and Wight gave them corn, melons, beef, and other goods.

One day, some one hundred Comanches rode into Zodiac while a sergeant from Fort Martin Scott was visiting. The sergeant asked Wight if he could put on a pistol-shooting exhibition for the guests. He then pulled two potatoes from his pocket and drew his pistol. He threw one potato high into the air, and after a brief pause threw upward the second spud. Just before the rising second potato passed the falling first one, he fired the pistol. To everyone's amazement, the bullet passed through both potatoes. Several of the Comanche braves attempted the trick with their bows and arrows, but none succeeded. They were highly impressed.

In 1850, Wight ran for Gillespie County chief justice and probate court judge. Wight lost the election to Johann Jost Klingelhoefer, but he contested the results on the grounds that Klingelhoefer was not a U.S. citizen (he had not yet been naturalized). The contest was decided in Wight's favor, and he took office in September. But since the rest of the county court was composed of Germans, Wight could not run the county as he pleased. After attending five court sessions, Wight refused to attend any more. He ignored summons from his fellow commissioners to attend, so the commissioners met, declared the office of chief justice vacant, and called a special election to fill the vacancy. The election was held in August 1851, and Klingelhoefer, by now a U.S. citizen, was elected to take Wight's place.

Despite the colony's industriousness, its debts seemed to grow larger and larger, owing to bad luck and Wight's bad financial management. Income from the mill averaged only fifty dollars a month in 1850. In July 1850, a flood on the Pedernales swept away much of the mill and crops in nearby fields and flooded the village. What to do?

Wight prayed for three days seeking guidance. Then he told the colony of the vision he had, that the mill should be rebuilt. Work commenced the next day, and in less than a month the mill was back in operation and the village was livable again. In the meantime, Wight and three other men began looking for another site.

There were several reasons for the move: Wight's inability to get along with the county commissioners; sickness in the colony; no more contract work at Fort Martin Scott; two nearby competing mills; a defect in land title that caused them to lose the land, necessitating repurchase; the flood that swept away their crops and mill; and, finally, Wight's seemingly insatiable wanderlust.

An even greater flood in February 1851 spurred Wight into action. The colony abandoned Zodiac for a new site in Burnet County. On their northeast path toward Hamilton Creek in Burnet County, they stopped briefly at the Colorado River near the Marble Falls.

To get to Marble Falls from Austin, take US 183 to Cedar Park; just after the intersection with RM 620, you can take either US 183-A (the toll road) or old US 183, and then turn left on FM 1431. Or, take I-35 north to Round Rock, and take the FM 1431 exit. Go west on FM 1431 to Cedar Park, where you cross the Balcones Escarpment and enter the Hill Country.

Cedar Park is located on Cluck Creek. In the early days, the community and the creek were named Running Brushy, after a heavy-flowing spring that formed Cluck Creek's headwaters. In 1873, George and Harriet Cluck bought the land that included Running Brushy Spring. A community formed around their ranch, and a post office was authorized in 1874. Harriet Cluck became postmistress later that year and served for eight years. In 1882, the Austin and Northwestern Railroad passed through Running Brushy, and the railroad company changed the community's name to Brueggerhoff, to honor William Brueggerhoff, a railroad company official. A picnic and public gathering ground for railroad excursionists was established on land donated by the Clucks. In 1887, the town was renamed Cedar Park. Limestone for building and cedar fence posts were Cedar Park's major industries for decades. Then, as a result of Austin's growth, area ranch land was converted to subdivisions starting in the 1960s, and between 1970 and 1980 the population of Cedar Park grew from 125 to over 3,000. In 1973, Cedar Park citizens voted to incorporate, and the town has grown like kudzu ever since, to more than 40,000 in 2010.

Cedar Park is also home to the Austin Steam Train, which runs to Bertram and Burnet on a seasonal basis. There are three levels of service on each train ride: coach class, excursion class, and first-class Pullman lounge. Coach cars are not air conditioned or heated. Ticket prices vary, and seasonal schedules vary, so it's best to visit the website, www.austinsteamtrain.org, or call 477-8468. You pass the station on your way out of town, located at 401 E. RM1431/Whitestone Boulevard.

From Cedar Park, FM 1431's path is forever restless.

The views from the hilltops may be beautiful, but wresting a living from this rugged land wasn't easy. It took a special breed of folks to survive here, stalwarts such as the Preece family, who came to Texas from Kentucky during the days of the Texas Republic. The Preece, clan owned three thousand acres of hill country that stretched from Lake Travis to Cedar Park, roughly along FM 1431. One of the sons, Richard Lincoln Preece, is said to have killed the last buffalo in Travis County, a bull buffalo, along what is now called Bull Creek in northwest Austin. The state of Texas voted to secede from the Union, but support for the Southern cause was far from unanimous. Unionist pockets were scattered across the Hill Country, including Preece country. During the Civil War, Richard Lincoln Preece served as a sharpshooter in a Union guerilla outfit, the Texas Mountain Eagles, which became the First Texas Cavalry of the Union Army.

Richard Lincoln Preece fathered twelve children, including David Preece, born in 1871. As an old man, Dave Preece wrote about his family's life and how the advent of barbed wire eventually drove them from the land they so loved. In 1876, Dave's Uncle Frank visited San Antonio, where he saw John Gates' famous demonstration of barbed wire in Alamo Plaza. The Preeces had no use for or love of barbed wire. "We share our grass like we share our bread," Dave's dad once said. The mountainous range where they lived was rocky and it dipped up and down, making fencing difficult. The Preeces considered themselves hill people and took pride in the fact that no one had ever penned them in yet.

Like most hill folk, the Preeces were stock raisers. The rough land wasn't fit for farming, although they found enough flat, fertile land for a family garden. Their post office, at Running Brushy, was run by Harriet Cluck, a tough woman who had taken a herd of longhorns with her husband up the Chisholm Trail in 1871. A feeder branch of the Chisholm Trail passed by their house. Trail bosses passing by bought mustangs they broke. Strangers stopped to bed for the night. It wasn't polite to ask a traveler who he was, because names, like brands, often got changed in Texas. It was in this spirit that the little ranch of cousin Joe Shannon on Brushy Creek was to become Sam Bass' hideout, prior to his death at Round Rock. Their neighbor, Deputy Sheriff Maurice Moore, was shot that day. Ironically, Dave's dad, as a Union soldier, had captured Moore, a Confederate soldier, in Louisiana in 1865.

In 1881, young Dave went with his dad to Austin. Inside Cap Richardson's hardware store,

> Dad was in the middle of a lot of men, talking mighty excited. Some of 'em had tough-looking clippers in their hip pockets, and they were talking mean and mad. I figured they were ranchers from the prairies below Austin, because I'd have known them if they'd been mountain men.
>
> Theirs was fighting talk. One of them said that 3 million acres of the best range land of Texas had already been fenced in, and that was just the beginning. It was shameful, all that they were grabbing up and enclosing. Little homesteads that the penned-up steers tramped down; bounty land deeded to old soldiers who didn't have anything else; state-owned grazing and school land that was our public domain.

"But it ain't going easy for the fence men," one fellow said. He pulled out a pair of clippers, sheared the air, and told how he'd chopped down 500 miles of the cussed barb up in Coleman County west of Fort Worth.

Another said they were blowing up the fences with buried bombs in the blackland country around Dallas. Bombs were connected with loose fence wire, and when the rider pulled at the barb to tack it up, they exploded. Two fence riders had thus been blown sky high.

Whereupon Richard Lincoln Preece retorted, "The Preeces held them hills agin the Secesh and we'll hold them agin the fence men." But while the Preeces held out, all around their neighbors were fencing in.

From 1885 to 1886, there were lots of mustangs to round up, because as the surrounding land was increasingly fenced in, the mustangs retreated to this last little stretch of free grass range. The next year, they were fewer and were being rounded up and slaughtered at glue factories for a dime per hundred pounds. "That was a devilish thing," Dave Preece observed, "because I can remember the days when they fined you ten dollars for killing a man, and hung you for stealing a horse."

By the time Dave turned sixteen, he had his own herd of longhorn cattle, and he drove thirty-five fat grass-fed yearlings down to Austin to the commission pen. His head was full of plans on how to spend all the money he'd get for them. But his longhorns brought him just seventy dollars. His bill at Schneider's store (which still stands in downtown Austin at Second and Guadalupe streets) was sixty-seven dollars, leaving him enough for some cartridges and a quart of cheap whiskey. The cattle buyer apologized for the low price and pointed to some sleek white-faced shorthorns in the pen. "Them's the cattle that sells now, Herefords, and along with 'em, Aberdeen Angus."

Dave studied them and realized that you could grow those breeds cheaper on less grass and make more than you could on the old longhorns. Hence, the final seeds were sown for the destruction of the Preeces' free-range way of life. "The fence men had us whipped before they ever laid a wire in the hills, because there was no money left in the breeds of the open range," Dave wrote. "I don't know what us mountain ranchers would have done if the older men hadn't been drawing their Union soldier pensions." And then came the depression of 1893, which let the fence people get into Preece country.

"Their smart town lawyers, crooked as a dog's hind leg, swarmed the hills talking about the dam to be built across the Colorado that would flood our range. They said we'd better sell our river bottom holdings while we could still get something for them." The family sold out and then bought poorer land on old rocky Bull Creek. "The dam was never finished, but we were [editor's note: the dam that formed Lake Austin was finished in 1893 but was washed away in the flood of 1900]. The town men bought more mountain land cheap and it all got fenced in." And the Preeces had to fence their new lands because everyone else did.

Life became crueler. They used to have church every Sunday and an eight-month school. But church played out when the deacons started tending stills to make ends meet. There wasn't enough tax money to keep a teacher more than four months. Men now went off every fall to pick cotton to earn some cash. Dave did that until 1905 when he married a cotton-patch woman who didn't like the Hill Country, so they moved to Austin and ran a truck farm until he moved his family to work on a ranch in Cochran County.

TRAVIS PEAK COMMUNITY

Travis County • About 13 miles from Cedar Park

Named for the nearby peak, this settlement got its start in 1851 when Herman Hensel built a cabin here. Hensel came to Travis County via Cape Horn and the California gold-mining camps of the great rush of 1849. He bought eighty acres here on Cow Creek and settled down to raising a family. He replaced his cabin in 1878 with a large two-story limestone house, and also donated land in 1880 for the one-room limestone schoolhouse. These buildings and the cemetery are located just off FM 1431 on Singleton Road, which runs off to your left down to Lake Travis, just past the Travis Peak community sign. The small, one room, rock schoolhouse is on your left just after the Travis Peak Church of Christ and before the Flat Creek bridge. To see it, take the "lower road," as per the sign. The house is on the right just after crossing Flat Creek. The Singleton family cemetery is on the right just before the entrance to Gloster Bend. At the end of this road is Gloster Bend Primitive Area, the first of several LCRA primitive areas located on Lake Travis, about 3.3 miles off FM 1431.

LCRA PRIMITIVE RECREATION SYSTEM ON LAKE TRAVIS

The Lower Colorado River Authority's Primitive Recreation System on Lake Travis is composed of seven tracts of public land managed by the LCRA. They are open year-round, but they are generally primitive (no toilets, no running water, no trash collection facilities). What you pack in, you must pack out. Camping is allowed in designated camping sites. You can fish at any of the sites. Many varieties of fish, including largemouth bass, sunfish, crappie, striper, and catfish, are in Lake Travis. All anglers must have a Texas fishing license. An admission fee is generally charged; check www.lcra.org for the latest information.

GLOSTER BEND

North side of Lake Travis, on Singleton Rd, off FM 1431

Singleton Road has beautiful, far-reaching vistas of Lake Travis and the surrounding, rolling Hill Country. At 840 feet, 640-acre Gloster Bend is the highest overlook above Lake Travis, with more than a mile of Lake Travis shoreline and a single-lane paved boat ramp. The topography is mostly rolling hills with some steep ravines. There are designated access roads. There is a paved parking area for vehicles and trailers, as well as composting toilets and trash collection sites.

TURKEY BEND (EAST)

North side of Lake Travis, about 3 miles west of Travis Peak Community • Shaw Drive dead-ends into FM 1431 from the south. Turn left on Shaw Dr. and go 1.8 miles to reach the Turkey Bend (East) Primitive Area

Turkey Bend (East) offers more than two miles of shoreline and one of the prettiest coves on the lake. The four-hundred-acre property has varied topography ranging from steep shoreline slopes to gentle flats. A looped trail along the upper plateau is for nonmotorized use only. Spectacular views of Lake Travis and the surrounding countryside make it popular with hikers and horseback riders. A trailhead parking area large enough to accommodate horse trailers is provided.

Two more LCRA primitive areas on Lake Travis are located in the Smithwick neighborhood. The first is Shaffer Bend, which is accessed via Burnet County Road 343A, about a mile off FM 1431.

SHAFFER BEND

North side of Lake Travis, off FM 1431, about 17 miles west of Lago Vista, near Smithwick community

This five-hundred-acre site exhibits two distinct topographies. The northern portion is very hilly with extensive exposed limestone outcrops and dense stands of cedar. There are several good views of Lake Travis and the surrounding countryside, and the area is accessible by a gravel road. The southern portion is gently sloping bottomland with large oaks and pecan trees along more than a mile of gently sloping shoreline. An improved gravel road provides access to the shoreline while avoiding the center of the property, which is habitat for black-capped vireos. Hiking, biking, and horseback riding are allowed in the interior portions of the property. Vehicles with good traction and high ground clearance are recommended.

Another mile west on FM 1431, and you come to the intersection with Burnet County Road 343, which runs down to Lake Travis and the Camp Creek Primitive Area.

CAMP CREEK

North side of Lake Travis, on Burnet County Rd. 343, 0.5 miles off FM 1431, near the Smithwick community

Camp Creek features sizable stands of pecan trees and unique creek bottoms. There is excellent diversity of vegetation and wildlife on the five-hundred-acre tract. A hiking trail follows Camp Creek and then climbs to a plateau. The trail provides many scenic opportunities and opportunities for nature study. The shoreline at Camp Creek is shorter and steeper than at many of the other sites in the LCRA's Primitive Recreation System. Burnet County operates and maintains a five-acre park along Camp Creek's waterfront. Overnight camping is permitted. The only public boat ramp on the upper north side of Lake Travis is here, along with tables, grills, and trash cans. An improved county road provides access to the park area. There is no running water or restrooms.

SMITHWICK COMMUNITY

Burnet County • About 11 miles from Travis Peak

Smithwick community is named after the Mormons' Webberville neighbor, Noah Smithwick. Smithwick was born in North Carolina on New Year's Day,

1809. He moved to Texas in 1827, working as a blacksmith and smuggling to-bacco across the Mexican border with "Dr." John Webber. After serving in the Republican Army during the Texas war of independence, Smithwick lived first in Bastrop, then in Webberville, where he served as blacksmith, postmaster, and justice of the peace. He moved to Fort Croghan (now Burnet) in 1848, then to the section of the country that now bears his name, located between Double Horn and Hickory Creeks, in 1855, where he built a mill. Double Horn Creek's name is derived from the interlocked antlers found near the source of the stream by early settlers. Two bucks, presumably having met at the spring to drink, engaged in battle. During the fight they managed to interlock their horns, and unable to extricate themselves, they starved to death. Here Smithwick built his first house and a mill on the Colorado River. His children were students at the nearby Frog Pond school in the newly formed village of Double Horn.

In 1858, a great grasshopper plague descended upon the countryside, and Smithwick described their onslaught:

> They came on the wing and in such numbers that the sun was literally darkened with them. Anyone who has ever looked toward the zenith during a snowstorm will remember that the snowflakes looked like myriads of black specks. That is just the appearance the grasshoppers presented when first discovered. Soon they began to drop, and the ground was alive with them. It was late in the fall, and they went into winter quarters, devouring every green thing in sight except the ragweed, which is intensely bitter, utilizing the denuded branches and weeds for roosting purposes. When the cold came on, they were frozen on their perches, and in this state they fell easy victims to the hogs, which devoured millions of them, but there were still enough left to seed the ground for the next season's crop, which they did by boring holes into the earth with their tail-ends. They did not distribute themselves evenly, some farms being almost free of them. On one such place there were only a few dropped down, and the owner thereof, mustering his whole family when the hoppers began to light, gathered tin pans, beating them energetically until the main body of pests passed over. After his neighbors had received the full force of the invasion he was wont to attribute their affliction to shiftlessness. "If you had just got out and fought them, as I did, you might have saved your crop." Pretty soon, though, there came on another detachment. When they began to drop our hero got out with his tin pans and brooms and "beat" and "shooed" till he was exhausted, but the hoppers kept on dropping, and lost no time in getting to work, cleaning out everything in sight.

With the coming of the Civil War, Smithwick, a Unionist, was threatened by his secessionist neighbors, so he sold his farm for $2,000, gave his mill—for which he had been offered $12,000 the year before—to his nephew John Hub-bard, and with some friends left Burnet County in April 1861 in a prairie schoo-ner, bound for California. But before leaving Texas, he paid a farewell visit to his old friend and fellow Unionist Sam Houston. Secessionists later murdered Hubbard and threw his body into a waterhole. Smithwick lived out the rest of his ninety-one years in California. Toward the end of his life, he wrote his memoirs of life in early Texas. Smithwick didn't let blindness halt his work; he dictated the text to his daughter.

The inhabitants of the Double Horn community seemed to be a pretty bad-assed bunch as indicated by their treatment of Smithwick and Hubbard, and this correspondence to the *Burnet Bulletin* from Cypress Mill in 1881:

The unenviable reputation of Bell County as the "outrage" district of Texas bids fair to be taken from it by Burnet County, and it remains to be seen whether the latter will prosecute the offenders with more vigor than the former. The ducking of Honey, the whipping of Dr. Russell and the Dow brothers and the lynching of Bell County prisoners are eclipsed in malevolence, if not in magnitude, by the actions of some twenty persons calling themselves the "Double Horn Mob," who broke up the Methodist camp meeting on Fall Creek last week. This meeting is an annual one and this year was conducted by the Southern Methodist Church, but has been attended by members of other denominations, and has heretofore been the occasion of a happy reunion of Christians, where peace and harmony have prevailed. I can ascertain no reason for the action of the self-styled mob, other than the devilish spirit which inspires some men to petty, dastardly actions. The impression prevails that they were drunk and armed on this occasion. They cut the saddles and stakeropes of those attending the meeting, threw rocks at those who went out to ascertain the cause of the disturbance; shot off pistols, beat a negro who was sleeping in a wagon on the campgrounds, cursed and mimicked the preachers, and made things so intensely unpleasant that it was resolved to break up the meeting, which had been in progress but a short time. Among the sufferers was one of the estimable young ladies of this community, whose saddle was cut literally to pieces and it was this cowardly act, more than anything else, has aroused the indignation of every good citizen. My informants are confident that several of these villains are known and they say that the sheriff of Burnet County is a terror when he goes on the warpath. Let us hope that these "bloods" will get the punishment (which is entirely too light), inflicted upon disturbers of religious worship and malicious destroyers of property.

MARBLE FALLS

7,000 (approximate) • (830) • About 9 miles from Smithwick

Marble Falls is covered at length in the Hermit of the Hills/Highland Lakes trip, so only a few pieces of trivia are offered here:

- Some people say that the area around Marble Falls was supposed to have been the first dry land in the world.
- After Colonel Charles J. Todd's ill-fated attempt to establish a town at Marble Falls (although he managed to sell several lots for $200 apiece), a Colonel Dale came down to Burnet County in the summer of 1860 to buy land. Representing a St. Louis manufacturing firm looking to build a woolen factory somewhere contiguous to the wool-producing section, Dale was attracted to the Marble Falls of the Colorado for their obvious power-producing capacity. But Colonel Todd held out for too dear a price, and Dale turned to Smithwick and his mill on the Colorado, offering him the aforementioned $12,000 figure. Itching for new worlds to conquer, Smithwick accepted this handsome offer. Dale went back to St. Louis to report to his company, get the cash for the purchase, and obtain the requisite machinery. That winter brought the victory of Lincoln and the first of the thirteen ordinances of secession passed by the rebelling states, and the Dale deal fell through.

- Noah Smithwick described the first Fourth of July celebration held at the Marble Falls, in 1854:

> Preparations on a scale proportionate to the place and the occasion were inaugurated several weeks in advance. Meetings were held, committees appointed with power to levy contributions indiscriminately, everybody cheerfully complying with the demands thereof and faithfully carrying out the parts assigned. The mills were called on for flour, and some of the Mormon ladies who were famous cooks manufactured it into bread. The Burnet merchants gave freely of their groceries. Old man Hirston, who lived on the creek which bears his name, a few miles below town, was put down for a wagon load of roasting ears; other farmers brought loads of watermelons and canteloupes, together with such vegetables as were on hand. Huntsmen brought in venison and wild turkeys, and beef and pork galore were advanced. Nor were more delicate viands wanting; there were pound cakes worthy of the name, warranted full weight, that deluding inflationist, baking powder, not having, as yet, found its way into that neck of the woods. There were wild grape pies and dewberry pies and wild plum pies; as yet there was no cultivated fruit to be had except dried fruit, which was very scarce and high.
>
> Several families from Burnet, among them the Vandevers and McGills, went down beforehand and camped on the ground to superintend the final arrangements. There was a wide spreading arbor covered with brush, beneath which seats and a speaker's stand were arranged, the ground being carpeted with a thick layer of sawdust, which served for a dancing floor. People came from far and near, on foot, on horseback, in carriages and farm wagons. None stayed away for want of conveyance, and the seating power of the spacious arbor was taxed to its utmost.
>
> The first number on the programme was a national salute fired from holes drilled in the rock. The band, consisting of a lone fiddle manipulated by Jabez Brown, then played "Yankee Doodle" and "Hail Columbia," the only national airs in his repertoire. The literary exercises began with the reading of the Declaration of Independence by the young son of the writer, a lad of fourteen, one of Professor Dixon's pupils, whom the professor had carefully drilled for the occasion.
>
> Dr. Moore, the orator of the day, then took the stand. He was as long winded as a silver senator. His stentorian voice rolled out from his perspiring visage, contesting supremacy with the falls, while his rotund figure shook with the energy of his gesticulation. The sun mounted the zenith, and stooping far over to the westward, peered curiously beneath the arbor to see what all the noise was about. Still the doctor's sonorous voice rang out the paean of liberty above the nodding heads of the weary audience, mingling with the roar of the water and reverberating among the distant hills. At last it was finished, and the famished multitude made a rush for the dinner which had long been waiting, the odor therefrom aggravating the impatience of the throng, to a large number of which the dinner was the principal feature of the occasion, they presumably having risen early and breakfasted on the anticipation of the feast. But there was enough and to spare for supper and breakfast for those who remained to participate in the sawdust dance which closed the performance. Long before night a space was cleared of seats and Jabez Brown took his place on the stand and sawed out reels, which he also called, until daylight the next morning, occasionally varying the programme by singing, in a strong, musical, though uncultivated voice, "The Maid of Monterey" and "The Destruction of Sennacherib."

Wight and the Mormons had earlier been attracted to the Marble Falls; a February 1851 scouting party had chosen a location on the river near the falls. But the colony didn't stay there long, as Wight related in a letter. "We stopped on the Colorado river which we anticipated was a pleasant place to stop till we made choice of a place on which to locate. In an unexpected moment the spring of water failed and weather being extremely dry and hot and not having nother but river water and being exposed to the heat for fear that sickness would again persue us we made a sudden effort to find good water which we found here in great abundance."

"Here" was a spot on Hamilton Creek about eight miles north of the Marble Falls, to be known thereafter as the Mormon Mills.

To continue the trip, go to the intersection of US 281 and FM 1431. Proceed two blocks north on US 281 to the intersection with Mormon Mills Road, marked by a four-way light, and turn right, and then immediately veer left to get to Mormon Mills.

MORMON MILLS

Burnet County • About 6 miles from Marble Falls

About six miles north of Marble Falls on Mormon Mills Road, you cross Hamilton Creek. The Mormon cemetery lies up on the west bank of the creek just north of this low-water bridge, hidden from sight on private property. It was here along scenic Hamilton Creek that the Mormons had settled by July 1851. Go another couple hundred feet and you see a wide blue pond, a historical marker on the left between the road and the creek, and a tree-obscured view of the Hamilton Falls, which form the pond.

Smithwick described the falls as follows: "A mountain had been cleft from north to south, to permit the stream to pass through, and then from east to west, the southern portion having been entirely removed so that the almost perpendicular walls between which flowed the creek, turned away at right angles at the mouth of the gorge, where the stream fell over a precipice twenty-eight feet or more in height into a deep pool below; thence rippling away between great banks, shaded by the various trees indigenous to the country."

Today you see a several-tiered limestone cliff, which is the breaking point of a long limestone chute. Several streams of water course over its edge, breaking into smaller rivulets on their stair-step path down to the 2.5-acre pool. The chute's east bluff is conveniently cut away for the roadside viewer; the west bluff continues on for a considerable distance. You have to settle for a partially obscured glimpse of the falls, for they are on private property very explicitly posted with "No Trespassing" signs, but fortunately there is no way for the signs to diminish the melodic tumbling of the waters. It should still be easy to see why the Mormons settled here.

This was the finest land along Hamilton Creek, originally granted to Conrad Rohrer, a German bachelor from Pennsylvania, in compensation for his services in the Texas Revolution. Rohrer, unfortunately, was killed by Indians in the same year of his grant, 1836, and never cast an eye on the land.

Once settled, the Mormon colony built a new set of mills and shops, but not without problems. They had lost their grain-grinding burrs in the Zodiac floods. Since they had no money to buy new ones, they went out to a nearby quarry and got out blocks of marble, from which they manufactured burrs that sufficed for grinding corn but required frequent dressing.

Smithwick picks up the story: "Old Lyman Wight, the high priest, set about the task of recovering the lost stones. After wrestling alone with the spirits for some little time he arose one morning with joy in his heart, and summoning his people, announced to them that he had a revelation, and bidding them take spades and crowbars and follow him, set out to locate the millstones. Straight ahead he bore as one in a dream, his divining rod in his hand; his awestruck disciples following in silence. Pausing at last in the middle of the sand bar deposited by the flood, he stuck his rod down.

"'Dig right here,' he commanded. His followers, never doubting, set to work, and upon removing a few feet of sand, lo and behold, there were revealed the buried millstones. Wight said he saw them in a vision and his followers believed it."

With the recovered stones in place, the Mormons increased their grinding activities, adding a sawmill and turning lathes, with which they manufactured chairs, tables, and all other manner of furniture, supplying the whole countryside. Most of their furniture was made from hackberry wood, which being so white in color required frequent washing to preserve its purity.

Smithwick told another story about this furniture. "One lady in Burnet, to obviate the necessity of such frequent cleaning, concluded to paint her chairs; that was before the days of chemical paint. We bought the pigment and reduced it with linseed oil. This lady, having no oil, and arguing that oil was oil and so was butter, during the summer, mixed her paint with butter and applied the combination to her chairs; the effect can be better imagined than described."

In addition to the furniture business, they operated a farm and the women made willow baskets for sale. Within two months of opening, customers' wagons were filling the campgrounds below the large pool, including some of his Zodiac customers. But Wight was dissatisfied with the small amount of business he received from nearby Fort Croghan. In spite of their industrious habits and frugal living, the Saints fell deeper into debt.

They were also plagued by Indian raids. Several times their horses and oxen were stolen and their milk cows were killed. Members of nearby families were slain or kidnapped.

Disease also plagued the colony. Wight did his best to stem its tide through the performing of "miracles," but in spite of his best efforts, twenty-three of the faithful ended up buried along the ridge half a mile downstream from the mill. Smithwick told of one of Wight's healing sessions, as described to him by an eyewitness.

A boy fell from a tree and broke his leg. He was taken to the council chamber and the elder and his council were summoned. They laid their hands upon the broken limb and prayed; the boy then arose and walked. When the narrator had finished . . . I looked him searchingly in the face and said:

"Did you feel of that leg and satisfy yourself that it was really broken?"

"No, I didn't; but 'the twelve' did and they said it was broken," he replied, with an air of wonder that any one should have the audacity to question a verdict rendered by such an authority.

"I'm glad you didn't," said I, "for if you had told me that you yourself felt of that boy's leg and found it broken, I should never believe another word you speak."

The poor dupe looked as if thunderstruck. I was not so much surprised at him, but there were some really intelligent men among them, and it was a mystery to me how they could lend themselves to such a course, when there was so little to be gained by it.

By the late fall of 1853, the faithful were on the move again. Wight had never obtained a deed from the land's owner, W. H. Magill, and so the site was sold to Noah Smithwick, who confessed to "having all my life had a penchant for mills." While a youth, Smithwick became fascinated with windmills and whirligigs and constructed a creek-driven circular saw that he used to turn out considerable quantities of cornstalk lumber.

Smithwick described his newly acquired mill, which stood

> just at the foot of the falls on the east [bank, the roadside bank you are just a stone's throw from], a three-story frame building, with which it was connected by a gangway. A patriarchal pecan tree lifted its stately head beside the building, caressing it with its slender branches. On the upper side, connected with the falls by a flume, rose the huge overshot wheel, twenty-six feet in diameter, which furnished the power for the mill. The machinery was mostly of the rudest, clumsiest kind, manufactured by the Mormons of such material as was obtainable from natural sources. Great, clumsy, rattling wooden cog wheels and drum and fly-wheels filled up the lower stories, the upper one containing a small corn crackermill and an old up-and-down sash saw, which, after all, had this advantage over the circular saw, that it could handle large timber.

Smithwick and nephew John Hubbard decided to throw out the sawmill, since there was no good milling timber in the vicinity. Then they reorganized the machinery, throwing out all the old wooden cog work and replacing it with cast-iron gearings, a ton's worth. While they were at it, they replaced the overshot wheel with another that was twenty-eight feet in diameter! They also built a rock store building here.

"We then put in a new set of burrs and added bolting works, the first flouring mill west of Georgetown," Smithwick related years later. "This gave a new direction to the farming interest, and soon the rattle of the [wheat] threshing machine was heard in the land, and the reign of the corn-dodger [corn pone] was over in those parts. People came from all points to have their grain ground, and the capacity of the mill being very limited, sometimes when the mill was crowded they had to wait several days for their turn. Those who lived at a distance, many of them thirty or forty miles, struck camp and stayed it out. The Germans came from Fredericksburg. Like other German colonists, they had a hard scramble for the first few years, their crops failing, and for want of a knowledge of the use of firearms they were unable to utilize the game. Many of them gave away their children to keep them from starving."

Farmers waiting for their grain to be milled were not the only visitors to the Mormon Mills while it was under Smithwick's ownership. Political candidates in the election of 1854 managed to penetrate the dense cedar brakes surrounding the mill, as did Gail Borden of condensed milk fame, whom Smithwick had known in San Felipe de Austin back in the 1820s when Borden was just a blacksmith. Lately, Borden had been to Europe in the interest of condensed milk, and he had also taken up the practice of homeopathic medicine and begun prefixing his name with the title "Dr." But Borden's business in Burnet County had to do with gold. He owned land located on Sandy Creek, and gold particles had been found in the creek, which had the good "doctor" excited and dreaming of vast wealth. But the gold mines didn't pan out.

While visiting Smithwick, Borden imparted to him the great secret of his school of medicine:

It is no use to be a doctor unless you put on the airs of one. Nine times out of ten sickness is caused by overeating or eating unwholesome food, but a patient gets angry if you tell him so; you must humor him. This I do by taking one grain of calomel [a purgative] and divide it into infinitesimel parts, adding sufficient starch to each part to make one of those little pellets (exhibiting a little vial of tiny white pills), then glaze them over with sugar. In prescribing for a patient I caution him about his diet, warning him that the pills have calomel in them. Well, the result is that he abstains from hurtful articles of food, which is all he needs to do anyway. But I have strong medicine to use in cases of need.

Sounds like good advice today.

Smithwick sold this property and moved in 1855 to the community that now bears his name. The mill was demolished in 1902; the wooden mill dam that turned the creek toward the flume burned the same year. The last of the old Mormon buildings burned in 1915. In 1935, the landowners sold the stone walls and chimney from Smithwick's store to the Daughters of the Republic of Texas, who used the stones to build a cabin in Houston's Hermann Park.

The placidly flowing creek we see here most of the time turns occasionally into a beast. Hamilton Creek drains quite a scope of country, and when swollen by heavy rains, the runoff becomes congested within the narrow gorge above the falls. The creek then rises rapidly, coming down in a solid wall of water that pours over the falls like a little Niagara. Smithwick related,

I have often seen the creek, which is ordinarily a trivial stream, become a torrent within a few minutes. On one occasion a party of sightseers had a narrow escape. Having wended their way up into the gorge, along the margin of the shallow stream, they were startled by a roar above them, and the guide being acquainted with the vagaries of the stream, ordered them to climb for their lives. Laying hold of the bushes in the face of the steep declivity, they scrambled up out of harm's way and watched the angry flood of waters rush past and leap the falls with a report like thunder, sending up clouds of spray.

But back to the Mormons. A few of them stayed with Smithwick at the mill; the rest moved on. Before we resume our retracing of their wanderings, let us listen to Smithwick's estimation of the Mormons.

I found them just the same as other people in matters of business. While some of them were honest and industrious, others were shiftless and unreliable; and this must ever prove a potent argument against community holdings—the thriftless got just as much as the thrifty. But though the industrious saint was still forced to contribute to the support of his idle brother, he drew the line to exclude the worthless dog that is generally considered an indispensable adjunct to thriftlessness, the canine family being conspicuous by its absence about the domicile of the Mormon. Nor was there anything objectionable in the Mormons as neighbors. If there were any polygamous families, I did not know of them. To still further emphasize the perfect equality of all members of the society, all titles of respect were discarded, men and women being universally called by their first names. And these first names, by the way, were perhaps the most striking peculiarity about the Mormons. The proselytes were permitted to retain their gentile names, but those born in the fold received their names from the Book of Mormon; and have no counterpart elsewhere. There were Abinadi, Maroni, Luami, Lamoni, Romali, Cornoman and many others equally original. The female children, however, were apparently not permitted to participate in this saintly nomenclature. It might be that women cut no figure in the Book of Mormon; at any rate, there was nothing distinctive in the names of girls.

So, the Mormons were on the trail again. For your part, return to Marble Falls and take FM 1431 west to Kingsland.

One last story as you leave Marble Falls. About four miles south of Marble Falls, on the old wagon road to Smithwick, is the infamous Dead Man's Hole, a 160-foot-deep cavern into which many a poor unfortunate's body is supposed to have been dumped during the Civil War, victim of the bushwhackers. Bushwhackers were a loose assortment of anti-secessionists, army deserters, draft dodgers, and lowlifes who used the war as an excuse to rob and kill anyone who crossed their path. Judge John R. Scott, robbed of $2,000 and thrown dead down the hole, was supposedly only one of many bushwhacker victims thrown into the hole. In early years, the cavern contained some type of deadly gas, which prevented its exploration. A few years after the war, however, it is said that an expedition successfully reached the bottom of Dead Man's Hole and brought up two sacks full of bones, of the human variety. More sober assessments of the hole's past question the number of men actually thrown into the hole; instead of seventeen victims, they cite only three known victims.

To visit Dead Man's Hole, take US 281 south from the Colorado River Bridge at Marble Falls for two miles to the intersection with RR 2147 East and turn left. Once on RR 2147 East, you cross Flat Rock Creek in half a mile. Immediately after crossing the creek, turn right onto County Road 401. In about another half mile, you'll see the entrance to the hole area on your left.

GRANITE MOUNTAIN

FM 1431, about 0.5 miles west of Marble Falls

Just west of Marble Falls you pass the Granite Mountain, home of the state capitol building's granite. Indians swapped the rock to its first white owners for a couple of acres elsewhere. To cut down on building costs, capitol contractors arranged for the use of convict labor at the quarry. Organized labor objected, so the contractors sent to Scotland for stonecutters. Over 15,000 railroad carloads of granite went into the walls and dome of the capitol. Early owner and Burnet County physician Dr. George Jackson McFarland traded it for a team of horses and a buggy, explaining that "There was not enough grass on the whole mountain to support one cow." Another owner, G. W. Lacy, once tried to trade this mountain of granite for a good saddle horse. He got no takers. That was bc (before the capitol). In 1890, he sold out for $90,000. Granite Mountain has furnished stone for buildings, monuments, the Galveston seawall, and other projects all over the state, the nation, and the world, yet the great dome looks barely disturbed. There are centuries' worth of granite left here in the largest quarry of its kind in the United States.

NIGHTENGALE ARCHEOLOGICAL CENTER

Burnet County Rd. 126, off FM 1431 • 800-776-5272, ext. 8001 • www. lcra.org • Guided tours on second and fourth Saturdays, February through November and by appointment • Donations accepted

This ten-acre wooded site on Lower Colorado River Authority land on Lake LBJ is the only public archeological site on the Colorado River and is administered by the Llano Uplift Archeological Society. Humans have inhabited this site for at least ten thousand years. It was discovered in 1988 when vandals were nabbed stealing artifacts and is now a state archeological landmark. Excavations have since turned up over one hundred thousand artifacts, including knapped stone tools, grinding stones, and bone fragments. The museum and education center displays prehistoric artifacts, a field-school excavation site is on display, and an outdoor trail goes through nomadic campsites that date back at least five thousand years.

KINGSLAND

Llano County • 4,500 (approximate) • About 13 miles from Marble Falls

Kingsland was first known as Kingsville and was named for Martin King, who bought this tract of land in 1877. By the 1880s, a store had been established here, along with a couple of saloons. In that decade, a great business rivalry developed between Kingsville and Buzzard Roost (aka Gainsville), located across the river and several miles northwest. Buzzard Roost had a post office, gin, and store. The rivalry between the towns was resolved in favor of Kingsville when Kingsville merchant J. F. Banks bought the Buzzard Roost gin and store and moved them to Kingsville.

Prosperity really caught up with Kingsville in 1892, when the Burnet-to-Llano branch of the Austin and Northwestern railroad came through town. J. F. Banks built a commodious stone store near the depot that same year. The town's name was changed to Kingsland sometime between 1892 and 1901; the post office already had a Kingsville in Kleberg County in South Texas. Kingsland became a hog-and-cattle shipping center with the railroad's arrival. Located at the confluence of the Llano and Colorado Rivers, this area has long been a popular fishing spot. The Austin and Northwestern began running excursion trains out here soon after the tracks were laid. Governor Hogg was among the avid anglers who made the trip out from Austin. In 1901, the Austin and Northwestern built a resort hotel here: the Antlers Hotel, named for the Antlers Hotel in Colorado Springs, Colorado.

THE ANTLERS HOTEL

1001 King St., just off FM 1431 • 800-383-0007 • www.theantlers .com • B&B

Families from across the state came to vacation at the Antlers, situated beside the railroad tracks on the shores of the Colorado River, where local families came to picnic. After a while, ownership of the hotel changed hands. It is about all that remains of old Kingsland. It is located on your right, just after you cross the railroad tracks on the western edge of Kingsland, a frame two-story affair, with twin front porches running the length of its front. Accommodations include several converted train cabooses, a surefire hit with kids. There is also a boat slip.

The Antlers Hotel is the anchor of the Kingsland Historic Railroad District, which also includes a railroad crew house (west of the hotel), the old Muldoon Station, and an old I&GN "combine" car.

The Kingsland Bridge that spans the Colorado River near the point where it joins the Llano River was built in the 1890s and rebuilt in 1963. The old granite piers of the original bridge were incorporated into the present concrete bridge.

Kingsland went into something of an eclipse until Highland Lakes tourists gave it a new shot of life several decades ago. Kingsland now relies on tourists, retirees, and its many second-home owners for business. But the railroad across the lake with its pink granite pillars still stands.

THE SLAB

At the end of FM 3404, about 1.5 miles west of FM 1431 • Open daily • Free • W

FM 3404 crosses the Llano River about eight miles above its junction with the Colorado and peters into an unimproved county road. At this point, the Llano runs over (and through) granite outcroppings and wide sandy beaches. This is a popular picnicking, swimming, and wading area. There are no restrooms or drinking water.

ANNUAL EVENT

JULY

AQUA-BOOM CELEBRATION

388-6211 (Kingsland/Lake LBJ Chamber of Commerce) • www.kingslandchamber.org • Weekend nearest July 4 • The celebration includes ski shows, a water parade, boat races, and fireworks.

Turn left on FM 2900 in Kingsland and cross the Llano River branch of the lake. Once across the bridge, take the first right (Packsaddle Mountain Road), a few feet past Lakewood Forest Subdivision and Comanche Rancheros.

Packsaddle Mountain Road turns to gravel after a bit but offers a great close-up view of Packsaddle Mountain as you skirt its edges, after about six miles on the road. This road can be very rough and washboarded after a rain, so be prepared to go slow. Packsaddle has a plethora of violent and romantic legends and stories surrounding it; these stories are told in the Hermit of the Hills trip.

Turn right onto SH 71 and head toward Llano.

Shortly thereafter you cross Honey Creek, upon the banks of which the Mormons camped on December 4, 1853, before resuming their journey toward the old German settlement at Castell. The road to Buzzard Roost/Gainsville, about four miles north of the Honey Creek Crossing and running east off SH 71, is marked only by a three-way intersection sign. Nothing is left at the old town site.

On your left is Riley Mountain, whose summit is Dancer Peak, named for the Reverend Jonas Dancer, who established a Methodist church on nearby Honey

Creek, which rises from several sources along the base of Riley Mountain. Dancer had purchased the Wight colony's mill in Austin in 1847. He attempted to make the mill more secure against flooding, but his solution only worsened the damage the next time the Colorado River flooded.

Noah Smithwick takes up the story at this point:

> When the flood subsided, Parson Dancer got out his machinery and prepared to set it up again. He went around among the citizens soliciting aid to rebuild the mill and raise the fender higher. Feeling the necessity of a mill, the people turned in and helped, raising the fender clear above the high water mark. But the Colorado was not a stream to be defied by man. The next large flood swept down against the imposing structure, sweeping it from its foundation and burying the mill under the debris. With indomitable courage, Dancer prepared to dig out his mill and set it up again; arguing that in watching the course of the flood, he saw where he had erred in his former plans, and felt sure he could make it secure next time. But the people were not so sanguine of the success of the scheme and refused to lend assistance.

With no help forthcoming, Dancer decided to move westward in 1852. Dancer was killed by Indians on May 23, 1859, probably the first white man killed by Indians in Llano County (see Click Community). Ironically, his daughter, Mathilda Friend, was killed in the infamous Legion Valley massacre of 1868 (see Oxford).

LLANO

Llano County Seat • 4,000 (approximate) • (325) • About 21 miles from Kingsland

Llano, which is (and always has been) the seat of government of Llano County, was founded in 1855. Several other settlements, including Castell, Tow, and Bluffton, had already been founded in the area. Among the first settlers of Llano were John Oatman Sr. and Amariah Wilson. Indians still raided the countryside, and in that first year the Llano pioneers lost their clothes to the raiders. Llano County was part of the vast Fisher-Miller tract, which was to have been settled by German Adelsverein Society colonists. That tract extended northward into San Saba, Menard, and other counties. Castell, which was as far north as the first wave of Germans got, was on the southern edge of this tract.

Llano County was created from parts of Bexar and Gillespie counties in 1856 and was named for the river that courses through it from west to east. Llano means "plains" in Spanish; although Llano County is ruggedly hilly, the Llano River rises in the flatland counties of Sutton and Schleicher. One explanation lies in an old (1711) Spanish name for the river, "Rio de las Chanas," or River of the Chanas. The Chanas were a band of Tonkawa Indians that lived in the area. In 1754, the Spanish explorer Pedro de Rabago y Teran identified the river on his map of Texas as the "Sanas" River. *Sano* means "healthy" in Spanish, and *sanas* would mean two or more healthy females. Over the years, the local explanation goes, the phonetic similarity between "chanas" and "llano" caused confusion and led to the present name, Llano.

The location of the new county seat was hotly contested. Clement Oatman was appointed commissioner of the new county, and as such was charged with holding an election to establish the county seat and to elect the first county officials. The contest narrowed to two sites: the present-day town of Llano built on land donated by John Oatman Sr. and Amariah Wilson, and a site on Wright Creek north of Llano that was advocated by Uncle Dave Cowan and the Tow Valley/Bluffton crowd, who wouldn't have to cross the Llano River to get to the courthouse. The Llano River was not always easy to cross.

Clement Oatman decreed that the county seat election be held under a live oak tree on the south side of the river (near the south end of the SH 16/SH 71 bridge across the river) on June 14, 1856. On the morning of the election, Oatman sent a boy down to the river to draw a bucket of water so that the thirsty arriving voters could refresh themselves. When Cowan and the Tow Valley/Bluffton crowd arrived, they were thirsty and sampled the bucket of water from the Llano. After tasting it very deliberately, Cowan said, "Boys, boys, it won't do to have our county seat here for this water is unhealthy, there are bugs in it." Whereupon he walked to his horse, rummaged about in his saddlebags, pulled out a quart of moonshine, and poured it into the bucket of water so as to "kill the bugs."

Theatrics notwithstanding, the Wright Creek faction lost the election, and the county seat ended up here on the river, which was probably just as well. In 1856, Wright Creek was a bold stream considered always able to supply a good-sized town. Now it only flows during the rainy season. Llano finally erected a bridge across the river for the convenience of southbound travelers (the courthouse is located on the south side of the river), but it was not needed on two recent occasions; the Llano River ran bone-dry in 1952 and 1956.

The county was plagued by Indian attacks from the very beginning, which is not surprising, since the Comanches regarded the white settlers as interlopers on their homeland.

On Saturday evening, April 19, 1856, three Indians were seen near Mr. Wright's, on Sandy Creek. On Monday night following, they drove off eight or ten head of horses from J. W. Riley (of Riley Mountain), in the same neighborhood. On Tuesday morning, two young men, David and George Riley, pursued them, two or three miles from this neighborhood, and found the horses secreted in a dense thicket. They took the horses but saw no Indians. Upon further examination by the Riley men, and Jonas Dancer, they found moccasin tracks leading off from the place where the horses were secreted.

The attacks were so frequent that in June 1858, Governor Hardin Runnels authorized Jno. Williams to raise twenty men, for sixty days, for the protection of Llano and San Saba counties from Indian hostilities. Robert Green, just from the Rangers' camp, presented Governor Runnels with a portion of the armor worn by Iron Jacket. It seems that the bullets fired at him from Colt revolvers did not penetrate the armor, but those fired from the Rangers passed through his shield, armor and body. A public demonstration was made by the Comanches residing on their North Texas reservation in vindicating themselves from the charges made against their fealty to Southern institutions.

On Tuesday, February 8, 1859, the village of Llano and the surrounding country were thrown into a state of excitement by the reports that the country was full of Indians, and that they had shot six or eight head of horses and driven off as many more, besides as many more were missing. A company was immediately formed of ten or twelve men, and on repairing to the ranch of Thomas Wright on the north side of the Llano river, about thirteen miles from the village of Llano, they found the report to be too true. Upon making search for the tracks, the company found that they directed to a certain pass in what is called the Narrows of the San Saba River, but the Indians had fired the grass, which completely obliterated their travel, and it was further discovered that the Indians separated and crossed over to the settlements on the south side of the Llano River, stealing B. Berry's cavayard of some twenty or thirty horses, and also Mr. Eacre's horses were taken, besides picking up the best horses in the settlement. The Indians were seen on Tuesday morning last about five miles from where the depredations were committed, by a person who was at a distance from them and was not aware that there were any Indians in the country and therefore took no notice of them and thought that they were the owners of the horses, drifting or moving them to a new range. They then passed up on the divide between the Sandys and Llano rivers, firing the grass behind them, entirely obliterating their sign.

On that same Tuesday, they made a break on Mr. Moss's horses on Hickory Creek and succeeded in capturing several fine horses, and killing two or three, while several more were missing from the same cavayard that were also thought to have been stolen, and two Indians were discovered by Moss and chased by him into the mountains. The supposition is that they would recross the Llano River and pass out by the San Fernando Mountain, thence by the mouth of the Concho, and then north to their homes.

A party of the same company of Indians made at the same time a break on the Smoothing Iron settlements and stole all, or nearly all, the horses, having taken some seventeen head from Mr. Rainbolt, that being the entire number of the horses he owned. The best estimates were that they had stolen at least one hundred head of horses, and if all the horses, or two-thirds of them, were stolen that were missing and could not be found, there had certainly been stolen from Llano County from 200 to 225 head of horses at least, worth at the lowest calculations from $12,000 to $15,000, there being scarcely a Spanish horse among them, besides killing several head of cattle.

The settlers had no idea how many Indians came into the country, but they guessed, based on some years' experience of Indian depredations on the frontier, that they came in bodies of from twenty to fifty, and they divided into smaller bodies of from three to six, when they got into the settlements, and after committing their depredations returned to a place of general rendezvous some two or three hundred miles from the settlements.

They seemed to be bolder than ever in that foray, from the fact that they had stolen all the horses in San Saba County and always managed to get away without being chastised or even pursued any distance, and it could be seen by a glance at the map of Texas that they had to pass through that country to get into the Llano country. There were seven or eight of them that walked around within ten feet of a house while the inmates were asleep, as discovered next morning by the moccasin tracks of the Indians.

Information relative to the Indians was given to Captain Williams and the Texas Rangers, who immediately started in what proved to be a fruitless pursuit, for he had an insufficient number of men. An independent company was again formed in the county and were pursuing them, but with little hope of finding them, as they were so poorly mounted, due to the fact that the Indians had stolen all of the best horses in the upper portion of the county.

Despite the travails, by 1860 Llano had stores, a hotel, and plenty of saloons, but no churches. In 1861, Llano County approved the Texas Ordinance of Secession by 65 percent, one of the largest percentages on the frontier. With the Civil War, Indian attacks increased. Three Confederate Army companies were raised in the county; so many of the men were away fighting, leaving many farms as easy targets for the Comanches. For instance, in July 1863, Comanches entered into Llano town itself and took off all they could and killed twenty-odd horses.

In December 1870, the district court at Llano was broken up by reports of Indian raids. Business was suspended by the judge to allow citizens to hasten to their homes. A number of horses had been stolen in Llano and adjoining counties.

A home guard was again formed to protect the county, but the county's schools were closed in April 1872 because of Indian attacks, and Comanche bands raged through the county until the decisive (but not the last) battle atop Packsaddle Mountain in 1873.

You would not expect a county known as the "Colorado of Texas" to be heavily farmed, and Llano County has never had more than 20 percent of its 941-square-mile area in cultivation. Llano County residents have traditionally been stock raisers, and many of the ranchers, such as the Moss brothers (see the Hermit of the Hills trip), drove thousands of steers north during the great cattle-drive era. Llano was at the edge of the frontier until 1875.

A correspondent for the *San Antonio Herald* did not have much good to say about the prospects of making a living in Llano County in the fall of 1876.

> It is enough for me to say that nearly the whole of Llano County over which we have roamed so far is good for nothing under the sun so far as heard from. In some portions of the valley there are enterprising and thrifty ranchmen engaged primarily in the cattle traffic. Among those we have met are the Moss brothers and they are all successful in their pursuits. There are four brothers located in different valleys and they all have comfortable and commodious houses, and possess in their surroundings evidences of thrift and industry not found in all the ranchos in this county. Few are engaged in farming and these only to raising what is actually necessary for home consumption, and Llano County will never be anything but a cattle and hog raising country unless the mines, which some claim are rich in gold and silver, should prove to be big bonanzas.

As was typical with Texas frontier towns and counties, Llano the city and Llano the county both had their share of banditry and rustling and feuding. "Llano boys," as they were called, thought themselves pretty tough, wherever they went.

On February 4, 1876, a shooting scrape occurred on Congress Avenue in Austin between a man named Hanna, of Llano, and Austin's infamous Ben Thompson. Three or four men of the rowdy order, claiming to be from Llano, had been hunting a fight during the day, and in the forenoon had pulled out their pistols in a saloon and bluffed around generally, saying that they wanted to show the Austin fighters the Llano style of fighting. They especially wanted to encounter someone in Austin that had a reputation for fighting, and they finally met up with Ben Thompson on the sidewalk outside of the saloon, where they used offensive language and threw out a general invitation for a fight. Thompson replied that he knew nothing of Texas fighters; that he was down here from Boston for his health, but that he did not apprehend that the

Llanoites could fight any better than anyone else. Hanna thought they could and said, "If you come up there we will show you how it is done." Thompson said, "If I should come up there I would serve the boys just so," drawing his hand across Hanna's face gently. Instantly Hanna struck Ben with his fist, knocking off his hat, whereupon pistols were drawn and the firing commenced. Some witnesses said that Hanna fired first, while others claimed that he attempted to fire but his pistol would not go off. Thompson at this time was on the sidewalk, and Hanna had stepped down into the gutter behind a post and seemed to be trying to get his pistol to revolve. While thus engaged, Thompson fired at him, the ball entering his neck and passing through one ear. Hanna then started across the street, and having reached the middle of the street, Thompson fired another shot, which passed through Hanna's side. Hanna then continued his retreat to the opposite sidewalk and the fight ended. Both men were taken to the mayor's office. Hanna's wounds, which were not considered dangerous, were dressed, and Thompson was put under bond for his appearance on trial.

Violence in Llano County was so commonplace that folks had trouble remembering the names of all the victims. On August 31, 1876, the *Austin Daily Statesman* commented,

Frank Bean of Llano reports the killing of a man whose name he can't remember last week. He was in the company of a stockman named Neal Cane, and got 30 buckshot in his breast, dying instantly.

That man was in fact Henry Burts. Burts was in Bell's saloon and had become somewhat intoxicated; he made some remarks derogatory to the character of Dept. Sheriff Joseph Leverett, when Henry Leverett, who was in the saloon, made some reply, and Burts commenced abusing him, telling him that he was as much a rascal and scoundrel as his brother. Leverett went out of the saloon, and Burts followed him, seeming to be trying to get a fight. Finally Burts drew his pistol and was in the act of shooting when Leverett fired at him with a double barrel shotgun, breaking his neck and killing him instantly.

Earlier that day, August 23, 1876, Robert Smith was found lying dead in the field where he had been gathering corn near Oatmanville (present-day Oak Hill). An inquest was held, and the verdict was that the deceased was stoned to death by Henry Burts. The evidence was strong enough to induce the governor to offer a $250 reward for his apprehension and delivery to the sheriff of Travis County. The murder was a very cold-blooded one, Burts having slight, if any, cause to commit the horrible deed.

In September, Burnet County Sheriff Strickland told the *Austin Daily Statesman* that there was a "bad state of affairs" in Llano County and it was probable that the governor would send Major Jones and a company of Rangers to the county. "A number of desperados and roughs have organized and they are defying all law and order. They have threatened the lives of Mr. Oatman and Mr. Rowntree."

On or about September 12, Nat Moore and his son had a shooting scrape with another man named Moore at their Llano County ranch. The latter Moore had rented land from Nat with the understanding that he would plow it for farming purposes, but he failed to comply with his promise. Nat requested him to vacate and asserted that he kept a lot of men about him who were thieves and were marking and branding other people's cattle and horses. During the day, one of those men called at Nat's house and, after some words, drew a pistol and shot young Moore in the arm and then shot Nat in the leg, at which point young Moore drew his pistol and shot the man dead.

Jones and his force would head for Llano in early October.

Just a few days before Strickland's comments, the *Statesman* ran a letter from a relative of a Joseph Graves Olney, who had recently shot and wounded deputy sheriffs S. B. Martin and Wilson Rowntree in Burnet County. The officers, Olney claimed, had not bothered to identify themselves as such when they stopped him and demanded, with much profanity, that he throw down his gun. Despite having the drop on him, Olney, who was a much better shot, wounded both men. Had they identified themselves, Olney said, there would have been no fight.

An article that ran in the *Burnet Bulletin* told a different story: Martin and Rowntree had gone to Joseph Olney's house to arrest him, but being unacquainted with him, they talked with him a while and passed on, intending to cross the Colorado River from Llano County and return to Burnet. Olney, suspecting that something was wrong, picked up his gun and remarked that he would see whether they crossed the river or not. Martin and Rowntree noticed him following and at once concluded that he was Olney. They rode back, met him, and ordered him to surrender. Olney quickly drew his pistol and fired, missing his aim. Martin and Rowntree then fired. Olney, who was on foot, jumped behind a tree and shot Martin, breaking his left arm above the elbow. Martin then told Rowntree to shoot Olney. Rowntree ran up, put his gun very close to Olney and pulled the trigger, but the gun snapped. Rowntree then attempted to draw his pistol, when Olney shot him. Martin's horse had turned around and was trying to run away, when Olney shot him again. The fight then ceased.

Martin and Rowntree came across the Colorado River and stopped at a vacant house where Rowntree helped Martin dismount. Rowntree moved on to another house and lay down. Sheriff Strickland had been just three miles away, watching for someone whom he wished to arrest. Martin died on September 11. Olney was still at large.

Joseph Olney was born in 1849, in Burleson County. In 1860, his family moved to Burnet County. He enlisted in Company O, Minutemen, in September 1872 and served through January 1873. During the spring of 1874, he became involved in a dispute over cattle and shot a man in Llano County. He was indicted for theft of cattle and assault with intent to murder. In 1875, he was drawn into the Mason County War by the killing of Moses Baird. During the rest of 1875 and 1876, he was opposed to the "mob" faction of Mason and Llano counties. After his gunfight with Martin and Rowntree, Olney fled to New Mexico. During the Lincoln County War in New Mexico, Governor Lew Wallace issued papers for his arrest for the Texas killing. In the fall of 1881, Olney moved to Bowie. There he was killed on December 3, 1884, when his horse fell on him.

Neal Cane, more commonly known as Neal Cain, was not your average "stockman." He was commonly considered to be a rustler, and in late October 1876, the Texas Rangers were very interested in finding him. They thought they would find him at his old man's place about twelve miles northeast of Austin.

At about sunset on October 26, Ed Stewart and Billy Thompson (brother of the famous gambler/gunfighter/Austin City Marshal Ben Thompson) were arrested by ten Texas Rangers commanded by Captain Sparks at old man Cain's, just as they were penning a drove of ninety head of cattle, which they, with several other parties, were driving in the direction of Rockdale for shipment. The Rangers stated that a drove of cattle had been stolen in the counties of Llano, Mason, and Gillespie, and that they had followed the drove from those counties. They did not say who had stolen the cattle, but that they had received a warrant for Stewart, who was known to be one of the principal men in charge of the drove. They arrested Thompson for the killing of a U.S. soldier in Austin about ten years earlier, and for the killing of a sheriff in Ellsworth, Kansas. The Rangers stated that the drove of cattle had been separated somewhere near Austin, and that one portion had been regularly inspected and passed near the city, and the other, which had all been stolen, had been passed around the city. Stewart and Thompson were found with the latter drove. The Rangers came upon the men at Cain's just as they were penning the cattle for the night, and when they rushed upon them, Stewart and several others attempted to escape, and a few shots were fired at Stewart, who then surrendered. He and Thompson had on no arms at the time of their arrest. The Rangers expected to find George Gladden but did not. They had also hoped to arrest Neal Cain, and though they got sight of him, he made his escape. Captain Sparks took charge of both droves of cattle and brought them into Austin the next day. Stewart and Thompson were brought to Austin and lodged in jail. Thompson was arrested on a warrant charging him with the theft of cattle, but he stated that he had no connection with the men who were suspected of driving stolen cattle out of the country. He said that he had been stopping at Neal Cain's for some weeks past, but that he had nothing to do with his cattle drives. He said that he made no effort at resistance or escape because he did not feel that he was one of the men wanted.

Burnet County Sheriff Strickland arrested Cain a couple of weeks later in Palestine, while Cain was on his way to Kentucky. Sheriff Strickland had passed through Austin, where Captain Sparks told him to be on the lookout for Cain, and fortunately Strickland happened to meet Cain at the railroad depot in Palestine and the arrest was made. A few days later, Cain, John Ringo, and George Gladden were brought to Austin and lodged in the Travis County jail. All three of these prisoners were held in the Austin jail until the courts convened in the respective counties where they were to be tried for the crimes committed.

Cain was assassinated at his home in Taylor, Williamson County, in April 1879, by person or persons unknown, but it was believed that one of the friends of a man whom Cain's brother Jeff had shot and killed about a month earlier did the shooting. Jeff was one of Austin's leading "sporting men."

On the night of June 11, 1877, arsonists torched the house of Llano County district clerk John C. Oatman. Oatman, who kept records at his home, saved the records. But life here was not as cheap as it was in neighboring Mason County, home of the infamous "Hoodoo War," a cattle feud between German-American and Anglo ranchers (see Hermit of the Hills/The Highland Lakes trip). Many early Llano County records were destroyed in the courthouse fire of 1892. But we do know that Llano County ranchers had their share of cattle rustlers to contend with, and that between fifty and one hundred Llano, Burnet, and San Saba ranchers banded together in a vigilante group to kill the rustlers and otherwise rid their country of outlaws.

Just over two months later, a mob shot and killed Walter Wadsworth in the Llano County jail. He was a young man, twenty-one or twenty-two years old, who had been many years in the stock business in the area. He had been arrested a few days earlier by a sheriff's posse from Llano County on a charge of unlawfully handling cattle and had been conveyed to jail, where he was shot through the grates of the prison with shotguns in the side and back. It is supposed that Wadsworth was asleep at the time. It was said by those who had an opportunity of knowing that a case could not have been made out against him.

A few days later, James Taylor was killed by the Rangers for resisting arrest at San Saba, and the day before Henry Hoy was killed by a party led by the sheriffs of Llano and Mason while resisting arrest. Hoy had been in the employ of Wadsworth and Taylor.

By May 1880, the cattle and sheep men of Llano County were at war, the sheep men on the defensive, and in February 1882, the adjutant general visited the scene of the troubles prior to stationing troops there.

On December 10, 1882, a detachment of six Texas Rangers went to Llano to maintain order during the sitting of the district court. Just six months earlier, a pitched battle between the Carter and Coggins families had broken out, the result of a feud that grew out of theft charges, one against the other. The Hatley family had sided with the Cogginses, and the Herridge and the McNutt families stood with the Carters. They had previously gotten very near to coming together several times but were prevented. But on June 14, while district court was going on, the thing came off. The area around the courthouse square was full of horses, wagons, buggies, and people; court trials were a favorite form of entertainment in rural Texas in those days. Members of the Coggins-Hatley party had come to town and had started collecting in the rear of Deputy Miles Barler's store. A group consisting of members of the Carter, Herridge, and McNutt families had also come to town. Word spread through the courthouse crowd that the boys were back in town, and most of the people fled for cover, while the braver ones picked out prime viewing sites. There were eight or nine men on each side, mostly armed with Winchester rifles. It is at this point that details of the shootout diverge, and my version is based on contemporary newspaper accounts. One of the Carter party walked out in open view and told the Coggins boys that if they wanted anything to just open up. It was about one in the afternoon. Sheriff R. A. McIness, from his office in the courthouse, saw that the thing was about to come off, and he told deputies Barler and Sam Stoudenmier (brother of the infamous Dallas Stoudenmier) to see if they could stop it. The two deputies went out in front of the Coggins men, who had their guns up and ready for business, and tried to get them to put their guns down. They said they would not. About that time, they leveled their guns to shoot. Barler and Stoudenmier sprang to one side, just in time to escape a volley from both parties. Since they were peace officers, they decided not to take any stock in the fight and ran around a saddle shop on the east side of the square to get out of harm's way. Barler was a little behind, and just as he turned the corner of the shop, two or three balls struck the corner close to his head. "Look here," Barler said, "do you reckon them devils are shooting at me?" Some men standing close by said it looked mightily like it. He turned and walked back to the corner and stood there a minute. Barler then looked at his pistol and saw there wasn't a load in it. He entered the shop and saw a man stretched out flat as a pancake, face down on the floor. He said he heard the balls striking the shop and threw himself down to avoid being struck by them. It was District Attorney Lessing. A stray ball had come crashing through the plank wall and lodged in the desk where he was working, missing him by about a foot.

Fifty or sixty shots were fired, and eight of them were known to have hit their mark. The rest went crashing through half a dozen houses, riddled a wagon, and killed one or two horses and some pigs. When the battle was over, Henry Hatley lay dead on the street, and "Little Johnny" Coggins was mortally wounded; he died that night. Jack Coggins, Little Johnny's father; Ben Carter; and Jack Herridge were wounded, as well as a bystander known only as Mr. Harwell. The district court had adjourned without any formality but was called ninety minutes later and proceeded with its business.

None of the participants in the pitched battle were brought to justice that day, but about a week later, most of the survivors rode into town, surrendered, and were released on $1,000 bond each.

A requisition for troops to protect the district court at Llano against "lawless bands" was made that same day to the state's attorney general.

Ten months later, Jack Coggins and one of his sons, were riding home to their ranch when they were ambushed by an unknown assailant. The boy was shot in the forehead while Jack was shot in the gut. Both of them lived, but Jack's wound never healed, and he died several years later of complications.

About a month later, on Sunday night, November 11, 1883, Mr. James McLeary, who had strolled a short distance from his house, "was seized by four negroes lying in ambush, thrown down and castrated. The parties were masked, but the unfortunate gentleman believed he recognized two of them. Llano has a tip top criminal record—men will steer around the county," the *San Antonio Light* advised in reporting the gruesome story.

In mid-December 1883, district court was again in session, and fear had been expressed that trouble would come with the court, but everything was quiet there for the time being. Eight Rangers were present to assist in keeping order.

On June 12, 1884, Deputy Stoudenmier shot it out with a local merchant named Swanson, seriously wounding him, for causes unknown.

In 1885, a detachment of Texas Rangers returned to Llano to help Sheriff George Shaw keep order during another trial stemming from the Carter-Coggins feud. The Rangers searched everyone for weapons and separated the Carter and Coggins factions by a neutral seating area. The two factions left the courtroom at separate times. A capable judge brought this Carter-Coggins trial to a peaceful close, aided by the Rangers' stern discipline.

The town of Llano did not have an honest-to-God church building until 1885. Prior to that year, services were held in private homes or in the local schoolhouse. Many of the town's young men and boys enlivened their Sundays by disrupting the worship services of the faithful. Owing to the disorganized state of organized religion on the frontier, God's children in Llano were administered to by an ever-changing assortment of circuit-riding preachers. One Sunday, the Reverend James Moore, a real frontiersman, came to preach. He entered the schoolroom, which had turned sanctuary for the day, with his saddlebags in one hand and his long-barreled Winchester rifle in the other. Drawing his Bible from his saddlebags and setting his rifle on the table-turned-altar, Moore gazed over the crowd calmly and announced, "By the grace of God and Winchester there will be no disturbance to the services today."

Llano remained a dusty, rough-edged cow town until 1886, when the Wakefield Iron and Coal Company of Minneapolis came to town in a big way. Prospecting trips had revealed large deposits of magnetic iron ores scattered across the county, the largest concentration of which was located at Smoothingiron

Mountain, about fifteen miles northwest of Llano as the crow flies. The Wakefield Company and other eastern capitalists who came in on Wakefield's coattails dreamed of making Llano the Birmingham of Texas. Over $300,000 was spent buying up area mineral leases—a considerable amount of money back then, when land sold for a couple of dollars, rather than thousands of dollars, an acre.

These vast iron beds were discovered by geologists Dr. Francis Moore and Dr. J. B. Buckley when engaged in the geological survey of Texas in the winter and spring of 1861.

Dr. Francis Moore wrote from Austin on January 10, 1861,

> I expect to start on a journey today to Llano and Mason counties to examine the Primary region there. I have received specimens of lead ore from that section, indicating that there are valuable deposits of galena in these and the adjoining counties; and I wish to ascertain the extent of the deposits. I want to make the survey as practicably as possible. Science should always be in advance of private enterprise; I cannot perform any duty well unless I continue almost continually in the field. I have been almost continually travelling lately, and camp out in all weather; but I find that I can bear the exposure and fatigues of the camp as well as I could in the army of 1836.

The unhappy war that shortly followed prevented any account of them from being published until 1866. The principal deposit of iron was on the San Fernando, a tributary of the Llano River. Buckley glowingly described it as

> apparently a solid mass of iron which has been upheaved by igneous agency, and extends to unknown depths below. Its elevation above the Llano river is about 300 feet, with a length of about 800 feet, and a width of 500 feet. Immense loose masses of ore lie scattered over its surface and near its borders. It is partly magnetic and partly specular iron ore, being similar to that of the celebrated iron mountains of Missouri, and also being in the Azoic rocks, or those which were made before the appearance of animal life upon our globe. Red felspathic granite, gneiss quartz, talcose and chloritic schists, are the prevailing rocks in its vicinity.
>
> A large deposit of similar ore occurs eight miles from this in a north-westerly direction. Granite ridges nearly surround this deposit, and veins of quartz traverse it in all directions. The chemical analysis of these ores shows that they are nearly a pure oxide of iron and that they contain from sixty to seventy percent of metallic iron, being equal to that of the best iron ore of any country.
>
> Excellent limestone for a flux is abundant within a distance of a few miles. Large deposits of steatite (soap-stone) suitable for furnaces, are in the same county. Post-oak, hickory and other timber, are common, on and around the premises. Iron, manufactured from wood and charcoal, is superior to that made from any other fuel. The abundance and purity of these ores, their situation at and near the surface, rendering the expense of deep excavations unnecessary, thus ensuring large profits to the manufacturer, will ere long, cause them to be worked, and furnish a huge amount of metallic wealth to the State. Here is iron sufficient to make all the railroads needed by Texas and the other Southern States, and also more than enough to build the Southern Pacific Railroad, leaving plenty to supply the wants of the state for ages to come.

Their report, coupled with stories of the region's legendary Spanish gold mines, brought prospectors streaming into Llano County, to the point that in June 1874, the *Fredericksburg Sentinel* declared Llano County "the Texas El Dorado." A Mr. Theodore Tuschinski had been investigating the mineral wealth of Llano and San Saba counties and said that he had found lead ores, their silver value varying from about 3 ounces to the ton to 15.32 ounces per ton, at the Babyhead mine, Wolf Creek, and on Cole Creek, amounting to almost 3 percent of silver—worth about $1,000 per ton.

Besides, he stated, there were fine prospects for gold in various parts of that district since several of its associates were found, for instance, those mineral characters which always indicated or formed the nature of gold, namely, the sulphuret of molybdenum and copper pyrites. The former was a body of an appearance similar to plumbago, but of highly metallic luster, and highly sulphurized.

The *San Antonio Express* said a few days later that the

silver mines of Western Texas are beginning more and more, to attract attention. The silver region seems to include the counties of Gillespie, Mason, Llano, San Saba and Menard. The last issue of the Fredericksburg *Sentinel* says that the editor has seen specimens of ore taken from a mine on Babyhead creek yielding at the rate of one thousand dollars silver per ton of the ore.

They are located in a country where water is plentiful, where timber is bountiful, and where roads can be built with comparatively little cost. The party who own the last named mines have negotiated in New York for a large amount of crushing machinery, which is being shipped directly to Austin for Llano county.

One great benefit in these which can not be found in other argentiferous ores is that their smeltable heat is extremely low when compared with other argentiferous ores, bismuth being a large component part. There is no reason to doubt that these mines will yield a handsome quantity of the precious metal, and when the day arrives for the development, which certainly is not far distant, these counties will be as populous and wealthy as the valley of the San Joaquin, Cal., is at present.

Think, says the *Sentinel*, of ores yielding $1000 per ton of pure silver not yet developed, and only one hundred miles from the State Capital. And it is a much shorter distance to San Antonio, where the railroad will soon extend.

By March 1876, the silver and copper mines of Llano County were being rapidly developed. The machinery to work three different mines on an extensive scale had arrived.

Barney Tiernan, who was working the "Sam Houston mine" in Llano County, sent the *Galveston News* some specimens of the quartz he was getting out. Experts told the *News* that they were what were termed "croppings" of "chloride ore," and that "bromide of silver" is apparent to the naked eye in some of the specimens, and promises of great richness are flattering.

Because of these and other reports, by 1877 Llano County was full of men prospecting for silver. But the promising results reported by these "forty-niners" were dismissed out of hand by state geologist S. B. Buckley after his geological survey of the area: "Much time and money had been uselessly spent for want of a knowledge of geology and mineralogy." He had not found a single good specimen of either gold or silver ore.

The many northern and eastern capitalists who came to Llano in 1886 brought a brand-new snobbish, ostentatious social life with them. The famous Algona hotel was built early in the boom, and it was the hub of the new social lifestyle for Llano and Central Texas. Countless fancy balls, dinners, and parties were held in the grand ballrooms and dining rooms. Of the Algona's eighty rooms, fifty were bedrooms. Built of red brick on the north side of the river, the Algona was named for its builder's hometown of Algona, Iowa. Typical of the vast and rapid changes wrought in Llano by big money, this grand edifice replaced a spread of muddy cattle pens.

Most of the stone and brick buildings in downtown Llano were built during this boom era, replacing the original wooden structures. The Llano Improvement and Furnace Company was organized to promote the north bank of the Llano River, plotting out a large tract of land with plenty of parks and green space. Lots were sold to speculators at highly inflated prices. Some of the streets were given steel-related names: Bessemer, Pittsburg, Sheffield, and Birmingham.

The town was full of hope and optimism. Smoothingiron Mountain was celebrated as "bearing the richest grade of magnetic ore to be found in the world." Then, of course, there was Barringer Hill—the greatest field of rare minerals to be found anyplace in the world—located east of Llano. An iron mine, the Olive Mine, opened about ten miles east of town and actually shipped out a few carloads of ore, one to the state prison's foundry at Rusk and the others to Birmingham, Alabama. The mine had a fat-enough payroll during its few years of operation to attract the attention of one bandit, who ambushed the mine's manager as he was driving the payroll wagon from town back out to the mine. The highwayman killed the manager, Captain Thomas Dunn, and made off with the loot.

Llano's granite industry began in 1888, when J. K. Finlay polished his first piece of Llano granite. In 1872, Finlay had built a gristmill on a bend in the Llano River eight miles west of Llano (round about present-day Scotts Crossing), using locally quarried granite for the dam, mill house, millstones, and millrace. In 1888, he began to use the mill to polish granite, installing a thirty-inch turbine and using a twelve-foot waterfall for power. While he polished granite, his oldest son and daughter operated the gristmill. But Llano granite remained a local commodity until the railroad came in 1892 and loads of granite began to be shipped out across the country. Shortly thereafter, Findlay abandoned this mill and built another one six miles closer to town. The railroad was greeted with great excitement as the next step toward making Llano the iron-and-steel capital of the Southwest. The line was a twenty-nine-mile-long extension of the Austin and Northwestern railroad from Fairland, which is located between Marble Falls and Burnet. The town was even more excited by the proposed San Antonio and Aransas Pass railroad spur, which was to run from Comfort through Fredericksburg up to Llano. Grading was started from both Llano and Fredericksburg, but the project went bust when Llano citizens couldn't scrape up the money to pay for the first ten miles of grading and the railroad company couldn't put together enough money to go over or bypass the Great Divide, the range of high hills south of Fredericksburg that separate the Pedernales and Guadalupe watersheds.

The steel boom went bust in 1894. Charcoal may have sufficed for making iron, but coal was preferred for making steel, and there were no significant deposits of coal to be found in Llano County or anywhere near it. Carrying it in cost too much. So the big capitalists left town. The Algona closed, the Llano Improvement and Furnace Company went bankrupt, and the Olive Mine shut down. Fires destroyed most of the north-side boom buildings, and Llano town, incorporated in 1892, disincorporated in 1895, not to reincorporate for many years. A tornado in 1900 did further damage.

With the steel boom gone bust, the granite industry took up some of the industrial slack. By 1920, Llano had six granite quarries and one marble works, sending out at least thirteen different varieties of granite. Llano's granite supply was called "the best and largest deposit of grey granite to be found in the U.S., not excepting the well-known deposits of Massachusetts and Vermont."

The granite industry peaked in 1935, at ten quarries and five finishing plants. The largest block of stone ever quarried (forty tons) here became the base for a statue of a Terry's Texas Ranger on the state capitol grounds in Austin. Increased rail shipping rates made it cheaper for many customers to use out-of-state granite, so the number of quarries declined, although commercially usable granite remains here in almost limitless quantities.

But even with the capitalists gone, tireless Llanoans continued to push their county as a metallurgical nirvana, where gold, silver, iron ore, serpentine, manganese, graphite, and all manner of rare and precious minerals awaited exploitation, so easily accessible that they would practically jump into their captors' hands.

One of the most energetic proselytizers was N. J. Badu, born in Nancy, France. Badu came to the United States via Mexico, where he had helped build that country's first railroad. In the United States, Badu first went to New Orleans, then to Paris, Texas, where he taught French and married an American, Miss Charlie Neal. A geologist for most of his life, Badu moved to Llano after hearing about its mineral wealth for two years in Paris. The "Prof," as everyone called Badu, managed the Algona Hotel for most of its short life, and later managed Austin's famous Driskill Hotel, while maintaining a permanent residence in Llano.

In Llano, Badu set up a laboratory, identifying many rare minerals found on prospecting trips. He also operated a manganese mine for several years. Geologists, miners, and capitalists from Washington, New York, and other centers of wealth and power came to visit Badu and to investigate the possibilities of tapping this potential great wealth, but the visits always ended on the same note: a polite no thank-you, based on the insufficient transportation facilities and power sources to support profitable mining operations. Badu sent mineral samples and displays to expositions and universities all over the country, but he died with his dream unfulfilled in 1936. Funeral services were held in the Badu House, and his obituary read in part, "It was more than a citizen that has passed. A landmark had crumbled into dust."

Promoters touted Llano as a sort of second Eden, to wit:

Lying hidden and protected from the hot, scorching winds of the plains, raised above the malarial infected district of the East, where the nights are too cool for the mosquitoes to thrive, where the plagues of Egypt are unknown, where nature has done more to promote the health, wealth, happiness, and prosperity of mankind than any other spot in the great Empire of the Lone Star State, we find Llano.

The altitude, together with the pure mountain breezes, causes the ruddy glow of health and youth to shine upon the cheeks of him who is so fortunate as to dwell therein. No healthier or prettier spot could be found anywhere.

The death rate of the county is lower in proportion to the population than any county in the State of Texas. Men of fifty and sixty are sprightly and walk with alacrity and have the same vigor and healthy appearance as the men and women who live at the altitude of Waco, Dallas and in Houston too, at the age of eighteen and twenty-two. So much for the health of the country.

The census bureau has at least partially confirmed these extravagant turn-of-the-century claims, recently rating Llano as the second healthiest town in the United States.

Turn right on SH 16 from SH 71 to enter Llano. SH 16/SH 71 becomes Ford Street within the city limits. A few blocks south of the Llano River you come to the courthouse square and main business district.

LLANO COUNTY COURTHOUSE

Ford at Main

A block for the courthouse was laid out and noted on the town plat soon after the county was organized in 1856, but it was a long time before a courthouse was built. The original building, completed in 1885, served Llano well until it was destroyed by fire on January 22, 1892. Built of tan-colored brick with pink granite columns and trim, its replacement is one of three original Texas courthouses unmarred by subsequent additions or remodeling. It was completed in 1893 at a cost of $35,000. Under the granite boulders on the west side of the structure is a time capsule to be opened in 2056, Llano's Bicentennial. Of the 288 county courthouses in Texas, only 66 built prior to 1900 remain. Llano's is the thirty-ninth oldest in Texas. Photos of old Llano are inside. On the grounds are several statues and monuments.

The Confederate Monument, dedicated to Texans who served in the Civil War, was sculpted and erected by James K. Finley and Sons. The two sons used their father as the model. Governor Jim Ferguson dedicated the imposing work in 1916. The Vietnam Monument was dedicated on Veterans Day 1987. "Charging Over the Top" is a bronze World War I monument sculptured by Frank Teich, a nationally famous artist who owned the nearby town of Teichville. Governor Dan Moody dedicated the monument in 1928.

Anchoring the corner of Ford Street and Main, at the northeast corner of the courthouse square, is the "Haynie Block."

THE HAYNIE BLOCK

101 W. Main at Ford

This grand (for Llano) two-story commercial building, which fronts on Main Street and stretches north for most of a block on Ford Street, was designed by prominent Austin architect A. O. Watson for Elizabeth Haynie of Llano in 1882. The first telephone switchboard in Llano was located here in the 1880s. This building, which has a series of storefronts on Ford Street, has housed professionals and merchants as well as a bank for thirty years. During the 1940s, the county hospital occupied the entire second floor.

Despite their appearance, the next three one-story buildings west of the Haynie Block (103–105 W. Main) are believed to be among the oldest on the courthouse square, perhaps dating to the late 1870s. The current brown-brick facades were tacked on to the stone buildings decades later.

THE ACME CAFE ON THE SQUARE

109 W. Main • 247-4457 • Open Monday through Saturday • W

This red-brick building was constructed in 1892 and housed a succession of dry goods companies, the longest lived of which was the Acme Dry Goods Company, which operated here for more than seventy-five years. The building was converted into a restaurant in 2001. The porch awning outside still sports its decorative, pressed-tin ceiling; the facade still bears "The Acme" name written in the original elegant hand-painted script. The old cash register and other old store fixtures are on display at the county museum.

OLD COMMERCIAL BUILDING

115 W. Main

Directly west of the old Lan-Tex Theater, erected in 1880, this plain, two-story brick commercial building is one of the earliest surviving, unaltered structures on the town square. It has been used as a meeting site for the Llano Masonic Lodge, and the back section of the cellar was used as a jail. For a while it housed Pessel's mercantile store, then J. Duff Brown's drugstore. A furniture store and undertaking business occupied the building until 1894. It has also served as the Martin Telephone Company, a hardware store, a confectionery store, a millinery shop, a grocery store, and as an annex for the Southern Hotel's overflow.

SOUTHERN HOTEL

201 W. Main at Berry • Currently houses Buttery Hardware offices

J. W. Owen built the first two stories of this structure in about 1880; the third story was added during the ownership of Colonel W. A. H. Miller, a lawyer who bought the establishment in 1883. The wide porches were a welcome resting spot for the hotel's many guests. It also served as a stagecoach stop. It was later operated as the Colonial Inn before closing in the 1950s. The old hotel was saved from the wrecking ball by the Buttery Hardware Company, which restored and remodeled the place for use as its offices. Buttery Hardware is one of the three oldest businesses in Llano still operating under the same name.

OLD ICE HOUSE

Berry St., 1 block north of the Southern Hotel, on the bank on the Llano River

In 1904, A. J. Zilker of Austin (for whom Austin's famous park is named) built this ice house and accompanying water-powered millrace to generate electricity for Llano. The smokestack was added later and never used.

ENCHANTED ROCKS AND JEWELRY/LLANO UPLIFT ROCK SHOP

805 Berry, on the west side of the courthouse square • 247-4137, 247-1987 • Tuesday, Thursday, Saturday

It's strange that the Central Mineral Region would have so few rock shops, but this is the place to come.

THE LLANO NEWS BUILDING

813 Berry

Another plain, brick, essentially unaltered commercial building dating to 1890, this one originally housed the Bon Ton Barber and Bath. It provided the only commercial bath facilities in town.

MASONIC TEMPLE

832 Ford at Sandstone

This interesting stone building at the southeast corner of the courthouse square was built in 1907 as the Masonic Temple. The lodge was organized in 1860 and still meets on the second floor. Members get up there in an old hand-cranked elevator.

CHARLIE'S STORE

800 block of Ford St., on the east side of the courthouse square

Charlie's Store stretches through a series of old storefronts in the 800 block of Ford Street. This series of buildings dates back to 1880. The large two-story building in midblock, constructed in 1890, first held a saddle and harness shop, followed by a dry goods store, a saloon, a drugstore, and the Tourist's Hotel. The building at the corner of Ford and Main (built by J. K. Finley) housed a dry goods business until 1908, and was then occupied by Llano National Bank.

To get to the old Llano County jail, go east on Main Street from the courthouse square.

CORNER DRUG STORE

101 E. Main

Although several architectural changes have been made, this site has operated as the Corner Drug since 1898. It is one of the three oldest businesses in Llano still operating under the same name.

OLD MASONIC LODGE

102 E. Main, just east of the courthouse square

The building was constructed for F. J. Smith and Company as a storage facility in 1883 and is one of the oldest buildings in downtown Llano. Beginning in 1887, the Masons used the second story as their lodge for twenty-one years. The lodge was organized in 1859 on Comanche creek southeast of Llano and moved to Llano the next year, where local merchant William Haynie joined. Haynie became the center of controversy nine years later, when an accused horse thief, a black man named Ned, was captured near Fredericksburg. He confessed to being of the party that played Indians and robbed the mail coach near Kickapoo Springs and murdered the driver, Mullen, one of the El Paso drivers. He said he belonged to a regular gang that extended all over the frontier, from the Brazos, in fact, to Monterey, Mexico, and the members were in every town. He gave the names of prominent men in San Antonio and elsewhere belonging to this gang. Among the things found on the prisoner's person were charts of the roads from every section of the frontier to Monterey, with various "stations" dotted thereon, and a letter of recommendation from W. H. Haynie, who, Ned stated, was a prominent member of the gang. Nothing ever came of Ned's charges, at least as far as Haynie was concerned.

Turn left on Oatman Street from E. Main Street, one block after Ford Street.

LLANO COUNTY JAIL

Oatman and Haynie • Open on a limited basis

A block east of downtown stands the old Llano County jail, built in 1895 by the Pauly Jail Building and Manufacturing Company of St. Louis. The gray granite was locally quarried, and the red roof of this Romanesque Revival hoosegow earned the jail its nickname, "Old Red Top." The first floor housed the jailer's office and living quarters. The second floor housed four cells and two drunk tanks. The third and fourth floors housed the gallows, which are still in place. Tours can be arranged by appointment. Call the visitor center for more information.

From the jail, return to Main Street and continue east on Main, past the Fraser House.

FRASER HOUSE

207 E. Main • 247-5183

Located in the same block as the "Red Top," the Fraser House was built in 1903 by William Fraser for his new wife Laura. He was one of the master stonecutters brought to Texas from Scotland to complete construction of the state capitol building in Austin. He came to Llano after the granite capitol was finished and he never left. This simply styled two-story granite blockhouse would be perfectly at home on a rugged Scottish moor.

HOLTZER HOUSE

107 E. Luce

A few feet west of the Oatman-Luce intersection is the one-story frame house built just before the turn of the last century by H. A. Holtzer. Holtzer was a saddle maker who lived here from 1896 through the 1920s. The gingerbread woodwork and ornate fireplace inside are original to the house.

Continue south on Oatman another two blocks to the intersection of Oatman and Brown.

GRACE EPISCOPAL CHURCH

1200 Oatman

Built in 1881 to house the Llano Academy, this simple one-story Gothic building made of locally quarried sandstone was purchased in 1883 by the Episcopal Church's West Texas Missionary District after the academy failed. It was the first building in Llano to receive a state historical marker.

Continue south another two blocks on Oatman to the corner of Oatman and College. To see the O. Henry School, you will have to walk another half block down Oatman; it becomes a one-way street going north here. Or, you can drive one block west to Ford/SH 16, turn left on Ford and continue two blocks, turn left on Lampasas, then left on Oatman, and you can drive right past the school.

O. HENRY JUNIOR HIGH SCHOOL

1400 Oatman, at Ollie

The original section of this two-story schoolhouse was completed in 1887 to serve Llano schoolchildren south of the river. Built of native sandstone and timber, it was known locally as "the college building" because of its stately style. The north side addition of locally quarried gray granite (with pink granite trim) was completed in 1902. It housed all grades until 1925, when a separate high school building was constructed.

From O. Henry School, return to Ford Street (one block west) and proceed north across the river. Ford Street becomes Bessemer Avenue across the river.

The last block of buildings to your left on Ford just before you cross the river looks almost exactly the way it did ninety years ago, down to the sidewalks out front.

LLANO COUNTY LIBRARY

900 block of Ford St., just before you cross the river • 247-5248

The three plain, brick, one-story buildings that make up the library were built in 1904. They have housed a variety of businesses, including Hargon Furniture, Lange Furniture, Goodman Liquor Company, Southern Mercantile (1908), Pessell's Dry Goods, Hackworth's Variety, C. Bailey's Domino Hall, S. Roundtree's Palace Bar (1916), and a Studebaker agency (1920s), as well as pool halls and cafes. Doll collectors will enjoy the collection of dolls from all over the world.

★

The Llano River, which flows so peacefully most of the year, goes into a fit of rage every so often. Perhaps the worst rampage occurred in 1935, when the raging waters swept the highway bridge away.

LLANO COUNTY MUSEUM

310 Bessemer/SH 16 • 247-3026 • June through August: open Tuesday through Sunday 10–noon, 1:30–5:30; September through May: open Friday through Sunday 1:15–5:15 • Free • W

Immediately across the bridge and on your right is the Llano County Museum, located in the buff-color, stuccoed old Bruhl's Drug Store. Many items from Llano County's past are on display, as well as a large collection of photos and clippings. You'll see pictures of the great flood of 1935 sweeping the bridge away and of the Lone Star Brewing Company, established here in 1892.

You'll also learn the fate of the magnificent Algona Hotel. Vacant from 1894 to 1898 in the wake of the mineral boom's demise, the Algona was acquired by the Texas Military Institute in 1898. Two years later, the building was sold to Mr. and Mrs. Ernst Marschall, who reopened it as a hotel. They sold it in 1907. From 1907 to 1910 it was the Franklin Hotel, and from 1910 to 1923 it was the Don Carlos Hotel. The block-sized building burned on February 11, 1926.

Probably the most interesting and once-controversial article in the museum is the "self-fitting eye-testing machine" that A. J. Bruhl kept in his drugstore. The Texas legislature declared the machine illegal in 1928, and Bruhl was tried and convicted when he refused to retire the machine. The case was appealed, and the law was declared unconstitutional. Bruhl reinstalled the machine, and it was used until the drugstore closed in 1957.

Another exhibit is devoted to the game of polo and one of polo's greatest players, Cecil Smith of Llano. Indian artifacts from the area, as well as rocks and gems, are also on display.

LLANO RAILROAD DISTRICT

400 block of Bessemer

Excursion train enthusiasts have been working several years getting the tracks from Llano to Kingsland in operating condition in order to run a tourist train similar to the Austin and Northwestern into Llano, which would be nice, since the best scenery on the route from Austin to Llano starts at Kingsland and culminates with about seven beautiful miles beside the Llano River just before you enter Llano. The route crosses several vintage trestle and steel-truss bridges and passes by different kinds of granite outcroppings. The district currently contains a reproduction depot/museum/visitors center, a red caboose, and an unrestored 1950s Long Island Railroad passenger car.

THE FILLING STATION

502 Bessemer

Built in the early 1920s as a Texaco station, this ex–gas station was famous at the time as the only covered gas station between here and San Antonio. (A November 1921 fire map has this building marked as a filling station. At that time no highways ran through town, so north-south or east-west were indicated. Ford Street crossed the river via the bridge and dead-ended into railroad right-of-way between Pittsburg and Bessemer streets and what used to be a public square.)

FINE ARTS GUILD INC.

503 Bessemer • Open daily • W

The Guild was founded in 1963 to promote the work of Llano artists. Works by members are on exhibit here.

CHRISSY'S HOMESTYLE BAKERY

501 Bessemer • 247-4564 • Open Tuesday through Saturday • W

This quaint little Mission Revival building was built in 1919 by T. Y. Hill to house the offices of his business, the Cassaday Grey Granite Company. The Cassaday Company was the first to use motor transportation for hauling granite. You can satisfy your sweet tooth here with a variety of sweet rolls, pastries, cookies, cakes, pies, and breads.

LLANO COUNTY CHAMBER OF COMMERCE AND VISITORS CENTER

100 Train Station Dr., in the Railyard Depot • 1-866-539-5535 • www
.llanochamber.com • Open Monday through Friday; visitor center open
Monday through Saturday

Hunting lease information, free walking-tour maps of Llano, and other local
information are available here. For more tourist-oriented information about
Llano, visit www.llanotx.com.

BADU HOUSE

601 Bessemer, at Tarrant

This blocky, two-story Italian Renaissance structure executed in stucco,
red brick, and gray granite was built about 1891 or 1892 as the First National
Bank of Llano. Professor Badu bought the place in 1898 at public auction
after the bank failed. Located directly across the street from the old Algona
Hotel block, the Badu house is the only boom-era building north of the
river that survives. The pride of the Badu house is the Llanite bar. The
bar top is inlaid with polished slabs of this rare (but commercially valueless)
rock, the blue quartz crystals glowing in the dark brown feldspar. Professor Badu discovered Llanite, and it is not encountered outside of Llano
County.

LODGING

DABBS HOTEL

**112 E. Burnet, just off Bessemer on the north bank of the Llano • 247-2200
• www.dabbsbnb.com**

The Dabbs Hotel is the last standing railroad hotel in Llano. It began operation
in 1907 for railroad crewmen who stayed overnight and returned to Austin the
next day. To travel any farther west, you had to go over to the Southern Hotel
to catch a stagecoach. It has a loose, funky, congenial atmosphere and is currently oriented to group events.

DINING

Llano, along with Taylor and Lockhart, is one of the three "capitals" of barbecue in Texas, the criteria being that each town has more than one stellar smoke
shack. I'll argue that Luling and Schulenburg also deserve consideration for the
same reason. Try them all and take your own side.

COOPER'S OLD TIME PIT BARBECUE

604 W. Young/SH 29 W. • 247-5713 • www.coopersbbq.com • Open daily • W

Brisket, chuck and club steaks, sausage, inch-thick pork chops, pork ribs, lamb, and cabrito are cooked over mesquite coals. Pick your meat off the outside pits and carry it inside to eat. Peel your own onions; white bread, jalapenos, and other condiments can be found on the long picnic tables. Beans and potato salad are also offered. Cooper's cooks up more than 1,200 pounds of meat year-round, except during hunting season, when the pounds become tons. Friends whose opinions I respect have come back from Cooper's with less-than-glowing reports, but I have had no such bad luck. If you don't like what you see on the pit, go elsewhere, and remember, the later in the day you come, the less choice you'll have and the greater the chances for dried-out meat. There is also beer.

INMAN'S KITCHEN

809 W. Young/SH 29 W. • 247-5257 • www.inmanskitchen.com • Open Tuesday through Saturday, breakfast, lunch, and dinner, except during deer season when hours are expanded • No Cr. • W

Inman's features turkey sausage, smoked turkey, ham, chicken, sausage, brisket, and pork ribs. Beans, slaw, potato salad, breads, and pies are made on the premises. Inman's is open at breakfast time but serves no breakfast food. It is very popular during hunting season.

KENNETH LAIRD'S BAR-B-QUE

1600 Ford/SH 71 • 247-5234 • Open Wednesday through Sunday • No Cr. • W

Kenneth Laird ran Cooper's back in the late 1970s and early 1980s and has been here at his self-named place since. Brisket, sausage, pork steaks, chicken, and pork ribs are slow smoked and served with the usual trimmings. Rib eyes and sirloins are cooked on order on Friday evenings. The pace here is generally much more relaxed than at Cooper's, where you "eat the fat." At Lairds, you can "chew the fat" with the entertaining Kenneth.

Barbecue is not Llano's only tasty food offering. Fain's Honey, a family business, has been producing raw natural honey here since 1951, and in Texas since 1926. The product line has been expanded in recent years to include honey-based spread, ribbon cane syrup, and sorghum molasses. Their honey is available in most grocery stores in the region, including Austin (www.fainshoney.com).

PARKS

Two parks offer free access to the Llano River. The Llano River (Badu) Park, on the northwest side of the river above the dam, has a nice walkway along the river, picnic tables, benches, boulders for climbing and sitting on, a covered pavilion, and a public restroom. The Leonard Crenwelge County Park, on the southeast side of the river just below the dam is more rustic, with hiking along the river and among the boulders. It has picnic tables and a public restroom.

To continue the trail of the Mormons west, return to the courthouse square and take FM 152 west toward Castell.

ROBINSON PARK

FM 152, about 2 miles west of the courthouse • 247-4457 • Open daily • Free, except for golf course

Just west of town on the Llano River is this city-owned park. A nine-hole golf course, swimming pool, playground, camping, RV campsites, community center, rodeo grounds, and picnic facilities are here, as well as drinking water and restrooms. Fishing is often good in the river, but the river is too shallow for large boats.

As you leave town, one last bit of Llano trivia. All of us who have ever enjoyed the ease and convenience of an electric typewriter, and more recently the fancy newfangled PCs and word processors, owe some thanks to Llano County native J. Field Smothers, who invented an electric typewriter back in 1912.

THE DUTCH SETTLEMENTS

Leaving Llano on FM 152, you again pick up the wandering Mormons' path west, along the fertile valley of the Llano River, toward the "Dutch settlements" where they were to briefly encamp before turning sharply south toward their eventual home near Bandera. Although you seldom see the river for the next eighteen miles, it is always there, just beyond the trees. The Dutch settlements were in fact the Adelsverein's final colonization attempts in Texas. Five projected communities were strung out for several miles along the north bank of the Llano River, which put the Adelsverein just inside the southernmost boundaries of the sprawling Fisher-Miller Grant. This toehold was as far as the Adelsverein would get in its grandiose empire-building scheme.

Despite its dubious claim to the grant land (by 1847, the Fisher-Miller Grant was void), the Adelsverein readied that year to make the final push into the three-million-plus-acre tract. That land was mostly stone and seldom tillable, and the scanty rainfalls were often months apart. Extremely isolated, it was also a Comanche stronghold. The principal instigators behind the settlements were John Meusebach, Prince Carl of Solms-Braunfels, H. Spies, and Count Carl of Castell.

Schoenburg was the easternmost of these settlements, followed by Meerholz, Leiningen, Bettina, and Castell. The first two were stillborn. Castell, Bettina, and Leiningen made a run at life, but only Castell actually made it, and it is the only Dutch settlement that exists today.

Bettina, the most controversial of these settlements, was composed of recruits from Darmstadt, Germany. Upon his return to Germany from New Braunfels in 1845, Prince Carl hit the university circuit to drum up enthusiasm for the Adelsverein's pretentious colonization project. He told students that there was no demand in the old country for all the young professional men the German universities were turning out. They had to find a new and growing country where their services would be in demand. That place was Texas.

The most receptive ears belonged to the members of a fraternity of communistic freethinkers in Darmstadt known as Die Vierziger (the Forty). Prince Carl described Texas to them as "a land of milk and honey, of perennial flowers, of crystal streams, rich and fruitful beyond measures, where roamed myriads of deer and buffalo while the primeval forests abounded in wild fowl of every kind."

After listening to his spiel, the Forty decided to turn their pipe dreams of a communistic utopia into reality. Early in 1846, they formed the Darmstaedter Kolonie and began to plan their colony in Texas, which was to be based on the motto "Friendship, freedom, and equality" and the cardinal principle "Let everyone do as they please." They "had no regular scheme of government," Vierziger member Louis Reinhardt recalled years later. "In fact, being communistic, the association would not brook the tyranny of a ruler. Instead there were guiding spirits by common consent. Being the youngest of the company—I was thirteen—I was, of course, rarely consulted."

The Forty made a contract with the Adelsverein to settle themselves and two hundred other families within the Fisher-Miller Grant boundaries. In return, they would receive $12,000 or the equivalent in livestock, tools, agricultural implements, wagons, and one year's provisions.

Seven of the Forty came down with cold feet; the other thirty-three sailed from Hamburg in February 1847. Their occupational makeup was quite diversified: physicians, architects, lawyers (seven of them), foresters, mechanics, carpenters, engineer, butcher, blacksmith, army artillery officer, shipbuilder, brewer, miller, botanist, hosteller, theologian, musical instrument maker, and agriculturalist. Only the ship's cook spoke English, and few of the thirty-three had ever actually worked for a living.

Their ship landed at Galveston on July 17, 1847, and there they paused long enough to name their colony Bettina, after the forward-thinking, controversial German author Bettina von Arnim, and to resolve that each man would do his share of the work, from tending the fields to building cabins. That done, the men of Bettina sailed again for Indianola—then called Carlshafen—where they disembarked for the long journey inland. Before leaving, they received financial assistance from the Adelsverein. The thirty-three men and their supplies filled up thirty wagons. The cargo included a complete set of mill machinery, barrels of whiskey, and their favorite dogs from back home. "We came prepared to conquer the world," one of them said.

The journey to New Braunfels took a leisurely four weeks. They camped out, drank, sang, and frolicked like the schoolboys they had until recently been. "We lived like the Gods of Olympus," one confessed. Their favorite traveling song commenced, "A life we lead, a life full of bliss." Quite a contrast to their countrymen's death-ridden experiences at Carlshafen and New Braunfels only a year earlier. The men of Bettina experienced no Indian hostilities along the way, courtesy of the recently signed Meusebach Treaty with the Comanches (see Fort Martin Scott, this chapter).

Bettina was first laid out under a large oak tree near the confluence of Elm Creek and the Llano River. A cannon was set up and a guard posted. The rest of the men sang and drank until the wee hours of dawn. "Lebe Hoch United

States, Lebe Hoch Texas" rang out drunkenly through the night. They started on a huge brush arbor the next day and followed it with pecan-shingled adobe huts.

Their Indian relations were harmonious. Whenever some raiders stole from the tenderfoot Germans, Chief Santanta tried to bring justice to the thieves. When the Germans visited the Indians, the Indians gave them pecans and spread out deerskins for their sitting comfort. They even tried to learn German.

"Heaven on earth" lasted a couple of months. Since everyone could work if and when he pleased, less and less work was done as time progressed. Some spent their time hunting; others chose to while away their days in deep philosophical debate. "Most of the professional men wanted to do the directing and ordering, while the mechanics and laborers were to carry out their plans. Of course, the latter failed to see the justice of their ruling, so no one did anything," one of the thirty-three later reflected.

By the summer of 1848, members had begun to drift away. Bettina, barely a year old, was a complete bust by the end of 1848. Some of the defectors went to New Braunfels, others to San Antonio, Austin, and Tusculum, which later became Boerne. Several went on to leave prominent marks on Texas history, among them Gustav Schleicher and Dr. Ferdinand Herff. Schleicher served as state legislator and U.S. congressman, and had a West Texas county named for him. Previously a distinguished Hessian Army surgeon, Herff performed a successful cataract operation on an Indian girl out here on the frontier and later became the first doctor in Texas to perform an operation with anesthesia, in 1854. Nothing remains of Bettina today.

Castell, the westernmost settlement, was named for Count Carl of Castell. Henry Lorenz was the first white man to settle on the north banks of the Llano, but he stayed only a short time, returning to the safety of Fredericksburg. Next came Ludwig Schneider and Henry Vasterling, who settled several miles east of present-day Castell, on the north side of the river. Thus Castell was born. In the coming years, Castell moved several times, first across to the south bank of the river, then a mile or so upstream to its present location.

Life here was not easy. For the first couple of years, Castellites depended heavily on supplies and support from Fredericksburg, which had problems enough of its own. A round trip to Fredericksburg—about fifty miles—took four days. Trips to Indianola were also necessary, and they could last from three to four months. Five or six wagons would band together to make the trek. If the wagon train were detained—by bad weather, high rivers, or bandits—the folks back home would suffer, sometimes coming close to starving. On one such occasion, two wives whose husbands were away, Mrs. Bader and Mrs. Steele, became so disconsolate that they agreed to divide what little cornmeal they had between them and starve together. To ease the hunger pangs, they gathered tender weeds and cooked them. Once, Mrs. Bader nearly died from eating poisonous weeds.

To survive, many of the German men became wagoneers, supplying the frontier forts. Hunger sharpened their business instincts. They would often spend their limited hard cash to buy whiskey, which they would trade to the soldiers for corn. Soldiers always had plenty of corn, but seldom did they have enough booze. Other times the Germans would comb the stable yards for stray kernels after the soldiers' horses had been fed. When times really got hard, the "Dutchmen" would feed their stock first, then salvage and wash off the corn kernels they found in the droppings.

Those who chose to hang on here had to work hard and imaginatively. Henry Vasterling established the region's first cheese factory, turning out huge wheels of the stuff and wagoneering it as far away as Austin to sell. Others made and sold bacon in a similar manner. Some even sold their children, or so their Anglo neighbors claimed. These few stalwart survivors were rewarded in a way by the state, which eventually awarded them legal title to the lands settled under terms of the defunct Fisher-Miller Grant. Its beneficence really didn't put the state out much, however; many years later, 320 acres of land out here was sold for a quart of whiskey. As one wit put it, "In those days a man could obtain title to 640 acres by filing on it and then living on it for 3 years," or in other words, "The state bets you 640 acres that you'll starve to death before 3 years are up."

Almost nine miles out of Llano, you come to an intersection with CR 102, running off FM 152 to your right, across the river. You're entering the Dutch Settlements now. In another four miles you come to a four-way intersection with CR 103. If you turn right here, in a few yards you come to a low-water crossing of the Llano, one of the most pleasantly pastoral river crossings in the Hill Country.

Just past the intersection you see almost immediately on your left the 1850s two-story fieldstone Oestrich home, one of the finest preserved pieces of early German Texas architecture north of Fredericksburg. It's now a private residence. Then, on your right, you'll notice a section of fieldstone fence as it rises up from Vasterling Creek.

★

It wasn't too many years after Castell's founding that Charley Lehmburg decided that the grass looked greener over on the south bank of the Llano, and so he moved across the river, near where St. John's Lutheran Church stands, on the eastern edge of Castell. Cattleman and drover, Lehmburg also ran the community's store and post office. Theodore Bucholz, newly arrived from Fredericksburg, bought the store in 1881 and moved it to the town's present location.

CASTELL

Llano County • 72 • About 18 miles from Llano

William Hermes Sr. was one of Castell's founders and, years later, wrote about life in early Castell and the Dutch Settlements.

The expedition to found the Dutch Settlements got under way in the middle of November 1847. The public announcement explained that instead of a quarter section of land, colonists would be given ten acres in a colony, furnished free board until a crop was made, and loaned the necessary utensils and draft oxen.

Crossing the Llano was not difficult, but some delay was caused by the time the last wagon had been brought across by Mr. Bickel's order that the wagons "stay together" as precaution against sudden Indian attacks.

After crossing the Llano, the expedition camped in the vicinity of the Bettina Colony, which consisted of one large building and a few smaller ones. That afternoon, a scouting party set out to find a suitable place for the proposed colony. A prairie a mile in extent and about a mile above Bettina running parallel to the river was chosen, and work began immediately. Bickel assembled all colonists for a council, and he organized the motley crowd into effective groups.

One group of seven was to fell trees, another to build houses, a third group to build fences, the fourth to do plowing, and two men were to watch the cattle. One out of each seven was to cook for the group. Each Sunday morning, an assembly was to take place for discussion of alternating the tasks amongst the groups. For each thirty colonists, a blockhouse was to be erected, and houses were to be thirty feet apart.

Tents were not available in Fredericksburg, and so a large tarpaulin was put up for the storing of baggage and sleeping quarters. This "shed" reached to within two feet of the ground and was open at both ends, so it was not much protection against cold winds. The winter of 1847–1848 was a severe and rough one. Sleeping on the ground under the shed, Hermes spent many a night shivering with cold—one of the most bitter experiences in his pioneer life.

Whenever a few houses had been finished, married men went to Fredericksburg to get their families. Each group had dissatisfied members, quarrels arose, and it was decided to discontinue the group cooking arrangement. From there on, each cooked for himself or jointly with friends.

The emigration company furnished provisions, and as long as they lasted, work went ahead with great briskness. But there came times when no provisions were brought. Those were trying times for the young single men who had to stop working as their strength failed; families mostly brought milk cows and chickens from Fredericksburg and thus could tide themselves over for a time. They searched the forests for orache to cook as cabbage, and the river bed for mussels as substitute for meat. The meat of the river mussel was tough and indigestible, but when cooked with cornmeal it made a tasty soup.

The corn came in the shuck, and each colonist had to grind his own meal using a hand mill fastened to a tree in the center of the colony. A hungry man who couldn't wait would roast a handful of the corn to quiet his growling stomach.

One time Hermes had hungered for three days before a wagon arrived with bacon. The bacon was rationed three pounds to the person. Hungry, hungry Hermes immediately consumed most of his ration raw and got sick, so he went to see Dr. Herff in Bettina, where he got an insight as to the difference in the prevailing conditions of the two colonies.

In Bettina he found an organization of mostly highly educated men unaccustomed to manual labor and who understood little about farming but loved the hunt, and classic lectures. They had a well-constructed roomy house in which all resided and slept jointly, well furnished with camp beds. A small building at the side served as the kitchen.

The Bettina organization was of communistic form. The cooking chores, like in Castell, were the first source of discord. Hermes found it interesting and instructive to see communism tried practically. At classical school in Hamburg, he attended Professor Wurm's lectures on communism and socialism and had there learned the beautiful reform ideals of Fourier and Louis Blanz. But in Texas, experience taught him that an organization of communism required a capable organizer and leader and that the old adage, "many heads, many-sided-ness," held true. Communistic Bettina did not last long. Its members gradually scattered, some going to San Antonio, New Braunfels, or Austin, and in the fall of 1848 a colonist of nearby Leiningen bought out the rest of the Bettina Colony.

Members of the Castell Colony were given the land promised to them in the summer of 1848. They went to Fredericksburg to look at a map, on which the various surveys of the land in the grant were shown and numbered, and selected their land. Shortly before going to Fredericksburg, Mr. Bickel ordered a number of Castell men to ride out in a radius of twenty miles and select the most favorable farming lands. These men selected the lands for the colonists from a map that Hermann Seele, in the name of the Governmental Commissioner Torrey, laid before them. Hermes later learned that the German Emigration Company had already lost all rights to the grant and that the colonists owed their thanks to the State of Texas for its generosity in giving them the land promised to them by the emigration company.

The emigration company, besides the furnishing of provisions and as a loan the furnishing of implements and draft oxen, had also, as a protection against Indians, given each colonist a rifle, and each colony a cannon. It was quite a necessity because the Indians became rather annoying. Even before the corn had ripened in the field, they at night turned their horses into the center of the fields and thereby wasted great quantities of the crop.

On a moonlight night, a horse belonging to a Mr. Simon who lived at the east end of the colony was stolen. Simon, hearing something unusual going on, ran out of the house in time to see Indians galloping off with the horse. In order to protect himself of a similar loss, Mr. Menges added a pen at the side of his house where he slept and kept his horse therein at night. As a precaution, he tied a rope around the horse's neck, brought the rope through an opening in the wall, and tied it around his wrist. But this precaution did no good; one morning he awoke with the rope in his hand, but the horse was gone.

For protection of the colonies, a company of Rangers under Captain Highsmith was ordered to the Llano, but strange to say, not to the north side where the colonies were, but on the south side. During floods, they were completely cut off from the colonies.

When the houses had been built, a drawing for the houses, with ten acres of land behind each, was arranged whereby each colonist received a house, on the land of which two and half acres had been planted with corn.

Soon thereafter, at the end of August, the Emigration Company went bankrupt. All agricultural implements and draft animals belonging to the company were sold, and the furnishing of provisions ceased. Hermes saw that neither his physical nor his financial circumstances would permit him a realization of a contented country life, so he sold his possessions, purchased a horse, saddle, and the necessary traveling items and journeyed to Galveston. A few weeks after he left, the Indians gave the colonists two days to evacuate the colonies, and they all fled to Fredericksburg.

Hermes had not been long in Galveston when one day he read in the *New Orleans Picayune* a legal citation citing the members in Germany of the German Emigration Company, headed by the Prince of Prussia, to appear on a certain date in court in defense of indebtedness charges. Naturally no one appeared; attachment was made on any properties still belonging to the company, and they were legally sold. That was the disgraceful ending of a once noble-intentioned and with fondest hopes begun undertaking.

Residential Castell today is composed of a couple of trailer houses and a dozen turn-of-the-century, millsawn-lumber Anglo German farmhouses, quaint but showing their age. The Castell post office (located in the old general store) and Randy Leifeste's Castell General Store (the old Sunshine Station) (325-247-4100, www.theranchman.com) comprise commercial Castell; its spiritual center is Trinity Methodist Church. Deer hunting and some fishing have been Castell's industries for decades, but the sleepy hamlet is waking up. You can rent kayaks now at the General Store, and there were six B&Bs in 2009 and more on the way; inquire at the General Store.

The Castell post office dates to 1900, give or take a few years, and still has its original beaded ceiling, but not much else of interest. The Sunshine Station dates to 1928, back when FM 152 was SH 29 and was the main road through these parts. Station owner Emil Holtzer actually set up shop a few years earlier next door, but the first station burned down. The little wooden building across FM 152 from the station was the meat market, and between it and the Castell Store stood one of Castell's cotton gins. Folks around here used to grow a lot of cotton.

The General Store sells Llano-style barbecue (pork loin, ribs, steak, beef brisket, sausage) on Saturdays, and all brands of beer sell for the same low price, from Natural Light to Negro Modelo. You never know who might show up; one Sunday the owner of Luckenbach and his wife were chilling and picking guitar. Ask Randy how to play "Castell Cattleguard"; even pieces of jewelry count in this stripped-down game. You can play it on any road with cattle guards (preferably on your way home from somewhere), but locals play it on Keyserville Road, a picturesque gravel road that runs off of FM 152 just west of the General Store down to Loyal Valley.

TRINITY METHODIST CHURCH

Just off FM 152

The Trinity congregation built a simple shotgun house of worship on these grounds in 1880, enlarging it to its present size and configuration over the next twenty years. The Victorian parsonage dates to 1899; the cedar-post-and-tin-roof arbor is at least as old. The old Castell schoolhouse completes the tableau.

A short trek across the windswept, flower-strewn meadow gets you to the burying grounds, where many of the German pioneers lie in eternal sleep. Among all the Vasterlings, Kothes, and Kowierschkes, there is the stone of Christian Oestrich, the first white child born in Llano County (in 1855) and the first man to string "bob wire" north of the Llano. Previous to his use of barbed wire, Oestrich had hired Mexicans to build rock fences for him. Oestrich noted that his employees slept on beds of leaves and ate beans flavored with "smoking tobacco." In all probability, the "smoking tobacco" Oestrich mentioned was the aromatic herb epazote, which is a common addition to boiled beans in Mexico. When dried, epazote looks very much like home-cured pipe tobacco.

Students of religious history will note the unusually strong presence of Methodism in this overwhelmingly German community. This is largely due to the efforts of one man, the pioneer preacher Charles Grote. Grote rode a regular preaching circuit from Fredericksburg north to the Dutch settlements during the 1850s, and he often spent the night in a cave near House Mountain, ten miles south of the river.

The Reverend Grote was not easily deterred from his evangelic mission. To honor one preaching commitment, Grote rode the twenty-five miles from Fredericksburg to Castell through stormy weather in one day, only to be halted by the rain-swollen, impassable Llano River. His flock waited just across the river. They sent three friendly Indians across to help the reverend over. Grote nearly drowned crossing the river, despite his experienced helpmates, but he finally made it across and immediately set about his task of saving souls. Preaching in the shade of a big live oak, Grote chose as the text of his message Jesus' words, "Ye must be born again." Before Grote had finished his sermon, his listeners were dropping to their knees and praying for pardon, as impressed by his preaching as by his tenacity. And within this story lies the ultimate reason for Castell's move south across the Llano. During the rainy season the river might be impassable for weeks at a time, no small inconvenience when the nearest civilization lay far south of the river. Every September, the German Methodist congregations of the Llano River Valley (Art, Castell, Hilda, and Mason) gather together to sing the old German hymns of their ancestors, usually on the fourth Sunday.

Speaking of the river, continue on FM 152 west from the church grounds, through the few short yards of commercial Castell. At the intersection, take FM 2768 across the Castell low-water bridge.

As you look out over the Llano River's granite-rifted channels and thicketed islands, it seems hard to believe that the Adelsverein officials had assured prospective colonists that steamboats would soon be running up and down the dredged and channeled Llano and Pedernales rivers. No wonder the society failed. So taken in were the German colonists by the Adelsverein's extravagant claims that at first, distant glance they fancied the omnipresent mottes of gnarled live oaks to be olive trees. How disappointed they must have been when they learned otherwise, and when they saw these rocky rivers for the first time.

A historical marker commemorating the Dutch settlements stands just north of the river, where FM 2768 veers off sharply to the right. If you're feeling particularly adventuresome and enjoy good river scenery, you can follow FM 2768's path from the marker, and shortly thereafter turn right onto CR 104, a mostly gravel road just yards north of the river.

This road takes you back east, toward Llano, through the Dutch settlements and along the river, which is sometimes only a few feet away. These miles of river, granite boulders notwithstanding, probably reminded the German émigrés of home, and the river and bank look very much the same today. This road makes a number of low-water creek crossings and one low-water river crossing, so it's not advisable to take it during rainy, flash flood weather. Grazing cattle wander at will along and across the road, so take it easy. Otherwise, the road is generally smooth but very dusty. Warning: it can be washboarded at times after heavy rains.

After several miles on CR 104, you pass on your right the bare shell of the 1850s two-story Peter Lang house, and then the original St. John's Lutheran Church on your left. The St. John's Church on FM 152 is the successor to this old rock church across the river, which is now used for hay storage and is on private property.

If you take CR 104, turn right when it comes to a T intersection with CR 103. Then turn left at the intersection of CR 104 with CR 103 about a mile later, in order to continue on CR 104.

About five miles later, turn right onto CR 102, go past the new Walden Plantation Bed and Breakfast (325-247-2046) and in a matter of yards you cross the river and return to FM 152. Turn right on FM 152 to complete the loop back to Castell.

From Castell, continue 9.5 miles west on FM 152 toward its junction with US 87. Turn right onto US 87, toward Fredericksburg. Five and a half miles later, turn left on FM 2242 so as to pass through Loyal Valley.

Once known as Cold Spring, this section of the Cold Spring Creek valley was settled by Unionist Germans, who named their settlement Loyal Valley to reflect their political beliefs. The outlaws George Gladden and Johnny Ringo, prominent players in the Mason County Hoodoo War, were the most infamous residents of Cold Spring.

LOYAL VALLEY

Mason County • 50 • About 15 miles from Castell

John Meusebach settled down here in 1869 to raise cattle and fruit. His orchards were locally famous. Fluent in five languages, Meusebach kept a store and served as postmaster and justice of the peace. He was wounded in an attack on his store during the Hoodoo War. The settlers at Loyal Valley suffered their share of problems with marauding bands of Indians, who were understandably upset about losing their lands. Given the warrior culture of the Apaches and Comanches, violence was inevitable, but the raiders didn't always kill their foes. Prisoners were often taken. Many escaped or were eventually freed. But a few stayed for life.

Herewith, the story of the Lehmann brothers, as told in the *San Angelo Standard-Times* on May 18, 1932, by Mrs. A. C. Bowman:

> Perhaps few Texas pioneers have had personal experiences to compare with those of William Lehmann, seventy, an interesting character of the Hill Country who lives on a ranch at Loyal Valley, Mason County.
>
> "Uncle Bill," as he is fondly called in this section, was captured by the Indians when he was eight years old. Although he was with them only six or seven days, the incident made such a deep impression on his youthful mind that he can relate the details as if they occurred but yesterday.
>
> His brother, Herman Lehmann, who died several months ago, was captured at the same time and lived as one of the Indian tribe for eight years.
>
> "My brother, Herman, and a sister and I were in the wheat field, and I had a baby on my lap," began Lehmann, when asked recently to relate the story. "The Indians slipped up on us and captured Herman and my sister. When they had gone only a short distance, one came back after me, leaving the baby behind unharmed.
>
> "The girl managed to fight herself away from the red men while they were trying to get her over a rock fence, but the young boys were unsuccessful in their struggle for freedom. They were placed on horses and forced to begin a long and weary march from home and loved ones.
>
> "I could have got away several times if I hadn't been so scared," continued Uncle Bill, as he told of camping at night and being placed on the ground to sleep near his Indian guard.
>
> "One night I rolled down a hill some distance from camp and could have slipped away but I was too scared. I was too little to know what to do; so I climbed the

hill and went back to sleep. Early the next morning I heard roosters crowing and I knew then that we were not far from a farm house."

His brother, Herman, who was eleven years old, was always kept tied and had no chance to escape. Uncle Bill remembers well the cruelties suffered during that eventful week.

"They just scared us to death," he said with feeling, "pointed pistols at us and made us think they were going to kill us."

He has his own idea as to why the savages abandoned him after he had been on the road with them for six or seven days. Apparently fearing that they were about to be overtaken by soldiers, or scouts, the group became separated, and the Indian on whose horse he was riding threw him off.

"To lighten his load, I guess, though of course I don't know," he explained.

The young German boy found himself alone in the wood, where he experienced real hardships, starvation and fright. For two days and a half he was without food or water, the only human in a wilderness of strange sounds and sights. He was in constant fear of being destroyed by the wild beasts that frequented his hiding place. He tells that longhorned deer often ran him into trees and that on one occasion he lay motionless while two large animals passed near him.

"I don't know what kind they were or what kept them from seeing me and eating me up. I was just scared to death."

One night during a rain he was able to moisten his parched throat by holding his mouth open and catching a few cool drops of water. He also drank from animal tracks which the rain filled.

One day a white man passed on the rough trail nearby, and although he saw the lost boy he went on without stopping to aid him.

"He said something to me in English, but I couldn't understand him."

A Fredericksburg teamster on the way to San Angelo finally rescued him. Digressing, Lehmann explained that while he was with his captors they made him wear a funny-shaped cap, the kind the Apaches wore. After the first passerby failed to stop, the youth decided that perhaps he had been mistaken for an Indian. So, hearing the approaching team, he threw the cap in the bushes and ran out in the road in plain view of the driver.

"I don't know what I'd give right now if I had that cap," he remarked, as he neared the end of his story. Seeing him in the road ahead, the teamster began shouting and calling to him.

"My! I was glad to see him. He hugged me and talked to me in German, and gave me so much water I almost died," the former captive related pathetically. "I was so thirsty and hadn't had anything to eat or drink in so long. Oh! I was sick."

But in spite of the emaciated condition of his body and the almost fatal illness caused by the treatment of the kind but overindulgent freighter, the child recovered and was soon able to tell where his family lived. After several days he was returned to them.

His experiences with the Indians, however, were not yet over, for he tells of another incident which occurred sometime later. His mother and eight children were alone at their home when they were attacked by a band of Apaches. Eleven holes were shot in the house, and large pieces of iron and rocks were thrown at the structure, almost destroying it. The members of the family managed to lock themselves securely in one room, and the brave mother routed the Indians by firing two shots from a shotgun.

For many years, Loyal Valley had a hotel and the usual secular and spiritual trappings of a Texas village. But when the new highway (now US 87) went through a half mile west, Loyal Valley withered down to the collection of ranch houses and ruins that you see today. At least one producing apple tree still stands in the yard of the old two-story stone house.

You shortly rejoin US 87 and begin to enter the hills again. Less than five miles later, you come to Cherry Spring. Several hundred yards after you see the Cherry Spring highway sign, you see a sign directing you to turn left to enter Cherry Spring, followed by a small Lutheran church sign. Turn left here, onto E. Cherry Spring Road. In the near distance you see the silvery spire and roofs of the Cherry Spring Lutheran Church and the Diedrich Rode homestead.

CHERRY SPRING

Gillespie County • 75 • About 5 miles from Loyal Valley

The three-story Rode home is one of the largest Hill Country limestone houses still standing, and its tall, shiny tin-hipped roof further heightens its prominence. Unfortunately, its new owners have surrounded it by a ten-foot pole fence, cutting off a view of the house to passersby. The energetic evangelic rancher Diedrich Rode founded the Cherry Spring community in 1853, naming it for the wild cherry trees he found growing along the creek. The settlement was located along the main highway between Fort Mason and Fort Martin Scott.

Rode had been here on the banks of Marschall Creek only a few months when the Mormons wandered through, camping first on the banks of Marschall Creek, and then on nearby Squaw Creek, from December 1853 through January 1854. They tended their livestock, repaired their wagons, and gathered wild honey, finding fifty bee trees in one month. Wight took twenty cattle into Fredericksburg, where he sold them for fifteen dollars each. The colonists must have made a strong impression, for Marschall Creek was commonly known as Mormon Creek for years thereafter.

Rode finished the large house in 1880 and followed it with the other, smaller limestone structures that dot the ranch-house grounds: carriage house, smokehouse, blacksmith shop, and sheep-shearing barn. A lay Lutheran preacher, Rode helped found the church at Castell and taught catechism classes in his home for years. Along the way, he became one of the region's biggest stock raisers and landowners.

Rode's dream was to see a Lutheran congregation organized here. Christ Lutheran Church was organized in March 1905, and Rode died less than four months later, at the ripe old age of seventy-seven.

The present limestone Gothic sanctuary, whose shiny tin steeple can be seen from miles around, was finished in 1907. It is immaculately kept, as is the old Rode ranch just across E. Cherry Spring Road from the church. All in all, they form one of the most unique and imposing collections of limestone buildings in the Hill Country.

Return to US 87 and continue on toward Fredericksburg. You can see the church and ranch house for several miles over your left shoulder, nestled in the Marschall Creek valley. In seven miles, you come to an intersection with FM 2323. Slow down here, then slow some more and turn right as per the "Old Mason Rd." sign, just before the "Fredericksburg 9" sign.

Driving this narrow, wandering road, it's hard to imagine that it, not that four-lane Johnny-come-lately drag strip you just turned off of, was once the main highway north from Fredericksburg.

Soon a creek comes into view: Barons Creek, named for Baron John Meusebach. A couple of miles later, on your right, you see another distinctive little farmhouse, two stories high, two rooms deep, covered completely by tin, with a tin-sheet roof and brick-patterned tin siding. You pass several more vintage stone ranch houses and cross a 1920s concrete bridge while on the old highway.

Continue your trek to Fredericksburg by turning right on US 87 when Old Mason Road runs into it. Continue into Fredericksburg on US 87, which merges with US 290 to become Main Street.

FREDERICKSBURG

Gillespie County Seat • 11,000 (approximate) • (830) • About 18 miles from Cherry Spring

Fredericksburg was not built by spendthrifts; the countryside, however pretty, has never allowed for such luxuries. Statistically, Fredericksburg averages just under thirty inches of rain a year. But statistics don't tell the whole story. Weather in this part of Texas is cyclical. Several wet years are followed by several dry years and so on. Spring and fall are the rainy seasons. Some years it won't rain a drop for months at a time; other years half the annual rain falls on one weekend. January's average temperature is forty-six degrees, but it may be ninety degrees one day and nineteen degrees the next. During summer, the daily high is seldom below ninety-five degrees.

Summer is the harshest of seasons here; winter is almost a blessing by comparison. But springtime is joyous. Bluebonnets and peach blossoms are the co-regents of spring in and around Fredericksburg. Bluebonnets favor thin, poor soil, which the Hill Country has in abundance, and peach trees thrive on the iron-rich soil of the Pedernales River Valley. Spring also brings flowering redbud trees, Indian paintbrushes, phlox, verbena, mountain laurel, yucca, and dozens of other blossoms that splatter and sometimes sweep over the newly green hills and valleys from early March through mid-June.

Fredericksburg's founders arrived here during the height of a banner spring and immediately fell in love with this valley. Miss Margaret Keidel (see Keidel Medical Complex Family) said that her great-grandfather Wilhelm liked it so much that he abandoned his plans to pursue advanced medical studies at Johns Hopkins to stay here.

Fredericksburg's founders were a diverse lot: doctors, professors, skilled craftsmen, noblemen, and artists. Some came searching for political freedom; many more came for the economic opportunities unavailable in the homeland. But to a person, they were romantics, Miss Keidel said. It took a healthy dose of romance to leave home—probably forever—and sail for three months to a country they really knew nothing about, other than what they had read in novels and travel books that often painted a milk-and-honey picture.

As contemporary chronicler Frederick Kapp put it in an 1855 letter to the *New York Tribune*, "The least that even the less sanguine ones expected was to find parrots rocking on the boughs and monkeys playing on the palm-trees."

Romance soon made room for determined resignation. The heat of summer came, as did deadly epidemics and Indian attacks. After the first few wet years, the dry years came. But the German settlers persevered. They had no other choice. The Adelsverein had collapsed, and they had no money to move elsewhere. They learned to save as much as possible during the fat years in anticipation of the lean ones, and they seldom threw anything away. Their peculiar blend of hardheaded practicality and romanticism was typified in the hotel built by Charles Nimitz, which stands today as the Admiral Nimitz Museum at the corner of Main Street/US 290 and Washington Street.

ADMIRAL NIMITZ MUSEUM

340 E. Main • 997-8600 • www.nimitz-museum.org • Open daily • Fee • W Variable

Charles Nimitz and wife Sophie founded the Nimitz Hotel back in 1852, beginning with four rooms and a huge fireplace in the central hall. Within a few years, it had been enlarged to thirty rooms. The place was always buzzing; after all, it was the last real hotel between Fredericksburg and San Diego, California, until the 1870s. And since it happened to be on the road west across the great American desert, everybody stayed there, eager to get their first bath in weeks or to get one last good meal before commencing the weeks-long trek west. Robert E. Lee, General Phil Sheridan, and Elisabet Ney were but a few of the hotel's distinguished guests. Part of the trek around the museum affords a glimpse inside the old bathhouse, with its line of hand-soldered tin bathtubs and center fireplace, where the water was heated.

The Nimitz had the frontier's first bathhouse, a cellar brewery, and a great concert/dance hall. Gardens behind the hotel produced most of the dining-room fare, even the table wine. Newcomers are invariably impressed by the Nimitz's fanciful, steamboat-like superstructure, complete with bridge and crow's nest. Nimitz added it during the 1880s as a nostalgic indulgence. He could well afford it. Despite the horrors of the Civil War, the decline in use of the Military Road, and the closing of the frontier forts, Fredericksburg prospered, slowly but steadily, as a self-contained community. Wagons hauled the region's excess produce down to San Antonio and hauled back luxury items like the town's first electric light plant (1896), ice cream-making factory (1907), wrought-iron filigree, and white elephants.

In November 1883, a traveler described the Nimitz as the best hotel in Western Texas in quality and price. "They give you fine meals and splendid beds at $1.75 per day. I asked one of the clerks what they did on Sunday. He said, 'Keep open, play pool and gamble.'"

Will Porter (O. Henry) visited Fredericksburg at least once during his Austin years (1884–1898) and used it as the setting for his story "A Chaparral Prince." He described it as "a pleasant little Rhine village. . . . They are all German people who live in Fredericksburg. Of evenings they sit at little tables along the sidewalk and drink beer and play pinochle and scat. They are very thrifty people." Nimitz family lore has it that Captain Nimitz regaled the ever-ready-to-listen Porter with a number of stories, one of which eventually grew into "A Chaparral Prince."

Charles' grandson, Chester Nimitz, spent his early years at the hotel and in Kerrville before entering the Naval Academy and eventually becoming America's highest-ranking seaman in World War II.

The old hotel is now headquarters for the Admiral Nimitz Museum, an approximately nine-acre day-use museum named for Admiral Chester W. Nimitz. At Admiral Nimitz's request, it is dedicated to the 2.5 million men and women who served with him in the Pacific. The motto of the museum is "We inspire our youth by honoring our heroes."

Several museums make up the center: the National Museum of the Pacific War, the George H. W. Bush Gallery, the Admiral Nimitz Museum, the Japanese Garden of Peace, the Pacific Combat Zone, the Plaza of the Presidents, the Surface Warfare Plaza, the Memorial Wall, the Veterans Walk of Honor, and the Center for Pacific War Studies. In addition to nearly 45,000 square feet of indoor exhibit space, the museum boasts an impressive display of Allied and Japanese aircraft, tanks, guns, and other large artifacts made famous during the Pacific War campaigns. The Japanese Garden of Peace, which was donated by the people of Japan in honor of Admiral Nimitz, is a painstakingly identical replica of the garden of the great Japanese admiral Heihachiro Togo, of whom Nimitz was a self-proclaimed disciple.

PIONEER PLACE GARDEN

Behind the Vereinskirche • Free • W

The Pioneer Place Garden is a quiet little green spot whose most obvious feature is the old wooden waterwheel. Said wheel was dedicated by the people of Fredericksburg to Lyman Wight's long-vanished Mormon colony at nearby Zodiac, in gratitude for the invaluable help given by the Mormons during the difficult early years here.

Most of the Germans who came to Texas had no idea what they were getting themselves into. For most, romantic optimism was soon replaced by a simple struggle to survive in a land harsher than any of them had imagined. William Hermes Sr. arrived in Fredericksburg early in 1847 and years later described his arrival in Texas and his subsequent journey to Fredericksburg.

He landed in Galveston in late 1846. The reception on the Galveston wharf was not very agreeable. A man, who probably was an agent for the Castro Colony, shouted in a loud, warning voice: "My country people, if you go to Indian Point, you enter into everlasting torment. The way to New Braunfels is strewn with bleaching bones of the colonists," and so on. He then recommended the Castro's Colony.

Frightened by such a reception and after being informed in Galveston that chances to be transported inland from Indian Point were questionable and that a great number of colonists were sick there, many decided to stay in Galveston; others decided to go inland to relatives and friends, or to New Braunfels via Houston. Hermes went to New Braunfels.

In New Braunfels, he learned that all of the land had already been given away, and he would have to go to Fredericksburg or Fisher-Miller Grant to receive free land. As he was deliberating how to get to Fredericksburg being minus funds, some colored wagoneers—slaves, from the Victoria neighborhood—proposed that he accompany them to Indian Point where they were to load freight for Fredericksburg. They wanted a white man to accompany them to feel more secure against annoyances from insolent whites.

Hermes accepted their proposition, so as to get to know the land and the people, and because he wanted to find out whether it was true, that the route was strewn with bleaching bones of emigrants marking the way from Indian Point to New Braunfels. He saw no human skeletons, but many carcasses of draft animals.

At Indian Point, he found a number of colonists unable to get away, partly because of sickness and partly because of lack of funds to pay the high freight to the colonies. He saw pitiable figures, wasted by intermittent fever and diarrhea. One family lived in a dugout made in the sand; for a roof they had spread all kinds of pieces of cloth sewn together. Several members of the family had died, others were sick.

Many colonists who had deposited their funds with the Emigration Company, in Frankfort or Bremen, with promise that it would be paid out to them in Texas, could not be paid out for lack of funds here. No wonder that under such evil conditions imprecations were hurled at the Emigration Company and its agents.

The journey of several weeks from Indian Point to Fredericksburg was without mishap except for an intermittent fever Hermes caught. He reached Fredericksburg, a stranger, sick, and minus funds. When he had recuperated a little, he began looking for work which was not hard to find, since laborers were scarce. Entire families were bedridden with sickness, and many who were recovering were yet too weak to work. Laying of the fence around the municipal garden often required two men to lift a fence rail.

At the beginning of 1847, the death rate in Fredericksburg was such that not enough coffins could be provided. Corpses were sewn up in sacks, placed on carts, and buried in the cemetery outside of town.

Logs had to be felled and hauled for construction of homes, rails for fencing fields and gardens, stone from Bear Creek for fireplaces, and so on. Hermes also found employment at the municipal warehouse whenever goods were to be moved from one room to another room.

Hermes got acquainted with the municipal officials. At the head was Director Schubert who before going on a hunting expedition distributed his orders and left the rest to Mr. P. Bickel. Bickel worked chiefly in the "Comptoir" with Th. Specht, under whom stood a Mr. Schildknecht, who managed the warehouse with the help of an assistant.

The municipal headquarters consisted of adjoining rooms with a spacious courtyard. The entrance was through a gate, to the right of which was the dining room, to the left the "Comptoir" (countinghouse), to both of which connected the warerooms, behind and to the right of the warehouse was a room for the commissariat officer, and next to it the kitchen. At the opposite side of the yard were rooms for the soldiers of the municipality, and at the rear of those, the stables. A house for the director was situated somewhat aside near the soldiers' quarters. The big cannon was mounted in front of the entrance.

Headquarters was arranged to protect the supplies stored in the warehouse against possible Indian raids.

Provisions were hauled from Indian Point and from Houston. Later a contract was entered into with Mr. Roeder for supplying corn and meal. Whenever wagons arrived with provisions, the words could be heard, "Tomorrow we get provisions." The news spread quickly from house to house throughout the colony, and the following morning one could see the mothers and children going to the warehouse with caldrons, baskets, and sacks to bring home the necessities of life.

For a long time the municipal warehouse was the only supply place. Mr. von Ransleben opened a store, and soon thereafter Louis Martin. They conducted exchange trade with the Indians, taking in trade both tanned and untanned skins, which the municipal officials did not do. Ready money was scarce. Whoever worked for the officials was credited with one-dollar-a-day wages on the company books. One then could issue a check against the credit amount, for which the recipient then drew supplies from the warehouse.

Whenever the wagoneers were detained by bad weather and roads, and supplies could not be brought in on schedule, famine would set in; also, when provisions were not sufficiently protected against rains, sicknesses developed from consuming spoiled articles of food. At times moldy ship bread and musty cornmeal were furnished.

Regarding the epidemic disease that demanded so many victims, it was not scurvy, as Dr. Schubert diagnosed. The wrong diagnosis was fateful for many. Instead of prescribing nourishing food and fresh meat, Schubert recommended wild portulaca as a remedy.

Food shortages caused people to try substitutes. Acorns from the live oak trees were used as a coffee substitute and for bread. The acorns were roasted, ground, and made into a dough, then baked.

When these famine periods were overcome, the young folks again lived a gaysome life. Fandangos were arranged, usually out in the open in front of a store or tavern, sometimes under an arbor improvised of green tree branches. At times the fandangos ended in quarreling, usually between North Germans, called Hanoverians, and the South Germans, Nassauers, for the two states from which the majority of the Fredericksburg colonists emigrated.

On Sundays, Bickel held divine services under a large live oak tree. He also performed marriage ceremonies and baptisms.

Effort was made to classify the many Indian tribes into friendly and hostile classifications, whereby the Comanche Indians were classed as friendly. Experience revealed that they were friendly when they were to be presented gifts, but the balance of the time they were not to be trusted. The Delawares and Shawnees only proved true to their word. They also spoke some English, while the Comanches, aside from their Indian language, understood Spanish. The Delawares and Shawnees had hunting grounds in the vicinity of Fredericksburg and brought venison, bear meat, and furs for barter.

Before Meusebach made the treaty with the Comanche Indians at the San Saba, the Fredericksburg colonists lived in fear of attack by Indians and organized themselves into a mounted company and a foot company to defend the colony. Mr. Bickel commanded the foot company and Mr. Ransleben the mounted company. A shot from the cannon was the signal for all colonists to assemble armed on the plaza before the municipal building.

The expected attack never occurred, in consequence of Meusebach's treaty with the Comanches and Lipans on the San Saba whereby the Indians permitted German colonists to establish colonies in the Grant Lands and promised to never attack the colonists.

In celebration of the event, and as compensation for that concession, the Indians were promised presents and a feast. At the appointed time, several hundred Indians came to Fredericksburg and camped in the vicinity of the municipal building where they received their presents. A number of oxen were killed in order to furnish meat to the Indians. At night the Indians, sitting in groups around their campfires, roasted the meat on sticks. Late into the night they made very great noise by alternatingly beating on drums and kettles accompanied with hideous monotonous singing that, at a distance, sounded like a muffled howling. The Indians also proved themselves quite annoying with their begging when they spotted some article which they desired. The Fredericksburg colonists were glad when after a few days they were rid of their uncanny guests.

Now, arrangements were to be undertaken to begin settling the so-called Grant. A little delay occurred here, probably by the dismissal of Director Schubert who was replaced by Mr. von Coll. An entirely different system of administration was begun, everything was placed on a more economical basis, a day's wages were reduced from a dollar to seventy-five cents, and so on.

Hermes tried to earn $1.50 a day as a carpenter at building the "coffee-mill" Vereinskirche, but on the second day he cut his foot with a broadaxe and had to give it up. Dr. Keidel sewed his wound up, and when his foot had healed he found employment for a short time as a bookkeeper and later in a barroom.

As you may have noticed, Main Street in Fredericksburg is one of the broadest streets in any Hill Country town or city. When Fredericksburg's town fathers laid out Main Street, they made sure that a sixteen-horse team and wagon could make a clean U-turn in it. One thing you may not have noticed is that, traveling east from the center of town on Main, the first letters of all the cross-streets combine to spell "all welcome." Traveling west from the center on Main, the combined first letters of all the cross-streets read "come back."

From the Nimitz Museum, continue east on Main Street/US 290. A little more than four miles east of the Gillespie County courthouse in downtown Fredericksburg, US 290 crosses the Pedernales River. Zodiac stood just upstream, in the fields to your left.

ZODIAC

Site on private property, not open to public

Nothing remains of Zodiac today except a one-acre cemetery plot that lies hidden away, north of the road, on the western banks of the river. Church officials from Salt Lake City visit the plot occasionally to keep it clean, but otherwise Lyman Wight and his followers buried here sleep on, undisturbed.

Shortly after the Mormons departed, a group of English, German, and Danish families moved in. Before and during the Civil War, the area was the site of the only Gillespie County cotton plantation to use slave labor; descendants of the slaves still owned land there as late as 1947. The town was renamed Rocky Hill after the local school, built in 1885.

In the spring of 1875, George Elam left Bandera with a herd of one thousand head bound for Ogallala, Nebraska. When they reached a farming settlement on the Pedernales near Fredericksburg (probably Rocky Hill), a German farmer living nearby thought he saw the family milk cow in the herd. "The news spread through the settlement like wildfire, and in a short while there must have been a hundred or more indignant neighbors of his around our herd. They had the effrontery to insinuate that Childs [Lige Childs, the trail boss] was trying to steal old Betsy. The result was that Childs was arrested by the Sheriff and taken to jail at Fredericksburg. However, just as they got him to the jail door, one of the boys suddenly reminded him that he had a bill of sale to that cow in his coat pocket. Whereupon Childs reached into his pocket and produced the paper which showed that he had bought old Betsy down in Atascosa County. There was a consultation among the irate farmers and the Sheriff. It didn't hardly look right to put a man in jail for stealing an animal when he had a bill of sale for it. So they told Childs he could go, but that the farmer would keep the cow."

Turn around, recross the river, and head back toward Fredericksburg. Shortly you see on your right Fort Martin Scott.

FORT MARTIN SCOTT

1606 E. Main, about 2 miles east of downtown Fredericksburg • 997-9895 • Open Friday through Sunday • Donation • W with assistance

General Zachary Scott led the Army of Observation into Texas in July 1845. In March 1846, Taylor's army established Fort Brown, the first permanent U.S. military installation in Texas, on the north bank of the Rio Bravo, across from the Mexican city of Matamoros. It was here that the war with Mexico over who owned Texas began.

With the end of the war in 1848, the army began constructing a line of forts along the Rio Grande from Brownsville to El Paso, and another line of forts along the edge of Texas' rapidly expanding western frontier, from Fort Duncan at Eagle Pass on the Rio Grande, north to Fort Worth. These forts were designed to protect settlers and travelers from attacks by Indians and brigands.

One of these frontier posts was Fort Martin Scott, established in December 1848, two miles east of Fredericksburg on Barons Creek. Folks called the place "the fort at Fredericksburg," or "Camp Houston," until December 1849, when the army officially named the post in honor of a U.S. Army officer killed in the war with Mexico. Established by Company D of the First U.S. Infantry, the fort was subsequently garrisoned by companies of the Eighth Infantry and the Second Dragoons, or mounted infantry. Mounted infantry was cheaper to fund than cavalry, which was important to the penny-pinching U.S. Congress.

At the tail end of 1850, the army finally decided to build permanent housing for the troops. The army regarded the fort as temporary, so it directed that the buildings be of the most economical character, consistent with the health and comfort of the troops. This meant an assortment of log and adobe buildings for the troops and officers, and a stout stone guardhouse for the prisoners.

The buildings may have been cheap, but they were well built, thanks to the meticulous German craftsmen from Fredericksburg who constructed them. Most of the lumber came from the Mormon sawmills at Zodiac, east of the fort on the Pedernales River. A government inspector noted in 1853 that "the buildings put up are of a better description than at most of the posts in Texas," where soldiers often lived in tents or stick-and-mud huts of their own construction.

Fort sites were carefully picked. Grassy meadows where the animals could graze, wood for fuel, and building materials had to be readily available. But the most essential factor in choosing a fort site was a location near good water—a spring or perennial, clear-running stream. The ideal site also had to have good drainage—standing water was to be avoided like the plague. Malaria, yellow fever, tuberculosis, cholera, dysentery, and breakbone fever were associated with poor drainage and stagnant water. Scientists didn't know enough yet about the nature of sickness to finger mosquitoes and microbes as the culprits; they blamed bad humors, spontaneous generation, or mysterious poisonous mists and vapors caused by rotting vegetable matter.

The fort played an important role in the lives of Fredericksburg and Zodiac, but the relationship between the soldiers and the settlers was not always gracious. The soldiers came from many different places, so it was inevitable that conflicts would flare up. One incident led to a fire that destroyed the earliest records of Gillespie County on July 1, 1850. John Hunter, the county clerk, kept all the county records at his store (located where the Bank of Fredericksburg now stands). Like most merchants of his time, Hunter sold whiskey. On the last night of June 1850, a young soldier cursed Hunter when Hunter refused to sell him any more liquor. Angered, Hunter threw the drunken soldier across a table and stabbed the soldier in the chest with a knife, killing him instantly.

Naturally, the killing aroused much resentment among the dead man's compatriots, and the next night about forty of them came to the store looking for revenge. Hunter wasn't there. Forewarned, he was hiding at a friend's place on Live Oak Creek. Since Hunter was not available for slaughter, the soldiers burned down his store. Efforts to rescue the county records were thwarted by the vengeful soldiers.

Penateka Comanches and Lipan Apaches regularly visited Fort Martin Scott. These visits were usually peaceful. Richard Irving Dodge was stationed at Fort Martin Scott from the spring of 1851 until February 1852. Then a second lieutenant, Dodge oversaw road construction between the fort and San Antonio. He wrote of one visitor,

> Years ago, when matches were not so universally used as now, a Lipan Indian was visiting Fort Martin Scott in Texas. One day an officer to whom he was talking took from his pocket a box of what, to the Indian, were merely little sticks, and scratching one on a stone, lit his pipe. The Lipan eagerly inquired into this mystery, and looked on with astonishment while several matches were lighted for his gratification. Going to his camp near by, he soon came back, bringing half a dozen beautifully dressed wildcat skins, which he offered for the wonderful box. The exchange was accepted, and he went off greatly pleased. Some time after he was found sitting by a large stone, on which he was striking match after match, holding each in his fingers until forced to drop it, and then carefully inspecting the scorched fingers, as if to assure himself that it was real fire. This he continued until every match was burned.

The basic dress of nineteenth-century Lipan and Comanche men was buckskin moccasins, leggins, and breechclout. In cold weather, a buckskin shirt was added, and a buffalo robe or blanket wrapped around the body. Women—both Lipan and Comanche—dressed in knee-length buckskin skirts, moccasins, leggins, and loose-fitting, poncho-like blouses fashioned from a single deerskin. These were often decorated with fringe, beadwork, and tin jingles.

Comanche men refused to do anything beyond eat, fight, and hunt. Lipan women, on the other hand, enjoyed a rough equality with the men. They maintained gardens, sewed, and decorated elaborate outfits. Lipan men, in addition to hunting and fighting, also did drudge work like hauling water and packing meat on the horses. Comanche men would never stoop to such tasks.

By 1853, Fort Martin Scott had been demoted to a forage depot for wagon trains that supplied the new upper frontier posts. The garrison consisted of a sergeant, a corporal, and sixteen men of the Eighth Infantry under the command of Lt. Theodore Fink. A government inspector noted that year, "An Ordinance sgt. is stationed here, but there is little for him to do, the only ordinance at the post being a 12-pounder mountain howitzer, with less than 100 rounds of fixed ammunition and 33 pounds of powder.

"Provisions are obtained from the San Antonio depot. Some 3,000 rations are on hand and they are in good condition. The cost of the rations delivered at the post is 17 and 1/2 cents. No parts of it could be bought on advantageous terms in the vicinity. On account of the smallness of the command, fresh beef cannot be obtained. It's sold generally at 5 cents per pound."

There was a notable absence of spit and polish at the fort, the inspector noted. "Black belts and white belts are intermixed; some are destitute of parts of their equipment. One was without arms and almost all had a very limited supply of clothing. They had not received much instruction and made but an indifferent appearance on parade."

Soon after this report, the army closed Fort Martin Scott; in its opinion, the frontier had been tamed. It was certainly swarming with Americans now, at the expense of the Indians. In just three years—between 1847 and 1850—Texas' non-Indian population increased by nearly 50 percent, to over 212,000 persons.

On the other hand, the total Indian population in Texas in 1849 was only about twenty-nine thousand souls, and rapidly decreasing. About twenty thousand of these were Comanches; the rest were Kiowas, Lipan Apaches, Tonkawas, Wacos, and other smaller groups. Bison and the other game that the hunting tribes of Texas depended on for food, clothing, and shelter had dwindled to the point that the tribes were frequently on the brink of starvation. Disease also hit hard. The Penateka Comanches, whose territory included Fort Martin Scott, were ravaged by epidemics of smallpox, cholera, and venereal diseases in 1848 and 1849. Thousands died, including the great chiefs Old Owl and Santa Anna, who had made peace with Meusebach and the Germans in 1847.

The widow of the great chief Santa Anna bucked the tribe's male supremacy and formed a semiautonomous band of seven women, all widows like herself. She owned a large herd of horses and was a successful hunter, having shot with her rifle fifteen deer in a morning's hunt.

Though acquainted with firearms, the Lipans and Comanches of the 1850s still preferred the bow and arrow. They used three-to-four-foot-long bows. The arrows had hardwood shafts and iron points cut from barrel hoops or other metal. Comanches also carried long lances decorated with feathers and other ornamentation, and tipped with long, sharp steel blades as wicked as any Bowie knife. As intimidating as these lances were, they could not hold back all the white people, who outnumbered the indigenous peoples twenty to one.

Faced with such odds, the tribes could either fight and die; accommodate the whites, which meant settling down and adapting the white lifestyle; or move on, into someone else's territory. In practice, they generally died or moved on.

In 1856, camels came to Texas, the vehicles of an army experiment to improve transcontinental travel. Fort Martin Scott was first considered, and then dismissed, as home base for the camel corps. Little of the fort remained. Many of its twenty-one buildings had already been dismantled and recycled into other nearby buildings, like perhaps an adobe wall in Fredericksburg's old Nimitz Hotel, which was a favored hangout for frontier soldiers. The camels, trainers, and troopers finally settled at nearby Camp Verde; you'll read about them in the Hill Country Rivers trip.

The fort was reoccupied sporadically by the Confederates during the Civil War before being closed for good by the U.S. Cavalry in December 1866. John T. Braeutigam bought the property in 1870. He and his family made the officers' quarters their home. Using materials salvaged from the fort's remaining buildings, Braeutigam built a dance hall and saloon up at the front of the property (alongside present-day US 290) and called it Braeutigam's Garten. It was possibly the county's first such hall; at any rate, the first annual Gillespie County Fair was held on the Garten grounds in 1881. This continued for several years, and then Braeutigam was robbed and murdered at the Garten in 1884 by a gang of four men led by Judd Roberts. A group of Texas Rangers that included Ira Aten was dispatched to hunt down the killers. They quickly captured Roberts and another man. The people of Fredericksburg were so enraged that the men were not safe in the town's flimsy rock and wood jail, so they were moved to San Antonio. A Fredericksburg posse caught a third suspect and put him in the local jail, which burned down shortly thereafter, the prisoner dying inside. After four months, Roberts and his partner escaped the San Antonio jail and headed for Travis Peak in Travis County. Aten went there to track him down. Roberts, who had been born and raised in Williamson County, headed north to join up with Butch Cassidy. After many days' frustration, Aten finally found Roberts, and they shot it out. Aten hit Roberts' right-hand trigger finger. Roberts missed. Roberts leapt on his horse and rode away. Aten chased him to a doctor's office on the Colorado River in Burnet County. The doctor had treated Roberts an hour earlier. Aten let him go for the time being. But Roberts returned to the area several months later, settling near Liberty Hill. Aten chased him down again, and Roberts again headed north. Aten caught up with him in 1887 in the Texas Panhandle. Roberts was working on one ranch and courting a girl who lived on another ranch. Aten and his partner John Hughes ambushed Roberts, filling him full of holes. Before dying in his sweetheart's arms, he confessed to the Braeutigam murder.

Following Braeutigam's death, the fair moved elsewhere; the family tried to keep the place going for a while, but it soon closed. The land stayed in the family until 1959, when Raymond Braeutigam sold the property to the city of Fredericksburg. It was closed to the public until 1989, when the old fort grounds were opened as a public park. Of the several buildings on the grounds, only the old guardhouse/stockade is original. The other buildings are reasonably faithful replicas, for example, the adobe, stuccoed officers' quarters, which consist of two rooms, each with a fireplace and a large shaded front porch. The fort's drill grounds were located across the creek, in what is now a meadow. Tradition says that this is where the county fair's horse races were later run. At any rate, we can be sure that everyone was well lubed. This stretch of Barons Creek is generously littered with the shards of ancient champagne bottles and glasses, long since shattered and worn smooth by 140 years of flowing water.

From Fort Martin Scott, go back to downtown Fredericksburg, to the junction of US 290 and SH 16. Turn left on SH 16, toward Kerrville. About 3.5 miles later, you pass the entrance to Lady Bird Johnson Municipal Park, located on Live Oak Creek.

Back in 1851, a German immigrant millwright named Carl Guenther came to Fredericksburg and built a gristmill on Live Oak Creek, taking up where the Mormons left off. At that time, the nearest mill was a several-day journey away. The millstones were imported from France. He built the waterwheel and carved the driving gears out of native woods, and through careful craftsmanship, Guenther was later able to boast that when "the various moving parts were assembled, they fit perfectly and ran like clockwork." But not long after its completion, a flash flood washed the mill away. Although dismayed by the loss, Guenther rebuilt it stronger than before and added a sawmill. By 1859, Live Oak Creek's flow began to diminish, and a steam-powered mill opened nearby, so Guenther and family moved to San Antonio where only one water-powered mill served a city of ten thousand. Guenther's mill prospered, and he became one of the wealthiest men in San Antonio, as well as a leader of San Antonio's sizeable German population. Guenther died in 1902 at the ripe old age of seventy-six. The company he founded, Pioneer Flour Mills, is the country's oldest continuously owned flour-milling business still operated by members of the same family.

Just over five miles from the center of Fredericksburg, you see on your right a state sign reading "Picnic Area 1 Mi." Go another tenth of a mile and turn left on the little paved road marked by "Old Kerrville Rd." and "Bear Creek" signs. After you cross the Pedernales, bear right at the road's fork (Old Kerrville Road). One mile after you leave SH 16, you pass an old limestone home sitting off to your left on a hill overlooking the Pedernales.

PETRI-LUNGKWITZ FARM

6 miles from Fredericksburg • Private residence

This is the old farm of German Texas' first great painters, Richard Petri and Hermann Lungkwitz. The pair had been classmates at the Academy of Fine Arts in Dresden, and Hermann married one of Richard's sisters, Elisabeth. The trio immigrated to Texas in 1851, part of the influx of "forty-eighters" seeking the freedom they could not get in Germany.

After living in New Braunfels, Petri and Lungkwitz bought this plot of land and began life as frontier painters and farmers. Both men painted scenes from everyday life: women milking cows, Indians, soldiers at Fort Martin Scott, and the mills at Comfort, Fredericksburg, and Barton Springs.

For his Mexican-American War services, William Keidel (see Keidel Family Medical Complex) was awarded a section of land along Bear Creek, adjacent to the Petri-Lungkwitz farm. Keidel family tradition says that Keidel granted them a fifty-foot-wide easement across his land so that their cattle could get water at Bear Creek. It was the neighborly thing to do; cooperation was the key to survival. Petri and Lungkwitz needed all the help they could get, for as Miss

Margaret Keidel (Wilhelm's granddaughter) observed, "They were patricians who were really out of place living with pigs and cows."

In 1856, Petri's sister Marie married Jacob Kuechler. Jacob Kuechler was born in the German state of Hesse-Darmstadt in 1823 and graduated from the University of Giessen with a degree in civil engineering and forestry. He emigrated to Texas in 1847 with the Darmstadt colony and helped found Bettina. After Bettina's collapse, Kuechler settled at Fredericksburg, working as a forester. He became a U.S. citizen in 1853. After his marriage to Marie Petri, Kuechler farmed with Hermann Lungkwitz.

The rigors of farm life proved to be too much for Richard Petri's frail physique. Delirious with fever, he wandered down the Pedernales and drowned in December 1857.

During the 1850s, Kuechler worked as a surveyor in Gillespie County. In the course of his work, he noticed that the growth rings of the trees he cut alternated between thin and thick. Intellectual that he was, he wondered why this happened. He wondered if this was linked in any way to the cycles of wet and dry years that the German pioneers had been experiencing during their first ten years in the Hill Country. They had arrived during one of the region's wet cycles and were unprepared when hit by drought in succeeding years. Some wondered if it would ever rain again. Kuechler compared dry and wet years from rings of post oaks going back to 1727 to prove that there would be extended periods, even years, of drought, but the rains would eventually return. His study was published as "Das Klima von Texas" in the German-language newspaper, *Texas Staats-Zeitung*, in 1859 and in the *Texas Almanac* two years later.

After Texas seceded from the Union in 1861, Governor Sam Houston commissioned Kuechler to enroll state militia troops in Gillespie County. Captain Kuechler signed up only German Unionists in his frontier company, which was then dismissed by Houston's Confederate successor, Governor Francis R. Lubbock. Kuechler then served as a guide to German Unionists fleeing to Mexico. He survived the battle of the Nueces and lived in exile in Mexico during the rest of the war and worked as a surveyor in northern Mexico until the end of 1867.

Lungkwitz found it impossible to make a living by painting during the Civil War, so he moved to San Antonio and learned photography. He served several years as photographer for the Texas General Land Office and then returned to painting and teaching art. He died in Austin in 1891.

Kuechler returned to Texas in 1867 and was appointed deputy collector of customs at San Antonio. Kuechler was elected and served as General Land Office commissioner from 1870 until 1874. Thereafter, he surveyed land for railroads in the Trans-Pecos region. Kuechler died in Austin in 1893 and was buried in Oakwood Cemetery.

The house that stands here was built by the folks who bought the land from Hermann Lungkwitz and his brother in 1869. The two-story limestone house was built in 1880 right next to the old Petri-Lungkwitz cabin, now vanished.

Continue on the Old Kerrville Road south. In about a mile you come to a small, paved road running off to your left. It is marked by a Center Point Road sign, a solitary mailbox, and a grove of pecan trees. SH 16 is just ahead across the river. Turn left on Center Point Road, aka Bear Creek Road. About eight miles out on this road, you begin to follow Bear Creek quite closely for about two miles.

Very quickly you are topping the Divide between the Pedernales and Guadalupe rivers. You get some great canyon views to the west (your right), and soon you are making a scenic descent toward the Guadalupe valley.

About five miles from the Divide, Bear Creek Road comes to a T intersection with FM 1341. Turn left and follow FM 1341 across I-10 and turn left onto the I-10 frontage road. Stay on I-10 about three miles, taking the Business 87 exit into Comfort. Turn right on FM 473 in the city, then veer right on SH 27 toward Center Point.

COMFORT

Kendall County • 2,400 (approximate) • About 25 miles from Fredericksburg

You cross Cypress Creek as you leave town. Back when the Mormons camped at this creek while on their way from Cherry Spring to Bandera, only the shingle makers down by the Guadalupe lived anywhere nearby.

Take SH 27 to Center Point, turning left onto FM 480.

CENTER POINT

Kerr County • 800 (approximate) • About 9 miles from Comfort

In January 1854, the wandering colony stopped on Verde Creek near Center Point, where they built a gristmill and sawmill. They stayed about six months and then moved on in search of a better location.

Center Point was also home after the Civil War to the "Fightin' Parson," Andy Potter. Sent to the rough-and-tumble Kerr County circuit in 1867, Potter chose to hold his first West Texas revival at Center Point. Local believers had been asked to erect an arbor for the occasion. But when Potter arrived he found no arbor, whereupon he told Bandera County Sheriff Buck Hamilton that if he couldn't get the lazy Methodists to build an arbor, he would get Buck and all the sinners to build it. The sinners laid aside their regular work and put up the arbor. Sheriff Buck even kicked in all the beef for the three-week meeting.

Potter has become an almost mythological character in Texas frontier history. Stories of his exploits abound, all of them entertaining. Most of them probably contain at least a kernel of truth, and this book, and its companion volume, *Lone Star Travel Guide to Central Texas*, are full of them.

Let's start with the facts of his life, as per the *Handbook of Texas*: Andrew Jackson Potter was born in Missouri in 1830. Orphaned at age ten, Potter became a jockey, running with a rough, undisciplined horse-racing crowd. He learned how to play cards and shoot straight, and somehow he also managed to learn how to read and write. Potter served in the Mexican War under General Sterling Price. His subsequent army service included driving ox teams to Santa Fe, fighting Indians and Mexicans, acting as a scout, and serving as a nurse at Santa Fe and Fort Leavenworth. Potter went to California in 1851 to prospect for gold but returned the following year to San Antonio, where he worked as a freighter. In 1853, he married Emily C. Guin, who bore the brunt of raising their fourteen children, since Potter spent so much time away from home. In 1856, while hauling lumber from Bastrop County to San Marcos, he was converted by Methodist circuit rider Rev. J. G. John at a camp meeting at Craft's Prairie (aka Alum Creek) and was immediately inspired to preach the Gospel.

Since his formal schooling had been brief, he had to study diligently in order to be licensed to preach by the Methodist Church. He preached with great enthusiasm and made special appeals to the rougher elements. He earned the nickname "fighting parson," according to his son T. W. Potter, "because he stayed when other preachers had been scared away."

In February 1862, Potter enlisted as a private in the Confederate Thirty-sixth Texas Cavalry. He participated in the Red River campaign of 1864 and was made chaplain of the Twenty-seventh Texas Cavalry. In 1866, he was assigned to the Methodist Church's West Texas Conference and appointed pastor of the Prairie Lea circuit. He served as a frontier minister and circuit rider until his death. At various times he headquartered at Bandera, Kerrville, Uvalde, Mason, Brady, and Boerne. During twelve years on the Kerrville circuit, he preached in homes, churches, camp meetings, saloons, and fort chapels. Potter frequently carried a gun, propping it against the pulpit when facing down drunken hecklers. He established a circuit at Fort Concho in 1880 and preached the first Methodist sermon at the site of future San Angelo. He founded the First Methodist Church in San Angelo in 1882. As a circuit rider, Potter rode an estimated 2,500 miles annually.

Potter may have been more flamboyant than most of his preaching peers, but no less resilient. Potter's friend Noah Smithwick once described the kind of preacher needed on the Texas frontier, although in this instance he was speaking of the Rev. Hugh M. Childress: "He was an expert with a violin, and even 'tripped the light fantastic.' For an all around useful man he had few equals, always bearing his full share of anything that came along, from a prayer meeting to an Indian fight. A preacher who could only talk found himself out of a job in these parts."

Potter was also a trail driver; he led his first herd of cattle to Kansas in 1861. Later, the Kendall County sheriff appointed him to escort trail drivers through the county. In 1883, he and another son, Colonel Jack Potter, laid out the Potter and Blocker Trail, a variant of the Western Trail. That year he moved his family to San Angelo but continued riding the circuit. In 1894, he was sent to preach the Lockhart circuit. He died in the pulpit while delivering a sermon at Tilmon Chapel in Caldwell County on October 21, 1895.

CAMP VERDE

Kerr County • 41 • About 6.5 miles from Center Point

Camp Verde is covered at length in the Hill Country Rivers trip, but while we're here, here's another Andy Potter story. Upon joining the Confederate Army, Potter was sent with his regiment to Camp Verde to guard prisoners of war.

Potter showed his comrades-in-arms just why he was called The Fightin' Parson early on when he tamed the regiment's bully, a muscular giant, dreaded by most of the men in the regiment. Being a bitter enemy of religion, he took great pleasure in hurling insults at the preacher. One morning the bully made a false statement about the parson within hearing range of the latter. Potter walked up to the man and said, "Sir, you are a liar, and if you take that, you're a coward." When the bully advanced belligerently, Potter just shoved him back and scoffed, "You won't fight." And the bully didn't; instead he became Potter's friend and was a terror no more.

Chaplain Potter had a private's pay and rations. In camp he conducted regular religious services, counseled, taught men to read and write, handled mail, and comforted the sick. He once whipped a newspaper editor for libeling the army. In battle, until the order to fire came, he had his Bible in hand, preaching to his men as they crouched "on the brink of eternity." He fought with his men to the end of battle and then took down the dying men's last words to send to family or friends, prayed for the passing souls, and aided the wounded.

At Camp Verde, turn left on SH 173.

SH 173 passes through the Bandera Pass into the valley of the Medina River and the town of Bandera. The Mormons no doubt crossed the Bandera Mountains via the pass on their way from Center Point to Bandera. This road was part of a winding one-hundred-mile trail from San Antonio to Kerrville traveled by nineteenth-century Texas Rangers in their attempts to guard pioneer settlers from Indian attacks.

BANDERA

Bandera County Seat • 1,200 (approximate) • (830) • About 13 miles from Camp Verde

The first settlers here on the Medina River were shingle makers who set up camp by the river in 1852. In 1853, John James, Charles De Montel, and John Herndon surveyed and laid out the city of Bandera and built a sawmill to make shingles and lumber from the many cypress trees then growing along the river. Shingle making was not exactly a get-rich-quick proposition; a good shingle maker could make a thousand shingles a day, and the thousand shingles would sell for about six bucks delivered in San Antonio.

Philip Mazurek, who came to Bandera in 1855 from Poland with his parents when he was eight months old, became an excellent shingle maker. Years later he described the shingle-making process: Cypress blocks were sawed into thirty-two-inch lengths (twice the length of a finished shingle). These blocks were hauled up from the river banks and then cut in two and marked off to the proper thickness. Then the blocks were split and rived with a froe knife and wooden mallet. Next they were taken to a shaving horse and trimmed to a feather edge with a drawing knife. The shingles were stacked in huge piles to season. Afterward, they were put up in bundles of a thousand and in due time were hauled to market. Big ox wagons hauled them, twenty-five thousand shingles to the wagon. In San Antonio, the shingles sold for about $4.50 per thousand. Thousands of shingles were produced around Bandera. One cypress could make thirty-thousand shingles.

The road to San Antonio was very bad, especially at a point known as "the slideoff," so-called because in crossing over the steep hill, the load would often slide off the back of the wagon. To prevent this, a big piece of cypress timber, called the binding pole, had to be placed across the top of the load to keep everything in place, but there was still the danger of the wagon turning over.

People started to join the shingle makers almost immediately. The Mormons came to Bandera from Verde Creek during the spring of 1854. At first they camped across the river from the young town. They set to work making shoes, nails, and shingles (including one order for one hundred thousand shingles) and tending the local sawmill. Evidently, they commuted by boat to work across the river at the sawmill each morning. But finally the Mormons bought lots in the little city, where they built a schoolhouse and a furniture factory. Lyman Wight performed the first marriage in Bandera County between his son Levi Lamoni and Sophia Leyland. But troubles dogged them. While delivering lumber and shingles to a customer in San Antonio, they had difficulties with the Comanches.

The Mormons left Bandera in December 1854 for a spot farther downstream on the Medina. We have no recorded reasons as to why they left Bandera, but we can surmise that their proselytizing was a probable cause, considering their earlier hassles at Webberville.

But Bandera suffered only temporarily from the loss of the Mormons. Sixteen Polish families settled here in 1855. Freshly arrived from the motherland, they came first to Panna Maria and then to Castroville, only to find that all the choice acreage had already been taken. Town builder Charles DeMontel found them scratching their heads and talked them into moving to his town of Bandera, promising them work at his saw and shingle mill. The Poles started to work almost immediately upon their arrival. The men worked at the mill and cleared land, while the women tilled the soil and dug a millrace for Bandera's first gristmill. The mile-long race diverted water from the Medina River, which powered the mill. The race took the women several months to complete, but they had the satisfaction of seeing families from seventy-five miles around come to get their grain ground for their daily bread. Even the basics of life were hard to come by. To get a milch cow in those early days, two of the Poles walked to Castroville and drove the cow back on foot, a round-trip of at least sixty miles.

Indian raids continued until almost 1880, up and down the Medina valley. The Indians were loath to give up this territory, for not only was it a favored hunting spot, but it was also the source of their paint supply. The Comanches had discovered in the land around Bandera deposits of clay that were natural paints. Blue and yellow clays were found a few miles south of town, while white and red clays were located northwest of Bandera. Once the Comanches were driven from Bandera County and eventually onto the Oklahoma reservations, they were cut off from their "Valley of Paint."

Banderans have long been connoisseurs of prime horseflesh, and the January 21, 1886, edition of the *Bandera Enterprise* went on at length about the previous Saturday's slate of races. Practically the whole town turned out. The principal race of the day matched Brown Jug and Hummingbird. But previous to that contest, doctors Sharpe and Rice ran a fifty-yard footrace, with Sharpe representing Hummingbird and Rice filling in for Brown Jug. Sharpe won by five feet, and Rice fell flat on his face at the finish line. In the real race, Hummingbird won by sixty-two feet. Betting was widespread. When pari-mutuel betting became legal in Texas a few years ago, Bandera Downs was one of the first tracks in the state to open. Bandera may be a horse-race-loving town, but the track couldn't attract enough out-of-town patrons to make a profit, and it became one of the first tracks to close.

Bandera was a fun-loving town in those frontier days, as J. Marvin Hunter wrote in the early 1920s:

> The 21st of April, San Jacinto Day, and the 4th of July were the great days of the year; rain or shine, there was feasting and revelry on those days. But there were other occasions for jollification during the spring, summer and fall months, and the smallest local happening of good fortune wound up with a barbecue and a grand ball. And at these barbecues, always held in some one of the great cypress groves on the banks of the Medina River—the prettiest river in Texas—there was no dearth of orators. Every man was called on for a speech, and even the boys were led forward and in most instances forced to "make a talk."
>
> John Pyka was the chef at all these functions, always aided by a full corps of able volunteer assistants. The pits were prepared under John's supervision, ample supplies of seasoned live oak wood were placed on the ground, and the fires were lighted on the evening before the day of the celebration. John's vigilant eye was on that meat from the time it was spitted on clean wooden skewers until the day following when it was removed to the carving tables, brown, crisp, tender, thoroughly cooked, and retaining all its nourishing juices. All night long he stood over those furnace-like pits, reducing the heat here, adding more fuel there, all the while turning and "basting." And that "basting"! To the novice it was a liquid compound, profoundly mysterious. It must not be inferred that John Pyka was the only barbecue expert in Banderaland. To barbecue meats properly was an important part of a boy's education in those days. In the cow camp, on the hunt, at the roundup, and on the Indian trail, all these afforded opportunities to learn, and all the pupils were apt.
>
> When a barbecue was suggested no one thought of carrying a paper around soliciting subscriptions to defray expenses. Ice cream, lemonade, cold drinks, and the merry-go-round were unheard of. Even ice water was unknown, save that quaffed from the pure sparkling fountains that gushed from the everlasting hills. Fat yearlings, goats, and sheep were delivered at the pits. To offer an old animal, however well conditioned, would have been regarded as an insult. When the feast was spread the tables were not roped off to prevent the onrush of the rude and untutored rowdy. The ladies dined first, and then became waiters. The rarest bread, cakes, pies, pastries, and preserves, besides fish, fowl and fruits, all combined in making a feast fit for kings and high prelates.
>
> There was good fellowship, comradeship, friendship, social relationship, and sometimes the "Fighting Parson," old Jack Potter, would come around and then they would have worship. When it was announced that Parson Potter or any other minister was in town and was going to preach that night or next day, no matter what was on foot—horse race or dance—everything was called off, and everybody went to church. Protracted meetings were often held, always well attended, always earnest and orderly, but it was hard to get up a great revival. Parson Potter said it was no use to tell these people of Paradise, they wanted no better place than Bandera.

Jack Potter often employed "advance men" to proclaim his arrival in a town, or to announce the place where he would preach. Once, on arriving in a frontier town to preach, he discovered that the only available building was a saloon. He made arrangements to use it for the service and then stationed a "cryer" outside to hawk the service in his somewhat typical fashion: "Oyez, Oyez, there's goin' to be some hellfired racket here this mornin', gents, by Fightin' Parson Potter, a reformed gambler, gents, but now a shore-nuff gospel shark. It's a-goin' to begin in fifteen minutes, gents; all ye old whiskey soaks an' card sharks better come on over an' learn to mend yer ways or the devil's gonna get ye quiker'n hell can scorch a feather."

Follow SH 173's route through town to Main (SH 16). Turn left on Main to the Bandera County courthouse, located at Main and Pecan.

BANDERA COUNTY COURTHOUSE

Courthouse square, Main St.

Bandera County was organized in 1856 but did not get its first permanent courthouse (built as such) until this one was built in 1891 in the Second Renaissance Revival style. The shiny tin roof and turret are visible for miles around. It is built from locally quarried limestone, but it did not go up easily. There were factions, well represented in the Bandera County Court, that wanted the county seat moved farther west from Bandera City and ostensibly closer to the county's geographical center. At that time, Bandera County was slightly larger than it is now, extending about eight miles farther west almost to Leakey. Although the "movers" ultimately failed (unlike those in Blanco County), they managed to delay the courthouse's construction by a year or so.

Several historical markers are in front of the courthouse. One is a great granite boulder with a plaque honoring Amasa Clark, Bandera County's first permanent Anglo settler. Born in 1825, Clark served in the Mexican War, and upon his discharge in 1849 he came to San Antonio. Clark next spent time on the Guadalupe River making cypress shingles. In 1852, Clark first visited the Medina River valley while on a hunting trip with friendly Delaware Indians. At that time there were only three families living on the river where Bandera now stands. They were also shingle makers, and they moved on soon after Clark's visit. Amasa Clark liked the Medina valley so much that he moved here as quickly as possible. Clark worked with the Camp Verde camels for fourteen months (1859–1860) and sheared some of them to get hair for a mattress and pillows. One of those camel-hair pillows was placed under his head in his casket, and the other was donated to the Frontier Times Museum. Clark established his farm four miles west of Bandera and worked the place until his death in January 1927 at the ripe age of 101 years and 5 months.

Then there is the "Cowboy Capital of the World" marker, honoring Bandera County's best-known champion cowboys, starting with the semi-legendary Toots Mansfield, seven-time world champion calf roper.

An (in)famous native son that Bandera doesn't talk as much about was Will Carver, who rode with Tom "Black Jack" Ketchum and the Wild Bunch. Ketchum, who came from Tom Green County, Texas, left Texas for New Mexico in about 1890, possibly because of a murder or train robbery. By 1894, his brother Sam and Will Carver had joined him in the Cimarron Mountains of New Mexico, and they commenced robbing post offices and holding up stages, trains, and a railroad station in New Mexico and Arizona. They also spent a lot of time across the border in old Mexico.

Carver also spent some time in El Paso, where he was the final link in an interesting chain of unrelated killings. John Wesley Hardin was killed in El Paso in 1895 by the cowardly city constable John Selman. Less than a year later, Selman was shot dead by deputy U.S. Marshall George Scarbrough. In 1900, Will Carver shot and killed George Scarbrough. In 1901, Carver's old boss, Black Jack Ketchum, became the first man to hang for robbing a train.

The historical markers across the street tell of the old Texas Ranger trail and the last Indian victim in Bandera County.

From the courthouse, proceed east on Pecan as per the signs to the Frontier Times Museum.

FRONTIER TIMES MUSEUM

506 13th at Pecan • 796-3864 • Monday through Saturday 10–4:30, Sunday 1–4:30 • Fee • W

Started by Marvin Hunter in the 1920s, the Frontier Times Museum is an incredible pastiche of relics and artifacts. An eight-inch Brahma fetus mummy, a one-armed man's combination fork and knife, a map of Texas executed in rattlesnake rattles, grisly photos of dead bandits, and a pair of locked deer antlers are just a few of the estimated thirty thousand diverse articles on display.

The fireplace in the middle of the room was built from hundreds of fossil snails and the millstone used by Lyman Wight and the Mormons here at the Bandera Mill and then at their camp by Lake Medina. It is the same one lost in the Zodiac flood and later recovered through Wight's "miraculous" vision. The museum is worth the admission fee. It is owned and maintained by the citizens of Bandera County. Besides the interesting exhibits, the museum sells many interesting and otherwise hard-to-find books and publications about Bandera and Texas history.

As you walk out of the museum, you'll notice that you are on a slight hill. You'd never know it, but this little rise has a lot of local history. It was first called Poker Hill, back when it was just a dense live oak thicket. 'Tis said that during district court sessions, the grand and petit jurors would retire to the thicket and play poker while they deliberated the case at hand. After the thicket was cleared away and the Baptist church was built, the hill became Baptist Ridge, which it stayed until the Methodists and the other denominations started moving up on the hill. They couldn't just call it Baptist Ridge anymore, and Baptist-Methodist-Presbyterian Ridge was too much to say, so the folks just started calling it Delightful Hill.

From the museum, return to Main and turn left. In three blocks, you come to Cypress, where SH 16 leaves Main and makes a ninety-degree turn to the left.

HUFFMEYER STORE

Main and Cypress

Bandera's oldest Main Street building, Huffmeyer Store was built in 1873 of native limestone and stands at Bandera's historic crossroads. The big fire of 1915 destroyed most of the north side of Main between Cedar and Cypress streets.

Next door is Bandera's chief culinary shrine, the O. S. T. Restaurant.

O. S. T. RESTAURANT

307 Main • 796-3836 • Open daily • Breakfast, lunch, and dinner • MC, V • W with assistance

In business since 1921, everything on the extensive Tex and Tex-Mex menu is made from scratch. Mexican and American breakfasts are served at any hour, and there is a blue plate special at lunch Mondays through Fridays. Half orders are okay. Biscuits, onion rings, french fries, chili, beans, and soup are made on the premises. It's not bad for this day and time. There is no beer.

And while we're on the subject of food—with absolutely no aspersions being cast on the O. S. T.'s fare—most all of us have a touch of trouble with our stomachs from time to time. An old-time Bandera saloon keeper offered this personally tested cure to his customers: "When I came here, I had stummick trouble bad. I cured it by eating powdered cedar charcoal mixed with honey. I have passed this information on to many of my friends, and it has helped all of them, that has tried it."

And while we're on the subject of cures, here are some other Bandera folk remedies:

- For arthritis, wrap a brass wire that has three knots in it around the sore area three times.
- For boils, remove thorns from a prickly pear pad and split it open. Scrape out the pulp and wrap it in gauze and place it on the sore.
- For burns, put on homemade molasses.
- To cure a cold, boil some onions and add honey to the liquid and take often. Or, pour boiling water over ashes from a wood stove and then soak your feet in the water as soon as possible.
- For colic, drink sheep-dropping or chicken-dropping tea.
- For coughs, put a spoonful of sugar in a rag, squeeze lemon juice on the rag, twist into a small ball, dip in kerosene, and suck on the rag.
- For croup, apply poultice of flaxseed and mustard.
- For diphtheria, have the sick person urinate on a cup of carrot greens. Hang them in the northwest part of the chimney for eight days.
- To cure hiccups, stand in the road and say, "Hiccup, stickup, not for me, hiccup, stickup."
- For hives, make a tea of agarita root and drink it at three o'clock.
- To relieve itching, take guajillo root and burn it in the dark of the moon. Skin a prickly pear, mix it with the root ashes, and apply it to the itchy area.
- For liver trouble, make some asafetida by putting one half of a white turnip on top of one half of a purple turnip and urinating on it. Hang this on the head post of the bed on the first night, then on the foot post on the second night, and so forth until you circle the bed.
- For poison ivy, rub ashes of guajillo root on it.
- For toothache, take a letter from a relative and burn it over a lamp that has been burning for thirty minutes. Put the ashes in a teaspoon and place them on your tooth.
- For warts, put cedar ends in a quart of kerosene. Rub them on the warts and in thirteen days they will go away.

OLD FIRST NATIONAL BANK

315 Main

This two-story limestone building was built in 1875 by W. J. "Short Bill" Davenport and first operated as a private bank.

From Main, turn right on Cypress (not left on SH 16). Drive five blocks on Cypress to Seventh Street.

FRANZ JURECZKI HOME

7th and Cypress • Private residence

Franz Jureczki built this stucco-over-limestone home in 1876. It is one of Bandera's oldest residences. Jureczki opened a store here. It is said that he sold whiskey for twenty-five cents a quart, or he would trade a gallon of "the oil of gladness" for a bushel of corn. With a picket fence out front and a woodshed and log barn out back, the Jureczki homestead still looks much as it did at the dawn of the past century.

Just across Seventh from the Jureczki home is the St. Stanislaus Catholic Church and convent school.

ST. STANISLAUS CATHOLIC CHURCH

7th at Cypress • 460-4712 • Open during daylight hours • Free

When the Polish immigrant families under the leadership of Father Leopold Moczygemba arrived in Bandera in February 1855, they bought the entire block on which the church stands from the James-Montel Company for one dollar and organized their congregation, making this the second-oldest Polish Catholic Church in the United States, after Panna Maria.

Soon the congregation built their first church, a twenty-foot by thirty-foot log building that no longer stands.

A series of priests served the community, including Father Felix Zwiardowski, who lived in Bandera from 1869 to 1870. He wrote in 1870, "I have only seventeen farmers on whom I can depend for means of sustenance, and half of these are infected with the teachings and doing of my predecessor and ex-Reformer. I have found here many Freemasons, Americans and Germans, even one Pole from Krakow by the name of Paul Martin. The water here at least can be had free of charge, unlike Panna Maria where I had to pay from twenty-five to thirty-five cents a barrel." Father Felix reluctantly returned to live in Panna Maria in 1870, but he came to Bandera once a month to conduct Mass, "armed because of the frequent encounters with the Indians."

In 1876, construction of the present limestone Gothic vernacular sanctuary began. It was completed in 1877. The steeple was not added until 1906, and in 1912 the baptistery and confessionals were added, bringing the church to its present size. Step inside to admire the high Gothic altar, stained-glass windows, and stenciling. The church was extensively restored in 2005.

Ironically, at the time the present church was built, many Texans mistakenly believed that the Poles of Bandera were remnants of Lyman Wight's Mormon colony.

In 1877, the congregation again received a stationary priest, Father Bronislaus Przewlocki. But Father Przewlocki died in January 1879 and was buried inside the church. Father Felix visited Przewlocki's grave in 1891: "Praying at the grave of our departed brother I noticed that his body, which can be seen through the glass, bears strange marks of preservation. His hands and his face, after these twelve years, have remained the same as in time of death, even the hair remained the same as in time of death, even the hair remains the way I combed it at the time of the funeral."

In 1882, the Sisters of Incarnate Word came to Bandera to teach. Father Felix led the three sisters from San Antonio to Bandera. He drove a buggy. One wagon carried bedding and furniture; another wagon carried the sisters. The first two days and nights were pleasant, but then the weather changed, as it often does in Texas. The rain began to fall so heavily that the hilly road was converted into a "respectable river."

"Slowly we plodded along," said Sister Mary Fink, "until it became evident that the horses could no longer draw the furniture wagon, and it was left by the side of the road. Only a mile or so were covered when it became impossible to move the second vehicle now buried to the hubs in mud; it, too, was abandoned. As a last resort, we exchanged the wagon for Father's buggy and continued thus until the torrents of rain compelled us to stop at a very small and poor-looking house. In answer to Father's request for hospitality the people, not without apprehension of their unknown and strange looking guests, silently consented. They seemed to be afraid of us and managed to keep out of sight. We were, however, grateful for the shelter and were wondering what we should do for supper since we had forgotten to provide ourselves with something to eat when we abandoned the wagons. Fortunately, Father had some meat in his buggy; this he brought and one of us summoned enough courage to ask for a frying pan. In response to the request, a woman stood in the doorway and at arm's length handed Sister the pan. We did justice to the meat without any bread or anything else. In spite of our strange surroundings we slept until Father called us at daybreak and said he was ready to start. Towards noon we reached Bandera after a three days trip."

The smaller limestone building on the church grounds was built in 1874 as a convent for the nuns and as a school. It now contains a museum filled with local parish memorabilia dating to the congregation's founding. The museum is open after Mass and by appointment.

The one-story limestone building directly across Cypress from the back of the church was built in 1897 as a rectory; previously the priests had lived in a wooden rectory mounted atop the church.

The cemetery contains the graves of most of the Polish immigrants. Stones date to the 1850s, many with Polish inscriptions.

From Cypress, go up two blocks to Hackberry. Turn right on Hackberry.

At the corner of Tenth and Hackberry (on opposite corners of Hackberry), you'll notice a pair of dressed-limestone block homes to your left. The first, a one-story house, was built in 1880 for Judge and Mrs. Charles Montague Jr., who raised twelve children here. The second, a two-story house over in the next block, was built in 1890 by H. H. Carmichel, a Columbia University graduate who came to Texas via Missouri. He married Mary Risinger of Helena, Texas, in 1876. (Helena was popularly called "Six-Shooter Junction" and was home of the Helena Duel. In this duel, two adversaries were tied together with a short length of leather strap and then they fought each other with bowie knives until one was dead.) They came to Bandera and established a store in the present Bandera Ranch Store Building.

Proceed another block to 11th and turn right; 11th Street was Bandera's original main street.

FIRST METHODIST CHURCH

Hackberry at 11th

Andy Potter was the first Methodist minister to preach in Bandera, starting in 1862. He was stationed at Camp Verde at the time. He brought with him from camp some of his boys who had begged to come along. They even promised, as Potter later remembered, that "if I would select my hymns and loan them my hymnbook, they would practice during the week." The group left Camp Verde at eight on Sunday morning, neatly dressed. Bandera was fifteen miles distant. They ran several horse races down the road along the way. Once in Bandera, Potter "told them they might walk about the town until the hour, but be sure and be there in good time" for preaching. At eleven o'clock, Potter walked into the preaching place and found a large congregation waiting. His boys were sitting together on one bench. "I gave out my hymns and started the tune, the soldiers joining in, to the admiration of all. I introduced them to the people of Bandera, who gave them an invitation to dinner. We returned to Camp Verde that afternoon, and the men gave a full detail of our trip."

Potter often got permission to preach out in the country, and the young soldiers vied for every opportunity to go with him so as to enjoy some home cooking and female pulchritude. Potter helped organize the town's first congregation and assisted in getting the congregation's first sanctuary built in 1867. The present venerable stone building has been enlarged and remodeled since its construction in the last century. Potter continued to visit Bandera and nearby Pipe Creek regularly on his postwar preaching circuit.

But even Potter had his failures: "I went to Fort Clark to preach several years ago, and started in without a member, and at the end of twelve months I quit without a member."

Continue on 11th across Cedar.

OLD FIRST STATE BANK

11th at Cedar

This two-story stone building dates to sometime before the Civil War. It housed a school from 1860 through the 1880s. During the 1880s it operated as the Bandera Institute, administered by a Professor Ryan, who was thought by some to be the fugitive assassin John Wilkes Booth. Later it served as a bank.

BOYLE STORE

307 11th

Built in 1908, this recently restored one-story frame shotgun building with false facade is a good example of early Texas commercial houses, as is the old Stevens Store (now Stein's of Bandera) across the street at 306 Eleventh.

OLD BLACKSMITH SHOP

305 11th

Built during the 1850s, this one-story stuccoed limestone building was used by John James and Charles de Montel while they were platting the town of Bandera. Andy Potter probably preached here, since local Methodists worshipped here before building their first church. It was later a cabinetmaker's shop, blacksmith shop, and doctor's office.

OLDEST STONE BUILDING IN BANDERA

11th at Cypress

Built in 1855 by P. D. Saner, this much-altered, field-dressed limestone building has been used as a courthouse, school, store, and funeral home.

Turn left on Cypress and go one block back to Main. Turn right on Main to reach the Medina River, which is just over a block away.

BANDERA RANCH STORE

Main at Maple, between Cypress and the river

On your left is the sprawling Bandera Ranch Store. The original limestone section was built in 1868 by Henry White, who operated a general store. It has been added to several times since. The store claims the oldest elevator west of San Antonio.

Turn right on Maple just before you cross the river.

The north bank of the river, up to Maple and west for several blocks, is city park land. You can follow the river on foot, however, for another half mile or so on the north bank only. Traces of the old Polish millrace can be seen upstream, just past the old low-water bridge at the foot of First Street where the river makes a sharp bend.

From Main and Maple and the city park, return to Main and Cypress. Turn right on Cypress/ SH 16. One block past Main on SH 16, you see a gas station and convenience store on your right, and a couple of old limestone buildings behind them. They are the old courthouse and jail.

OLD BANDERA COURTHOUSE AND JAIL

12th near Cypress

Stonemason Henry White built the old courthouse from native limestone in 1868 as a store. By 1877, it housed a store on the first floor and the Masonic Lodge on the top floor. That year the county bought it to serve as Bandera County's first permanent courthouse. The county continued to use it even after the current courthouse was occupied in 1891. It currently houses some county offices.

Designed by Alfred Giles, the jail was built of native limestone in 1881. It has ornate window arches and a castellated roof, giving it a very Bastille-like appearance. Such fortress-massive construction was not happenstance. Cowmen began trailing their market-bound herds through Bandera right after the Civil War, and Bandera served as a major supply and rest center right through the big cattle bust of 1893, when practically all trailing ceased.

Bandera welcomed the cowboys' dollars but not their excesses. Any jail built here had to be not only strong enough to corral a dozen drunken cowboys, but also massive enough to resist the assaults frequently launched by their liberation-minded buddies on the outside. This jail was in use as such until after World War II.

Rowdy cowboys weren't the only disturbers of Bandera's peace; pigs wreaked their own peculiar havoc. Wild hogs were a valuable crop in Bandera County's early days. During the 1890s, hog buyers would come through the county and announce the places and times that they would receive hogs. Each hog weighed between two hundred and three hundred pounds when sold and brought three or four cents a pound on the hoof. This amounted to a considerable piece of coin to most Banderans. Not surprisingly, hog rustling was common, and each term of district court (held twice yearly) at Bandera saw lots of pig theft cases on the docket. Many prominent citizens were among the accused. Most townspeople owned hogs—it's said one man owned two hundred—and most of the porkers roamed Bandera streets and riverbanks at will, "rooting up gardens, scavenging the premises of townspeople for watermelon rind and eating the offal of the back alleys," as one contemporary put it.

It's also said that on one occasion a Methodist "protracted meeting" was broken up because of the fleas infesting the building to an alarming degree, caused by so many hogs bedding down under the church. Considerable friction was created whenever an election was called to "vote out the hogs," that is, to prohibit them from running loose within the city limits. But since hog owners outnumbered citizens without hogs, the "hog law" propositions were consistently voted down for years.

SCHMIDTKE-CALLAHAN HOUSE

Cypress/SH 16 at 13th

This one-story limestone Greek Revival cottage was built during the 1870s by James Henry White for Charles F. Schmidtke, an early-day merchant as well as sawmill and gristmill operator. It was later owned by J. C. Callahan, who operated a store next door. His grandson bought the house in 1927, and it stayed in the Callahan family until the 1970s.

OTHER ATTRACTIONS

THE SILVER DOLLAR

308 Main • 796-8826

This place dates back to 1901. Popular regional country music bands play dancing tunes. Put on your boots.

BANDERA VISITORS BUREAU

800-364-3833 • www.banderacowboycapital.com

Call or visit the website for the latest information about rodeos and other local events, river sports, and new B&Bs. Walking and driving tours of Bandera County are available. You may also contact the Bandera County Chamber of Commerce at www.banderatex.com.

LH7 LONGHORN RANCH TOUR

5 miles from downtown Bandera • 796-4314

This is a working Texas Longhorn ranch, one of the state's oldest. The Marks family helped save the breed. Call for a tour.

RODEOS

Open rodeos are generally held twice weekly from Memorial Day weekend through Labor Day weekend, on Tuesday and Saturday nights. On Memorial Day weekend, the Cowboy Capital Rodeo Association sponsors a CCRA Rodeo at Mansfield Park.

AREA PARKS

BANDERA PARK

On the banks of the Medina River • 796-3765

This seventy-seven-acre park offers free, easy access to the river for swimmers and fishers. Picnic areas have grills; bring your own wood or charcoal. Day use only is allowed. Several local businesses rent canoes, kayaks, and tubes; some offer shuttle service.

From Bandera, travel south on State Highway 173, go across the Medina River, and continue for approximately 0.25 miles to State Highway 1077; turn right and go 8 miles on State Highway 1077 to the end of the blacktop. Continue on the caliche road, crossing two cattle guards to the park entrance.

HILL COUNTRY STATE NATURAL AREA

830-796-4413 • Open daily February–November; Friday–Sunday in December and January • Fee • W Variable

This 5,370-acre site has rocky hills, flowing springs, broad creek bottoms, oak groves, grasslands, and steep canyons up to 1,900 feet in elevation. West Verde Creek has several spring-fed streams, and tanks provide several swimming holes and fishing for catfish, perch, and large-mouth bass. Spring water is available for horses, but people need to bring their own drinking water. Reservations are recommended for large groups. Fires are permitted in fire rings only; bring your own wood. Campers must pack out all trash for disposal, including all hay and animal by-products.

Recreational activity centers around forty miles of designated, multiuse trails that are open to backpacking, horseback riding, and mountain bicycling. Other activities include primitive and equestrian camping. Various adjacent ranches offer horse rentals, tours, and other accommodations. For information, call the Bandera County Convention and Visitors Bureau at 800-364-3883, or go to www.banderacowboycapital.com.

LODGING

RIVERFRONT MOTEL

1004 Maple at Main, by the Medina River Bridge • 800-870-5671 • www. theriverfrontmotel.com • Cr.

The best place to stay in downtown Bandera is on the river. Campers can stay at the private campgrounds on the north side of the bridge; city slickers can bed down at the Riverfront Motel, a collection of cottages overlooking the river. The house that serves as an office was built in the 1880s. Reservations are strongly recommended during the summer. There is air conditioning, television, and eleven cottages.

DUDE RANCHES

Bandera is famous for its dude ranches. Bandera's dude ranch industry dates to 1920, when some Houston folk engaged room and board for a few weeks in the home of Ebenezer and Kate Buck, who owned a large ranch on San Julian Creek a few miles south of Bandera City. The Houstonians returned home and told their friends about the wonderful time they had. In 1921, several groups came to stay with the Bucks. The good home-cooked food, plus the Buck's cordial western hospitality, became increasingly well known in Houston. To accommodate the increasing numbers of guests, the Bucks had to add on to their already large house. Through the next two decades, the Buck Ranch was so popular that reservations had to be made months in advance, if they could be obtained at all. With the Bucks' deaths (within seven months of each other in 1941), the ranch was sold to W. E. Tedford, who declined to continue taking guests. But others took up where Tedford left off.

DIXIE DUDE RANCH

Nine miles out of town (southwest) on FM 1077 • 796-4481, 800-375-YALL (9255) • www.dixieduderanch.com • PO Box 548, Bandera 78003 • Cr.

This is Bandera's oldest dude ranch, since 1937. But it is also a working ranch of over seven hundred acres, home to a herd of registered Texas Longhorns. Guests stay in cabins. There are about nineteen rooms. Activities include horseback riding, swimming, fishing, and hayrides. There is a playground and live entertainment. Other interesting features are an old barn and a cemetery with graves that date to the area's post–Civil War range wars.

MAYAN RANCH

From the courthouse square on Main, take Pecan down to 6th, turn right on 6th, and cross the Medina River • 796-3312, fax 796-8205 • www.mayan-ranch.com • PO Box 577, Bandera 78003 • Cr.

This 324-acre dude ranch offers access to the lovely Medina River, which is great for swimming, tubing, and fishing. There is also horseback riding, tennis, volleyball, barbecues, hayrides, and cowboy breakfasts on the trail.

TWIN ELM GUEST RANCH

SH 470, off SH 16 N. • 796-3628, 888-567-3049 • www.twinelmranch. com • PO Box 117, Bandera 78003 • Cr.

In the dude—pardon, guest—ranch business since 1939, Twin Elm has rustic, air-conditioned cabins and activities like swimming, tubing, fishing, horseback riding, campfires, hayrides, and outdoor chuck-wagon meals. The Medina River runs through the ranch, and there is an outdoor pool as well. The ranch property includes one of the highest of the Bandera Hills, which means lots of nice scenery on your horseback rides. It was previously a stock ranch. It features a full American plan; some meals are in the dining room, others are outdoors, with real range grub: barbecued beef, biscuits, and more.

You leave Bandera on SH 16, heading toward San Antonio. The good views start about four miles out of town and bring to mind several of Bandera's many nicknames: Land of Pure Delight, Switzerland of Texas, Cowboy Capital of the World. Do the nicknames fit the terrain? You be the judge.

Bandera may have been far from the battlefields of the Civil War, but blood was shed here in the name of the Confederacy, and under circumstances far from honorable, as J. M. Hunter described in a 1922 story for the *San Antonio Express.*

During the days of the Civil War, Bandera County was the scene of several tragedies, the most prominent of which was the execution of eight men one night in the summer of 1863, on Julian Creek, four miles east of town. While Lawhorn's company was stationed at Camp Verde in 1863, it became known that a small party of supposed "bushwhackers" was passing through the country en route to Mexico to avoid service in the Confederate Army. There were eight men and one boy in the party who hailed from Florence in Williamson County. The assumption was that they had taken part in bushwhacking operations and had been forced to leave Williamson County. Word of their passage was carried to Camp Verde, and a troop of twenty-five men under command of Major W. J. Alexander started in pursuit.

The eight men passed through Bandera several days before the soldiers began to pursue them. They were well mounted, well armed, and well provisioned and made no secret of their destination, saying that they did not care to become involved in the war, and when it was over they expected to return to Williamson County. They seemed quiet and peaceable, paid for everything they secured in Bandera, and went on their way.

Several days later, Alexander and his men came through Bandera trailing the men and headed south to Hondo. Picking up the bushwhackers' trail there, they followed it to Squirrel Creek, some ten miles beyond Hondo, where they discovered the Williamson County men's camp. The eight men were unaware that they were in danger of being captured. Approaching under cover to the edge of the camp, Alexander stepped out and, swinging his saber over his head, bade them surrender, telling them that they were surrounded with no chance for escape, and that if they would peacefully surrender he would pledge a fair trial by court-martial in Camp Verde.

The Williamson County eight surrendered their arms, saddled their horses, and started back to Camp Verde with their captors. The trip was uneventful until the second night, when, camped on Julian Creek east of Bandera, some of Alexander's men decided to hang the prisoners. Some of the Confederates objected and refused to participate, but the rest were determined to have their deadly way and marched them away from camp and hanged them one by one. When dead, the victims were let down and the rope was cut, the nooses still around their necks. One of the victims begged to be shot instead of being hanged. His wish was granted. Someone fired a rifle at him, wounding his arm. He fell, but another man placed the muzzle of his gun against the man's body and shot him through the body with a full charge, leaving the ramrod in the gun, which went through him and into the ground. The boy in the party, a lad about sixteen years old, is supposed to have escaped, but he too may have been murdered, as he was never heard of again.

The next morning, the hangmen rode through Bandera on their way to Camp Verde, some of them hinting to citizens that they had rid the country of some more bushwhackers. They had their victims' horses, saddles, bedding, clothing, and shoes.

Joseph H. Poor, who lived on West Verde Creek, was camped near the place of execution, and the next morning he went to look for his horses and discovered the bodies just as Alexander's men had left them. He hastened to Bandera and notified the authorities. The Justice of the Peace and a number of others went to investigate. An inquest was held, and the verdict rendered: "We, the jury, find that these men [giving their names] were killed by Maj. W. J. Alexander's company." They dug a common grave and rolled the bodies of the eight unfortunate men into it and covered it up.

The men in Alexander's party who refused to help execute the helpless prisoners talked freely about it for months afterward, telling all particulars, and even giving the names of the men who had participated. After the war ended, district judges all over the state were instructed to charge their respective grand juries to investigate such matters. G. H. Noonan was judge of this district at that time, and in 1866 he directed the Bandera County grand jury to thoroughly investigate the hanging of these men. As soon as the grand jury's investigation became known, a number of the Alexander detail left the area.

The grand jury indicted W. J. Alexander and others for the murder and highway robbery of the men. But Alexander had disappeared, and not one of the men charged in the indictment was ever arrested. One of them, Dan Malone, was killed in New Braunfels by officers while resisting arrest. According to Hunter, who declined to name names, the men who had urged the execution of those prisoners and had carried it out were not citizens of Bandera County.

Turn right on FM 1283 at Pipe Creek.

PIPE CREEK

Bandera County • 66 • About 9 miles from Bandera

Pipe Creek, the settlement, started in about 1872 as a trading post. Pipe Creek, the stream, takes its name from an incident in which a pioneer returned to the creek to retrieve his pipe in spite of the fact that he and his party were being pursued by hostile Comanches. He made his recovery safely, and the creek got itself a name. Many of Pipe Creek's first settlers were charcoal burners. They hauled it down to San Antonio where it sold for twenty-five cents to one dollar per forty-pound sack depending on the supply. Ladies used it to heat their irons, among other things. Robert Buck, son of an early Pipe Creek settler, described the charcoal making procedure.

The cedar trees were cut down and into poles and were hauled to the burning spot. The bark was peeled from the posts, and the poles were set up on end, leaning in at the top like a teepee. At the top, a small opening would be left so that smoke could escape while the wood burned slowly. The bark would be piled on the poles, along with dirt, to form a three-to-four-inch-thick coat over the stacked poles. Another small opening was left at the bottom of this "kiln" so that the burner could light a fire in the center. After the fire was started, the opening was closed, and the cedar poles would slowly smolder as the fire ate its way through and charred the wood as desired. It took at least four days and sometimes a week to properly char the mass of poles; the slower the fire, the better the coals. Flames were an anathema to charcoal burners. If air got inside the kiln, the fire would break into flames, which had to be hurriedly put out with dirt or water, or the cedar would burn too fast and the charcoal would be ruined. When the charcoal was ready and the fire put out, all the charcoal was raked out from the pile of dirt and sacked. It was now ready to be hauled to market by wagon, fifty sacks to the wagon. The round-trip to San Antonio and the time spent peddling it took about a week. So, for about two weeks' work, the burner and his helpers got about twenty-five dollars or less. But in times of drought and crop failure, it was the only income for many families.

Will Carver, outlaw partner of Tom Ketchum, was reared in the Pipe Creek community. Carver worked as a cowboy in Bandera and Medina counties before riding up to Tom Green County to work. He loved the cowboy life. He met Black Jack Ketchum at Knickerbocker and went west to become an outlaw. He rode first with Black Jack Ketchum and then threw in with Butch Cassidy. On the run late in 1900 (or early 1901), Carver, Ben Kilpatrick, and Harvey Logan (Kid Curry) visited the Carver family in Bandera County and then went north to Concho County. Shortly after his visit, Carver's stepfather paid cash for a one-hundred-acre farm. Will Carver was shot and killed in Sonora, Texas, by Sheriff Lige Briant and his deputies on April 2, 1901, when local authorities tried to arrest him. Kilpatrick was wounded fourteen times but lived, only to die eleven years later near Sanderson, Texas, during an unsuccessful train robbery, the last train robbery in Texas.

Continue on FM 1283, 3.5 miles to Bandera Falls, which is a relatively recent residential development. FM 1283 then takes you through rugged, wide-open ranching country. Follow FM 1283's sharp bend left at Bandera Falls and continue almost six miles to the intersection with Park Road 37. Turn right onto Park Road 37 to reach Medina Lake and the Mormons' last stand in early-day Texas. You experience an abrupt change in terrain after you turn onto Park Road 37, which takes a wild and twisting path along the hillsides filled with cedar and the vacation homes that ring Medina Lake.

MEDINA LAKE

Medina and Bandera Counties

Completed in 1912, Medina Lake is the oldest large reservoir in Texas, unless you count Lake Austin, whose dam had to be rebuilt two times after its initial failure in 1900. The main dam across the Medina River is 1,580 feet long and 160 feet high, and the lake it created covers over five thousand acres. The dam was built and is still owned by private interests. During the two years of its construction, 1,350 workers lived in nearby campsite barracks with their families. This camp city had electricity, a hospital, baseball teams, and even movies. It also had a steady stream of unsavory visitors—whiskey peddlers, gamblers, and prostitutes—all of whom endeavored to separate the workers from their hard-earned pay, $1.25 for a ten-hour day. At its completion, Medina Dam was the largest dam in Texas, but seventy men, women, and children had died of accidents, sickness, and violence in the process of building it. Medina Lake submerged Mountain Valley, the site of the last organized stand of the Lyman Wight colony in Texas.

Continue on Park Road 37, following the contours of Medina Lake down to Medina Lake Recreation Park where Park Road 37 ends and you are treated to a head-on view of jewel-like Medina Lake.

MEDINA LAKE PARK

At the end of Park Rd. 37 • Open daily; day use only

Medina Lake Park offers swimming, picnicking, fishing, and boating; there is a boat ramp. Medina Lake Park is about as close as you can get to the old Mormon colony of Mountain Valley, which their gentile neighbors called Mormon Camp. The great flood of 1900 destroyed the few buildings that remained, and Lake Medina put the site forever under water in 1913 (in 1989, many of the structures that made up Mountain Valley could be seen on the lake floor when the lake water level was low). But you can still appreciate the beauty of the Medina valley, and it should be easy to see why Wight settled his colony down here in December 1854. In Wight's own words,

We are placed in a valley between several lofty mountains, on a beautiful prairie bottom. The Medina River, a stream a trifle smaller than the Genesee River [in New York State] runs within thirty steps of our doors. Our houses are spaced at a proper distance apart in two straight rows, our gardens lying between, which makes it very pleasant. We have mechancks of allmost all descriptions. We make bedsteads and chairs in large quantities, and they sell as well as the finest quality of work brought from the east. We sent off one hundred and thirty chairs and eight or ten bedsteads yesterday and can send as many more in three weeks. We send them sixteen miles and get one dollar apiece for chairs by the thousand. We have a good horse mill to grind for ourselves and neighbors. We have a black smith and white smith. We raise our own cotton and make our own wheels to spin it on; and with all we have a share of farmers . . . our corn is mostly up and growing finely, we have lettice, and in a few days we will have radishes.

The Mormons also had Indian problems. Raiding Comanches hit the colony often, stealing or killing the disciples' horses and mules, firing their crops, and driving off their cattle. Wight wrote pleading letters to Indian agents, the legislature, and even the governor, asking for protection. Wight even offered the colony's assistance in civilizing the Indians, in teaching the Indians how to use a plow, make wagons and chairs, and handle the blacksmith's furnace and tools. But protection was slow in coming, and the raids continued. The Mormons' stock losses mounted, and so did their indebtedness to area merchants.

Wight started dreaming of yet another move, down to Mexico where, in Wight's words, "they have established a pure republic and put down the priests with their craft and made many of them pay one hundred thousand dollars for their lives; they have given free toleration to all sects and denominations and have invited all classes to come, and as the inhabitants are more than three-quarters Indian blood, I shall seek the earliest opportunity of laying the book of Mormon before them, which treats of many anticuities with which they are perfectly acquainted." (Remember, Smith had been told by God that the Indians were the remnants of the House of Israel.) Wight further hoped that he might find there enough converts to make a republic in Jackson County, Missouri, from which he and the faithful were driven in 1833. But before Wight could turn his Mexican dream into a reality, he received a vision from God in March 1858. Wight claimed God warned him in a vision of a coming war between the North and the South, and further that God told him to move back north. Of course, continued financial reverses and the resultant litigation may have been additional incentive to move, but Wight would never have admitted to any such mundane pressures. Wight announced the plans to move the following day, but his decision to move all the way back to Missouri met with considerable opposition.

Levi Lamoni wrote:

In the spring of 1858 my father planned another move. Of course we must all go. Here came quite a test of faith in the technicalities of his religion. I told my wife that I was not going to follow those wild moves any longer. We consulted about the matter for several days and came to the conclusion that we would rebel, and arranged to stay where we were and risk the consequences, and went to plowing. I thought over the matter seriously. My father and mother were getting old and feeble and we could not tell what might happen to them, and finally thought it our duty to follow them once more, so we arranged to go along. On the second day's journey after our start my father suddenly died [eight miles north of San Antonio].

The emigration moved on north as far as Bell County, forty miles south of Waco. Myself and my two brothers concluded to drop the project and remain in Texas. My mother, of course, dropped out with us; the emigration moved on, and we finally drifted back as far as Burnet County.

Wight's body was taken for burial to Zodiac, where he still rests. With Wight's death, the expedition fell totally apart. Some drifted back to Mountain Valley and Bandera, while others dropped off at various points on the route north, such as Burnet County. The persistent ones ended up in Shelby County, Iowa, in the spring of 1861. Practically all of them became affiliated with the Reorganized Church of Jesus Christ of Latter-Day Saints, which established its headquarters in Independence, Missouri. Of Wight's sons, Levi Lamoni served in the Confederate Army and settled afterward at Medina City, Loami Limhi served the Confederacy and afterward lived in Bandera, Orange Lysander lived in Llano County before moving to Utah, and Lyman Levi lived in Burnet County before moving to Missouri.

Thus the Mormon colony of Lyman Wight passed into the history books.

In March 1861, R. H. Williams camped briefly at Wight's final stand and described it in his book, *With the Border Ruffians: Memories of the Far West, 1852–1868:*

About the middle of March I joined a company mustered in by T. Paul. Directly we were mustered we went into camp on the Medina River, in an old Mormon settlement, where there were several solid stone houses and a mill. The Mormons had established themselves on the Medina at the time that the main body of their curious co-religionists were settled in Nauvoo; but when the general movement was made against that body in the States, these folks, like the rest of them, had to trek to Salt Lake.

Whatever else they are, the Mormons are first-class organisers in a new country, and know how to make themselves comfortable. Nothing could be better than the spot they had chosen here, and they had made the most of it; and we could not but be grateful to them for the excellent shelter the old fellows had provided for us against the keen, cold norther blowing.

From Lake Medina, retrace your route on Park Road 37 to its junction with RM Road 1283. Here you can return to Bandera or continue on Park Road 37 to SH 16, which takes you to San Antonio.

HILL COUNTRY RIVERS

Limestone and granite are the body of the Hill Country, and the rivers are its lifeblood. Anglo and German pioneers conquered the Hill Country by threading up the valleys of its great rivers—the Colorado, the Llano, the Guadalupe, the Pedernales, the Blanco, and the Medina—and then fanning out along the lesser tributaries like Cibolo, Little Blanco, Turtle, Cypress, and Verde. They depended on these flowing waters for food, drink, and industrial power. Life was impossible without them.

Until the introduction of mechanical drilling rigs and the Halladay windmill during the 1870s and 1880s, settlers had to depend on surface water supplies, which meant that the great arid interfluves that comprise most of the Hill Country could not be settled. Now, all you had to do was drill until you hit water and then build a windmill, which could haul water up from previously unreachable depths.

These days, as urban sprawl envelops the Hill Country, many Central Texans view these streams as little more than seductively beautiful playthings. And they are beautiful, perhaps more beautiful than they were during those pioneer days, when the waters powered grist-, saw-, and shingle mills and served as laundry tubs and garbage dumps.

Many of the miles on this trip are river miles, where the water is within view or earshot, and they lead ultimately to one of Central Texas' few remaining natural treasures, the Lost Maples of the Sabinal River Canyon.

The trip begins in San Marcos, home of the famous San Marcos (Aquarena) Springs, the headwaters of the San Marcos River. Still issuing millions of gallons per day, these springs, along with the Comal Springs in New Braunfels, are the most prolific springs in Central Texas. But that may not be true for long if current groundwater usage rates continue.

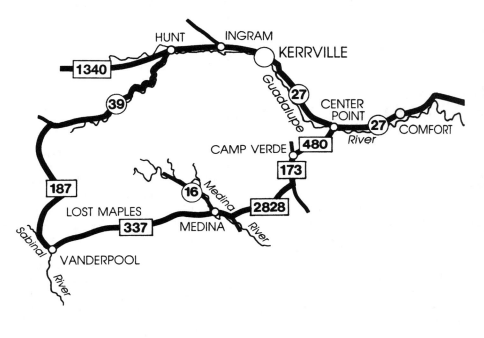

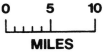

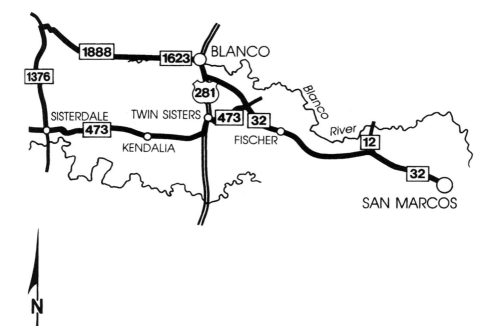

HILL COUNTRY RIVERS

SAN MARCOS

Hays County Seat • 51,000 (approximate) • (512)

Located on the headwaters of the San Marcos River, San Marcos was a favorite Indian campsite long before the appearance of European settlers.

In 1691, Domingo Teran de los Rios crossed the southern edge of Hays County on his way to the East Texas missions and the Red River, but he evidently missed the springs. The first Europeans to see the springs were probably members of the Espinosa-Olivares-Aguirre expedition of 1709. The Apaches attacked Louis Juchereau de St. Denis in 1714 at the San Marcos River crossing. A mission to be called San Marcos was authorized in 1729 near present-day San Marcos, but the authorization was later rescinded in favor of San Antonio. Nevertheless, the springs were an important stop on the Old San Antonio Road that ran from northern Mexico to Nacogdoches.

In August 1755, the San Francisco Xavier missions, which had been located on the San Gabriel River near present-day Rockdale, were briefly moved to the San Marcos Springs because of drought and disease. A truce with the Apaches had eliminated the need for a presidio, or fort, at San Xavier. Shortly after the missionaries arrived at San Marcos, one thousand Apaches joined the missions. The site could not support so many people, and in 1756 all property from the San Xavier missions and the presidio were reassigned to Santa Cruz de San Saba Mission (near present-day San Saba), which would serve the Apaches in their own territory. San Xavier neophytes were transferred to San Antonio missions. A small group of San Xavier Indians, the Mayeyes, persuaded the missionaries to set up a new mission on the Guadalupe (present-day New Braunfels), but it lasted only until 1758.

With the United States' purchase of the Louisiana Territory in 1803, the Spanish government became worried about American citizens moving into Texas and decided to establish more Spanish settlements between San Antonio de Bexar and Nacogdoches. The governor of the province of Texas, Manuel Antonio Cordero y Bustamante, approached a friend, Felipe Roque de la Portilla, to organize and oversee the venture.

Felipe Roque de la Portilla was born in 1766 in Spain. He went to Mexico as a captain in the Spanish Army, and in 1799 he married Maria Ignacia de la Garza Montemayor, a native of Mier, Nuevo Santander (now Tamaulipas), Mexico. They had eight children, including Dolores and Tomasa, both of whom were later married to empresario James Power.

In 1807, after extracting promises from Cordero that he would receive a substantial land grant and that the government would assist the settlers financially, Portilla headed for the San Marcos River with a small group of settlers. The exact number of settlers is disputed—some say ten; others say as many as fifty-two. There is also disagreement as to whether Portilla's family was in the original group or whether they arrived in the fall of 1808.

Portilla recruited his colonists from south of the Rio Grande, and the first group left Refugio (now Matamoros) in December 1807 and by February 1808 had settled near the San Marcos River crossing of El Camino Real. In April, Governor Cordero issued an official order establishing San Marcos de Neve. He appointed his military representative, Lt. Juan Ygnacio de Arrambide, as justicia (magistrate) of the town, with power to issue titles to land. He promptly issued thirteen titles to town lots. A central plaza was laid out, and homes were built, only to be washed away by floods. Throughout the summer and fall, the settlers rebuilt their town.

Portilla left the colony in September 1808 to get more settlers and returned with six new families in late October. Portilla's census of 1809 counted 73 persons and 1,771 animals. Over the next three years, the settlers made a valiant effort to maintain their new homes, but it wasn't easy. The promised priest never arrived, and seed and a farm irrigation system did not materialize. Frequent raids by Comanche and Tonkawa Indians and the failure of the government to send soldiers for protection forced them to abandon the settlement in 1812.

Portilla, in ill health and heavily in debt since he had extended loans to many of the settlers and had never been reimbursed by the government, resettled his family in Matamoros, Mexico. Maria died 1819, and Portilla later married the daughter of Jose Antonio de la Garza Falcon. Portilla held the position of alcalde of Matamoros and served as a lieutenant of the Provincial Militia and Cavalry until 1829, when he left Mexico to help his son-in-law, James Power, and Power's associate, James Hewetson, establish their colony at Refugio, near Copano Bay in what is now San Patricio County. Portilla received land there in 1834, but in 1836 he left the Power and Hewetson colony and returned to Matamoros, where he died in 1841.

Because he invested his own fortune in the colonizing effort, he is sometimes called the First Empresario of Texas and is recognized as a forerunner of Stephen F. Austin, "the Father of Texas."

After Mexico gained its independence from Spain, the government of Coahuila Y Texas encouraged settlement by issuing land grants in the area to Juan Martin Veramendi in 1831, Juan Vicente Campos in 1832, and Thomas Jefferson Chambers in 1834. Thomas G. McGehee was issued a league of land in 1835. But because of the Texas War for Independence and Indian domination of the region, the McGehees didn't take physical possession of their land until 1846.

Thomas McGehee, born in Oglethorpe County, Georgia, in 1810, belonged to one of the state's prominent families. He married Minerva Hunt of Hunt Springs (now Huntsville), Alabama, in 1832. In 1833, McGehee and his brother John brought a load of lumber by boat to the mouth of the Brazos, saw the luring promise of Texas, and decided to move here. In 1834, Thomas and Minerva moved to Texas. They brought with them their one child, their household goods, a few faithful servants, and some equipment for their new pioneer life.

For a few years they lived in Bastrop, where they had several more children. In 1836, McGehee joined Jesse Billingsley's company of Rangers, where he attained the rank of captain. When Santa Anna reached San Antonio and besieged the Alamo, Captain McGehee, with fifteen men, was stationed five miles east of where New Braunfels now is. From there he was ordered to join Houston's army and remained with Houston until after the Battle of San Jacinto.

Minerva and two small children were part of the "Runaway Scrape," in which Texian settlers fled from the advancing Mexican army. McGehee had ridden away on the only horse they owned, but Minerva and a young slave girl built a rude cart in which they carried the two small children (one of them a month-old baby) and a few household treasures. Two young steers provided motive power, and thus they joined the flight east. Mrs. McGehee walked beside the cart on their plodding retreat toward the Trinity River to safety. The despair and weariness were often overwhelming, and the way was rough and long. Some perished along the way, but Mrs. McGehee and her little family survived, and they eventually returned to their home at Bastrop. Captain McGehee and his compatriots joined the refugees on the Trinity after the successful battle of San Jacinto.

In 1846, the McGehee family finally took possession of their land in the San Marcos River valley and built the first home and tilled the first farm in Hays County, which was then part of Travis County. The family's move from Bastrop to San Marcos was a thrilling adventure for sons George and John, aged eight and ten, respectively, who walked the whole way, driving the family's plentiful flock of chickens and turkeys. The boys started out with the idea that they would drive the chickens and turkeys, but they soon realized that the chickens and turkeys were driving them. When the fowls got tired or saw an enticing spot to roost for the night, they took charge, thus compelling the boys to camp at that particular spot whether they wished to or not.

McGehee chose his league of land near where the Blanco and San Marcos rivers come together, and there he built his home, within five hundred yards of the old San Antonio and Nacogdoches road. Except for the little colony of settlers just establishing themselves in New Braunfels, there was no other settlement between Austin and San Antonio.

Early-day San Marcos included, besides the McGehee home, a small cabin owned by William Moon, and another owned by Mike Sesson, both of whom belonged to Captain Jack Hays' company of Rangers, which was camped nearby. Between San Marcos and Bastrop there was only one house on Cedar Creek, and down the San Marcos river none nearer than within nine miles of Gonzales.

The McGehees' first home was a three-room log house with a wide porch. It was no cheap or temporary affair—trees were left to shelter the house, and shrubs and flowers were planted to adorn the place. The big living room had a beautiful floor of solid walnut boards fashioned from logs cut on the place. The wide hall had a smooth polished red cedar floor. Captain and Mrs. McGehee had come from homes of comfort and refinement and were determined to make their home as near to their ideal as the possibilities of the wilderness would allow. Their furniture was of solid walnut from their farm and was made by a German cabinetmaker named Westervelt, who made much of the early furniture in this section of Texas. Captain McGehee loved trees and never failed to plant a tree where he saw a place for one.

On December 23, 1846, William, the first white child born in Hays County, was born to the McGehees. They had a total of nine children. Life was not easy; Minerva dipped tallow candles by which to read the Bible to her children at night, teach them the alphabet, and light her babies to bed, and spun and wove the cloth for their pants and jackets, while Thomas toiled in the fields to break the virgin land and grow the crops needed to make a living for his family.

The community's first schoolhouse was near the head of the San Marcos River, and going to school could be a perilous journey. It was not considered wise to start the children to school until they were old enough and clever enough to kill a bear or elude a prowling Indian. The schoolhouse was finally moved from that beautiful location on account of those dangers.

To tree a bear or sight an Indian was not an uncommon occurrence, and it was near the old McGehee home that Mrs. Cheatham killed a bear there. The McGehee children were often turned back from their walk to school or to Sunday school by the sight of a bear or an Indian in the brush. One story has Mrs. McGehee taking two of her small children and hiding on the river bank from pursuing Indians—determined to sell her life dearly, even if it meant jumping with her babies into the river's icy water and taking her chances of swimming to safety with her children, rather than be captured and perhaps seeing her babies tortured and killed before her anguished eyes.

Captain Thomas McGehee died at age eight-one, his wife having died about twelve years before.

After McGehee and his family had settled on the banks of the San Marcos, more Anglos began to join them, and in 1851 William Lindsey, Edward Burleson, and Dr. Eli Merriman platted out the town site of San Marcos. San Marcos had already been the center of Hays County for several years, ever since the day Dr. Caton Erhard opened up his general store here. His original stock consisted of one barrel of flour, one barrel of whiskey, one sack of coffee, a few pounds of tobacco, a few shingles and nails, and some ten or fifteen pieces of calico at sixteen yards to the piece. Eight yards was needed to make a dress in those days, and no less than eight yards would Erhard sell. His store served as post office, county clerk's office, and general gathering place.

In 1848, Messrs. Tarbox and Brown (who had started the Houston and Austin Mail Stage Line, a biweekly service via Washington on the Brazos, Independence, La Grange, and Bastrop) started up a line of four-horse stagecoaches between Austin and San Antonio. Each coach carried a sack of mail along with the passengers, and the journey took three days each way. Stage stands were placed at twelve-mile intervals, and horses were changed at each station. Coming from Austin, a station stood beside the Blanco River, on the north side of present-day San Marcos, with the next stand at Stringtown, just south of San Marcos. With the coming of the stage line, San Marcos became a commercial center for the wagon trade between area farmers and ranchers and the Texas coast. The powerful springs (Aquarena Springs) drove gristmills, sawmills, and cotton gins, making San Marcos the regional center for ginning and milling local agricultural products.

San Marcos has been the seat of Hays County government ever since the creation of Hays County in 1848, but not without controversy. As the population of western Hays County grew, there became an ever-increasing demand that the county seat be moved nearer to the geographical center of the county. (San Marcos sits in the southern tip.) Inhabitants of the county's western hills had a difficult and long journey to San Marcos.

William Cannon had spent a couple of years accumulating thousands of acres in central Hays County, and in 1859 he platted the town of Cannonville and offered it as the site for a county seat. He even went so far as to outline the town's lots with logs and build the county's first courthouse. (After ten years, Hays County still didn't have a proper courthouse at San Marcos; county officials met in rented buildings.) An election was held in 1860, and Cannonville won over San Marcos by less than ten votes. A couple of court sessions were held there, but the county records were never moved to Cannonville. Cannon's death and the Civil War hampered relocation efforts, and by war's end, county officials had purchased enough land from Comal County to make San Marcos' location a legal one.

In the meantime, Hays County got its first courthouse, courtesy of a defendant in a local murder case who jumped bail after his trial had been transferred to Travis County. The $2,000 sum he forfeited was used to build San Marcos' first courthouse, a 36-by-40-foot two-story pine structure that also served as a church, Masonic Lodge, and school. It burned in 1869.

San Marcos and Hays County had voted in favor of secession from the United States in 1861, and after the Civil War some local citizens organized a Ku Klux Klan group to counteract "lawlessness," such as the following incident, reported by a gentleman just returned to San Antonio who had passed through San Marcos a few days earlier, in mid-April 1868:

> Great excitement was prevailing there, on account of an apprehended outbreak among the negros of the vicinity, caused by a warning given by a negro to his employee to take care of himself and his property, as a plot threatening to burn the town had been introduced into the Loyal League by a white man, a stranger, who immediately on the alarm being given betook himself to parts unknown. The citizens, about 40 strong, came together and paraded the streets, night and day, Thursday, armed and ready to defend themselves. Some thirty or forty negros during the night were discovered banded together in the vicinity of the town, approaching it, but a negro ran out to them, telling them of the citizens being on the alert, and they ran. The whites pursued and captured three of the ring-leaders, one a deserter from the 9th Cavalry, colored—confined them and sent for the bureau agent at Lockhart, who declined to interfere with the civil authorities though by request of the citizens he remained and was present during the examination.

Slowed by the Civil War, the population of San Marcos had grown only to 742 by 1870, but in the decade following the arrival of the International and Great Northern Railroad in 1881, it reached 2,335, and the town boasted two banks, an opera house, and a variety of stores, saloons, and other businesses. Cattle and cotton production in the area fueled the gradual but steady growth of San Marcos as a center for commerce and transportation.

Texas State University was founded in 1899 as San Marcos Normal School. Located atop old Chautauqua Hill, university buildings rather than Chautauqua Hill dominate the skyline today.

There's a lot to see in San Marcos these days, and the place to begin is the courthouse square. To get there from I-35, take Loop 82 from either its north or south confluence with I-35. Either way you end up at the courthouse.

HAYS COUNTY COURTHOUSE

Loop 82 at SH 80 • Guadalupe at Hopkins

The locally quarried soft-limestone building that replaced the pine courthouse had to be razed only ten years later. It, in turn, was replaced by a harder limestone two-story building designed by noted architect F. M. Ruffini. It was also razed after burning in 1908. The present courthouse was built in 1909. It is basically of the Greek Revival school, buff brick with a limestone rock foundation. The three-story courthouse is capped with a red tile roof, four corner cupolas, and a large center dome. Massive limestone columns with Corinthian capitols guard the entrances. The roofline's cast-metal cornice and pediments are similarly Corinthian.

The courthouse is the most imposing building on the square. In the last few years, many of the older commercial buildings on the square have had their modern facades stripped away and been returned to more or less their original appearances, and there is an increasing number of dining establishments and interesting shops.

LBJ MUSEUM OF SAN MARCOS

131 N. Guadalupe St. • 353-3300 • www.lbjmuseum.com • Open Thursday through Sunday afternoons • Donations accepted • W

Lyndon Johnson attended Texas State from 1927 to 1930, and the museum, located in a renovated movie theater, focuses on his formative years, and how his early experiences as a college student and schoolteacher impacted San Marcos, Texas, and the nation. Permanent and rotating exhibits are featured.

OLD SAN MARCOS STATE BANK AND TRUST BUILDING

100 West Hopkins at Guadalupe

This rather plain looking two-story brick building is most famous for having been robbed by the Newton Brothers in the early morning hours of January 4, 1923. They poured so much nitroglycerine in the vault door that the side of the bank was partially blown away, and coins showered across the street. They gathered up what they could and made a leisurely escape. The building was used in 1972 for the movie *Getaway*, starring Steve McQueen and Ali McGraw.

HARPER'S HALL

139 Hopkins

This simple, two-story building, dating to 1873, is the square's oldest surviving structure. Built by Willie Harper, it was San Marcos' first "opera house," hosting traveling and local amateur entertainment shows, local events, and gatherings. As was common at the time, the first story was occupied by a livery stable. In succeeding years, the building has housed a variety of businesses.

A fire in January 1872 burned down all the buildings on the eastern side of the square at a loss estimated between $15,000 and $20,000, and from that point on, stone and brick buildings like Harper's Hall began to replace the original wooden structures.

HAYS COUNTY COURTHOUSE ANNEX (OLD FIRST NATIONAL BANK)

San Antonio at LBJ, on the courthouse square

This building was originally the First National Bank, which was established here in 1879. On May 22, 1933, the bank was robbed by four men with Thompson submachine guns who got away with $7,040. Hostages were taken, but they were soon released at the Blanco River bridge five miles north of town. Sometime later, the bank's president saw an account of Machine Gun Kelly's trial and said, "That's the man." When the FBI brought him a photo lineup, he picked Kelly's picture, identifying him as one of the robbers.

OLD CITY HALL AND FIRE STATION

224 N. Guadalupe • Currently houses Texas State University offices

Downtown San Marcos has a couple of nice examples of early twentieth-century Spanish Renaissance buildings, one of which is the 1915 City Hall and Fire Station, one-half block north of the courthouse square. Brick, two-story, with a red tile roof, it has been remodeled into private office space, and the new firehouse is just around the corner.

FIRST UNITED METHODIST CHURCH

129 W. Hutchison

Located one block north and west of the courthouse, this 1894 vintage church is a fine example of Gothic Revival church architecture. Its outstanding features are the bell towers and the tin roof. The congregation dates to 1847 and included in its membership General Edward Burleson, Republic of Texas vice president under Sam Houston.

JACKMAN FORD DEALERSHIP

215 E. Hutchison

A few blocks east of the First United Methodist Church, old car buffs will enjoy the restored second-story facade of the 1920 Jackman Ford dealership, complete with the classic "Ford" script. The building is no longer an auto dealership.

BELVIN STREET HISTORIC DISTRICT

San Marcos' finest concentrations of vintage homes are in the Burleson Street Historic District and in the three blocks of the Belvin Street Historic District, located one block below Burleson Street. Several houses on Belvin Street were built by the children of Thomas and Minerva McGehee. One block above Belvin Street and paralleling it is Burleson Street, which is also lined with several blocks of Victorian-era mansions and houses and is a recently designated historic district.

To get to the Belvin Street Historic District from the courthouse, take Hopkins (FM 2439) west through the SH 80 intersection. Two blocks past the SH 80 intersection, turn right on Scott. Belvin begins one block later, running parallel to Hopkins and Burleson streets.

G. T. MCGEHEE HOME

727 Belvin • Private residence

Son of original settler Thomas McGehee, George McGehee built this eclectic, rambling house in 1895. A highly pitched shingle roof sprouting gables in several directions, a shingled side turret, and a wraparound porch add distinction to this wood-frame dwelling.

ROBERT H. BELVIN HOME

730 Belvin • Private residence

Robert H. Belvin, a Methodist minister, is the namesake for this street and historic district. This two-story, Victorian-influenced Greek Revival wood-frame house was originally a one-room building, built just before the Civil War as a private school by Professor Charlton Yellowley. Professor Orlando Hollingsworth bought the property in 1866 and renamed the school the Coronal Institute, so named for its situation crowning a beautiful hill overlooking the beautiful San Marcos valley. Belvin purchased this house and the institute in 1871.

Hollingsworth had built several limestone buildings to house the growing school and its students, so Belvin built the existing two-story house around the one-room schoolhouse for his family. It was enlarged again in 1890 by Rev. J. W. Vest. The Methodist Church bought the institute from Belvin in 1879, who died in San Marcos in 1888. The institute closed in 1918, and all the buildings were razed during the 1930s.

GEORGE H. TALMADGE HOME

802 Belvin • Private residence

Farmer and carpenter George Talmadge built this Victorian Gothic house of cypress in 1889. Its shuttered windows, porch balustrades, and porch column brackets reflect Talmadge's skill and taste in carpentry.

JOHN F. MCGEHEE HOME

832 Belvin • Private residence

John F. McGehee built this house in 1889 from Bastrop pine and cypress siding, along with handmade brick. This home is most notable for its elaborate Eastlake-style gingerbread porch and gable trim.

JOSEPH EARNEST HOME

833 Belvin • Private residence

Merchant and cattleman Joseph Earnest built this frame house in 1892. Constructed according to a stair-step floor plan, each of the three progressively deeper "pens" has its own separate roofline-central French tower overlapped by flanking gables. Other Second Empire details adorn the gables and lintels of this house.

CROOKWOOD

227 N. Mitchell at Belvin • Private residence

This mansion in the Classic Revival style is unique among Belvin Street's collection of Victorian buildings. Merchant and banker Ike Wood built this imposing residence in 1908. A row of massive Corinthian columns and a hanging second-floor balcony dominate the house's classical facade.

You have now reached the end of the Belvin Street Historic District. There are more fine old houses to see. Continue past the old Masonic Temple several more blocks to Bishop. Turn left on Bishop, cross Hopkins/FM 2439, and turn left on San Antonio one block later. Proceed up San Antonio back toward downtown San Marcos. San Antonio is also lined with many fine old houses; one is of particular note.

RAGSDALE-JACKMAN HOME

621 San Antonio • Private residence

This simple, white frame two-story home is one of San Marcos' oldest still-occupied homes. Texas Revolution veteran Peter Ragsdale built it in 1868. Colorful Hays County Sheriff W. T. Jackman bought it in 1891.

W. T. "Bill" Jackman was born in Missouri in 1851. At the end of the Civil War, Jackman's father, who had served in the Confederate Army, decided to head for Mexico rather than submit to Union rule. After being told that it wouldn't be a good idea to take his family into Mexico with him, he left his family in a tent on the Blanco River and headed for Mexico alone. At age fourteen, Bill was head of the family. He rented some land to raise cotton, which he had never done before. But daddy Jackman didn't like Mexico and soon returned to his family on the Blanco. Bill left home in 1870 to become a cowboy, trailing herds north to market.

On his first cattle drive, in 1870, the herd started from a Uvalde County ranch and took a course through Bandera, Mason, and Llano counties. About four miles before reaching Bandera, the herd was stopped one day at noontime. The herd was rounded up so that the cowboys could brand a few head that hadn't been branded at the ranch. After finishing the branding and eating dinner, the cowboys and herd were drifting along when a stranger rode up and started talking with Bill. He was a nice young fellow, and after they had chatted a while, he asked Bill where he had gotten one of the yearlings that had just been branded. Bill told him it had come from the ranch. The young cowboy then said, "I would be sorry to see you get in trouble, but that yearling belongs to an old Dutchman who lives down the creek and he is as mean as hell. There is one trail boss in jail at Bandera now for driving one of his yearlings." He then rode away. Bill saw no reason to disbelieve him, so he and the yearling took the high road for the next few days until they were safely away from Bandera, and then they rejoined the herd. Jackman became a rancher but was driven out of the business in the mid-1880s by drought, low cattle prices, and the like. He was elected sheriff of Hays County in 1892, a position he held for twenty years, after which he became marshal of San Marcos and then postmaster.

Follow San Antonio's wandering path past the courthouse to its dead end into C. M. Allen Parkway. Turn left onto Allen Parkway. Just after you do, you see on your right the Charles Cock Home.

CHARLES COCK HOME

Allen Pkwy. and E. Hopkins • 392-1111/392-3410 • Open all day the first Friday of each month • Open for lunch every Friday • Open by appointment to groups • W variable

Built by Charles Cock in 1867, this little cottage is the only stone building of its period left in San Marcos. It was completely restored and furnished in 1976. Owned by the city, the house is maintained by the Heritage Association of San Marcos, which serves a home-cooked lunch each Friday. Some of the furnishings are from the Cock family; the rest come from all over Central Texas.

Adjacent to the Cock House is the Eli Merriman cabin, which was moved here from its previous location in the old Pioneer Village complex at Aquarena Springs. Built in 1846 by Dr. Eli Merriman, the cabin is San Marcos' oldest standing home and was originally located near the courthouse square. It served as office, operating room, and home to Eli, Jenette, and their six children. Merriman also served as postmaster and tax collector. He left San Marcos in the 1850s and moved to south Texas. Merriman served as a doctor/officer in the Confederate Army and died in Corpus Christi in 1867 of yellow fever.

OTHER ATTRACTIONS

AQUARENA CENTER AND RIVER SYSTEMS INSTITUTE

Loop 82 at Aquarena Springs Dr., follow signs around town • 245-7575 • Open daily • W variable

Aquarena Springs is San Marcos' bubbliest tourist attraction, built around the prolific (millions of gallons per day!) headsprings of the San Marcos River. They were discovered by Franciscan monks on St. Mark's Day (April 26) in 1709, hence their original name, the San Marcos Springs. In 1926, A. B. Rogers started a park here, which gradually grew into a full-fledged tourist trap complete with Ralph the diving pig and an underwater submarine theater with mermaids from SWTSU who drank soda water underwater.

Acquired by Southwest Texas State University in 1994, the park has been transformed from hokey commercial resort to the Texas Rivers Center. Ralph and the mermaids have been put out to pasture. The pioneer village and the sky tram that you rode across Spring Lake to reach it have been dismantled. The chief attraction here is again what it originally was: the glass-bottom boat tour of Spring Lake, the lake that is fed by the hundreds of springs—large and small—located here on one of the Balcones Fault lines. There is a fee for the cruise. Pay it; the ride is worth taking. The rest of the park is free. On the entrance side of Spring Lake, there is an endangered species exhibit.

The Texas Rivers Center now occupies the hotel A. B. Rogers built in 1928 at the springs' head. San Marcos' first tourist-trade entrepreneur, Rogers had started out in the furniture and undertaking business, which was a common combination in those days.

The Texas Rivers Center explains our rivers' important role in maintaining Texas' many ecosystems. The center features a restored native wildlife habitat, and educational and entertaining exhibits. One exhibit details archeological findings, including Clovis points, mastodon bones and teeth, and more recent human detritus. Several interactive, multimedia kiosks teach archeological history and early San Marcos history. Researchers from throughout the world participate in rivers studies at the center. Sponsoring partners include Texas State University, Texas Parks and Wildlife, the U.S. Fish and Wildlife Service (USFWS), the Wetlands Project, and the City of San Marcos.

Some naturalists would like to see Spring Lake drained and the springs restored to something approaching their natural state. The dam suffered major damage during the October 1998 floods, and some think it should be removed, arguing that the dam is actually a threat to the endangered species present and that the most educational thing that could be done would be to let the area revert to its natural state. But the USFWS argues that the endangered species have adapted to Spring Lake and would be worse off without it.

SPRING LAKE HISTORICAL SITE

Spring Lake was created in 1850 with the construction of a wood-and-stone dam 1.3 miles below the San Marcos Springs by William Alexander Thompson. Thompson (1803–1879) had been a planter in Mississippi and Louisiana before moving his family and slaves to Texas in 1850. He established a plantation in Caldwell County along the San Marcos River, including a cotton gin powered by eight mules.

In 1850, Thompson decided to build a mill along the San Marcos River. Slaves dug a ditch and a wasteway by hand; they isolated two areas of land that came to be called Thompson's Islands (historical marker at Conway and River Road). The ditch carried water diverted by the dam to the waterwheel. The wasteway led from the main ditch west to the San Marcos River and carried excess water back into the river during periods of high flow, or when the machinery was not in use.

The slaves also built an irrigation system of hollow log pipes, headgates, and a large, overshot waterwheel using cypress wood. A wheelhouse, millhouse, and several bridges were constructed near the ditch. The waterwheel generated power for a gristmill, sawmill, shingle machine, and cotton gin.

The present dam dates to 1867. Its core consists of cypress wood frames sunk into the riverbed and filled with gravel from the Blanco River. Shortly after construction of the new dam, William A. Thompson Jr. became increasingly involved in the mill's operation, gradually buying out his father's and partners' interests and accumulating additional nearby land on which cotton was grown.

The Texas legislature passed an act in 1895 "to encourage irrigation and to provide for the right to the use of water." William A. Thompson Jr., together with many other persons along the San Marcos River, filed for water rights. About this time, William Jr.'s son, William Hardeman Thompson, began to participate in the family business. He built a house in 1898–1899 that still stands with a historical marker.

In 1909, a new owner made extensive improvements. In 1914, the gin burned down, and the plant was replaced. The gin burned again in 1936, and was replaced once more. In 1935, the Rural Electrification Act was passed, and inexpensive electrical power soon became widely available. In 1942, the gin was converted to electrical power, and the dam, ditch, and turbines fell into disuse. Today the waterworks are preserved in a semipublic park, while water diverted from the San Marcos River still flows through the ditch, wasteways, and wheel pit.

TEXAS STATE UNIVERSITY

LBJ Dr. and University • 245-2111 • W+, but not all areas

A summer normal school was held in San Marcos at least as far back as 1886. In 1899, the Texas legislature authorized the establishment of a normal (teacher training) school at San Marcos, to be called the Southwest Texas Normal School. The citizens of San Marcos donated eleven acres of land on Chautauqua Hill, where the citizenry had long gathered to listen to lectures on various subjects and to the preaching of evangelist extraordinaire, the Reverend Sam Jones, as well as to marvel at "sun pictures" ("sun pictures" was an early name given to photographs, including daguerreotypes invented by Louis J. M. Daguerre, calotypes/Talbotypes invented by W. H. Fox Talbot, and ambrotypes, which were an improvement on the daguerreotypes). They were probably presented in a "magic lantern show" put on by a Professor Tremaine. Popularly known as the Texas Chautauqua, it was an institution similar to the one held at Chautauqua, New York.

Southwest Texas Normal School opened in September 1903 with 303 students. In 1918, it became a full-fledged senior college; in 1969, it became a university. The campus now covers over 360 acres and counts about twenty thousand students. Lyndon Johnson received his bachelor's degree and permanent teaching certificate here in 1930. Visitors must obtain a pass at the gate during school hours. The visitors center presents a multimedia show about the university and also features some LBJ memorabilia.

WONDER WORLD/WONDER CAVE

1000 Prospect St. just off FM 2439/Hopkins St., about a mile south of downtown San Marcos; look for and follow the signs around town, or take the Wonder World exit off I-35 • 392-3760 • www.wonderworldpark.com • Open daily, except Christmas Eve and Christmas Day

Wonder Cave is billed as America's only commercial dry-formed cave. That means it was formed in a matter of seconds during an earthquake, during the creation of the Balcones Fault. It also means that you don't see any spectacular stalactite and stalagmite formations. You do see the Balcones Fault line running along Wonder Cave's ceiling and the waters of the Edwards Aquifer at the "wishing well." Don't go expecting to be visually dazzled; this is more of a thinking man's cave. It was discovered in 1896 when a water well was being drilled, and it housed a distillery and gambling den before the authorities shut down cave discoverer Mark Beavers' illicit operations. Public tours began in 1903 for a nickel a head. Wonder World also features an observation tower and a quaint little wildlife park stocked with llamas, all sorts of exotic deer, and other peaceful, feedable animals.

THE CALABOOSE AFRICAN AMERICAN HISTORY MUSEUM AND OLD HAYS COUNTY JAIL

Corner of Martin Luther King and Fredericksburg

Constructed as the first Hays County jail in 1873, this small brick structure was later an annex for black prisoners. Known locally as the "Calaboose," in the 1940s it was enlarged with a wooden addition and served as a USO center for black World War II servicemen. In later years, the Calaboose became a community recreation center. Almost torn down in 1990, it is now a museum and part of a complex that includes the Eddie Durham House and the First Baptist Church across the street, The unoccupied, deteriorating, two-story, limestone, second-empire-style Hays County jail (used from 1884 to 1936), immediately behind the Calaboose, was most recently used in the movie *The Newton Boys*, and efforts are being made to stabilize and restore it.

Eddie Durham is San Marcos' most famous citizen, although the town took a relatively long time to recognize it. Durham, one of the most important Swing Era composer-arrangers, was born in San Marcos in 1906. He was of mixed African American and Native American ancestry. His father, Joseph, played the fiddle at local square dances, and his oldest brother, Joe, who served as musical director for Teddy Roosevelt's Rough Riders Cavalry Band during World War I and played cello briefly with Nat King Cole, took correspondence music lessons and taught Eddie and his other brothers to read and notate music. Joe Jr., with his brothers Eddie, Earl, and Roosevelt, formed the Durham Brothers Orchestra in the early 1920s and were occasionally accompanied by their sister Myrtle, who played piano. Their cousins Allen and Clyde Durham later joined them. In Dallas, they were joined by another cousin, the great tenor saxophonist Herschel Evans. According to Eddie, he became a professional musician at age ten; at eighteen he was with the 101 Ranch Brass Band playing for circuses in the Southwest and traveling as far as New York City, where he performed in Yankee Stadium. In 1926, he joined a jazz group and toured the Southwest before joining the Oklahoma-based Blue Devils in 1928. He then moved to Kansas City and played with Benny Moten from about 1929 to 1933 before moving to New York in 1934.

Durham's training in music theory led to his work during the 1930s and 1940s as a composer-arranger for four prominent jazz bands: the Blue Devils, Bennie Moten, Count Basie, and Jimmie Lunceford. Among the tunes Durham composed or arranged are the classics "Swinging the Blues," "Topsy," "Time Out," "Out the Window," "Sent for You Yesterday," "One o'Clock Jump," "Jumpin' at the Woodside," "Harlem Shout," and "Pigeon Walk." He also arranged music for white bands led by Artie Shaw and Glenn Miller, contributing to Miller's best-known hit, "In the Mood."

Durham played guitar and trombone. By 1929, he had begun experimenting with homemade resonators and megaphones to enhance the projection of his guitar. He was the first person to record an amplified guitar when he was featured on the 1935 Jimmie Lunceford recording of Durham's arrangement of "Hittin' the Bottle." Durham influenced fellow Texan Charlie Christian, the most important guitarist in jazz history, who recorded electric guitar the following year. In 1938, Durham was the leader for a historic combo recording session with Lester Young, Count Basie's star tenor saxophonist.

In the 1940s, Durham organized his own band, directed the all-girl International Sweethearts of Rhythm, and brought together a number of important Texas jazzmen from the Kansas City era, including Joe Keyes, Hot Lips Page, and Buster Smith. During the 1950s and 1960s, he performed less but still worked as an arranger for various groups. In England, albums were released under Eddie Durham's name in 1974 and 1981. In the 1980s, Durham toured Europe with the Harlem Blues and Jazz Band. He died in New York City in 1987. San Marcos subsequently declared August 19, his birthday, as Eddie Durham Day, and in 2003 began an annual Eddie Durham Day Musical Tribute and Festival.

DINING

CAFE ON THE SQUARE AND BREW PUB

126 N. LBJ • 353-9289 • Open daily, breakfast, lunch, and dinner • Cr. • W

The cafe started in the 1897 T. A. Talbot building, which still has the original pressed-tin ceiling, skylights, and wood floor. Then it moved into the 1896 store building next door and opened a brew pub. The owners have a good collection of vintage Texas beer signs and paraphernalia. American and Tex-Mex breakfasts are served. The lunch and dinner menu is heavy on burgers and sandwiches but also has steaks, fajitas, wild game, and more exotic fare. Try a pint of any of the several house brews, or choose from a fairly extensive selection of domestics and imports. Live music is another feature.

FUSCHAK'S PIT BAR-B-Q

920 SH 80, east of I-35 • 353-2712 • Open daily, lunch and dinner

Look past the fake log cabin decor and concentrate on the brisket, chicken, and fajita meat.

JOE'S CRAB SHACK

100 Sessoms Dr. at the dam below Spring Lake • Open daily, lunch and dinner • Cr. • W

You come for the view of the San Marcos River from the outdoors back porch. The food is merely an excuse to drink in the beauty of the nascent river on a warm, sunny day. The beer, at least, is good and cold. It is a popular college-student hangout; the more adventuresome ones may be diving off the porch's rails into the drink.

WOODY'S BAR-B-QUE

2601 Hunter Rd. • Open Monday through Saturday, lunch and dinner • Cr. • W

Normally this book does not include dining establishments less than five years old because of the failure rate of many new places. But Woody's meat is of such high quality that we broke the rule. Woody's features oak-smoked brisket, pork ribs, pork-loin chops cut to order, chicken, turkey breast, and their own Lockhart-Luling style beef-pork ring sausage, juicy and coarsely ground, with a nice peppery bite. The standard side dishes and desserts are available. See www.woodysbbqtx.com.

LODGING

CRYSTAL RIVER INN

326 W. Hopkins • 326-3739

Just three blocks from the courthouse square, this B&B is located in a Greek Revival house built about one hundred years ago by William D. Wood, who was a newspaper editor, lawyer, legislator, and judge. The fourteen guest rooms are named for the various Hill Country rivers.

Close by the Crystal River Inn is the Cope House (316 W. Hopkins), built in 1902 for businessman John Matthew Cope. Its two-story wraparound galleries, festooned with gingerbread, make it the equal of any of the Belvin Street houses.

SPORTS AND ACTIVITIES

CANOEING AND TUBING

T. G. CANOES

About 2 miles out SH 80, 353-3946

Canoes and kayaks can be rented here.

LIONS CLUB TUBE RENTAL, CITY PARK

Aquarena Springs Dr. and Bugg Ln. • 396-LION • May through September, Sunday through Friday 12–7, Saturday 10–7

They have more than one thousand tubes in various sizes. There is shuttle service back from Rio Vista Park, which is about a ninety-minute float. Profits go to Lions' charities.

ANNUAL EVENTS

MAY

VIVA CINCO DE MAYO STATE MENUDO COOK-OFF

Hays County Civic Center, I-35 south • 353-VIVA • www.vivacincodemayo .org • Weekend nearest May 5 • Free

The menudo cook-off highlights this weekend of beauty pageants, folklorico dances, a parade, live entertainment, arts and crafts, and lots of food and beer.

JUNE

TEXAS WATER SAFARI

Aquarena Springs, Loop 82 • 693-1107 • www.texaswatersafari.org • Starts second Sunday in June • Entry fee

Beginning at Aquarena Springs, the race course follows the San Marcos and Guadalupe rivers to the Gulf of Mexico at San Antonio Bay. The event is considered one of the world's toughest canoe races. Contestants must carry all supplies in their craft. The race draws canoe teams from as far away as Alaska.

TOURISM INFORMATION

SAN MARCOS CHAMBER OF COMMERCE

202 N. C.M. Allen Parkway • 393-5900 • www.sanmarcostexas.com

SAN MARCOS CONVENTION AND VISITOR BUREAU

617 IH 35 North • 888-200-5620 Toll Free • www.toursanmarcos.com

Leave San Marcos on FM 2439, heading south to its junction with RR 12. Turn right onto RR 12 and head west. As you leave San Marcos, notice how quickly the landscape changes. About ten miles out of town, RR 12 suddenly veers north toward Wimberley. You continue straight ahead on what is now RM 32. Less than five miles later, you are climbing the Devil's Backbone, a particularly rugged, long hill that helps define the Guadalupe and Blanco rivers' watersheds. The views from the roadside park at the top are worth a pull over.

FISCHER

Comal County • 20 • About 22.5 miles from San Marcos

To reach Fischer, turn right on FM 484 as per the Fischer Store sign. Return to RM 32 via FM 484 and continue west.

About five miles past Fischer, RM 32 comes to an intersection with SH 473. Turn left on SH 473 toward Twin Sisters. You begin to parallel the delightful Little Blanco River on your left. Quite a collection of vintage stone houses and barns are strung out along this, the old Little Blanco Road, such as the two-story limestone house on your left at 3470 SH 472, about two miles after you have turned onto SH 473. After five miles, you come to Twin Sisters.

TWIN SISTERS

Blanco County • 78 • (830) • About 11 miles from Fischer

In 1853, when the first settlers were coming up the Blanco River valley from New Braunfels and San Marcos, Joel Cherry built a house here on the banks of the Little Blanco River. A number of German settlers soon joined Cherry, and before long a general store and Blanco County's first post office were established. In those days, the area was known as Moureau's Valley, for Franz Moureau, a New Braunfels lawyer who owned much of the area's land. But since Moureau was an absentee owner who eventually sold off his holdings, the community came to be called Twin Sisters, named for two look-alike peaks in a string of hills to the south.

There are no signs for Twin Sisters on SH 473, but 4.5 miles after you've turned onto SH 473, at 1295 SH 473, you'll see a huge limestone barn on your right, the old Bruemmer Barn, built by Heinrich Bruemmer, one of Twin Sisters' early settlers. Sixty feet long and twenty-five feet tall, the barn contains its own water system. If ever a Hill Country barn was spectacular, this one is. It's doubtful you'll find one larger. Just a few feet farther on your right are St. Mary's Help of Christians Catholic Church and the Twin Sisters School.

ST. MARY'S HELP OF CHRISTIANS
CATHOLIC CHURCH

1051 SH 473 • Church building not open to the public

Unlike their free-thinking, intellectual neighbors in Comfort and Sisterdale, the Germans who settled around Twin Sisters were good Catholics. For the first thirty years, they met in local homes or at Twin Sisters Hall. But in 1887, land was donated for a permanent church, and it was built in 1889. The little white frame church is so forthrightly simple in appearance that it tends to stand unnoticed by the speeding traveler, just a big white box with a tin roof and simple little steeple and wooden cross atop. But you can better appreciate its spareness when you realize that the millsawn lumber for the building itself was hauled by wagon over thirty miles of rocky roads and trails. The foundation is of locally quarried limestone. The church is locked up, but you can get a good look inside through the screened windows. Worshipers sit on a dozen rude, homemade, wooden backless benches. The altar is a simple homemade one, with two statues of Jesus and the Virgin Mary, in marked contrast to the opulent interiors of some of the other Catholic churches you'll see in Central Texas. There is no electricity either. Except for the tin roof, the church looks exactly as it did one hundred years ago.

Next to the church is the Twin Sisters School (993 SH 473). This is Twin Sisters' second school building, built in 1881 by public subscription. The porch was added in 1906. Classes were last held in 1953, but the school still serves as a community center and polling place.

In a mile you come to an intersection with US 281. Turn right to reach Twin Sisters Hall and a look at the cemetery, a few hundred feet north.

TWIN SISTERS HALL

Open for dance the first Saturday night of each month; otherwise the front gate at US 281 is locked and the hall is inaccessible • Fee

The center part of this sprawling hall was built in 1867; the wings were added later, as was the embossed tin siding. It still has its original vaulted and beaded wooden ceiling, wooden dance floor, and homemade wooden tables and benches, as well as slightly more modern oscillating fans. An advertising board of area businesses dating from the 1930s still hangs. It is a timeless place; except for the beer prices and cans, it could be the 1920s or 1930s in here. Come here for a Saturday-night dance for the real old-time flavor of Texas. Forget the claims of that dancehall-turned-tourist-trap in Gruene; this is the oldest dance hall in Texas.

Across the highway from the Twin Sisters Hall entrance is the old Twin Sisters cemetery, where many of the old stones' inscriptions are in German.

From the hall and cemetery, double back on US 281 and cross the Little Blanco River. After nearly two miles with US 281, SH 473 turns away again to the west. Follow SH 473 to Kendalia.

KENDALIA

Kendall County • 76 • (830) • About 9 miles from Twin Sisters

Kendalia was named for George Wilkins Kendall, the world's first war reporter. He joined the ill-fated Texan Santa Fe Expedition in 1841 as a reporter, was imprisoned with other expedition members, and lived to write a book about it. In 1846, Kendall joined American forces fighting in Mexico as a foreign correspondent, filing his reports via a pony express–style courier service. Kendall was wounded in the knee during the storming of Chapultapec Castle. Kendall got into the sheep business in 1852 with three partners. He had a ranch on the

Nueces River as early as 1841 and another on the Brazos, but he decided to move elsewhere to raise sheep. In November 1852, he found a tract in Comal County four miles above New Braunfels at Waco Springs. He brought his sheep from the Nueces and bought some more from General Pitts, who lived about ten miles away. He was unable to purchase the property, so in the summer of 1854 he moved to Post Oak Springs, a dry, hilly tract six miles east of Boerne. He had his share of hard times, including blizzards, grass fires, and disease, until 1856, when he began making a profit. In 1856, he began moving his family to Texas, first to Waco Springs and then to Post Oak by 1861, despite the menace of Comanche raids. His herders took turns standing sentry each night. Each herder oversaw eight hundred sheep and was armed with a double-barrel shotgun, a Colt six-shooter, and a Bowie knife.

In 1859, his friends encouraged him to run for governor, but he demurred. With the war, his market for wool dried up. He sold one clip in Mexico during the war and evaded federal troops to sell a clip in New Orleans, but otherwise the wool rotted. He did manage to sell more than three hundred improved rams at a profit in Mexico in 1862, but after that the market declined. He couldn't keep herders, and the Indians raided. Kendall's family had to barricade themselves in their house several times during the war. The scab hit him hard in 1864. So he built a big vat for dipping, which other sheepmen copied. The market improved after the war, but Kendall died on October 21, 1867, having helped shift the emphasis from mutton production to wool production.

A town had been laid out here by 1883, and contemporary promotional sheets urged readers to "buy a mountain home in the sunny South" in Kendalia, "a great health resort in Kendall County, Tex." Farseeing promoters had set aside blocks for the Kendalia Steam Mill and Cotton Gin, Mountain College, Vogel Square, and Spring Garden. Five of the original twenty streets exist today.

For the grand tour of Kendalia, veer left on FM 3351 at the Y intersection when SH 473 continues to the north.

GEORGE ELBEL BUILDING

FM 3351

A few yards down RM 3351 you see on your left the 1911 George Elbel general store building. Elbel was perhaps Kendalia's most prominent businessman in the early 1900s. Built of rough-finish limestone blocks, this building's calling card is its cast-iron ground-story facade and imposing pressed-tin false second-story facade. The house next door has some nice gingerbread detailing. Elbel built this house for his family in about 1900.

KENDALIA HALLE

1135 FM 3351 North • 833-4902 • www.kendaliahall.com

Kendalia Halle, on the other side of the Elbel building, was built, barn-raising style by the community, in 1903 on land donated by George Elbel. The red fir wood used to build the dance hall was shipped from Oregon by railroad to Boerne and hauled here by wagons. It was first used for community events and concerts by the town's brass band, the Nicholas Syring Musical Club, and was subsequently used for dances, wedding receptions, graduation ceremonies, reunions, and school plays. A small area to the right of the stage was fenced off with chicken wire. Nonpaying customers sat here and watched, and paying customers bedded down their children here while they continued to dance. Dances began early and went far into the night, so folks brought their dinners with them. A family atmosphere predominated, but the occasional unruly patron was chained to the oak tree out front until he had sobered up. Back in Kendalia's heyday, a bowling alley, barbershop, and cotton gin stood by Kendalia Halle. A cedar yard and mill stood across FM 3351.

Dances are held once a month with free barbecue served; call or check the website for dates, prices, and bands. The hall is also available for private functions.

Continuing on FM 3351 from Kendalia Halle, in two blocks you come to Loeffler Street and see a sign directing you to turn right to reach the Kendalia Community Church.

KENDALIA COMMUNITY CHURCH

Loeffler at Arthur St. • Open to the public and still in use

This simple, white frame church with green trim and louvered window shutters was built about 1887 after Boerne newspaper editor Carl Vogel deeded this lot to a newly formed Methodist congregation.

From the church, continue in the same direction, on Arthur Street, toward SH 473.

To your left at the stop sign one block past the church, at 105 Arthur (corner of Arthur and Martin streets), the one-story limestone building with the Alamo arch is the old Longhorn General Store, built in the 1890s. It also served as a school and is now a private residence. The town's hotel stood out back of the store; it was torn down years ago.

From the old Longhorn Store go one more block to SH 473, turn left, and continue on SH 473 to Sisterdale.

SISTERDALE

Kendall County • 63 • (830) • About 14 miles from Kendalia • Sisterdale is located in the valley of the Sister Creeks, near their confluence with the Guadalupe River.

Nearly every settlement in America founded by Germans between 1830 and 1860 had a "Latin" community, comprising scientists, artists, noblemen, and others who desired to distance themselves somewhat from the ordinary hardworking class and devote most of their time to cultural advancement. They read all the best and latest literature and could speak several languages, including, obviously, Latin. They generally did not have to work, at least not too much, to survive, because they were financially well off. Such a settlement was Sisterdale, on the upper Guadalupe, in Bexar County, before the Civil War.

The father of the Latin community at Sisterdale was Captain Nicholas Zink. Born in Bavaria in 1812, Nicholas Zink came to Texas in 1844 with his wife,

Louise. They came as part of the Adelsverein colonization scheme. Zink was a civil engineer and former Bavarian Army officer. Considered eccentric by some, he had built roads for the Greeks during their war for independence. From December 1844 to March 1845, he supervised the move of approximately half of the German immigrants from Indianola to New Braunfels. Once they had arrived at the site that would become New Braunfels, Zink supervised the construction of a log palisade, or fort, to protect the immigrants' temporary tent city. This fort was called Zinkenburg. Zink also surveyed the original town site and surrounding farmland.

By 1846, Zink was hauling freight and passengers back and forth from Houston to New Braunfels. In 1847, he and Louise divorced for "unhappy differences," and he decided to start a new life, so he left New Braunfels in an ox wagon and headed for Fredericksburg along the recently established "Government Road." On the night of March 3, 1847, he made camp on the banks of the Guadalupe, forty miles north-northwest of San Antonio. The next morning, Zink crossed the river at the mouth of Sister Creek. The area looked so appealing that he decided to stop and settle here. With the help of his teamster and one or two laborers, he began to build a two-story log house, about three hundred yards from the river just above the high-water level, the first building in what would become the Latin community of Sisterdale.

He was soon joined by a group of intellectual refugees from Germany known as "forty-eighters," forward-thinking men who had seen their dreams evaporate with the failure of the revolution of 1848. Disillusioned with the world, these men had retreated to the Texas hills, having "decided that the quest for learning was the only occupation in this world." Each of these gentlemen farmers had a library, and they met weekly at the little log schoolhouse to discuss the latest in literature, often in Latin. Indians sometimes came to listen at the door. In spite of their erudite backgrounds, these men had to hunt and work the fields for their daily bread. This combination of lifestyles presented a bizarrely contrasting sight to visitors.

Frederick Olmstead visited Sisterdale in 1854 and wrote for his monumental travelogue, *A Journey through Texas*:

> You are welcomed by a figure in blue flannel shirt and pendant beard, quoting Tacitus, having in one hand a long pipe, in the other a butcher's knife; Madonnas upon log walls; coffee in tin cups upon Dresden saucers; barrels for seats, to hear a Beethoven's symphony on the grand piano; "my wife made these pantaloons, and my stockings grew in the field yonder"; a fowling piece that cost $300, and a saddle that cost $5; a bookcase half-filled with classics, half with sweet potatoes.

Olmstead was referring to the home of Baron Ottomar von Behr, son of the prime minister of Anhalt-Kothen and friend of Bettina von Arnim (see Dutch Settlements) and the scientist Alexander von Humboldt. Von Behr came to Texas in the mid-1840s, and the book he wrote for prospective German farmers in Texas served as sort of a bible for many German immigrants. Von Behr was the second settler here and is usually credited with naming the village. Behr came up from New Braunfels a few months after Zink and built a log cabin on the south side of the Guadalupe, on land he purchased from Zink.

A man of many interests, he maintained what was probably Texas' first lending library in his house, and he served as justice of the peace and postmaster. A meteorologist and naturalist, he made and recorded extensive observations about the area. Von Behr was one of the first Texans to raise and upbreed sheep. After settling in Sisterdale, he began to mate German Merino (Saxon) rams with chaurros he bought for a buck a head. The chaurros were an inferior breed from Spain, lean and gaunt, almost goatlike in appearance, and producing 1 to 2.5 pounds of coarse open wool. But they were survivors. By 1854, he had a small but growing herd of quality sheep grazing unpenned in his pastures.

He made regular trips back to Germany to collect rents on property he owned there, and he died of yellow fever in 1856 while on one of his trips. His wife remarried and remained in Texas to raise their four children; their descendants still live in the area.

During the next two years, a number of educated Germans also settled at Sisterdale.

Dr. Ernst Kapp was a geographer-historian-philosopher turned physician. He had been a teacher in the College of Minden, Westphalia, and was the author of a scientific book, *Comparative Geography*. Imprisoned briefly in 1849 for a book he had written advocating a more liberal, democratic government, Kapp immigrated to Galveston in December 1849. At Sisterdale, Kapp farmed and operated a mineral-water-cure sanatorium called Badenthal, offering "Dr. Ernest Kapp's Water-Cure." His treatment included hydrotherapy and gymnastic exercises. The Kapp log home and the adjacent patient quarters survive and have been restored. The front door of his home was constructed of stout planks in which an iron nail was driven every inch in order to resist Indian tomahawks and battle axes. This door is now in the Comfort Historical Museum. In 1853, Kapp was elected president of the Freier Verein, an organization of mostly German intellectual liberals. They held a convention in 1854 in San Antonio at which they demanded the abolition of slavery. It was the first open convention for abolition held in the South.

Edward Degener was a member of the first, short-lived German National Assembly in 1848. Degener, sent by his parents to learn English at an English college in Europe, immigrated to the United States in 1850 and settled at Sisterdale, where he purchased the original Nicholas Zink farm and homestead.

Dr. Adolph Douai, imprisoned for treason as a result of his participation in the revolution of 1848, arrived in Texas in May 1852 and first settled in New Braunfels, where he founded a school. After a brief spell at Sisterdale, he moved to San Antonio to edit the German-language newspaper, the *San Antonio Zeitung*, which he transformed from a literary publication into an abolitionist platform. In 1856, as revenues declined and ill feeling among proslavery Americans grew, Douai was forced to sell his interest in the paper to Gustav Schleicher and leave the state. He moved to Boston and then a series of other northern cities until his death in New York in 1888.

Dr. Ferdinand von Herff, from the defunct colony of Bettina on the Llano River (see the Mormon Trails trip) also spent time at Sisterdale.

The social life of Sisterdale reached its height in 1849 with a visit from Prince Paul of Wurtemberg, the king's brother. Prince Paul was a distinguished naturalist and botanist and spent several weeks on the upper Guadalupe studying the flora and fauna. He was astonished and greatly pleased to find drawing-room conversation on the Texas frontier.

Indians seldom molested the settlers. In the fall of 1853, some horses were stolen from the farms of Dr. Ernst Kapp, Ernst Altgelt, and Julius Dressel. In 1855, Herman Runge, the twenty-year-old son of Dr. W. J. Runge, was killed and scalped on the farm of A. Dressel, and all the horses of the farm were taken away by Comanches. This same band killed some oxen belonging to Julius Dressel and stole several horses from W. Rhodius. The Indians were pursued but could not be overtaken. The Comanches roamed through the country at will, and large bands of them visited the settlement frequently. So far as is known, however, this is the only murder they ever committed in the old community. The last raid they made on stock at Sisterdale was in the year 1871.

A vocal quartet composed of leader A. Stemerling, Ottomar von Behr, Louis von Donop, and W. Rhodius, organized in 1852, existed until about 1857. This quartet participated in the Saengerfest held by all the German settlements in New Braunfels in 1853.

In the 1850s, some of the original settlers began to drift away. Among the first to leave was the newly remarried Nicholas Zink in 1850. During a particularly favorable year, Zink made three thousand bushels of corn on his river-bottom land. But he and his new wife were restless to move on, so he sold his entire holdings to Edward Degener.

Zink opened a gristmill on Baron Creek, south of Fredericksburg, which he operated for some years, but he finally settled at Spanish Pass between Comfort and Boerne, where he lived until his death in 1890. Zink Street in New Braunfels is named for him. You can read more about Zink in the chapter "Take a Ride on the Fredericksburg and Northern."

The men of Sisterdale joined in with the rest of the region in petitioning for the creation of a new county from bits of Bexar, Blanco, and Comal counties in 1859. Kendall County was organized in 1862, and in the election to determine the location of the county seat, Sisterdale lost to Boerne by less than ten votes. This loss, plus the forty-eighters' gradual disenchantment with the country life and the cruelties inflicted by the Confederacy, signaled the end for Sisterdale as a prominent town and major cultural center.

The Ordinance of Secession was passed by a vote of the people of Texas on February 23, 1861. But Union sentiment was strong in Southwest Texas. Secession barely carried in San Antonio, but in the Hill Country, including Fredericksburg, Boerne, and Comfort, the vote was twenty to one in favor of remaining in the Union. On July 4, 1862, about five hundred Germans favoring the federal government organized into frontier defense companies near Fredericksburg. The Confederate authorities in Texas declared the counties of Gillespie, Kerr, Kendall, Edwards, and Kimble to be in open rebellion against the Southern States and sent a detachment of about two hundred soldiers to deal with the situation.

On learning of the action taken by the Confederates, the Germans disbanded. Major Fritz Tegener, who had organized the "Union Loyal League," called for all those who did not care to submit to Confederate rule to meet him on Turtle Creek, in Kerr County, the first day of August, and follow him into Mexico. From this place they were pursued by the Confederates and were overtaken on August 10, on the banks of the Nueces River, in Kinney County, where they were ambushed and defeated by the Confederates in a battle that will be covered in more detail in a few more pages.

Many of the Sisterdale settlers had been part of Tegener's movement, and after the Nueces battle, they moved to live in the more thickly settled districts around San Antonio and New Braunfels. The general exodus from Sisterdale included practically all of the original settlers, and all of the more recent arrivals. About the only ones remaining during the war were Ottomar von Behr's widow, Louise, and their four children, and a few bachelors. The golden period of the Latin settlement of Sisterdale had come to an end.

During the Civil War, Edward Degener had been the head of the "Union Loyal League's" advisory board, which included his two sons, Hilmar and Hugo. For his devotion to the Union cause, Degener was court-martialed and imprisoned. After his release, he moved to San Antonio and operated a wholesale grocery business.

But in September 1871, the *Austin Democratic Statesman* accused Degener of importing lead and inferior powder from Mexico for sale to the Confederate Army, and then after the war, of taking the "Ironclad Oath" that he had not aided the Rebel cause. Why, the *Statesman* asked, should Republicans of West Texas vote for Degener who was not a Union man by virtue of his acts during the Civil War, and not vote for John Hancock, who had served in the Union Army? After the war was over, Hancock stopped fighting his fellow Southerners who had chosen the Rebel side, while Degener chose that moment to show his devotion to the Union by voting to disenfranchise the men he had imported lead and powder for during the war.

Degener became a prominent Republican politician after the Civil War, associated with the party's ultraradical wing and one of the few white men in Texas to openly advocate giving blacks the right to vote. During the Reconstruction era, Degener was elected and served as congressman from the Fourth Congressional District from 1870 to 1874, and later as a San Antonio city councilman. He died in San Antonio in 1891.

A few of the old-timers came back to Sisterdale after the Civil War, but not to revive the Latin "Kultur" community. The old log cabins became barns and storage houses for the new settlers, who built more comfortable homes of stone and sawed planks. The old inhabitants had been content to endure rude cabins without floors or windowpanes, to sleep on rough platforms spread with corn husks, and sit on crude frames covered with deerskin as chairs, so long as they could mingle together and discuss the higher arts, drink fine liquors, read the best in literature, and sing the songs of the Fatherland at the old Kapp home, where Kapp himself accompanied them on a fine harpsichord.

Kapp returned to Germany for a visit in 1865 with the end of the Civil War and never came back, writing books and finally dying in Dusseldorf in 1896.

Other, more practical-minded German immigrants came along to take their places, like Andreas Langbein. Langbein came in 1863 and bought the Kapp place at about the close of the Civil War; at one point he owned most of the valley.

To see the old von Behr homestead, turn left at the junction with RM 1376, headed toward Boerne. Shortly you cross the Guadalupe River, and the entrance to the von Behr compound is the first driveway to the right after crossing the river. A prominent sign, "Ottmar Von Behr, 1847" stands behind an old rock fence. This is private property, but the large, two-story stone house, wooden barn, and outbuildings are clearly visible.

To see "downtown" Sisterdale, reverse your path and continue straight ahead on what becomes SH 473/RM 1376/Sisterdale Road.

SISTER CREEK VINEYARDS

1142 Sisterdale Rd. (SH 473) • 324-6704 • www.sistercreekvineyards .com • Open daily (afternoons) • W

The vineyard, located between East and West Sister Creeks, is planted with Chardonnay, Pinot Noir, Cabernet Sauvignon, Cabernet Franc, and Merlot grapes. Sisterdale's old cotton gin houses the winery. It was built in 1885 and closed in 1927. Sister Creek's wines have won several silver medals in the annual North American International Wine Competition.

SISTERDALE GENERAL STORE AND BAR

SH 473, just up the road from Sister Creek Vineyards • 324-6767 • Open Tuesday through Sunday, closed Monday • No Cr. • W

Up on the wall just inside the front door is a large framed history of Sisterdale. Several of the pioneer buildings depicted still stand but are not accessible or easily visible from the road. You will also notice old beer signs and a beautiful hand-carved curly-pine bar, brought to Sisterdale from Fredericksburg in 1919. It used to be across the road in the old dance hall-saloon, but it was moved here when this store was built in 1954.

Gus Langbein (Andreas's son) built the dance hall-saloon across the road between 1884 and 1890, as well as the long, white, one-story house next to it with all the front doors. It served as home, boarding house, general store, post office, and stage stop, hence all of the separate entrances. The property was purchased in 2010 by a San Antonio lawyer with plans to preserve the property and turn it into a special events/community center. As you leave Sisterdale and continue toward Comfort, the small limestone building immediately on your right is the old Sisterdale School, built at the tail end of the glory days, supposedly the best primary school in the state. You can see the old Kapp Sanatorium by taking the small road just before the school. Private property.

From Sisterdale, continue west on SH 473 to Comfort. Between Sisterdale and Comfort, SH 473 takes you through the fertile Guadalupe River valley.

Just past the River Bend Road turnoff to your left, you pass the Seidensticker Ranch compound on your right, which dates back to 1855 and is marked by the magnificent two-and-a-half-story limestone mansion.

THE BAT ROOST

SH 473, 11 miles west of the SH 473/RM 1376 intersection at Sisterdale • Private property

Malaria was one of many scourges in early Texas, especially in low-lying areas. After it was discovered that mosquitoes spread the disease, health professionals began searching for ways to control the mosquito population. Since bats are voracious insect eaters, experimental efforts were made between 1907 and 1929 in the United States and Italy to promote bat populations in problem areas through the construction of "hygieostatic bat roosts." According to plans drawn up by Dr. Charles A. Campbell, San Antonio's health officer, one of the few roosts in America was built near Comfort in the Guadalupe River bottoms in 1918, on land owned by the family of San Antonio mayor Albert Steves. Seven roosts were eventually built in Texas, and this site is the only one still in existence. The roost consists of three wooden towers resembling Dutch windmills without blades. Only one tower is visible from the road. The tower is located in an orchard just a few feet to your left, directly opposite the intersection with Flat Rock Creek Road.

COMFORT

Kendall County • 2,400 (approximate) • (830) • About 13 miles from Sisterdale

The first white men to settle the area were shingle makers who set up camp along Cypress Creek and the Guadalupe River in 1852. A league and labor of land (4,605 acres), which covers the Comfort of today, was first given by the Republic of Texas to Jose Maria Regalado, who probably never even saw the land. The tract changed hands several times and by 1854 belonged to John F. C. Vles, a New Orleans cotton merchant and real estate speculator. Theodor Wiedenfeld; his brother-in-law, Heinrich Schladoer; and their families were the first German settlers in the area, having traveled up the Guadalupe from New Braunfels. Not wishing to remain a squatter, Theodor wrote a letter to Vles regarding sale of the land. In response, Vles sent twenty-two-year old Ernst Altgelt, a newly arrived Prussian employee, to check the tract out. It was spring, and Altgelt fell in love with the Comfort valley the first time he laid eyes on it, deciding to build a town here. Vles approved, and Altgelt surveyed and laid out a town.

The camp that Altgelt set up for his surveying crew on the west bank of Cypress Creek was called Camp Comfort, but no one is quite sure why they chose the name Comfort. Altgelt was so sold on the developmental possibilities that he wrote to his father in Dusseldorf for enough money to buy a thousand-acre tract that adjoined Vles' tract. Vles paid Altgelt off with land, giving Altgelt 2,500 acres to play with. Vles also gave Altgelt power of attorney to sell his land off to settlers. After three hundred lots were laid out, Altgelt declared the town alive and for sale on September 3, 1854. Thirty lots sold immediately, under a grove of oaks (now gone) at the corner of Main and Seventh. Eight houses were immediately built.

Soon after the village's founding, Altgelt erected a sawmill and gristmill, which came to be called Perseverance Mill. More than sixty families and as many individuals followed Altgelt here in the first year of Comfort's existence. Many of them were highly educated "freethinkers" of the same ilk as their intellectual compatriots at Sisterdale and Bettina. In that way, these settlers were unlike the Catholic and Lutheran farmers, tradesmen, and shopkeepers who left Germany in the 1840s to escape famine and unemployment and settled New Braunfels and Fredericksburg. These later comers quite openly told people that they left Germany to escape not only the political persecution that followed the liberals' failure in the revolution of 1848, but also religious oppression. From 1854 to 1892, no church was built in Comfort; you could scarcely find a

Bible in any of the homes. There were no prayers, and at funerals, sentimental German ballads replaced hymns. Vera Flach wrote in *A Yankee in German America*: "Funerals were always as large as they would be with so many relatives near at hand. The service was conducted by a German lodge and its message was 'Rest in Peace.' The life of the deceased was told and sometimes there was a eulogy read by a man skilled in public speaking. There was no mention of immortality because no one believed in it. We live in our children. That is our only immortality." Comfort still has a small but active group of freethinkers. The arrival of the railroad in 1887 and other factors led to the establishment of a sizeable Christian community and the establishment of the first church in 1892.

So how did Comfort get its name? One story says early settlers wanted to call their settlement "Gemuetlichkeit," a hard-to-spell, pronounce, and translate German word expropriated in the 1960s by the New Braunfels Wurstfest, which handily translates it as "good times." But the word means more, implying a sense of tranquility, serenity, peace, happiness, and comfort.

The erudite backgrounds of many of the Germans here caused another story to be told on them, that "these Freiburg and Heidelberg professors had made a vow to give their descendants a thorough education and therefore to speak only in Latin and German during the intervals of their hard work." At any rate, these hardworking Germans wasted no time in providing themselves with all the comforts of life, including the luxury of wheat flour ground at their own local mill starting in 1860.

Comfort was the county seat of Kerr County for two brief years, from 1860 to 1862. Comfort had wrested away this honor—seventy-eight votes to Kerrville's twenty-two votes—in an 1860 election. Kerrville regained its county seat status with the creation of Kendall County in 1862. Comfort was found to be just inside the new county of Kendall.

Cotton came to Comfort in a big way after the Civil War, for the nearby Guadalupe River bottomland is rich and black. The soil was locally known as the "mulatto" land and was considered capable of withstanding the severest and most continued droughts.

The arrival of the San Antonio and Aransas Pass Railroad (SAP) in 1887 made Comfort a major cotton shipping center, over more isolated Fredericksburg, which didn't get a railroad until 1913 (see "Take a Trip on the Fredericksburg and Northern"). Because of its high altitude relative to the Gulf Coast and much of the rest of populated Texas, Comfort was promoted as a cool summer resort; hunters found it to be a "Mecca of the Nimrods." Tuberculars and other respiratory sufferers came for the dry air and mild winters. They liked the clean water and lack of mosquitoes and malaria. By 1910, three hotels were serving hundreds of guests a week. Others stayed at boarding houses or on ranches with guest quarters; many others just pitched tents and lived off the bountiful local provender: fresh milk and butter, fish, fresh meat and game, and lots of fruit and vegetables.

The hospitable climate here was also deemed by E. T. Hall in 1914 to be "more ideal for ostriches than anywhere else in the country, with the exception of Phoenix, Arizona, where the largest ostrich farm in the world is located." Hall was in charge of Hot Wells Development Company's ostrich farm operation. In 1914, Hot Wells bought one thousand acres along the Guadalupe near Comfort in order to raise enough ostriches to supply the contemporary demand for "French plumes" for ladies' hats. You see, ostriches grow 160 of the plumes every nine months, 80 on each wing. All you have to do is pluck them. The ostrich farm never really got off the ground because the plumage craze was already at its peak and was soon to crash. Ostrich raising may never have caught on here, but armadillo ranching surely did. Beginning in 1898, Charles Apelt, who had been a supervisor in a wicker furniture and basket-weaving factory in Germany before coming to Texas, operated his armadillo farm—the only one in the world—about five miles out of town on SH 27. Apelt began trapping armadillos, breeding them, processing them, and turning their shells into baskets, lamp shades, and other novelties. A Depression-era pamphlet said of the farm: "Comfort's farm, the only one in the word, has probably done as much as any agency to put this lively 'hill country' town on the map. Not only does the world come to see it whenever it gets a chance, but it buys armadillo baskets in great numbers from the Comfort farm." Notice that back then they put Hill Country in quotations. Apelt died in 1944, but family members continued to operate the farm until it closed in 1971. New owners have restored parts of the property, although armadillo products are no longer sold.

As pleasant a place as Comfort is to live in today, nature still strikes some hard blows. Disastrous floods swept through in 1870, 1900, and 1932. In 1976, a tornado blew through town, most notably razing the old gazebo. August 2, 1978, brought the worst flood yet. Old-timers had long warned of what would happen if the headwaters of Cypress Creek, Verde Creek, and the twin forks of the Guadalupe all received heavy rains simultaneously. On that date, it happened, with the greatest concentration between Bandera and Center Point estimated at as much as forty-three inches of rain in forty-eight hours. Cypress Creek exploded into town and ran into the Guadalupe, which had already crested. The floodwater ran up to Main Street, and even High Street in one block. The water was up to twelve feet deep in places, and in the park, only the roof of the gazebo could be seen. Three people died, and many low-lying homes were destroyed. The July 1987 Guadalupe River flood stranded two summer-camp buses trying to escape and carried ten of the young campers to their deaths as they tried to evacuate the inundated vehicles.

Comfort is full of things to see, reminders of a Teutonic past. There are about one hundred pre-1910 buildings within walking distance of the center of town. For a town with so much to see, Comfort remains relatively unspoiled, compared with New Braunfels and the increasingly Disneyland-like Fredericksburg.

Take SH 473 across US 87 to SH 27. Turn right on SH 27, and then after one block turn left onto High Street (the name Comforters gave to their stretch of the Old Spanish Trail), which was until 1933 the main highway through the Hill Country to California, tracing the same path that I-10 follows today. US 87 and SH 27 eclipsed High Street as the main drag through town, but it remained Comfort's principal "downtown" street. The street's name refers to its altitude relative to Main and the streets below, which are closer to Cypress Creek.

OTTO BRINKMANN HOUSE

601 High St. • Not open to the public

Otto Brinkmann built this cottage in 1860 and lived here with his twin brothers until he married in 1867 (hence the house's nickname, "Bachelor Bude"). This house is one of Comfort's best examples of the "fachwerk" construction technique; that is, half-timbered walls filled in with native stone, in this case limestone. The cottage was enlarged in 1879 and restored in 1973.

OLD COMFORT STATE BANK (COMFORT HERITAGE SOCIETY'S ARCHIVES AND MUSEUM)

7th at High • Very limited hours • W

The old Comfort State Bank, a delightful mix of Romanesque Revival and castle Gothic, was built in 1907–1908. Richard Doebbler, survivor of the 1862 Nueces River Massacre, built it of rough-polished limestone blocks with pink granite pillars. It was Comfort's first formal, chartered bank. Previously, local merchants had provided banking services, beginning with August Faltin in 1856. Peter Joseph Ingenhuett began offering the same services for his customers in 1869. Although this caused a rift in the community, with inhabitants divided between the two mercantile families, there was little local interest in organizing a formal bank until a bank officer from San Antonio came sniffing around in 1906 to investigate the possibilities of opening a branch bank here. When they got wind of this, the rival Faltin and Ingenhuett families joined forces with three other Comfort men to organize the Comfort State Bank. The bank stayed in this building until 1960, when it moved to its present location. The building was then donated to the Comfort Independent School District, which in turn made it available to the Comfort Public Library, now located in the Arno Schwethelm Building (1916) across the street. The museum has various exhibits on display, including the armadillo farm, early clothing and housewares, and the Treue Der Union monument, including an original 1866 copy of *Harper's Weekly* about the monument.

The Chamber of Commerce and the Comfort ISD Board of Trustees are the closest thing Comfort has to local government; Comfort is one of the oldest and largest unincorporated towns in Texas and proud of it. "Live and let live," "We'll take care of our own," and "The less government the better," are the town's philosophical linchpins, and the direct heritage of Comfort's freethinking founders. A freethinkers society, the Texas Hill Country Freethinkers, is still active; anyone who approaches belief systems from a skeptical and rational point of view is welcome. Volunteerism and personal donations built the schools, hospital, theater, and park facilities, and founded and funded the public library, museum, volunteer fire department, and emergency medical services. This "benevolent anarchy," as it has been called, seems to have worked pretty well for nearly 150 years now.

Not too many other towns in Texas have a Bolshevik Hall. Comfort's Bolshevik Hall was a small frame building originally located behind the bank where the old men gathered to play dominoes, skat, pinochle, and other card games and to engage in philosophical argument or debate, depending on how many pilsners and lagers were consumed. It has moved several times in recent years and is now located on Main Street, near the corner with Seventh Street, next to the waterworks and across from the Faltin General Store. It currently houses the Comfort Little Theater.

From the old bank, go south one block on Seventh to Main.

Founder Altgelt had intended that the main business district be located around the two town squares on Main, but early flooding made most businessmen move up to High Street. High, between Sixth and Eighth streets, became the main business district, although the Faltins and Brinkmanns remained in business across from each other at Seventh and Main.

FALTIN HOMESTEAD

400 block of 7th, between High and Main • Not open to the public

On your right, in the middle of the block, is one of the oldest buildings still in its original location in Comfort. Brothers Theodore and Fritz Goldbeck built it in 1854 and operated Comfort's first general store next door, at the corner where the Faltin Store now stands. Fritz, a member of Altgelt's surveying party, also wrote poetry about early German pioneer life in Texas. Tired of the pioneer life, they sold the cabin and store in 1856 to August and Clara Faltin and moved to San Antonio. Faltin added the fachwerk section, and the house has remained in the Faltin family ever since.

FALTIN GENERAL STORE

Main at 7th

Born in Danzig, Prussia (now Gdansk, Poland), in 1831, August Faltin came to Comfort in 1856 and took over operation of the Goldbeck store on the corner, next to the cabin. In 1879, he built this imposing Italianate limestone building, designed by noted San Antonio architect Alfred Giles. It was Giles' first building outside San Antonio. The sheet-metal cornice and heavy consoles were to be repeated two years later in the Giles-designed Gillespie County courthouse. The store was downstairs, the family lived upstairs, and merchandise was stored in the basement. August retired in 1889 and turned the business over to his sons, who sold it to their brother-in-law, Dan Holekamp, in 1907. He decided to tear down the old Goldbeck store and build the simpler 1907 addition that sits directly on the corner, also designed by Alfred Giles. The second story was used for community meetings.

The Faltin Store started a trend toward limestone construction, as the community recovered economically from the ravages of the Civil War. The limestone was quarried from nearby ranches and hauled in by wagon. Limestone is sedimentary rock, built up layer by layer over the millennia. To split the limestone into manageable blocks, quarriers drilled holes into the rock at regular intervals, pounded round cypress or cedar poles into the holes, and then saturated the poles with water. The wood swelled with the water, and their expansion split the limestone along even lines. Holes were also chipped into the sides of the big blocks so that the giant tongs used to lift the stone blocks had something to grip on to. This explains the holes and grooves you see in the stones of many of the old stone buildings here and throughout the Hill Country.

They also had to make their own mortar to stick the stones together. Lime, sand, and water made a fine mortar and plaster. To make the lime, they built a kiln by digging an egg-shaped hole in the ground, preferably on a hillside where there would be a good draft for the fire. The hole was then filled with broken limestone rock, but with a hole in the center (like a Bundt cake) into which enough burning charcoal was dropped to fill the hole. After burning for three days, the limestone was broken down to a lime component suitable for mortar. More permanent lime kilns were also built into the hillsides, with round stone walls like a well. A good example for public view is on FM 165, eight miles north of Blanco at a roadside park in the Peyton Colony area. Peyton Colony was a farming community of freedmen families that developed after the Civil War, similar to St. John's Colony near Red Rock (see *Lone Star Travel Guide to Central Texas*).

BRINKMANN AND SONS STORE

405 7th at Main • Currently houses an antique store

Otto Brinkmann, whose "Bachelor Bude" you have already seen, built these adjoining store buildings beginning in 1883. The larger section was a general merchandise, hardware, and appliance store. Otto also had a lumberyard. The family lived in the gabled section, before the house next door (facing Main) was built in 1894. Otto's sons joined him in the business as they came of age. Otto's brother Walter, a tinsmith, built the tinwork building next to the corner store in 1894. A furniture store addition came in 1911. Walter lived in the house (1896) next to the tin shop.

From the Faltin General Store, proceed two blocks south on 7th (away from downtown) and turn right onto Water. Go one block, to the corner of 6th and Water.

COMFORT TURN VEREIN

700 Water, 6th at Water

This simple one-story white frame shotgun building until recently housed one of the few bowling alleys in Texas where pin boys manually set up the pins after each ball. The Turn Verein was Comfort's first organized social club (organized by Carl Brinkmann) and dated to 1860. The front part of the building was built in 1870. The organization reorganized in 1901, the same year the bowling alley was built at the back.

From the Turn Verein, return to the Faltin General Store. From the Faltin Store, return to High and the Chamber of Commerce.

The south side of the 800 block of High Street is cited as one of the most complete nineteenth-century business districts still standing in Texas.

PETER JOSEPH INGENHUETT HOUSE

812 High

Peter Joseph Ingenhuett came to the Comfort area in the 1850s and tried his hand at farming before moving into town in 1867 to try shopkeeping. He and his family lived in the small fachwerk cottage (built in 1863) at the back of this property. A better businessman than farmer, he quickly began to prosper and expand, buying his partner out in 1868 and branching out into a variety of businesses. As his four sons reached maturity, each one took over at least one of his concerns. Ernst took over the hotel; Hubert, the saloon; Paul, the general store and cotton gin; and Herman, the livery stable. In 1888, Peter Joseph built the larger, unpretentious, stucco-over-limestone, one-story house that sits out front.

OLD POST OFFICE

814 High

Alfred Giles also designed Comfort's first proper post office, built in 1908. Herman Ingenhuett was postmaster at the time. Giles did not often work in brick; this little building, built of red brick with limestone accents, shows off Giles' ability to work with mixed media and is in the same simple style as his Center Point School (1911).

INGENHUETT/FAUST HOTEL (THE COMFORT COMMON)

818 High • 995-3030 • www.bbhost.com/comfortcommon • Open daily • W with help

The original eight-room wing of this hotel was designed by Alfred Giles for Peter Ingenhuett, who built it in 1880. The hotel's size was doubled by the addition of a back wing in 1894. Out back, wide verandas open onto a courtyard brightened by hanging baskets and flowerbeds. A charming turn-of-the-century gazebo sits in the middle of the courtyard and provides a nice resting spot. Various members of the Ingenhuett family operated the hotel until about 1903; Louis and Mathilde Faust operated it from 1909 to 1946. It was restored in 1985 and is now home to a complex of antique shops and an above-average bed and breakfast establishment.

INGENHUETT STORE

830–834 High

Until it was destroyed by fire on March 15, 2006, Ingenhuett Store could lay claim to being the oldest general store in continuous existence in Texas, spanning five generations of the same family. The painted sign hanging from the porch read, "Peter Ingenhuett • Fancy Groceries • Hardware & Implements • Cash Grocery." The store was still all of these things. If you needed service or parts for your 1920 Lavalle cream separator, you could get them here, along with canned tamales, fresh meat, and overalls. The walls were covered with an amusing 1940s cowboy mural. The oldest, second-story section of the store building dated to 1880 and was designed by Alfred Giles. Efforts to rebuild the store were abandoned after the fire when it was discovered that the store's fire insurance did not cover the building, and without insurance compensation, rebuilding costs were prohibitively high. The cause of the fire was never determined. At press time, a Texas couple had announced plans to rebuild the store.

The original store stood where the Ingenhuett/Faust Hotel now stands. Peter Joseph ran his private bank inside the store; the post office was also located here until 1898. He was postmaster nearly twenty-five years. In addition to this store and the hotel, Peter Ingenhuett also established a livery stable, cotton yard, opera house, and saloon. In 1891, son Paul Ingenhuett assumed operation of the store and expanded the banking business and the marketing of grain and farm implements. He also got into the wool and mohair business in a big way and added the store's east wing in 1900.

In 1891, Alfred Giles also designed the saloon next door at 828 High Street. Church services were held here occasionally before 1900, and the building has also served as a dance hall, grocery store, meat market, and cabinet shop.

Paul's son, Peter C. Ingenhuett, ran the store from 1921 until 1955, when he was succeeded by his daughter and son-in-law, Gladys and James Krauter, and then their son Gregory. Gregory Krauter committed suicide on November 10, 2007.

A cenotaph honoring the role of freethinkers in Comfort's history stands between the burned-out store and the Comfort Historical Museum. Gregory Krauter was a prime mover in the cenotaph's erection, which was opposed by certain of the town's intolerant Christian elements.

COMFORT HISTORICAL MUSEUM

838 High at 8th • The museum is open by appointment; call Roy Perkins Jr. at 995-3807 • Donations accepted

This two-story limestone block building was built by Jacob Gass in 1891. During its construction, he walked in from Sisterdale each week, walking back to spend weekends with his family. He lived upstairs and had his blacksmith shop below. Paul Ingenhuett bought it in 1903 for storage for the store next door and then made it available to house the Comfort Museum when the museum was created in the 1930s. The museum consists of natural history artifacts, Indian relics, and historic memorabilia of the early German settlers.

Just around the corner from the museum, to your right down Eighth from High, is the Paul Ingenhuett home.

INGENHUETT HOUSE

8th, just south of High, on your right • Private residence

Paul Ingenhuett was born on this block and succeeded his father, Peter Joseph, in the mercantile business. Young Paul also expanded into farming and stock raising and helped found the Comfort State Bank. After noted architect Alfred Giles had designed several buildings in Comfort, Ingenhuett commissioned him to design this house in 1897. Of limestone quarried from Ingenhuett's property, the house is simple yet tasteful in its lines. Its only extravagance is the recessed center porch with its Greek pediment and twin supporting pillars. Unaltered, it is currently occupied by the fifth generation of Ingenhuetts.

One of the family reminisced about a hailstorm that struck Comfort in about 1928 or 1929: "I was just a little girl then. Hail stones the size of softballs crashed right through the window shutters, screens, and glass. Mother pulled me out of bed just before the hail pounded through, and it was a good thing too, because my bed was left full of broken glass." Her husband remembered that he spent most of the storm under his bed.

Behind the family home, almost hidden from view, stands the old Ingenhuett Opera House, built of native limestone in about 1890. It is not open to the public but was Comfort's social center before the Comfort Theatre was built.

Continue east on High Street. In another few yards you come to the old Meyer Hotel complex on your right, marked by a state historical marker.

THE MEYER BED AND BREAKFAST

845 High • 888-995-6100 • www.meyerbedandbreakfast.com

Frederick Meyer came to Comfort in 1862. A wheelwright, he also operated the town's first stagecoach stop and way station (a small log building built in 1857), located here on the banks of Cypress Creek. After purchasing the property, he added a sleeping loft to the cabin, in the style of the Fredericksburg Sunday houses, where passing travelers could spend the night. He built the two-story limestone cottage you see out front here in 1869. The upstairs rooms were rented to stagecoach passengers; he and the family lived downstairs.

In 1872, Meyer built a two-room frame cottage for his wife, Ernestine, who was a midwife and needed birthing rooms for her patients who came into town from area farms and ranches. When the railroad came through in 1887, he built the two-story frame hotel with double galleries to accommodate the rail passengers. The Meyers met the passengers at the station and took them by carriage to the hotel. Guests could eat a bountiful fifty-cent dinner in the dining room or enjoy a picnic on the grassy banks of Cypress Creek, behind the hotel. Although Frederick Meyer died in 1889, his wife, Ernestine, and then his daughter, Julia Ellenberger, continued to operate the hotel. Julia built the two-story stucco hotel in 1920 to handle the increasing business, and she ran the hotel until her death in 1956. It was Comfort's favorite eating place.

The complex changed hands several times before restoration and renovation began in 1973. All nine units are now air-conditioned and have private baths and cable TV, but otherwise they retain their original charm. Complimentary country-style breakfast is available. Call for rates and reservations, or visit the website.

If you continue east on High Street, you will cross the Guadalupe at the same point as the pioneers on the Old Spanish Trail. The scenic 1920s low-water bridge was damaged by the 1987 flood and was replaced by the current low-water bridge. In the 1930s, SH 27's route through town was modified; the sharp corner at High and Fourth was replaced with two blocks of curved road, which accounts for Comfort's apparently somewhat confusing layout. It's actually a very geometric, German town. Turn around and head back up High to Third Street to visit the only monument to the Union located in the South.

TREUE DER UNION (LOYALTY TO THE UNION)

High St., between 3rd and 4th • Open to the public • W

This simple monument, erected in 1865, memorializes the Union sympathizers killed at the Battle of Nueces on August 10, 1862. Most of the men in Comfort were Unionists, and when Confederate enrolling officers began conscripting young Germans in the summer of 1862, many of their fathers sent a petition to the governor denouncing the draft as a "despotic decree" and asking that the Texas government protect their "indisputable rights" as "free citizens" and refuse to comply with the draft laws.

On July 4, 1862, Unionists in Kerr, Kendall, and Gillespie counties formed the Union Loyal League. Three companies of men, one from each county, were organized. When word of this meeting reached General H. P. Bee, commanding this particular subdistrict of Texas, he declared the counties of

Gillespie, Kerr, Kendall, Medina, Comal, and Bexar to be in a state of open rebellion against the Confederacy and dispatched Captain James Duff's company to enforce martial law and protect enrolling officers. Duff, commonly held to be a cruel, hard-driving officer (although there is at least one modern-day researcher who disputes his reputation as a sadist and hanger of men), set up headquarters near Fredericksburg, whose inhabitants were "Unionists to a man," and promptly hanged anyone he suspected of having anti-Confederate sentiment.

After learning that the Confederate authorities had declared their counties to be in open rebellion and thus subject to martial law, the Union Loyal League decided to disband so as to assure the Confederate government that no rebellion was imminent. All those who did not wish to submit to Rebel rule decided to meet at Turtle Creek in Kerr County on August 1, 1862, in order to go to Mexico. Sixty-eight men gathered that day, many of them from Comfort. They left the same day for Del Rio and the Rio Grande. Although heavily armed, the Unionists were treating their trip as a holiday ride, apparently unworried about Confederate reprisals. But riding with them was a Confederate spy who left signs along the way for a body of pursuers—a Confederate cavalry patrol under Lieutenant C. D. McRae—which was about a day's ride behind.

The Unionists reached the Nueces River, about twenty miles from Brackettville, on the evening of August 9. There they camped for the night without choosing a defensible position or posting a strong guard. The Confederate cavalry, ninety-four strong, attacked before dawn the next morning. Nineteen of the Germans were killed on the field; nine of them were captured and shot a few hours later. Of the forty who escaped, six were later captured and shot, twenty made it to Mexico, and eleven sneaked back home. The men slain in battle were mutilated and left for the buzzards. Their bones were brought to Comfort after the war and buried in a common grave.

Back at Fredericksburg, Lieutenant McRae reported to Captain Duff that "they offered the most determined resistance and fought with desperation, asking no quarter whatever; hence I have no prisoners to report."

The massacre precipitated Unionist uprisings in the Fredericksburg area and especially in San Antonio, where men cried out in protest, threatening to resist by force of arms and posting notices around the city:

German brothers, are your eyes not opened yet? After the rich took every picayune away from you, and the paper is worth only one-half what you so hard earned, now that you have nothing left, now they go about and sell you, or throw you out of employment for Dunhauer, who left his wife and children, wants to do the same with you to the poor you might leave. Now is the time to stay the heads of Dunhauer, Maverick, Mitchel, and Meager to the last bone. We are always ready. If the ignorant company of Newton fights you, do as you please. You will always stay the God damn Dutchman. Do away with that nuisance, and inform everybody the revolution is broke out.

It is a shame Texas has such a brand. Hang them by their feet and burn them from below.

Nearly 150 years later, the Nueces battle is still a very emotional issue in Comfort. People sometimes shed tears almost as if the battle took place yesterday.

Across High Street from the Treue Der Union monument is the Immanuel Lutheran Church. Behind it is Comfort's first church, the 1892 Deutsche Evangelische Kirche, a simple white frame sanctuary that has been used by all denominations. Before this church was built, services were held in a saloon. The second and third generations of Comfort established the church; Comfort's founders remained freethinkers to the end.

Return to SH 27 and head west toward Center Point. As SH 27 makes its bend to the southwest leaving Comfort, you see on your left Comfort Park and on your right the Faltin home.

COMFORT PARK

SH 27 between Main and Broadway

Comfort Park is one of the original blocks laid out as a park by Ernst Altgelt, and a plaque and bust honor him here. After founding Comfort, Altgelt went on to develop San Antonio's prestigious King William Street neighborhood, naming the street and building its first house in 1867. In the center of the park is a gazebo, built in 1904, the site of countless summer band concerts, speeches, and celebrations.

Germans tend to be passionate gardeners, and a farmers market operates here on Saturday mornings from May through August, offering a wide variety of locally grown foodstuffs. Comfort also has a number of commercial horticultural and herb businesses, as well as dozens of pretty, carefully tended home flower and vegetable gardens.

Across the park on Main Street, almost at the corner of Main and SH 27, are the Wilhelm Heuermann homes. The fachwerk cottage out front was built in 1857; the one-room log cabin in back was built in 1854 or 1855.

FALTIN HOUSE

SH 27 at Broadway, across from Comfort Park • Private residence

August Faltin commissioned Albert Beckman to design this grand, multi-gabled, two-story limestone residence in 1890. Faltin had come to the Hill Country as a prosperous banker, late of Prussia, and the money he brought with him financed the growth of Comfort and Kerrville. Faltin was especially interested in helping mercantile businesses and industry get started. One of the men he staked was young Charles Schreiner. With Faltin's money, Schreiner established a general store at Kerrville in 1869 and went on to become a millionaire.

Near the Faltin home, at the corner of Main and Fourth, across SH 27, is the home of Ernst Flach, one of Comfort's great entrepreneurs, who built and owned the mill complex one mile upstream on the Guadalupe. It powered a cotton gin, made ice and electricity, cut lumber, and ground grain. The house is an interesting mix of construction styles, showing how additions were attached to houses following the original construction. The fachwerk section in the back is the oldest section, post-Civil War. The front part of the house has a limestone center section flanked by wings of whitewashed, millsawn lumber.

DINING

CYPRESS CREEK INN

400 block of SH 27 • 995-3977 • www.cypresscreekinn.com • Open Tuesday through Saturday, lunch and dinner; Sunday, lunch only • W

The Inn is Comfort's oldest restaurant, although it dates only to the mid-1950s. Still, it has a loyal clientele of locals and long-time Hill Country travelers. The food is uncomplicated country-style cooking, though not extraordinary. The pies are homemade, the vegetables frozen. There is a daily lunch special, and the Sunday lunch menu includes roast beef, baked ham, barbecued chicken, and steaks.

DOUBLE D FAMILY RESTAURANT

1004 Front/SH 27, west of the Guadalupe River bridge • 995-2001 • Open daily, breakfast, lunch, and dinner • W

The Double D serves what most folks call the best hamburgers in Comfort. With a daily ("all-you-can-eat") buffet, this is a place for hearty eaters. Everything, down to the hot rolls, is made in-house. Beer only.

TOURISM INFORMATION

COMFORT CHAMBER OF COMMERCE

630 SH 27 • 995-3131 • www.comfortchamberofcommerce.com, www.comfort-texas.com

Pick up your local tourism information here. The office is well marked by a highway sign.

ANNUAL EVENT

JULY

HOMECOMING

Comfort Park • July 4 • Features a noon barbecue, contests, games, traditional German band music, dancing, and arts and crafts show

SH 27 west out of Comfort continues to carry you through the flat, rich farmland of the Guadalupe River valley. Although you seldom see it along this five-mile stretch of road, the river is never more than a few hundred yards away. You can see what little is left of Charles Apelt's armadillo farm, which is located 1.5 miles inside Kerr County, on your right at the turnoff for Legacy and Bryce lanes. Look for the small stone house by the road, which served armadillo barbecue, and the larger brick house set back from the road.

Turn left off SH 27 onto RM 1350 5.5 miles west of Comfort. RM 1350 takes you into Center Point.

CENTER POINT

Kerr County • 800 (approximate) • About 9 miles from Comfort

In 1856, Dr. James Crispin Nowlin settled at the juncture of the roads leading to Camp Verde and Kerrville, off the San Antonio Road. Nowlin, a slaveholder born in Kentucky, grew the first cotton in Kerr County.

In 1858, Dr. Charles Ganahl, his family, and slaves moved here from Savannah, Georgia. He had tuberculosis and sought the drier climate of West Texas to prolong his life. They built a home using locally harvested cypress logs on the north bank of the Guadalupe River, across from the present town of Center Point. The 1860 census stated he owned four thousand acres of land and twenty-one slaves.

Center Point was originally called Zanzenberg, after the Ganahl family ancestral home in the Austrian Tyrol. Ganahl opened a post office inside his home in 1859. His wife, Jennie, served as postmistress. The community was often referred to as Ganahl.

Dr. Ganahl was a fervent secessionist, serving in the Texas Secession Convention. Most families in Kerr County did not own slaves, and the vote for secession in the county was very close.

Ganahl, trained in surgery in Germany and in Paris, joined the Confederate Army as a surgeon. At the end of the war, Dr. Ganahl refused to take the oath of allegiance to the Union and fled to Mexico where he practiced medicine in Matamoros for several years, until it was safe for him to return to Texas. In the meantime, Jennie moved to Galveston with their daughter. Upon his return to Texas, Ganahl moved to Galveston to practice medicine, where he remained during much of the 1870s, before returning to Kerr County in 1879. During 1881–1882, he practiced medicine in Eagle Pass, but, growing weaker from tuberculosis, he returned to Kerr County, where he died in 1883.

As more settlers moved into the area, a village grew on the opposite bank of the Guadalupe, which was named Center Point in 1864 due to its central location between Kerrville, Comfort, Fredericksburg, and Bandera. Center Point and Comfort were neighbors, but their relation was anything but friendly during the war. Center Point was cotton-growing, slave-holding, and every bit as pro-Southern as Comfort was pro-Union. The animosity continued long after the war, as the following story illustrates:

In November 1879, robbery charges were brought against a count Keroman, who had been staying with Dr. Ganahl's family. Keroman was charged with robbing a safe in the Faltin, Schreiner and Below store at Center Point one night in October. The only evidence was the fact that two fifty dollar bills were found in his possession, and two fifty dollar bills were stolen from the safe. It was not pretended that they had been identified as the same notes at all. The examination before the justice was conducted in English, which the count did not speak. He had no lawyer and no friends present. He was jailed in default of a two thousand dollar bond but paid eight dollars a day to three men who guarded him in jail until friends in San Antonio could come to his rescue. The store proprietors subsequently confessed that they were mistaken. The count provided a complete alibi.

To understand this case, you must understand the state of society existing in most frontier counties. In cities, most people attended to their business first and that of their neighbors afterward. In the country the reverse was the rule. If a stranger moved into a neighborhood and was not hand-in-glove with Tom, Dick and Harry, those worthies regarded it as a personal insult and endeavored to make life as disagreeable as possible to the intruder. A favorite mode to gratify private spite was to make an affidavit for theft or some other offense against the obnoxious individual. In most cases it was not seriously believed that the party had been guilty of any offense, but it was a very good way to put an enemy to considerable expense and annoyance. Count Keroman's troubles grew out of the fact that he lived with a family against whom a ring of Kerr county officials had a spite. Dr. Ganahl, for some reason, possibly his Confederate past, was the object of bitter hostility on the part of the crowd who were most prominent in annoying Keroman. It was openly boasted in Kerr County that Ganahl would be run out of the county, and this Keroman affair was a part of the proceedings.

It was alleged by no less a personage than the sheriff of Kerr County that Keroman had stolen money on a number of occasions. One of the parties mentioned as having been robbed promptly made a written document, attested by witnesses, that he never made any such allegations. The count then engaged lawyers to push the investigations in the federal court until he was satisfied.

In 1872, the post office moved from Ganahl's house to Center Point, which grew into a sizable town, spurred on by the local cypress lumber industry, and the arrival of the railroad in 1887, which, to the town's great consternation, located its station, which it named Ganahl, on the opposite bank of the Guadalupe on property donated by Mrs. Ganahl. As the Bandera Enterprise wrote at the time, "Mrs. Ganahl is a very energetic lady, and it seems she is determined to build a town for herself."

But Ganahl never grew beyond its depot status and Center Point became the shipping center for most of Bandera County and once boasted two banks and over a dozen commercial establishments. Development of the Texas highway system diminished Center Point's importance as a trade center; it is now a sleepy little farm and ranching town. Center Point was incorporated in March 1913, but its charter was dissolved that same October, probably making Center Point the shortest-lived city in Central Texas.

The Ganahls' home stood in its original location until 1967, when it was moved to the Y.O. Ranch at Mountain Home, along with the log building that served as Center Point's first school.

Ganahl is buried in the Center Point Cemetery, along with thirty-two or thirty-three Texas Rangers, the most in any cemetery in Texas. Also buried here is Stacy Sutherland, guitarist for the psychedelic rock band the 13th Floor Elevators. He died under mysterious circumstances in 1978. Fans visit the site, leaving guitar picks and other remembrances. His gravestone features some of Stacy's poetry.

CENTER POINT SCHOOL

219 China/RM 1350, between Ave. A and Ave. C

Indicative of Center Point's former economic prowess is the old Center Point School, still in use and part of a larger, newer Center Point ISD complex.

Alfred Giles designed this two-story limestone building, constructed in 1911. Although much simpler in design than earlier Giles buildings, it still bears his distinctive touch. For reference, see his old post office (1910) in Comfort, and the Kendall County courthouse addition (1909) and Boerne High School (1910), both located in Boerne.

When RM 1350 dead-ends into RM 480, turn left onto RM 480 toward Camp Verde. RM 480 follows Verde Creek to Camp Verde.

CAMP VERDE

Kerr County • 41 • (830) • About 6.5 miles from Center Point

Camp Verde was one of four camps established in 1855 to accommodate the newly organized U.S. Second Cavalry, under the command of Albert Sidney Johnston, and Joseph E. Johnston's First Cavalry. The camp was named after the creek, Verde, where it was located. Verde means "green" in Spanish. The place was first referred to as Green Valley.

Camp had barely been set up when the camels came marching in. These "ships of the desert" were part of then-Secretary of War Jefferson Davis' quest to improve the quality of long-distance transportation on the western frontier, where water was scarce and forts few and far between. Davis envisioned the camels as "gunships of the desert," thinking that the camels might carry mounted infantry and small howitzers. Thirty-four camels, mostly single-hump Arabian dromedaries, arrived at the port of Indianola in May 1856. Major Henry Wayne, who had sailed to Africa to purchase them, brought them to Texas, complete with native handlers and detailed plans for the construction of an authentic caravanserai. The camels quartered first in San Antonio, where they were joined by another forty-one camels in February 1857. San Antonio was no place to raise camels, so Wayne began searching for a permanent home. He visited Fort Martin Scott near Fredericksburg, which had been abandoned in 1852, and left unimpressed. More impressed by a visit to newly established Camp Verde, Wayne soon moved the camels here. George W. Kendall, who was interested in innovative animal husbandry, visited Camp Verde, where one of the native handlers told him that a two-year-old camel raised in Texas was larger that a three-year-old at home, and better formed. Some of Camp Verde's camels were included in a wagon train that set out for California in June 1857. These animals carried supplies for U.S. Army posts in Arizona and California during the Civil War.

The camels performed well in several long journeys west, except that their feet, accustomed to sandy terrain, were cut and bruised by the rocky terrain. The soldiers used the camels only as pack animals, but the officers' wives occasionally used them as mounts to travel to camp meetings, six women to an animal.

Confederate troops took over Camp Verde in March 1861 with the outbreak of the Civil War. R. H. Williams, one of the attacking Confederate force, described the capture of Camp Verde in his book, *With the Border Ruffians: Memories of the Far West, 1852–1868:*

> About the middle of March I joined a company mustered in by T. Paul. We were forty in number, all good men and well armed, and reported at Castroville.
> Paul had, in bygone times, held a commission in the Texas Navy; he was an old frontiersman and a fighting man. He was the only commissioned officer in the

company, and appointed me at once orderly sergeant. Directly we were mustered we went into camp on the Medina River, in an old Mormon settlement, where there were several solid stone houses and a mill.

That night Paul told us his orders were to march at daybreak to Val Verde, forty miles distant, to attack that post, which was held by a detachment of U.S. cavalry. How many of the enemy he would find he didn't know, but thought there were not many more than our number. It seemed rather a large order, but the "Boys" were in high spirits and eager for a fight. Before daybreak our small bugler had roused the camp, and by sun-up we had drunk our coffee and were off on our long ride.

Our route lay, for the most part, by bridle-paths alongside the Medina River, which ran swift and clear between high cedar-clad ridges. We took all proper precautions, and had scouts well ahead, whilst every man rode with his loaded rifle across the horns of his saddle and his six-shooter in his belt ready for use. But perforce we had to ride in single file, and a dozen plucky men, properly posted in some of the narrow defiles, could easily have wiped us out. However, we were not molested, and camped that night about two miles from the post.

That night we lay on our arms, and our pickets and those of the enemy were almost in touch. It passed without any attack on either side, and at daybreak we fell in and marched to within a mile of the fort. There Paul left his command in charge of the next senior sergeant, an old fighting frontiersman, whilst he and I rode on to the post, I bearing a white flag. A sergeant's guard received us and escorted us inside the fort, outside which I saw strong picket-defences had been thrown up, and I made sure we were in for a fight. Lieutenant Hill, the officer in command, received us very stiffly, and said he meant to hold his post to the last. He had really received orders to retire, as we afterwards learned, but put a bold face on it to gain better terms.

Paul assured him that though he might hold his post against us for a time, reinforcements were coming up and eventually he must surrender; fighting would only mean useless waste of life. Our crafty friend was deaf to all reason for some time; but when Paul offered to let the officers and men march out with their horses, arms, and personal property, which was what he had been fighting for, he at once agreed, and terms were forthwith settled. Hill was to march out next day and report his command at San Antonio.

So at two o'clock that day he marched out and we took possession of the post, the stores, ammunition, twelve mules, eighty camels, and two Egyptian drivers, for all of which I had to give a receipt. The camels had been purchased in Egypt by the U.S. Government for transport across the prairies in the dry season, and answered very well. They were very little trouble to us as far as the females were concerned (do they call them "mares?"—I don't know), but some of the males were the mischief, especially an old gentleman they christened "the major." He was evidently possessed by "Shaitan," and bit and fought like a demon; but we chained him by the foot to a strong picket-post, and peace reigned in the camel-corral.

The camels soon were widely scattered; some were turned out on the open range near Camp Verde; some were used to pack cotton bales to Brownsville (two bales to a camel, mounted on each side); and one was commandeered by Captain Sterling Price, who used it throughout the war to carry his company's baggage.

Some of the camels were kept in San Antonio, where John S. "Rip" Ford tried but failed to render them serviceable, reporting to General Magruder: "The camels have been sent to the Guadalupe for corn. Two are reported to have died on the trip. They can live best on grass, and it is not certain they will live on corn. Captain (William) Prescott will send them to Camp Verde for the present."

Union Army prisoners were also kept at Camp Verde, in Prison Canyon, which is southwest of the headquarters and surrounded on three sides with very steep cliffs that were practically impossible to scale. When the Confederates took over the frontier forts, they didn't repatriate the U.S. soldiers but imprisoned them in

Prison Canyon. They were joined by other captured soldiers, perhaps as many as six hundred. At this point, some of them were exchanged for Rebel prisoners.

The Confederate soldiers at Camp Verde didn't have much use for the camels. One young soldier, annoyed at the slow pace of one old camel, pulled out his dirk and stabbed the beast to death at the Bandera Pass, where the camel died by the grave of the Indian chief who had died in the battle at Bandera Pass. The soldier and a colleague partially dug up the chief's grave and took some beads as souvenirs. The grave is along the old road through the pass that leads down into the valley following Mico Creek. They did use camels to haul cotton to Matamoros. Another time, three or four Rebel soldiers pushed an uncooperative camel off a cliff.

J. W. Walker, who came to Camp Verde in 1862 as a fifteen-year-old Ranger, worked as a camel herder. He says that one night while he was guarding the camels, he heard some noise (oxen and dogs) and went down to the creek to investigate, where the Camp Verde store stands. There he found an "Old Marster" and three hundred negroes. This was in 1863. He said he was going with his negroes to Mexico. He left the next day and was later seen near Bandera, and his campfire was later seen about one day's travel from Bandera. But as far as Walker ever heard, the old marster was never overtaken.

Andy Jones was born in Bexar County in 1853. His family came to Bandera County in 1864 and settled on Myrtle Creek.

> One day we hobbled three or four of our horses and turned them loose near the house, and fourteen of those old camels came lumbering along. The horses took fright at the sight of them, and we did not see those horses again for many days. My brother and I penned the camels, all of them being gentle except one. We roped the wild one, but never wanted to rope another, for the old hump-backed villain slobbered all over us, and that slobber made us deathly sick. We had a jolly time with those camels when we got rid of the foul, sickening slobber, and as often we rode broncos and wild steers we rode those camels too. The camel has a swinging pace and is easy to ride when you catch the motion of its gait. They could easily travel 100 miles in one day. The Indians seemed to be afraid of the camels, and, of course, never attempted to steal any of them.

Another of the Confederates' camel handlers was Cuba Blanks, who had come to the area with Dr. Ganahl as a slave. Toward the end of the war, a couple of musically inclined black men came to Camp Verde to play for a dance for the white folks. The blacks had their own dance, at the camp hospital. They had lots of whiskey and dancing, but no trouble, Cuba said. The end of the war brought no joy to Blanks. One day he returned to the slave quarters at the Ganahl Ranch to find the white overseer skipping out. The other white folks had fled, leaving just the blacks. When the Yankees rode up, Cuba greeted them in his best clothes and invited them to partake of the ranch's watermelons, which had just ripened. The Yanks ate all of Cuba's melons, cut the shiny buttons off Cuba's coat, and left him standing in his drawers. He never thought much of the Union after that and never did take the Union Loyalty Oath.

After the war, the federal government lost interest in the great camel experiment and in 1866 auctioned off the beasts that remained in captivity in Texas. Austin lawyer Bethel Coopwood bought several dozen, hoping to use them to haul freight between El Paso and Chihuahua City, as well as from San Antonio to Los Angeles. He rode one from Austin to court in San Antonio one morning at a record-breaking pace. But he soon realized that the profits to such a venture were small and the risks high, and he sold his interests to others. He sold the camels to circuses, fairs, and anyone else sufficiently adventuresome. Escaped camels roamed the hills around Camp Verde for several decades thereafter, scaring the wits out of travelers and newcomers. Comanche Indians named them "goats of the devil."

The camel experiment failed, not because they were inferior transport animals, but because the soldiers wouldn't accept them. The camels smelled horrible, spat foul-smelling cud indiscriminately, frightened horses, and did not passively accept their handlers' abuse the way mules did. They could defend themselves, and did. One day, a private overloaded a camel, and the camel started groaning and bleating. The soldier kicked the camel in the belly, whereupon the camel spit a wad of cud in his face. The enraged soldier grabbed a club and aimed for the camel's head. He missed, but the camel didn't. It quickly ripped open the man's arm to the bone with its sharp incisors. The soldier got off lucky; the camel could just as easily have nipped off his arm or his kneecap.

Camels have a good memory, especially for those who harm them; "the 'camel's temper' is a proverbial expression used by the Arabs to denote a vindictive and unforgiving disposition," scientist, traveler, and camel enthusiast George Marsh wrote in his 1856 book, *The Camel*. If sufficiently angry at someone, the camel would bide its time until it had a chance to knock him down and lie on the man, crushing him.

Some of the camel handlers returned to their native countries; others headed west. According to J. Marvin Hunter, one of the handlers, a Turk named Elias, settled first in New Mexico and then moved into the Mexican state of Sonora, where he ranched, married a Yaqui Indian girl, and raised a family. One of his children was Plutarco Elias Calles, born in 1877, who was President of Mexico from 1924 to 1928. As a youngster he was known as El Turco ("The Turk"), and while president of Mexico he recalled hearing his father speak of herding camels for the U.S. Army.

Elias' origins are obscure, and his enemies would later claim that he was a Turk or a Jew. Actually, he was neither. As near as can be ascertained, he was the natural son of a woman named Maria de Jesús Campuzano and Plutarco Elias, a member of a prominent local family of Lebanese descent. The boy grew up in poverty as Plutarco Elias, and according to Fernando Torreblanca, who was both his secretary and his son-in-law, he took the name Calles from his maternal uncle, who befriended and raised him after his mother's death. Historians suggest that this background of illegitimacy and deprivation had much to do with shaping Calles' morose nature and fanatic hostility toward his enemies.

The army abandoned the fort in 1869, and the lumber from the khan was hauled to San Antonio for sale. The headquarters building passed to W. H. Bonnell, who rented rooms to folks looking to get away from it all. On March 26, 1910, the place burned. The fire is believed to have started in the room occupied by Thomas Blair of Hamilton, Ohio. He had spent several summers there with the Bonnells. By three in the morning, the house was afire. Would-be rescuers of Blair were driven back by the flames' intensity, even though they could see his body lying on the floor. Blair and a friend had been up until at least midnight, drinking from a bottle of Green River whiskey. The house was rebuilt from the remains.

CAMP VERDE STORE

RM 480 at SH 173 • 634-7722 • www.campverdegeneralstore.com • Open daily • MC, V

This store first opened in 1853 as the Williams Community Store, located about one mile south of Camp Verde. The store had been opened principally because the army forbade the sale of liquor inside military reservations. Because of the meager population, the store was only open on army paydays. Charles Schreiner and Caspar Real bought the store in 1857 after Mr. Williams' health began to fail, supplementing their store business with army beef and wool contracts. Caspar Real was lured here by J. C. Nowlin, and Real brought Charlie Schreiner here. Schreiner moved on to bigger and better things in nearby Kerrville after serving in the war.

But the store at Camp Verde persevered, even after the camp itself was abandoned. A post office was established here in 1858, was abandoned in 1892, and was reestablished in 1898. Today the store contains an inventory of arts and crafts, souvenirs, antiques, and other items designed to appeal to the tourist. Most of the store's fixtures are original, although they are largely obscured by the prodigious inventory.

From the FM 480/SH 173 intersection and the Camp Verde store, proceed south on SH 173 toward Bandera. In two miles you cut through the Bandera Pass, the ancient path through the hills that divide the Guadalupe and Medina river watersheds.

BANDERA PASS

SH 173 • About 2 miles from Camp Verde

The Bandera Pass is the logical pass for all travel from the Medina valley northward, as steep barriers obstruct the progress of anyone who would follow another route across the Bandera Mountains. It has been used since prehistoric times. It is possible that the Old Spanish Trail passed through this pass. The Spaniards who discovered Bandera Pass were members of Captain Jose de Urrutia's 1739 expedition against the Apaches, according to historian Robert Weddle. The Apaches used the pass on their raids from their camps in the San Saba country to San Antonio, and Urrutia was able to surprise the Indians in their camp near the present-day town of Menard and took many captives, who were then enslaved.

The origins of the name of Bandera Pass are clouded, but one story goes something like this: Spanish troops from San Antonio de Bexar met Apache warriors in battle at the pass in 1732. The battle was very bloody, and afterward the Spanish and Apaches held a council and signed a treaty. The Indians would not tread south of the pass, and the Spanish agreed never to set foot north of the pass in Indian hunting grounds. In token of this agreement, a red flag (*bandera* in Spanish) was placed on the highest peak by the pass to remind both sides of their promises.

Others, including J. Marvin Hunter, say the Spanish commander in this battle was named Ciro or Manuel Bandera. A Manuel Bandera owned property at the confluence of the Arroyo de Alazan and the Arroyo de San Pedro near Nuestra Senora de la Purisima Concepcion de Acuna Mission at San Antonio. But various popular accounts crediting Bandera as the Spanish general cannot be corroborated, says the *Handbook of Texas*, nor has his name been found on any Bexar muster roll.

In 1922, J. Marvin Hunter recounted the 1843 battle of Bandera Pass, basing his story, in part, on A. J. Sowell's 1900 account of the battle in *Texas Indian Fighters*:

In 1843, while Captain Jack Hays' company of Rangers was stationed on Leon Creek, west of San Antonio, he got word that a large band of Comanches had been seen in the Guadalupe River region near present-day Kerrville. Anticipating a raid on the settlements near San Antonio, Hays, with a force of about forty men, rode out to intercept the Indians, if possible, and engage them in battle. The plan was to go up to the head of the Guadalupe and then down some of the canyons and back to camp if they did not discover the Indians. Among his squad of Rangers were Ben McCulloch, Sam Walker, Ad. Gillespie, P. H. Bell, Ben Highsmith, Tom Galbreath, Lee Jackson, and Mike Chevalier. Many of these men had been members of the ill-fated Mier expedition to Mexico. Sam Walker was of this number, having made his escape from a Mexican prison and just returned in time to rejoin Captain Hays. Bigfoot Wallace was also a member of Hays' Rangers, but he was still in prison in Mexico City.

The Rangers struck the Medina River at a point about where the Castroville colony would soon be established and followed the river to the present location of Bandera, where they camped for the night. Early the next morning, they headed north toward Bandera Pass, which they entered at about ten o'clock. The Comanches had seen the Rangers as they rode through the open country and laid an ambush for them, concealing themselves among the rocks and gullies on both sides of the pass, which is about a mile long and about 150 yards wide. The high and steep hills and the narrow pass were an excellent place for the attack, which began as soon as the Rangers, who were riding in groups of two and three, were almost halfway through the pass. The Comanches' sudden and furious fire momentarily confused the Rangers riding point, and their frightened horses tried to turn and run back, but Hays quickly rallied his men and prepared to make a stand. The Indians had guns and bows and arrows, and they wounded several of the Rangers and horses, but Hays assured his men that they could "whip the redskins." At this point the Indians left their places of concealment and collected at the north end of the pass, charging down upon the Rangers, who had dismounted and were ready to receive them. This part of the fight took place at close quarters, and the Rangers used their pistols with telling effect. There was hand-to-hand conflict, and in one of these the Comanche chief was killed.

After the death of the chief, the Indians withdrew to the north end of the pass, and the Rangers went the other way, carrying their dead and wounded, and camped at a waterhole near the south end of the pass. Nearly one-third of the Rangers received wounds, and five Rangers were killed; they were buried at a point near where the present road enters the pass.

The Indians remained at the north end of the pass and there buried their chief but did not molest the Rangers further. It is not known how many were killed, but many were carried off the field of battle. Jack Hays and his men, after burying their dead comrades, carried the wounded Rangers to San Antonio where they all recovered.

For many years, the bleached bones of the killed horses lay scattered about for all to see. During the 1850s, early settler Fabian Hicks found the chief's skeleton, which someone had dug up. Beads and other things belonging to the dead warrior were scattered about. Hicks gathered up his bones and placed them back in the grave, covering it with dirt and loose stones.

The approximate site of the battle is marked by a state historical marker.

In 1874, Captain John Lytle established the Great Western Trail, which began in Bandera and passed through Bandera Pass into Kerr County, following SH 173's path through Camp Verde, crossing the Guadalupe River in Kerrville, and running along Town Creek toward Harper in Gillespie County, where it crossed the Pedernales River, and on through Mason and Brady on its way north. More than three hundred thousand longhorns, seven thousand horses, and one thousand men passed annually through the pass, into and through Kerr County, to railways in Kansas and Nebraska for shipment to markets in the northeast. Captain Charles Schreiner was an instrumental figure in the trail's history, and his store in Kerrville became a major stop for trail outfitters to replenish supplies on the journey north.

In April 1883, the first herd of the season left Bandera, fully a month later than the previous year. It numbered 4,200, belonged to Lytle and McDaniel, and was under the care of Gus Black. It was mostly composed of steers, and their condition was not good. Lytle had several partners, including Captain Charley Schreiner, who said that he and Lytle would drive about twenty-five thousand head of cattle that year, apart from the twelve-thousand-odd head that would be driven by the firm of Lytle and McDaniel.

Schreiner went on to buy full control of the business from Lytle.

By 1886, the trail had passed into history for several reasons, including the extension of the railroads, the fencing in of the open range, an oversupply of cattle, and the introduction of "improved" breeds like the Hereford, which were incapable of making the long walk north.

As you descend Bandera Pass, you come to an intersection with RM 2828. Turn right here to reach Medina. Once you are on RM 2828, you are in the rugged "mountains" of Bandera County, high hills that have earned Bandera County the nickname "The Switzerland of Texas." RM 2828 runs into SH 16 after nine miles. Turn right onto SH 16 to reach Medina.

MEDINA

Bandera County • 515 • (830) • About 14 miles from Camp Verde

Medina dates itself to 1880, when the post office was established. It was first called Medina City. The "city" was dropped when it failed to become one. No one knows who named Medina, which was presumably so named for the river that runs through town. The area was a popular hunting and camping site fought over by several Indian tribes who also fought off non-Indians who tried to settle here.

At public auction on July 1, 1841, John James, who surveyed and platted Castroville, D'Hanis, Quihi, Boerne, and Bandera, bought several thousand acres here and sold about half of the acreage to the famous Confederate general John Bell Hood in 1864. White families tried to settle the area in the 1850s and 1860s, but all but a few were killed or run off by Indians. The property changed hands several times until 1879, when B. F. Bellows purchased and divided the property into town lots and began selling them off. People started moving here as news spread that the Indian raids had ended.

The village declined with the development of Texas' high-speed road system, but it received a shot in the arm in recent decades from the vacation trade. Medina is the capital of Texas' fledgling apple industry, which explains all the red apples you see hanging or nailed up around here. The harvest begins in late July and continues through September, so be sure to stop by any of the local stands and stores for apples, fresh-pressed cider, and other apple treats.

Medina only has a few historical landmarks left; most have been destroyed by floods or fire, have been torn down, or have been drastically remodeled. The Stanard House, which overlooks the river, is on the left as you come into Medina. Charles Parker built the house in 1878 and sold the property to Bellows in 1879. In 1889, Harvey Stanard bought the property from B. F. Bellows, and it stayed in his family until in 1973. The native limestone Hatfield Store on Main Street dates to 1888. It had several owners before the Hatfield family took it over in 1909. It was your typical general store.

For a good look at the river, turn left on Patterson (before you get to downtown) at the "First Baptist Church 1 Block" sign and go two blocks to the low-water bridge.

The small white frame church behind the Baptist Church is the Methodist Church, organized here in 1881. The West Prong Methodist Church was established in 1881. It later became the Medina Methodist Church. Harvey Stanard donated land for the church, which was built here by the river in 1889. The church has been expanded and remodeled a number of times so that it no longer resembles its original state.

THE APPLE STORE (FORMERLY THE CIDER MILL AND COUNTRY STORE)

14024 N. SH 16, downtown Medina • 830-449-0882 • www.lovecreek orchards.com • Open daily

Besides cider, you can buy apple jelly, apple jam, apple butter, apple syrup, apple shampoo, and apple ice cream. The Patio Cafe located in the back of the store serves burgers, sandwiches, and salads.

LOVE CREEK ORCHARDS

800-449-0882• www.lovecreekorchards.com

Texas' apple industry dates to the early 1980s, when Baxter and Carol Adams began growing dwarf apple trees in the fertile valley of Love Creek, west of Medina. Full-sized apple trees take seven years to produce a crop; dwarf trees yield full-sized apples in less than two years. Varieties grown include Red Delicious, Gala, and Crispin. Hill Country apples don't redden as much as their northern relatives, but they are delightfully sweet and crisp, the equal of apples grown anywhere else. Call for tour availability. Harvest starts in late July and runs through August.

From SH 16, turn left on RM 337 to reach Vanderpool and the Lost Maples. RM 337 closely follows the route of the Medina River for the next nine or ten miles, through and over breathtakingly beautiful but ruggedly desolate hills and valleys. You are forever catching glimpses of the silvery Medina, sometimes beside you, sometimes far below. The best time to drive this road is at sunrise or sunset when the fifteen miles of RM 337 are some of the most pleasant you'll find in the entire state.

Turn right on FM 187 when RM 337 dead-ends at Vanderpool.

VANDERPOOL

Bandera County • 20 • About 20 miles from Medina

Vanderpool, named for early settler L. B. Vanderpool, has never been anything more than a wide spot in the road. Today it consists of two churches, some homes, and the Lone Star Motorcycle Museum (www.lonestarmotorcyclemuseum.com). This was one of the last sections of Central Texas to be settled, for the valleys of the Medina and Sabinal rivers were home to the Comanches. The almost impenetrable hills through which these streams thread made the Indians nearly impossible to root out. Once the Indians were gone, there was little the Anglo settlers could do for a living other than run livestock over this devil's playground.

Take FM 187 the last five miles to the Lost Maples through the chute that is the Sabinal River Canyon.

LOST MAPLES STATE NATURAL AREA

FM 187, about 4 miles from Vanderpool • 830-966-3413 • Open daily • Fee • W variable

This area is best known for its stands of Uvalde bigtooth maples, trees that aren't normally found in this section of the country, hence the name Lost Maples. They're not really lost; they're just a relict population from thousands of years ago when the weather was cooler and the trees more widespread. The microclimate of the Sabinal River valley retains the characteristics of this lost climate, hence the trees line the river for most of its fifty-eight-mile length. This 2,900-acre park is the only place along the river where the public can commune with the trees. If the weather conditions have been right, the trees go out in a blaze of glory sometime in late October or early November. Conditions vary year to year, so call ahead. Some years, there is no show. In good years, the park is filled to capacity on weekends; weekday visits are more pleasant. Parking capacity is 250 cars and is enforced. The park gets approximately two hundred thousand visitors a year. Because of the crowds of visitors, the maples are in danger of extinction. Like the cypress trees at Pedernales Falls, the maples' roots don't like compacted soil, and that's what we do when we hike. Each step compacts the soil a bit and makes it less capable of absorbing water. That's why it's important to stay on the designated paths; the trees need their space and loosely packed soil.

Lost Maples is beautiful and interesting any time of the year, with steep, rugged limestone canyons, springs, plateau grasslands, wooded slopes, and clear streams. More than ten miles of trails wander through a variety of habitats and offer glimpses of most of the 350-plus plant species found here. The natural area contains three state champion trees: escarpment chokeberry, Texas ash, and bigtooth maple. The birding is good here. Rare species of birds, such as the green kingfisher, can be seen year-round. The endangered black-capped vireo and golden-cheeked warbler nest and feed in the park in spring and early summer. Wild animals include gray foxes, white-tailed deer, armadillos, raccoons, bobcats, rock squirrels, and javelinas.

This area was inhabited by prehistoric peoples at various times; artifacts that go back twelve thousand years have been found. In historic times, which began with Spanish exploration and colonization efforts in the late seventeenth century, the Apache, Lipan Apache, and Comanche Indians ranged over the land and posed a threat to settlers into the 1870s.

Visitors can picnic, camp, backpack, sightsee, hike, photograph, watch birds, fish, swim, and otherwise study nature. Many natural hazards exist due to the steep and rugged terrain, so do not hike or climb on rocks or hillsides. Facilities provided include restrooms with showers, picnic sites, primitive camping areas, a comfort station, campsites with water and electricity, and a trailer dump station. The busy season is October, November, and March through May.

Continue north on FM 187 from the Lost Maples.

Soon you climb out of the river valley and do some ridge running for the next few miles through semiarid grazing country. Little more than one hundred years ago, this land was commonly referred to as the "rim of the great American desert." Sinkholes, which are porous basins that feed rainwater into the Edwards Aquifer, are found throughout the Hill Country. You can see a textbook example of a sinkhole at the western edge of FM 187, exactly 8.9 miles north of Lost Maples.

When FM 187 finally dead-ends into SH 39 in the headwaters area of the south fork of the Guadalupe River, turn right onto SH 39.

In the next twenty twisting miles to Hunt, you cross the south fork no fewer than fourteen times as it grows into a full-fledged river. As you draw closer to Hunt, the road is increasingly lined with entrances to resort and summer camps, plush vacation retreats, and little fishing cabins. This stretch of the Guadalupe has been a favorite with vacationers for seventy-odd years.

HUNT

Kerr County • 708 • (830) • About 39 miles from Vanderpool

Within two or three years of Kerrville's founding in 1856, folks began to move up the Guadalupe River valley, first stopping at "the forks," where the north and south branches of the Guadalupe come together. Soon a sawmill, a gristmill, and a cotton gin were built here. The neighborhood's first post office was located three miles north of present-day Hunt and was called Japonica. Hunt came into existence in 1912, when R. F. Hunt opened a grocery and general merchandise store. The post office was moved from Japonica to Hunt's store that same year, and the settlement took his name. Tourism has been Hunt's major industry since the Great Depression. Perhaps the most illustrious resident was World War I flying ace Eddie Rickenbacker, who owned the nearby Bear Creek Ranch. Hunt today is a collection of homes, a dance hall, and a couple of stores and cafes.

CRIDER'S

3.5 miles west of Hunt • 238-4441 • Open Friday and Saturday nights, Memorial Day through Labor Day weekends

This fair-weather dance hall, actually a dance platform, located above the Guadalupe River, first opened in 1925. Live bands play C&W dancin' music on Saturday nights. Friday night is rodeo night, in the little ring across the parking lot from the dance platform. They have catfish on Friday nights; burgers, Frito pie, nachos, and such on Saturday nights. Beer and setups are also available.

At Hunt, RM 1340 merges with SH 39. Take RM 1340 west to see the scenic, northern branch of the Guadalupe River. Several county parks offer access to the river. Continue west on FM 1340, for as long as you wish, up to its dead end into SH 41 some twenty miles from Hunt.

Whether or not you take the Rm 1340 detour, from Hunt, continue on SH 39 to Ingram. You cross the south fork of the Guadalupe one last time; the forks are just a few hundred yards north, and it is a united Guadalupe River you cross and follow from here on out.

The historical marker you see a couple of miles east of Hunt marks the former site of pioneer John Sherman's water-powered mill. It was in operation until destroyed by flood in 1932. Ten mills, grinding corn and wheat, cutting lumber, and powering cotton gins, were once located on the Guadalupe between Hunt and Comfort.

INGRAM

Kerr County • 1,800 (approximate) • (830) • About 6.5 miles from Hunt

Ingram is located on the Old Spanish Trail, on a site originally owned by Abner Morriss. The land was sold to the Reverend J. C. W. Ingram in 1872. He opened up a store, a church, and a post office here on the Guadalupe near its confluence with Johnson Creek. A community grew up around the store and church, serving as a commercial center for ranchers, shingle makers, and cedar choppers. The rough country up Johnson Creek was a favorite outlaw and cattle rustler hangout in olden days. During the Civil War, three German Unionists were hanged on the banks of Johnson Creek above Ingram, their bodies then thrown into the rocky creek bed seventy-five feet below. The last recorded Indian massacre in Kerr County took place in 1878 on Johnson Creek, when four children of the James Dowdy family were killed while tending the family's sheep. The town moved slightly north during the 1930s when SH 27 was built, but much of old downtown Ingram still stands.

As you come into Ingram, you first pass the Lake Ingram dam on your right, a popular public recreation spot, open daily. Just before crossing Johnson Creek, you see the Hill Country Arts Foundation complex on your right.

POINT THEATRE/HILL COUNTRY ARTS FOUNDATION

The entrance is well marked, and the complex is just yards from the road • 367-5121, 800-459-4223 • www.hcaf.com

Theatrical productions are staged on summer evenings in the Smith-Ritch Point Theatre's outdoor amphitheater. Located alongside the scenic, rushing Guadalupe, this used to be a skating rink. Concerts and other events are presented during the nonsummer months in the intimate Elizabeth Huth Coates

Theatre. Art studios are located inside the Arts Foundation Building, and well-known artists teach art classes. The foundation offers youth theater and art summer camps. The Duncan-McAshan Gallery hosts exhibitions that range from classroom work to national juried shows.

Moved to the foundation's grounds in 2010 are Stonehenge II and the Easter Island replica statues from their original location on FM 1340, two miles west of Hunt. Stonehenge II is 60 percent as tall and 90 percent as large in circumference as the original. The "stones" are made of steel rebar, wire mesh, and cement. You can get out of the car and walk around it. Easter Island–type statues are also here. If you build it, they will come.

After crossing the Johnson Creek bridge, take the first possible right, on a street identified as the Ingram Loop, to see old Ingram.

OLD INGRAM

Old Ingram today is a collection of mostly rock buildings dating to the early 1900s that house a variety of arts, crafts, and antique shops.

Only several hundred feet long, the Ingram Loop rolls you right back onto SH 39. When you come to SH 39, you will see in front of you a multi-panel mural on the walls of the T. J. Moore Lumberyard warehouse depicting various events and eras in Kerr County history. Park the car and take a closer look, as each of the fifteen panels is accompanied by written commentary. From the Ingram Loop, turn right onto SH 39 and continue straight on what becomes SH 27 E. into Kerrville.

KERRVILLE

Kerr County Seat • 23,000 (approximate) • (830) • About 6.5 miles from Ingram

Joshua Brown was the first permanent Anglo settler here. A member of the original Anglo colony at Gonzales, Brown had moved west to Curry Creek by 1844, where he made shingles. By 1846, the cypress trees around Curry Creek (Kendall County) were about played out, and Brown started up the Guadalupe looking for a new source of cypress timber for his shingle-making operation. He ended up at a spring on the Guadalupe where he made camp and resumed his shingle making.

Indians soon began to attack his camp, so Brown and his coworkers had to move back to Gonzales after just a couple of months here. But in 1848, Brown returned to the camp and started making shingles again. The settlement that grew up around the camp was first called Brownsborough. Brown had acquired legal title to the land by 1856. That same year, Kerr County was created from Bexar County, and Brownsborough, consisting of a shingle mill and a couple of log cabins, became Kerrsville, county seat. Kerrsville did not exactly take off like a fast-growing weed. In fact, it lost its county seat status in 1860, when Comfort partisans beat the Kerrsville backers in a special election, and the government of Kerr County moved to Comfort. Kerrsville regained its position in 1862, when Kendall County was formed and Comfort was found to be just inside the Kendall County line.

Kerrville (the s was officially dropped from Kerrsville during the Civil War) is named for a man who never lived here, James Kerr. In fact, Kerr died six years before "his" county was created.

Kerrsville hung on by a thread during the Civil War; Indians and bushwhackers terrorized the whole county. They hid out in the hills north and west of town. During the years before a jailhouse was built, the few offenders who were caught were chained to trees. The lawlessness continued after the war's end; cattle and sheep rustlers ran roughshod over the countryside. Disguised as Indians, the rustlers would steal cattle and horses, commit murder and arson, and then head back to the many caves and thick cedar brakes located along the south fork of the Guadalupe.

The opportunities for mischief attracted men from all over Texas, such as Philip "Doboy" Taylor. Doboy was a son of Creed Taylor, principal in the infamous Taylor-Sutton feud of south-central Texas. In 1867, he and his brother, Hays, got into an argument in Mason with soldiers from Fort Mason. They killed two of the soldiers. By November 1871, Doboy was living in Kerrville. A man named Sim Holstein got a job as an agent for New York cattle buyers that Doboy had wanted, and one day Doboy called him out of his hotel and threatened him. Doboy fired his pistol and missed, whereupon Sim jumped over a low gate and tackled Doboy. Sim tore the gun out of Doboy's hand and shot him. Doboy got up, and Sim shot him again, and then a third time. Doboy got up yet again and staggered away, whereupon Sim shot him a fourth time. Doboy lived six more hours, cursing Sim before dying at eleven p.m.

By 1873, the rustling problem was so out of hand that Kerr County stock raisers organized a vigilante group. One night the anonymous vigilantes stormed the county jail after overpowering the sheriff and deputies and took three prisoners accused of cattle rustling from their cells. One was shot at the jail. The other two were taken to the outskirts of town and hanged from a live oak tree. Shortly thereafter, Texas Rangers arrested another man as a suspected cattle rustler, and again the vigilantes stormed the jail. They took the suspect to Goat Creek four miles west and shot him.

Time and again the local vigilantes followed the gang into the mountains, and several times they shot and hanged a number of them. By July, it was reported that the vigilantes had killed twenty outlaws.

But by September 1873, affairs at Kerrville were assuming such a serious aspect and so much of the vigilantes' time was been taken up by these excursions that they became tired of them and were reluctantly compelled to ask the aid of General Auger, the commanding general of the Department of Texas, in breaking up this lawless gang and either killing them off or driving them out of the country.

Grave troubles were apprehended from the outlaws on the river. They were congregating there in larger numbers than ever, and they had lately made several attempts at assassination. The majority of the people of that section had been forced to neglect their farms almost entirely in order to keep these fugitives from justice from harming them. It was reported that many of the Haynie-Davidson gang had selected a strong ambush on the north and south forks of the Guadalupe, where an attempt to dislodge them with a small force would have been futile.

By early October, a full company of cavalry had been stationed at Kerrville to hold the outlaws of the section in awe or to drive them into old Mexico.

The outlaws' excesses were finally quelled, but the rugged country along the Guadalupe continued to attract fugitives from the law, such as the Semnalt-Walton gang of Gonzales County. In January 1878, Rube and James Semnalt, and William Walton, stole three horses on Peach Creek, Gonzales County, and headed for Kerr County. They robbed a store along the way at Prairie Lea, in Caldwell County. They were followed by a local posse, which had to travel at night in order to take them by surprise. A week later, the posse overtook them at their uncle's, Adam Semnalt, in Kerr County, above Kerrville. The house was surrounded that morning, and with the assistance of citizens the outlaws were compelled to surrender. The posse found all the stolen goods and horses. Rube Semnalt, the leader of the gang, gave the posse the names of others who were still at large who were connected with them in horse stealing. The prisoners were brought in irons back to Gonzales and turned over to the sheriff. They had been a terror in Gonzales County for some time, stealing horses, robbing stores and post offices, and burning a school.

The driving force behind Kerrville's rise to preeminence among Hill Country cities was Charles Schreiner. Schreiner came to Texas from France in 1852. He became a Texas Ranger at age sixteen, and by 1857 he had staked his government service claim on Turtle Creek, near Kerrville. Charles Schreiner served in the Confederate Army during the Civil War and wasn't noted for any heroism or other exploit during his war service, but he was the best forager in his outfit, his commander said. Schreiner walked home from the Civil War flat broke.

But Comfort merchant and banker August Faltin recognized Schreiner's business acumen and decided to grubstake young Schreiner's first postwar venture. In 1869, Schreiner moved into town and opened a mercantile store on Christmas Eve inside a small lumber shed made of cypress slabs with three-inch planks covering the seams between the slabs, board-and-batten style. During the first month, he averaged fifteen dollars in sales a day, with cash sales amounting to $2.50 a day. Most of his business was done on credit. He kept his money under a loose board in the floor with a barrel rolled over it. Commonly known as the Captain, Schreiner had a simple business motto: Live and let live. He did not discourage competition; he had confidence in his ability to judge character, and he seldom bet on the wrong horse. He did not hesitate to lend advice to those seemingly on their last knees.

At the store, Schreiner often accepted other types of goods for payment instead of cash. He took in tanned hides, honey, beeswax, bear oil, and cypress shingles. He would resell them to other folks for cash or for goods he needed. He also milled flour. He gradually got into banking. People trusted him to keep their money. Whenever he had accumulated enough of his own and others' money, he had it sent to a San Antonio bank. In 1898, he formally organized a bank to accommodate his customers' needs. But it was unincorporated and issued no capital stock. Folks just trusted the Charles Schreiner Bank.

Schreiner was so successful and so much a part of the lives of the people of Kerrville that the following joke was told on him.

A Socialist organizer came to Kerrville and told a man, "We are going to organize a Socialist Party here and we want you to join."

The citizen asked, "What's the purpose?"

The organizer replied, "We're going to divide everything up."

The prospect said, "Sure, I'll join. Who's going to shoot Charles Schreiner?"

"Why, nobody," said the organizer. "Why do you ask that?"

"Because if you don't shoot him, even if you divide everything up, he'll have it all back inside of a year."

Horace W. Morelock, one-time superintendent of Kerrville schools and later president of Sul Ross University, told the following story.

In the early days, Joseph Pierce owned a ranch near London in Kimble County. But times were hard and he became discouraged. Late one afternoon, he and his wife came to Kerrville with the avowed purpose of transferring their holdings to Captain Schreiner. But the captain had a different idea: "Go back to the ranch, save every nickel, and the next time you come to Kerrville, do not stop at the St. Charles Hotel; bring your blankets along, and stay in the camp yard." Within a few years Pierce paid off the debt he owed the captain, sold his ranch at a profit, moved to Crockett County and became a millionaire.

Schreiner soon became a millionaire himself, largely due to innovative thinking and his sense for good deals. Schreiner observed that cattle were so cheap that people wouldn't bother to brand the calves, and in some parts of Texas the maverick yearlings were killed for their hides. Schreiner believed that raising sheep for wool could be highly profitable out here, and so he set out to prove his hunch. By 1900, his Charles Schreiner Company owned six hundred thousand acres of land, which stretched continuously from Kerrville to Menard, a distance of over eighty miles. He instituted a co-op market and warehouse system for wool growers so that their wool would not be subject to the vagaries of the market. Schreiner was generous with credit to sheep ranchers; he believed in sheep raising so fervently that one of his loan requirements to ranchers was that they use at least half the loan for sheep raising.

The Hill Country around Kerrville never experienced the violent cattlemen versus sheepmen wars as elsewhere, partly because many of the stockmen raised both types of animals, thanks in part to Schreiner's loan policy.

One of Schreiner's many beneficiaries was Captain Herman Steiler. Steiler was born in Germany in 1853 and came to Texas three years later. His family settled in Kendall County in 1863 where he learned sheep raising from Schreiner. After the war, he served as captain of a volunteer home defense organization that responded to Indian attacks. In the late 1870s, he claimed three sections of land near Comfort and started raising sheep and angora goats, coming to hold twenty-five sections. His four sons carried on the business, and one of them, Adolf, became known as the Goat King of Texas.

Schreiner made Kerrville the Mohair Center of the World. He was instrumental in bringing the railroad to Kerrville (having donated $15,000 for its construction), as well as establishing the Schreiner Institute. The railroad was an essential part of Schreiner's grand scheme for Kerrville; it was the only form of transportation that was capable of handling the export traffic he had envisioned. But Fredericksburg also coveted the San Antonio and Aransas Pass (SA&AP) spur line, and it took every bit of influence Schreiner had to win the rails. The first train arrived in Kerrville on September 20, 1887.

Kerrville was determined to outdo Boerne and Comfort in its welcoming celebration, which was originally scheduled for September 20, 1887, but had to be postponed until October 6. The *Kerrville Eye* promised: "The citizens of Kerrville do not propose to give a barbecue a la Boerne. The people of San Antonio who come up here will get a square meal for once in their lives. Come to the barbecue at Kerrville, you San Antonio dudes. We will swell you out so with ozone and good grub that you will have great difficulty in crawling out of your umbrella-socket like pants when you get home. The scenery along the road to Kerrville is well worth a trip to see. No expense has been spared by the people of Kerrville to make the barbecue and celebration a grand success."

The *San Antonio Daily Express* sent a reporter along for the ride:

For at least 3,000 people; it is safe to say that October 6, 1887, will be long remembered as a red letter day in experience. At last, that number attended the barbecue celebration at Kerrville yesterday, and where all were the recipients of unbounded hospitality, and were feasted to the limit of human power with well-cooked, tender and delicious meats, flanked with the usual "trimmings" of a well appointed dinner, liberally served and eaten in joyous companionship, the dinner being followed by sports, games, races, tournaments and shooting matches, it is not too much to say that all present had a general good time and as such will cherish its memory in after years.

Though once postponed and hampered by rumors of railway washouts and a very early hour for starting, the excursion train from this city left the depot of the SAAP railway with over two hundred excursionists aboard. The start was made at 7:30 a.m., just thirty minutes late. Had the advertised time for starting been 7:30 o'clock and the start been on time instead of being advertised to start at 7 o'clock the attendance would have been much larger.

The recent rains having caused several washouts and developed weak places in the road bed the run was necessarily slow. But with Engineer Thomas McGuire at the throttle, and with Conductor S. G. Warner in command, the engine A. C. Schryver with the six new Pullman coaches well filled with their human freight safely made the trip.

The San Antonio delegation included some of our leading and representative citizens, among whom were about 75 ladies. Every line of business, including the city's breweries, and nearly all the professions were represented, from the weighty insurance man, who thinks he is a thorough sportsman, to our city fathers and worthy chief of police. But businessmen did not restrict their enjoyment nor mark their brows with care. It was a picnic for all from the youngest clerk to the oldest representative power of the "Future Great."

The Little Joker, who takes in everything, of course went to the Kerrville barbecue. If his country constituents didn't see him they certainly heard him or heard of him, as he went well supplied with samples ["Little Joker" was a famous brand of smoking tobacco] and other advertising matter [such as colorful playing card sets]. Mrs. B. accompanied him to take care of that sore arm of his.

Boerne was reached at 9:30 o'clock and an addition of 149 made it to the party. The train pulled up at 10:10 o'clock and a further addition of 141 were added. Seats now commanded a premium and the capacity of the coaches was further drawn upon at Ganahl by the addition of 30 more. This was the last stop before arriving at the objective point, and at 11:15 o'clock Kerrville was reached, and the inhabitants of the town and surrounding countryside assembled on either side of the track and at the depot and gave a shout of hearty cheers, while a salute of seven guns and the lusty music of the Fredericksburg Mexican brass band enthused both guests and hosts. The total attendance was not less than 3,000 and without delay they were formed into a procession headed by the band and led by the genial master of ceremonies, Mr. Charles Schreiner, ably assisted by the members of the various committees, and marched to the barbecue grounds, which were conveniently near to the railway tract and depot.

On arriving at the grounds the preparations for dinner were found to be well advanced and 14 beeves and 20 sheep and a number of kids were found already roasted and ready to be taken from the trenches over which they had been cooked.

Watching the carvers prepare the meats for the feast, comparatively few of the guests heard the admirable address of welcome delivered in the arbor near the tables. The guests appreciated the welcome, but the appetizing odors wafted from the cooking pits set their stomachs strongly against any wind pudding.

A steady advance was now made for the tables, which forming the four sides of a square, afforded ample accommodation. The generous supply can best be appreciated by the fact that after the dinner and fully 3,000 people had been fed, there were great sides of beef, legs of mutton, carcasses of kids, a huge pile of bread, cake, etc., gallons of delicious coffee, to say nothing of the sugar, pickles, etc., to be distributed among the poor, if there be any, of Kerr County. Every committee man was a self-constituted and untiring waiter on the wants of his guests. Mrs. Ganahl dispensed her hospitality with that delicacy and grace of manner for which she is so justly esteemed.

Dinner over, the afternoon was devoted to the various sports, races, prize shooting, rides about the pretty little town and the romantic surroundings, and in genial enjoyment.

The return trip was very pleasant, and was made in better time than the up trip. Leaving Kerrville at 6:45 p.m. amid the cheers of the inhabitants, the stirring strains of the band, and a general waving of handkerchiefs and hats, and hearty God speeds, San Antonio was reached at the West Commerce street crossing at 10:15 p.m., and the well pleased excursionists were home again.

A number of San Antonio pilgrims remained over at Kerrville to attend the ball there last night.

The Kerrville depot, a sturdy brick structure built in 1915, is now a restaurant: Rails, a Café at the Depot (www.railscafe.com). The original wood-frame depot burned in 1913. Located at 615 Schreiner Street, it is one block west of the intersection of Sidney Baker Street (SH 16) and Schreiner Street, just north of downtown Kerrville, and is easily seen from Sidney Baker. As the line's terminus, there was a roundhouse, which no longer stands.

The news spread across the rest of Texas that Kerrville was a healthy place to live (a fact still borne out by the census bureau), and soon it was a regular pilgrimage for consumptives seeking a cure. Morelock told of his first trip to Kerrville, via the SA&AP in 1905: "I observed that many passengers were coughing violently and I inquired of the conductor as to its significance. He replied blandly: 'Well, you know the passengers on this train usually go up to Kerrville coughing, and they come back in a coffin.' When I arrived in Kerrville, the first man I met at the station inquired, 'Are you here for your health?' I stammered: 'No, I am here for the other fellow's health.'"

In 1921, the U.S. Health Department declared Kerr County to be "the healthiest spot in the nation."

Kerrville's most famous pilgrim in search of a cure was Jimmie Rodgers. Born in Meridian, Mississippi, in 1897, Rodgers grew up on the railroad. His father was a railroad gang foreman, and Jimmie started work as a water carrier at age fourteen. He eventually worked up to brakeman. Working on railroads throughout the South, he learned songs from the black workers, who also taught him how to play guitar and banjo. He contracted a severe case of tuberculosis in 1924 and was forced to leave railroad work for something less strenuous.

He took up entertaining and in 1927 signed a record contract with the Victor Talking Machine Company. Soon he was a star, recording 111 songs altogether and selling twenty million records before his death. To seek relief from his steadily worsening TB, Rodgers moved to Kerrville in 1929 and built a $25,000 house that he called "Blue Yodeler's Paradise." Financial difficulties forced him to move into a modest home in San Antonio in 1932. Rodgers died on May 26, 1933, in his hotel room in New York City while on a recording trip. He was buried in his hometown of Meridian.

Besides being a major wool and mohair shipping center, Kerrville has also been a major exporter of cedar posts. In fact, the cedar chopper's favorite axe was invented here in the early 1920s. About that time ranchmen of the cedar section of Texas began to hire cedar choppers to clear out the excessive growth on their land. Most of the choppers were Mexican migrants who complained about the traditional forest axe they were forced to use. They said the forest axe was too heavy, the handle too long, and the blade too short.

Henry Weiss of Kerrville wanted to produce a better axe for cedar cutting. Collaborating with local blacksmith Frank Krueger, Weiss was able to produce a better cedar axe. Using the Weiss-Krueger axe as a model, a company started to make a cedar axe in commercial quantities. Instead of naming the new axe the "Kerrville Axe," the company marketed it as the "Grey Gorge" model. It sold like wildfire, and experienced woodsmen say that this specially designed axe cuts cedar 25 percent more effectively than the old forest axe.

Tourism is now Kerrville's biggest industry. Long recognized by the census bureau as the healthiest place in America to live, Kerrville is now the Hill Country's largest city. This is very much the result of Kerrville's distinct pro-growth mentality. Kerrville has elected to pursue the tourist-retiree-weekend homeowner dollar, rather than run after industry coin, but in the end it doesn't matter. Little of "old Kerrville" remains, and what does remain stands obscured by Kerrville's ebullient, ever-expanding present. It is certainly the Hill Country's liveliest city.

Continue east on SH 27, which becomes Main Street. When you come to the intersection with Sidney Baker (SH 16), turn left onto Baker/SH 16. After a long five blocks, turn right onto RM 1341 (Wheeless) and follow it out of town. After a little more than a mile on RM 1341, you come to a historical marker and a gravel road winding up the steep hill on your right. This is Tivy Mountain, and the marker memorializes Captain Joseph Tivy.

TIVY MOUNTAIN

RM 1341

Joseph Tivy came to Texas in 1837 with his two sisters. After serving as a Texas Ranger, Tivy joined his sisters in California during the great gold rush. The trio returned to Texas in the 1850s, and when Texas went to war, Tivy fought for the Confederacy, attaining the rank of captain. Tivy and his sisters moved to Kerrville in about 1870. Soon after arriving, the Tivy siblings made a pact never to marry. Much to the sisters' disappointment, Tivy broke the vow a few years later, marrying Ella, the widow of his departed best friend. She died shortly after their marriage, and her last request was that she be buried atop this high hill. Four days were spent carving a road to the summit. The top of Tivy Mountain is solid rock, and it had to be blasted out to make the grave. The blasting could be heard for miles around. The casket was taken to the top in a hack pulled by two mules. Mourners had to walk to the top for the services. Captain Tivy and his younger sister eventually joined Ella up here. Take the effort to climb up the hill to the gravesite and you'll see why they wanted to be buried here. An expansive view of Kerrville and the Guadalupe valley unfolds before you.

Tivy served as a state legislator, Kerrville's first mayor, and a town surveyor. When the railroad came, he built the Tivy Hotel nearby. While mayor, he donated land for the city's public school system. The local high school is named for Tivy. The old Victorian limestone Tivy High School building still stands at the corner of Tivy and Barnett streets, beneath Tivy Mountain.

From Tivy Mountain, return to downtown Kerrville by retracing your path on RM 1341 to Sidney Baker/SH 16. (If you wish to see the old Tivy school, leave Tivy Mountain on RM 1341, but when RM 1341's route turns right onto Wheeless a few blocks later, continue straight ahead on what is now Tivy Street. In three blocks you come to the Tivy school. From the Tivy school, return to RM 1341 and proceed to Sidney Baker/SH 16.) Turn left onto Sidney Baker and return to the courthouse and center of town. Proceed one block past Main/SH 27 and turn left onto Water.

Water Street was Kerrville's main business street during the railroad era. Several of the old buildings from that age remain.

PAMPELL'S DRUGSTORE/OPERA HOUSE

701 Water

This Spanish Renaissance two-story brick building replaced an earlier frame structure in the early 1900s. Like that old building, this one had an opera house on the second floor and a pharmacy with soda fountain below. The pharmacy closed in the late 1980s but reopened in 1989 as a gift store with the old soda fountain still intact. That store closed, and the building has housed a variety of restaurants since. The soda fountain is gone.

The building at 709 Water is of two-story cut-limestone block construction, with a nice cast-metal cornice. At the end of this block, anchoring the corner of Earl Garrett and Water, is the now-closed Schreiner Store, the cornerstone of Charles Schreiner's empire since 1869. For years, it was one of the Southwest's largest country stores. Across Water from it was the Schreiner Bank, the town's major financial force until its failure in the mid-1980s.

CHRISTIAN DIETERT MILL HISTORICAL MARKER

800 block of Water St.

Christian Dietert was born in Tesen District of Magdaburg, Germany, in 1827. He was a millwright and miller. In early manhood he left his homeland, accompanied by his brother, William Dietert, who later settled in Boerne. After eight weeks, their ship landed at Galveston. They came to Texas to try their fortunes with the much-talked-of new country and to gain political freedom. Their destination was New Braunfels. There were at that time only two routes to New Braunfels, one by way of Houston, which was a long and perilous journey, and another by way of the seaport of Indianola. This route was somewhat shorter, so they shipped in a two-masted sailboat to Indianola. Dietert's first civic act upon arriving in Texas was to take out naturalization papers and begin learning English.

After some weeks of delay, waiting for transports, they boarded mule-drawn wagons and were conveyed over tractless miles of territory covered with water from six to twelve inches deep. This, together with the scarcity of camping places and the danger of Indian raids, wild animals, and the like, was a most arduous journey. They reached New Braunfels in July 1854, after weeks of slow travel. In August, Christian Dietert joined a company of thirteen men who journeyed to the place where Cypress Creek joins the Guadalupe River, where they surveyed, laid out, and named the town of Comfort.

In the beginning, shingle making was the only industry. The shingles, which were made by hand, were freighted to San Antonio by ox wagon. Early in 1855, a saw- and gristmill was built under the direction of Christian Dietert and financed by Ernst Altgelt. The power was furnished by a huge waterwheel fed by the waters of Cypress Creek. The little stream that gushed from the hills, no doubt fed by copious rains the preceding seasons, dried out after a year or two of droughts, and as a result the mill had to be abandoned for lack of water power less than two years after its completion.

Dietert married Rosalie Hess in 1855, who had come to Comfort a short time before from Jena, Germany. Dietert's father and mother, two brothers, and a sister came from Germany in 1856 to settle in Comfort. The Dieterts had twelve children, four sons and eight daughters, all of whom grew to adulthood, except one daughter who died in infancy. The Dieterts moved to Fredericksburg early in 1857. Later that year they moved to Kerrville. The young millwright bought the tract of land along the banks of the Guadalupe River southwest of Water Street, from what is now Earl Garrett Street south to A Street. He established a shingle mill, using horsepower until he could construct a water wheel, with which he later sawed lumber from the cypress trees lining the banks of the river. It was washed away by a great flood after a year or two of operation.

Dietert, without funds to rebuild his mill, moved back to Fredericksburg to build a saw- and gristmill for C. H. Guenther on Live Oak Creek. This venture was short-lived, but they did saw lumber from local pecan and walnut trees for the building of homes and furniture. After only a few months' operation, torrential rains softened the sandy land of that section to such an extent that the earth crumbled before the onrushing waters and took the mill, waterwheel, and everything else, to be buried and lost miles down the creek.

Dietert moved his little family and belongings back to Kerrville where he again built a mill on the old site. This mill was destroyed by fire. Offered mill-building work in the vicinity of Comfort, and to be near a school for his children, Dietert moved to Comfort. He also built a mill for his brother, William Dietert, near Boerne.

Dietert's sympathies, like most of his German compatriots, were with the Union during the Civil War. But he hauled freight to and from Mexico for the Confederate government. Heavy wagons drawn by four to eight yoke of oxen were used. These trips usually took several months and were filled with dangers and hardships. Necessary provisions and clothing for the home were bought with each return trip. The groceries consisted mainly of coffee, tea, sugar, flour, rice, and dried fruits. Cloth was bought by the bolt and was a coarse white material. Lengths of this cloth were dyed by the women with herbs, roots of the agarita and sumac, and the bark of the pecan and live oak tree, and were then made by hand into garments for the men and children according to their needs.

The Dieterts moved back to Kerrville in 1866, and Dietert again set up a waterwheel to operate a sawmill and steel gristmill. The waterwheel was also washed away by a flood. In 1868, Dietert put in an underwater iron turbine for power and a flour mill. People came from many miles around to have corn and wheat ground, and also to have lumber sawed by the sawmill into suitable lengths for building purposes.

Christian Dietert was appointed postmaster at Kerrville in 1868 and served until 1888. He was elected to fill the office of justice of the peace in 1869 and filled the place of county judge in the absence of the regular judge. Dietert also served on the school board for some time. Women were not appointed to office in those days, but Mrs. Dietert was made assistant postmistress and took over all responsibilities and all transactions pertaining to the office during Mr. Dietert's tenure of office.

The Dietert home was the center of social activities. Young couples danced in the large living room to the tune of fiddle and accordion. Being accomplished in the art, Mrs. Dietert taught the young men and the very few girls to dance and waltz. The Dieterts had the first Christmas tree in Kerrville. People came from miles around to see the wonderful tree. Its homemade decorations consisted of festoons of chains, the links of which were cut and made from brightly colored paper. There were also nuts, covered with gold and silver paper, apples brought from San Antonio, and cookies cut into shapes of birds and animals and decorated with colored sugar. The candles were tallow dips.

The nearest trading place was San Antonio, and trips, which were made by wagon, took about a week. The nearest doctor was also in San Antonio. In case of sickness, the neighbors assisted each other with home preparations, mainly potions of roots and herbs.

In 1885, Dietert sold his mill site and interests to Chas. Schreiner and bought a farm across the Guadalupe, opposite the town, where he lived with his family until his death in May 1902. Mrs. Dietert lived to the ripe old age of ninety-six.

Turn left on Earl Garrett. This first block of Earl Garrett contains two buildings of note, the Schreiner Mansion and the Masonic Hall.

SCHREINER MANSION/THE HILL COUNTRY MUSEUM

226 Earl Garrett

Charles Schreiner moved into a small frame house on this lot in 1869. The south portion of this house was built in 1879; Schreiner copied the design of his grandfather's house in Alsace, France. The house was enlarged in 1895, and in 1897 it was remodeled by Alfred Giles to its present Romanesque Revival appearance. The first house in Kerrville to have electricity and indoor plumbing, it originally had thirteen rooms and two bathrooms. Schreiner imported masons from Germany to lay the stone walls. Brass light fixtures for the house and the bronze fountain for the formal gardens were imported from France. French immigrant John Michon laid the parquet floor, which uses ten kinds of wood. Upon the Captain's death in 1927, the local Masonic Lodge bought the house to use as a lodge hall. The Masons sold the house in 1973 to a couple that sold it to the Hill Country Preservation Society in 1975, which donated it to Schreiner University in 2009. The house has been completely restored and contains a collection of Kerr County and Schreiner family memorabilia.

At press time, Schreiner University had closed the museum for cleaning, to inventory artifacts, and make repairs, including making sure the building is up to current codes, and to seek grants to make improvements to the structure. No date for reopening had been announced.

MASONIC HALL

211 Earl Garrett

Designed by Alfred Giles and built in 1890 of rough-finish limestone blocks with a cast-iron cornice and arch, the Masonic Hall followed the common practice of retaining the second floor for lodge use while leasing or selling the ground floor to local merchants. The C. C. Butt Grocery Store (predecessor to H. E. B.) occupied the ground floor from 1916 to 1926.

Turn left onto Main/SH 27 from Earl Garrett, and then turn left again after one block onto Sidney Baker/SH 16, which takes you across the Guadalupe and out of Kerrville. Turn left on SH 173 at the Kerrville outskirts. Soon you come to the Museum of Western Art.

THE MUSEUM OF WESTERN ART

1550 Bandera Hwy. (SH 173) • 896-2553 • www.museumofwesternart.org • Closed Sunday and Monday • Fee • W with assistance

The Museum of Western Art is a showcase for Western art and artists, Anglo and Native American, past and present, and provides art and history education focusing on the American West. It exhibits art by today's best-known western artists as well as rotating exhibits featuring famous past masters. Displays include period artifacts, and there are western art and history education programs. The museum also includes a library, auditorium, and museum store.

It was designed by noted architect O'Neil Ford and was the last nonresidential building in which he was personally involved before his death. Heavy timbers and dry-stack limestone retaining walls are part of the entry gardens. There is a heavy Mexican influence throughout. The most impressive feature of the main entrance is the ceiling, composed of eighteen boveda brick domes. The construction of boveda domes dates back to the Moorish occupation of Spain. Boveda domes use light Mexican brick and are positioned without supporting forms or wires. Only a few artisans from the beautiful colonial Mexican towns of Guanajuato and San Miguel de Allende still construct the domes. The gallery floors are of mesquite. Tree trunks were cut into slices, squared off, glued together, and polished.

OTHER ATTRACTIONS

KERRVILLE CONVENTION AND VISITORS BUREAU

2108 Sidney Baker St. • 800-221-7958 • www.kerrvilletexascvb.com

BLUE YODELER'S PARADISE

617 W. Main

Jimmie Rodgers' mansion on the hill was finished in May 1929. Mounting medical costs and the price of luxurious living forced Rodgers to sell Blue Yodeler's Paradise and move to San Antonio. In his last two years of life, Rodgers recorded, appeared on radio, and performed in tent shows around Texas, health permitting. His birthday is celebrated each September with the Texas Heritage Living History Day (www.texasheritagemusic.org).

JAMES AVERY CRAFTSMAN

145 Avery Dr., turn right from FM 783 (Harper Rd.) about 1 mile north of I-10, exit 505 • 895-6800 • www.jamesavery.com • W

The business James Avery started here in his garage now has stores all over the Southwest and sells nationally by mail. There is a small factory and retail store here. You can see a short video and watch jewelry being made.

Y. O. RANCH

Take I-10 west to SH 41 (exit 490) at Mountain Home, then 18 miles south (left) to ranch entrance sign • 830-640-3222 • www.yoranch.com • Fee • W variable

This is a working ranch with cattle, sheep, and goats, plus the cowboys who do all the herding, roping, and other daily ranch chores. Founded by Charles Schreiner in 1880, it is home to over one thousand longhorns, champion quarter horses, and free-ranging native wildlife, plus exotic animals such as axis deer, American elk, antelope, zebras, giraffes, and ostriches. Several historic buildings have been moved to the ranch and restored, including an 1850s stagecoach stop, Wells Fargo office, and pioneer schoolhouse. In addition to the tour (which includes a ranch lunch), you can arrange photo safaris and year-round hunting. Tours can be customized. There is a summer camp for boys and girls ages nine to fifteen. Lodging is available in the lodge or in century-old cabins. There is also a general store, swimming pool, and restaurant. Entrance is by reservation only.

DINING

BILL'S BARBEQUE

1909 Junction Hwy./SH 27 • 895-5733 • www.billsbbq.net • Tuesday through Saturday 11–7; closed Sunday and Monday • W

Bill's cooks up brisket, ribs, sausage, pork loin, turkey, and chicken. Homemade side dishes and pies, plus cold beer. Bill's often sells out early.

LODGING

Y. O. RANCH HOLIDAY INN

2033 Sidney Baker (SH 16), about 2 blocks south of I-10 • 877-YO RE-SORT • www.yoresort.com • W+ 10 rooms • No-smoking rooms

The Holiday Inn has two hundred rooms and suites, including thirty-two no-smoking rooms. Cable TV, room phones, and Internet access are included. Pay transportation is available to San Antonio airport. There is a restaurant, two bars, and live entertainment on weekends. An outdoor heated pool, a hot tub, and a tennis court are also featured. The hotel adjoins a municipal golf course. A large lobby is decorated with chandeliers made of 350 branding irons and a bronze statue of a cowboy on horseback struggling to herd a longhorn. Rooms have custom-made furnishings. There is also a gift shop.

ANNUAL EVENTS

MAY/JUNE

KERRVILLE FOLK FESTIVAL

Quiet Valley Ranch • Take SH 16 (Sidney Baker St.) south 9 miles • 257-3600 • www.kerrville-music.com • About 3 weeks at the end of May, beginning of June • Fee • W variable

More than one hundred musicians and groups playing folk, blues, soul, and a smattering of other styles make this outdoor festival something to listen to. Many performers are Texas songwriters singing their own songs. There is a folk Mass on Sundays. Bring lawn chairs to sit on. Single-day and multi-day tickets are available. Many festivalgoers camp out.

TEXAS STATE ARTS AND CRAFTS FAIR

River Star Arts and Event Park, 4000 Riverside Dr. East • 792-3535 • www.tacef.com • Memorial Day weekend • Fee • W variable

The artists and craftsmen are carefully selected for their work, and the number of exhibitors is limited to two hundred. Demonstrations and free crafts instruction are offered. There is also music, entertainment, and a children's area.

AREA PARKS

KERRVILLE-SCHREINER PARK

2385 Bandera Hwy. • 257-7300 • www.kerville.org • Fee • W variable

Kerrville-Schreiner Park, 517 acres along the Guadalupe River, began as a city park in the 1930s built by the Civilian Conservation Corps. It subsequently became a state park and was transferred back to the city in 2004. SH 173 splits the park into two sides, the Hill Side (larger side) and the River Side (smaller side, on the Guadalupe River). Activities include boating, fishing, camping, picnicking, unsupervised swimming in the river, bird-watching, hiking, walking, and cycling. Recent improvements include sewer connections to both RV camping loops on the river side of the park, twenty-three new mini-cabins, and a butterfly garden. The park hosts a bicycle tour every Easter weekend. The park has a typical Hill Country landscape; juniper, live oak, and Spanish oak trees populate the hills and arroyos. Other plants include redbud, sumac, buckeye, pecan, mesquite, and several varieties of flowers. Bluebonnets usually abound in spring. White-tailed deer are plentiful, along with squirrels, armadillos, turkeys, jackrabbits, mallard ducks, and several species of birds. You can fish in the Guadalupe River for crappie, perch, catfish, and bass.

LOUISE HAYS PARK

Enter from Thompson Dr. west of Sidney Baker South • Open daily • Free

The Guadalupe River flows through the park, located in the heart of downtown, and makes a delightful natural pool. Amenities include shaded picnic tables, public restrooms, and a footbridge that crosses the river to Tranquility Island where cypress trees tower over gently sloping grassy banks.

RIVERSIDE NATURE CENTER

150 Lemos St. at the junction of the Guadalupe River and Town Creek (the Lemos St. bridge is closed, so you must reach the center from Water St.) • 257-4837 • www.riversidenaturecenter.org • Open daily

Riverside Nature Center is a former farm converted into an urban wildlife and native plant sanctuary. Its arboretum features 200 species of wildflowers and over 140 species of trees, as well as cacti, shrubs, native grasses, birds, insects, and other animals. Walking trails meander through the center and down to the Guadalupe River.

Gardens and trails (self-guided) are open daily from dawn to dusk at no cost. The visitors center and many of the walks are wheelchair accessible. A sensory garden has Braille signs for the visually impaired. Guided group tours are available with advance notice. The Lawson store, a restored turn-of-the-century grocery store, serves as office and gift shop. Many students and adults participate each year in educational programs at the center.

To continue the trip, leave Kerrville on SH 173 (aka the Bandera Highway). As you leave town, you pass the entrance to Kerrville-Schreiner Park. Slightly over two miles from the park entrance, you come to an intersection with Wharton Road. Turn left here onto Wharton Road, which is the original river road to Zanzenberg (Center Point).

Wharton Road is named for William Wharton, one of Kerr County's earliest settlers. He bought 640 acres and moved here in 1857 with his wife, Thankful, and their three sons. They rest now in the family cemetery across the road from the river. The Wharton crossing of the Guadalupe River is one of the finest of the dozens of river crossings you make on this trip. The Guadalupe abruptly narrows from a sluggish, sprawling fifty-foot width so that it can squeeze under this low-water bridge and then rush out and into a jagged limestone chute, about twelve feet wide and several hundred churning feet long, before it finally spreads out and calms down in the woodlands below.

Once inside Center Point, Wharton Road is called River Road, and you enter town on it through old Zanzenberg. Follow its path to the right, on what is now Park Street, crossing the Guadalupe River on the old (1925) low-water bridge, known locally as the "Crossing Street bridge," just below the dam. At press time, the Crossing Street bridge was scheduled for replacement by a wider, safer bridge, but the project was meeting with considerable local resistance, with some suggesting that the bridge remain in place and be converted to a pedestrian-only crossing. Just after you cross the river, take the first left onto Skyline Drive, which is marked by a stop sign. Then turn right in another few yards on RM 480/San Antonio Street.

Several nice old stone buildings from Center Point's golden days still stand along this downtown stretch of RM 480/San Antonio Street, notably the old Center Point Bank, a two-story Romanesque Revival cut-stone building with four front windows, and the Woolls building next door, at 218 San Antonio Street at Skyline, a two-story, limestone-block-and-rubble building with full-width wooden balcony and exterior stairway. The Woolls building was built in 1873–1875 to house George Woolls' mercantile business. Woolls died in 1876. A variety of retail businesses subsequently operated out of the first floor, with fraternal organizations using the upper story for their meetings. The Rising Star Masonic Lodge, which counted many Texas Rangers among its members, met upstairs from 1875 to 1900.

Turn left on RM 1350 toward Comfort, then right on SH 27, which takes you into Comfort.

As you round the bend on SH 27 in Comfort, you pass on your left the old yellow San Antonio and Aransas Pass (SAP) depot, a simple wooden shed built in 1917 after the original one burned in December 1916. Hotels sent buggies and wagons to pick up their guests and luggage.

Comfort celebrated the railroad's arrival with a grand barbecue on August 27, 1887, held in a beautiful grove of trees along the Guadalupe River, only a short walk from the railroad. The *San Antonio Express* sent a reporter along.

The gray clouds that gathered at nightfall on Friday, heaped together by the norther that had sprung up, were all there yesterday morning, only they had spread themselves and covered the blue sky with a mantle of leaden hue. Those who intended to go to the Comfort barbecue and excursion made the journey to the Aransas Pass depot yesterday morning, accompanied by the freshening south breeze and a cheerful expectancy of spending an enjoyable day. Shortly before 8 street cars and hacks commenced bringing excurters, who after purchasing their tickets, $1.50 for the round trip, whiled away the time by watching the operations of the employees of the City, Lone Star and San Antonio Breweries, who were busily occupied by filling the baggage car with kegs of beer and large chunks of ice, which were handled by them with a muscular ease that commanded admiration. Seventy-five kegs of beer and ice in proportion. The breweries knew they had a thirsty crowd to deal with, and liberally they catered. By the time the baggage car was packed like a refrigerating box the platform of the depot was alive with people. Anxious looks were cast upward at the threatening clouds and various weather sages were consulted as to the probability of rain, notably the One Horse-Farmer who was prepared for the excursion. He predicted against rain, and his prediction, in addition to removing the doubts of the excursionists, was also eminently correct, for no rain fell during the day. Half past 8 arrived, and all the passengers were soon summoned on board, and though there was a goodly number, still the three cars provided for the excursion were not by any means filled. It was evident that the dull day had kept many from taking advantage of the excursion. The train drew out of the depot about 9 o'clock, and then all went well. The excursionists were somewhat dull at first, but soon a gentleman was seen to issue from the baggage car with such a bland smile that a general inquiry was made as to the cause of it. He whispered it to several, and then there was a general exodus. Liege lords left their spouses and retired to the baggage car, where Messrs. Beckman and Koebler, wearing genial smiles, invited the visitors to have some beer. It was quaffed heartily and a general feeling of good fellowship soon pervaded all.

The journey to Boerne was uneventful, although the country was seen under a new phase. The earth throbbed with relief; everywhere could be seen the signs of heavy rains; creeks that had been dry for months were rushing with water sportively; pastures that but a week before looked as if they had been seared with an immense hot iron had assumed a tinge of green—eloquent testimony that the drought had gone, and that vegetation was revivified. Here and there cotton patches showed that though backward, the stands were looking vigorous, giving promise of fair fruit. Boerne was reached a few minutes before 11 and the depot of this quiet hamlet presented an unusually lively appearance. Every inhabitant had turned out to meet the excursionists and there could not have been fewer than 200 people who received the incoming train. After the train had drawn up at the platform the cars were soon swarming with those who minutes before had received the San Antonians with effusive greetings. They also were "excurters" and the majority of them were of the fair sex. At Boerne the norther became more than pleasantly fresh. It became chilly, and the San Antonio ladies looked enviously at the wraps their sisters from Boerne had provided themselves with. Once more the train started over the newly laid track toward Comfort, about 20 miles distant.

Comfort is a small place, and as tranquil a spot as can be found, but the advent of the iron horse into her midst has roused the little latent enthusiasm she possessed. The shrill scream of the locomotive thrilled her. The placid life she has led for the last 30 years has gone forever, and Comfort is now naturally exercised. As the train neared the village yesterday the visitors were greeted by the village brass band playing lustily, "Hail Columbia," and a series of hearty shouts of welcome by a large number of people assembled, accompanied by an indiscriminate waving of hats and handkerchiefs, while the stars and stripes fluttered more vigorously than ever from several flagstaffs erected for the occasion. The barbecue grounds are located about a mile below the town proper, contiguous to the railroad track, and here the train stopped to discharge the passengers, who were soon mingled with those who were prepared to receive them. Some went to the trenches, where 10 huge beeves and the like number of muttons were roasting merrily in the most approved barbecue style. Others took advantage of the several beer stands erected, and others strolled around listlessly. There was a strange unanimity of opinion concerning one thing. All expressed themselves as being hungry. The keen air of Comfort, which is 1,400 feet above the level of the Gulf, and the norther, which by this time was somewhat tempered, had made everyone's gastronometer register abnormally.

It was not long before smoking joints of barbecued mutton were placed before the guests. They did justice to the feast, eating with such a sense of enjoyment that the Comfortites felt their labors had not been in vain. The repast went on for some hours and still the pangs of hunger were not appeased. More beeves and more muttons were brought from the cooking trench and they disappeared with wonderful rapidity.

There is an end of all things says the chestnut, and finally, all seemed satisfied. Then they were ready for the next item on the programme, which they awaited with a good humor born of good digestions. This took shape in an address of welcome delivered by Mr. A. Wertheim.

This was all the speechifying and once more the crowd looked for something new. A sudden scream from the locomotive startled the ladies' nerves and caused that necessary and respected individual, the oldest Inhabitant, to nearly have a fit. This, it was found, to be the signal that the train was ready to escort "the barbecuers" to the new depot ground in the centre of town. All flocked on board, and, reaching the depot, the few inhabitants still remaining in the hamlet were amazed at the sea of humanity that was turned loose. Comfort had never seen the like before. It is from the roof of Karger's hotel that the visitor is best able to appreciate the beauty of the valley in which Comfort is situated. To this point of vantage the genial host, Mr. Charles Karger, invited several of the visitors, and the trouble taken to reach the roof was well repaid. Stretching on all sides except the south is a chain of verdure clad mountains, at the bases of which rich agricultural country teeming with produce of the soil is apparent. Toward the north runs the Guadalupe River, and Cypress Creek embedded in rich foliage, here and there are dotted vineyards, while standing out in bold relief is the white column which marks the last resting place of those who were massacred in the lamentable disaster of the 10th of August, 1862.

The air of Comfort is wonderfully bracing and the country is as fertile as the climate is healthful. One thing that strikes the gazer from the hotel roof is the absence of any church. Comfort possesses neither churches nor lightning rods, a somewhat singular fact.

At 6:30 the warning whistle was again heard and those who did not stay over to attend the dance that was given that night in Karger's hotel, seated themselves in the cars in readiness for the homeward journey, which was accomplished safely and quickly The visitors generally declared they had enjoyed themselves at the barbecue and their journey to and fro.

The track beyond Comfort is being laid as rapidly as possible and will reach Kerrville, 20 miles distant, the 13th prox. The character of the grading is by no means so difficult as the 20 miles preceding it from Boerne, which was exceptionally heavy. The citizens of Kerrville are also preparing to give a barbecue shortly, for which purpose $500 has been subscribed for the purchase of fatted calves, etc. wherewith to regale the many visitors they expect to have on that momentous occasion.

Across the highway from the depot is the Frederick Werner home; the fachwerk section of the house visible from the highway was built in the late 1860s and was later added onto.

The SAP brought a lot of business to Comfort, but it helped put Peter Ingenhuett out of the beer-brewing business. Peter Ingenhuett's Cypress Creek brewery was said to brew as good a beer as San Antonio's famous Menger Hotel brewery. His beer was very popular until San Antonio's breweries began shipping their ice-cold product up on the SAP, and Comforters succumbed to the lure of "imported" beer, leaving Ingenhuett and his home brew high and dry.

When it came to beer, the Germans in Comfort were practical minded above all else, even to the point of celebrating the Fourth of July a day early. One July, Comfort's Goldbeck brothers were responsible for the glorious Fourth being celebrated on the third. Confronted with the delivery of several kegs of Menger Hotel beer a day early, the brothers realized that the beer would spoil if not drunk quickly. Wasting no time, the Goldbecks fired the cannon reserved to call residents together in case of emergency. The town folks, who quickly responded, soon lost their indignation at the ruse and began the annual celebration a day early.

Continue on SH 27 and turn left onto RM 473, as per the RM 473 sign, and go back to Sisterdale. At Sisterdale, turn left onto RR 1376 from RM 473.

Frederick Law Olmstead quite enjoyed his visits to Sisterdale and provides us with a good idea of what life was like there in 1854:

> Sisterdale is a settlement of eight or ten farms upon the Guadalupe, at the junction of the Sister creeks and the crossing of the Fredericksburg road. The farmers are all men of education, and have chosen their residences, the first by chance, the latter by choice, within social distance of one another. Up and down the Guadalupe, within long walking range, are a dozen or twenty more, single men, living in huts or caves, earning a tough livelihood chiefly by splitting shingles. They are of the same stamp, but of less social disposition, disheartened, or tired of circumstances, a sort of political hermits, who have retired into the woods, and live with one companion, or in complete solitude.
>
> The gentlemen we met were two of these singular settlers; one of them, the schoolmaster, a Berlin student; the other a Baron, over whose Texan "domain" we were actually passing. He took us to his castle, which was near by. It was a new log-house. The family occupied a lean-to in the rear, as the roof was not quite finished. Here we were presented to the lady, who received us with cordial politeness, holding up, in commendation of the climate, a bouncing baby, seven days old, weighing, she said, three times as much as babies at home.
>
> During a luncheon of bread and broth, we were interrupted by the clatter of hoofs. On looking out, we found a dozen men on horseback, partly Americans, from the next settlement. They were on their way to the Dale, to attend a Justice's Court. Draining our cups we joined the cavalcade.
>
> A few minutes brought us to the judge's house, a double log-cabin, upon a romantic rocky bluff of the Guadalupe. He came out to receive us, and after converting his dining-room into a temporary court-room, for the reception of the legal arrival, resumed his long pipe, and gave us a special reception in his own apartment. We had interrupted him at work at notes upon a meteorological table, and availed ourselves of his judicial absence to look over his observations, and to make notes of such as interested us.
>
> Court over, our host rejoined us. The case had been one of great simplicity, requiring a few words only, to fix the value of a dog which had been shot and to reconcile all parties. This function of a peacemaker, we found, was one that was a habitual blessing to the neighborhood, with the judge—a certain largeness in his nature sufficing to quell all expressions of ill-feeling and put an end to silly discords.
>
> He was partly bald, but seemed to have an imperturbable and happy good-nature that gave him eternal youth. A genial cultivation beamed from his face. He had been a man of marked attainments at home (an intimate associate with Humboldt and a friend of Goethe's Bettina), and kept up here a warm love for nature. His house was the very picture of good-nature, science, and back-woods. Romances and philosophies were piled in heaps in a corner of the logs. A dozen guns and rifles, and a Madonna, in oil, after Murillo, filled a blank on the wall. Deer-skins covered the bed, clothes hung about upon antlers, snake-skins were stretched to dry upon the bedstead, barometer, whisky, powder-horns, and specimens of Saxony wool, occupied the table.
>
> The dinner was Texan, of corn-bread and frijoles, with coffee, served in tin cups, but the salt was Attic, and the talk was worthy of golden goblets.

We passed, as may be imagined, a rarely pleasant day. A stroll to the Guadalupe showed us the corn-field and the sheep—a small flock of the finest Saxony. They had been selected with care, had arrived safely, and had now been, for two or three years, shifting for themselves. They had thriven well, but the flock of twelve had not much increased, owing to the depredations of panthers and Indians. A German shepherd had been shot by Indians in the early days of the settlement, and it was afterwards impossible to give, to so small a flock, the constant attention they needed. They had been, however, very profitable for their numbers, from the constant demand for thorough-bred bucks.

In the afternoon, several neighbors had dropped in, and there was some pleasant dispute as to what roof should offer us shelter. We were, finally, carried off by Mr. T., whose farm lies uppermost on the Guadalupe. The farm lies in a bend of the river, and has an agreeable proportion of timber and of rich meadow. The house, of logs, is large, warm, and substantial.

The evening's talk ran upon the principles of government, and kept us late. Mr. T. had been a member of the Frankfort Parliament. He had arrived in this country with little else available than a hopeful energy, but with this capital had become, in a few years, what, in Texas, was considered a wealthy man, owning large tracts of land, and able to live freely upon his rents.

We rode with him, next day, over the Dale. The land is much broken, but well wooded and drained. In each little valley are one or more small prairies adapted to cultivation, and the hills are thickly covered with grass. It is here not the mesquit, but a taller and coarser leaf, rich in summer but affording poor nourishment in winter. Cattle, however, manage to find their own subsistence through the year, browsing, during the cold, in the river bottoms, where there is always some verdure as well as protection from the wind. The soil for cultivation is excellent. The principal crop is corn, the yield, being thirty to sixty bushels, from what would be considered at the North a very small outlay of labor. Wheat has been introduced with such success as to induce the settlers to send for harvesting and thrashing-machines. One of the greatest sources of profit is from droves of hogs, which increase with remarkable rapidity, and pick their living from the roots and nuts of the river bottoms. The distribution of a few ears of corn at night brings them all every day to the crib. Tobacco is cultivated by the settlers for their own use, but none has yet been prepared for market.

We called upon several of the settlers. The first house was a surprise—a neat, stuccoed, Swiss cottage, almost the only thing of the kind we had seen in Texas. Its proprietor came from the plough to welcome us—literally, a free laborer. We found within, a thousand evidences of taste such as the exterior led us to expect. Another short ride took us to a large stuccoed log-house, near the bank of one of the Sister creeks. Here lives a professor who divides his time between his farm and his library. The delicious brook water has been turned to account by him for the cure of disease, and his house is thrown open to patients. To any friend of mine who has faith in pure air and pure water, and is obliged to run from a Northern winter, I cannot recommend a pleasanter spot to pass his exile than this.

Evening found us in the largest house of the settlement, and a furious norther suddenly rising, combined with the attractive reception we met to compel us to stay two days without moving. Mr. D., our host, was a man of unusually large education, and, having passed some years at school in England, spoke English in perfection. Before the Revolution he had controlled an estate on which the taxes were $10,000. He had become a popular leader, and was placed at the head of the temporary government of his Duchy. When the reaction came, all was swept away, and, exiling himself, he came to settle here. Now, working with his own hands in the Texan backwoods, he finds life not less pleasant than before.

He had this year cultivated sixty acres, and with the help of the forenoons of his two sons, of fourteen and fifteen, who are at school the rest of the day, had produced 2,500 bushels of corn, besides some cotton, wheat, and tobacco.

After supper, there were numerous accessions of neighbors, and we passed a merry and most interesting evening. There was waltzing, to the tones of a fine piano, and music of the highest sort, classic and patriotic. The principal concerted pieces of Don Giovanni were given, and all parts well sustained. After the ladies had retired, the men had over the whole stock of student-songs, until all were young again. No city of fatherland, we thought, could show a better or more cheerful evening company. One of the party said to me: "I think, if one or two of the German tyrants I could mention, could look in upon us now, they would display some chagrin at our enjoyment, for there is hardly a gentleman in this company whom they have not condemned to death, or to imprisonment for life."

RR 1376 takes you into the region between the Sister creeks, a broken-up country once favored by outlaws and marauding Indians. It also takes you up and over the High Hills, the Great Divide, the string of hills that separates the Guadalupe and Pedernales watersheds. Few people live in this sparsely watered region.

After almost fourteen wide-open miles on RM 1376, turn right onto RM 1888 to Blanco.

The country continues to be sparsely settled, and the homes along the way are mostly well-aging limestone ones.

After eight miles on RM 1888, you see on your left the small, whitewashed frame Lindendale School, all that remains of that community. It was named for the linden trees that grew along the Blanco River. Settlement began in the 1860s, when the Gates family arrived and established an apple orchard. J. C. Hoge donated five acres with a log cabin for the Mount Glen school, which was later renamed Lindendale. The school closed upon consolidation with the Blanco school system in 1951.

RM 1888 picks up the Blanco River in its infancy and follows its ever-strengthening flow. At first the south banks of the Blanco are high sheer bluffs, and then both banks lie low for the rest of the trip to Blanco. Blanco means "white" in Spanish and refers to the river's white limestone bed. There is a legend to the effect that if a person gets a drink of Blanco water, he will never be content in any other place under the sun but will always have a desire to again quaff the waters of the Blanco River.

When RM 1888 runs into RM 1623, take RM 1623 into Blanco.

BLANCO

Blanco County • 1,600 (approximate) • (830) • About 27 miles from Sisterdale

Blanco was first settled when James Callahan and E. C. "Uncle Clem" Hinds moved to the Blanco River valley and built cabins on opposite sides of the river in 1854. Callahan came to Texas as a sergeant in the Georgia Battalion, which arrived at Velasco just before Christmas in 1835. Callahan escaped the Goliad Massacre, probably because he was in a labor detail at Victoria. He helped establish Walnut Springs (now Seguin) in 1838. During the 1840s he moved to Caldwell County, where he operated a 350-acre farm and a store. He also held government land grants in Lavaca and Kimble counties. He married Sarah Melissa Day in 1841; they had four children.

Callahan remained an active soldier and, like many others who had fought in the revolution, was vigorously anti-Mexican. From 1839 to 1841, he commanded a group of minutemen in Guadalupe County who chased and fought Indians and Mexicans accused of stealing horses. Callahan served as a first lieutenant in Mathew Caldwell's Ranger company in 1840 and became a company commander during the incursion of Rafael Vásquez in 1841, in which he led a retreat from San Antonio. In 1842, his sixty-man company fought in the battle of Salado Creek and helped expel the Mexican force that had invaded Texas and captured San Antonio. Later that year, Callahan also served as a lieutenant in the Somervell expedition. His military activities then ceased until 1855, when he commanded the punitive expedition into Mexico that bears his name.

Callahan had come through the Blanco valley in 1836 and fell so in love with the place that he moved his family out into what was then the wilderness eighteen years later. Others followed, so many that Callahan and real estate entrepreneur John Pitts laid out a town on the south side of the river in 1855, calling it Pittsburgh.

In 1855, Governor Elisha M. Pease ordered three companies of Texas Rangers under Callahan's command to protect the Texas-Mexico border from marauding bands of Lipan Apaches and Kickapoos. On October 1, the Rangers arrived at Fort Duncan (present-day Eagle Pass) and crossed the Rio Grande into Mexico in pursuit of the Indians, and probably in pursuit of runaway slaves as well. At first, Mexican authorities cooperated with the Rangers, because the Mexicans suffered even more than the Texans from Indian raids. But then the Mexicans joined with the Indians to drive the Texans back across the Rio Grande. To cover his retreat, Callahan burned the Mexican border town of Piedras Negras on October 6. The commander at Fort Duncan covered the Texans' retreat back across the river. For burning the town, Callahan was dismissed from the service. He returned to his piece of paradise on the Blanco.

Apart from his military exploits, Callahan was a violent man, as this story from the *Seguin Mercury* (from about 1855 or 1856) illustrates:

We understand that a negro, the property of Mr. Geo. Smith, of this county, was killed by Capt. Callaghan, at his place on the Blanco a few days ago. We learn that Capt. Callaghan had been molested several times, for two or three nights, by persons attempting to break into his house. The noise he made in arising scared them away, and each time he found the negro man in question near a woodpile. This probably excited his suspicion. In the mean time he learned that the negro was armed. He therefore ordered him to give up his arms—a six-shooter and an unearthly, long sharp steel blade. The negro refused to do so. The Captain then drew his six-shooter, and told him he must give up his arms or be shot. The boy drew his pistol, and told him to shoot, and seemed careless of his life. The Captain then sent his little son to the house for his shot gun, and as the little fellow approached with the gun the negro broke and ran towards a horse which he had staked out, with a view to mounting him and escaping. The Captain discharged his fowling-piece at him without serious effect, and, the boy still running, he plumped him in the back with his six-shooter and that was the last of "Poor Old Edward." The Captain's experience with the "Injins" doubtless assisted him in this affair.

Callahan's penchant for violence meant that he would enjoy just a few more months of his paradise on earth. Because Callahan was absent from home for long periods on expeditions with the Rangers, he hired a young man named

Calvin Blassingame to work his farm. This was in 1856, and not long afterward, Callahan and Blassingame had a violent argument. Callahan dismissed Blassingame, and a bitter feud started between the two families. Once, two of Callahan's dearest friends heard the boy's father, Woodson Blassingame, make some very disparaging remarks about the Callahan family. These men were Clem Hinds and W. S. "Maulheel" Johnson. The peace-loving Hinds chose to let the remarks go unnoticed, but Johnson thought it his duty to tell Callahan.

When Callahan returned home in April 1856, Johnson told him what he had heard. The captain was very upset and went to Hinds for advice. He also asked Hinds if he had heard Blassingame. Hinds answered that he had, and that Blassingame had said just what Johnson had told Callahan. Callahan told Hinds that he and Johnson had to go with him to see Blassingame about his remarks.

The three mounted their horses and rode to the Blassingame home. As they rode, they discussed the matter, and Hinds and Johnson persuaded Callahan that the best thing to do was to act as civil as possible under the circumstances. About twenty feet in front of the Blassingame's log cabin was a fence, and when they got to it, they stopped and called. Mrs. Blassingame came to the door and said that father and son were at home.

"Well, tell your husband that I want to see him," replied Callahan. As he finished speaking, two double-barreled shotguns answered from the cracks between the logs of the house. Callahan and Johnson both fell. Callahan died instantly with a load of buckshot in his breast, and Johnson lived only a few minutes. Hinds, severely wounded in the face, neck, and arm, clung to his horse, which carried him back to Callahan's house. There he fell from the horse, and almost too weak to whisper, he gasped out the grim story.

A warrant was issued immediately, and John M. Watson was made a special officer in order to arrest the Blassingame men. Many men wanted to go after them in a group, but Watson preferred to handle the situation alone. He went to them, cool and confident, and arrested them without any trouble, assuring them that they would get a fair trial. They had expected to be hunted out with a posse like dogs.

The excitement over the murders spread like wildfire down through Texas to San Marcos and Seguin. Dozens of Callahan's old friends and comrades rushed to Blanco. There was no jail, but the prisoners were under guard at Little Blanco, where Justice of the Peace George Lang lived. About this time, Watson was called to Lockhart on business but was almost afraid to leave the prisoners for fear of violence from the crowd. At about midnight that very night, a crowd, estimated at one hundred men, overran the guards and shot the two Blassingame men to death.

The trouble did not end there, however. "Uncle Clem" Hinds was crippled for life, and Callahan's wife and infant child died soon afterward from shock and grief. Immigrants to Texas, looking for a place to settle, shied away from Blanco as news of the murders spread. The entire population was on the verge of dividing up into factions over the matter.

In October 1857, there was a camp meeting held at Pittsburg on the Blanco, at which a number of families were encamped. On Saturday night, October 10, at about nine o'clock, while the services were still proceeding at the stand, the sheriff of Comal County, with two sons of Woodson Blassingame, rushed suddenly up to the tent occupied by the families of two men named Day and Pharr for the purpose of arresting Pharr, against whom the grand jury of Comal

County had found a bill of indictment, charging him with being concerned with the mob that killed Woodson Blassingame eighteen months earlier. Pharr was seized, but he extricated himself and ran off between the line of tents and the preaching stand, pursued by one of the Blassingames with a double-barreled shotgun, who was in the act of shooting him when some person shot Blassingame with a six-shooter. He fell instantly, but his wound was not considered fatal. The other Blassingame ran around the tents and shot at Pharr with a double-barreled shotgun but missed him. The line of tents was about thirty steps from the preaching arbor where the services were going on, and the whole affair occurred in the midst of men, women, and children, to the imminent danger of innocent persons being killed. The entry of the sheriff was sudden and unexpected, and in the dim light of the camps it produced a great confusion and excitement. The meeting was broken up the next day. All families were unwilling any longer to remain there. The sheriff had never before attempted to arrest Pharr, nor had he any reason to expect any resistance. Pharr, with his family, was encamped on this ground, and he was unarmed. There was no disposition whatever on the part of the people there to respect the sheriff, and they regarded him as in every respect reprehensible for the time, place, and manner of attempting to arrest Pharr, but particularly for bringing the Blassingames along as a posse, armed with double-barreled shotguns. He had repeatedly promised never to bring them as assistants to act in arresting persons charged with participating in the killing of Calvin and Woodson Blassingame.

But the tensions gradually eased, and the following story is told of the hospitality of the early settlers of Blanco in 1860: A young man was riding through the region when nightfall came. He was still miles from his destination and did not know where to go. In the settlement at Blanco, he was directed on his way and told of a place where he could spend the night. When he rode up, he thought he must be looking at one of the outhouses, but a jovial-looking man appeared and told him to "get down, hobble his horse, and come in." This he did, finding what he had thought to be a barn to be a house sheltering a large family of four boys, two girls, and the man and woman. He was given a hearty supper of coffee, venison, bread, and honey, and he began to feel better but still could not understand where he could sleep that night. Soon, however, the woman went to a corner and began pulling down a large pile of tanned deerskins. Then she went to the one large bed and took off mattress after mattress. Soon she had enough comfortable beds for the entire family as well as their guest, and the young man afterward declared it to be one of the best nights he had ever spent.

Blanco County was created in 1858, and an election that year located the county seat at a spot just across the river from Pittsburgh. So the town site was moved across the Blanco River and renamed Blanco. The Pittsburgh Land Company gave the new town 120 acres of land. The court met for the first couple of years under a tree, then in the log schoolhouse. Their approach to law enforcement was equally casual and realistic. Take the case of "Dr." McKinney, who settled down four miles above Blanco and started to practice his own brand of medicine, which to his neighbors was quackery. He was also a bigamist, for which illegal practice he was indicted. But when the sheriff and posse rode out to arrest him, McKinney barricaded himself in the house, while his wives sallied forth to meet the posse with a double-barreled shotgun and an axe. The two women looked so determined that the sheriff deemed it prudent to retire from the scene. Shortly thereafter, the good doctor and his entourage left Blanco County for Utah.

Many Blanco County voters favored secession in 1861, but there was a sizable Unionist element. While the Rebels were away at war, the Unionists managed to divide the county through an election. Western Blanco County became a part of the new Kendall County. Such division in sentiment made for trouble. Bushwhackers scoured the countryside, molesting anybody they chose, and their Confederate pursuers were very liberal in their definition of "bushwhacker," tormenting and killing German farmers who were neither anti-Rebel nor pro-Union; they merely wished to be left alone. The Comanches were also on the warpath, but the bushwhacker was feared more than the Indian; you knew an Indian was your enemy, but how could you tell whether a strange white man was your friend or foe?

In the fall of 1865, the district court here held its first postwar session. The grand jury went over the various wrongdoings of the past four years, the consequence of which was seventy-three indictments returned for murder, all of a political nature; that is, involving the killings of bushwhackers and soldiers.

In March 1868, the *Austin Republican* and the *New York Times* printed a report purportedly filed by the Blanco County district clerk concerning the county's criminal docket. It stated that since June 1865, grand juries had issued 178 indictments, 83 of which were for murder, and 61 for theft and robbery, while the number of registered voters was only 120, because of all the murders. The June 10, 1868, edition of the *San Antonio Daily Herald*, however, reported that the clerk indignantly declared that his report had been falsified, that not a single murder had been committed in Blanco since June 1865, but that all of the eighty-three murder indictments had been returned by Union-loyal grand juries for the killing of seven "bushwhackers" during the war, and that most of the other charged offences had also been committed before June 1865. The small number of voters, he declared, was due to the ignorance and politics of the registrars.

The quarrels and trouble did not abate. Nearly all of the county's men were stock raisers, and they had left most of their stock on the range with little or no care. After four years of little attention, there was much stock neither marked nor branded. Some of the returning soldiers argued that this unbranded stock was the natural increase of the stock they had left. This was partly true, and if there had been a fair divide, the harm would have been less, but the man who was most expert with the rope and branding iron got more than his share, and the man with a conscience often got none. This led to hard feelings, and, even worse, it led greedy men into the habit of branding what they knew was not their own. What they were doing was wrong, but could one expect that after four years of the demoralizing effects of camp life, and the fraud and corruption in many government departments, they would not become demoralized and corrupt too? Government corruption had been so bad during the war that one soldier declared that "honest men would steal."

Indian attacks continued into the 1870s. In September 1871, the citizens of Blanco County, "expecting a heavy Indian raid to desolate their county and murder their people," solicited the State Arsenal in Austin for arms but were coolly told that it had only five hundred arms, and that all of them were necessary to keep the peace during the upcoming elections. This was during the administration of the largely unpopular Radical Reconstructionist governor,

Edmund J. Davis, and the people of Blanco County were upset, needless to say, with him and his regime, referring to him as "Edmund I," "Granny Davis," "little pettifogging tyrant," and "Your Imperial Majesty" in a letter of protest that appeared in the *Austin Democratic Statesman*.

On the evening of August 15, 1876, someone set fire to the Blanco County courthouse. All the benches, chairs, and other furniture were piled up and lit by the arsonist. None of the county records were saved, and the total loss was valued at $18,000. The Masonic Lodge, which had its hall on the courthouse's second story, also lost everything. The next morning, books, papers, and the county seal were found some distance from town on the riverbank.

Three months later, William Winkleman, a farmer, was burned out and shot at because he spoke his opinion about thieves. He managed to recover from his wounds.

That same month, William Marshall visited the county to look at a tract of 14,070 acres of land, he being one of the three heirs owning it. It lay on Pedernales Creek, twelve miles north of Blanco City, in the center of the county. He proposed to remove the county seat to this tract, promising to give every alternate lot in the survey of the town for public use. Marshall's efforts failed, but it proved to be the first of a series in attempts to move the seat of Blanco County government elsewhere.

But despite the turmoil, by 1876 Blanco City had a debating club, a university, and two amateur bands, a brass and a string one.

In early November 1876, the citizens of the northern portion of Blanco County were startled by a report resembling the discharge of a cannon, and at the same time the earth was jarred as by an earthquake. The report was also heard at Fredericksburg, and some gentlemen visited the mountain from whence it was supposed the report came, and there found a pool of water.

The creation of Kendall County came back to haunt Blanco in 1879. That year the residents of the newly organized Johnson City and the northern part of the county called for an election to relocate the county seat to Johnson City. Blanco residents laughed, until the votes were counted. Johnson City had lost by only 10 out of 660 votes cast.

In December 1884, the second election for the removal of the seat of government from Blanco to Johnson City resulted in favor of the former by a majority of sixteen votes. One hundred guns were fired in Blanco in honor of the victory. By this time the county was polarized over the issue. Men were ready to fight at any time over the courthouse location; fistfights and gunfights were not uncommon. Many families even divided over the issue, causing the *San Antonio Daily Light* to observe: "Blanco County has just got through with a very disagreeable duty, being the permanent location of the county seat in which Blanco City was the point selected. County seat wars are generally never ending, and they have the effect to unsettle values, make enemies, and otherwise create trouble among peaceful people, and to this end Blanco City and Blanco County are to be congratulated on the result of the recent election there."

Johnson City finally wrested away the county seat from Blanco in a third election, held in January 1890. The Johnson City faction won by a majority of sixty-six votes. In an election row at Johnson City that day, Ben Casey shot and killed George Loyd and wounded Deputy Sheriff Crosby in the thigh. The former was an advocate of Blanco City, the latter two of Johnson City, which won in the election. Casey was arrested and taken to Blanco City, lynching being expected.

Less than six months later, District Clerk J. M. Martin of Blanco County was killed at Johnson City in the trouble over the recent county seat contest.

Within hours of the declaration of Johnson City's victory, all the county records were loaded onto wagons for removal to Johnson City, despite the lack of a courthouse, or jail, for that matter.

The ill feeling over the county seat removal was so bad in November 1890 that the dissatisfied parties were making plans to propose the creation of a new county to the next session of the legislatures, carving out parts of Blanco and the neighboring counties of Hays, Travis, and possibly Comal counties, with Blanco as the county seat. But the plan was doomed from the beginning, since the state constitution prohibited the creation of any county measuring less than seven hundred square miles, nor the reduction of any existing county below that size, which meant that the neighboring counties of Hays, Kendall, and Comal could not be reduced, and Blanco could be by only seventeen square miles. So, the new county could only use parts of the larger, border counties of Travis, Burnet, Llano, and Gillespie, which would defeat the object of those interested in placing Blanco near the center of the new county, since a central location within the county was another requirement. Never mind that an almost-new courthouse and jail already existed in Blanco, while Johnson City had nothing.

The county seat battle went on sporadically for decades. In May 1915, a petition was circulated in the south end of Blanco asking the commissioners court to order an election to determine whether or not the county seat should be removed from Johnson City to Blanco. Since Johnson City was in the center of the county and it would take a two-thirds majority to remove the county seat, a second petition was circulated asking the court to order an election to determine whether or not the county should issue bonds in the amount of $30,000 for the purpose of erecting a new courthouse on the public square in the town of Johnson City. The bond issue passed, resulting in the courthouse we see there today.

Ironically, Blanco long remained the larger town, although the respective populations now are practically identical. And to this day, each town tends to keep its own company.

Cotton came to Blanco in the 1870s, and 1882 was a bumper year for Blanco County and Texas. Blanco farmers grew an astounding number of bales of cotton per acre. It was one of those years that prompted Uncle Clem Hinds to say, "Some years Texas floats in grease."

But then the drought years came. During the dry summer of 1886, a deserted farmhouse near Blanco had the following words chalked onto the board nailed across the door: "250 miles to the nearest post office, 100 miles to wood, 20 miles to water, 6 inches to Hell. God Bless our home! Gone to live with wife's folks." An old farmer remembered, "The corn crop was sorter short that year. We had corn for dinner one day and Paw ate 15 acres of it."

For decades, Blanco was a sleepy little town largely ignored by tourists and travelers. Many of the buildings on the courthouse square stood vacant and forlorn, including the old courthouse. By the 1980s, the courthouse was in danger of being torn down and rebuilt elsewhere. This bleak existence began to change in the 1990s. Thousands of urban refugees from Austin, San Antonio, and elsewhere have been moving into sparsely populated Blanco County. By 2000, a number of restaurants, antique shops, art galleries, B&Bs, a coffee and juice bar, a health food store, and even a microbrewery had opened to serve them, and the trend has continued since.

RM 1623 becomes Fourth Street/Loop 163 in Blanco. When you cross Main Street/US 281, you come to the old courthouse and square.

OLD BLANCO COUNTY COURTHOUSE

On the square

Built in 1885 for $27,000, the old courthouse served its intended function only five years before the county government moved to Johnson City. Designed by noted architect F. M. Ruffini, who crowned its relatively unadorned square limestone body with an elaborate mansard roof, the courthouse was Blanco's pride and joy. Blanco citizens schemed for years after the Johnson City move to reinstate Blanco County government within its walls, but their efforts ultimately failed. In the meantime, the courthouse served as a bank, newspaper office, opera house, hospital, school, union hall, and museum. Recently restored after years of community effort, the old courthouse is now open as a visitor/community center.

The west side of the courthouse square (300 block of Main/US 281) is composed mostly of vintage, courthouse-era limestone buildings that are part of the "Uptown Blanco" arts and dining project. The most interesting, and well-hidden, building of the lot is the old Blanco County jail. Built in the mid-1870s, this squat, square, no-nonsense limestone blockhouse is one of the oldest surviving buildings in town. It served as county jail until 1890, when the county seat moved to Johnson City, accompanied by the jail's steel cells.

The jail's most notorious occupant was Al Lackey. In 1885, Lackey decided to kill his family. After fatally shooting six family members in succession, Lackey was captured in Johnson City and transferred to the Blanco County Jail. A few days later, a mob snatched Lackey from the jail and lynched him from a large live oak north of town, which still stands. The jail is located behind the Uptown Blanco Restaurant at 317 Main and is accessible to the public through the restaurant. On the north side of the square, the venerable Blanco Lumber and Hardware Store (412 Fourth) now features antiques, dolls, and a Blanco rain chart that goes back to 1900.

BINDSEIL PARK

On Town Creek, by City Hall, just off the courthouse square

This short little linear park connects you to Blanco State Park. A couple of footbridges cross the creek.

BLANCO UNITED METHODIST CHURCH

Pecan at 1st, 2 blocks south of the courthouse square

The congregation dates to 1854; the present limestone-block sanctuary dates to 1883, with subsequent additions.

ADRIAN EDWARDS CONN HOME

3rd and Main

The little cottage was built before 1873 with sixteen-inch-thick limestone walls, a rock-walled cellar, and an underground cistern. Remember that Indian raids continued here until at least 1874.

DINING

RILEY'S BAR-B-Q

318 4th, catercorner to the old courthouse • 833-4166 • Open daily, lunch and dinner • www.rileysbarbq.net • W

They have brisket, pork ribs and loin, sausage, turkey breast. The usual sides are available, as well as deviled eggs. Cobblers and banana pudding are for dessert. Beer is offered.

BLANCO BOWLING CLUB CAFE

4th St., next to Riley's, just east of the courthouse square • 833-4416 • Open daily, breakfast, lunch, and dinner • W

The Blanco Bowling Club Cafe is full of anachronisms. Take for instance the made-from-scratch doughnuts and sweet rolls served every morning, and the homemade coconut, lemon, chocolate, apple, and pecan pies, and the hand-breaded chicken-fried steak. Or take the old-fashioned burgers and homemade onion rings and french fries.

OTHER ATTRACTIONS

REAL ALE BREWING COMPANY

231 San Saba Ct. • (830) 833-2534 • www.realalebrewing.com

Real Ale Brewing reminds me of the Spoetzl Brewery way back when it could legitimately call itself "Texas' Little Brewery." This little brewery works sixty barrels at a time, making four year-round brews and a variety of seasonal specials. Their Rio Blanco Pale Ale, Full Moon Pale Rye Ale, Brewhouse Brown Ale, and Firemans #4 Blonde Ale are as fine as you'll quaff anywhere, within Texas or without.

Tours are given, and the tasting room is open on a limited basis; it's best to call ahead or send an e-mail to info@realalebrewing.com to check on current schedules or to arrange a special visit.

To paraphrase the Frank Zappa quote on their website home page, "You can't be a real [Hill] country unless you have a beer and an airline—it helps if you have some kind of a football team, or some nuclear weapons, but at the very least you need a beer."

BLANCO PIONEER MUSEUM

418 Pecan St., just off the Blanco Square, across from the old mohair warehouse • Open weekend afternoons; call Blanco Chamber of Commerce, 833-5101

Opened early in 2010, the museum, located in the newly restored white frame Pat Ryan building, is furnished as it would have been in the mid-1800s, with antique furniture and accessories.

BLANCO RIVER DINOSAUR TRACKS

Just off RM 1623, 3.2 miles west of the old courthouse • Free

Dinosaur fossils are rarely found in central Texas, which was covered by a shallow sea for tens of millions of years. But here in the limestone bed of the Blanco River, you can see the huge, bathtub-sized, roundish footprints of sauropods (brontosaurus), dating back to the Cretaceous (66 million to 144 million years ago). After 3.2 miles on RM 1623, you come to Trainer-Wuest Road (County Road 103) on your left. Parking along this road and by the river is strictly prohibited. So if you want to see the tracks, you'll have to take your chances by parking on the RM 1623 right-of-way, walking down Trainer-Wuest Road to the river, and then heading downstream (toward Blanco) about two hundred feet to find the first of several sets of tracks.

BLANCO STATE PARK

4 blocks south of the town square; take US 281 south, then turn onto Park Road 23 • 833-4333 • Open daily • Fee • W variable

Blanco State Park is 104 pleasant acres along the Blanco River. More than two hundred thousand people visit the park annually, which opened in 1934. The area had been used as a campsite by early explorers and settlers. Koch Springs feed Koch branch, which flows through the park. They were probably the abundant springs yielding a "buey de agua" ("a lot of water") described by Bernardo de Miranda y Flores on his inspection trip from San Antonio to Los Almagres silver mine in Llano County in 1756. The park's hilly terrain is dotted with cedar, pecan, and other trees. Animal life includes nutrias, mallard ducks, raccoons, armadillos, and squirrels. Fish include rainbow trout (in the winter), perch, catfish, and bass. Park activities include camping, swimming, picnicking, hiking, nature study, boating (electric motors only), fishing, and paddle boat rentals (seasonal).

ANNUAL EVENT

JUNE

Blanco Valley Jamboree • 833-5101 • Second weekend in June • Free • W

The event begins with a Friday night dance, unwinds with the chili cook-off on Saturday, and includes a band contest and fiddlers competition sanctioned by the Texas Old Time Fiddlers Association. Other activities include a cow chip (cowboy Frisbee) toss, armadillo races, a jalapeno-eating contest, egg throwing, an armadillo beauty contest, washer pitching, and a Miss Blanco beauty pageant, all climaxed by a street dance.

PEYTON COLONY

From Blanco take RM 165 eight miles northeast to a roadside park on west side of the road.

The limekiln located in the roadside park was built by Peyton Roberts and his neighbors to provide high-quality lime, which was used to make mortar for buildings in Peyton Colony and elsewhere in Blanco County, some of which still stand. The kiln was restored in the 1960s during construction of the roadside park.

Peyton (Payton), formerly known as Peyton Colony and Board House (Boardhouse), started as a freedmen's community established about 1865 under the leadership of former slave Peyton Roberts. White inhabitants of the area called the settlement Freedman's Colony. The community included a school and Mount Horeb Baptist Church.

Born a slave in Virginia, Peyton Roberts was owned by Jeremiah Roberts, who came to Texas as a member of DeWitt's Colony. Jeremiah Roberts came to own fifty slaves and many acres of land in Bastrop and Caldwell counties. At the dawn of the Civil War, he gave his slaves to his children. The son who received Peyton, his wife, and five children gave them their freedom in 1863, on the condition that they remain as hired hands until the war's end. Peyton agreed, on the condition that he be paid, not in money, but in all the goods necessary to start his own farm: a wagon, oxen, a bull and cow, some hogs, chickens, and furniture.

Soon after the end of the war, Roberts acquired public land in southeastern Blanco County by preemption. Late in the summer of 1865, he started building a log home for his family, filling the cracks with a mix of mud and grass. Early in 1866, he brought his family to their new home, only to discover that his mud mortar had frozen, cracked, and started to fall apart. To adequately insulate his family from the cruel winters, he would have to remortar the cabin with a mix of lime, water, and sand. He built a lime kiln using mud and grass to close up the holes and gaps, but the mud mortar failed in the face of the kiln's intense heat. Whereupon Roberts sought the advice of his former master, who came out to Blanco County with some of his own lime to help construct a proper kiln.

To make lime, chunks of limestone were placed in the kiln in such a way that the heat would spread evenly. The rocks were fired for 15 days and nights and then allowed to cool down. The baked rocks were then placed on a heavy cloth and tapped gently all over. The dust that fell from the rock was the lime, in its unslaked state. For use, it had to be slaked, or placed in water, and stirred vigorously.

Other freedmen followed Roberts to this hilly section of Blanco County, and though preemption technically ended in 1876, land patents in the area continued to be issued as late as 1880. In 1872 or 1874, a church was built on land donated by Jim Upshear, who had come with his wife to Peyton by wagon train from Virginia. A small log schoolhouse was built. The colonists chose the most intelligent member of their lot to be teacher. A post office operated from 1898 to 1909. Another post office operated from 1918 to 1930, but it was officially named Board House because it was located in A. V. Walker's board house, the first such house in the community.

Life wasn't easy in those postwar days, especially if you were as poor as these ex-slaves were. Matches were one of the community's scarcest commodities. Folks normally used flint to light their fires. Since there was little flint to be found in the vicinity, families jealously guarded their pieces. No one normally had more than two pieces of flint at any given time, and there was more flint than guns or horses. The nearest doctor was in Blanco, about eight miles away, which a runner might cover in two hours.

The Comanches made no distinction between whites and blacks. Milk cows were easily pilfered, and when one of the colony families finally got a horse, it was soon stolen. The raiding troubles were such that Roberts asked a white friend in Blanco for help. They didn't have much in the way of firearms, horses, or experience, but they were willing to learn if someone would care to equip and lead them. The next day a wagon loaded with guns and food, and a remuda of horses arrived from Blanco. Ten or twelve colonists saddled up and followed their leader single file into the wilderness. They found the Indians camped about twenty miles distant and rode pell-mell through the camp, scattering the raiders. They didn't kill anyone, but they burned and pillaged the camp beyond use.

The *Blanco Star-Vindicator* summed up the white community's benevolent and progressive (at the time) view toward the colonists in 1884: "The negroes down in the colony seem to be about the most thrifty, industrious and peaceable people of this race we ever saw. They attend to their own business and are getting along well. The negroes down in the colony are building a good substantial Methodist church for which they deserve great credit. The citizens of Blanco are helping them along very liberally, too, with the good work."

To see Mount Horeb Baptist Church, go about one mile north on CR 409.

In 1874, under the direction of the Reverend Jack Burch, residents of the community established the Mount Horeb Baptist Church. Early worship services were held in a log building also used as a school. Since the Reconstruction era, Mount Horeb has served as a focal point for the community and for a widespread rural area.

To leave Blanco and continue the trip, go east from the courthouse square on Fourth Street/ Loop 163 across the Blanco River. When Loop 163 runs into US 281, turn left on US 281. In a half mile you come to the junction with RM 32. Turn left on RM 32 and head for San Marcos.

As you roll through these arid hills, consider these remarks by an early settler about the same land:

> [We] were dependent in many respects upon each other, but especially for mutual protection and the care of each other's stock, as stock was about all the property we cared for, or counted as property. What did we care for who owned the broad acres while our horses and cattle had the free use of it? A man with large stock did not care for more than land enough on which to build his cabin and pens, with plenty of water convenient. So the men with large tracts of land were to be pitied, for they had their taxes to pay and the land brought no income.

So far was this practice carried that the teller claimed to know of a rancher "that claimed to control 10,000 head of cattle on a 160 acre preemption claim, and that not patented; in fact the owner was not willing to pay even the patent fees." What do you think he would say about the four- and five-digit land prices of today?

Remember that RM 32 becomes Ranch Road 12 ten miles out of San Marcos.

ENCHANTED ROCK

Enchanted Rock is the Hill Country's most awe-inspiring natural landmark, a 640-acre bald dome of pink granite rising 325 feet above the bed of Sandy Creek and 1,825 feet above sea level. It is the second largest exposed batholith in the United States, behind Georgia's Stone Mountain, and it is one of the oldest geological rock exposures in Texas, formed nearly a billion years ago. The rock's rugged surface conceals entrances to caves and subterranean passages far below.

A correspondent for the New York Mirror wrote in 1838 of an "enchanted" or "holy" mountain, which the Comanches regarded with religious veneration and where they frequently assembled to perform "paynim" rites. Modern Texans still flock to Enchanted Rock each year, probably just as awestruck as those Comanches.

Leave Austin on Bee Caves Road (FM 2244) west, toward Bee Cave.

The explosive growth that Austin has undergone is typified by Bee Caves Road. In 1970, a few scattered houses and the Eanes School stood along the road, and the surrounding hills were mostly green. Now Bee Caves Road is lined with dozens of business establishments, and the once-verdant hills are brown with McMansion rooftops.

This four-lane highway was a winding dirt wagon trail through an isolated cedar choppers' neighborhood called Panther Path back in 1902. That was the year our Central Texas version of the Abominable Snowman appeared in Panther Path. Our "Bigfoot" first frightened a group of young people who were fishing and hunting several miles above the old McDonald Dam. The eight-foot-tall hairy man-monster flourished a large club and, uttering blood-curdling screams, started to attack. The young people ran for their wagons and managed to escape. The beast followed them for some distance, however, before abandoning the chase and disappearing into a large canyon. Measurements of Bigfoot's tracks showed his feet to be twenty-two inches long and seven inches wide, with four toes on each foot. Hunters reported feeling unsafe for quite some time thereafter and organized a hunting party to effect Bigfoot's capture.

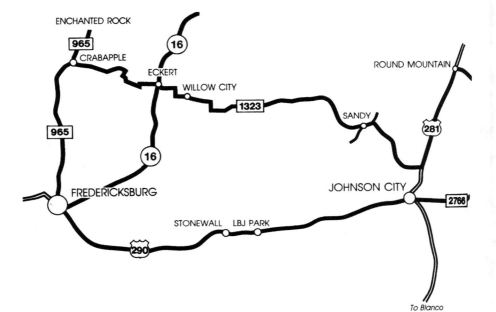

ENCHANTED ROCK

965

CRABAPPLE

16

ECKERT

WILLOW CITY

1323

ROUND MOUNTAIN

SANDY

281

965

16

FREDERICKSBURG

JOHNSON CITY

2766

STONEWALL   LBJ PARK

290

To Blanco

ENCHANTED ROCK

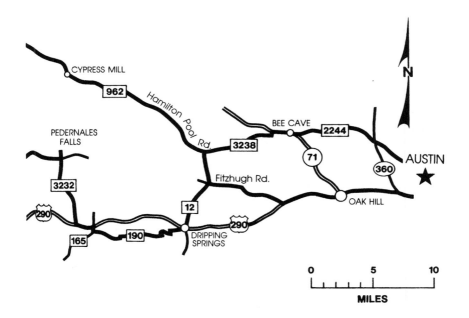

They were unsuccessful, and perhaps Bigfoot still lurks in the Bee Creek and Barton Creek valley.

Bee Caves Road twists and turns, up and down, offering an occasional glimpse of Lake Austin all the way to its junction with SH 71 at the village of Bee Cave.

BEE CAVE

Travis County • 2,200 (approximate) • About 12 miles from Austin

Bee Cave, or Bee Caves as it is sometimes called, was named for a large cave of wild bees found nearby. According to Jack Holly, who grew up there, the early settlers at Bee Cave stayed loyal to the Union during the Civil War, while the nearby hamlet of Snuff Box sided with the Confederacy. Located just east of Bee Cave, Snuff Box was also known as Brewton Springs School. The school closed in the late 1930s or early 1940s.

A post office opened at Bee Cave in 1870. By 1871, Will Johnson was operating a trading post. By 1885, the community had a steam gristmill, cotton gin, general store, church, school, and twenty residents. The population fell to ten in the early 1890s but rose to fifty-four by 1914. The post office closed in 1915, and Bee Cavers had to go to nearby Cedar Valley for their mail. The Bee Cave school closed in the 1940s. The population stayed pegged at about fifty through the 1980s, until Austin's relentless growth began to reach it. In 1990, the population had risen to 241. It had roughly sextupled by 2009.

Dietrich Bohls was one of the early settlers, and you pass a Bohls homestead on your right just before you come to the SH 71 intersection located on the grounds of a restaurant and next to the entrance of Bohls Ranch subdivision. Slow down if you wish to see the old rail fences and the several vintage rock and log buildings, since they are practically obscured by the newer development.

If you think Snuff Box is a funny name for a town, try these other Texas town names: Poverty Slant, Shake Rag, Gourd Neck, Frog Level, Flat Heel, Short Pone, Steal Easy, Po Boy.

Turn right onto SH 71.

The Trading Post, at the intersection of SH 71 and Bee Caves Road, was founded at the turn of the century by Will Johnson's son, Wiley, back when this intersection was just a crossing of two dirt wagon roads. Continue on SH 71, noting the beautifully preserved zigzag rail fence on your right across from the Trading Post, in front of Compass Bank.

The Baptist Church on SH 71 on your right still has its open-air arbor out back, which was used for revivals, church social functions, and in the summer when it was too hot to hold services inside the sanctuary.

Continue past the RM 620 turnoff for another couple of hundred yards; then turn left on Hamilton Pool Road (RM 3238).

Early settler Carl Beck set up shop at the old Hamilton Pool/Marble Falls crossroads in 1873. A lot of cotton was grown in the fertile Colorado River valley back then, and Beck soon built a gin, mill, and cigar factory at this crossroads. Beck produced a locally famous stogie using tobaccos imported from New Orleans. He also served as postmaster here for forty-five years. Two small stone buildings remain on what was his property.

Continue west on Hamilton Pool Road/RM 3238, past the turnoffs to Fitzhugh and Dripping Springs. At this point the road loses its state ranch-road status and narrows. Hamilton Pool Road also becomes much twistier and slightly rougher at this point.

MILTON REIMERS RANCH PARK

Hamilton Pool Rd. • About 13 miles from Bee Cave • 854-PARK (7275)

This pristine parkland, with almost three miles of continuous frontage along the Pedernales River, comprises 2,427 acres of parks and open space. Central Texas rock climbers consider Reimers Ranch to have world-class rock climbing. Local mountain bikers enjoy more than eighteen miles of trails. Local anglers have come to Reimers' for generations to fish for white bass in the river. The park's Pogue Springs Preserve/Hogge Reserve component is less known but equally spectacular, with Pedernales River frontage, deep canyons, and panoramic views of the Texas Hill Country.

HAMILTON POOL

Hamilton Pool Rd. • About 14.5 miles from Bee Cave • 264-2740

Hamilton Pool is named for a natural pool where a one-hundred-foot waterfall furnishes a constant supply of water. The area was first settled in the 1880s, and over the years Hamilton Pool has become a favorite swimming hole. It is now a Travis County park. User capacity is strictly limited to one hundred cars, so it's best to call ahead to check. Hamilton Pool, the stretch of the Pedernales River you are about to cross, West Cave, and the nearby Dead Man's and Dead Cow holes have been tourist destinations since at least the early 1880s.

Shortly past the Hamilton Pool turnoff, you will plunge into the Pedernales River valley. The road takes a hairpin course down and across the narrow one-lane low-water bridge, so take it easy and enjoy the scenery.

WESTCAVE PRESERVE

Hamilton Pool Rd. • About 15.5 miles from Bee Cave • 830-825-3442 • www.westcave.org • Open Saturday and Sunday; tours at 10, 12, 2, and 4 in good weather. Open weekdays by appointment only • Entrance to the Environmental Center is free; fee for guided canyon tours

As you climb out of the valley you pass the Westcave Preserve. This semitropical preserve includes a waterfall and collapsed grotto. The grotto was formed 150,000 or so years ago when falling water washed away enough sand and shale beneath a limestone cliff to make it collapse. The river canyon within the preserve grows a number of unusual plants—for the Hill Country—such as columbine and orchids. Two distinct ecosystems meet on the preserve. The nonprofit Westcave Preserve Corporation operates the preserve. Confirm tours by calling, or write Westcave Preserve, 24814 Hamilton Pool Road, Round Mountain, Texas 78663.

The Warren Skaaren Environmental Learning Center includes a sun aperture in the ceiling above the solar exhibit where sunlight is projected on the floor and crosses a meridian at local noontime each day. It functions as a visitor center and has classroom space for public and school programs. Integrated exhibits illustrate how the elements, forces, and cycles of nature have interacted to create and sustain the preserve and its plants and animals.

After you cross into Blanco County, Hamilton Pool Road resumes its state-maintained status as RM 962. RM 962 roughly parallels Cypress Creek through fertile bottomland, pastureland that once grew bales and bales of cotton.

CYPRESS MILL

Blanco County • About 50 • About 23 miles from Bee Cave

William Evans was the first settler and built the first water-powered mill in Blanco County on swift-flowing Cypress Creek. People came from miles and miles in all directions to have their corn ground and their timber sawed into rough though usable lumber. Life was good, for the creek flowed strong and there were many springs in the area. The abundance of cypress trees along the creek—the source of the creek's name is still obvious to the modern traveler—made for a bustling business at the mill. One fly in the ointment was Indians. Blanco County was a favored hunting ground, and they resented the white settlers' presence. They made their displeasure known by dozens of raids over the years, the most tragic of which occurred in 1869. Thomas Felps and his young wife Eliza were ambushed and killed by Comanches on July 21 at a spot along Cypress Creek. They were visiting her father's ranch at the time. Thomas was found unscalped; the superstitious Indians refused to take his redheaded scalp. Eliza was found some distance away savaged and scalped. Her discoverers speculated that the raiders had planned to take her away as a hostage, but Eliza had fought them so stubbornly that they decided to slay and scalp her and be done with it. The couple left two young children. They are buried in the scenic Miller Creek Cemetery located in between Miller Creek and US 290 between the intersection with US 281 and RM 3232.

The Indian attacks subsided in the 1870s, and the locals grew prosperous raising cotton, cattle, and sheep in these fertile bottomlands. But over the years, the once-plentiful springs dried up, and Cypress Creek no longer flowed with its former force. Rains no longer fell with the same frequency, and the land became barren. The cotton farmers left, and the land was given a chance to rest. It is now the almost exclusive domain of cattle and goats. All that remains now of Cypress Mill is the old schoolhouse, which most recently housed the post office and store. To reach it, take Spur 962 at the T in the road.

One evening in November 1882, as Julius Kellersburger was closing his store, two roughly dressed men rode up. One man entered, asking for some sardines and tobacco. He tendered a ten dollar bill in payment. Kellersburger noticed that the man had change and, feeling suspicious, declined to open his safe, telling the man he could not change the bill until morning. The man then thrust a pistol in Mr. K's face, saying, "So, you won't change it, eh?" Mr. K dodged and darted out the door in the direction of his house, hallooing to his wife for his gun, whereupon the pistolero ran to his horse, mounted, and then he and his partner galloped off into the night toward Austin. Mr. K fired a farewell shot with his gun and held on to the bill subject for demand.

Continue north on RM 962 through the fertile Cypress Creek valley toward Round Mountain.

ROUND MOUNTAIN

Blanco County • 120 (approximate) • About 7 miles from Cypress Mill

The Round Mountain community is named for nearby Round Mountain, about five miles northeast. Joseph Bird was the first settler, in 1854. Bird came here to the Cypress Fork of the Pedernales from Arkansas, buying a full league (640 acres) of land, on which he raised cattle. A Baptist minister, Bird organized the community's first church. The place was called Birdtown until the post office was established in 1871, when it took the name of the nearby hill.

MARTIN COMPLEX

426 RM 962 • Not open to the public

One of Round Mountain's biggest entrepreneurs in those early years was the widow Martin. She came here from Llano County after the death of her husband in 1869, and with the help of her children built a two-story hotel (the Birdtown Inn), with limestone extracted from a quarry located about a mile away on the old Marble Falls Road, and from cypress wood milled at Julius R. Kellersburger's Cypress Mill. An existing two-story rock building was converted into a livery stable. The hotel and livery stable still stand a little over one hundred yards to the east of the historical marker and are easily visible from both this place and RM 962. The hotel is now a private residence. The Martin clan next built a blacksmith shop and a general store. Mrs. Martin was appointed postmaster at Round Mountain in 1879 and served until 1896, operating the post office out of her store. Round Mountain was on the old stage-coach road west from Austin to Fredericksburg (you have been on it since turning onto Hamilton Pool Road), and Mrs. Martin did quite a business. She and son David established Blanco County's first telephone company. When the main road west shifted north, Round Mountain became a predominantly ranching community.

OLD ROUND MOUNTAIN SCHOOL AND CHURCH

RM 962 at Church Rd. • Not open to the public • Historical marker

Just before you get to the intersection with US 281, you will see on your left a simple stark white frame building with an equally utilitarian steeple. This structure served as community church and school for many years. The school was established in 1871 and had up to two hundred students at one time. Before Johnson City was founded in 1878, Round Mountain was the only town in the northern half of Blanco County and was larger than Johnson City when the county seat was moved to the latter town in 1891.

Turn left on US 281 toward Johnson City.

The land is gently rolling, wide-open, sparsely populated ranch country. As you approach Johnson City and the Pedernales, you'll see a wall of hills looming in the distance, the Great Divide that separates the watersheds of the Pedernales River to the north and the Blanco River to the south.

Eight and a half miles south of Round Mountain and just a long mile north of the Pedernales, turn right onto RM 1323.

SANDY

Blanco County • About 25 • About 15.5 miles from Round Mountain

The first settlement you come to is Sandy, named for the deep sandy soil. Never more than a ranching community, Sandy's only identifiable center today is the now-closed Sandy Store and post office.

Continue on RM 1323 from Sandy toward Willow City.

You are on the Texas Department of Transportation's Hill Country Trail. This is typical Hill Country ranching country, and houses are usually tucked away in the rolling hills well away from the road. One, just inside Gillespie County on your right, stands as a vintage limestone dwelling next to an aging windmill. Rectangular, one story, with cedar doors and window frames and severe, unadorned lines, this house was long abandoned but still stood strong, waiting for someone to come along and fill it with human warmth. Renovation had started in 2009. Cattle fill the pastures prominently, but even more evident are the flocks of sheep and the shaggy, curved-horn, unmistakably Angora goats. Mount Hudson looms large in front of you.

WILLOW CITY

Gillespie County • (830) • About 75 • About 17 miles from Sandy

Willow City was named by a group of Southern, Scotch/Irish-American families who, in the 1870s, settled in the valley of a creek bordered by button willows. The first school, a one-room log building with a dirt floor, was built in about 1879. It was also used as a church on Sundays; three denominations shared it on a rotating basis. The town soon had a blacksmith, druggist, mill, post office, and store. An early 1880s flood washed much of the town away. Folks rebuilt the town farther away from the creek, in its present location. Cotton became an important crop, and the gristmill became a cotton gin.

A two-story limestone school (located just west of Hohmann's General Store) was built in 1905 and served until 1961. It looks larger from the outside than it really is. Two classrooms are located on the first floor, with one large classroom upstairs that also served as an auditorium. The upstairs stage still sports its 1930s-era hand-painted curtain with advertisements from area merchants. Perhaps because of the community's Scotch-Irish/Southern settlers, discipline was a problem at the school. Pulling a knife at school was a common student offense, and at least once teachers had to wrestle a six-shooter away from a boy. Today, the Willow City Community Club gathers on the first Friday evening of each month to play "42" and socialize. Visitors are welcome.

HOHMANN'S GENERAL STORE

RM 1323 • Monday through Thursday 8–5, Friday 8–3, Saturday 8–2:30

Hohmann's is a typical Hill Country store, selling more ranch supplies than groceries; most folks just drive into Fredericksburg to shop, where food prices are cheaper. The store is usually full, though, mostly with good ol' boys in to pick up some feed, salt blocks, bob wire, and the like. Snake hunting—of the rattlesnake variety—is a favorite topic of conversation. There are a lot of rattlers in the rocks, and almost as many different ways of hunting them. Some guys lure them out of their rocky holes by pouring gasoline down the openings, while others use a mirror to reflect sunlight into their dens. There's a market for the hides, meat, bones, rattles, and heads. Cedar talk also fills the air. Cedar chopping is a major pastime. To kill cedar and keep it killed, you either have to strip off all the needles or cut the tree down at ground level; if even one leaf is left on the tree, it will resprout. And they swear that some days the cedar pollen is so dense out here that it looks like thick smoke boiling off the ground. A lot of mesquite is chopped here too, much of which goes to barbecue joints and smokehouses around the area.

Rain (or the lack of it) is also staple talk. Most of the talk is in "points"—Hohmann's may have recorded a spotty "10 or 15 points" (0.10 to 0.15 inches), while nearby Bell Mountain may have been deluged by "an inch and thirty" (1.3 inches). But bring up the subject of bluebonnets and you're likely to get some harrumphs and raised eyebrows. "I wouldn't want to live in a pasture of them. You know what they smell like? I can stand it about five minutes and then I want to mow 'em down. Old so-and-so's house sits in a pasture full of bluebonnets, and he'd just as soon burn them up as smell 'em any longer—but the state law won't let him," is the way one fellow put it. For those of you who don't know, the odor of a bluebonnet changes on a day-by-day basis, starting with a delicate almost indistinguishable scent and ending with a heavy, sickeningly sweet smell like shoe polish.

As the name Hohmann implies, German settlers soon began supplanting the original Scotch/Irish settlers. By 1898, Willow City was noted for its many camp meetings, and its German population ensured a good time.

Like so many other locales in the Llano Uplift, Willow City was once touted for its potential mineral wealth, to the point that it had its own newspaper, the *Willow City Miner*, by 1888. It declared that in and around Willow City could be found "some of as fine mineral lands as can be found in the world; the magnetic ore is to be found in large quantities; also there is to be found here good specimens of silver, lead, gold and asbestos. Also an abundance of granite, some four or five different kinds; soapstone, marble, limestone and stone coal."

By April 1891, prospecting for gold and silver was all the rage around Fredericksburg, and a rich find had been reported at Willow City. But this was all flash in the pan, as had been the case in so many other places throughout the Llano Uplift. But Willow City is not without its riches; you are about to experience one of the greatest treasures the Hill Country has to offer: the Willow City Loop.

WILLOW CITY LOOP

Backtrack from Hohmann's Store and the schoolhouse a few hundred feet east on RM 1323 to the ninety-degree turn you took to get to the store. Here at this T intersection you see a sign reading "Willow City Loop." Turn left here to drive one of the most wildly beautiful roads in Texas. If Willow City Loop is impassable due to high water, continue on RM 1323 from Willow City west 2.7 miles to RM 1323's intersection with SH 16 at Eckert. RM 1323 ends here. Turn right on SH 16, then in several feet turn left onto Eckert Road, marked by "To Crabapple" and "Rabke's" signs.

You ridge run the first few miles out of Willow City, and then suddenly you dive-bomb down into the brakes of Coal Creek where great gray and pink granite boulders lay tossed about the countryside. This is known as Hell's Half-Acre, the Devil's Kitchen, or the Dungeon: a great trough-like depression where stars fell many centuries ago, leaving many smooth meteoric stones. The brush is almost impenetrable and was a favorite hiding place for raiding Indians and Civil War bushwhackers. The narrow road twists through the Coal Creek valley, crossing the creek several times in the shadows of the hundreds-of-feet-high, sheer northern and eastern cliffs of Coal Creek. In the spring this valley is awash in miles and square miles of bluebonnets, which flood the bottomlands and rise high up the inclines of Cedar Mountain, where the blooming yuccas stand guard.

Cedar Mountain is the only hill in the Hill Country to have merited its own poem, "The Ballad of Cedar Mountain," by Carlos Ashley.

> Did you ever hear the story
> Of that famous hog of mine?
> She's a razor back and spotted,
> Black and white from hoof to spine.
>
> With a snout made outta granite,
> She can root just like a plow,
> And the fence ain't been invented
> That can turn that spotted sow.
>
> Born and bred on Cedar Mountain,
> She is wilder than a deer,
> And she's known by reputation
> To the ranch hands far and near.
>
> Though a sow of mine had raised her,
> On that mountain she was free,
> And I always kinda doubted
> That she really belonged to me.
>
> She might be picking acorns
> On the banks of Sandy Creek;
> Or in somebody's turnips
> Cultivating, so to speak;
>
> But let the foot of dog or man
> Disturb the morning dew,
> And you might as well a-phoned her,
> Cause somehow she always knew.
>
> She'd light out for Cedar Mountain,
> Where the land and sky divide
> There ain't no spot on earth nowhere
> A better place to hide.

Well, the Fall froze into Winter,
And the Winter thawed to Spring.
April watered hill and valley,
Maytime painted everything.

Late one evening just at sundown
I was riding home right slow,
When I passed a lonesome waterhole
And saw—it was a show!

Ole Spot was trailing down the hill
And right behind her trotted
Ten baby pigs not ten days old,
And everyone was spotted.

I stopped and stared; she studied me;
My eyes filled like a fountain;
And there I gave Ole Spot a deed—
A deed to Cedar Mountain.

She's still on Cedar Mountain—
Though I seldom see her now,
You can bet that's one dominion
Where the queen's a spotted sow.

Carlos Ashley—lawyer, rancher, and cowboy poet—was born and reared in San Saba County. His maternal grandparents, R. W. and Susan Gray, had settled on Cherokee Creek in San Saba County in 1860. His parents came to San Saba County in 1870. His father, Alf Ashley, became a well-known rancher and hog producer.

Carlos went to Fort Worth for four years of college at Texas Christian University where he was president of the student body, sports editor of the university paper, and lettered in baseball. And he won the coveted Bryson Poetry Prize. But when he graduated from TCU in 1926, he returned home as fast as he could.

Carlos Ashley was a high school physical education teacher and coach for three years before he went back to college and got his law degree. He practiced law in Llano for many years. All the while, he engaged in his real love—ranching and writing poetry. He wrote two books, *Front Seat in Heaven* (about his family and his life) and *That Spotted Sow and Other Texas Hill Country Ballads* (first published in 1941 and revised in 1975).

Carlos Ashley was the district attorney in District Thirty-three from 1935 to 1944 and from 1961 to 1968. He held the title of poet laureate of Texas from 1949 to 1950. And he was the first assistant attorney general of Texas in 1944. He was a Texas state senator for ten years.

"That Spotted Sow, or The Ballad of Cedar Mountain," is his most famous poem. Another one of my favorites is called "The Cedar Whack."

The North Wind howls like a timber wolf
As it snaps at the flapping door
On the duckin shack of the cedar-whack
And his kids on the damp dirt floor.

A hardy man is the cedar-whack—
No part of the artful faker—
He clears the lands with his leather hands
For sixty cents an acre.

The rain and snow and the blazin sun
All lash at his hungry frame,
As he whacks away at the brush all day
In Winter and Summer the same.

He wields his ax with the skillful wrists
Of a sculptor carvin' wood;
Now new grass frills on a thousand hills
Where the cedar brake once stood.

He sorts and stacks the posts and staves,
Then hauls them to the yard
In his Model-T where he sells them to me
For his beans and a can of lard.

Eight miles from Hohmann's Store, you'll pass the entrance to Texas' only serpentine quarry, at the foot of Cedar Mountain. Although relatively soft, Texas serpentine takes a beautiful, lustrous polish. It is widely used for terrazzo floors, decorative objects, and as wainscot in office buildings and hotel lobbies. While there are many deposits, the largest outcropping is here. The Coal Creek serpentine mass is over 3.5 miles long and 1.5 miles at its widest point. It extends over into Blanco County. The importance folks out here attach to rain is best summed up by this sign that used to be along the loop: "K and L Ranch, where a good rain and a baby calf are always welcome." This is all private property, so don't trespass. The Willow City Loop is a very popular springtime weekend "drive," so be prepared for traffic on Saturdays and Sundays during bluebonnet season. Better yet, go on a weekday.

Cattle wander at random along many of this road's thirteen miles, so you must keep your speed down. In the fall you must also contend with dozens of deer, which cross your path every half mile or so during the late afternoon. After you've turned west, things calm down a bit and you are out of the Dungeon and into more gently contoured pastureland.

Turn left when you reach SH 16 in about fourteen miles. In three miles you pass between Mount Nebo on your right and Bell Mountain on your left. Soon you come to Eckert.

ECKERT

Gillespie County • (830) • About 20 miles from Willow City

Eckert was named for W. R. Eckert, in whose store the post office was established in 1900. Previously the settlement had been known as Nebo, after the mountain. The original Mount Nebo is the summit of Mount Pisgah, a mountain ridge in ancient Palestine from which Moses viewed the Promised Land. Nebo dated to 1875 when eight Anglo families built a log church named Mount Zion, around which they settled. Not much is left here these days, except for the vacant rock store and a couple of old farmhouses.

Turn right on Eckert Road, which is the small road to the right and which is also marked by a sign reading "Rabke's: 4 miles." In four miles, you cross Riley Creek and come to Rabke's Table Ready Meats.

RABKE'S TABLE READY MEATS

Crabapple Rd., 4 miles from Eckert • 830-685-3266 • No Cr. • W with assistance

Sandwiched between Crabapple Road's crossings of Riley and Crabapple creeks is Rabke's, home of some of Texas' best beef jerky and other smoked meats. Leroy and Geneva Rabke started the business about sixty years ago. Leroy's ancestors bought this place, four hundred acres along Crabapple Creek, in 1880. The barn was built before 1850, and there is another, smaller log-and-rock building from that era. Rabke's processes deer for hunters and offers a variety of excellent and reasonably priced meats, such as turkey sausage and breast rolls, whole turkeys, hams, beef brisket, bacon, beef and pork sausage, turkey jerky, and beef jerky, all slow smoked over mesquite and hickory fires. Leroy and Geneva have both passed on, and son Stanley now runs the business. Rabke's also makes and sells homemade pear relish, bread-and-butter pickles, and plum, wild grape, and agarita jellies, all made from fruits and vegetables grown in their garden or picked from the fields. Write PO Box 17, Willow City 78675.

From Rabke's proceed west to Crabapple community after paralleling scenic Crabapple Creek for several miles. Cattle wander at will across this pencil-thin road, so take it easy. Less than a mile west of Rabke's you will come to a T intersection. Turn right onto "Lower Crabapple Road."

CRABAPPLE COMMUNITY

Gillespie County • About 4 miles from Rabke's

This settlement along fertile Crabapple Creek began to grow almost as soon as Fredericksburg got its feet firmly planted on the ground. Both New Braunfels and Fredericksburg initially were laid out according to the traditional German farm village plan, where early settlers were granted town lots of about a half acre in size, and outlying farms of ten acres. It was assumed that the immigrants would locate their houses, barns, and other homestead structures on their town lots and then go out to work in their nearby ten-acre fields each day. The farm village plan was a failure in both places from the beginning. Large numbers of cattle and unwise prairie burning quickly exhausted the supply of natural forage nearby, so the settlers began to fan out in search of better grazing lands. The dispersal from town was further aided by cheap land prices. So the Germans fanned out from Fredericksburg, making their homes in the fertile stream valleys scattered throughout the Hill Country.

Heinrich Grobe was one of these expansionists. He moved his family from the New Braunfels area to the Crabapple Creek bottomlands in 1857. Life was good to the Grobes during their first five years at Crabapple. But on the morning of April 4, 1862, Heinrich Grobe went out to work on a rock fence. His older sons did the morning chores at home and went to help their father. As they approached his place of work, the boys spotted their father's body in a bush, stripped of all raiment save his shoes, eleven arrows buried in his chest. The boys ran home to get mother, and together they wrapped father's body in linen and dragged him home on a sled, for the Indians had stolen all their horses. A neighbor took poor Mr. Grobe to Fredericksburg for burial. "Widder"

Grobe persevered here several more years before moving to the comparative safety of Rheingold community, which was more densely populated and less prone to Indian raids. But her neighbors stayed on, and Crabapple grew.

CRABAPPLE COMMUNITY BUILDINGS

Feel free to roam the grounds, but all the buildings are locked.

Today Crabapple community is one of the nicest collections of unaltered limestone buildings to be found in the Hill Country, kept neat as a pin. The centerpiece of the collection is St. John's Lutheran Church. Built in 1897—the date is prominently inscribed in a date stone above the front door—the sanctuary is a cleanly constructed, high-gabled rectangular box. A tin steeple with a weathervane crowns St. John's. The Germans who settled the area were practical above all else; the church steeple is the neighborhood's tallest and therefore most visible manmade point, so where else would you put the weathervane?

Scattered across the community-center grounds are the limestone schoolhouse, featuring equally simple lines, and the old teacherage, of similar design with a shed attached to it, covered with pressed tin in the design of large limestone blocks. In your Central Texas travels, you will be amazed at the diversity in patterned-tin designs that you will see; several different types are found here at Crabapple alone. You may hear wild turkeys in the distance, too.

The Crabapple school dates to January 1877. Neighborhood families were so eager to have a school that a footrace decided the question of who would donate the schoolhouse land. Mathias Schmidt outran Crockett Riley for the privilege. Construction immediately began on the school, located in the house next to the current schoolhouse. It was originally two rooms, one for instruction and one for the teacher's living quarters. School opened on January 5, 1878, and Mathias Schmidt died four days later on January 9, having seen his dream of a school come true.

As enrollment grew, a larger building was needed, and so in 1882 the present school was built for $600. After this, the original school served as the teacherage and as the Crabapple post office from 1887 to 1910. At this time the school enjoyed its highest enrollment, around forty pupils. The second schoolhouse doubled as a church building until the present St. John's sanctuary was built. Inside, the school is one of the best-furnished examples of a rural, one-room school remaining in the Hill Country, down to the old student desks and picture of Abraham Lincoln hanging above the original blackboard. The school closed in 1957 due to declining enrollment.

The whitewashed wood-frame hall attached to the schoolhouse was built during the 1920s and is still used on a monthly basis by the Crabapple Community Club as well as for wedding receptions and family reunions. The 1882 school also serves as neighborhood polling place at elections. The community club normally meets in the hall on the first Friday of each month to play dominoes and cards, and to chat. Visitors are welcome. While St. John is no longer an active congregation (worship services were discontinued in 1962), the church is still a popular wedding locale. The St. John Lutheran Community Association holds a homecoming celebration on the fourth Sunday of September each year; visitors are welcome.

Continue west on Crabapple Road a few hundred yards to the point where the road divides into two forks. Either fork takes you to RM 965, but if you take the low road, you get to cross Crabapple Creek twice. Turn right on RM 965.

WELGEHAUSEN RANCH

Crabapple Rd. at RM 965 • Not open to the public

Just after you cross the creek, you will see on your left another great collection of vintage log and stone buildings. This is the old Welgehausen homestead. Frederick Welgehausen came here in 1856, back when Crabapple Creek was on the very edge of the western frontier. Welgehausen's first log cabin still stands slightly east of the main residence, restored for use as a guesthouse.

The main house, a large two-story limestone structure in the center of the group, also began life as a simple one-room log cabin with an outside stairway to the loft. Over the years, as the family grew, rooms were added downstairs, and gradually the little cabin became the core of a larger limestone one-story house. Finally the second story was added, and this expansion is very obvious in the different-sized rocks used. There are many other similarly evolved houses throughout the country, dwellings that had their start nearly a century and a half ago as rude cabins. Sometimes the owners are not even aware of this history until they decide to do some interior work and stumble upon the old log walls, long covered with plaster. Several other restored log cabins and ranch buildings are scattered across the ranch. Welgehausen family members are buried in the cemetery just north and west of the ranch.

Continue north on FM 965 toward Enchanted Rock. In a scant couple of miles, as you top a hill and turn a corner at its summit, the Enchanted Rock formation unfolds before you.

"Awesome" is the only adequate word to describe this great bald knob and its smaller companions.

Fredericksburgers realized the tourism possibilities of "this freak of nature," as they called it, as early as the summer of 1921, when the chamber of commerce, citizens, and ranchers living along the way pitched in to improve the road there from Fredericksburg, making it more accessible to thousands of predicted tourists. The farmers and ranchers along the road contributed the mule teams and plows, while eighty volunteers were assigned to work on different parts of the road. In one day they improved the road to the point that the (then) twenty-mile trip from Fredericksburg could be made in ninety minutes.

ENCHANTED ROCK

16710 Ranch Rd 965; About 18 miles north of Fredericksburg on FM 965, about 7 miles from Crabapple Community • 830-685-3636 • Open daily • Fee • W variable

Enchanted Rock State Natural Area, which contains Enchanted Rock, consists of 1,643.5 acres on Big Sandy Creek north of Fredericksburg on the border between Gillespie and Llano counties. Humans have been coming to marvel at the rock for over eleven thousand years.

Legends surround the rock like a fog. Tonkawa Indians believed that ghost fires flickered at the top, and they heard weird creaking and groaning, which geologists now say results from the rock's heating by day and contracting in the cool night. A Spanish conquistador captured by Tonkawas escaped by losing himself in the rock area, giving rise to an Indian legend of a "pale man swallowed by a rock and reborn as one of their own." The Indians believed that he wove enchantments on the area, but the Spaniard explained that the rock wove the spells. "When I was swallowed by the rock, I joined the many spirits who enchant this place." The first well-documented explorations of this area began in 1723 when the Spanish intensified their efforts to colonize Texas. During the mid-1700s, the Spaniards made several trips to the north and northwest of San Antonio, establishing a mission and presidio on the San Saba River and carrying out limited mining on Honey Creek near the Llano River.

Writing in 1834, W. B. Dewees described "a large rock of metal which has for many years been considered a wonder. It is supposed to be platinum. The Indians have held it sacred for centuries, and go there once a year to worship it. They will not permit any white person to approach it. It is almost impossible to make any impression on it with chisel and hammers. When struck it gives forth a ringing sound which can be heard miles around. The party was successful in finding the rock, but were unable to break off any specimens to bring home."

Some legends state that Indians, Comanches in particular, came here once a year to hold their sacred rites at the summit. But many more stories tell how the Indians held the rock in fearful veneration, refusing to venture much farther up it than the rocky, broken base. They believed it to be haunted, for a variety of reasons, but on occasion some of them evidently used one cave whose entrance is on top of the rock and whose exit is far below on the backside of the rock.

One tale tells of a few brave warriors, the last of a tribe now long extinct, who defended themselves here from the attacks of their enemies for many years, until they were finally annihilated. From that time Indians looked upon the rock as the exclusive haunt of the phantom warriors. Others say that a tribal chief sacrificed his daughter on one of the boulders to please the gods. The gods became angry at the sacrifice, struck the chief down, and forced his spirit to walk the rock forever. The depressions you see dotting the rock at its summit are his footprints.

Local historian Julia Estill wrote of Enchanted Rock:

At night spirit fires dance on the summit, and by day millions of isinglass stars glint in the sunlight. During an early morning shower in the hills, when the sun shines out from under the passing cloud, the streams of water coursing down the sides of the boulder resemble sheets of molten silver. Then above the gigantic dome there forms a rainbow path which will lead the seeker directly to a mine of gold, so the old legend goes. In fact the sands of the sluggish stream winding lazily around the base of the rock testify of gold in the vicinity. And the oldest pioneer in the neighborhood will tell you that there is a lost mine somewhere near the rock, the shaft having been sunk by Spaniards in the eighteenth century.

In earlier years it was said that a basin on the top of the dome filled with water and trickled down the sides of the mountain. On moonlight nights this gave the mountain a ghostly appearance, and hence the Indians called the place the Enchanted Rock.

The Indians were further convinced of the rock's spirit infestation by the strange creaking noises you hear on cool nights following hot days. The Comanches are said to have regularly offered human sacrifices in the boulder yards at the base of the rock in order to appease these powerful spirits and win favor for their raids. According to a story told by a Reverend Hoermann, a missionary at the San Antonio missions, some of the Indians at the Mission of San Jose were absent one night, and the Comanche chief Tehuan saw therein a grave omen. He had an interview with Don Jose Navarro, commander of the Spanish troops stationed at the mission, communicating to him his fears in regard to an attack by the Indian renegades. Navarro began preparations of the defense. While the preparations were in progress Don Jesu Navarro arrived from Spain. Tehuan's daughter, who had been baptized and given the name Rose, lived at Comandante Navarro's home. While the preparations for the defense were going on, Don Jesu made love to Rosa, and when the attack finally came, the young people were very much in love. After great slaughter, the Indians gained entrance to the mission, killing all inhabitants except Rosa and another Indian woman, whom they took with them to sacrifice to the spirits at the Enchanted Rock.

Don Jesu Navarro had been among those who had gone out of the mission to drive the attacking Indians from the stockade and had been knocked unconscious by a tomahawk blow during the mission attack. When he awoke, he staggered back into the mission to find all the inmates murdered, and he was distraught to find his beloved gone. From an Indian boy, he learned that she was on her way to her imminent death at the Holy Rock.

Realizing that single handedly he could not save her, Don Jesu rushed to Goliad for aid and recruited an impetuous band of Spaniards and colonists, whom he paid with valuables that escaped the loot of the Indians at the mission. They pursued the raiders to their camp in the Guadalupe. Don Jesu proposed to attack immediately, but his companions persuaded him to wait until dark so as to play on the Comanches' superstitious beliefs. So that night the rescue party surreptitiously harassed the Indians by stampeding their horses and assaulting their guards. Believing the gods to be incensed with their recent raid, the Comanches found their horses and galloped off with their hostage to the rock, even more determined to appease the spirits with their sacrifice.

Don Jesu and company followed as best they could and reached the rock only to find Rosa already bound to a sapling in the ravine between Enchanted Rock and the peak to the right, faggots piled high around her. The rescuers divided into two parties, one group skirting the peak so as to surprise the Indian camp from the north, while Don Jesu and the rest rushed the guards stationed in the sacrificial gulch from the south. Driven to frenzy by the sight of his beloved about to be immolated, Don Jesu fought like a demon, killing the Indian guards, and managed to rescue Rosa, with whom he fled south, eventually falling in with an expedition from Mexico. He and Rosa settled on the Medina River, where those of his few companions who had escaped in the fight at the Enchanted Rock visited him often.

Enough of legend. Enchanted Rock has been a state natural area since 1978 and a popular recreational spot for many more decades. In addition to Enchanted Rock, it includes the smaller formations known as Little Rock, Turkey Peak, Freshman Mountain, Flag Pole, and Buzzard's Roost. Sandy and Walnut Springs creeks flow through it. The "inselberg" (island mountain) we call Enchanted Rock is just one small exposed (albeit the most famous) part of the Enchanted Rock batholith, which covers about one hundred square miles. Other outcroppings, which rise as high as 1,800 feet above sea level, occur throughout the area.

The batholith is a gigantic mass of molten rock, or magma, which intruded the earth's crust and cooled below the surface millions of years ago. This batholith, as such large igneous rock structures are called, did not initially erupt through the earth's surface, but it did create a "bump" about seventy miles across and one thousand feet high. This molten rock cooled and became the pink and gray granite that we see throughout the uplift. Through millions of years of erosion, this granite bedrock was exposed. The exposed granite then began to erode, and the granite knobs, of which Enchanted Rock is the largest, were formed throughout the uplift. A process called exfoliation, caused by the development of joints or fractures parallel to the rock surface, produced the smooth, rounded onionlike shape of Enchanted Rock. Huge sheets of rock break away (exfoliate) from the main dome along these curved joints and start inching down toward the base. Its granite is too coarse for commercial quarrying, which has saved it from the fate that has befallen other domes such as Bear Mountain and Granite Mountain.

From a distance, the rock appears barren and devoid of plant life. But once you've started the mile-long climb to the summit, you'll be surprised at the amount of life that Enchanted Rock supports. Gnarled, wind-twisted oaks grow alone and in little island forests. Lichens of varying shades of orange, red, black, yellow, gray, and green mottle the granite; they are the shock troops of the erosion process. Dozens of little seasonal pond, marsh, and prairie ecosystems dot the rock, hosting a variety of grasses, cacti, wildflowers, water bugs, lizards, and the like. Weathering has produced a variety of features, including small circular depressions with raised rims (called rock doughnuts) and shallow depressions up to fifty feet in length (called gnammas, or weather pits). Many of these depressions function as temporary rain collectors called vernal pools. As repeated rains dissolve the rock, and soil begins to develop, pools that were once devoid of life begin to support algae, quillwort, and fairy shrimp. As more soil accumulates, annual and perennial herbs take over these depressions. Finally grasses take root, and soil islands form, which support larger animal life and trees.

The four major plant communities of Enchanted Rock are open oak woodland, mesquite grassland, floodplain, and granite rock community. Live oak, post oak, and blackjack oak dominate the oak woodland, with black hickory in moister areas. Texas persimmon, agarita, white brush, and prickly pear are common shrubs. Bluestem, three-awn, and grama grass grow in the shade of the oaks. American tripogon is common on gravelly slopes that are seasonally wet. The mesquite grassland, once an area of bluestem grass, is now covered with three-awn, grama, Texas wintergrass, panicum, and sandbur, along with invading mesquite. Elm, pecan, hackberry, black hickory, soapberry, and oak grow in the floodplains. White buckeye, agarita, Texas persimmon, Roosevelt weed, and buttonbush are commonly found shrubs. Grasses and sedges, as well as annual and perennial herbs, form the ground cover. Some of these are water bentgrass, late eupatorium, Indiangrass, bushybeard bluestem, frost weed, and switchgrass. In the spring, bluebonnets, Indian paintbrush, yellow coreopsis, bladderpod, and basin bellflower bloom.

Rock and fox squirrels are common, as are armadillos and rabbits, lizards, turkey vultures, and white-tailed deer. The park's birdlife is varied and abundant. Ask and you will receive a bird checklist for the park.

The various rock formations are favorite hangouts for serious rock climbers and recreational hikers. Visitor activities include primitive backpacking, camping, hiking, technical and rock climbing, picnicking, geological study, bird-watching, and stargazing (minimal light pollution). Do not disturb plant or animal life, geological features, or Indian or historical artifacts. These park resources are protected by law. Bring your own firewood. Rock climbers must check in at headquarters; route maps and climbing rules are available.

A four-mile trail winds around the granite formations, and a short, steep trail leads to the top of Enchanted Rock. Park occupancy is limited to minimize park deterioration from overuse; it is wise to call ahead. Parking along FM 965 is now prohibited. The park is busy year-round, especially during spring, fall, and winter.

Near the summit is a state historical marker commemorating Jack Hays' victory over a band of Comanches in 1841. Hays was heading up a surveying party that fall. Their work took them to the Indians' sacred rock. Hays and company had two strikes against them from the beginning, in the Indians' eyes. They were violating the sanctuary of the sacred rock, and they were surveyors. Indians hated the white surveyors, for they believed the white man's compass was the device that stole their land. Off on his own one day, Hays was surprised by three Comanches. He fled toward a rendezvous point prearranged with his men, pursued by a growing number of Comanches. Hays arrived at the point alone; his men were already fighting for their lives with another band of Indians. He sought refuge atop Enchanted Rock, where, heavily armed and well protected, he managed to repulse his tormentors, killing their war party chief in the process.

This was just the first time that Jack Hays found himself in a pinch and managed to get out alive. During the Mexican American War, Hays' regiment was trapped during the battle of Palo Alto. Whereupon Hays is supposed to have prayed: "Oh Lord, we are about to join battle with vastly superior numbers of the enemy, and, Heavenly Father we would mighty like for you to be on our side and help us. But if you can't do it, for Christ's sake don't go over to the Mexicans, but just lie low and keep in the dark, and You will see one of the dangdest fights you've ever seen." Instead of ending his prayer with "Amen," Hays yelled, "Charge!" His men charged and lost only three men dead and four wounded.

From the summit you can look to the north and gaze out upon a vast expanse of the Hill Country, which looks almost the same as it did in Hays' day. The entrance to Enchanted Rock Cave is near the summit, down the north slope a little ways. One of the largest known granite caves, it goes for about one thousand feet. It developed under talus blocks along a sheeting joint—that is, debris comprised of house-size chunks of exfoliated granite slid down and lodged against a raised joint below and, after centuries of settling, a "cave" evolved. Smaller structures called A-tent caves have also been formed at various places on the Rock by sections of exfoliated sheets.

The rock was a tourist attraction for Anglo Texans even back in the 1850s, and in 1860, Joe Walker's curiosity cost him his life. He and his wife Annie, living in the newly minted town of Llano some twenty-three miles to the north, had heard of the wondrous knob and were determined to see it. Riding to nearby Legion Valley, where they spent the night with friends, the Walkers started early the next morning to the Rock. Within a couple of miles from their destination, they encountered half a dozen Indians on horseback. The Walkers made a run for it, but the Indians caught up and surrounded the pair, shooting hundreds of arrows at them almost as fast as you can snap your fingers. But the arrows had little effect, for the hard wind blowing that cold Sabbath day made them flutter and fall short of their mark.

But one of the Indians had a gun and shot Mr. Walker, wounding him in the back. Killing one Indian, Walker held them off with his six-gun for over half an hour until their arrows were exhausted. Then one came walking toward the Walkers with a gun. He stopped at a tree with a waist-high fork in its trunk, placed the rifle in the fork, and took careful aim at the wounded Walker. Mrs. Walker later related:

> My poor husband laid his pistol on the ground and put his cold, trembling arms around my shoulders and said, "Kiss me goodbye dear wife, may God protect you now, for I must go." I could not cry, nor sob, but kissed him and then took the pistol and put its muzzle to my heart. "Oh, Annie what are you going to do?" he asked. I told him that I intended to go with him in case he was killed, as he had told me the savages would carry me off if they could kill him, and I did not want to go with his murderers. "Oh my brave and true little Annie," exclaimed he, "Please do not commit such a deed. Oh God stay her hand that she may not take her own life." During this time, which was only a few seconds, everything else was perfectly quiet. What caused that Indian not to shoot is more than I can tell.
>
> "I had held my breath until I was all in a tremble. As he did not shoot I arose, laid the pistol on the ground, and went toward him. I went within a few yards of the savage, could see his dark clear eyes and into the muzzle of his gun, I then threw up my hands and cried out loud, "O gracious God of Heaven have mercy and protect a poor helpless woman." I begged the hostile Indian to please spare my poor husband, that he was already deadly wounded and to please not shoot him in my presence. He took down his gun; stood it against the tree. After pleading until I sank to the ground almost lifeless, my head went up but saying nothing, they all went back to their horses. They layed the dead man across one horse, the others mounted their horse and led our poor bleeding animals away, disappearing over the hill.

Annie returned to her weakening husband, who told her to leave him and try to save herself, that she would find a house about a mile away, and if anyone was home she could get help. Reluctantly agreeing with him, Annie found a thick cluster of bushes by the cliff of a rock where he could hide and be protected from the drizzling rain that had begun to fall.

> He begged me to leave him there, but I said "No." He put his arms around my shoulders and I carried him twenty steps at a time until he was on the spot. Giving him the pistol and taking his quirt and bidding him a loving farewell, I left him without water, help or doctor and almost no bed. It was after three o'clock and I started on a run, asking God to protect him. Hearing him crying aloud, I stopped a moment and heard him say, "Oh, my God, how can I bear to see her go?"
>
> I dashed off again like mad through the thorny brush, tearing my flesh and clothes in numberless places. I soon reached the house but not a soul was there. (Mr. Walker heard me hallooing and thought the Indians had caught me.) So on I ran. There were a great many cattle near the road. They scented the blood on my dress and followed me in droves, bellowing, screaming and fighting. Often I had

to strike them with the quirt to make them give the road: after running a long time I came to a creek which must be crossed. It was waist deep and my clothes were so wet and heavy that it made running very difficult. I broke loose my clothes and dropped them in the road. My shoes becoming untied were also dropped. Travelling was easier for awhile, but soon my feet began to hurt for they had been cut on sharp stones. Nothing could stop me however.

Just before dark I reached a deep creek on the other bank of which stood the house where help was certain. Oh how glad I was. I hallooed again and again, the answer that came was the barking of a pack of fierce dogs, that ran down to the crossing. What could be done? I found a long pole with which to steady myself in the water, crossed over, the dogs did not even growl at me. I reached the house, pushed open the door, but found nobody at home. Tired and weak I sank upon a chair. Darkness was fast approaching, and it was three miles to the next house where lived Mr. Walker's sister. A little after dark I reached the house and found help, and told what had happened and where.

The neighborhood was soon wild with excitement, and a party was organized to search for my poor husband. I wanted to go along but they forbade me, saying they knew the spot better than I. They reached the place by two o'clock, but as they had no idea of finding him alive, search was deferred till daylight. Then they started out in different directions. Tom Cox, one of the party called out "Oh, Joe." Immediately he answered, "Here I am Tom!"

He was sitting up against the tree. He shook hands with them, and asked "Is Annie safe?"

"Yes."

"Thanks be to God. He has answered my prayers. Now lay me down and let me die."

They brought him home alive, but he died that day before sunset.

We buried him in a pretty green valley where the long green mesquite grass would wave over his grave.

A correspondent for the *San Antonio Herald*, in the fall of 1876, dismissed the Enchanted Valley that we find so beautiful today as

one rough mass of great piles of granite rocks. Now and then can be found a few acres of tillable soil in the open glades between the rough craggy mountains. But there is an immense amount of wasteland scattered promiscuously through the southern section of Llano County, and it is neither fit for cultivation nor grazing purposes. The Maverick estate own most of the desirable land in the neighborhood of Enchanted Rock and Watch Mountains, while the balance is principally "State" or "railroad" lands. The ranchmen in this county know three classes of land. The first is land fit for cultivation, and is known as farming land. The second class is rough land, worth something perhaps, but not much, for grazing purposes, and for the timber that is upon it. This they call State land, while the third class is that great pile of granite found all through the southern portion of the county, and this they call railroad land. It is enough for me to say that nearly the whole of Llano County over which we have roamed so far is railroad land and good for nothing under the sun so far as heard from.

There was at one time a scheme to create a Texas Rushmore here by carving the faces of famous Texans in the rock.

Owner Tate Moss opened Enchanted Rock to picnickers and hikers in 1927, and it was immediately popular with tourists. On June 22, 1929, Governor Dan Moody was in attendance here to proclaim Enchanted Rock "Texas's most wonderful summer resort." That day, another man drove his new Pontiac automobile to the summit. Moss's grandson Charles later owned the rock. It was acquired by warranty deed in 1978 by the Nature Conservancy of Texas Inc., from the Moss family. The state acquired it in 1984, added facilities, and reopened the park in March 1984. Enchanted Rock was designated a National Natural Landmark in 1970 and was placed on the National Register of Historic Places in 1984.

From Enchanted Rock park headquarters, head back south to Fredericksburg on FM 965.

As you speed comfortably along the road today, enjoying the scenery, be thankful for the fruits of progress we enjoy today. Back in 1877, the journey north on FM 965 past Enchanted Rock and on to Llano on what is now SH 16 was a veritable ordeal:

> From Fredericksburg to Llano forty miles of roughest road had to be traveled that an ambulance, wagon, or coach ever rolled over without an accident. The many mountains seemed one solid boulder of rock. The rocks alternated with sand in the valleys, which is more disagreeable and difficult to pull through, especially mid-day, when the sun is fiercest and the breeze cut off by the high hills on every side. Passing through the coarse granite hills and sandy valleys that extend far from Fredericksburg into the county of Llano, it was quite a relief to the eye and refreshing to the mind to behold the beautiful rolling mesquite lands that extend for miles around Llano and far up the Llano River, even to its source.

As you continue south on FM 965 toward Fredericksburg, you come to Bear Mountain, located on the east side of FM 965.

BEAR MOUNTAIN

FM 965 • About 14 miles south of Enchanted Rock

Bear Mountain is another of the Llano Uplift's granite hills, and home of the Bear Mountain Quarry, famous for its red granite. Many buildings in Fredericksburg and the surrounding Hill Country are built with stone from the prize-winning Bear Mountain Quarry. Bear Mountain is not marked as such, but as you pass by you'll recognize it from the tall masts and guy wires on your left, part of the hoisting apparatus for the huge stone blocks, some of which litter the hill's slopes. There's also a roadside park alongside Bear Mountain. Up until 1986, you could park here and hike up Bear Mountain to see one of the area's natural wonders, Balanced Rock, a large granite boulder delicately balanced on three strategic points in a manner seemingly defiant of the basic laws of gravity. That year, vandals blew Balanced Rock off its delicate perch with explosives and sent it tumbling down. Afterward, the trail was closed off to the public, depriving us of a great panoramic view of the Palo Alto Valley as well.

On the northern outskirts of Fredericksburg, on the west side of FM 965, is Cross Mountain.

CROSS MOUNTAIN

FM 965, just north of Fredericksburg • About 17 miles from Enchanted Rock

John Christian Durst found an aged timber cross at the summit of this hill in 1847. He raised the old cross up as a sort of sentinel overlooking the young city, and a cross has stood up here ever since. Spanish missionaries traveling from San Antonio to their San Saba Mission probably first raised the crucifix. Cross Mountain lay on the Pinto Trail, and both Indians and the Spanish used the mountain, as well as Enchanted Rock, as a point of reference in their journeys. When the settlers began replacing their rude log cabins with more substantial stone ones, they often went to Cross Mountain to quarry its soft limestone. Many of the tombstones in Fredericksburg cemeteries came from Cross Mountain limestone.

Cross Mountain is also the home of the annual Easter fires, a tradition here since 1847. In Germany, Easter fires are symbolic of burning the old growth to make way for new life, signaling the dawn of Easter and Christ's resurrection. Here in Fredericksburg, the fires have a different meaning. In 1847, Adelsverein commissioner John Meusebach negotiated a treaty of peace with the Comanche nation, allowing the German colonists to live in relative peace. But the days before the treaty was signed were tense ones. On Easter eve, the hills surrounding Fredericksburg were filled with Comanches awaiting the final negotiations. Their campfires lit up the hills. Frightened by the fires, mothers calmed their children by telling the little ones that the Easter Bunny and his helpers were tending the fires, boiling the big cauldrons of dye used to color the traditional Easter eggs. With the successful treaty signing, the Easter fires became a celebration of this landmark event as well as of the most sacred Christian holiday.

You can park at the bottom of the hill and walk up the well-marked trail to the top for a great view of the city and a look at the latest cross now standing guard over Fredericksburg.

Leave Cross Mountain (and Fredericksburg) by continuing south on PM 965 to its junction with US 290; then take US 290 east toward Austin.

ROCKY HILL

Gillespie County • About 5.5 miles from Fredericksburg

Rocky Hill is located roughly where Lyman Wight's "Zodiac" colony of Mormons settled in 1847. The Mormons were gone by 1853, and the area was settled by German, Danish, and English families. Gillespie County's only cotton plantation employing slave labor operated here. After the Civil War, many of the ex-slaves remained here on land granted to them. The hamlet's name came from the school built in 1885, and the source of the name should be obvious. The old rock school still stands on the north side of US 290 and was in use as such through the early 1970s.

There are a number of period stone houses along this stretch of US 290 between Fredericksburg and Stonewall. You can usually discern the national origin of the builder by looking at the houses' rooflines. A shallow-pitched roof with a slight break where the porch joins the house often indicates an Anglo American builder. A steeply pitched and gabled roof is typical of German builders. Deep porches running the length of the house reflect a Deep South influence.

WILDSEED FARMS

US 290, approximately 7 miles east of Fredericksburg • 830-990-1393 • www.wildseedfarms.com • Open daily • Free • W+

Dozens of species of wildflowers are grown commercially for seed on two hundred acres here, providing gorgeous, car-stopping views practically year-round. Bluebonnets, poppies, Indian blankets, coneflowers, phlox, primroses, Mexican hats, verbena, blue sage, and gay feathers are just a few of the familiar Texas wildflowers grown here. Walking trails lace the fields, and you may picnic as well. Pick your own bouquets or buy seed to plant at home. And visit the gift shop.

Continue on US 290 east to Blumenthal.

BLUMENTHAL

Gillespie County • About 3 miles from Rocky Hill

Blumenthal is one of Gillespie County's youngest communities, founded about 1900 by two brothers from Grapetown, Max and Eugene Hohenberger. The hamlet received its name either from nearby Blumenthal Creek or from a German town of the same name. Blumenthal means "blooming valley" in German, which it certainly does in the spring. Original buildings here include a general store, saloon, house, and cotton gin.

A number of wineries have been established along this stretch of US 290. Shortly after Blumenthal, you come to the entrances to the two best-established ones, Grape Creek Vineyard and Becker Vineyards.

GRAPE CREEK VINEYARDS

10587 US 290, 10 miles east of Fredericksburg • 800-950-7392 • www .grapecreek.com • Open daily • Free • W variable

One of Texas' older modern vineyards, grapes were first planted in 1986. There is a gift shop, tasting room, and B&B. Tours and tastings are given.

BECKER VINEYARDS

464 Becker Farms Rd., off US 290, 10 miles east of Fredericksburg • 830-644-2681 • www.beckervineyards.com • Open daily, closed holidays • W

This vineyard was planted in 1992 on the site of an old stand of native mustang grapes, which were used by the Germans to make wine. The native limestone winery stands beside an 1880s log cabin and well. Wines are aged in French oak barrels. The appropriately named "Iconoclast" Merlot and Cabernet Sauvignon honor the late and great Austin artist Tony Ball, whose self-portrait graces the label. Bell was a member of the *Texas Ranger* magazine humor staff and a driving force behind the Vulcan Gas Company, precursor to the Armadillo World Headquarters, in the 1960s. Both varieties offer tremendous value for the money. The long, antique bar came from San Antonio's old Green Tree Saloon. The old, mirrored bar back was made in St. Louis.

Continue east on US 290 to Stonewall and the intersection with Ranch Road 1. Turn left onto Ranch Road 1.

STONEWALL

Gillespie County • 400 (approximate) • (830) • About 5 miles from Blumenthal

This section of the Pedernales was first settled in the 1840s by German immigrants, but the town of Stonewall was not established until after the Civil War and was named for Civil War Confederate hero Thomas J. "Stonewall" Jackson. Major Israel Moses Nunez can be considered the father of today's Stonewall.

According to family history, Nunez' parents came to Florida from Spain, where he was born in 1841, as Israel Moses. He added the last name "Nunez" when he came of age. After serving in the Confederate Army, Nunez and his wife, Maria, came to Texas in 1868. They settled in Fredericksburg. During the six months they lived there, he established a stagecoach line that ran from San Marcos to points beyond Fredericksburg. Needing a stage stop east of Fredericksburg, he bought almost five thousand acres south of the Pedernales River for fifty cents an acre. He built a house for his family, a stage stop, and post office about two miles south of present-day Stonewall. In 1870, he laid out a town along the Pedernales which was called Millville. Nunez donated land for a saw- and gristmill, plus two acres each for a cemetery and school. In 1879, a mill was built on the banks of the Pedernales. In 1882, Nunez moved his operations to Millville and requested that the post office be named for Stonewall Jackson, under whom he had served in the Civil War, and so the name Stonewall was chosen. The Nunez family moved to Austin in 1890, where he operated a dairy.

Local farmers raised cotton, and later turkeys and chickens. When commercial peach growing began in the Hill Country during the 1920s and 1930s, Stonewall farmers adopted the crop, and today Stonewall peaches are recognized as the Hill Country's best. Stonewall celebrates the peach with its annual Peach Jamboree, held the third Friday and Saturday of each June. Events include a rodeo, dance, parade, and lots of peaches and ice cream.

Depending on weather conditions, the yearly Hill Country peach crop ranges from nonexistent to bountiful. A number of peach farmers have roadside stands, offering their peaches and other fruit. One of the oldest and largest stands is Burg's Corner (open daily May–September, weekends through Christmas; 800-694-2772; PO Box 281, Stonewall 78671; www.burgscorner.com), located on US 290 in downtown Stonewall. Even in marginal harvest years, Burg's will have peaches when competitors don't, along with plums, blackberries, and other garden produce (in season), as well as delicious frozen peaches and peach preserves, butter, salsa, and ice cream year-round.

Burg's Corner dates to 1892, when John and Elizabeth Burg moved to Stonewall and built a store and saloon. He hauled cotton and cotton seed to Comfort and on the return trip carried the merchandise that had been sent to him by train from San Antonio. Burg built a dance hall in 1894. Dances were held three times a year, from sundown to sunup. Drinks were sold all night long, and a family-style supper was served at midnight. The store changed hands several times over the years among family members as one generation retired and another took over operations. Marcus Burg closed the mercantile store in 1946 and opened a lumberyard and feed store in the building that now houses Burg's Corner.

Emil Sauer was Stonewall's first famous native son. Born here in 1881, Sauer earned degrees from the University of Texas and Harvard before joining the consular service in 1911. He served all over the world, including Turkey, Venezuela, Canada, Brazil, and Germany. While serving in Canada in the 1930s, he was appointed consul general. Author of several books on international finance, Sauer retired from the consular service in 1941 and died in 1949.

Stonewall is more famous as the birthplace of Lyndon B. Johnson. As such, Stonewall was quite a tourist attraction during the LBJ presidential years. Most of the tourist traffic today centers around the LBJ National Historic Site and the LBJ State Historical Park, established as a cooperative effort by the late president and Mrs. Johnson and federal and state planners. The Texas Parks and Wildlife Department operates the state park located on the south side of the Pedernales River, while the National Park Service operates the LBJ Ranch area directly across the river.

LBJ NATIONAL HISTORIC PARK

Headquarters at the LBJ State Historical Park • 868-7128 • www.nps.gov/ lyjo/index.htm • Open daily except Thanksgiving, Christmas and New Year's Day • Daily guided and self-guided tours; check website for current schedule • Small fee for some activities • W

The LBJ National Historic Park was created when president and Mrs. Johnson deeded two hundred acres of the LBJ Ranch to the National Park Service. Johnson wanted the site to be more than just a memorial to himself or to the abstractions of history. He thought of it as a place where people could enjoy the Hill Country as he had—a place to get away, to relax. And he wanted visitors to be aware of the heritage that had been his—of land-taming pioneers, cattlemen, farmers, and overcomers.

Four historically significant sites are located within the LBJ National Historic Park: the LBJ ranch house, the Johnson birthplace, the Junction school, and the Johnson family cemetery. A free, self-guided driving of the tour lasts about two hours and requires a free driving permit obtained at the LBJ State Park and Historic Site Visitor Center.

LBJ RANCH HOUSE

Then-Senator Johnson and Lady Bird bought the limestone and frame ranch house from Frank Johnson Martin in 1951. The original two-story limestone core was built sometime before 1900 by Wilhelm Meier Sr. The house and acreage surrounding it changed hands several times before Clarence and Frank Johnson Martin—Lyndon's uncle by marriage and aunt by blood—bought the place in 1909. The Martins enlarged the Meier house, adding the frame structure to the limestone house. Johnson visited the Martins often as a youth and was so impressed by the grandeur of their house that he vowed to own it someday. Martin practiced law in Blanco and Gillespie counties and was a district judge for many years.

JOHNSON BIRTHPLACE

Just downriver from the big ranch house is a faithfully reconstructed replica of the little white farmhouse in which Lyndon Johnson was born on August 27,

1908. The original house was torn down in 1935. Lyndon's grandparents Sam Ealy Johnson Sr. and wife Eliza bought the land on which the house stands in 1882. Sam built the house in 1889, and in 1907 son Sam Ealy Johnson Jr. brought his new bride, Rebekah Baines, home to this dogtrot house. He had just finished serving his second term in the Texas House of Representatives, and his new wife was the daughter of his predecessor at the statehouse. The family occupied this simple whitewashed one-story L-shaped home through 1913 and the birth of two more children after Lyndon. Today the house is furnished with many articles original to the home or identical to them, such as the telephone and some of the president's childhood toys, including his first teddy bear. The place actually has a lived-in look, in spite of the roped-off sections in several of the rooms. The grounds are immaculately kept up with flowers and plants appropriate to that era.

JUNCTION SCHOOL

Further east from the birthplace is Johnson's first school, the Junction school, so named because it sat at a junction of country roads. The simple one-room embossed-tin structure was completed in 1910, although the school itself had operated in a variety of locations since 1881. Johnson started his education here at the age of four. He began hiking over to the school to play with his cousins and the other children during recess. This practice worried his mother no end, since Johnson loved the Pedernales, and the path to the school ran along the river; she was forever fearful that he might fall in and drown. So finally she asked the teacher, Miss Kate Deadrich, to please take on one more pupil even though he was a bit young. Miss Kate agreed, and fifty-three years later they were reunited at the old schoolhouse when Johnson signed the Elementary and Secondary Education Act into law with Miss Kate as his witness.

JOHNSON FAMILY CEMETERY

Lyndon and Lady Bird Johnson are buried here under the great live oaks overlooking his beloved Pedernales. They rest here with his grandparents Sam Sr. and Eliza Johnson, his parents Sam Jr. and Rebekah, and other members of his family in what is surely one of the most beautiful cemeteries in the Hill Country.

LBJ STATE HISTORICAL PARK

Ranch Rd. 1, about 2 miles east of Stonewall • 830-644-2252 • www.tpwd. state.tx.us/spdest/findadest/parks/lyndon_b_johnson/ • Open daily, except Thanksgiving, Christmas, and New Year's Day • W variable

The visitor center has a room filled with some of the many gifts sent to the president during his administration, ranging from ornate handcrafted jewelry boxes given by heads of state to seed-and-corn-kernel portraits sent by admiring Americans. The rest of the center contains exhibits relating to the Hill Country and its people, past and present, memorabilia from Johnson's boyhood, a variety of maps, photographs, and assorted paraphernalia from the presidential years, and finally an auditorium in which a slide show is presented, a show that attempts to explain all the influences on Johnson's character formation, his family, and his life.

Attached to the visitor center is the two-room dogtrot cabin built by German immigrant Johannes Behrens during the 1840s. It is furnished with items typical of the era. Located to the west of the visitor center is the Danz log cabin, one of the oldest in the area. It was discovered when a newer home built around it was being dismantled. Because of its age and historic importance, officials decided that it should be restored and furnished to the period of its use. Johann Casper Danz emigrated to Texas from Germany in 1846. He and his wife first settled in the Grape Creek area. In 1860 he purchased seven hundred acres in the area that includes Stonewall, of which he can be considered the founder. The whole of LBJ Park is located on the Danz tract.

To the east of the visitor center is the "living" Sauer-Beckmann farmstead, with all the animals, gardens, buildings, and equipment common to the Texas farm of 1900–1918. Park employees in clothes of the period perform the daily chores and show visitors how life was back then. Spring at the farm is garden-planting time, fall is butchering and sausage-making time, and Christmastime sees an old-time Christmas tree and tables laden with goodies for the visitors.

Johan Friedrich Sauer bought 188 acres, including the land on which these homes stand, in 1869 from Casper Danz. Born in Nassau, Germany, in 1838, Sauer came to Texas with his parents in 1845. Married in 1865, Sauer and his wife built a one-room log cabin. As his family grew, Sauer added a cellar, a stone shed at the rear of the cabin, and finally two rooms on either side of the original cabin pen. The front room is now the "summer kitchen."

The next home Sauer built is the cut-and-dressed limestone house immediately east of the log cabin. Featured in this house is a functioning turn-of-the-century farm kitchen with a blue enamel wood range. Emil Sauer, the youngest of Johan's ten children, was born in this house. Another daughter, Augusta Lindig, was the midwife in attendance at the birth of Lyndon Johnson.

The Sauers sold their farm to Herman Beckmann in 1900 and moved to the Doss community in northwestern Gillespie County. Beckmann had bought the farm for his two sons, Emil and Otto. Emil lived in the log cabin, and Otto lived in the limestone dwelling. Emil later bought out Otto's interest and married Emma Mayer in 1907. A good cotton crop in 1915 allowed Emil and Emma Beckmann to build a new barn, add a frame room onto the old rock structure, and construct porches connecting to a lovely Victorian-style house covered with fashionable pressed tin.

In 1966, Edna Beckmann Hightower sold the site to the Texas Parks and Wildlife Department, and the farm opened to the public in 1975. The L-shaped house is furnished according to the period, down to the period wallpaper. The big house is connected to the smaller stone house by a Durchgang, or open hallway. In the Durchgang are a long table and benches, used by the family on summer days and when feeding the neighbors and hired hands who came to help with the threshing and harvesting.

Behind the big house is the stone smokehouse where the bratwurst, liverwurst, blood sausage, beef, pork sausage, and Schwademagen hang to cure. In front of the house is the stone tank house that supports the cypress water tank next to the windmill. Beckmann's big frame barn and battered chicken house stand nearby, still functional. Depending on the day and season in which you visit, you may find the farm staff planting, harvesting, canning, or preserving their garden crop, butchering, or washing the weekly laundry in the big black cast-iron wash pot.

Tours of the complex, including the Sauer-Beckmann farm with its smokehouse, Victorian-style house, garden, and log house, last approximately an hour; group reservations are accepted. A nature trail wanders through woods and meadows. No entrance fee is required, but donations are appreciated. LBJ Ranch Tram Tours begin at the state park's Visitor Center Complex and are operated by the National Park Service. Tours are offered by the National Park Service and depart from the LBJ State Park Visitor Center. Tours run daily except Thanksgiving, Christmas Day, and New Year's Day; check the website for the current schedule. Individuals and families can take the tour on a first-come, first-serve basis. There is a small fee. Call for group tours.

Facilities include restrooms, picnic sites, refreshment vending machines, interpretive center with exhibits, auditorium, amphitheater, swimming pool (open during summer), playgrounds, Creek Walk Nature Trail, ADA nature trail, tennis courts, baseball field, dining hall (capacity 70), group picnic area (capacity 200), bookstore, and Texas State Park Store. The park is famous for its spring-blooming wildflower fields.

Just a few hundred yards east of the LBJ State Historical Park on Ranch Road 1 is Trinity Lutheran Church.

TRINITY LUTHERAN CHURCH

Ranch Rd. 1, about 3 miles from downtown Stonewall

Lean, tall stained-glass windows with white frames punctuate the walls and bell tower of this soaring Gothic sanctuary, which are covered with pressed-tin siding in a brick pattern. The church looks blue from all but the shortest of distances, thanks to immaculate care. The congregation organized in 1902. The lumber to build the first church was hauled by wagon from Marble Falls. The present church was built in 1928. The Lyndon Johnson family worshipped here occasionally while staying at the ranch.

LODGING

STONEWALL VALLEY RANCH

North of Stonewall, near the LBJ Ranch • 830-644-2380, 512-454-0476 • www.stonewallvalleyranch.com

This ranch-style B&B is located on a scenic, working Texas Longhorn ranch that also has antelope and a herd of bison. The guesthouse, which is the original ranch house, sleeps five to six and has one full bath. You can hike, ride bikes, fish in one of the many stock ponds, or help with ranch chores. Families with children are welcome.

Continue east on Ranch Road 1. Just past Trinity Lutheran Church, Ranch Road 1 ends. Turn left onto US 290.

HYE

Blanco County • 105 • About 6.5 miles from Stonewall

Hye is the next hamlet east on US 290. Hye was named for Hiram "Hye" Brown, who established the first store here in 1880. The post office was established in 1886.

DEIKE STORE AND HYE POST OFFICE

US 290

Hye's chief attraction is the Deike Store and Hye post office. White with green-and-red trim bringing out the highlights of the elaborate Bavarian-style, cast-metal facade, the Hye store was built in 1904. Young Lyndon Johnson mailed his first letter here at the age of four, and Johnson's appointee as postmaster general of the United States, Lawrence O'Brien, was sworn into office on these very steps on November 3, 1965.

ROCKY CREEK

Blanco County • About 2.5 miles from Hye

You enter the Rocky Creek neighborhood when you pass the intersection with Rocky Road (CR 205) followed by Rocky Creek about a mile later. Rocky Creek, or Rocky, was a small farming community named for a nearby creek. The settlement began in the 1880s, according to the *Handbook of Texas*.

But in fact, the neighborhood was being called "Rocky" by September 1877, when a stock dealer named Stoops was robbed near there by two men who stopped him, six-shooters drawn, and made him take off all his clothes in the road. Then they made him walk away from them until they could search every garment. He started to walk away with his hat on after stripping, when they made him return and hand them his hat. While Stoops was undressing, his horse got away, and the robbers, at his request, caught the horse for him after they had finished searching his clothes and pocketed $314; they had missed seventy-five cents. A small store had been started there recently, and from what Stoops could learn he thought he had been robbed by some rough characters who generally hung around that store.

The community cemetery was established by 1880, and a schoolhouse was built by the late 1880s. After the school closed, the building was used for church services and eventually became a community center. The Rocky Creek community was associated with the neighboring Pleasant Hill school, and the area is often referred to as Rocky-Pleasant Hill. The Pleasant Hill-Rocky Creek School building is located just off Highway 290 West, on Rocky Road. The cemetery is a little farther down the road.

JOHNSON CITY

Blanco County Seat • 1,670 (approximate) • (830) • About 10 miles from Hye

Prior to 1850, the land between Austin and Fredericksburg was mostly uninhabited wilderness. The area that was to become Johnson City was first settled in 1856 by James and Martha Provost, back when this was still Hays County. John L. Moss had the first cultivated land here in 1861. Life was hard here in those early years. Indian attacks were frequent. Few Indians lived in Blanco County, but they regarded it as one of their prime hunting grounds, and they looked particularly askance at the white men who came and plowed up their land and drove away the game. During their brief stay here, James and Martha Provost built a log cabin and several modest outbuildings. These structures became the core of the Johnson settlement.

As you come into town, on your left you will see the tiny Captain Perry log cabin.

CAPTAIN PERRY CABIN

404 Main/US 290 • For more information or a tour, call 868-7800

This single-pen log cabin was the home of Cicero R. (Rufe) Perry, born in Alabama in 1822. He came to Texas in 1833 with his parents. They settled at Bastrop. Perry participated in the siege of San Antonio in late 1835 and became an Indian fighter at age fourteen. Perry helped repulse the Adrian Woll invasion of Texas in 1842 and served in the subsequent Somerville Expedition. He joined John C. Hays' Texas Rangers in 1844, fought against Indians in Concho County in 1865, and was commander of Company D, Frontier Battalion, as late as 1874. It is said that he could point out twenty bullet, arrow, and spear wounds on his body. Perry died in Johnson City in 1898.

SUGAR PLUM COTTAGE

US 290 at Ave. J • Private residence

On the western edge of Johnson City, on your right a few hundred yards east of the Johnson City historical marker, you see the Sugar Plum cottage, one of Central Texas' most distinctive dwellings. This frame cottage has been rocked over with a variety of regional rocks and stones. The window casements are concrete, with tiny rocks punctuating the stucco. Ditto for the edging along the porch roof in front. In the center of the porch awning edge, the words "Sugar Plum" are spelled out in the same tiny rock chips. The porch awning is held up by two vastly dissimilar rock posts. The east post is built of little rocks stacked up on top of each other, while the west post is a stack of much larger stones, altogether a very yin-and-yang effect.

LBJ NATIONAL HISTORICAL PARK

Visitor center is south of US 290 at 100 Ladybird Lane (corner of Ave. G) • 868-7128 • www.nps.gov/lyjo/index.htm • Open daily, except Thanksgiving, Christmas, and New Year's Day • Free • W

The Johnson Settlement and Lyndon Johnson's boyhood home are part of the LBJ National Historical Park. The Johnson Settlement is accessible via the visitor center. You can see the settlement from US 290 as you enter Johnson City.

The visitor center has two film auditoriums, permanent and temporary exhibits, and a sales area. Multimedia exhibits (including a thirty-minute film) tell the story of Johnson and his presidency in the context of the isolated little Hill Country town that he grew up in. Lady Bird Johnson isn't slighted either. She has her own exhibit and documentary film.

JOHNSON SETTLEMENT

By 1862, the Provost property had changed hands twice, and the latest owner was an absentee proprietor. His agent was Jesse Thomas Johnson, better known as Tom. Tom Johnson was Lyndon's great uncle. Tom Johnson occupied the cabin till 1866, adding an east room and breezeway during that period. The next year, Tom's newly married brother (Lyndon's grandfather), Sam Ealy Johnson Sr., set up housekeeping in the cabin with wife Eliza.

In 1868, the two brothers became partners in a cattle-driving business. Due to a cutoff from normal northern markets during the Civil War, the numbers of unattended cattle on the vast open Texas ranges had increased greatly. At war's end, there was great demand for Texas meat from the northern markets. A steer worth six to ten dollars on the hoof in Texas might bring thirty to forty dollars at the railheads in Kansas.

The first year of business was so good that Sam bought 320 acres and the cabin in 1869. Soon after, the Johnsons bought an adjoining 640-acre tract. Located in the valleys of the Blanco and Pedernales rivers, the land was ideal for their operation, with plenty of good pasture and water. There was no need for big barns or an elaborate ranch headquarters, just corrals and pens to hold the cattle. The cabin served as headquarters, and the pens stretched from the cabin to the Pedernales, virtually covering what was to become Johnson City. Individual owners would deliver their herds to the Johnsons, and the longhorns were held in the pens until the trail boss and drovers were ready to start for the northern markets. Between 1868 and 1871, the brothers made four drives up the Chisholm Trail to Abilene, Kansas, with herds numbering between 2,500 and 3,000 head. They were the largest trail-driving outfit in Blanco and six surrounding counties. In 1870, Sam Ealy drove 7,000 head to Kansas and returned with more than $100,000.

The Johnson brothers operated on credit. Buying cattle on credit during the spring, they would return home in the autumn with mules to sell and gold to pay for the cattle they had driven north. They had little trouble buying on credit because of the great price differential between range and marketplace.

But in the end, the high market prices led to their business's demise. The high prices inspired thousands of others to enter the cattle business, which resulted in a flooded market and significantly lower prices paid by buyers. By 1871, the brothers could scarcely sell their beeves for the money they would have to pay upon their return home. After losing their shirts, the brothers dissolved their partnership; sold their holdings to nephew, former ranch hand, and drover James Polk Johnson, and left Blanco County. Sam Johnson moved to Caldwell, then Hays County, before returning to the Pedernales and Stonewall in 1889. With the acquisition of the land and a bride, James Polk made the transition from drover to farmer and rancher. Accordingly, he built a small stone barn northwest of the cabin in which to shelter his horses.

During the years he owned the ranch, James Polk Johnson built a large frame house, which was destroyed in 1918. It was located near the still-standing windmill and water tower erected in 1896. The smokehouse Johnson built stands next to the water tank. In 1882, Johnson sold the south portion of the ranch to German immigrant John Bruckner, who built the large, German-style stone barn west of the original cabin. These buildings today make up the Johnson Settlement, a "living history" project similar to the Sauer-Beckmann farmstead at the LBJ State Historical Park.

Perhaps more than anything else in his life, Lyndon Johnson wished he had been born in a real log cabin, as had his grandfather. He was enthralled with the pioneer exploits of Sam Sr. and Eliza. If it had not been for Eliza's coolheadedness one day in 1869, Lyndon Johnson might never have been born. Sam was away from the Johnson Settlement Ranch that day, and Eliza had been left alone with her baby daughter. Out in the yard with Lyndon's young aunt, she looked up to see a Comanche raiding party approaching the house. Scooping up the baby, she ran for the little cabin without being seen and crawled into a low crawl space beneath the cabin. There the terrified mother and daughter hid from the Indians, not coming forth until hours after the Indians had left.

LBJ BOYHOOD HOME

100 E. Elm, between Aves. G and F, one block south of US 290

In addition to the Johnson Settlement, the LBJ National Historic Site here includes the modest frame home that the Johnson family moved to in 1913. It is a typical middle-class home of its time: six rooms, a screened porch, a front porch swing, and a bit of gingerbread trim on the gables and front porch.

The Johnson home was seldom empty. There were five children to be raised, and State Representative Sam Ealy Johnson Jr. always seemed to be bringing friends home. The parents conducted regular debates and speaking bees, determined that their children would learn to think on their feet. Mrs. Johnson was one of the few college-educated women in Blanco County, and she took her family and civic responsibilities seriously, giving elocution, debate, and declamation lessons on the east front porch and in the parlor of this house. She also wrote a column for the weekly newspaper, directed plays at the opera house, organized a Browning Society (as in Elizabeth Barrett Browning), and joined the local temperance society (Sam Ealy Jr. liked to drink). Lyndon Johnson lived here until he started college at Southwest Texas Normal Institute (now Texas State University) in San Marcos.

The house has been restored to look much as it did during Johnson's boyhood, including many of the original furnishings. It has a comfortable lived-in look: toys are scattered on the floor of Lyndon and brother Sam's room, papers and magazines lie casually on the parlor table, the kitchen is full of all the boxes and cans and foodstuffs that you would expect to find. All these little touches make the house like a place where the owners are expected home at any minute.

Stop by the visitor center first to sign in and look at the displays there; then await one of the free guided tours of the boyhood home.

From the LBJ Boyhood Home, proceed north on Avenue G across US 290 to the courthouse square.

BLANCO COUNTY JAIL

Ave. G at East Pecan • Not open to the public

Its tall, lean, totally spare appearance perfectly symbolizes the builders' attitudes toward the law and its breakers.

BLANCO COUNTY COURTHOUSE

Ave. G at E. Pecan (east side), Cypress at Nugent (west side) • One block north of US 290

The present Blanco County courthouse, a two-story limestone Greek Revival structure, was built in 1916. It replaced Johnson City's first courthouse (see below). Construction was supervised by James Waterstone, a Scottish stonemason who came to Texas in 1883 to work on the state capitol.

JOHNSON CITY BANK/OLD COURTHOUSE

7th and Nugent

James Polk Johnson had this two-story limestone building erected in 1885. It served as a store for the first five years, then county courthouse from 1890 to 1916. Since then, it has been a store, a hotel and restaurant, a movie and opera house, a community center, and a bank. During its time as the Withers Opera House, Rebekah Baines Johnson wrote several plays that were presented there.

OLD PEARL HOTEL

201 N. Nugent, at Pecan St.

Catercorner to the old courthouse is another one of James Polk Johnson's edifices, the two-story, double-front-porched old Pearl Hotel. Johnson built this hotel in the early 1880s in anticipation of the travelers who would come to Johnson City when it became county seat. It served as city hall for a number of years.

James Polk Johnson was Johnson City's namesake and principal promoter. He had the town laid out in 1878 on his land, and he intended that his town would become the seat of Blanco County. He didn't wait long to begin his crusade.

The creation of Kendall County came back to haunt Blanco in 1879. That year the residents of the newly organized Johnson City and the northern part of the county called for an election to relocate the county seat to Johnson City. Blanco residents laughed, until the votes were counted. Johnson City had lost by only 10 out of 660 votes cast.

In December 1884, the second election for the removal of the seat of government from Blanco to Johnson City resulted in favor of the former by a majority of sixteen votes. One hundred guns were fired in Blanco in honor of the victory. By this time the county was polarized over the issue. Men were ready to fight at any time over the courthouse location; fistfights and gunfights were not uncommon. Many families even divided over the issue, causing the *San Antonio Daily Light* to observe: "Blanco County has just got through with a very disagreeable duty, being the permanent location of the county seat in which Blanco City was the point selected. County seat wars are generally never ending, and they have the effect to unsettle values, make enemies, and otherwise create trouble among peaceful people, and to this end Blanco City and Blanco County are to be congratulated on the result of the recent election there."

A third election for the removal of the seat of government from Blanco to Johnson City was announced in the fall of 1889. Tensions again rose in both towns, perhaps contributing to the following Christmas Eve tragedy in Johnson City: A serious shooting affray occurred, in which four persons were seriously wounded. It seems some trouble was caused by the firing of roman candles on the streets, and a quarrel followed in which two men, one boy, and a lady received gunshot wounds, the lady being shot accidentally.

Johnson City finally wrested away the county seat from Blanco in the third election, held on January 21, 1890. The Johnson City faction won by a majority of sixty-six votes. In an election row at Johnson City that day, Ben Casey shot and killed George Loyd and wounded Deputy Sheriff Crosby, in the thigh. The former was an advocate of Blanco City, the latter two of Johnson City, which won in the election. Casey was arrested and taken to Blanco City, lynching being apprehended.

Less than six months later, District Clerk J. M. Martin of Blanco County was killed at Johnson City in the trouble over the recent county seat contest.

Within hours of the declaration of Johnson City's victory, all the county records were loaded onto wagons for removal to Johnson City, despite the lack of a courthouse, or jail, for that matter. Johnson City also needed a good hotel and dwelling houses, the *San Antonio Daily Light* noted a couple of weeks later.

That began to change with a few months, so that by December, the *Johnson City Star* indulged in this snatch of doggerel: "Rip goes the saw, whack goes the hammer, up goes the house, on goes the boom, Johnson City is on the move."

The ill feeling over the county seat removal was so bad in November 1890 that the dissatisfied parties were making plans to propose the creation of a new county to the next session of the legislatures, carving out parts of Blanco and the neighboring counties of Hays, Travis, and possibly Comal counties, with Blanco as the county seat. But the plan was doomed from the beginning, since the state constitution prohibited the creation of any county measuring less than seven hundred square miles, nor the reduction of any existing county below that size, which meant that the neighboring counties of Hays, Kendall, and Comal could not be reduced, and Blanco could be by only seventeen square miles. So the new county could only use parts of the larger, border counties of Travis, Burnet, Llano, and Gillespie, which would defeat the object of those interested in placing Blanco near the center of the new county, since a central location within the county was another requirement. Never mind that an almost-new courthouse and jail already existed in Blanco, while Johnson City had nothing.

The county seat battle went on sporadically for decades. In May 1915, a petition was circulated in the south end of Blanco asking the commissioners court to order an election to determine whether or not the county seat should be removed from Johnson City to Blanco. Since Johnson City was in the center of the county and it would take a two-thirds majority to remove the county seat, a second petition was being circulated asking the court to order an election to determine whether or not the county should issue bonds in the amount of $30,000 for the purpose of erecting a new courthouse on the public square in the town of Johnson City. The bond issue passed, resulting in the courthouse we see there today.

Ironically, Blanco long remained the larger town, although the respective populations now are practically identical. And to this day, each town tends to keep its own company.

One of the reasons Johnson City remained so small was because of a series of disastrous fires during the first two decades of the twentieth century; by 1920, the town's population was only five hundred, and there had been no growth in the previous ten years. Locals finally organized a volunteer fire department in 1949 after fire destroyed the Johnson City School in 1944 and three businesses and the Masonic Lodge in 1948.

Besides building the Pearl Hotel and the old courthouse, Johnson also built the big cotton gin and mill located on the south side of US 290 at the US 290/ Nugent intersection. In earlier times, farmers also brought their corn and wheat here to be ground into flour.

These are just several of the historically significant or interesting structures in Johnson City. For a more complete guide to the city, pick up a copy of *Johnson City Walking Tour* at the LBJ National Historical Park visitor center.

From the Courthouse Square, head back south on Nugent to reach the old feed mill and visitors center.

THE FEED MILL

U.S. 290 at Nugent • 868-7299 • Open daily

Little Lyndon Johnson and friends used to sneak into this old mill to play; it dates to about 1880. About one hundred years later, it was renovated and turned into a retail/restaurant complex. Inside, the old Fairbanks Morse generator that powered the mill and supplied electricity to parts of Johnson City in the pre-REA (Rural Electrification Authority) days has been restored to its original appearance, and much of the old machinery remains inside. Up until Lyndon Johnson, as president of the United States, put Johnson City on the map, Johnson City was proud to call itself the home of the largest Rural Electrification Authority in the world—the Pedernales Electric Cooperative. Congressman Lyndon Johnson was the driving force behind its creation in 1939. Johnson never forgot the folks back home.

The driving force he was famous for in achieving his many legislative aims often involved threats, intimidation, humiliation, and bullying. This was perhaps in reaction to his teenage years in Johnson City. In the days before radio, TV, video games, and iPods, children had to amuse themselves in other ways, and for boys, a favorite form of entertainment was fighting, wrestling, boxing, or something in between. According to one of Lyndon's playmates, who went on to a distinguished career that ended with a professorship at the graduate school of Johnson's name in Austin, Johnson's strategy in such matches was to fall on the ground, kicking and flailing his gangling arms and legs, screaming bloody hell the whole time.

JOHNSON CITY CHAMBER OF COMMERCE AND VISITORS CENTER

U.S. 290 (100 E. Main St.) and Nugent • 868-7684 • www.johnsoncitytex-aschamber.com • Open daily

Located in the restored Withers-Spauldings General Merchants Building, the center offers the usual visitor maps and brochures of local businesses and attractions, plus some locally oriented exhibits. Back in 1913, turkey drives passed the store and the bank next door on their way to Fredericksburg or Cain City to catch the Fredericksburg and Northern train to San Antonio.

ANNUAL EVENT

LIGHTS SPECTACULAR

Late November through January 1 • Free

The Blanco County courthouse is wrapped in a hundred thousand tiny lights and brilliantly lighted for the holiday season. There are various special events during the Christmas season, such as concerts and a parade. Contact the Chamber of Commerce for more information.

PARK

PEDERNALES RIVER NATURE PARK

North of Johnson City, just off US 281 on Pedernales River

The 222-acre Pedernales River Nature Park is one of the Lower Colorado River Authority's newest parks, open at publishing time for limited public recreational day use, such as fishing and picnicking. As with other LCRA nature parks, admission fees will be charged and rental fees collected for facility usage once the new recreational facilities are constructed and available for public use. For more information about Pedernales River Nature Park, send an e-mail to parkinfo@ lcra.org.

Leave Johnson City via US 290 east toward Austin. On the east edge of town, you come to the junction with US 281. Turn right here, and then prepare to turn left in a hundred or so yards onto FM 2766 and head toward Pedernales Falls State Park. The road is pleasantly rolling, and you cross Miller Creek, which is still lined with the majestic cypress trees that were cut down so long ago from the banks of other Hill Country creeks by shingle makers and such.

About ten miles east of Johnson City on FM 2766, you encounter the turnoff to Pedernales Falls State Park. Follow the signs into the park.

PEDERNALES FALLS STATE PARK

FM 2766; 2585 Park Rd. 6026 • About 10 miles east of Johnson City • 830-868-7304 • Open daily • Fee • W variable

This 5,211-acre park stretches along both banks of the Pedernales for six miles and along the south bank for an additional three miles. Pedernales Falls is the park's main attraction and may be viewed from a scenic overlook at the north end of the park. Here the emerald-clear river stretches out through a boulder-strewn gorge, tumbles down a pair of stone ledges, and finally spills into a deep, wide placid pool. In this area, the elevation of the river drops about fifty feet over a distance of three thousand feet, and the falls are formed by the flow of the water over the stair-step-like, layered limestone, which belongs to the three-hundred-million-year-old Marble Falls formation and is part of the southwestern flank of the Llano uplift. These layers of limestone were tilted by the uplift and then eroded long before early Cretaceous seas (120 million to 100 million years ago) covered this part of Texas and deposited sands, gravels, more layers of limestone, and marine fossils.

Well-marked trails pass through hills dotted with oak and juniper woodlands; they provide access to more heavily wooded areas of pecan, elm, sycamore, walnut, and hackberry in the major drainages. Ash, buttonbush, and cypress grow on the terrace adjacent to the river. A short trail winds through upland, river bottom, and canyon habitats to an overlook on the Pedernales that is particularly beautiful at sunset and sunrise, when thick, vaporous clouds float up off the river and bathe the valley in a dreamy haze. Farther on are the Twin Falls of Regal and Bee creeks, where the two creeks meet just prior to entering the Pedernales.

Visitors to the Twin Falls are restricted to an observation deck overlooking the falls. When the park opened, the flat area below the deck was covered with knee-high grass. Excessive visitor foot traffic caused soil compaction, which killed the grass as well as the bald cypresses that once grew abundantly in the canyon bottom. Soil compaction prevents proper aeration and water percolation. The lower walls of the canyon cut by these creeks are lined with a variety of mosses and ferns.

The Wolf Mountain Trail offers a good look at some of these canyon habitats, as well as a great view of the Pedernales River valley. A primitive camping area is on the trail. There is also a horseback-riding trail and a rugged 3.5-mile hiking trail that runs along sixty-foot-high rock bluffs and offers panoramic views and access to rock caves.

Wildlife in the park includes white-tailed deer, coyotes, rabbits, armadillos, skunks, opossums, and raccoons. Over 150 species of birds have been seen in the park; about one-third of these are permanent residents. Commonly seen birds include hawks, buzzards, herons, quail, doves, owls, roadrunners, and wild turkeys. The endangered golden-cheeked warbler nests in the park.

Activities at the park include camping, picnicking, river swimming, tubing, and wading, mountain biking, fishing, bird-watching, and horseback riding. River recreation is in a limited area. Facilities include 19.8 miles of hiking, biking, and equestrian trails. It's wise to make campsite reservations during peak season, March 1 through Thanksgiving. Wildlife management activities sometimes dictate closure of all or part of the park.

Leave Pedernales Falls State Park via RM 3232, climbing out of the Pedernales valley toward US 290. You are rewarded with a good five miles of panoramic views. At the intersection with US 290, turn left.

You are presently in the Henley neighborhood, now most notable for New Canaan Farms. Henley was established in the 1880s and was named for the owner of the town site. It had a post office, a justice of the peace, and a couple of businesses in its heyday but never amounted to much more than a wide spot on the rocky road between Austin and Johnson City.

One of Henley's most colorful early residents was "Uncle" Dave Wonsley, who was memorialized shortly after his death in 1929:

Uncle Dave was a picturesque old character with a history behind him that is highly engrossing. He was to be seen around Johnson City or Blanco or other towns around Blanco County nearly every day in his buggy. He was a picturesque old figure—white beard, tall, big hat and boots. There was never a reunion within miles of his farm near Henley that was complete without Uncle Dave. He attended all the reunions, barbecues and picnics and usually took part in many of the entertainment features. He was an old Ranger and attended conventions of the Ranger association this year at Colorado City and the previous year at Ranger.

There was a kindly twinkle in Uncle Dave's eye. Around Johnson City, they will tell you how Uncle Dave has ridden for miles to see some veteran of the Confederate war or some widow that he believed entitled to a pension. He worked with Sam Johnson, former member of the legislature, and between them, they managed to secure more pensions for the veterans or widows than any other team in Texas.

Uncle Dave Wonsley came to Blanco County in 1870. One of the first things that he did was to join Capt. Cox's Ranger company on the year of the arrival. In the ranks of the company, Uncle Dave saw a great many battles against Indians that made life in Texas miserable. He did a large amount of scout work in Blanco County when to scout was flirting with death.

Uncle Dave always had a story for his friends about some of his escapades. He was cutting cedar on Cold Branch near Miller's Creek one day and had left his horse tied to a tree nearby. His saddle, lunch, gun and red overshirt were lying on the ground near the horse. A band of Comanches came up and stole the horse and other belongings of the old Indian fighter. Uncle Dave concealed himself in the bushes, and made his get-away down a hollow.

To add to the danger and excitement of the incident, two young hounds that he had following him commenced yelping and barking. Uncle Dave enjoyed telling this incident more than any other in his career. He would jestingly say that he ran all the Indians out of the country, but that he was "working a little bit in the lead of the pack."

Soon after this escape, he returned to his post and led a party of men in pursuit of the Indian outlaws. Sight of the band was picked up near the scene of the robbery. The leader was riding Uncle Dave's horse and wearing his red shirt. A skirmish took place. Several of the red skins bit the dust, the rest were captured and the stolen property was retaken. Dave Wonsley was noted for his bravery, daring and fighting ability. He was always willing to assist any friend or any acquaintance when they were in trouble.

Uncle Dave was a splendid old-time fiddler. He always won honors at old fiddlers contests. It was seldom that a contest was held anywhere in the vicinity of where he happened to be that Uncle Dave was not in the heat of the fiddling. He was greatly attached to his old violin which was over 100 years old.

He was born in May 1849 in Anderson County. He had a host of friends in Blanco, Guadalupe, Travis and Coryell counties. He had lived in all of them. He was married in 1877 to Miss Amada Kent. Uncle Dave lies buried in the scenic Miller Creek Cemetery located in between Miller Creek and US 290 between the intersection with US 281 and RM 3232. He was a prominent Mason and asked that the Masons have charge of his funeral. It was impossible at the time because so many of the Dripping Springs lodge were ill, but memorial services were held shortly afterwards.

NEW CANAAN FARMS

5956 US 290, about 1 mile east of the intersection with FM 165 • 800-727-JAMS • www.shopncf.com • Open Monday through Saturday • W

New Canaan Farms has been making country-style jams, preserves, and sauces since 1979. It is located on the site of the old Henley Picnic Ground. Lyndon Johnson gave his first political speech here on July 4, 1930, under a massive spreading oak that is actually five large trunks growing from a single root system. If you go to New Canaan Farms, go back toward Fredericksburg on US 290 to the intersection with FM 165 to continue this trip.

Slightly a mile after you have turned onto US 290 from FM 3232, you come to the junction with FM 165. Turn right on FM 165 toward Blanco, and then turn left on Creek Road, less than one hundred yards south of US 290.

Onion Creek is one of Central Texas' largest and most scenic creeks, rising in southeastern Blanco County, flowing twenty-two miles across Hays County, and emptying into the Colorado River in southern Travis County. Creek Road follows Onion Creek for a baker's half-dozen of those twenty-two miles. This narrow lane takes you past rock fences, pecan groves, and the high bluffs of Onion Creek. Several of the ranchers along the way have dammed up the creek so that it alternates between wide placid pools and a narrow rock-broken path. The first stream you cross is the Millseat Branch of Onion Creek, almost a mile past the Mt. Gainor Road turnoff.

Louis Capt built a gristmill along this little stream in the 1860s, but it was washed away by floods, as were other mills he built both before and after the Millseat Branch one. There was a post office here at the turn of the century, but never an identifiable town.

After crossing Millseat Branch, you come to a Y intersection with Roger Hanks Parkway, marked by a large sign for Roger Hanks Park. Veer right to continue on Creek Road, which dead-ends into US 290 in Dripping Springs.

DRIPPING SPRINGS

Hays County • 1,770 (approximate) • About 16 miles from Pedernales Falls State Park

The area's first permanent resident was a man named Fawcett who arrived in about 1849. Late in 1853, three kin families set out from Mississippi and arrived here late in January 1854, settling down at a spot along the wagon road from Austin to Fort Martin Scott and Fredericksburg.

The three families comprised Dr. Joseph and Sarah Pound, John L. and Indiana (Nannie) Moss, and John Lee Malvina Wallace. The Pounds were newlyweds, but the Wallaces and Mosses already had children. Sarah Pound and Indiana Moss were sisters. The Wallaces and Pounds lived on their properties for the remainder of their lives. Descendants of Dr. and Mrs. Pound lived in the Pound House until 1983. Many of the Pound descendants and a few of the Wallace descendants still live in the area.

The Mosses moved from Dripping Springs to Blanco County by 1860. Their brief stay, however, was meaningful in the history of Dripping Springs. On June 5, 1857, John Moss was appointed the first postmaster. In order to have a post office, the community needed a name. Nannie Moss officially named it Dripping Springs.

In the next few years this section was rather thickly settled, as the people were drawn to the plentiful timber, easily obtained water, and fertile soil of the hills and valleys here. In contrast to the collection of predominantly German communities to the west and south, Dripping Springs' early settlers were almost exclusively of Anglo-southern stock.

Like much of the Hill Country and Central Texas in the five-county Austin Statistical Metropolitan Area (SMSA), Dripping Springs has experienced explosive growth since the late 1990s.

At Creek Road's dead end into US 290, turn left on US 290, go a couple of hundred feet, and then turn right onto Mercer Street (marked by a "City Offices" sign) to enter downtown Dripping Springs. Just a few feet down Mercer Street, you see a white frame-and-limestone house on your left, located on the west bank of Milkhouse Creek. This is the Marshall-Chapman home, bearer of a state historical marker.

MARSHALL-CHAPMAN HOME

500 Mercer • Not open to the public

The original John Moss property changed hands several times before Burrell J. Marshall purchased it in 1870. In 1871, Marshall added rooms constructed of native limestone to an existing wooden structure. Marshall, who was local postmaster, used his home briefly as the Dripping Springs post office until his death in February 1872, leaving the property to his wife, Martha Ann, and five children. William Thomas Chapman arrived in the community soon thereafter, and within a year he wed the Widow Marshall. He took over as the town's postmaster and is considered by locals to be the true founder of the town of Dripping Springs. Chapman donated land on which to build the Dripping Springs Academy, which opened in 1881 and operated as a private boarding school until 1905 when it became a public school. Chapman, a real estate agent, laid out the town of Dripping Springs just south of the academy. His original 1881 plat established a dozen 200 × 300 foot blocks. Six streets divided the blocks. Over the years he added four more additions to the original plat. Mercer Street, named after Chapman's son, became the main street of Dripping Springs.

Next to the Marshall-Chapman home on the west bank of Milkhouse Creek is a historical marker explaining the origins of Dripping Springs' name.

DRIPPING SPRINGS MARKER

500 block Mercer

The marker reads as follows,

> Where the Tonkawa once prowled, the cool clear waters of the Edwards Aquifer burst forth along this brook (Milkhouse Branch) and drip musically from the limestone overhang. About 1850, the Moss, Wallace, and Ponds families settled near the Dripping Springs. Mrs. Nannie Moss named the community for the Dripping

Springs. Dripping Springs became a stage stop and post office in 1857. The Pedernales Baptist Association operated a boarding school which grew out of an aborted attempt to establish a military academy. During this period (1880s) a town was laid out with names for streets that were bordered by flagstone sidewalks in 1854.

Over the years, several different dripping springs have been offered up as the source for the town's name, but as of 1980, these springs along Milkhouse Creek have been declared the official, original "dripping springs." You can see the springs by parking at the far east end of the city offices parking lot, across the street from the Marshall-Chapman home; take the cobblestone stairs down the creek bank and follow the dripping sounds upstream several yards to the fern-covered overhang where the springs emanate.

Continue on Mercer St. into downtown Dripping Springs. The Dripping Springs business district is a collection of old and not-so-old stone buildings dating from the 1870s up through the 1930s, the most notable of which is the old Dripping Springs Academy, located next to the Dripping Springs post office and bearing a state historical marker.

DRIPPING SPRINGS ACADEMY

Mercer St. downtown • Not open to the public

A rude log school had been erected early on, but the citizens of Dripping Springs yearned for a true institute of higher learning. This dream began to be realized in 1880, when W. M. Jordan moved to Dripping Springs. He was determined to establish a great boarding school in this place of healthful clime and superior moral caliber, despite the area's general poverty and considerable distance from the great centers of population from which the boarding students would have to come.

Despite the odds against his success, Jordan was determined to build his school, and the townspeople pitched in to help. Farmers quarried the limestone from nearby hillsides and carried it to the site. They constructed a lime kiln and burned the lime necessary for mortar. The sand for the mortar came from nearby creek beds. Cash for the necessary lumber could not be raised readily, but respectable citizens pledged their credit for the amount needed. When the requisite building materials were at hand, the structure was erected by men whose only knowledge of masonry was that learned by the construction of rock fences around their farms. They were supervised by a single mason.

The academy building was completed in time for the 1881 term. Two boarding houses were erected, and when the school opened both were filled with students, while every house in the village and on the adjacent farms with a spare room was filled with boarders. By the second year, the academy's enrollment was around two hundred. After its first year of operation, the academy was taken over by the Pedernales Baptist Association. Jordan moved to Kyle in 1883 to found the short-lived Kyle Seminary. The academy remained a church school until becoming a public school in 1905. The second story was added to the academy in 1920, and it became the home of the local Masonic Lodge in 1952.

From the Dripping Springs Academy, continue east on Mercer Street and turn left on RR 12.

At the edge of town, on your right, is the entrance to Founders Memorial Park.

FOUNDERS MEMORIAL PARK

27908 RR 12 • 694-0874, 858-4057 • www.drpoundpioneerfarmstead. com • W

Of principal historical interest at this thirty-acre, multiple-use park is the home of Dr. Joseph M. Pound and his wife Sarah. The first, log portion of this house was built in 1853 using slave labor. Pound served as a private in the Mexican-American War and was a Confederate Army surgeon in the Civil War. Methodist circuit-riding preachers stopped here and held services. The home was expanded over the years and served as a hospital to Dr. Pound's patients. The Pounds had nine children. Four generations of the family occupied the farmstead until 1983. The property was donated to the City of Dripping Springs in 1987, and restorations on the house began in 1990. The Dr. Joseph M. and Sarah Pound Historical Museum opened in May 2003 and is part of Founder's Park.

Like most country folk, Dr. Pound had occasion to visit Austin, and on October 15, 1884, he and a friend checked into the Avenue Hotel. Their room looked out on East Hickory (Seventh) Street, and to the pavement below was a distance of some fifteen feet. After registering, they then went out and returned to their room at a late hour. At about four a.m., Pound fell from the window to the hard stones on the street below, receiving severe injuries in the fall. One of his wrists was broken, and the other was badly strained. His kneecap was terribly bruised, his face badly cut up, and there were possible internal injuries. He was unconscious when found and was treated by three of Austin's most prominent doctors. Whether the fall was the result of a fit of somnambulism or of too convivial a time in the early part of the evening could not be ascertained. He did recover, and he died at home in 1914, just short of his eighty-eighth birthday.

With no large, strong-flowing streams nearby, there was no water-powered mill to grind the corn and wheat that settlers grew. But for two years (1883–1885), Pound and other area settlers could have their corn ground at Phelps' Wind-Powered Gristmill. It was a windmill like those that pumped water all over the Southwest, except that it was fitted to grind corn instead of pump water. Wind speed determined how fast the millstone turned and how finely the meal was ground. The faster the wind blew, the finer the meal was ground. But according to John Woods, "A person could eat bread almost as fast as the wind-powered mill could grind the corn. There was no danger of meal becoming overheated by rapid grinding."

According to Dr. Pound's daughter, Mrs. Georgia Cavett, "You would take your corn and wait for the wind. Customers learned to leave their grain early in the week, to be sure of having meal by Monday."

People brought their corn in sacks, and their initials or cattle brand were marked with charcoal on the sacks. A storm tore up Phelps' windmill in 1885, leaving him only the millstones, which he sold before moving to San Antonio.

One of Dripping Springs' newest enterprises is the distillation of Dripping Springs vodka. Now, most people would not associate the Texas Hill Country with moonshiners and white lightning, but the fact is, the rugged country between here and Austin was once dotted with stills, which reached the height of their production during Prohibition.

Prohibition may have closed Austin taverns, but that wouldn't stop partying in the roaring 1920s. The good old, pre-Prohibition, bottled-in-bond whiskey went for prices comparable to the best "sinsemilla" marijuana fifty years later—when it could be found—but homemade hooch was about as easy as water to buy. The rough hills just west of town, as yet untamed by modern civilization, were one of the best places in Texas to hide a still, and dozens of them were tended by rustic cedar choppers who spoke a flavor of English more familiar to Milton than to O. Henry. Bootlegging was such a problem that Frank Hamer, the celebrated Texas Ranger who would later kill Bonnie and Clyde, was anointed special Prohibition enforcement agent for Travis County. He may have been able to track down and kill Bonnie and Clyde, but he was not able to keep booze out of Austin.

Alcohol consumption was so blatant that a Summer Texan ad on July 2, 1920, for an upcoming "student affair" dance at the KC Hall closed with an early variation of the well-known acronym: P.B.Y.O.B. Folks were more polite back then; they said "Please" first.

Desperate for something stimulating to drink, folks were drinking all kinds of concoctions, sometimes with fatal results, such that good jokes about the dangers of bad booze were soon a humor staple, such as these two from the May 1920 issue of Scalper:

"First you take a cocktail shaker,
Add wood alcohol,
Neighbors get the undertaker;
Pretty flowers. That's all."

"Formerly hair tonic was good for shampoo; now it is also good for shambooze."

About that time, the state chemist, E. H. Golax, warned the public that the average corn whiskey commonly known as "moonshine," "white mule," or "shinney" was unfit for human consumption.

Moonshine is seldom harmless and seldom a violent poison. It is mostly a nasty, filthy beverage. The manufacture of moonshine is simple enough. It consists of one or two barrels of mash and a distilling apparatus or still. The mash generally consists of a mixture of cornmeal, sugar, and water, with yeast added to it to induce fermentation. Through the process of fermentation the mash will develop about 7 to 8 percent alcohol, which is then concentrated to 30 to 50 percent by means of distillation. The whole process is in theory harmless enough. The nature of the still itself, whether made of copper, tin or lead, has no bearing on the finished product.

It is the condition that surrounds the manufacture that introduces the element of danger. The illicit still by its very nature must be clandestine—it hides itself in thickets, fields and barns—the containers consist of old barrels unspeakably filthy and ill smelling after repeated use. The unprotected fermenting mixture attracts animal life—flies, cockroaches, mice, rats and bugs of every description feed upon the material and often drown in it.

The still used to concentrate the alcohol from the mash is mostly, by force of circumstances, a crude affair, defying all average precautions taught by experience and practice. The condensing tube or 'worm' is placed directly upon the boiling liquid, and alcohol and aqueous vapor pass together with foam, scum and other parts of the boiling mass to be condensed by cold water.

The simplest expression of a still seen by the writer consisted of a common boiler covered with a filthy blanket—the alcohol vapors passing from the boiling liquid were retained in the blanket and wrung out of same into a bottle. In another instance, a torn-up mattress had furnished the necessary cotton for the straining of the finished product.

The result of the distillation, "singling" or "doubling" in bootleg parlance, is therefore a mixture of water and alcohol together with many byproducts of putrefaction and a large amount of "fussel oils" which impart to the stuff its distinctive and repulsive odor. Fussel oil is the common name given to a group of higher alcohols formed simultaneously during the process of fermentation with the better known grain alcohol. Most of these higher alcohols are distinctively toxic. The symptoms they provoke are headache, giddiness, double vision, staggering, and unconsciousness. In repeated and frequent doses, they may cause acute nephritis and affect the composition of the blood.

The whiskies sold in the years gone by were kept under strict control under the Federal and State Food and Drug Laws and only traces of fussel oil were present in the brands offered for sale on the open market. Moonshine, made in violation of all laws, cannot be supervised and the purchaser must assume all responsibility as to the wholesomeness or the purity of the article he purchases.

It is hard to believe that man would find a bottle in a street corner and drink its contents because it smells of booze; and still the "white mule," "shinney," or "white lightning" handled mysteriously by some unknown go-between is certainly no safer.

Dripping Springs vodka is, of course, as far removed from Golax's "shinney" moonshine as bilge water is from bottled water, but it is handcrafted in a copper still, in the classic manner.

SHOPPING

DRIPPING SPRINGS FARMERS MARKET

Intersection of US 290 and RR 12; enter off of RR 12 for free parking • Saturday mornings, spring through mid-November; dangerous weather may cancel the market • 858-4725 (City Hall) • www.cityofdrippingsprings.com

You'll find here locally and regionally grown/produced seasonal and heirloom produce, grass-fed lamb and beef, bread loaves, baked goods, farm-fresh eggs, salsa, teas, olive oil, home and bath products, plus local arts and crafts.

From Founders Memorial Park, continue north on RR 12. In about 4.5 miles you come to a four-way intersection with Fitzhugh Road. Turn right here on E. Fitzhugh Road to reach Fitzhugh.

FITZHUGH

Hays County • About 6.5 miles from Dripping Springs

Fitzhugh was known as Barton Creek until 1898, when an English widow named Mrs. E. A. Brewer established a post office here and named it Fitzhugh for the creek that runs through the community. The old Austin-Llano road used to run through here, and the main cattle trail from points west to Austin also ran through Fitzhugh. The post office was discontinued in 1914. The Fitzhugh

Baptist Church is all that remains. Worshippers first held services under a brush arbor, repairing to the little log schoolhouse when the weather turned nasty. The Methodists organized next, and they alternated services with the Baptists in the schoolhouse. A new sanctuary has been built, but the old tin-roofed arbor still sits out back. To see it, turn left on Crumley Ranch Road, as per the Fitzhugh Baptist Church sign, just before the stop sign at the intersection with Trautwein Road.

Continue east on County Road 101 from Fitzhugh. Once in Travis County, the road becomes Fitzhugh Road. The narrow road twists and turns over numerous seasonal streams and arroyos on its way to US 290. Once the exclusive domain of ranchers and cedar choppers, some of whom still hang on, Fitzhugh Road is becoming increasingly contaminated by subdivisions and gated McMansions.

Turn left on US 290 and head for Oak Hill. On your left, you'll see the old San Saba railroad depot, moved here and restored in the late 1980s.

OAK HILL

Travis County • About 11 miles from Fitzhugh

The Oak Hill area was first settled in the 1840s and was being called Live Oak Springs by 1856. The name was changed to Shiloh in 1865. The area was later known as Live Oak and Oatmanville before the present name of Oak Hill was adopted around 1900. After the capitol building in Austin burned in 1881, it was decided that native limestone from the giant limestone hill owned by Tom Oatman would be used for the giant structure.

A railroad spur was built to the quarry site so that the giant limestone slabs could be hauled back to Austin. Sweating convicts cut the stone under the eyes of watchful armed guards. Ten carloads of stone were shipped out of here daily. But capitol contractors soon found out that the Oatmanville limestone was unfit for exterior use—the iron pyrite nuggets it contained rusted when exposed to the elements—so they turned to the harder granite from Granite Mountain near Marble Falls. The Oatmanville limestone was used in the basement and inner walls of the capitol building instead. Eight convicts died on top of this hill and are buried nearby, their graves unmarked and lost now. The quarry has been called Convict Hill ever since, and it is the hill whose sheer walls line the south side of US 290 (on your right) as you drive through Oak Hill.

Farther east on US 290, on your left and just east of the Williamson Creek bridge, is the two-story limestone Old Rock Store, which bears a state historical marker.

OLD ROCK STORE

6266 US 290

James Patton built the store over a period of nineteen years with rock quarried from his land, finishing it in 1898. Patton's father came to Texas in 1836 and fought in the Texas Revolution. Young Patton, born in 1853, joined the Texas Rangers and fought the Comanches before settling down here several miles east of Oatmanville. He later helped consolidate Oatmanville and Oak Hill into one town. Patton established a store here in 1879 in a small frame building and then began work on the rock store. He became postmaster in 1886, serving until the post office closed in 1910. Patton was known affectionately for years as the "Mayor of Oak Hill," although the never-incorporated Oak Hill has never had a mayor. Oak Hill has experienced explosive growth in the last twenty years as a result of Austin's expansion westward and little remains of the old village.

Continue east on US 290/SH 71, which turns into a freeway just east of Oak Hill, into Austin, and you're done.

INDEX